PARRY & HARDY:

EEC LAW

by

ANTHONY PARRY, M.A., PH.D. (CANTAB.)

Licencié spécial en droit européen (Brussels)
of the Middle Temple, Barrister
Assistant Legal Adviser, Foreign & Commonwealth Office, London

and

JAMES DINNAGE, M.A. (CANTAB.)

Licencié spécial en droit européen (Brussels)
of the Inner Temple, Barrister
Legal Adviser, Du Pont (U.K.) Ltd.

SECOND EDITION

LONDON
SWEET & MAXWELL
1981

Published in 1981
by Sweet & Maxwell Limited
of 11 New Fetter Lane, London
and printed in Great Britain by Thomson Litho Limited
East Kilbride, Scotland

British Library Cataloguing in Publication Data

Parry, Anthony.
  EEC law.—2nd ed.
  1. Law—European Economic Community Countries
  I. Title   II. Dinnage, James
  341'.094   KJ

  ISBN 0–421–260904
  ISBN 0–421–261005 Pbk

PREFACE

The first edition of this work sought to give a concise account of EEC law in its entirety as it stood on January 1, 1973, the date of the accession of the United Kingdom to the Community. The second edition aims similarly at the presentation of an overall survey of Community law as it stands following the accession of Greece on January 1, 1981.

Many great changes and developments in the substantive law have occurred in the eight years since the first edition was written. This is true in particular of the competition policy, external relations, agriculture, customs and of environmental matters. The Court, moreover, has greatly expanded its case law. But, in striking contrast, the establishment of political cooperation and the setting up of the European Council (see Chapter 4) apart, development in relation to the Community political institutions has been slight and the impact of Community action in politically sensitive areas such as agricultural structures, regional policy and industrial policy has been correspondingly fairly marginal. Indeed, it may be that the vigorous jurisprudence of the Court is in part a product of reaction to the weakness of the Community's legislative and political institutions.

A reader familiar with the first edition will find that its broad structure has been retained. Nevertheless, except in the chapters on the Community institutions (now all consolidated into Part 2, with appropriate updating, including a discussion of direct elections and, equally, treatment of the new budgetary arrangements), this edition consists largely of new material. Thus Part 3, on the Community legal order and the Court, has been re-worked and extended. In Chapter 6 a complete treatment of the sources of community law (including fundamental rights) is now offered. Chapter 7 deals in detail with the supremacy and direct applicability of Community law within the legal systems of the several Member States. But we have, with some regret, decided for reasons of pressure on space to omit the original chapters on the European Communities Act and the reception of Community law at national level. We would argue, however, that these matters fall to be considered by works on national rather than on Community law.

The chapters on the substantive law (in Parts 4 and 5) have likewise been reworked and in some instances entirely rewritten to take account of new developments. But the absence of progress in the development of a true "Community" company law seemed to us to justify the omission of a complete chapter on this topic, and its relegation to treatment under the head of Establishment and

Services. On the other hand, there are new chapters on intellectual property and on energy.

We have omitted separate consideration of certain areas where the Community has initiated action (*e.g.* consumer protection) or proposed action but none has as yet been taken (*e.g.* industrial policy). While some measures, particularly in the field of harmonisation, may be viewed as giving substance to aspects of these policies there is as yet no body of law reflecting a coherent strategy.

Part 6 (*External Relations*) again consists almost entirely of new material, reflecting the great changes which have taken place in the general range and extent of Community activity and the case law of the Court originating in the celebrated *AETR* case.

We are heavily indebted to all those who helped us to prepare this new edition, with advice on many aspects and with practical skill in converting the manuscript. We particularly acknowledge with thanks advice on economic questions from Stella Paterson. Responsibility for content and for views and opinions expressed lies of course entirely with us.

London A.P.
July 1, 1981 J.D.

TABLE OF CONTENTS

Table of Contents

Table of Contents

TABLE OF CASES

COURT OF JUSTICE OF THE EUROPEAN COMMUNITIES

Table of Cases

xiv

Table of Cases

Table of Cases

Table of Cases

Table of Cases

ALPHABETICAL LIST OF CASES

Table of Cases

COMMISSION DECISIONS ON COMPETITION

Table of Cases

NATIONAL COURTS

France

Germany

United Kingdom

COMMUNITY TREATIES

COMMUNITY ACTS

Community Acts

Community Acts

1

INTERNATIONAL AGREEMENTS

For Community Agreements with Third States and International Organisations see Appendix 3, Part 1

li

NATIONAL CONSTITUTIONS AND LAWS

ABBREVIATIONS

AASM	Associated African States and Malagasy
AETR	Accord européen relatif au travail des équipages des véhicules effectuant des transports internationaux par route. Also: ERTA
A.F.D.I.	*Annuaire Francais de Droit International*
AG	Aktiengesellschaft
A.J.C.L.	*American Journal of Comparative Law*
A.J.I.L.	*American Journal of International Law*
Ann.Eur.	*Annuaire Européen*—European Yearbook
Art.	Article
BGBl.	Bundesgesetzblatt
B.J.E.	*Bulletin des Juristes Européens*
BKA	Bundeskartellamt
BLEU	Belgo-Luxembourg Economic Union
Brinkhorst and Schermers	*Judicial Remedies in the European Communities*, A case book, by L. J. Brinkhorst and U. G. Schermers, Kluwer, Deventer, Stevens, London, 1969.
Bulletin	Bulletin of the European Communities. EC Commission, monthly
CAP	Common agricultural policy
CCH	Commerce Clearing House
CCT	Common customs tariff
C.D.E.	*Cahiers de Droit Européen*
C.E.D.	*Cahiers économiques de Bruxelles*
CET	Common external tariff
Cie	Compagnie
Cin.L.Rev.	*Cincinatti Law Review*
C.M.L.Rev.	*Common Market Law Review*
Cmnd.	Command Paper
COCOR	Comité de Coordination
COREPER	Committee of Permanent Representatives to the European Communities (in fact abbreviation of comité des représentants permanents)
D.E.T.	*Droit Européen des Transports*
EAEC	European Atomic Energy Community
EAGGF	European Agricultural Guidance and Guarantee Fund
ECE	Economic Commission for Europe
ECMT	European conference of Ministers of Transport
E.C.R.	European Court Reports
ECSC	European Coal and Steel Community
ECU	European Currency Unit
EDF	European Development Fund
EEC	European Economic Community
EFTA	European Free Trade Association
EIB	European Investment Bank
E.L.Rev.	European Law Review
EP (or PE) doc.	European Parliament document
ERTA	European Agreement concerning the work of the crews of vehicles engaged in International Road Transport. Also: AETR
ESF	European Social Fund
E.T.L.	*European Transport Law*
EUA	European Unit of Account
Eur.	*Europarecht*
Euratom	European Atomic Energy Community
Europe Bulletin	Daily bulletin produced by Agence Europe, Brussels-Luxembourg

Abbreviations

EVSt	Einfuhr- und Vorratstelle
FA	Finanzamt
FAO	Food and Agriculture Organisation
FEOGA	Fonds européen d'orientation et de garantie agricol (European agricultural guidance and guarantee fund)
GATT	General Agreement on Tariffs and Trade
GmbH	Gesellschaft mit beschränkter Haftung
GNP	Gross national product
H.A.	High Authority of the ECSC
H.I.L.J.	*Harvard International Law Journal*
H.M.S.O.	Her Majesty's Stationery Office
HZA	Hauptzollamt
I.C.L.Q.	*International and Comparative Law Quarterly*
ILO	International Labour Organisation
J.C.M.S.	*Journal of Common Market Studies*
J.O.	*Journal officiel* (des Communautés Européennes)
J.T.	*Journal des Tribunaux* (Belgium)
J.W.T.L.	*Journal of World Trade Law*
K.G.	Kommanditgesellschaft
K.S.E.	*Kölner Schriften zum Europarecht*
L.G.D.J.	Librairie Général de Droit et de Jurisprudence
MCA	Monetary Compensatory Amount
Misc.	Miscellaneous series of treaties published by H.M.S.O.
Mod.L.Rev.	*Modern Law Review*
NATO	North Atlantic Treaty Organisation
N.J.W.	*Neue juristische Wochenschrift*
NV	Naamloze Vennootschap
OECD	Organisation for Economic Co-operation and Development
OEEC	Organisation for European Economic Cooperation
OHG	Offene Handelsgesellschaft
O.J.	*Official Journal of the European Communities*
PE (or EP) doc.	European Parliament document
R.B.D.I.	*Revue Belge de Droit International*
R.C.A.D.I.	*Recueil des Cours de l'académie de droit international*
R.D.E.	*Rivista di Diritto Europeo*
Rec.	*Receuil de la jurisprudence de la cour de justice des communautés européennes*
R.G.D.I.P.	*Revue générale de droit international public.*
R.I.D.C.	*Revue International de Droit Comparé*
R.M.C.	*Revue du Marché Commun*
R.T.D.E.	*Revue Trimestrielle de Droit Européen*
SA	Société anonyme
S.a.r.L.	Société à responsabilité limitée
S.E.W.	*Sociaal-economische Wetgeving*
Soc.	Société
S.p.A.	Società per Azioni
S.P.R.L.	Société de personnes à responsabilité limitée
Stan.L.Rev.	*Stanford Law Review*
Tex.L.Rev.	*Texas Law Review*
u.a.	unit of account
U.N.	United Nations Organisation
UNESCO	United Nations Educational, Scientific and Cultural Organisation
Valentine	*The Court of Justice of the European Communities.* 2 Vols. 1965. Stevens.
VAT	Value Added Tax
Wash.L.Rev.	*Washington Law Review*
WEU	Western European Union
WHO	World Health Organisation
Y.L.J.	*Yale Law Journal*

Part 1

INTRODUCTORY

Chapter 1

THE CONTEXT:

Scope and Method of this Book

1—01 European integration has been a constant theme in Western Europe since the end of the last world war, and the United Kingdom has throughout been more or less closely associated with such efforts as have been made in this direction. Nevertheless, it was only with her accession to the European Communities that the United Kingdom became a member of the organisations in which this integration is most advanced. The Communities have seen a substantial evolution since the accession of the United Kingdom together with Denmark and Ireland in 1973.[1] With the accession of Greece on January 1, 1981,[2] and accession of Spain and Portugal envisaged in the near future, the Communities are again at an important threshold in their development.

There are three European Communities, the Coal and Steel Community (ECSC) set up by the Treaty of Paris of April 18, 1951 and the Economic Community (EEC) and the Atomic Energy Community (EAEC or Euratom) set up by the two Treaties of Rome of March 25, 1957. The signatories of the Treaties and original Members of the Communities were Belgium, France, the Federal Republic of Germany, Italy, Luxembourg and the Netherlands.

1—02 The United Kingdom, Denmark and Ireland became parties by virtue of a Treaty and Decision and Annexed Act of Accession of January 22, 1972,[1] Greece by comparable instruments dated May 28, 1979.[2]

Each Community is a distinct legal entity, but the three are closely allied; from their inception the EEC and Euratom have shared a common Court of Justice and a common parliamentary Assembly with the ECSC, these institutions taking the place of those created for the ECSC by virtue of the Convention on Certain Institutions Common to the European Communities. The same Convention provided for an Economic and Social Committee common to the EEC and to Euratom. The close alliance between the three Communities was further consolidated by the Treaty signed at Brussels on April 8, 1965, establishing a single Commission and a single Council for all three Communities.

Of the three Communities, the EEC, extending as it does to

---

[1] T.S. No. 1 (1973), Cmnd. 5179 and see *infra*, para. 2–01.
[2] E.C. No. 18 (1979), Cmnd. 7650 and see *infra*, para. 2–02.

very broad spheres of economic and social activity, is far the most important, the other two being essentially specialised. It is with the EEC, therefore, that this book is primarily concerned. It is beyond its scope to go into a detailed description of the workings of the ECSC and the EAEC, and the discussion of these latter Communities is limited to those aspects having an importance for the three Communities as a group.

1—03   This book sets out to touch on all major aspects of EEC law. An understanding of the workings of the Community institutions is essential to any analysis of the rules laid down by the Treaty governing the various sectors of the economy. The Community institutions are therefore discussed first. This is followed by an examination of the nature and sources of Community law and the principles of judicial review. The various provisions of the Treaty governing economic activity are then discussed, dealing firstly with the foundations of the Community and then with the policies. The various chapter headings are self-explanatory. All aspects of external relations, including commercial policy are discussed together in Part 6 "External Relations."

Changes made to the Community Treaties, and the secondary legislation made thereunder, by the Treaties of Accession, the Decisions of the Council concerning accession and by the Acts of Accession ("the accession instruments") are referred to where necessary in this book. The accession arrangements for the United Kingdom, Denmark and Ireland are now of course largely spent, with the expiry of the five-year transitional period on December 31, 1977.

Chapter 2

WHERE TO FIND COMMUNITY LAW

1. *The treaties*

2–01   The main treaties governing the three European Communities are the following:

1. *Treaty Establishing the European Coal and Steel Community*, Paris, April 18, 1951.[1]
2. *Treaty Establishing the European Economic Community*, Rome, March 25, 1957.[2]
3. *Treaty Establishing the European Atomic Energy Community*, Rome, March 25, 1957.[3]
4. *Treaty Establishing a Single Council and a Single Commission of the European Communities*, Brussels, April 8, 1965.[4]
5. *Treaty amending certain Budgetary Provisions of the Treaties establishing the European Communities and of the Treaty Establishing a Single Council and a Single Commission of the European Communities*, Luxembourg, April 22, 1970 (and own resources decision of April 21, 1970).[5]
6. *Treaty concerning the Accession of the Kingdom of Denmark, Ireland, the Kingdom of Norway and the United Kingdom of Great Britain and Northern Ireland to the European Economic Community and the European Atomic Energy Community including the Act concerning the Conditions of Accession and the Adjustments to the Treaties (with Final Act) and Decision of the Council concerning the Accession of the said States to the European Coal and Steel Community*, Brussels, January 22, 1972.[6]
7. Council Decisions of January 1, 1973, adjusting the instruments concerning the accession of new Member States, alter-

---

[1] Unamended text, T.S. No. 2 (1973), Cmnd. 5189. Amended text, T.S. No. 16 (1979), Cmnd. 7461.
[2] Unamended text, T.S. No. 1 (1973)—Part II, Cmnd. 5179—II. Amended text, T.S. No. 15 (1979), Cmnd. 7460.
[3] Unamended text, T.S. No. 1 (1973)—Part II, Cmnd. 5179—II. Amended text, T.S. No. 17 (1979), Cmnd. 7462.
[4] T.S. No. 1 (1973)—Part II, Cmnd. 5179. Incorporated in T.S. Nos 15 to 17 (1979), Cmnd. 7460 to 7462, *supra*. Notes 1 to 3. Also printed separately in T.S. No. 15 (1979), Cmnd. 7460, p. 173.
[5] *Ibid.* but not reprinted in T.S. No. 15 (1979). Own resources decision is reprinted in T.S. No. 18 (1979); Cmnd. 7463, p. 285, *infra*, note 6.
[6] T.S. No. 1 (1973)—Part I, Cmnd. 5179—I. Text as amended by item 7 (*infra*, note 7) issued as T.S. No. 18 (1979), Cmnd. 7463.

ing the number of Members of the Commission and increasing the number of Advocates General.[7]

8. Council Decision of November 26, 1974, on the adjustment of Article 32 of the Treaty establishing the European Coal and Steel Community, Article 165 of the Treaty establishing the European Economic Community and Article 137 of the Treaty establishing the European Atomic Energy Community.[8]

9. *Treaty amending certain provisions of the Protocol on the Statute of the European Investment Bank*, Brussels, July 10, 1975.[9]

2—02 10. *The Treaty amending certain financial provisions of the Treaties establishing the European Communities and of the Treaty establishing a Single Commission of the European Communities*, Brussels, July 22, 1975.[10]

11. Council Decision of September 20, 1976, with annexed Act concerning the election of the representatives of the Assembly by direct universal suffrage.[11]

12. *Treaty concerning the Accession of the Hellenic Republic to the European Economic Community and European Atomic Energy Community and Act concerning the conditions of Accession of the Hellenic Republic and the Adjustments to the Treaties*, Athens, May 28, 1979.[12]

13. Council decision of May 24, 1979, concerning the Accession of the Hellenic Republic to the European Coal and Steel Community.[13]

Items 2 to 5 were drawn up in Dutch, French, German and Italian. They and all the subsequent items now exist in authentic texts in English, Danish and Greek as well. The ECSC Treaty (Item 1) remains authentic in French only.

The principal Treaties are compiled in Sweet & Maxwell's *"European Community Treaties"* (4th ed.). The EEC, ECSC and

---

[7] T.S. No. 43 (1973), Cmnd. 5277. Incorporated into T.S. No. 18 (1979), Cmnd. 7463, *supra*, note 6.

[8] T.S. No. 63 (1975), Cmnd. 6013. Incorporated into T.S. Nos. 15 to 17 (1979), Cmnd. 7460 to 7462, *supra*, notes 1 to 3.

[9] T.S. No. 7 (1978), Cmnd. 6986. Incorporated into T.S. No. 15 (1979), Cmnd. 7460, *supra*, note 2.

[10] T.S. No. 103 (1977), Cmnd. 7007. Incorporated into T.S. Nos. 15 to 17 (1979), Cmnd. 7460 to 7462. *Supra* notes, 1 to 3.

[11] E.C. No. 23 (1976), Cmnd. 6623. Incorporated into T.S. Nos. 15 to 17 (1979), Cmnd. 7460 to 7462, *supra* notes, 1 to 3. Also printed separately in T.S. No. 15 (1979), Cmnd. 7460, p. 201.

[12] E.C. No. 18 (1979), Cmnd. 7650, O.J. 1979, L 291.

[13] E.C. No. 28 (1979), Cmnd. 7735, O.J. 1979, L 291.

Euratom Treaties and 1972 Accession instruments as amended were published by HMSO in 1979.[14]

Other treaties relating to the Communities have been published in the *Official Journal* and *Special Editions* and in English in *European Communities Treaties and Related Instruments.*[15] Most of these are also published as Command Papers by HMSO in the European Communities (EC) Series, Treaty Series (TS) and Miscellaneous (Misc) Series.

2—03 **2. *Acts of the institutions of the Communities***

Acts of the institutions of the Communities[16] are published in the *Official Journal.* Most of those in force upon accession of the United Kingdom were published in authentic English texts in *Special Editions* of the *Official Journal* and in *European Communities, Secondary Legislation.*[17]

Citation: The legislative acts of the institutions are referred to as follows:

Regulations: Regulation number followed by year: thus—Regulation 1009/68. (Prior to 1963; thus—Regulation 17 of 1962 (or 17/62).

Decisions: ECSC-Council of Ministers; date only prior to 1968, thereafter as for EEC and Euratom decisions.
ECSC—High Authority; as for Regulations. EEC and Euratom; year followed by decision number; thus 64/221. (Prior to 1963: by date only).

Directives: As for EEC and Euratom decisions.

ECSC Recommendations: as for Regulations.

Other instruments are generally referred to by date, although many are in fact numbered.[18]

2—04 **3. *Judgments of the Court of Justice***

The judgments of the Court of Justice are now published in all official languages - Danish, Dutch, English, French, German and Italian. Judgments given after Greek accession will also be available in Greek.
Only the text in the "language of procedure"[19] is authentic. Translations of the principal judgments (along with translations of

---

[14] *Supra*, notes 1 to 3 and 6.
[15] 10 volumes, HMSO 1972.
[16] *Infra*, para. 6–03.
[17] 42 volumes HMSO 1972.
[18] See *infra* para. 2–05, on citation of the *Official Journal.*
[19] See *infra*, para. 8–12.

7

judgments of domestic courts on Community questions) are also published in English in the *Common Market Law Reports*[20] and in the *Common Market Reporter.*[21] Both series begin with judgments given in December 1961.

Citation: Judgments of the Court of Justice are cited as follows, *e.g.* "Case 219/78 *Hans Michaelis* v. *Commission.*" The Case number is assigned by the Court. References to the Official European Court Reports are given as: "[1979] E.C.R. 3349." (*Common Market Law Reports* citations are given in the tables but, for the sake of brevity, are not used in the footnotes in this book.)

2—05 Note on the Official Journal

Most Community instruments are published in the *Official Journal,* which appears more or less daily. Not all instruments so published are legislative in character.[22] The *Official Journal* of the European Coal and Steel Community appeared between December 30, 1952 and April 19, 1958. The *Official Journal* of the European Communities replaced it as from April 20, 1958. As from January 1, 1968, the *Official Journal* was divided into two parts: *Legislation* (L) and *Communications* (C).

Citation: References to pre-1972 acts are to the French text of the *Official Journal*—whether of the ECSC or of all three Communities. It is cited as follows:

1952—June 30, 1967	: *e.g.* J.O. 1961, 408
July 1, 1967—December 31, 1967	: *e.g.* J.O. 1967, 295/6
January 1, 1968, onwards	: *e.g.* J.O. 1968, L 148/1
	and J.O. 1968, C 22/3
January 1, 1973, onwards references are to the English Edition, cited	: O.J. 1974, L150/1

(Pagination was continuous within each year, until July 1, 1967, when the system was adopted of paginating within each daily part only).

Acts published in the *Special Editions of the Official Journal*[23] are cited as follows: O.J. 1968, 1235, the latter being the page number, each volume being continuously paginated. References to the Second Series of *Special Editions* are designated "2nd."

The L part publishes notably Community acts referred to in Article 189 EEC and international agreements. The C part contains reports of the sessions of the European Parliament, including written questions and answers, and notices of proceedings of the

---

[20] Published by European Law Centre, Ltd., London.
[21] Published by Commerce Clearing House, Chicago.
[22] See *infra*, para. 6–20 as to the obligation to publish.
[23] Translation of acts in force at the time of British Accession.

Court of Justice. It also contains Commission proposals and opinions thereon, besides various other types of notices and opinions. Monthly index volumes covering both the L and the C series appear somewhat in arrears, followed by an annual consolidation.

The *Official Journal* appears in all seven official languages, the English version being entitled *"Official Journal of the European Communities."*

2—06   Other Community publications

The Community institutions publish a vast amount of material on all aspects of the Communities. Most of these publications are produced by the Commission.[24]

Particularly useful are the monthly *Bulletin of the European Communities* (separate editions for the ECSC and for the EEC prior to 1968), the annual *General Report* (separate editions for each Community prior to 1968), and special reports on particular policies, such as competition.

The *Bulletin* contains documents and articles or studies on the Communities, a general survey of Community activities, and, in earlier years, a monthly index to the *Official Journal*. To the *Bulletin* are annexed various supplements, containing longer documents or Commission proposals. In recent years notices of new publications have been annexed also.

> *Citation*: Bulletin, followed by number and year.
> Supplement to Bulletin, followed by number and year.
> Bulletin Supplement, followed by number and year.

The annual *General Report* contains a rather more detailed survey of the main achievements of the year.

> *Citation*: *e.g.* Fourteenth General Report (1980), point 387.

Of importance also are the reports presented to the European Parliament by the various committees and sub-committees. These are referred to as session documents or EP Documents.

Documents referred to with a code number (*e.g.* Sec (71) 600 Final) are cyclostyled on A4-size paper. They are not generally produced in more permanent form, being generally proposals or plans, but they sometimes appear in whole or in part in the *Bulletin* supplements or in the C part of the *Official Journal.*

---

[24] Numerous catalogues of Community publications, general and special exist. Assistance in tracing particular documents can be obtained from The Library of the European Commission Office in London, 20 Kensington Palace Gardens, London W8 (01) 727 8090.

2—07 Other sources of information on Community law

Probably the most useful work is the *Encyclopedia of Community Law* published by Sweet & Maxwell which contains current texts of Community legislation and annotations, together with extensive cross-referencing and an updating service. The *Common Market Reporter*, published by Commerce Clearing House (CCH) contains a more limited range of legislative texts and also reports of major cases (indexed in the table of cases at the beginning of this book).

There are now two indexes of Community instruments (apart from the "yellow pages" of the *Official Journal* indexes); the Guide to EEC - Legislation, North - Holland Publishing Company 1979, compiled by T. M. C. Asser Institute - The Hague, with an updating service, and the Register of Current Community Legal Instruments, European Communities, 1980, compiled from CELEX, showing the position at July 1, 1979, with promise of annual revision.

The Court of Justice have announced that a Digest of Case Law relating to the European Communities is in preparation. This will supersede the Compendium of Case Law relating to the European Communities by Eversen, Sperl and Usher, published for the years 1973 to 1976, which continued on from Eversen and Sperl's Répertoire de la jurisprudence relative aux traités instituant les Communautés Européennes and Europäische Rechtsprechung.

A number of computerised Community law search systems are now being developed. First in the field is EUROLEX, Thompson Publications, which so far covers only Common Market Law Reports and not European Court Reports. Butterworths will be putting these two series of reports and other Community material onto the well-tried and very powerful LEXIS system from the end of 1981. The Community operates its own CELEX system. This may ultimately be accessible through EURONET/DIANE, operated through British Telecom.

Part 2

THE INSTITUTIONS OF THE COMMUNITIES

Chapter 3

THE INSTITUTIONS OF THE EUROPEAN COMMUNITIES

Provisions for Institutions

3—01 The Treaties of Rome provide that the tasks entrusted to the Community shall be carried out by an Assembly, a Council, a Commission and a Court of Justice, each acting within the limits of the powers conferred upon it by the relevant Treaty.[1] The ECSC Treaty simply states that the institutions of that Community consist of a High Authority, a common Assembly, a special Council of Ministers and a Court of Justice.[2] Although the institutions of all three Communities are constituted on broadly similar lines, and exercise broadly similar functions, the Rome Treaties did not provide that the institutions of the ECSC should serve the EEC and Euratom equally, but chose rather to provide for separate Commissions and Councils, acting independently of each other and of the organs of the already established ECSC. Provision for an Assembly and a Court of Justice is made on a rather different basis; pursuant to the Convention on Certain Institutions Common to the European Communities, concluded simultaneously with the Rome Treaties,[3] the powers and jurisdiction conferred in the Rome Treaties on the Assembly and on the Court of Justice were to be exercised by a single Assembly and a single Court of Justice from the inception of the EEC and of Euratom.[4] Upon taking up their duties these institutions took the place of their ECSC predecessors.[5] The same Convention provides that the functions conferred on the Economic and Social Committee in the Rome Treaties should be exercised by a single such Committee.[6] The Coal and Steel Community Consultative Committee was not amalgamated with the Economic and Social Committee, but continues its separate existence.[7]

3—02 The first few years of experience with three European Communities indicated that the interests of the region would be better served if not by the creation of a single Community, embracing all three existing ones,[8] then at least in the short-term by the creation

[1] Arts. 4 (1) EEC, 3 (1) Euratom.
[2] Art. 7 ECSC.
[3] *Supra*, para. 2–01, notes 2 & 3.
[4] Arts. 1 and 3.
[5] Arts. 2 and 4.
[6] Art. 5.
[7] Art. 18 ECSC.
[8] An aim adumbrated by the Merger Treaty, Preamble and Art. 33.

of a single Council and a single Commission for all three Communities. The Treaty establishing a single Council and a single Commission, commonly known as the Merger or Fusion Treaty, achieving this result, and making consequential amendments to the three original Treaties, was signed on April 8, 1965, and came into force on July 1, 1967.[9] Since that date a single Commission has exercised the functions of the High Authority of the ECSC and of the two Commissions, and a single Council has exercised those of the three Councils of Ministers.

The Merger Treaty clearly represents a step towards the eventual merging of the three Communities. Consequential features of the merger of the Councils and Commissions are provision for a common budget[10] and provision that officials and other servants of the three Communities should form part of a single administration of those Communities.[11] In addition, new provision is made in respect of privileges and immunities of all three Communities.[12]

No further progress towards setting up what would in law amount to a single European Community has been made, and the accession of new states to the Communities as they now stand has postponed, rather than accelerated, the possibility of such a development, for it is hardly feasible to carry out a revision of the Community Treaties while transitional provisions of accession arrangements are in force. The provisions of those arrangements have, it is true, some effect on the institutional structure of the Communities, but only in so far as they operate to enable the new Member States to participate in the activities of the institutions of the Community.

Discussion of institutional improvements has nevertheless been very active. The ill-fated Tindemans Report was largely set aside by the European Council but the Spierenburg Report of September 1979 on reforming the Commission, and the Report on European Institutions presented by the Committee of Three Wise Men (Mr. Biesheuvel, Mr. Dell and Mr. Marjolin) presented to the European Council in October 1979 seem likely to receive a more favourable hearing.

The Notion of "Institution"

3—03 It is to be noted that the relevant article of each of the three Treaties provides for four institutions only. The better view would appear to be that the notion of Community "institution" is to be confined to those four bodies alone, and does not for example include the Economic and Social Committee. The point is not

---

[9] *Supra*, para. 2–01, note 4.
[10] Merger Treaty, Art. 20 *et seq*.
[11] *Ibid*. Art. 24.
[12] *Ibid*. Art. 28 and annexed Protocol on Privileges and Immunities of the European Communities, *infra*, paras. 5–12 *et seq*.

entirely free from doubt, but this view is supported by the fact that the Economic and Social Committee and the European Investment Bank are for certain purposes expressly assimilated to the institutions.[13] The distinction between the institutions proper and the subsidiary bodies is potentially of importance, for only the institutions of the Community (and bodies assimilated thereto) may be represented before the Court of Justice pursuant to Article 17 of the Protocols to the EEC and Euratom Treaties on the Statute of the Court, and its equivalent in the ECSC Protocol, Article 20. The Court has not yet been called upon to give an express ruling on the status of bodies which might otherwise fairly be described as institutions, but it has held that clearly subsidiary bodies such as the Commission Secretariat are not institutions.[14] Some guidance as to the attitude the Court would be likely to take if faced with a less clear-cut case is perhaps to be derived from those cases where the question of the designation of the Community defendant has been discussed; the Court has always referred to the institution appointing the official concerned as being the appropriate defendant.[15]

The Relationship between the Institutions

3—04   The Treaties setting up the Communities do not elaborate on the nature of the relationship between the institutions *inter se*, and a brief comparative analysis of the institutions is therefore necessary before going on to examine each institution individually. The institutions play broadly similar roles in each of the Communities, although the relative importance of each institution varies; this must be borne in mind in what follows.

The Council in relation to the other institutions

3—05   The Council, consisting of representatives of the Member States, constitutes the final expression of the political will of the Member States within the legal framework of the Treaties. The so called European Council (as opposed to the Council of the European Communities established by the Treaties) and the political co-operation machinery exist outside that framework and for the most part deal with matters not coming within Community competence, although the European Council meetings do in fact provide guidance for Community development. Under the ECSC Treaty the role of the Council of the European Communities is apparently quite limited. Most of the decisions of ECSC policy require no more than the prior assent of the Council, administrative authority at least resting almost invariably with the Commission, although the Council, by its very power to withhold assent, in fact exercises

---

[13] *Cf.* Case 79/70 *Müllers* v. *Economic and Social Committee* [1971] E.C.R. 689.
[14] See, *e.g.* Case 66/63 *Netherlands* v. *HA* [1964] E.C.R. 533.
[15] Cases 79 and 82/63 *Reynier* v. *Commission* [1964] E.C.R. 259.

considerable influence. The difference in the position of the Council under the ECSC Treaty on the one hand, and the EEC Treaty on the other, is thus not perhaps very great, the two systems having if anything grown more alike over the years. The wording of the articles of the Euratom Treaty, defining the duties of the Council and of the Commission[16] suggests that the position of the Council under this Treaty is similar to its position under the ECSC Treaty, but in practice the position under the Euratom Treaty is closely assimilated to that under the EEC Treaty. The Council is, under the latter, invested with the major share of political and regulatory power; and can, with some justification, be described as the Community legislature. No new departure or important decision (with the possible exception of action on competition matters) can be taken without the agreement of the Council. Some idea of the power of the Council over the Commission is provided by the fact that the former has a large degree of control in the drawing up of the Community budget although final control here is now to be in the hands of the Assembly. To some extent the latter also has control over expenditure.[17] The Council also has the final word in international negotiations.[18] The powers specified in Article 160, enabling the Council to suspend a Commissioner and to replace him, pending an application to the Court of Justice for his compulsory retirement on grounds of misconduct or that he no longer fulfills the conditions required for the performance of his duties have been repealed by the Merger Treaty,[19] and no significance is to be attached in this context to Article 152, enabling the Council to request that proposals be made to it by the Commission; for it is not a power of coercion, but rather a provision for mutual co-operation.

The position of the Commission

3—06 If the Council is the legislature, then the Commission is the executive of the Communities. Under the ECSC Treaty it has very wide powers, and is not only able to propose policy, but to promote it as well. It is subject to relatively limited control by the Council in its activities, and its independence is guaranteed. The Commission's powers under the EEC Treaty (and under the Euratom Treaty) are materially narrower than those that it enjoys under the ECSC Treaty. Its own power of decision is limited in the main to executive matters. There is no doubt, however, that the Commission is the motor of the EEC and of Euratom, in that virtually all important decisions taken by the Council must be on the basis of proposals made by the Commission.

---

[16] Arts. 115 and 124 respectively.
[17] *Infra*, paras. 3–69 *et seq*.
[18] Arts. 113, 228 and 238 and see generally Part 6.
[19] Art. 19.

The Assembly (European Parliament)

3—07   The Assembly, now officially called the European Parliament, pursuant to its own resolution, is not a parliament in the true sense of the term, in that it possesses no direct legislative powers. It must, however, be consulted on certain matters, and in practice the Commission refers to it the vast majority of its proposals of any importance where these are made public. It is to this body alone that the Commission is responsible.[20]

The Court of Justice of the European Communities

3—08   The Court of Justice can most nearly be compared to a national administrative court; indeed its practice and powers are closely modelled upon those of the French *Conseil d'Etat.* It has jurisdiction in relation to matters concerning individuals, the institutions and the Member States. In an institutional context it is relevant to note that it has jurisdiction to rule upon the *vires* of the acts of the institutions of the Communities, and it can compulsorily retire members of the Commission.

The Institutions Analysed

3—09   The discussion in the following sections deals in turn with:

The Commission;
The Council;
Consultative Bodies;
The European Parliament;
Financial Provisions;
The European Council and Political Co-operation are covered in Chapter 4; location and territorial application and legal personality and privileges and immunities in Chapter 5.

The Court of Justice is considered in Part 3.

The Commission

The Functions of the Commission

3—10   The Commission of the European Communities combines the role of initiator of action with that of an executive. In this its functions do not differ from those of a national central administration, acting with the Government of the day, but the Commission is exceptional, in that it acts as a proposer of policy not simply as a matter of practice, but in the execution of its prescribed duties. The duties of the Commission under the EEC Treaty are set out in Article 155, and under the Euratom Treaty in Article 124. In order to ensure the proper functioning and development of the common

[20] Art. 144 EEC.

market and of nuclear energy the Commission is, in virtue of these articles, which are, *mutatis mutandis*, in identical terms:

(a)   to ensure that the provisions of the Treaties and the measures taken by the institutions pursuant thereto are applied;

(b)   to formulate recommendations or deliver opinions on matters dealt with in the Treaties, if they expressly so provide or if the Commission considers it necessary;

(c)   to have its own power of decision and to participate in the shaping of measures taken by the Council and by the Assembly in the manner provided for in the Treaties;

(d)   to exercise the powers conferred on it by the Council for the implementation of the rules laid down by the latter.

Each point will be taken in turn.

(a) The Commission as "watch-dog" of the Treaties

3—11   The function of the Commission as watch-dog of the application of the Treaties divides into two distinct parts: detection of breaches of the Treaties and remedial action.

So far as detection is concerned, Member States are under a general duty to facilitate the achievement of the Community's tasks.[21] In addition a number of articles impose specific obligations to give information of one kind or another.[22] Various items of Community secondary legislation also call for the supply of information of all kinds.[23] A Member State cannot, however, be obliged to supply information the disclosure of which it considers contrary to the essential interests of its security.[24]

On a general level, Article 213 EEC[25] empowers the Commission to collect any information and to carry out any checks required for the performance of the tasks entrusted to it, subject to limits and conditions laid down by the Council in accordance with the provisions of the Treaties. No general rules have as yet been laid down, but the article has been used as the legal basis for statistical exercises and the like.[26] Specific powers of control are contained in Articles 79 and 89 EEC, relating respectively to transport and competition. Some check on fraud is provided by rules on origin of goods, designed to ensure that Community rules on free circulation are not evaded.[27] Additionally, a certification system designed to combat fraud is associated with agricultural support measures.[28]

[21] Arts. 5 EEC, 192 Euratom and *cf.* Art. 86 ECSC.
[22] Arts. 14 (6), 15 (1), 31, 72, 73 (2), 93 (3), 109 (2), 111 (5) and 115, EEC.
[23] See, *e.g.* Reg. 17/62 (Competition) *infra*, Chapter 20.
[24] Art. 221 (1) (*a*).
[25] And Art. 187 Euratom.
[26] *e.g.* Directive 64/475, J.O. 1964, 2193.
[27] *Infra*, paras. 13–18.
[28] *Infra*. Chapter 15.

Matters may also come to the attention of the Commission through complaints from Member States, by way of written question from the European Parliament,[29] and by way of complaints of individuals—whether informal or under specific provisions—*e.g.* complaints procedure under Article 3 (2) of Regulation 17/62 (competition). This would not appear to exhaust the matter; the attention of the Commission was initially drawn to the celebrated Quinine Cartel by the activities of the U.S. Department of Justice anti-trust division.[30]

3—12   Where an individual has committed a breach of a Treaty provision, it will usually be a Member State which will take steps to punish the offender, but the Commission itself has certain powers to punish breaches, notably under Regulation 17/62 (competition) and Regulation 11/60 (transport). The powers under Regulation 17/62 are now being used increasingly, particularly as regards agreements containing bans on export from one Member State to another. The Euratom Treaty itself contains provisions for sanctions in Articles 83 and 145.

In case of a breach of a Treaty provision by a Member State, the Commission was originally able to take direct action, notably under Article 97 EEC and (possibly) Article 89 (2) EEC, but these provisions are now spent for all practical purposes.

The usual procedure by which the Commission takes action against a Member State is contained in Article 169, providing for the issue of a reasoned opinion on the matter; in the event of non-compliance, the matter can be brought before the Court of Justice.[31] Often, however, threat of proceedings will have the desired effect, or else the action may be dropped at the opinion stage or even later.

Responsibility for the preparation of "infraction dossiers" lies with the legal service of the Commission, the same service also dealing with the preparation of cases for the Court of Justice, and generally taking the case before the Court itself.

(b) The Commission as guide of national, and therefore of Community action through the power of recommendation

3—13   Article 155 EEC, second hyphen, enables the Commission to formulate recommendations or to deliver opinions if the Treaty expressly so provides, or if the Commission considers it necessary. In so far as Article 189 confers on the Commission the facility to make recommendations or deliver opinions in accordance with the provisions of the Treaty, the first limb of Article 155, second hyphen, duplicates that facility. A number of substantive articles[32]

---

[29] As provided for by Art. 140 EEC.

[30] Cases 41, 44 and 45/69, *infra*, para. 3–64, note 57.

[31] See generally *infra*, Chapter 11. The Commission need show no "legal interest": Case 167/73 *Commission* v. *France* [1974] E.C.R. 359.

[32] Notably Arts. 14, 15, 27, 35, 37, 64, 71, 72, 81, 91, 102, 111 and 118.

provide for recommendations or opinions. The real interest of the relevant sub-paragraph of Article 155, however, lies in the fact that the power conferred shall be exercisable where "the Commission considers it necessary." In so far as this power is general, it contributes to the influence the Commission may exercise in the direction of integration, despite the fact that it is not a provision for the issue of binding acts. In practice its greatest utility probably lies in the fact that it enables the Commission to prepare the ground for the promulgation of a binding act by way of preliminary recommendation or opinion, whether under a substantive provision of the Treaty, or under Article 235 (the residual decision-making power). The power in effect provides a diplomatic way of making proposals where a formal proposal would be inappropriate, or where a formal power is not provided in the Treaty.

(c) **The Commission as decision-maker and as participant in the shaping of measures taken by the Council and by the Assembly**

1. *The Commission as decision-maker*

3—14   Under Article 189 the Commission is to make regulations, issue directives, take decisions, make recommendations or deliver opinions in order to carry out its task.[33] On the face of Article 189 the Council has a coextensive facility to issue such acts. In reality, however, the power of the Commission is much narrower than that of the Council. The competence of the Commission (and indeed of the Council) is one of attribution and the Commission may issue one of the binding acts referred to in Article 189 only where a substantive article of the Treaty confers upon it the power so to do. This state of affairs is implicitly recognised by Article 189 itself, referring to the issue of the types of acts mentioned "in accordance with the provisions of this Treaty."[34]

The distinction between the "power of decision" referred to in Article 155, and the power to "take decisions," conferred by Article 189 is quite clear-cut; the former expression describes the power to issue any of the types of acts listed in Article 189; it amounts to a power to take action of any kind. A decision *stricto sensu* is a particular kind of act.[35]

2. *The Commission as participant in the shaping of measures*

3—15   The reference in Article 155 to the Commission participating in the shaping of measures requires some clarification. The measures referred to are acts of the Council and of the Assembly. In the nature of things the most important part of this work relates to the decision-making power *sensu lato* of the Council, exercised in

[33] See generally *infra*, paras. 6–03 *et seq.*
[34] See, *e.g.* 12/63 *Schlieker* v. *H.A.* [1963] E.C.R. 85 and 44/65, *Hessische Knappschaft* v. *Singer* [1965] E.C.R. 965.
[35] See further *infra*, paras. 6–03 *et seq.*

accordance with the substantive provisions of the Treaty. In the vast majority of cases decisions thus provided for are required to be taken on the basis of proposals of the Commission; the Commission can thus be described as the initiator of the Community decision-making process, and therefore as the motor of Community action. The power in question is not simply a legislative initiative, since under Article 149 the Council cannot, where it is required to act on a proposal of the Commission, amend that proposal except by unanimous agreement; the Commission on the other hand can, if the Council has yet to act, alter its original proposal, in particular where the Assembly has been consulted on that proposal.[36]

In the formulation of its proposals, the Commission is not to be taken as acting *in vacuo*; Article 15 of the Merger Treaty requires mutual consultation between Council and Commission, and also the working out of methods of co-operation on the basis of a common accord. Despite the resolution on the point, contained in the Luxembourg Accords of January 31, 1966,[37] no general arrangement has emerged, although, of course, *de facto* forms of co-operation exist.[38] Co-operation is also aimed at by Article 152, enabling the Council to request the Commission to undertake studies or to submit proposals. This does not impinge on the Commission's powers; rather it provides for a two-way flow of ideas.

3—16   The members of the Commission are required to be selected so as to ensure that they will fulfil their functions in full independence and will not be influenced by partisan views in the formulation of Community policies, relatively secure tenure of office itself apparently ensuring a continuity of policy line in their proposals to the Council. (It is true that the Commissioners are appointed only for four years at a time, but provision is made for renewal of office, a facility often used.) In the formulation of its proposals the Commission may be conceived of as having the role of honest broker. The Luxembourg Accords[39] opined that consultation with the Governments of the Member States through their permanent representatives was desirable before the adoption of proposals of special importance. Practice, however, goes considerably beyond this, in that the Commission in fact has contacts with national administrations direct.

In addition, the Commission is obliged in a limited number of cases to refer to consultative bodies in the formulation of its proposals. Thus Article 107 requires consultation of the Monetary Committee set up by Article 105, and Article 118 requires consultation of the Economic and Social Committee. Apart from consultations with bodies set up by the Treaties, the Commission is

[36] Art. 149, second paragraph.
[37] EC Bulletin 3, 1966 p. 5.
[38] *e.g.* the conciliation procedure: *infra*, para. 3–75.
[39] *Infra*, para. 3–37.

advised by various committees of experts on specific topics; their views are not necessarily binding on it.[40]

3—17   In practice the European Parliament is at least kept fully informed of all important Community proposals, whether or not it is officially consulted. The information processes are freer and wider ranging than formal consultations, and indeed if such formal consultations were demanded on all occasions this would constitute a curtailment of the powers of the Commission and the Council. The Parliament asked for prior consultations on Commission proposals as a general rule in the early 1960s, but the Commission resisted such a move, as derogating from its autonomy and authority.

3—18   *Where no proposal power is provided.* In relation to certain matters the Commission has no formal power of proposal, but has power to intervene in the decision-making process in some other way. Article 8 (3) required a report from the Commission. Article 109 (3) requires a Commission opinion, Article 195 (2) requires consultation of the Commission, Article 203 (4) second sub-para., required discussion with the Commission, and Article 212 requires the co-operation of the Commission.

Still other provisions enable the Council to act without any intervention at all from the Commission, *e.g.* Article 28, first sentence.

3—19   *Other proposals.* Even in the absence of formal powers the Commission may suggest to the Council that it is opportune to take action. This may be done informally or on the basis of recommendations or opinions under Article 155, second hyphen, second limb.

More formally the Commission may make proposals under Article 235,[41] which enables the Council to take appropriate measures if action by the Community should prove necessary to attain, in the course of the operation of the common market, one of the objectives of the Community, and the Treaty has not provided the necessary powers. This article is now frequently used by the Community, in particular where new policies are being mapped out.

Otherwise the Commission is, on its own admission, closely associated with the preparation and elaboration of the Decisions of the Representatives of the Member States meeting in Council and similar acts.[42]

3—20   *Other powers of communication with the Council.* The specific

[40] See notably management committee procedure, discussed *infra*, para. 15–12.
[41] Art. 203 Euratom: Art. 95 ECSC requires unanimous Council assent to proposed action by the Commission.
[42] WQ 140/64, J.O. 1964, 898 and *infra*, para. 6–23.

provisions discussed above do not exhaust the possibilities of contact with the Council. Apart from informal contacts, the Commision *inter alia* addresses communications, memoranda and reports to the Council. These have no official status as part of the decision-making process, but are nevertheless a significant part of that process, in that they express the Commission's thinking and describe Commission action in various fields.

(d) The Commission as agent of execution of the Treaty

3—21   The Commission's executive functions fall into two parts: it has powers conferred directly by the Treaties, and also by the Council for the execution of decisions of the Council.

Execution of Council decisions

3—22   The power specified in Article 155,[43] enabling the Commission to exercise the powers conferred on it by the Council for the implementation of the rules laid down by the latter, is the only provision for delegation by the Council contained in the Treaties themselves. In principle it is the Council which must ensure that the objectives of the Treaty are attained and to this end it has a power to take decisions.[44] In practice, however, the Council has no means of executing the details of its decisions, and does not set up the machinery for their implementation. These two tasks are generally left to the Commission.[45] In a number of areas the Commission acts on its own initiative, albeit generally within Council guidelines; *e.g.* setting agricultural levies under market organisation regulations.[46] Other provisions require the Commission to act in liaison with,[47] or with the agreement of,[48] national authorities. Yet other provisions require the Commission to seek the opinion of a committee.[49] A very common procedure is the so-called management committee procedure.[50] Most agricultural market organisation regulations provide for action by the Commission on the basis of a request of a Member State in connection with safeguard clauses.[51]

Execution of the Treaty pursuant to powers conferred by the Treaty

3—23   The chief powers of execution conferred on the Commission by

---

[43] Art. 124 Euratom.
[44] Art. 145 EEC: Cases 25/70, *Evst* v. *Köster* [1970] E.C.R. 1161; and 9 and 10/56 *Meroni* v. *H.A.* [1957 and 58] E.C.R. 133 and 187.
[45] *Ibid.* and see 57/72, *Westzucker* v. *Evst Z* [1973] E.C.R. 321. The power is to be interpreted widely: Case 23/75 *Rey Soda* [1975] E.C.R. 1279.
[46] *Infra*, para. 15–15.
[47] *e.g.* Art. 11 (2), Directive of October 23, 1962, J.O. 1962, 2645 (food standards).
[48] Art. 3, Reg. 3/64, J.O. 1964, 50 (frontier communes).
[49] *e.g.* Reg. 17/62, J.O. 1962, 204; (Committee on Monopolies and Dominant Positions).
[50] Legality confirmed by Case 25/70 *Evst* v. *Köster* [1970] E.C.R. 1161.
[51] *e.g. infra*, para. 15–17.

the Treaty are contained in Chapter 1 of Title I of Part II, on the establishment of the customs union, and in Chapter 1 of Title I of Part III, on competition. Other provisions in the Treaty are of a less general nature. Particular responsibilities are, however, conferred on the Commission in its role as watch-dog of the application of the Treaty, and for receiving information for various purposes. In addition the Commission has a largely exclusive control over Community finance and over the application of safeguard provisions. Discussion of these powers is to be found in the context of the relevant Community activity.

The Function of the Commission Under the ECSC Treaty

3—24 The Commission of the European Communities, which took the place of the High Authority of the European Coal and Steel Community,[52] and which now exercises the powers and jurisdiction conferred on that institution by the ECSC Treaty, fulfils in relation to the Coal and Steel Community the same role that it fulfils in respect of the Rome Treaties, but its duties are expressed rather differently; it is the High Authority (*i.e.* now the Commission) whose primary duty it is to ensure that the objectives of the Treaty are attained in accordance with the provisions thereof,[53] whereas it is the Council that has this duty under the EEC Treaty.[54] This in itself indicates that the High Authority was intended to play a leading role in the ECSC, and indeed it was provided with much broader powers of execution than were the Commissions under the Rome Treaties, and it enjoys much wider residual powers. The attribution of such greater general powers to the High Authority than to the Commissions is accounted for by the fact that the ECSC has relatively limited, and therefore well defined, objectives, and that the ECSC Treaty is much more detailed than are the Rome Treaties in setting out the powers and duties of the institutions. The position of the ECSC executive in the day-to-day running of the Community is thus much stronger than that of the Commissions under the Rome Treaties, and since most decisions taken under the ECSC Treaty are taken by the Commission, and not by the Council (although many are taken with the assent of the Council), this strength is apparently reinforced. True, the powers of the High Authority are, as under the other two Treaties, only powers of attribution, but the Court of Justice has held that the High Authority nevertheless enjoys a certain autonomy in relation to deciding on measures of execution called for in order to realise the objectives of the Treaty.[55]

3—25 The discussion above of the powers of the Commission centred

---

[52] Merger Treaty, Art. 9.
[53] Art. 8 ECSC.
[54] Art. 145: Art. 115 Euratom.
[55] Case 8/55 *Fédéchar* v. *H.A.* [1954–56] E.C.R. 245.

upon the terms of Article 155 of the EEC Treaty;[56] the ECSC Treaty contains no directly comparable clause, but within the sphere of operations of the ECSC the High Authority fulfils much the same roles of watch-dog, adviser and honest broker, and initiator of legislation, subject to the limitation, contained in Article 5 ECSC, that the task of the Community is to be carried out with a limited measure of intervention. Such a limitation is comprehensible in a Treaty setting up a Community with limited objectives. With these reservations, then, this discussion applies generally to the role of the Commission under the ECSC Treaty. The similarities in the institutional structure (discussed below) are even greater.

Whether, on the general level, the Commission is a more independent body under the ECSC Treaty than it is under the Rome Treaties is a moot question. The difference is probably more apparent than real.

Composition of the Commission

3—26 Article 157 (1) of the EEC Treaty as originally formulated provided for a Commission of nine members, to be chosen on the grounds of their general competence and whose independence is beyond doubt.[57] On the merger of the executives as from July 1, 1967, provision was made initially for 14 Commissioners, this number to be reduced to nine within three years.[58] The operative provision of the Merger Treaty, Article 10 (1), itself amended by Articles 15 of the Acts of Accession, provides for a Commission of 14 as from the accession of Greece. No Member State may appoint more than two Commissioners, and all appointees must be nationals of Member States.[59] In practice the four largest States of the Community will have two Commissioners each, and the others one each.

The device of a small number of Commissioners "acting by a majority of the number of members provided for in Article 10" of the Merger Treaty[60] was felt to have considerable advantages, further reinforced by the secrecy in which Commission decisions are taken. The Commission is able to present a united front to the outside and takes collective responsibility for its acts. Internal consultation between Commissioners is considered to have worked well.

3—27 Commission members are nominated by common accord of the Governments of the Member States under Article 11 of the Merger

---

[56] Art. 124 Euratom.
[57] Art. 9 ECSC is to similar effect. Art. 126 (1) Euratom provided initially for a five-member Commission, to be chosen on a similar basis having regard to the objectives of that Treaty.
[58] Art. 32, together with Art. 10, Merger Treaty.
[59] Art. 10, Merger Treaty.
[60] Art. 17.

Treaty. In practice the usual procedure is for members to be appointed by accord of the Representatives of the Member States meeting in Council (appointment by the Council itself would suggest dependence on that body). In general Member States do not oppose the candidates of other Member States, but a certain amount of mutual consultation takes place before final nominations are made.

The terms of office of members of the Commission are not staggered in the same way, for example, as those of members of th U.S. Senate (the only exception to this being the pre-merger provisions of Article 10 ECSC) but rather the mandate of the Commission as a whole is for four years, and is renewable. Vacancies caused by resignation, compulsory retirement or death are filled for the remainder of the mandate unless the Council decides, unanimously, to leave the post vacant until the end of the mandate.[61]

Provision is made for the appointment of a President and Vice-Presidents of the Commission, the current provision being Article 14 of the Merger Treaty, amended by Article 16 of the 1972 Act of Accession, providing for one President and five Vice-Presidents, to be appointed from among the members of the Commission for a renewable term of two years in accordance with the same procedure as that laid down for the appointment of members of the Commission. Save where the entire Commission is replaced, such appointments are required to be made after consultation of the Commission. This consultation has limited scope, however, in that the person selected has already been appointed a Commissioner.

Status of Commission Members

3—28   The key provision relating to the status of the Commission is Article 10 (2) of the Merger Treaty which provides that the members of the Commission shall, in the general interest of the Community, be completely independent in the performance of their duties. The independence of the Commission is reinforced by the injunction to the members in the same article neither to seek nor take instructions from any Government or from any other body. They are to refrain from any action incompatible with their duties (the ECSC Treaty, Art. 9, described these duties as having a supranational character). Each Member State undertakes to respect these principles and not to seek to influence the members of the Commission in the performance of their tasks. The Commissioners for their part further undertake[62] not to engage during their term of office in any other occupation (the French is more specific here; the term used is *activités professionelles*), whether gainful or not. The interpretation of "occupation" is not altogether without difficulty. Teaching work is not, apparently, considered to be

[61] *Ibid.* Art. 12.
[62] *Ibid.* Art. 10 (2), third sub-paragraph.

excluded. Acceptance of a parliamentary seat would be considered to be incompatible, but perhaps not the act of taking part in an election campaign. Retention of political interests, and even of a seat in local government is apparently acceptable. By the same paragraph the Commissioners are required to give a solemn undertaking to respect the obligations arising from their duties and to behave with integrity and discretion as regards the acceptance of certain appointments or benefits after they have ceased to hold office. The Court of Justice can punish breaches of this undertaking by making an order under Article 13 of the Merger Treaty, which provides for compulsory retirement on application by the Council or the Commission where any member of the Commission no longer fulfils the conditions required for the performance of his duties, or has been guilty of serious misconduct. Alternatively there is a similar power to remove pension rights etc.[63]

3—29   It is certain that none of the restraints placed upon members of the Commission can deny them the right to promote the European idea or the general right of comment. An attempt was made on at least one occasion to restrain the Commission in its criticisms of national policy, but the Council came to recognise that it could not legitimately take any action in the matter.

Individual compulsory retirement aside, the Assembly may pass a motion of censure on the Commission as a whole.[64] If this be carried on a two-thirds majority of votes cast, the Commission resigns as a body, remaining in office only to complete current business. This provision is to be contrasted with Article 12, third para., of the Merger Treaty which provides that save in the case of compulsory retirement under the provisions of Article 13, members of the Commission shall remain in office until they have been replaced. Article 12 therefore covers the case of end of mandate as well as individual retirement.

Salaries, privileges, etc.

3—30   The salaries, allowances and pensions of the President and members of the Commission are fixed by the Council acting by qualified majority.[65] The Commissioners enjoy the privileges and immunities specified in the Protocol on Privileges and Immunities.[66]

Internal organisation of the Commission

3—31   By virtue of Article 16 of the Merger Treaty the Commission adopts its own Rules of Procedure so as to ensure that both it and

[63] *Ibid.*
[64] Art. 144 EEC: this provision has been invoked on a number of occasions, but not pressed by the Assembly to conclusion.
[65] Art. 6, Merger Treaty.
[66] *Infra*, paras. 5–12 *et seq*.

its departments operate in accordance with the provisions of the Treaty.[67] Salient points are majority decision-making, and that discussions and meetings are held *in camera*.

Decisions are often not in fact discussed by the Commissioners face to face, a written procedure playing an important role here. Proposals of any single Commissioner are circulated, and are deemed adopted unless objection is lodged within a week.[68] For purely administrative matters the President and Vice-Presidents have the control of current business. Here too a written procedure is much used.

These methods of decision-making are not generally considered to amount to delegation of responsibility, but delegation of responsibility is made to individual Commissioners (with the possibility of sub-delegation in some cases) in certain relatively limited areas.[69] The Commission may not effect a complete delegation of its responsibilities.[70] There can never be a delegation of more than predetermined and controlled executive powers.[71]

So far as concerns the position of the Secretariat of the Commission, it goes without saying that the prohibition on delegation of responsibilities does not prevent the Commission from entrusting the task of preparation of action to its own staff. In practice each Commissioner has responsibility for groups of departments, called Directorates General, headed by one or more Directors General. The Directorates work through the responsible Commissioner to the Commission as a whole. The Commissioners also have personal staffs, or *cabinets*, which play an important political role in advising their Commissioners.

The Council

3—32 The merger of the Councils of the European Communities was in some sense a less radical departure than the merger of the Commissions and the High Authority. The Councils had always tended to have rather similar methods of operation, and had from the inception of the EEC and Euratom shared a single Secretariat. Although, therefore, merger meant, as it did for the Commissions, a changeover to a single system, effectively that of the EEC, where three systems had existed previously, the changeover was more one of form than of substance for the Council.

The Council consists of representatives of the Member States. It acts not merely as a group of representatives of Member States, however; its mission is to ensure that the objectives of the Treaty are attained (Art. 145 EEC) and in fact the Council can be said to

---

[67] 67/426, J.O. 1967, 147/1, last amended by 81/2, O.J. 1981, L 8/16.
[68] *Ibid*. Art. 11.
[69] *Ibid*. Arts. 24 to 27.
[70] Case 66/63 *Netherlands* v. *H.A.* [1964] E.C.R. 533.
[71] Cases 9 and 10/56 *Meroni* v. *H.A.* [1957–58] E.C.R. 133 and 157 (Scrap equalisation).

work in two distinct ways; on the one hand, it acts as the representative of Community interests, and on the other, it brings together national interests. It follows that it further acts as a forum for the confrontation of national and Community interests and ideas.

3—33   The individuals who attend meetings of the Council are generally ministers. The Treaty provides that each Government shall delegate to the Council "one of its members," but the Treaty does not define the latter phrase. It is accepted in practice that representation is not confined to, *e.g.* cabinet ministers, but will include *secretaires d'état* with political responsibility. In terms of British practice a Permanent Under-Secretary would probably be excluded, but a Minister of State or a Parliamentary Under-Secretary would be considered eligible to attend meetings of the Council discussing matters falling within his field of activity. It is also permissible to send a non-voting alternate, in which case the member of the Council absenting himself may depute another member to vote on his behalf[72] but a proxy may vote on behalf of one absentee only.[73]

The individual sent to any particular meeting of the Council may vary with the subject-matter of the meeting; thus ministers of agriculture will go to meetings on the Common Agricultural Policy, transport ministers to meetings on the Common Transport Policy, and so forth. It is also possible to arrange Council meetings at which the Member States are represented jointly by, for example, ministers of agriculture and ministers of finance; this would be appropriate where matters concerning the financing of the CAP are under discussion. The foreign ministers, apart from attending meetings on external relations, generally attend sessions on the directions of Community policy in general, being naturally the ministers with the main national responsibility for the European Communities. It has been suggested that there should be ministers for Europe, who would deal with all aspects of national policy at the Community level.

3—34   Meetings of the Council are presided over by a President. Under Articles 11 of the Acts of Accession, which amend Article 2 of the Merger Treaty, the office of President is to be held for a term of six months by each member of the Council in turn; the order in which this is to take place is the "absolute" alphabetical order of States, that is to say, the order that they would be listed, were the name of each State written in the national language or languages; thus, Belgique-België, Danmark, Deutschland, and so on. The President is frequently relieved of the duty of representing the viewpoint of his own State, so as to be enabled to devote himself to the tasks of co-ordination of viewpoint, but it is recognised that whether or not he is so relieved, the incumbent of the office can be relied upon, in greater or lesser degree, to defend and express

---

[72] Art. 150 EEC and Art. 4, Council Rules of Procedure, *infra*, note 75.
[73] *Ibid.* and Art. 5, Council Rules of Procedure, *infra*, note 75.

the Community point of view rather than the purely national one, particularly in contacts with third countries. This has greatly reinforced the institutional identity of the Council.

Internal functioning of the Council

3—35   The Council meets when convened by its President, or at the request of one of its members, or of the Commission.[74] There is no exact calendar for these meetings, but there is generally at least one meeting each month.

The meetings of the Council are, in the terms of the Council's own Rules of Procedure,[75] held *in camera*[76] but the rule is not an absolute one. In the first place, the Council may decide otherwise by unanimous vote. Secondly, the Commission is, again subject to contrary decision, invited to attend.[77] Thirdly, the members of the Council and of the Commission may bring officials with them, to assist them in their work.[78] Periodic attempts have been made to reduce the numbers to the minimum commensurate with the smooth running of the sessions.[79]

3—36   The course of business follows an agenda drawn up in accordance with the Rules of Procedure[80] by the President and fixed by the Council. The voting procedure depends in theory on the type of instrument to be voted upon, and the majority stipulated in the governing primary source of law. As stated in Article 148 (1) EEC, the normal rule is that the Council should act by simple majority, but special majorities are in fact more frequently required than not. Thus certain articles of the Treaties require the Council to reach a decision by a qualified majority, others by a unanimous vote.

The authors of the Treaty clearly intended that unanimity should be the rule at first, but that more "European" voting majorities should be used later in the development of the Communities. Thus quite a number of articles provide initially for unanimity, and for, *e.g.* qualified majority subsequently. It is in keeping with this aim that there should be no rule preventing members from abstaining. In some circumstances abstention will, however, block the adoption of acts requiring unanimity under the ECSC Treaty.[81]

Article 148 EEC as amended by Article 14 of the Acts of

[74] Merger Treaty, Art. 3.
[75] 79/868, O.J. 1979, L 268/1. See generally Houben, Les Conseils de Ministres des Communautés Européennes.
[76] *Ibid.* Art. 3 (1).
[77] *Ibid.* Art. 3 (2).
[78] *Ibid.* Art. 3 (3).
[79] There is a power to fix numbers: *ibid.* Art. 3 (3).
[80] *Ibid.* Art. 2.
[81] Art. 8, Merger Treaty.

Accession sets out the procedure for voting by qualified majority, which really amounts to a weighting of votes, giving the greatest *appui* to the largest States—France, Germany, Italy and the United Kingdom all being on an equal footing in this respect.

Where acts of the Council are required to be adopted by a qualified majority on a proposal from the Commission, 45 votes in favour are required.[82] On this basis, the measure can be carried by a minimum of five States. Where the act in question is required to be carried by qualified majority other than on proposal from the Commission at least six States are required to concur. Article 28 ECSC as amended by Article 7 of the Merger Treaty and by Article 12 of the Greek Act of Accession, achieves similar result, but the weighting is in terms of value of coal and steel output. The purpose of these formal requirements, quite apart from the obvious purpose of preventing States losing sight of reality, is to ensure that the will of the larger States shall not prevail over that of the smaller States, and vice versa.

3—37   The formal position as regards voting in the Council is as set out above. The question arises how far the voting procedures of the Council were affected by the so-called Luxembourg Accords, and how far the formal position reflects the reality.

The Luxembourg Accords[83] constitute the political settlement which terminated the crisis in the Communities of 1965. The work of the Communities came to a virtually complete standstill for a period of months during which the French absented themselves from the Council. Part of the "price" for the return of the French was the Luxembourg Communiqué, known as the Luxembourg Accords, dealing with many of the complaints of the French about the running of the Communities. "Accord" is something of a misnomer; to some extent the communiqué amounts to an agreement to disagree.

One of the matters on which the French delegation pressed for a statement related to the Council voting procedures. The statement of the Council as a whole was to the effect that:

> "where, in the case of decisions which may be taken by majority vote on a proposal of the Commission, very important interests of one or more partners are at stake, the Members of the Council will endeavour, within a reasonable time, to reach solutions which can be adopted by all the Members of the Council while respecting their mutual interests and those of the Community, in accordance with Article 2 of the Treaty."

To this the French delegation added a rider to the effect that it considered that:

> "where very important interests are at stake the discussion

[82] Art. 14, Greek Act of Accession.
[83] Bull. EC 1966 No. 3, p. 5.

must be continued until unanimous agreement is reached."

The six delegations as a group noted that there was a divergence of views on what should be done in the event of a failure to reach complete agreement.

3—38   It is generally accepted that the Accords have no force in law. The British Government has attached some importance to the Accords, but this is in recognition of their political reality rather than of their binding force. It must in any case be noted that the Council rarely in fact votes on a proposal, decisions in effect being taken by consensus. Where matters coming before the Council are controversial, and are not likely to meet with general acceptance, it is the practice to remit the issue to the Committee of Permanent Representatives or to a special working group to try to work out a solution which will be acceptable to all. It is only when the issue is ripe for decision that the Council will take a formal decision.

In order to expedite the discussion of matters before it, the Council resorts to two principal devices:

1. a division of the agenda into "A" and "B" points;[84] and
2. the use of a written procedure.[85]

Under the system of dividing the agenda into "A" and "B" points, the items submitted as "A" points are the points upon which the delegations of the Member States have already reached agreement in principle. At the political level of the Council very little remains to be done in relation to these matters except to approve the action proposed. If any difficulties arise, discussion is postponed. "B" points are the points presented to the Council on which an attempt to reach agreement is to be made in discussion at the Council meeting itself. These form the substantive part of the discussions.

The written procedure is generally reserved for matters which are urgent, and which require a simple affirmative.

3—39   As has already been indicated in the discussion of the Commission,[86] the vast majority of Council decisions require, under the Rome Treaties, to be taken on the basis of Commission proposals. The Commission thus exercises a decisive influence over the subject-matter of Council discussions, except where the Council is empowered to act on its own initiative. Although it can request that proposals be submitted to it[87] the Council cannot amend a Commission proposal except by unanimous vote,[88] a circumstance which theoretically makes it easier to adopt a proposal than to amend it. On the other hand, the Commission may alter its

[84] Art. 2 (6) and (7), Rules of Procedure.
[85] *Ibid.* Art. 6.
[86] *Supra*, para. 3–15.
[87] Art. 152 EEC.
[88] Art. 149 EEC.

original proposal as long as the Council has not acted, in particular where the Assembly has been consulted on that proposal, *i.e.* where the Assembly has suggested acceptable and desirable amendments.[89] This power is double-edged, in that it enables the Commission to keep improving its proposals, but it also enables it to act as a conciliatory body, mediating between national positions.

The arrangements under the ECSC Treaty are rather different, in that it is in general the Commission (High Authority) which takes the decision, but there are many circumstances in which the Council must first approve the Commission's proposal. There is much to be said for the argument that the difference between prior approval (or disapproval) and decision-making by the Council is more apparent than real.[90]

Apart from the proposal and approval mechanisms, there are, as already mentioned, various provisions in all three Treaties authorising action by the Council of its own motion. These represent the exception rather than the rule, and in no case do they relate to major questions of Community policy-making, but relate primarily to national policy and politics.[91]

3—40   Clearly, when a proposal comes before the Council a vast amount of work has to be done behind the scenes to reconcile points of view, and at least part of this work is done by the Commission, but the Commission is not in reality the body best adapted to reconciling national positions if it is to retain its position of independence. It is through Council machinery, therefore, that the task of attempting to arrive at a consensus amongst the Member States is undertaken before the Council itself votes upon the proposal. The body which in fact carries out the preparatory work is the Committee of Permanent Representatives of the Member States.[92] In addition, the Council is assisted by various committees and working groups, whether set up under specific articles of the Treaties, or otherwise, and of course by a Secretariat General, which initially served the ECSC special Council of Ministers, and was then expanded to serve the other two Councils. This body carries out the technical back-up work for the Council.

At least some assistance to the decision-making process should derive from the provision for mutual consultation under Article 15 of the Merger Treaty, but no institutionalised arrangement has as yet emerged. The consultation provided for under Article 26, second para., of the ECSC Treaty is, however, quite similar on its face, and many of the plans which fall within the autonomous powers of the High Authority are submitted to the Council under this provision through the Committee of Permanent Representatives, so that its eventual decision will reflect the general con-

---

[89] *Ibid.*
[90] *Cf. supra*, para. 3–24 and see *infra.*
[91] *e.g.* Arts. 84 (2), 136 and 217 EEC.
[92] *Infra*, para. 3–45.

sensus of views. This type of consultation, which certainly does not amount to an abnegation of existing High Authority powers (for the submission is to discussion, and not to decision or approval), does not differ materially in kind from that existing in fact within the ambit of the Rome Treaties between the Commission and the Committee of Permanent Representatives.

Powers of the Council

3—41   As has already been explained, the powers of the Council under the ECSC Treaty on the one hand, and the EEC and Euratom Treaties on the other, are dissimilar, in that the Council ostensibly plays a secondary role to the High Authority under the ECSC Treaty, while it is the dominant body under the Rome Treaties.

Under the EEC and Euratom Treaties[93] the Council is entrusted with tasks of co-ordination and with powers of decision. Under the ECSC Treaty it possesses similar responsibilities and powers[94] with the difference that it in general agrees with Commission proposals, rather than decides on them. Nevertheless, the High Authority has a large measure of independence, and the real limitation on this independence is not the veto of the Council, but the fact that, as must inevitably be the case in a Community with limited aims, the Member States have considerable concurrent powers.

3—42   The powers of the Council under the Rome Treaties are from all points of view much wider, and it is through the Council that all important decisions on a vast range of topics must be channelled. The powers of the Communities themselves are nevetheless powers of attribution, so the powers of the Council ultimately have limits set to them by the Member States. The Court of Justice has recognised that under the ECSC Treaty the Council has implied powers enabling it to execute specific requirements of the Treaty, even when methods of execution are not provided.[95] It seems evident that this principle would apply equally to the single Council of the Communities, but it is not clear how far it would go. Some indication is given by the cases on implied powers in external relations,[96] but the analogy is not exact. The line of reasoning in those cases is open to considerable extension, but could in no circumstances enable the Community to act, for example by regulation, where only a power of recommendation is granted.

3—43   The jurisdiction of the Council under the ECSC Treaty is not defined in the clear way that the functions of the Commission are

---

[93] Arts. 145 and 115 respectively.
[94] Arts. 26 and 28 ECSC.
[95] Case 8/55 *Fédéchar* v. *H.A.* [1954–56] E.C.R. 245. See also Cases 20 and 25/59 *Italy,* and *Netherlands* v. *H.A.* [1960] E.C.R. 325 and 355.
[96] *Infra*, paras. 29–43 *et seq*.

set out in Article 155 EEC, and indeed it is questionable how far an attempt to define the areas of responsibilities of the Council can serve any purpose. There are three factors involved here; in the first place, the Council itself possesses the power of decision if not perhaps in the absolute majority of instances, certainly nearly always where a decision going beyond the merely technical is concerned. Secondly, the Council is in any case the repository of any residual powers which may lie with the Community. A fair illustration of this is to be found in Article 235, which provides that it is for the Council to decide upon appropriate measures where the necessary powers to attain one of the objectives of the Community are not provided by the Treaty. Lastly, even assuming it were possible to provide a definitive list of Council powers by inspection, the cases on implied powers[97] show that these powers are capable of expansion, while practice indicates that they may not always be as wide as they may at first sight appear. Thus Article 238 states that association agreements are to be concluded by the Council, but a number of the agreements were concluded by the Council together with the Member States. This intervention, which does not appear to be provided for by the text of the Treaty, is justified legally by the fact that the subject-matter of these agreements extended beyond the powers of the Community. The justification is not perhaps entirely convincing but there is here a clear indication that the powers of the Council are neither totally clear-cut nor unchanging.

3—44   It is possible to indicate a number of areas in which the Council has primary responsibility for action under the EEC Treaty, even though it may only be able to act upon a proposal from the Commission. Thus Article 145, which itself sets out the Council's responsibilities, states that the Council is to ensure the co-ordination of the general economic policies of the Member States, and there are a number of other articles involving co-operation and co-ordination for which the Council bears some responsibility, although generally acting on proposals from the Commission where a power of action is given.[98] Secondly, it is invariably for the Council to lay down the rules for the expansion of Community activity: the Treaty itself contains guidelines, and the Council is to expand upon these on the basis of Commission proposals, or on its own motion in certain cases.[99] Thirdly, there is a group of powers exercised by the Council either of its own motion or on proposals from the Commission, which are of an *ad hoc* nature, generally involving discretionary powers to combat economic difficulties at

[97] *Ibid.*
[98] *e.g.* Arts. 6, 56 (2), 57 (2), 70 (1), 103, 105, 112, 116 (220).
[99] *e.g.* Arts. 84 (2), 126 (b), 136, 217, 223 (3), 227 (2), 228, 237 and 238.

a national level, and requiring the political, rather than the purely administrative touch.[1]

Consultative Bodies

*The Committee of Permanent Representatives of the
Member States*

3—45 The responsibilities of the Committee of Permanent Representatives, generally known as COREPER, in abbreviation of the French *Comité de Representants Permanents*, are stated in Article 4 of the Merger Treaty to be the preparation of the work of the Council and the execution of the tasks assigned to it by the Council.

COREPER was not set up by any of the Treaties establishing the Communities, but a similar body, known as COCOR (*Commission de Coordination*) was established under Article 10 of the ECSC Council Rules of Procedure, permitting the creation of commissions. Article 151 EEC provided for the creation of a similar committee for the Rome Treaty Communities, its task and powers to be defined by the Council. COCOR, and the single COREPER which had served the Councils of the EEC and Euratom, have been combined in a single COREPER, whose existence is recognised rather than provided for by Article 4 of the Merger Treaty. In so far as that article sets out the responsibilities of COREPER, it does no more than institutionalise Article 16 of the EEC Council Rules of Procedure[2] and does not clarify the Committee's legal position. Article 16 of the Council Rules of Procedure thus still provides the basis of the powers and duties of the Committee. Its powers are primarily confined to the preparation of the work of the Council, but it may set up working groups to do preparatory work or to undertake studies. Co-operation with the Commission is built-in, for the Commission is normally to be invited to be represented at the Committee and on its working groups.

3—46   The internal workings of the Committee are described as being at the pre-political stage, that is to say that its function is to narrow and clarify areas of dispute and difficulty, and to prepare issues for eventual political decision. Its members are diplomats rather than politicians and, as is indicated by the name of the Committee, they are the Permanent Representatives of the Member States to the Community. In this capacity they constitute an integral part of the Community decision-making machinery. Some

[1] *e.g.* Arts. 8 (3), 8 (5), 25 (1), 28, 45 (3), 70 (2), second sub-para., 73, 76, 93 (2), 98, 108, 109 (3). Arts. 115 and 226 are conspicuous by their absence from this list, but both are concerned with essentially temporary situations.
[2] The origins of this provision antedate the Merger Treaty: the current rules, 79/868, O.J. 1979, L. 268/1, effectively reproduce the old so-called provisional rules of the Communities on this point.

36

doubt has been expressed as to the possibility of delegation of powers to the Committee. Although one of the functions of the Committee is to carry out the tasks entrusted to it by the Council, it would seem that no delegation of substantive powers is possible. The Committee is not a group of alternates for the Council, and its members have no voting power when acting as substitutes. In the same way the Committee, not being a politically responsible body, cannot be and is not entrusted with powers of decision. Its prime function must rather be to provide the element of continuity between Council meetings, and to prepare the way for the actual decision-making process by exploring the area of possible compromise, or at least through informal contacts.

3—47   Specific aspects of the work of the Committee are dealt with by special committees or working groups, set up by COREPER itself. Other special committees are set up directly by the Council and stand in the same relationship to the Council as COREPER. The most important of these are the Special Agriculture Committee,[3] and the so-called Article 113 Committee[4] appointed by the Council to assist the Commission in the negotiation of commercial agreements.

The regular aspects of the work of the Committee are directed by the President of the Committee, who presides over it, and gives it considerable directional force. The office of President rotates with the office of President of the Council, thus emphasising the close links between the two bodies.

3—48   The meetings of the Committee do not follow the form of Council meetings, for the purpose of its meetings, which may be of a quite informal nature, is to attempt to arrive at a general consensus with the assistance of national experts and with the Commission (the outcome going down as "A" points on the Council agenda—which can be agreed upon by the Council without discussion), rather than to take preliminary decisions by some system of majority vote. Nevertheless, the conclusions arrived at by the Committee have considerable decisional force. This decision-making process, carried out by a body which is not politically responsible to an elected body, has been questioned in some quarters, but the Commission has stated that the function of co-ordination played by the Committee is most valuable[5] and it is undoubtedly this function which justifies the existence of the Committee.

[3] Initially set up under Art. 5 (4), acceleration decision of May 12, 1960, J.O. 1960, 1217.
[4] *Infra*, para. 29–17.
[5] Hallstein, *L'Evolution des Communautés Européennes*, Ann. Eur. Vol. VI, p. 8.

Consultative Committees

3—49   As already mentioned, the Communities are assisted in various ways by a proliferation of other committees. Perhaps the most important of these are the Economic and Social Committee[6] common to the EEC and Euratom, and the Consultative Committee, discharging substantially similar functions in the context of the ECSC.

ECSC Consultative Committee

3—50   The ECSC Consultative Committee[7] comprises equal numbers of producers, or workers and of consumers and dealers, appointed by the Council. The members, although to greater or less extent nominees of representative organisations[8] enjoy independence of those bodies in the exercise of their functions.

The conduct of the Committee is in the hands of a chairman and officers, elected for one year, assisted by a Secretariat. The Committee itself has four standing committees on general objectives, on markets and prices, on labour and on research and development. *Ad hoc* committees can also be appointed for special problems.

The Economic and Social Committee

3—51   In the same way that the Consultative Committee of the ECSC is singled out for special mention in Article 7 of the Treaty of Paris, so the Economic and Social Committee receives individual mention in the Treaties of Rome: Article 4 (2) EEC, Article 3 (2) Euratom; both articles state that the Council and the Commission are assisted by an Economic and Social Committee acting in an advisory capacity. It is clear that there is here in question only one Economic and Social Committee, for this is one of the common bodies in terms of Article 5 of the Convention on Certain Institutions Common to the European Communities.[9]

The Committee is set up by Article 193 EEC,[10] which gives it an advisory status. It consists of representatives of the various categories of economic and social activity (particularised in the EEC Treaty as including producers, farmers, carriers, workers, dealers, craftsmen, professional occupations and representatives of the general public). Members of the Committee may not be bound by any mandatory instructions whatsoever.[11] Members are appointed by the Council, on the basis of lists produced by the Member States, after consultation with the Commission.[12] There

[6] Rules of Procedure O.J. 1974, L 228/1.
[7] Arts. 18 and 19 ECSC, amended by Art. 144, 1972 Act of Accession.
[8] *Cf.* Arts. 18 ECSC.
[9] *Supra*, para. 2–01, note 2 for reference.
[10] Art. 165 Euratom, Rules of Procedure, J.O. 1968, L 42/1.
[11] Art. 194 EEC, third para.
[12] Art. 195 EEC.

is also the possibility[13] of obtaining the opinion of European bodies which are representative of the various economic and social sectors to which the activities of the Communities are of concern. This facility has not been extensively used. Article 17 of the Greek Act of Accession, amending Article 194 EEC, first para., fixes the number of members of the Committee at six for Luxembourg, nine each for Denmark, Norway and Ireland; 12 each for Belgium, Greece and the Netherlands, and 24 each for the United Kingdom, France, Germany and Italy. In allotting seats account is to be taken of the need to ensure adequate representation of the various categories of economic and social activity.[14] In practice the system of representation by category works well, and there is considerable solidarity within the groups.

3—52   The internal structure of the Committee, based upon its Rules of Procedure[15] is similar to that of the Consultative Committee, but the mandate of chairman and officers is for two years instead of one.[16] The most notable new feature lies in the institutionalised creation of specialised sections of the Committee for the principal fields covered by the Treaties, in particular for transport and agriculture.[17] The sections can be consulted only through the main committee. Sub-committees can also be created within the Committee for the preparation of draft opinions for the Committee itself.

In addition, members of the Committee may form groups representative of the various categories of economic and social life.[18] In practice on the basis of this provision the Committee is divided into three groups: employers; workers; and "others." These groups serve primarily as *fora* within which common positions to be taken in plenary meetings are elaborated, but the groups do not, with the exception possibly of the workers' group, display any marked cohesion.

3—53   The Committee must be consulted by the Council or the Commission wherever the Treaties so provide.[19] It may be consulted in all cases which are considered appropriate.[20] Where a specialised section of the Committee is seised of the question by the Committee, that section's opinion goes forward with that of the plenary Committee.[21]

The Economic and Social Committee is in theory weaker than the Consultative Committee, in that its rules of procedure are

---

[13] *Ibid.*
[14] *Ibid*, para. 1.
[15] *Supra*, note 10.
[16] Art. 196 EEC.
[17] Art. 197 EEC, Art. 169 Euratom.
[18] Rules of Procedure, Art. 19.
[19] Art. 198 EEC.
[20] *Ibid.*
[21] Art. 44, Rules of Procedure.

subject to approval by the Council (as are the rules of procedure of all the committees provided for in the EEC Treaty),[22] and in that it cannot convene its own sessions.[23] Nevertheless, it enjoys greater influence than its ECSC counterpart, and in practice the second of the above difficulties is overcome in that the Committee can indicate that it is interested in a question, whereupon a reference will generally be made to it under Article 198 EEC. Additionally, under Article 20, third para., of its own Rules of Procedure, the Committee may, with the prior approval of the Council or of the Commission, be convened to make a study of matters on which, under the Treaties, it must or may be consulted.

The Committee is nevertheless not an autonomous institution of the Communities and does not possess any powers of its own, but it has proved most valuable as a platform for discussion.

Other Committees

3—54   A wide variety of other committees of an advisory character has been set up either under specific Treaty provisions or under secondary legislation, especially in the agricultural sector.[24]

The European Parliament

3—55   As already mentioned, the Assemblies provided for in the three Treaties[25] are constituted by a single Assembly. Provision for a single Assembly is made by Articles 1 and 2 of the Convention on Certain Institutions Common to the European Community.[26] The Convention provides that the powers and jurisdiction conferred upon the Assembly by the Rome Treaties are to be exercised by a single Assembly, taking the place of the ECSC Common Assembly, and exercising its powers and jurisdiction. After the establishment of the Rome Treaty Communities the Assembly initially called itself the European Parliamentary Assembly,[27] but now calls itself the European Parliament.[28]

3—56   Article 137 EEC provides that the Assembly is to exercise the advisory and supervisory powers conferred upon it by the Treaty. Article 20 ECSC omits mention of any advisory capacity, but such

---

[22] Art. 153.
[23] Art. 196 EEC.
[24] For a comprehensive list of Council and Commission committees see Bull. Supp. 2/80.
[25] Arts. 7 and 20 *et seq.* ECSC, Arts. 4 and 137 *et seq.*. EEC, Arts. 3 and 107 *et seq.* Euratom.
[26] Annexed to the Treaty of Rome.
[27] Resolution of March 20, 1958, J.O. 1958, 6.
[28] Resolution of March 30, 1962, J.O. 1962, 1045.

is implicit, inasmuch as the Assembly is required to be consulted in various contexts.

If a parliament is to be defined as an elected legislature with real powers of decision, the European Parliament does not as yet qualify. True, it is now an elected body, but it is certainly not a legislature, and although it is an autonomous institution, its powers are not extensive.

3—57   Article 137 EEC[29] states that the Assembly is to consist of representatives of the peoples of the States brought together in the Community. This phrase indicates that representatives are to be more than mere national nominees and it also contains a germ of the idea of direct election to the European Parliament, but in fact members were designated by their respective national parliaments from among the members of those parliaments in accordance with a procedure laid down by each Member State[30] until the installation of a directly elected Parliament under the Decision and annexed Act concerning the Election of the Representatives of the Assembly by Direct Universal Suffrage of September 20, 1976.[31] Following direct elections held in June 1979 the directly elected Parliament met for the first time in July 1979.

In accordance with Article 2 of the 1976 Act as amended by Article 10 of the Greek Act of Accession the number of representatives elected in each Member State is: Luxembourg 6, Ireland 15, Denmark 16, Belgium and Greece 24, Netherlands 25, and the United Kingdom, France, Germany and Italy 81 each: total 434.

Representatives are elected for five years, running from the first session following each election.[32]

3—58   Article 4 of the 1976 Act requires members of the European Parliament (MEPs) to vote on an individual and personal basis. They may not be bound by any instructions and may not receive a binding mandate. It is still possible for an MEP to be a member of a national Parliament at the same time (the so-called dual mandate),[33] but not to be a member of the Government of a Member State.[34] Membership of or being a staff member of a Community institution, body or committee is similarly incompatible.[35] The 1976 Act envisages creation of a uniform electoral procedure.[36] For the time being national electoral procedures apply[37] (including by-election procedures),[38] only the period of the election being

[29] And Arts. 20 ECSC and 107 Euratom.
[30] Under Art. 138 (1) EEC.
[31] *Supra*, para. 2–02, note 11.
[32] Art. 3, 1976 Act.
[33] Art. 5, 1976 Act.
[34] *Ibid*. Art. 6.
[35] *Ibid*.
[36] *Ibid*. Art 7. (1).
[37] *Ibid*. Art 7. (2).
[38] *Ibid*. Art. 12.

regulated by Community rules.[39] Credentials of representatives are examined by the Assembly.[40]

Sessions of the Parliament

3—59 The Rules of Procedure, which in this regard more or less follow the applicable Treaty dispositions[41] provide for a single annual session of the Assembly, meeting without requiring to be convened on the second Tuesday in March. The Assembly may also meet in extraordinary session at the request of a majority of its members, or at the request of the Council or of the Commission.[42] In practice the Parliament meets about 10 times a year for up to a week or more at a time, but a continuity in its working is preserved as a result of the fact that its standing committees work during the intervals. The standing committees are responsible primarily for the preparation of debates on topics falling within their terms of reference (foreign affairs, agriculture, social policy, transport etc.) but they may also report on any other matters coming before the Parliament which they may consider to be of concern.

The running of the Parliament

3—60 The Assembly elects its own President and officers from amongst its Members. Provision is currently made for a President and 12 Vice-Presidents (together constituting the Bureau)[43] and at least three "Quaestors."[44] The President, as is usual in the Community bodies, provides much of the direction to the work of the Parliament.[45] Unlike the President of the Council, however, the President of the Parliament is required to act with total impartiality, and in the chamber fulfils many of the functions fulfilled by the Speaker of the House of Commons. Day to day running of the Parliament is conducted by its officers, assisted by a Secretariat. The running of the Parliament is governed generally by the Rules of Procedure,[46] laid down by the Parliament itself under Article 142 EEC, and not subject to any confirmation, *e.g.* by the Council. The Rules represent in some sense a synthesis of national procedures. The proceedings of the Parliament are published.[47] All

---

[39] *Ibid*. Arts. 9 and 10.
[40] *Ibid*. Art. 11 and Parliament Rules of Procedure Rule 3.
[41] Art. 22 ECSC, Art. 139 EEC, Art. 109 Euratom as amended by Merger Treaty, Art. 27 (1). Current Rules of Procedure adopted November 1979, O.J. 1979, C 309.
[42] Art. 139 EEC, second para.
[43] Parliament Rules of Procedure Rule 5 (1).
[44] Rule 7A: Quaestors are members of the Bureau in advisory capacity: they are responsible for administrative and financial matters directly concerning MEPs. There are in fact five quaestors.
[45] *Cf.* Rules 8 to 11, 50A and 53: under the latter provisions the President is the Parliament's legal representative.
[46] *Supra*, note 41.
[47] In the manner laid down in the Rules: Treaty, Art. 142.

the written questions appear, with their answers, in the Communications and Information (C) Series of the *Official Journal of the European Communities*, as do minutes of all its debates, which are required to be published in the *Official Journal* within one month.[48] The full debates appear in a separate annex to the *Official Journal*, entitled "Debates."

Political groupings

3—61   The sittings of the Parliament follow the form of the sittings of a normal parliamentary body. The delegates do not, however, sit as members of national political parties, but rather as members of political groupings which are supposed to transcend national frontiers. The political groupings are constituted on a formal basis, with a minimum number of adherents, depending on the number of countries embraced by its membership.[49] In general the groups, besides sitting together, are represented by spokesmen speaking for the whole group. The chairmen of the groups have a certain official status. In particular they are members of the enlarged bureau,[50] which determines the agenda and treatment of questions.[51] MEPs are not required to belong to a group, although most do. Non-attached MEPs designate two of their number to the enlarged bureau.[52]

Powers of the Parliament

3—62   Article 137 describes the Assembly as exercising advisory and supervisory powers. Its advisory powers are those enabling it to give its opinion on projects which must (or may) be submitted to it before the Council takes a decision thereon.

The right to be consulted for an opinion

3—63   The power to give an opinion, which is more accurately expressed as the right to be consulted, stems from a large number of provisions in the Treaties, and in particular in the EEC Treaty.[53] Each of these provisions confers a power of decision on the

---

[48] Rule 17 (4).
[49] Rule 36 (5). On December 31, 1980, the then 410 seats in the Parliament were distributed as follows Socialist Group 113; European People's Party 107; European Democratic Group 63; Communist and Allies Group 44; Liberal and Democratic Group 40; Group of European Progressive Democrats 22; Technical Co-ordination Group for the Defence of the Interests of Independent Groups and Members 11; Non-affiliated 10. Several Greek parliamentarians attended Parliament's proceedings as observers. (Fourteenth General Report (1980), point 16).
[50] Rule 5 (2).
[51] Rules 12 and 46 to 47A.
[52] Rule 38A (2): without right to vote.
[53] EEC Treaty, Arts. 7, 14, 43, 54, 56, 57, 63, 75, 87, 100, 126, 127, 201 (203) 228, 235, 236, 238.

Council, but the exercise of that power is made in each case dependent upon prior consultation with the Parliament for its opinion. The Commission is not generally required to consult the Parliament, but under certain provisions of the ECSC Treaty, it is so obliged.[54] Quite apart from any obligation to this effect, however, the Commission of all three Communities has found it convenient to consult the Parliament more or less informally on a wide range of topics, although without ever going so far as to concede the demands of the Parliament itself, which has expressed the desire to be consulted on all matters. The Commission has held out against this, arguing correctly that this would amount to a usurpation of its decision-making and proposal powers, which would in effect be *ultra vires*. A limitation was in any case placed on informal consultations by the Luxembourg Accords of January 1966, which *inter alia* forbade the publication of Commission proposals before their communication to the Council.[55]

3—64   Whether or not the Parliament is consulted formally (and it is clear that even where there is no duty to consult, it may nevertheless be consulted and give an opinion), the opinion of the Parliament is without binding force. Decisions must refer to any proposals or opinions which are required to be obtained pursuant to the Treaties,[56] but it is open to the Council to ignore the substance of the opinion, and the Commission may even alter its proposals after the Parliament has been consulted, although this liberty is subject to certain limits.[57] But the Council may not forego the formality of consulting the Parliament and actually obtaining an opinion.[58]

Nevertheless, the functions of the Parliament are not confined merely to giving opinions on matters on which it is consulted, for it may discuss any matter it chooses, and its resolutions have not been without influence on matters which would otherwise have been outside its sphere of competence. The Parliament has now acquired the last word on the adoption of the Community budget. The Parliament's budgetary powers are considered in the next section, on the financial provisions of the Treaties.

Supervisory powers

3—65   Apart from its new powers in budgetary matters, which contain a strong supervisory element, the Parliament has a degree of supervisory power over the other Community institutions. For, in the first place, the Commission is required to submit to the Assembly an annual General Report on the three Communities,[59]

---

[54] Arts. 95 and budget provisions.
[55] See generally *supra*. para. 3–37.
[56] Art. 190 EEC.
[57] EP doc 110/67, Cases 41, 44 and 45/69 *Quinine Cartel cases* [1970] E.C.R. 661, 733, 769.
[58] Cases 138 and 139/79 *Roquette*, and *Maizena* v. *Council* [October 29, 1980].
[59] Merger Treaty, Art. 18.

which the Assembly discusses in depth.[60] Secondly, in so far as the Parliament may discuss any matter and issue an opinion on any matter, a spontaneous discussion of a matter, subsequently brought to the attention of the Council or Commission, entails a supervisory element.

Thirdly, provision is made for Members of the Commission to attend all meetings of the Parliament and for them to be heard on behalf of the Commission.[61] The Council also has a right to be heard in accordance with the conditions laid down in the Council's Rules of Proceudre.[62] Under these it is represented by the President or any of its members but it may also present its view by means of a written statement.[63]

Both the Council and the Commission are expected to keep abreast of Parliamentary affairs. In so far as this requires the two institutions to follow its activities fairly closely, the Parliament itself is able to engage in a process of dialogue with them, which, if not involving an element of control, at least enables the three bodies to form an idea of each others' thinking. This dialogue is in some degree institutionalised by annual colloquies between all the institutions, but the exchange is perhaps of too formal a character to be of any real value.

3—66   Associated with the dialogue resulting from the right to be heard are the now very elaborate provisions in the Parliament's Rules on questions. Under the Treaty the Commission is required to reply orally or in writing to questions put to it by the Assembly or by its members.[64] The Council has in practice accepted a similar obligation. The mechanism now also applies to the Foreign Ministers meeting in political co-operation.[65]

There are in effect four distinct procedures. Commonest are questions for written answer,[66] which any MEP has a right to put down without scrutiny. There are then questions to be dealt with by oral procedure without debate[67] and a right to one or two supplementaries. The Bureau, enlarged by the Chairmen of the Political Groups, can decide to convert this type of question into a question for written answer or for oral answer at question time.[68] The question time procedure,[69] first introduced by the Parliamentarians from Westminster, essentially opens the oral procedure without debate to single supplementaries from any MEP.

[60] Art. 143 EEC.
[61] Art. 140 EEC.
[62] *Ibid.*
[63] Council Rules of Procedure 79/868, O.J. 1979, L 268/1, Art. 19.
[64] Art. 140.
[65] Paris communique, December 9 & 10, 1974, Bull. EC 12–1974 point 1104, 4.
[66] Rule 45.
[67] Rule 46.
[68] *Ibid.*
[69] Rule 47A.

Questions for oral procedure with debate[70] can be set down only by a committee, a political group or five or more MEPs. Each political group has the right to have not more than one question dealt with by this procedure during each part session. Again, this type of question can be converted to one of the others by the enlarged Bureau.[71] A short debate of this type can also be called immediately after question time.[72]

Paradoxically, the answers to written questions probably reach the widest public since they alone are published in the "C" series of the *Official Journal*, and not in the special European Parliament supplements.

3—67   The final supervisory power of the Parliament consists in the motion of censure. Provision is made[73] for the tabling of motions of censure on the activities of the Commission. The Assembly may not vote thereon until at least three days after such a motion has been tabled and then only by open vote. If the motion is carried by a two-thirds majority of the votes cast, representing a majority of the members of the Assembly, the members of the Commission must resign as a body, but they are to continue to deal with current business until replaced. Motions of censure have now been put down on several occasions but have either subsequently withdrawn or not been carried. Setting down of a motion and its subsequent withdrawal only emphasises, however, that it is far too crude a means of controlling the day-to-day activities of the Commission. It is doubtful whether the existence of the power has even deterrent force.

Conclusions

3—68   If the judgment that the influence of the Parliament is about as telling as that of an annual general meeting of a joint stock company seemed unduly harsh in 1973,[74] it cannot be said to have any reality now. The MPs from Westminster who arrived in 1973 may not have been as successful as they hoped in breathing life into the European Parliament, but attitudes certainly began to evolve. The two decisive changes have been the move to direct elections and the new budgetary procedures. If it is still early days for drawing firm conclusions on the effect of direct elections, it is already apparent that budgetary powers have become the focus of debate on the extension, express or tacit, of the Parliament's powers. Legally these powers can only be extended by Treaty (which, in the United Kingdom must be endorsed by Act of Parliament, and not under the affirmative resolution procedure of section 1 (3) of

[70] Rule 47.
[71] *Ibid.*
[72] Rule 47B.
[73] Treaty, Art. 144.
[74] 1st edition of this work, para. 6–13.

the European Communities Act 1972[75]). But the differences of interpretation of the conciliation procedure[76] are a pointer to how changes may come about informally.

Financial Provisions[77]

3—69 The financial provisions of the EEC Treaty are Articles 199 to 209 as amended.[78]

All items of Community revenue and expenditure (including those relating to the various more or less autonomous Community funds) are included in an annual budget on the basis of estimates.[79] In principle the budget is to be balanced.[80] Community expenditure is now met entirely from Community own resources, provided for by the Council Decision of April 21, 1970.[81]

From January 1, 1975, the revenue from all charges and duties applied in trade with third countries became own resources of the Community, to be entered directly in the budget of the Communities, subject only to a 10 per cent. refund in respect of collection expenses.[82] In addition provision is made[83] for the Community to receive an amount not exceeding 1 per cent. of the total "take" in value added tax in the Member States. This provision became fully operative with the 1980 budget.

Even before accession in 1973, and despite transitional provision both in the 1970 Budget Treaty and in the 1972 Act of Accession, it was recognised that straight application of the own resources provisions was likely to mean that the United Kingdom's net budget contribution would remain consistently higher than its percentage share of Community GNP.

---

[75] European Assembly Elections Act 1978, s. 6.

[76] *Infra*. para. 3–75.

[77] On this section, see in particular the valuable article by Sir Charles Sopwith, *Legal Aspects of the Community Budget* 17 C.M.L. Rev. 1980, 315–347 and "EEC Budget," House of Lords Select Committee on the European Communities, session 1979–80, 2nd Report, June 19, 1979.

[78] Notably by the Budget Treaties of 1970 and 1975, *supra*. paras. 2–01 & 2–02, notes 5 and 10.

[79] Art. 199. Identical procedures apply to supplementary budgets, under the Financial Regulations, *infra*, note 90. European Development Fund finance is dealt with separately, with an ad hoc key of contributions. The ECSC budget is also entered separately.

[80] *Ibid.*

[81] J.O. 1970, L 94/19 and *supra* para. 2–01, note 5, Art. 4 (1). Implementing Regs. 2891/77 & 2892/77, O.J. 1977, L 336/1 & 8. Enforcement is nevertheless for Member States: Cases 178–180/73 *Belgium & Luxembourg* v. *Mertens* [1974] E.C.R. 383 and Cases 265/78 *Ferwerda* v. *Produktschap* [1980] E.C.R. 617 and 66/77 *Ammin. delle Finanze* v. *Salumi* [1980] E.C.R. 1237. Greece receives a transitional rebate inversely proportionate to the rate of application of the Community rules: Arts. 124 to 127 of the Act of Accession.

[82] *Ibid.* Arts. 2 to 4.

[83] *Ibid.* Art. 4.0.73% in 1980: 2.654 MEUA.

3—70   As the corner-stone of the United Kingdom's renegotiation of
terms of entry in 1974 a so called financial mechanism was
established,[84] without doing injury to the own resources principle,
whereby a Member State with below average productivity and
growth and above average contributions relative to GNP can claim
a corresponding payment from the budget. In practice the financial
mechanism did not really serve to alleviate the net burden on the
United kingdom because up until the end of 1979 the gap between
the UK gross contribution and GNP was never wide enough to
trigger the mechanism, this gross contribution being held down by
the operation of transitional arrangements under Article 131 of
the Act of Accession. Meanwhile the UK level of receipts from the
Community budget had fallen so low (£947 million by 1979) that
the net position was regarded as unacceptable.

In 1980 after particularly long and difficult negotiations various
hurdles in the basic regulation were removed or suspended in
favour of the United Kingdom pending a fundamental review to
take effect in 1983 at the latest.[85] At the same time supplementary measures were adopted, specifically for the United
Kingdom, for 1980 and 1981 with provision for extension into
1982.[86] These are to consist in financial assistance for programmes
of domestic public expenditure designed to improve the country's
social and economic infrastructure.

3—71   Expenditure under the budget is authorised for one financial
year (corresponding with the calendar year) and carry-overs are
permitted to the next year only,[87] although practice varies from
budget chapter to chapter. If no budget has been voted at the
beginning of the financial year (as occurred in 1980) a system of
"provisional twelfths"[88] of the previous financial year's appropriations is applied. Under this system a sum equivalent to one-
twelfth of the budget appropriations for the preceding financial
year may be spent each month in respect of any budget chapter or
other subdivision. These appropriations are financed by monthly
contributions from the Member States, again on the previous
year's scales. Subject to any necessary Council decision, the Commission is responsible for implementing the budget[89] in accordance with financial regulations laid down by the Council, acting
unanimously on a proposal from the Commission and after consulting the Assembly and obtaining the opinion of the Court of
Auditors.[90] There is a limited power to transfer appropriations

[84] Reg. 1172/76, O.J. 1976, L131/7.
[85] Reg. 2743/80, O.J. 1980, L284/1. Both this regulation and Reg. 2744 (note 86) are
   supplemented by Reg. 284/81, O.J. 1981, L32/1, to compensate Greece for the pre-
   accession period.
[86] Reg. 2744/80, O.J. 1980, L284/4.
[87] Art. 202 EEC.
[88] Art. 204.
[89] See Ehlermann, "Article 205 of the EEC Treaty" 1980 FIDE.
[90] Art. 209: Financial Regulation of December 21, 1977, O.J. 1977, L356/1, last amended
   by Financial Reg. 80/1176 O.J. 1980, L345/23.

from one budget-heading to another.[91]

The Commission submits annual accounts to the Council and to the Assembly relating to the implementation of the budget.[92] These accounts and the accounts of subsidiary bodies are examined by the Court of Auditors,[93] in effect an accounting body. Discharge of the accounts is given by the Assembly acting on a recommendation from the Council, which itself acts by qualified majority.[94] For this purpose the inputs for the Assembly and the Council are the accounts and financial statement provided by the Commission and the report of the Court of Auditors and any replies of the institutions under audit to the observations of the Court of Auditors.

Court of Auditors

3—72   The court of Auditors, established by the 1975 Budgetary Powers Treaty, is constituted along by now familiar lines.[95] It consists of 10[96] members appointed by the Council acting unanimously after consulting the Assembly for a renewable term of six years. (When the first appointments were made four members were appointed for four years only so as to provide for staggering). Membership is chosen from among persons who belong to or have belonged in their respective countries to external audit bodies or who are especially qualified for this office. Provisions on independence, outside appointments, replacement and compulsory retirement, etc., closely parallel those applying to the Commission. Other conditions of employment, etc, are laid down by the Council. Members enjoy those provisions on Privileges and Immunities applying to the Judges of the Court of Justice.

The audit is based on accounts and records.[97] It may if necessary be performed on the spot in the institutions of the Community and in the Member States, in the latter event in liaison with national audit bodies.[98] The Court of Auditors draws up an annual report. The first such report seems to have been fairly critical.[99] Furthermore procedures for carrying out audits have not been without difficulties.[1] Besides the audit function the Court of Auditors

[91] Art. 205. Towards the end of the financial year such adjustments have in practice to be made weekly.

[92] Art. 205a.

[93] Art. 206a.

[94] Art. 206b.

[95] Art. 206 EEC as introduced by the 1975 Treaty. The Court of Auditors replaced the Audit Board and Auditor of the separate Communities: Art. 22, Merger Treaty, as amended.

[96] As amended by Greek Act of Accession, Art. 18.

[97] Art. 206a (1) and (3).

[98] *Ibid.* para. (3).

[99] *Ibid.* para. 4 and see "Financial Control in the Community," House of Commons HC 159 xxxi (May 7, 1980). Annual Report for 1980, O.J. 1980, C242.

[1] *Cf.* Case 267/78 *Commission* v. *Italy* [1980] E.C.R. 31: a Member State may not contest the Commission's power to exercise its supervision over own resources.

may submit observations on specific questions and deliver opinions at the request of one of the institutions.[2] It has an overall duty to assist the Assembly and the Council in exercising their powers of control over the implementation of the budget.[3]

Budgetary Procedure

3—73   The central area of interest both as regards the financial provisions and more generally as regards the scope of powers of the Assembly lies in the procedures now contained in Article 203 for adoption of the budget.

The Commission presents a preliminary draft budget to the Council. The Council, consulting the Commission and other institutions concerned where it intends to depart from the Commission draft, establishes the draft budget and forwards it to the Assembly.

The draft budget as presented consists essentially of two types of entry: items relating to "expenditure necessarily resulting from the Treaty or from acts adopted in accordance therewith" (*i.e.* for the most part under regulations creating a right to payments in connection with the agricultural policy); and other items to which no such legal obligation or commitment attaches. This distinction is usually referred to as relating to obligatory and non-obligatory expenditure.

Acting within 45 days, the Assembly can propose modifications in relation to obligatory expenditure but real powers arise in relation to non-obligatory entries. Here the Assembly can itself amend the budget, subject only to a ceiling, called the maximum rate of increase, declared by the Commission after consulting the Economic Policy Committee as it results from the trend in terms of volume of national GNPs, the average variation in national budgets and the trend of cost of living. (The maximum rate usually becomes relevant at the second reading by Council and Assembly (below)). In practice therefore amendments relate to changes within the limits of the proposed budget while modifications relate to proposals for new expenditure. If the Assembly approves the budget or fails to act the budget is adopted or deemed adopted at this stage.

3—74   The amendments and modifications proposed by the Assembly are next put before the Council. The Council can modify any of the amendments and it can reject any of the modifications. In theory if the Council does not act within 15 days the budget is deemed to be finally adopted. In practice, however, the Council further modifies the draft budget and sends it back to the Assembly. The Assembly then has a further 15 days in which to amend or

---

[2] Art. 206a (4): a power used in relation to the 1980 package of financial mechanisms: *supra*, notes 85 & 86.
[3] *Ibid.*

reject the modifications to its amendments (non-obligatory expenditure) made by the Council and to adopt the budget accordingly. If the Assembly has not acted the budget is deemed to be finally adopted. Exceptionally ("if there are important reasons") the Assembly can reject the entire draft budget and request a new draft budget.[4] In summary, therefore, the Assembly now has a substantial say over obligatory expenditure and the last word on non-obligatory expenditure.

These are the formal mechanisms. Their operation is, in theory, facilitated by a process of annual negotiation or "concertation" which takes place between Council and Parliament, with the Commission participating. In practice, this is an occasion for formal statements: no matters of substance are resolved.

3—75   Having regard to the new powers conferred by the 1970 Budget Treaty, which became fully effective on January 1, 1975, and to the further amendments to Article 203 which were to be agreed in the Budgetary Powers Treaty of July 22, 1975, the Joint Declaration of March 4, 1975,[5] instituted a procedure which might be invoked by Council or Parliament in respect of proposals "for Community acts of general application which have appreciable financial implications and of which the adoption is not required by virtue of acts already in existence." In other words, it is designed to apply to instruments usually of a procedural/financial nature with significant financial implications relating to non-obligatory expenditure. The procedure is to be initiated if the Council intends to depart from the opinion adopted by the European Parliament on the Commission's proposal. The object of conciliation is to reconcile the position of the two institutions. After a slow start, the Parliament seems to have come to regard the conciliation procedure as an important battle-ground for the extension of its powers. The Council has been equally adamant that the procedure has a limited purpose relating to financial instruments. It seems that both parties regard the mechanism as being of limited value at present.

Units of account

3—76   Article 207 provides for the budget to be drawn up in a unit of account determined in accordance with the Financial Regulation.[6] Initially this unit of account (u.a.) was tied to a fixed parity equal to 0.88 mgs of fine gold (itself then equal to one US dollar). However, with the currency movements in the early 1970s this system ceased to be appropriate. The situation became extremely complicated with a number of different units of account being used in different areas.[7] Proposals were therefore made to harmonise on

---

[4] This actually occurred with the 1980 budget, which was not adopted until July 9, 1980: Bull EC 7/8 1980 point 2.3.70 and refs.
[5] O.J. 1975, C 89/1.
[6] *Supra,* note 90.
[7] See WQ 61/76, O.J. 1976 C158/35.

51

a single unit of account, the new unit of account being designated European Unit of Account (EUA) to distinguish it from the earlier u.a. system. The EUA was introduced gradually into the various areas of Community activity. It was applied to the budget by the new Financial Regulation of December 21, 1977.[8] The European Monetary System (EMS)[9] brought with it a new unit of account, the European Currency Unit (ECU). From January 1, 1981, the ECU replaced the EUA in all Community legal instruments.[10]

[9] Regs. 3180 and 3181/80, O.J. 1980, L379/1 & 2 and see generally paras. 24–24, *infra.*
[10] Reg. 3308/80, O.J. 1980, L345/1. See also Financial Reg. 80/1176, O.J. 1980, L345/23. Rates of conversion into national currency are published at frequent intervals in the C Series of the *Official Journal.*

Chapter 4

EUROPEAN COUNCIL: POLITICAL COOPERATION[1]

4—01   The final communiqué of the Paris Summit of December 9 and 10 1974,[2] established the European Council. Recognising the need for an overall approach to Community internal problems and the external problems facing Europe, provision was made for the Heads of Government "to meet, accompanied by the Ministers of Foreign Affairs, three times a year and, wherever necessary, in the Council of the Communities and in the context of Political Co-operation."

Under this formula, the occasional European Summits were institutionalised. The mechanisms already established for political co-operation in the field of foreign affairs became both responsible to the European Council and the initiators and co-ordinators of its work. (Loose rules of procedure for European Council meetings as such were laid down in 1977).[3]

The political co-operation machinery was established on the basis of the Davignon or Luxembourg Report of 1970[4] and the Copenhagen Report of the Foreign Ministers of 1973.[5] The Foreign Ministers meet in Political Co-operation four times a year and consult as necessary in the intervals. Their work is prepared by the Political Committee, composed of the national Political Directors. Support, implementation and follow-up are provided by a group of so called correspondents in foreign ministries. No Secretariat as such exists, but secretarial functions are in effect fulfilled by the Member State for the time being exercising the Presidency of the European Communities. Direct contact between participants is provided on a separate communications network (COREU).

4—02   From the outset careful consideration was given to the relation-ship of the political co-operation machinery to the institutions provided for by the Treaties. In particular, four colloquies are held each year with Members of the Political Committee of the European

---

[1] Literature on this subject appears very limited. See in particular O. von der Gablentz, "Luxembourg Revisited or the Importance of European Political Co-operation," 16 C.M.L. Rev. 1979, 685–699; J. Charpentier, "La Co-opération politique entré les Etats membres des CE." 1979 A.F.D.I., 753. See also, "Le Conseil Européen, origine, rôle et perspectives," 1975 A.F.D.I., 815 and Mortelmans K.J., "The Extramural Meetings of the Ministers of the Member States of the Community," 11 C.M.L. Rev. 1974, 62.
[2] Bulletin 12–1974, p.6.
[3] Bulletin 6–1977, p.83.
[4] Bulletin 11–1970, p.9.
[5] Bulletin 9–1973, p.12.

Parliament. In addition, an annual report is made to the European Parliament.[6] Parliamentary Questions are now answered on Political Co-operation.[7] The Copenhagen Report described the machinery as "distinct from and additional to the activities of the institutions of the Community which are based on the juridical commitments undertaken by the Member States in the Treaty of Rome." It nevertheless recognised that there would inevitably be a coincidence of interest. The Commission is therefore given an opportunity to make known its views and the Council is kept informed.

The objects of Political Co-operation are described in the Davignon and Copenhagen Reports. Political Co-operation envisages consultation among Governments on all important foreign policy questions with a view to arriving at common policies and common positions on matters of European concern. For their part, the Heads of Government at the Paris Summit of December 9/10, 1974,[8] "reaffirm their determination gradually to adopt common positions and co-ordinate their diplomatic action in all areas of international affairs which affect the interests of the European Community." In practice, it has also concerned itself with certain internal questions as well (*infra*). If Political Co-operation has been criticised as concentrating on "traditional diplomacy,"[9] nevertheless the existence of the "reflex" of consultation and co-ordination[10] has enabled the Nine to bring their considerable influence to bear on world events.[11]

4—03   In addition, Political Co-operation has produced concrete results in the form of written instruments in two areas already.

In 1977 the Foreign Ministers in Political Co-operation approved a Code of Conduct for companies with subsidiaries, branches or representation in South Africa.[12] The Code is principally concerned with desegregation and pay and working conditions. It has proved something of a model in relations with Southern Africa.

In the same year the European Council initiated within Political Co-operation study of proposals for the creation of a European Judicial Area.[13] As a first step a draft convention dealing mainly with extradition is being considered. Other matters in the criminal field are to be examined.

---

[6] See, *e.g.* Bulletin 10–1979, p.129.
[7] Bulletin 12–1974, p.7.
[8] *Ibid.* p.6.
[9] See Von der Gablenz, *supra,* note 1, p.697.
[10] Report on Political Co-operation 1979, Bulletin 10–1979, p.129, Col. 2 and Copenhagen Report Bulletin 9–1973, p.14, Col. 2.
[11] See 1979 Report, *supra,* note 10, in which the Irish Foreign Minister surveyed the previous five years of political co-operation. 1980 Report Bulletin Suppt. 4/80.
[12] Bulletin 9–1977, p.46, Cmnd. 7233.
[13] See J. Charpentier, "vers un espace judiciaire européen," 1978, A.F.D.I., p.927.

Following the European Council Declaration of July 1976 on International Terrorism,[14] the Ministers of Justice of the Nine on December 4, 1979, signed an agreement concerning the application of the European Convention on the Suppression of Terrorism among the Member States of the European Communities.[15] Under the agreement, the Member States agree to apply the European Convention between themselves pending the Convention's entry into force for all Member States without reservation. The Community agreement itself is subject to ratification.

Although falling partly within Community competence, Political Co-operation is also the context of the Euro-Arab Dialogue, intended to provide comprehensive arrangements comprising co-operation on a wide scale for the economic and industrial development of the oil producing countries, industrial investments and stable energy supplies.[16] Financing of studies and discussions was budgeted at approximately 4 million dollars at the end of 1978[17] with the Community meeting about 25 per cent. Of late the dialogue has been stalled.[18]

4—04   In still another field, the Declaration by the Foreign Ministers of the Nine on January 15, 1980, on Afghanistan led directly to the cancellation of Community aid to Afghanistan and the substitution of emergency aid to refugees coupled with the adoption of measures to prevent Community agricultural exports filling the gap in Soviet trade created by termination of US exports.[19]

4—05   The Declaration of the Foreign Ministers of the Nine of April 22, 1980, made public the decision "to seek immediate legislation where necessary in their national Parliaments to impose sanctions against Iran in accordance with the Security Council Resolution on Iran of January 10, 1980 which was vetoed" by the Soviet Union. In the United Kingdom this was reflected in rapid enactment of the Iran (Temporary Powers) Act 1980 and the subordinate Export of Goods (Control) (Iran Sanctions) Order 1980. A number of measures were introduced in concert immediately, notably reductions in embassy staffs in Teheran and cutting off of defence supply contracts. The emergency powers adopted under the April resolution were activated following a further resolution of May 17/18.[20] These measures embargoed sale, supply or transport of goods to Iran other than food and medicines: new credits

[14] Bulletin 7/8–1976, p.120.
[15] Bulletin 12–1979, p.90.
[16] Bulletin 12–1973 point 1106; see also Bulletin 5–1976, p.6, Bulletin 2–1977, p.64, Bulletin 12–1978, p.18 (meetings of the General Committee).
[17] Bulletin 12–1978, p.24.
[18] See Bulletin 9–1979, p.69 and Bulletin 10–1979, p.136. The dialogue was nevertheless "reactivated" at the 1980 Venice Summit: 1980 Report p.10, *supra,* note 11 and W.Q. 768/80, O.J. 1981, C49.
[19] See Bulletin 1–1980, p.7.
[20] See generally Bulletin 4–1980, p.20–26.

or loans, etc: and new service contracts as well as existing contracts concluded after November 4, 1979, the date on which the hostages had been taken, which triggered the crisis. The United Kingdom was unable to comply with this element of retroactivity,[21] in adopting the Iran (Trading Sanctions) Order, S.I. 1980 No. 737, under the 1980 Act. (These measures were revoked following the end of the hostage crisis in January 1981.)

4—06   So far as concerns the functioning of the Community as such, the European Council itself has been decisive in elaborating the proposals for direct elections to the European parliament (*supra*, para. 3-57) and has played an important role in the dialogue on fundamental rights (*infra*, para. 6-31). The discussions on European Union are conducted by the European Council, although in practice with the shelving[22] of the Tindemans Report,[23] the subsequent Annual Reports on European Union are largely in the nature of ritual. More recently it has been central in resolving budgetary difficulties.[24] It has of course discussed questions of Community interest generally at each of its sessions, especially energy, economic questions and the European Monetary System.

[21] See generally Bulletin 5–1980, p.26–28.
[22] Bulletin 11–1976, p.93.
[23] Bulletin Suppt. 1/76.
[24] See Commission Communication on budgetary questions, Bulletin 11–1979, p.121; "Comprehensive Agreement between the Nine," Bulletin 5–1980, p.7 and Bulletin 6–1980, p.23.

Chapter 5

LOCATION AND TERRITORIAL APPLICATION: LEGAL PERSONALITY AND PRIVILEGES AND IMMUNITIES

Location of the Institutions of the Community

5—01 No definitive assignment of locations for the various institutions has ever taken place. This is due partly to political and partly to practical considerations. Thus although Article 77 ECSC, Article 216 EEC and Article 189 Euratom state: "The seat of the institutions of the Community shall [will: ECSC] be determined by common accord of the Governments of the Members States," the Community has enjoyed only "provisional locations" for its institutions.

When the ECSC was set up it was simply declared that the High Authority and the Court would start work at Luxembourg, and that the Assembly would meet at Strasbourg. The ECSC Council Secretariat was set up at Luxembourg in 1952.

With the setting up of the EEC and of Euratom it was recommended that the Commission meet at Val-Duchesse (near Brussels) or at Luxembourg, while it was stated that the Council and the Bank would meet at the residence of their presidents, and that the Assembly would meet in Strasbourg. The Court of course remained in Luxembourg. The Assembly Secretariat and services were also set up in Luxembourg.

Certain changes were made in these arrangements by the decision of the representatives of the Member States of April 8, 1965, on the provisional location of certain institutions and departments of the Communities[1] which was required to enter into force on the same day as the Merger Treaty. Article 1 of the decision states that Luxembourg, Brussels and Strasbourg remain the provisional places of work of the Community institutions. In particular, however, to compensate Luxembourg for the fact that the ECSC institutions were merged into those of the EEC and Euratom, the Council sessions of April, June and October were to be in Luxembourg, while the Court of Justice remained in Luxembourg. Other Community departments were moved to Luxembourg.

5—02 The Parliament meets in Strasbourg, in the chamber which it shares with the Consultative Assembly of the Council of Europe, but it may, exceptionally, decide to hold one or more sessions elsewhere.[2] Its General Secretariat and Departments are located

---

[1] J.O. 1967, 152/18.
[2] Rules of Procedure, Art. 2(2).

in Luxembourg pursuant to Article 4 of the decision of April 8, 1965.

The new directly-elected Parliament has more than double the number of members which attended the old delegated Assembly. This has significantly complicated the practice of holding some sessions in Strasbourg and some sessions in Luxembourg. Furthermore, the present Parliament feels greatly the need to be closer to the "executive" of the Communities which is located principally in Brussels. Poor communications between the centres and between Strasbourg and Luxembourg and other European cities have not helped either.[3]

The Parliament thus has tended to hold its Committee hearings (which not being plenary sessions, are not covered by the decision of 1965) in Brussels and sometimes elsewhere (*e.g.* a special hearing in Paris in 1979 on environmental matters).

5—03　　The European Monetary Co-operation Fund and the Court of Auditors are located in Luxembourg, their provisional place of work for the purposes of the decision of 1965.[4]

Territorial Application

5—04　　The basic provision on territorial application is Article 227 EEC. This article was extended by the 1972 and 1979 Acts of Accession to take account of the circumstances of the acceding states.[5]

The key passages are paragraph 1 read with paragraph 4. Paragraph 1 states that the Treaty "shall apply to" and names each of the Member States by its formal designation. By itself this paragraph is enough to indicate that the territory to which the Treaty applies will be as defined by each Member State in accordance with its national law[6] and notably with the inclusion of declared territorial waters and superadjacent air space.

The better view is probably that the Treaty does not apply to the continental shelf beyond territorial waters, if only because the Member States only "exercise sovereign rights" over the shelf.[7] In a Memorandum of September 18, 1970,[8] the Commission

---

[3] See EP doc. 65–291.

[4] Decision of the Representatives of July 24, 1973, on the provisional location of the European Monetary Co-operation Fund, O.J. 1973, L207, Cmnd. 5740, TS No.54 (1974) and Decision of the Representatives of April 5, 1977, on the provisional location of the Court of Auditors, O.J. 1977, L104/40. The latter also has an office in Brussels; W.Q. 175/80, O.J. 1980, C183/43.

[5] Articles 26 and 20 respectively. See generally J-L Dewost; "L'Application territoriale du droit communautaire," societé française pour le droit international, colloque de Poitiers (May 17–19, 1979) "La Frontière."

[6] Case 61/77 *Commission* v. *Ireland* [1978] E.C.R. 417.

[7] Geneva Convention on the Continental Shelf, April 29, 1958, Article 2. T.S. 39 (1964), Cmnd. 2422; 499 U.N.T.S. 311.

[8] SEC (70) 3095 and see A. Wenger, "La CEE et le Plateau Continental," R.M.C. 1971 No. 143 and W.Q. 489/73, O.J. 1973, C49.

asserted the contrary in relation to the directives on establishment and services relating to mining and quarrying and to prospecting and drilling for oil and gas and the regulation on rules of origin. The Council has not endorsed this view.

5—05   But for paragraph 4 the Treaty could also be regarded as applying to *all* non-metropolitan territories for whose external relations a Member States is responsible. Paragraph 4 of Article 227 provides that the Treaty applies to the European territories for whose external relations a Member State is responsible. (This category would appear to exclude Monaco, San Marino, the Holy See (Vatican City) and Andorra, though the first two apply the Common Customs Tariff *de facto* by virtue of their customs unions respectively with France and Italy).

    Gibraltar falls within Article 227 (4) EEC, but Article 28 of the 1972 Act of Accession expressly provides that the Community rules on agriculture and on value added tax are not to apply in Gibraltar unless the Council, acting unanimously on a proposal from the Commission, decides otherwise. The CCT does not apply either because Gibraltar is omitted from the customs territory of the Community. Gibraltarians do, however, benefit from the free movement provisions of the Community Treaties, for they are included within the declaration of the United Kingdom on the term "nationals" contained in a declaration annexed to the Final Act. And all other Community rules apply in Gibraltar by virtue of the European Communities Ordinance which tracks the United Kingdom Act.

    Gibraltar is not eligible for aids from Community funds essentially because it does not fall to be defined as a development area by the United Kingdom. It has no formal representative in the European Parliament but an ad hoc committee of six British MEPs looks after Gibraltar's interests.

5—06   The remaining paragraphs of Article 229 deal with special cases. Paragraph 2 deals with Algeria and the French overseas departments. Paragraph 3 deals with the beneficiaries of Part Four Association. Paragraph 5 deals with exceptions from the general regime provided for by Article 227.

    Paragraph 2 provided that with regard to Algeria and the French overseas departments,[9] the general and particular provisions of the Treaty relating to free movement of goods, agriculture (save for Article 40 (4), the juridical basis for the setting up of the European Agricultural Guidance and Guarantee Fund), services, competition, the protective measures provided for in Articles 108, 109 and 226, and the institutions, should apply as soon as the Treaty entered into force. The manner of application

---

[9] The Departments concerned (known as the DOMs—Départements d'Outre-Mer) are Martinique, French Guyana, Guadeloupe, St. Pierre et Miquelon and Réunion.

of the rest of the Treaty to these same territories was to be determined within a further two years. The Treaty ceased to apply to Algeria when the latter achieved independence on July 1, 1962, and Algeria is now treated as a third State, although some Member States continue to maintain the status quo.[10] So far as the overseas departments are concerned, limited parts of the Treaty were made applicable within the two year period. Case 148/77 *Hansen*[11] nevertheless ruled that Community law applies generally and the two year period was in effect only transitional.[12]

Paragraph 3 annexes the list of overseas countries and territories to whom the special arrangements for association set out in Part Four were to apply. This annex is Annex IV.[13]

5—07   Annex IV itself is extended by Article 24 (2) of the 1972 Act of Accession so as to include most of the remaining non-European territories "having special relations with the United Kingdom of Great Britain and Northern Ireland." The principal omissions were Hong Kong and Rhodesia (the former because of its rather advanced economy, the latter because of the then continuing state of rebellion there pertaining).

Article 26 (2) of the 1972 Act of Accession makes it clear that the EEC Treaty (in particular the special arrangements for association set out in Part Four) is not to apply to those overseas countries and territories "having special relations with the United Kingdom of Great Britain and Northern Ireland" which are not included in the list contained in Annex IV, by adding a further sub-paragraph to this effect to Article 227 (3) EEC.

The Treaty does not apply to the Faroe Islands, an option to include them being rejected (Article 227 (5) (*a*)). Instead a special fallback regime applies (Protocol 2 to the 1972 Act of Accession). Nor does it apply to the Sovereign Base Areas in Cyprus.[14]

Article 227 (5) (*c*) applies the Treaty to the Channel Islands "only to the extent necessary to ensure the implementation of the arrangements for those islands set out in" Protocol 3 to the 1972 Act of Accession. This, as amplified by Regulation 706/73,[15] applies the rules on free movement of goods reinforced by elements of the rules of competition. The Islands are also within the customs territory of the Community under Article 1 of Regulation 1496/68.[16]

[10] See Written Question 298/68, J.O. 1969, C73/1, and "Syndicat général de fabricants de semoules de France" (Conseil d'Etat) [1970] C.M.L.R. 395.
[11] Case 148/77, *Hansen* v. *HZA Flensburg* [1978] E.C.R. 1787.
[12] And see W.Q. 1783/79, O.J. 1979, C.160/27.
[13] See generally *infra*, para. 29–24.
[14] Article 227 (5) (*b*): the Joint Declaration on the Sovereign Base Areas appended to the Final Act of the 1972 accession arrangements states the intention of defining the arrangements applicable in the projected association agreement with Cyprus. In fact this seems not to have occurred.
[15] Reg. 706/73, O.J. 1973, L68/1.
[16] See *infra*, next section.

Greenland is included in the Community under arrangements contained in Protocol 4 to the 1972 Act of Accession.

Customs territory

5—08   As already mentioned, Regulation 1496/68[17] defines the customs territory of the Community, the definition not corresponding exactly with that to be expected from Article 227. The territories included in the definition of the customs territory are the territories of all the Member States, with the express exclusion of the island of Heligoland and the territory of Büsingen (Germany), the French overseas territories, the Italian communes of Livigno and Campione d'Italia and "the national waters of Lake Lugano which are between the bank and the political frontier of the area between Ponte Tresa and Porto Ceresio." The Austrian territories of Jungholz and Mittelberg, the Principality of Monaco and San Marino are expressly included within the customs territory (Annex 1 of the Regulation). Gibraltar is excluded.

German Democratic Republic and Berlin

5—09   So far as other areas of Europe are concerned, the Protocol on German Internal Trade and Connected Problems and the Declaration on the definition of the expression "German National" are of particular interest. The Protocol confirms that since trade with East Germany is part of German internal trade, "the application of this Treaty in Germany requires no change in the treatment currently accorded this trade." While the importation of goods from the GDR does not constitute importation from a third state, this of course does not make the GDR part of the Community.[18] In particular the CAP financing provisions do not apply to goods of GDR origin. Moreover, Member States are permitted to take appropriate measures to prevent any consequential difficulties arising. The effect of the Declaration on German Nationals is to assimilate persons from East Germany to nationals of the Federal Republic. By the declaration by the Government of the Federal Republic on the application of the Treaties to Berlin, Germany reserved the right to declare, when depositing its instruments of ratification, that the EEC and Euratom Treaties should apply equally to Berlin. Such a declaration was duly made. Note was taken of a similar declaration to the Final Act of the Conferences at which the instruments of accession were signed. The latter declarations relate to all three Communities.

---

[17] Reg. 1496/68, O.J. 1968, L238/1 as amended by Annex I to the 1972 and 1979 Acts of Accession.
[18] See Cases 14/74 *Norddeutsches Vieh und Fleischkontor* v. *HZA Hamburg-Jonas* [1974] E.C.R. 899 and 23/79 *Geflügelschlachterei Freystadt* v. *HZA Hamburg-Jonas* [1979] E.C.R. 2789.

The Legal Personality of the Community

5—10   Article 210 of the EEC Treaty states that the Community shall have legal personality. This personality has two distinct aspects: one concerns the Community as an international person (considered *infra*. para. 29-01); the other concerns the Community's status in the Member States. Article 211 elaborates on the latter aspect, providing that

> "in each of the Member States the Community shall enjoy the most extensive legal capacity accorded to legal persons under their laws."

The power in particular to acquire or dispose of movable and immovable property and to be a party to legal proceedings is expressly conferred. Other powers, such as to receive gifts (mentioned expressly in Article 49 ECSC) are to be inferred. The inference to be drawn from Article 211 with its non-limitative list of powers is not so much that the nature of Community powers shall vary from Member State to Member State as that the Community should not be subject to limitative rules on the capacity of certain types of legal as opposed to natural persons, *e.g.* non-profit bodies.

5—11   Although personality is conferred on the Community as a whole, this personality is exercised for most purposes by the Commission ("to this end the Community shall be represented by the Commission" - Article 211, last sentence). Nevertheless, distinct personality is conferred on the European Investment Bank (Article 129) as a body run on commercial lines and having autonomous powers. Similar autonomous bodies exist under the Euratom Treaty (Articles 49 and 54) where the basic pattern is the same. The ECSC differs from the EEC/Euratom pattern in providing that "The Community shall be represented by its institutions, each within the limits of its powers" (Article 6). But even here, personality as such is granted only to the Community; *Algera*[19]. Usually the personality conferred on an international organisation is described as functional; thus Article 104 of the United Nations Charter provides that "the organisation shall enjoy in the territory of each of its members such legal capacity as may be necessary for the exercise of its functions and the fulfilment of its purposes." This idea is not express in Articles 210 and 211 but in *Von Lachmüller* and *Fiddelaar*,[20] the Court stated that the Commission (s.c. Community) when acting within the limits of the attributions conferred on it by the Treaty, enjoys the legal personality conferred by Article 210. The concept of a functional legal capacity therefore applies to the Community also.

[19] Case 7/56 *Algera* v. *Common Assembly* [1957/58] E.C.R. 39.
[20] Cases 43, 45 and 48/59 *Von Lachmüller* v. *Commission* [1960] E.C.R. 463 and 44/59 *Fiddelaar* v. *Commission* [1960] E.C.R. 535.

Privileges and Immunities

5—12   Article 28, first paragraph, of the Merger Treaty, repealing and re-enacting Articles 76 ECSC, 218 EEC and 191 Euratom, states that the Communities shall enjoy in the territories of the Member States such privileges and immunities as are necessary for the performance of their tasks, under the conditions laid down in the Protocol annexed to the Merger Treaty. The annexed Protocol on the Privileges and Immunities of the European Communities[21] likewise replaces the Protocol on the same subject annexed to the Treaties setting up the three Communities. The European Investment Bank has its own particular disposition on privileges and immunities: "The property of the Bank shall be exempt from all forms of requisition or expropriation."[22]

The new Protocol annexed to the Merger Treaty specifies broadly speaking the usual privileges and immunities which are traditionally accorded to States and which now attach to international organisations.

5—13   Article 1 states that the premises and buildings of the Communities shall be inviolable and that the property and assets of the Communities shall not be subject to any measure of constraint without the authorisation of the Court of Justice. Requests for permission to exercise a measure of constraint form a particular type of jurisdiction of the Court.[23]

The archives of the Communities are to be inviolable (Art. 2). The Communities are to be exempt from direct taxes and indirect taxes are to be rebated where possible (Art. 3). They are further to be exempt from customs duties and other import and export restrictions, in particular on Community publications (Art. 4). With regard to communications and the transmission of documents, the Community institutions are to enjoy in the territory of each Member State the treatment accorded by that State to diplomatic missions. In particular official correspondence and communications are not to be subject to censorship (Art. 6).

Article 7 provides for the use of *laissez-passer* as travel documents to be issued to members and servants of the institutions of the Communities by the presidents of these institutions. These documents are automatically valid within the Member States. The Commission may negotiate for the recognition of these *laissez-passer* by third countries.

Articles 8 to 16 are concerned with the privileges and immunities granted to different categories of persons concerned with the functioning of the Community. Articles 8 to 10 set out the privileges and immunities of members of the European Parliament

---

[21] See *Supra*, Chap. 2, note 4.
[22] Art. 28 (2), Statute of the EIB.
[23] See, *e.g. 4/62 Application for authorisation to enforce a garnishee order against the High Authority of the ECSC* [1962] E.C.R. 41.

who do not benefit under the privileges granted to the employees of the Community. Article 8 provides for unrestricted movement on official journeys to or from the Assembly, and for customs and exchange control exemptions. Articles 9 and 10 provide for the normal parliamentary privileges granted to the members of the Parliaments of most States, exemption from arrest, legal proceedings, etc, and to members of the Advisory bodies of the Communities.

5—14   Articles 12 to 16 concern officials and servants of the Communities. Article 12 (*a*) gives these persons immunity "from legal proceedings in respect of acts performed by them in their official capacity," although this is subject to the jurisdiction granted to the Court of Justice in such matters by the Treaties. The meaning of this provision was considered in case 5/68 *Sayag* v. *Leduc*[24] where a Euratom official, Sayag, having been asked to take two guests of the Commission to a plant at Mol, Belgium, took them in his own car. He was involved in a collision, for which he was responsible, and in which he and his two passengers were injured. One of his passengers, Leduc, brought domestic legal proceedings against Sayag, who pleaded immunity under Article 11 (*a*) of the Protocol on Privileges and Immunities annexed to the Euratom Treaty (now Article 12 (*a*) of the Protocol annexed to the Merger Treaty). Athough the Commission waived Sayag's immunity, the case was fought up to the Belgian *Cour de Cassation*. The latter court asked the Court of Justice for a preliminary ruling (under Art. 150 Euratom) on whether immunity may be invoked when the acts giving rise to legal proceedings were carried out by officials during the performance of their duties and have some relationship with their vocational activities or whether the immunity only covers acts constituting the actual performance of their normal duties or those prescribed under the Staff Regulations.

The Court held that this immunity "only covers acts which, by their nature, represent a participation of the person entitled to the immunity in the performance of the tasks of the institution to which he belongs."

On the facts, Sayag, not being a Commission chauffeur, was not performing his official duties when driving guests to a plant and therefore could not benefit from the Community immunity.

5—15   Article 12 (*b*) to (*e*) lay down privileges and immunities with respect to immigration restrictions on families, exchange regulations and duty free imports. Article 13 provides that the Community employees shall be exempt from any national personal taxation on salaries paid by the Communities,[25] but that they

---

[24] [1968] E.C.R. 345.
[25] See Cases 6/60 *Humblet* v. *Belgium* [1960] E.C.R. 559, 23/68 *Klomp*, [1969] E.C.R. 43, and 7/74 *Brouerius van Nidek* v. *Inspecteur* [1974] E.C.R. 757.

shall be liable to pay a similar tax to the Communities. Article 14 is a special provision to alleviate any problems arising from transfer of "domicile" consequent on Community employment, with regard to income tax, wealth tax or death duties. The employee of the Community is for these purposes to be regarded as having maintained his original tax domicile if that is within the Community. The same applies to a spouse not otherwise employed and to dependent children.

Article 15 requires the Council to lay down a special scheme of social security benefits for Community employees and their dependants.

5—16   Article 16 permits the Council to establish categories of employees to whom Articles 12 to 14 shall apply. The Community is under an obligation to inform the governments of Member States of the names and addresses of the employees contained in such categories.

By Article 17 the Member State in whose territory the Communities have their seat shall accord the customary diplomatic immunities and privileges to missions accredited to the Communities. In practice, this has meant that missions of any State, Member or non-Member, have received the normal diplomatic privileges, as now codified in the Vienna Convention on Diplomatic Relations of April 18, 1961.[26] The missions of third states conduct what might be described as a relatively traditional form of diplomacy. Accreditation is to the Community represented by the Council and the Commission acting jointly.[27] Missions of Member States, normally described as the offices of the Permanent Representatives, staff the Council at official level, supported of course by the General Secretariat of the Council, composed of officials of the Community (see further *supra*, para. 3-40).

5—17   The general provisions regarding the application of the privileges and immunities (Arts. 18 to 21) recite that the privileges granted are solely in the interests of the Communities (Art. 18, first para.) and provide that the institutions are to waive any immunity given to personnel when the interests of the Community demand it (Art. 18, second para: as in *Sayag*). To ensure efficient application of the Protocol, the institutions of the Communities are to co-operate with the relevant bodies in the Member States (Art. 19). Article 22 applies the Protocol to the European Investment Bank without prejudice to provisions in its own Protocol and adds exemption from taxation on the increase of its capital or on its dissolution or liquidation. The Bank's activities are not to be subject to any kind of turnover tax.

[26] Cmnd. 2565.
[27] Luxembourg Accords, Bulletin 3 1966, p.5.

By Article 20, Articles 12 to 15 and Article 18 of the Protocol apply to members of the Commission.

Privileges and immunities and the Court of Justice

5—18   By Article 21 of the Protocol on Privileges and Immunities, "Articles 12 to 15 and Article 18 shall apply to the Judges, the Advocates-General, the Registrar and the Assistant Rapporteurs of the Court of Justice, without prejudice to the provisions of Article 3 of the Protocols on the Statute of the Court of Justice concerning immunity from legal proceedings of Judges and Advocates-General." Article 3 of the Protocols on the Statute of the Court of Justice are identical in their first three paragraphs. They provide that:

> "The Judges shall be immune from legal proceedings. After they have ceased to hold office, they shall continue to enjoy immunity in respect of acts performed by them in their official capacity, including words spoken or written.
>
> The Court sitting in plenary session, may waive the immunity.
>
> Where immunity has been waived and criminal proceedings are instituted against a Judge, he shall be tried, in any of the Member States, only by the Court competent to judge members of the highest national judiciary."

Article 3 of the ECSC Statute has a fourth paragraph, granting to the Judges the privileges set out in Article 11 (*b*), (*c*) and (*d*) of the ECSC Protocol on Privileges and Immunities. The latter privileges are now contained in Articles 13, 12 (*b*) and 12 (*d*) respectively of the current Protocol on Privileges and Immunities. As such the fourth paragraph of Article 3 of the ECSC Statute adds nothing to Article 21 of the current Protocol on Privileges and Immunities.

5—19   Persons appearing before the Court of Justice also enjoy certain privileges and immunities: by the third paragraph of Article 17 of the EEC Statute (*cf.* Article 20 of the ECSC Statute) "such agents, advisers and lawyers shall, when they appear before the Court, enjoy the rights and immunities necessary to the independent exercise of their duties under conditions laid down in the rules of procedure." Article 32 of the Rules of Procedure[28] grants immunity in respect of words spoken or written concerning the case or the parties to agents, advisers and lawyers appearing in proceedings, also exemption from search and confiscation in respect of papers and documents relating to the proceedings, entitlement to currency allocations, and the necessary freedom of movement. The persons

---

[28] O.J. 1974, L350/1, O.J. 1975, L102/24.

enjoying these privileges are required to give proof of status (Art. 33) and the privileges are granted solely in the interest of the proper conduct of the proceedings, and may be waived by the Court when it considers that this would not be hindered thereby (Art. 34). Privileges in relation to documents, communications with counsel, etc, are emerging.[29]

Court of auditors

5—20 By Article 206 (10) of the EEC Treaty, as amended by the 1970 and 1975 Budget Treaties, the provisions of the Protocol on Privileges and Immunities applicable to the Judges of the Court of Justice apply also to the members of the Court of Auditors.

---

[29] See Case 2/54 *Italy* v. *HA* [1954–56] E.C.R. 37 (confidential documents) Case 267/78 *Commission* v. *Italy* [1980] E.C.R. 31 (non-disclosure of documents in criminal proceedings) Case 155/79 *AM & S Europe Ltd.* v. *Commission* (not yet decided) (communications with counsel).

Part 3

THE COMMUNITY LEGAL ORDER AND THE COURT

Chapter 6

SOURCES OF COMMUNITY LAW

1. *The Treaties*

6—01   The primary source of EEC law is the Treaty of Rome of March 25, 1957, establishing the European Economic Community,[1] as from time to time amended notably by subsequent Treaties.[2] The Treaties establishing the Coal and Steel[3] and Atomic Energy Communities[4] are relevant to the application and interpretation of the EEC Treaty. This is because much of the earlier jurisprudence was developed on the similar language and concepts contained in the earlier Coal and Steel Treaty. The Atomic Energy Community Treaty, of the same date as the EEC Treaty, also has many similarities with it.

6—02   Apart from Treaties concluded with third countries under powers express or implicit in the Treaties establishing the Communities (considered *infra*, Chapter 29) there is a further class of Treaty, concluded among the Member States, which exists outside the framework of the Treaties establishing the Communities. Most notable among these are the Treaties envisaged under Article 220 of the EEC Treaty.[5] By virtue of subsequent Protocols[6] the Court of Justice has jurisdiction to interpret the two Article 220 Conventions so far concluded.[7] Nevertheless because the obligations contained in the Conventions derive from the Conventions alone, they cannot be considered as forming part of Community law as such, albeit they are equally clearly primary sources of law, linked, in the words of the Preamble to the European Patent Convention,[8] which is comparable in status, with the legal order of the Community, but not part of it.

2. *Legislation*[9]

The types of legislation - Treaty provisions

6—03   Article 189 EEC provides:

[1] [4] See generally *supra*, para. 2–01.
[5] See generally *infra*, Chapter 23.
[6] *Ibid.*
[7] On mutual recognition of companies and on recognition and enforcement of judgments.
[8] Community Patent Convention, Luxembourg December 15, 1975, O.J. 1976, Ll7, Cmnd. 6553, EC No.18 (1976).
[9] As to this section see generally R. H. Lauwaars, *Lawfulness and Legal Force of Community Decisions* (Sijthoff 1973).

71

"In order to carry out their task the Council and the Commission shall, in accordance with the provisions of this Treaty, make regulations, issue directives, take decisions, make recommendations or deliver opinions.

A regulation shall have general application. It shall be binding in its entirety and directly applicable in all Member States.

A directive shall be binding, as to the result to be achieved, upon each Member State to which it is addressed, but shall leave to the national authorities the choice of form and methods.

A decision shall be binding in its entirety upon those to whom it is addressed.

Recommendations and opinions shall have no binding force."

6—04   Article 189 describes the various types of acts that both the Council and the Commission may issue in order to carry out their tasks. The article does not itself confer power to issue an act: this must be sought in a substantive provision elsewhere in the Treaty. The article merely lists the types of acts that either institution may issue as being regulations, directives, decisions, recommendations and opinions. These descriptions cannot be taken to be definitions for they only describe the effect of the act issued. Formal requirements for the various instruments are considered *infra*, para. 6-19 *et seq*.

The list of available forms of Community act contained in Article 189 is not exhaustive; various types of rules of procedure exist and use is made *inter alia* of communications, memoranda, guidelines and programmes. None of these instruments is binding within the meaning of Article 189. Decisions of the representatives, which present special difficulties, are considered *infra*, para. 6-23 *et seq*. The differences between the various types of non-binding act, decisions of the representatives apart, are probably not very significant, the name being descriptive of content rather than indicative of particular effects.

The binding instruments - regulations, decisions and directives - are considered first, then the distinction between binding and non-binding acts. Formal requirements are considered in the third section. Decisions of the representatives are considered in the final section.

(i) The binding instruments

Regulations and decisions distinguished

6—05   To summarise the effect of Article 189, A *regulation* is described as having general application. The implication is that it should be

72

regulatory in character; in fact akin to a law. A *decision* is binding on individual addressees. A *directive* (considered in the next section) is binding as to the result to be achieved, while leaving choice of form and methods.

/The distinctions between the different types of instrument are important because of the powers they place in the hands of Community institutions by virtue of substantive provisions of the Treaty - power may be conferred to proceed by directive, but not by regulation, as under Article 100.[10] From the point of view of the individual, however, what is of greater interest is the effect a given instrument will have on him, and the remedies available to him in the event he feels injured or his rights impaired by Community action/

Article 173 of the EEC Treaty permits a natural or legal person to institute proceedings against a *decision* addressed to him or against an act in the form of a *regulation* or a *decision* addressed to another person. In the latter case, however, he must demonstrate that the act in question is of direct and individual concern to him.[11] Conversely he may "complain to the Court of Justice that an institution of the Community has failed to address [to him] any act other than a recommendation or an opinion," under Article 175.

The Court has never accepted that the characterisation of an act by the Community institution issuing it should be decisive. The issue arose first in relation to decisions under the ECSC Treaty.

6—06   The provisions of the ECSC Treaty conferring powers of decision on the High Authority (*i.e.* now the Commission) are similar to but not identical with the provisions of the EEC Treaty. Article 14 ECSC provides for decisions, which are binding in their entirety (corresponding both to EEC decisions and regulations), recommendations, which are binding as to the aims to be pursued but leaving the choice of the appropriate methods for achieving these aims to those to whom the recommendations are addressed (these correspond to EEC directives), and opinions, which have no binding force. Where a given ECSC decision can be assimilated to a regulation, in that it is intended to have general application and to be binding in its entirety and directly applicable in all Member States, it is described as a general decision. ECSC decisions addressed to undertakings or associations, and thus having a more limited character, are described as individual decisions.

The concept of individual act was developed not so much from Article 14 or Article 15 and Decision 22/60[12] implementing it, which requires decisions and recommendations which are individual in character to be notified to the party concerned and in all other

[10] *Infra,* Chapter 23.
[11] Article 173, second paragraph.
[12] J.O. 1960, 1250.

cases to be published. Rather it was derived from Article 33 ECSC. Like Article 173 EEC this provision confers a right on individuals to challenge acts of the institutions. However the latter article refers on the one hand to decisions concerning undertakings or associations which are individual in character, and on the other to general decisions; undertakings and associations may attack individual decisions under Article 33 on any of the four grounds of illegality there set out, but may attack general decisions for misuse of powers only.

6—07   The Court has held that a decision cannot be individual in character in relation to the undertakings to which it is addressed and at the same time a general decision, in relation to third parties.[13] In the same case it held, moreover, that general decisions are quasi-legislative measures which issue from a public authority and have a legislative effect *erga omnes*. Identification of a given act will not generally depend on the form of the act but upon the object and content.[14] A disguised individual decision remains an individual decision.[15]

6—08   The Court first had to consider the effect of the limitation on individual rights of action under Article 173 in Cases 16 & 17/62 *Confédération Nationale des producteurs de fruits et légumes* v. *Council* and 19-22/62 *Fédération Nationale de la boucherie* v. *Council.*[16] It held:

> "the Court cannot restrict itself to considering the official title of the measure, but must take into account its object and content.
>
> The criterion for the distinction [between regulations and decisions] must be sought in the general 'application' or otherwise of the measure in question.
>
> The essential characteristics of a decision arise from the limitation of the persons to whom it is addressed, whereas a regulation, being essentially of a legislative nature, is applicable not to a limited number of persons, defined or identifiable, but to categories of persons viewed abstractly and in their entirety. Consequently in order to determine in doubtful cases whether one is concerned with a decision or a regulation, it is necessary to ascertain whether the measure in question is of individual concern to specific individuals."

In other words, the only valid test as between *regulations* or *decisions* is to ascertain whether provisions of an act apply to

---

[13] Case 18/57 *Nold* v. *H.A.* [1959] E.C.R. 41.
[14] Cases 22 and 23/60 *Elz* v. *H.A.* [1961] E.C.R. 181.
[15] Case 8/55 *Fédéchar* v. *H.A.* [1954 to 1956] E.C.R. 245.
[16] [1962] E.C.R. 471 and 491.

objective situations, even if the number of persons actually affected is very small. In practice this has meant an examination of the effect on individuals' legal positions. If the act has a particular effect on the legal position of a closed class of individuals as opposed to a theoretically undefinable number, it will be a decision. A particular example of this is the case where an act affects individuals retrospectively.[17] Unfortunately the simplicity of this test was put in doubt by several cases[18] where emphasis was placed on the intention of the legislator; the Court has since adopted a somewhat ambivalent approach, sometimes looking at the objective nature of the act,[19] sometimes examining the intention of the legislation.[20]

6—09   In some instances a regulation properly so called may contain elements which concern a defined group of individuals.[21] In such cases the rest of the regulation would continue to apply unimpaired even if the particular provision in question was struck down. The converse would no doubt apply in relation to a directive, of which parts had been held directly effective.[22] The effect of regulations and directives is considered *infra*.

The regulation is the prime means of achieving uniformity of rules throughout the Community. This type of instrument has been resorted to far more than any other, some 4,000 per year now being issued.

It is not usual for regulations to legislate on methods of control or execution inside the Member States, nor to provide for penalties (the principal exceptions being in the competition field), this being left to the Member States to implement, subject to Commission supervision.

Directives

6—10   / Since directives are described as binding as to the result to be achieved, but leaving to Member States the choice of form and methods (Art. 189) they are not usually used as a direct instrument for achieving precise legislative harmony. They have been used primarily where uniformity is unnecessary or where national interests prevent the adoption of a regulation or else where the aim is to lay down a standard rather than a precise procedure. Legislation by directive is always something of an exceptional procedure because of the relatively limited efficiency of the instrument for laying down common rules. Regulations have always been issued in far greater numbers except where no other instru-

---

[17] *e.g.* Case 25/62 *Plaumann* v. *Commission* [1963] E.C.R. 95.
[18] Cases 63 to 65/69 *The French Franc Devaluation cases* [1970] E.C.R. 205, 221, 229.
[19] *Ibid.*
[20] See further *infra*, paras. 11–21 *et seq.*
[21] Case 30/67 *Molitoria Imolese* v. *Council* [1968] E.C.R. 115.
[22] *Infra*, para.7–21.

ment is provided for in the Treaty (*e.g.* under Art. 100). Even so, the directive is now relatively less common than it was as a vehicle for legislation of more than a routine character.,

The ECSC recommendation corresponds broadly to the EEC directive, with the difference that the former may be directed to undertakings and associations. The distinction between directives and regulations has been somewhat undermined on the one hand by prescribing rather precise objects in certain directives and on the other hand by corresponding rulings of the Court holding provisions of certain directives to have direct effects (*infra*, para. 7-21 *et seq*).

Further types of binding act? International agreements concluded by the Community

6—11   Initially there were doubts as to whether international agreements entered into by the Community were binding Community acts within the meaning of Article 189 and therefore amenable to the jurisdiction of the Court. Because such agreements are concluded by an act of one of the institutions of the Community the Court has been able to hold that the agreement is an act of one of the institutions of the Community for the purposes of the Court's jurisdiction to give preliminary rulings under Article 177 (1) (*b*).[23]

Amendment or repeal of binding acts

6—12   If Community legislation is repealed or amended, it is presumed that the relevant amending or repealing act will apply to the future consequences of existing situations[24] but will not abolish private rights already acquired.[25]

Acts held to be illegal

6—13   In terms of Article 174 (considered further *infra* para. 9-06) an act struck down by the Court pursuant to Article 173 is declared void. There seems to be no doctrine that the act should be regarded as non-existent. The earliest cases under the ECSC Treaty talk in terms of revocation of illegal acts, this doctrine being derived from an examination of the laws of the Member States.[26]

Is there a difference in effects as between the institutions?

6—14   There is no difference in law between acts adopted by the Council and those adopted by the Commission. Nor is it material whether the act was adopted by the Council alone, on a proposal

---

[23] Case 181/73 *Haegeman* v. *Belgium* [1974] E.C.R. 449. A community decision is not an international agreement: Case 91/79 *Commission* v. *Italy* [1980] E.C.R. 1099.
[24] Case 143/73 *SOPAD* v. *FORMA and FIRS* [1973] E.C.R. 1433.
[25] Case 34/73 *Variola* v. *Amministrazione Italiana delle Finanze* [1973] E.C.R. 981.
[26] Case 7/56 *Algera* v. *HA* [1957 and 1958] E.C.R. 39.

from the Commission, by the Commission acting alone, etc.

(ii) The distinction between binding and non-binding acts

6—15   The first section examined the distinctions between different types of binding act, their importance for the legislator and the effect of the relevant characterisation on remedies. The distinction between binding and non-binding acts is important for the same reasons. Just as a regulation may disguise a decision, so a decision may be disguised by an apparently non-binding instrument, which normally could not be challenged.

Thus in Case 90 & 91/63 *Commission* v. *Luxembourg and Belgium*[27] a resolution of the Council was held to have no binding force since it was a statement of intent and no more. In case 22/70 *Commission* v. *Council (AETR)*,[28] on the other hand, the Court held Council "proceedings" to be susceptible of annulment since they "had definite legal effects."

A number of classes of act fall to be considered.

a) *Acts communicated by officials*

6—16   An act may not clearly be that of the Commission as opposed to that of its officials, as for instance where a letter was signed by the Director-General of Competition and indicated only that he or his office had come to a particular decision. The Court has held that such a communication may be a decision if it indicates that the Commission has actually taken it, even though signed by a subordinate.[29] In staff cases it may be that in some cases a subordinate may have delegated to him certain powers of decision.[30]

(b) *Acts which purport to have legal force*

6—17   General announcements and internal directives in respect of policy appear to have been regarded occasionally as binding acts. In Case 14/59 *Pont à Mousson* v. *High Authority*[31] the Court appeared to take the view that a statement by the High Authority as to the legal position of an individual undertaking could be regarded as a decision. Although an internal directive may not be legally binding, it may nevertheless set forth a rule of conduct indicating the practice to be followed, which should not be departed from without giving reasons.[32] A confirmation of an earlier decision is not itself a new decision.[33]

---

[27] [1964] E.C.R. 625. See also 59/75 *Manghera* [1976] E.C.R. 91.
[28] [1971] E.C.R. 263.
[29] 48/69 *ICI* v. *Commission* [1972] (II) E.C.R. 619.
[30] Case 56/72 *Goeth* v. *Commission* [1973] E.C.R. 181.
[31] [1959] E.C.R. 215.
[32] Case 148/73 *Louwage* v. *Commission* [1974] E.C.R. 81.
[33] Case 26/76 *Metro* v. *Commission* [1977] E.C.R. 1875, 1898.

(c) *Acts which purport to have no legal force*

6–18   The fact that an act purports to be only a "preliminary determination" does not deprive it of legal force if it transpires that the addressee's legal position is altered by it. The most prominent example is that under Article 15 (6) of Regulation 17/62[34] where the individual loses his immunity to fines as a result of a preliminary determination that Article 85 (1) may be applicable and that an exemption may be available under Article 85 (3); the Court has held that such a determination constitutes a decision even though the determination may be preliminary.[35] The *AETR* case has already been referred to (*supra*, para. 6-15) as showing that Council deliberations may in fact have legal effects. In Case 81/72 *Commission* v. *Council*[36] the question arose as to whether the Council was bound by a statement in its own minutes as to how staff salaries were to be calculated over the next three years. For the Court the decisive element was that "the Council had gone beyond the stage of preparatory consideration and had entered on the phase of decision-making"; "Both the antecedents and the terms of the decision taken make it clear that the Council intended to bind itself to observe fixed criteria."

(iii) Formal requirements for Community acts

6–19   The formal requirements are set out in Articles 190 and 191 of the Treaty, as amplified in the Council's Rules of Procedure.[37]

Publication

6–20   Although directives, decisions and recommendations are all normally published in the *Official Journal*, together with regulations, it is only to the latter that an obligation to publish attaches, under Article 190. Regulations enter into force on the date specified in them or if no date is specified, on the twentieth day following publication. There is a presumption that the date of publication is in fact the date appearing on each issue of the *Official Journal*. If this is not in fact so, the actual date of publication is taken.[38] Article 191 requires directives and decisions to be notified to the addressee. They take effect upon notification.[39]

Form

6–21   Articles 10, 11 and 12 of the Council Rules of Procedure[40] lay

---

[34] *Infra*, para. 20–44.
[35] Cases 8 to 11/66 *Cimenteries CBR* v. *Commission* [1967] E.C.R. 75.
[36] [1973] E.C.R. 575.
[37] 79/868, O.J. 1979, L268/1.
[38] Cases 98/78 *Racke* v. *HZA Mainz* and 99/78 *Decker* v. *HZA Landau* [1979] E.C.R. 69 & 101.
[39] Article 191.
[40] Note 37, *supra*.

down certain requirements as to form of regulations. Article 14 applies Article 11 (enacting formula and reasons) *mutatis mutandis* to directives and decisions. In practice all binding acts also follow the form laid down for Council regulations in Article 10; namely that they should include in their title the word "regulation," followed by a serial number,[41] by the date of their adoption and by an indication of their subject-matter. They are all also usually dated and signed (Art. 12). Commission instruments in practice follow the same forms.

Reasons

6—22   Binding acts of the Council and of the Commission must state the reasons on which they are based and must refer to any proposals or opinions which were required to be obtained pursuant to the Treaty (Art. 190 EEC). The manner of recital of these matters is laid down in Articles 11 and 14 of the Council's Rules of Procedure. Commission acts in practice comply with the same rules. By Article 11 a Council act must indicate the dispositions in virtue of which it is adopted in a paragraph preceded by the words "having regard to," and must similarly refer to any proposals or opinions which were required to be obtained, these references being followed by the reasons on which the act is based, introduced by the word "whereas" and concluded with the formula "has adopted this" regulation, directive or decision.

The requirement of recital of reasons applies only to binding acts in the EEC, but it extends equally to non-binding opinions under Article 15 of the ECSC Treaty. (For a discussion of the degree of reasoning required see below, Article 173).

(iv) Decisions not provided for in Article 189: Decisions of the Representatives of the Member States meeting in Council

6—23   Section (iii) above considered the distinction between binding and non-binding acts. Some of the non-binding instruments may not be nullities, but for example mere expressions of intent. Decisions of the representatives of the Member States meeting in Council fall into a separate category. They may well be intended to have binding force but they exist outside the immediate framework of the Treaties in general and Article 189 in particular.

Most, if not all, of these acts[42] are either measures taken in execution of Community obligations or measures taken to complement the provisions of Community law.[43] Their exact nature is, however, uncertain. The majority of them are described as being decisions of the representatives of the Member States, or as

[41] See *supra*, para. 2–03 as to the numbering systems.
[42] There is no current list of these decisions but for examples see W.Q. 336/68, J.O. 1968, C38/5 and EP doc. 215/69. See also Cmnd. 4862–I p.137.
[43] *Cf.* acceleration decisions, J.O. 1960, 1217 and 1962, 1284.

agreements of the representatives, etc.[44] There are other minor variations in terminology which are probably immaterial in law. Nevertheless, the contents of the acts vary considerably, some amounting to little more than extracts from the Council minutes. Others resemble fully fledged decisions, and indeed were in some cases taken at the suggestion of the Commission. The vast majority are published, as any ordinary Community act. Still others of these acts, on the other hand, resemble ordinary multilateral treaties. Thus, it would appear that the weight to be attributed to a particular instrument will depend upon its content and not upon its form. But it would be wrong to draw conclusions as to the nature of an act purely from its subject-matter; whether or not the subject-matter is one in which the Community already has powers, and whether the act executes the Treaty or enlarges upon it must be examined together with the question whether a binding obligation is intended.

6—24   The Court of Justice has not yet had occasion to pronounce upon the nature of these acts; a very few of them specifically confer jurisdiction on the Court of Justice, but most are silent on the point. The Commission, in answer to written question 336/68[45] described these acts as having the character of international agreements, a view which is generally accepted. This suggests that they may be outside the jurisdiction of the Court, but the point is far from certain. It seems now that the test the Court would adopt will not be whether the act is in the form of one of the types of acts referred to in Article 189, but rather whether in substance it can be said to be intended to produce legal effects.[46]

There has been some question as to whether acts of the representatives can derogate from Treaty obligations or even effect Treaty revisions. The generally accepted view is that this is not possible, since revision is only possible subject to certain clearly defined conditions, and indeed if one accepts the view that the Court could in appropriate circumstances take jurisdiction over these acts, then it would seem to follow that the Court would be obliged to ensure that the terms of the Treaty were respected. Where, however, the subject-matter of the decision of the representatives in question is strictly outside the powers and obligations set out in the Treaty or in binding acts in the sense of Article 189, the Court might possibly be forced to come to the conclusion that it had no jurisdiction, even though the act had the characteristics of, for example, a decision.

6—25   Many of the decisions of the representatives have been ratified in accordance with the applicable national constitutional require-

---

[44] These latter are usually associated with Agreements with third countries, see *e.g.* Lomé II: *infra*, para. 31–19.
[45] *Supra,* note 42.
[46] Case 22/70 *supra,* note 28.

m'ents. The question thus arises whether, assuming that the Court of Justice could be said to have jurisdiction over these acts coming within the criteria set out in the *AETR* case,[47] ratification within the Member States negates the "Community character" of the act for the purposes of that jurisdiction. No clear answer can of course be given to this question, but it may be pointed out that the Court of Justice referred explicitly to the acts of ratification deposited by the Member States as being the starting point for consideration of the autonomous nature of Community law in Case 9/65 *San Michele* v. *H.A.*[48] It would appear therefore that ratification ought not to impair the Community nature of decisions of the representatives, although it may make it difficult to accept that a given decision of the representatives has the characteristics of, for example, a regulation once ratified.

3. *Decisions of the European Court*

6—26   The legal force of decisions of the Court under its different heads of jurisdiction is considered *infra*, para. 9-04 *et seq.* This question apart, there can be no doubt that the jurisprudence of the Court has had an immense impact upon the development of Community law. In fact, a number of the most radical developments in Community law are judge-made law, *e.g.* direct applicability of Treaty provisions, first outlined in Case 26/62 *Van Gend en Loos*[49] or implied competence in external relations, first described in Case 22/70 *AETR.*[50] The Court recognises no doctrine of binding precedent although in references for preliminary rulings the Court has pointed out that if a question has already been answered by the Court, there is no need to ask it again: Case 28/62 *Da Costa.*[51]

In many instances the Court has also referred expressly to principles or rulings in earlier cases. Frequently, one may detect passages in judgments which are tacit quotations from earlier cases. Lack of a doctrine of binding precedent has nevertheless permitted substantial deviations from earlier case law in some instances (*e.g.* in relation to provisional validity under Regulation 17/62).[52] It may be, however, with the tendency of judgments to become fuller and with the already substantial body of case law that such departures will become less likely.

6—27   Even before the accession of Member States with common law jurisdictions (England and Wales and the two jurisdictions in Ireland) there was a strong tendency for litigants to rely on earlier

---

[47] *Ibid.*
[48] [1967] E.C.R. 27, 30.
[49] [1963] E.C.R. 1.
[50] [1971] E.C.R. 263.
[51] [1963] E.C.R. 31.
[52] *Infra*, para. 20–46.

case law where there was any. This tendency has undoubtedly grown with the very development of that case law. In the practice of the institutions and of the Member States extensive use is made of case law in argument both before the Court and in other contexts.

In arguing on the basis of Community case law no distinction is made between decisions, opinions or rulings given under different heads of jurisdictions: all are relied on in the same manner. Opinions have been the vehicles of far-reaching developments in external relations law. Opinions of the Advocates - General as opposed to those of the Court are more in the nature of an *amicus* brief. They are not themselves authority.

4. *Textbooks, etc.*

6—28   Article 38 (1) (*d*) of the Statute of the International Court of Justice refers to "the teachings of the most highly qualified publicists of the various nations" as subsidiary means for the determination of rules of law. Such writings probably enjoy a not dissimilar status in the eyes of the European Court: textbooks and the like are often cited but it seems unlikely that any case has turned on the force of such a citation.

5. *International law*

6—29   There are two distinct issues here: the extent to which the Community is bound by obligations of an international law character, (considered in Part 6, External Relations, Introductory and in relation to Article 234) and the extent to which the Court will apply principles of international law for the purposes of developing Community law. In some instances,[53] the Court has applied international law principles of treaty interpretation. In later cases, however, the emphasis has been on the Community system as a new legal order in international law.[54]

On the other hand, in the human rights/fundamental rights cases the Court has shown a willingness to be "inspired" by international conventions.

6. *General principles of law*

6—30   Article 215, second paragraph, relating to the non-contractual liability of the Community, is the only provision to refer to the general principles common to the laws of the Member States. In practice the Court has always been ready to have recourse to national laws for the purposes of discerning an appropriate Com-

---

[53] *e.g.* 8/55 *Fédéchar* v. *H.A.* [1954–56] E.C.R. 292, 299; 10/61 *Commission* v. *Italy* [1962] E.C.R. 1. See also Case 41/74 *Van Duyn* v. *Home Office* [1974] E.C.R. 1337, 1351.

[54] 26/62 *Van Gend en Loos* [1963] E.C.R. 1. See also Cases 90–91/63 *Commission* v. *Luxembourg and Belgium* [1964] E.C.R. 625 and 52/69 *Geigy* v. *Commission* [1972] E.C.R. 787, 823.

munity rule.[55] In the context principally of Article 173, which *inter alia* allows it to annul Community acts which infringe the Treaty or "any rule of law relating to its application," the Court has in addition developed a series of general principles of Community law, derived for the most part from notions of domestic law. These general principles have no clear counterpart in English law but elements of them can be identified in public policy and the rules of natural justice. They fall into a number of different categories.

Constitutional Rights and Fundamental Human Rights

6—31 / Litigants attempted to assert rights based on national constitutional law at a fairly early stage in the development of the Community.[56] It was only in 1969, however, that the Court expressly stated that fundamental human rights form part of the general principles of Community law.[57] The classic statement of the position occurs in the *Handelsgesellschaft* case,[58] where the Court held that Community rules cannot be affected by national constitutional principles including those relating to fundamental rights, but:

> "In fact, respect for fundamental rights forms an integral part of the general principles of law protected by the Court of Justice. The protection of such rights, whilst inspired by the constitutional traditions common to the Member States, must be ensured within the framework of the structure and objectives of the Community."[59]

A concept having its basis in national principles of law was thus carried over and "naturalised" into the Community system. In Case 4/73 *Nold* v. *Commission*[60] the Court went a good deal further, holding that in safeguarding these rights, it was bound to draw inspiration from the constitutional traditions common to the Member States, and that it cannot therefore uphold measures which are incompatible with fundamental rights as recognised and protected by the constitutions of the Member States. Further it held that human rights conventions "on which Member States have collaborated or of which they are signatories, can supply guidelines which should be followed within the framework of Community law."

6—32 Between 1974 and 1978 the Court's attitude seems to have been somewhat ambivalent: in *Nold* itself the Court measured

---

[55] 7/56 *Algera* v. *H.A.* [1957–58] E.C.R. 39.
[56] See Case 18/57 *Nold* v. *H.A.* [1959] E.C.R. 41.
[57] Case 29/69 *Stauder* v. *Stadt Ulm* [1969] E.C.R. 419.
[58] Case 11/70 *Internationale Handelsgesellschaft* v. *Evst* [1970] E.C.R. 1125.
[59] *Ibid.* p.1134.
[60] [1974] E.C.R. 491.

rights of ownership against national constitutional laws. In Case 41/74 *Van Duyn* v. *Home Office*[61] the Court referred to a principle of international law as precluding a Member State from refusing a right of entry to its own nationals, although this is more properly a right deriving from the European Convention on Human Rights and Fundamental Freedoms of November 4, 1950, and its subsequent Protocols.

In Case 36/75 *Rutili* v. *Minister for the Interior*[62] the Court found that limitations on the powers of Member States in respect of control of aliens were "a specific manifestation" of the general principle enshrined in the European Convention and its Protocol 4. But in the slightly later Case 118/75 *State* v. *Watson and Belmann*[63], also on aliens control, the Court referred only to fundamental principles contained in the Treaty.

In other cases the Court entertained actions asserting freedom of trade union activity recognised under the Staff Regulations in accordance with "the general principles of labour law";[64] freedom of religion guaranteed by the European Convention;[65] even an action asserting a right of protection from expropriation without compensation.[66]

In Case 149/77 *Defrenne* v. *Sabena*[67] the Court held that elimination of discrimination based on sex forms part of Community fundamental rights, referring to the European Social Charter and ILO Convention No. 111 as recognising the same rights.

6–33   Whatever the long-term importance of these cases in the intervening period, the general approach of the Court in *Nold* was endorsed and embraced by the other three institutions in a common declaration on Fundamental Rights of April 5, 1977,[68] referring specifically to national constitutional guarantees and the European Convention as underlying respect for fundamental rights in the activities of the Community institutions. Citing *Handelsgesellschaft* and *Nold* and the 1977 declaration, the Court in Case 44/79 *Hauer* v. *Land Rheinland-Pfalz*[69] held that "The right to property is guaranteed in the Community legal order in

---

[61] [1974] E.C.R. 1337.
[62] [1975] E.C.R. 1219.
[63] [1976] E.C.R. 1185.
[64] Case 175/73 *Union Syndicale* v. *Council* [1974] E.C.R. 917.
[65] Case 130/75 *Prais* v. *Council* [1976] E.C.R. 1589.
[66] Cases 56–60/74 *Kampffmeyer* v. *Commission and Council* [1976] E.C.R. 711.
[67] [1978] E.C.R. 1365.
[68] O.J. 1977, C103/1; Bulletin 3–1977, p.5; with which the European Council associated itself in its Declaration on Democracy of April 7 and 8, 1978, Bulletin 3–1978, p.5, declaring respect for and maintenance of representative democracy and human rights in each Member State to be essential elements of Community membership.
[69] [1979] E.C.R. 3727. Also 41/79 *Testa* [1980] E.C.R. 1979.

accordance with the ideas common to the constitutions of the Member States, which are also reflected in the first Protocol to the European Convention for the Protection of Human Rights."[70]

The Court then proceeded to analyse Article 1 of the Protocol in so far as it might be relevant to the facts of the Article 177 reference before it. This decision seems to have heralded a more or less direct application of the European Convention in the most recent cases, first in relation to Article 6 (right to a fair hearing) where the Court held that it did not appear necessary to consider the application of that provision since Directive 64/221 could be considered as fulfilling the requirement of Article 6.[71] In Case 136/79 *National Panasonic* v. *Commission*[72] the Court, citing *Nold*, considered directly whether there was a violation of Article 8 of the Convention (right to privacy), in the event finding none.

It may be noted that in 1979 the Commission proposed that the Community should become a party to the European Convention.[73] Apart from the technical problems involved in Community adherence, it may be doubted whether it in fact serves any real purpose following the Court's most recent decisions. The Court can now reasonably be expected to extend fundamental rights at least to the full extent of the European Convention and its Protocols.[74]

Procedural rules of justice

6–34   The rules of natural justice familiar in Common Law systems are examples of such rules, *i.e. audi alteram partem*[75] and *ne bis in idem.*[76] "Good faith"[77] and "equity" ("fairness")[78] have also

---

[70] *Ibid.* p.3745. See also cases 154, etc/78 and 39, etc/79 *Valsabbia* v. *Commission* [1980] E.C.R. 907, confirming *Nold*: the guarantee afforded to ownership of property cannot be extended to protect commercial interests.

[71] Case 98/79 *Pecastaing* v. *Belgium* [1980] E.C.R. 691.

[72] [1980] E.C.R. 2033.

[73] The Community and the European Convention on Human Rights, Bulletin 4–1979, p.16 and Commission Memorandum entitled "Accession to the European Convention on Human Rights", Bulletin Suppt. 2–79.

[74] The *Nold* formula quoted *supra* and *Rutili, supra,* note 62, acknowledge that not all Member States are parties at least to Protocols 1 and 4, but this did not inhibit the generality of the Court's remarks in *Hauer.*

[75] 35/67 *Van Eick* v. *Commission* [1968] E.C.R. 329, 342; 7/69 *Commission* v. *Italy* [1970] E.C.R. 111, 117; 30/68 *Lacroix* v. *Commission* [1970] E.C.R. 301, 311; 41/69 *Chemiefarma* v. *Commission* [1970] E.C.R. 661, 687, 691; 48/69 *ICI* v. *Commission* [1972] E.C.R. 619, 650; 51/69 *Bayer* v. *Commission* [1972] E.C.R. 745, 770; 54/69 *Francolor* v. *Commission* [1972] E.C.R. 851, 871; 55/69 *Cassella* v. *Commission* [1972] E.C.R. 887, 912; 63–69/72 *Werhahn* v. *Council* [1973] E.C.R. 1229, 1248; 17/74 *TMPA* v. *Commission* [1974] E.C.R. 1063, 1080; 75/77 *Mollet* v. *Commission* [1978] E.C.R. 897; 36/78 *Rutili* [1975] E.C.R. 1219, 1232.

[76] 14/68 *Wilhelm* v. *BKA* [1969] E.C.R. 1, 15; 7/72 *Boehringer* v. *Commission* [1972] E.C.R. 1281, 1290.

[77] 36/72 *Meganck* v. *Commission* [1973] E.C.R. 527, 534.

[78] 64/74 *Reich* v. *HZA Landau* [1975] E.C.R. 261, 268; 31/75 *Costacurta* v. *Commission* [1975] E.C.R. 1563, 1570; 78/77 *Lührs* v. *HZA Hamburg Jonas* [1978] E.C.R. 169, 180.

made an appearance. Other principles are less familiar, in particular the principle of proportionality[79] by virtue of which the scope or severity of an administrative measure must be justified having regard to the importance of the Community object served: the principle of equality of treatment;[80] and the principle of legitimate expectation,[81] protecting an individual against sudden changes in rules without transitional measures covering acquired rights.

Rules of interpretation

6—35   In England these are often presumptions in statutory construction. In Community law those rules of interpretation commonly encountered are that against retroactivity of Community rules[82] (a presumption usually rebutted); and in particular the requirement of legal certainty.[83] In some instances the result has been the opposite to that originally intended by the legislator.

[79] 62/70 *Bock* v. *Commission* [1971] E.C.R. 897; 5/73 *Balkan* v. *HZA Berlin-Packhof* [1973] E.C.R. 1091, 1111; 63/72 *Werhahn* v. *Council* [1973] E.C.R. 1229, 1250; 99/76 *Beste Boter* v. *Bundesanstalt* [1977] E.C.R. 861, 872; 8/77 *Sagulo, Brenca and Bakhouche* [1977] E.C.R. 1495, 1506; 52/77 *Cayrol* v. *Rivoira* [1977] E.C.R. 2261, 2281; 166/78 *Italy* v. *Council* [1979] E.C.R. 2575, 2601.
[80] 14/68 *Wilhelm* v. *BKA* [1969] E.C.R. 1, 16; 36/75 *Rutili* [1975] E.C.R. 1219; 117/76 *Ruckdeschel* v. *HZA Hamburg-St. Annen* [1977] E.C.R. 1753, 1769; 8/77 *Sagulo, Brenca* v. *Bakhouche* [1977] E.C.R. 1495 1506; 265/78 *Ferwerda* v. *Produktschap* [1980] E.C.R. 617, 628.
[81] 81/72 *Commission* v. *Council* [1973] E.C.R. 575, 584; 1/73 *Westzucker* v. *Evst-Z* [1973] E.C.R. 723, 731; 74/74 *CNTA* v. *Commission* [1975] E.C.R. 533, 550; 95/74 *Cooperatives Agricoles* v. *Commission* [1975] E.C.R. 1615, 1636; 5/75 *Deuka* v. *Evst-G* [1975] E.C.R. 759, 770; 126/76 *Dietz* v. *Commission* [1977] E.C.R. 2431, 2442; 68/77 *IFG* v. *Commission* [1978] E.C.R. 353, 369; 90/77 *Stimming* v. *Commission* [1978] E.C.R. 955, 1005; 112/77 *Töpfer* v. *Commission* [1978] E.C.R. 1019, 1032.
[82] 32/70 *Rewe Zentrale* [1971] E.C.R. 23, 36; 88/76 *Exportation des Sucres* v. *Commission* [1977] E.C.R. 709; 98/78 *Racke* v. *HZA Mainz* [1979] E.C.R. 69; 99/78 *Decker* v. *HZA Landau* [1979] E.C.R. 101.
[83] 17/67 *Neumann* v. *HZA Hof* [1967] E.C.R. 441, 456; 26/67 *Fink Frucht* v. *HZA München* [1968] E.C.R. 223, 233; 10/69 *Portelange* v. *Marchant* [1969] E.C.R. 309, 316; 43/69 *Bilger* v. *Jehle* [1970] E.C.R. 127, 136; 24/69 *Nebe* v. *Commission* [1970] E.C.R. 145, 151; 44/69 *Buchler* v. *Commission* [1970] E.C.R. 733, 751; 12/71 *Henck* v. *HZA Emmerich* [1971] E.C.R. 743, 751; 40/71 *Richez-Parise* v. *Commission* [1972] E.C.R. 73, 79; 48/69 *ICI* v. *Commission* [1972] E.C.R. 619, 653; (also the other dyestuffs Cases—49/69 and 52–57/69); 48/72 *Brasserie de Haecht* v. *Wilkin-Janssen* [1973] E.C.R. 77,86; 1/73 *Westzucker* v. *Evst-Z* [1973] E.C.R. 723, 731; 120/73 *Lorenz* v. *Germany* [1973] E.C.R. 1471, 1481; 146/73 *Rheinmühlen* v. *Evst* [1974] E.C.R. 139, 147; 15/73 *Schots-Kortner* v. *Council, etc* [1974] E.C.R. 177, 191; 66/74 *Farrauto* v. *Bau-Berufsgenossenschaft* [1975] E.C.R. 157, 162; 78/74 *Deuka* v. *Evst-G* [1975] E.C.R. 421,433; 5/75 *Deuka* v. *Evst-G* [1975] E.C.R. 759, 771.

Chapter 7

THE COMMUNITY LEGAL ORDER : SUPREMACY AND DIRECT APPLICABILITY

7—01   In Case 26/62 *Van Gend en Loos*,[1] the Court held that:

> "the Community constitutes a new legal order of international law for the benefit of which the states have limited their sovereign rights . . . and the subjects of which comprise not only Member States but also their nationals."[2]

The Court went on to conclude that:

> "according to the spirit, the general scheme and the wording of the Treaty, [certain provisions] must be interpreted as producing direct effects and creating individual rights which national courts must protect."[3]

With this decision, therefore, the Court laid the foundations for two fundamental and interrelated doctrines of Community law:

(1) *Supremacy of Community law* over national law, predicated by limitation of sovereignty in favour of the Community.

(2) *Direct applicability or direct effect* of Community law at the national level without requirements for further enactment.

Supremacy of Community law

7—02   /The first case in which the Court had to deal with the relationship of Community law to national law was 6/60 *Humblet* v. *Belgium*.[4] The consequences were considered of a European Court ruling that a national measure is contrary to Community law. It concluded that the Member State would be obliged to rescind the measure and possibly make reparations. The reasoning was based on a fairly conventional monist view of international law:

> "This obligation is evident from the [ECSC] Treaty and from the Protocol [on Privileges and Immunities] which have the force of law in the Member States following their ratification and which take precedence over national law."[5]

---

[1] Case 26/62 *Van Gend en Loos* v. *Nederlandse Administratie der Belastingen* [1963] E.C.R. 1.
[2] *Ibid.* p.12.
[3] *Ibid.* p.13.
[4] [1960] E.C.R. 559.
[5] *Ibid.* p.569.

This statement seems a little bald, especially perhaps to the English lawyer, who is familiar with a dualist system which recognises individual rights under treaties only where those rights have been transformed into domestic rights by legislative enactment. Nevertheless, the statement of the Court reflects constitutional theory in the six original Member States, the theory of the matter being that ratification itself creates rights. Express conversion of treaty rights into domestic law is thus not an automatic requirement. The status to be accorded to a treaty once ratified is a separate issue but is clearly linked with the question of supremacy at the Community level.

The domestic enactment at issue in the *Humblet* case was the Belgian Income Tax Act of 1948, and the Court of Justice was not therefore faced with the problem of a later national law; an application of the rule *lex posterior derogat priori* would thus have sufficed for the purposes of national law, had the Court considered that the rule was in point.

7—03   In the next Case, 26/62 *Van Gend en Loos*,[6] the Court held, as we have seen,[7] that the Community constitutes a new legal order of international law for the benefit of which states have limited their sovereign rights.[8]

In 6/64 *Costa* v. *ENEL*[9] the Court elaborated on the line it had taken in *Van Gend en Loos*, holding that:

> "By contrast with ordinary international treaties, the EEC Treaty has created its own legal system which, on the entry into force of the Treaty, became an integral part of the legal systems of the Member States and which their courts are bound to apply.
>
> By creating a Community of unlimited duration, having its own institutions, its own personality, its own legal capacity and capacity of representation on the international plane and, more particularly, real powers stemming from a limitation of sovereignty or a transfer of powers from the States to the Community, the Member States have limited their sovereign rights, albeit within limited fields, and have thus created a body of law which binds both their nationals and themselves."[10]

7—04   / This statement represents an advance on *Van Gend en Loos* in that the Court contemplates not merely a limitation of sovereign

[6] [1963] E.C.R. 1.
[7] *Supra.*
[8] *Ibid.* p.12.
[9] [1964] E.C.R. 585.
[10] *Ibid.* p.593.

rights, but also possibly a transfer of powers to the Community. The real advance, however, is contained in the next sentence:

"The integration into the laws of each Member State of provisions which derive from the Community, and more generally the terms and the spirit of the Treaty, make it impossible for the States, as a corollary, to accord precedence to a unilateral and subsequent measure over a legal system accepted by them on a basis of reciprocity."[11]

The Court thus rejected any attempt to make a later law prevail over the EEC Treaty, invoking its acceptance by the Member State on a basis of reciprocity. This approach is further justified by the assertion that:

"The executive force of Community law cannot vary from one State to another in deference to subsequent domestic laws without jeopardizing the attainment of the objectives of the Treaty.... The obligations undertaken under the Treaty ... would not be unconditional, but merely contingent, if they could be called in question by subsequent legislative acts of the signatories."[12]

This line of argument is based upon the requirement of uniformity and also upon a need to give effect to the Treaty. The Court also regarded the reference to direct applicability of regulations in Article 189 as providing further support. Summing up, and referring to the "special and original nature" of Community law, the Court held:

"The transfer by the States from their domestic legal system to the Community legal system of the rights and obligations arising under the Treaty carries with it a permanent limitation of their sovereign rights, against which a subsequent unilateral act incompatible with the concept of the Community cannot prevail."[13]

7—05   One of the next cases to come before the Court of Justice on this subject was 9/65 *San Michele* v. *HA*.[14] In this application the Court was asked to suspend judgment pending a decision by the Italian Constitutional Court as to the constitutionality of law No. 766 of 1952, which gave effect to the ECSC Treaty. The Court, referring to its duty, mentioned in Article 31 ECSC, to ensure that the law is observed in the interpretation and application of the Treaty and of the rules laid down for the implementation thereof, refused to consider law No. 766, and would agree only to consider the instrument of ratification deposited by the Italian

[11] *Ibid.* p.593–4.
[12] *Ibid.* p.594.
[13] *Ibid.* p.594.
[14] [1967] E.C.R. 27.

Government "which, together with the other instruments of ratification, brought the Treaty into force," and went on to refer to the autonomous nature of the Community legal order and to the need for a uniform application of Community principles, holding that adherance by the Member States to the Treaty substantially without reservation and on the same conditions meant (presumably for the purposes of the European Court) that "any claim by a national of a Member State questioning such adherence would be contrary to the system of Community law."[15]

In Case 14/68 *Wilhelm* v. *BKA*[16] the reasoning of the Court seems to have been very close to that in *Costa* v. *ENEL*: it concluded:

> "Consequently, conflicts between the rules of the Community and national rules . . . must be resolved by applying the principle that Community law takes precedence."[17]

7—06 / In Case 106/77 *Simmenthal*[18] concerning the conflict of a later national law with a directly applicable Community rule the Court seems to have gone a step further. Apparently confirming the doctrine in *Costa* and *Wilhelm* of "new legal order", "uniformity" and "effectiveness", coupled with the unconditional nature of acceptance by the Member States of the Treaty, the Court did not rule that Community law made the subsequent measure void but that directly applicable provisions of Community law:

> "preclude the valid adoption of new legislative measures to the extent to which they would be incompatible with Community provisions."[19]

The operative part of the ruling is as follows:

> "A national court which is called upon, within the limits of its jurisdiction, to apply provisions of Community law is under a duty to give full effect to those provisions, if necessary refusing of its own motion to apply any conflicting provisions of national legislation, even if adopted subsequently, and it is not necessary for the court to request or await a prior setting aside of such provision by legislative or other constitutional means."[20]

This needs some qualification: in particular it could not (at least in United Kingdom constitutional law) preclude a Member State

---

[15] *Ibid.* p.30.
[16] [1969] E.C.R. 1.
[17] *Ibid.* p.14.
[18] [1978] E.C.R. 629.
[19] *Ibid.* p.643.
[20] *Ibid.* p.647.

from depriving its courts of the relevant jurisdiction, notably by amending the legislation providing for the acceptance of Community law (in the United Kingdom the European Communities Act 1972)./

Consequences of supremacy

7—07   In the almost 14 years separating *Simmenthal's* consolidation of *Costa* v. *ENEL*, and since, the Court has elaborated a number of related doctrines which flow as a necessary consequence from supremacy of Community law.

Autonomous character

7—08   /It follows from the supremacy of Community law that it constitutes an autonomous system.

In particular the validity of Community measures can only be judged in the light of Community law. Community law cannot be overridden by rules of national law without it being deprived of its character as Community law. Therefore the validity of a Community measure or the effect in a Member State cannot be affected by assertions that it runs counter to either fundamental rights as formulated by the constitution of a Member State or the principle of national constitutional structure.[21]

/ This doctrine, less startling than it seems, especially since the Community itself safeguards fundamental rights,[22] is itself the child of a more general doctrine that Member States may not, in implementing directly applicable obligations, purport to re-enact them or alter their effect.[23]

The doctrine of supremacy of Community law is clear enough in the instances discussed above: there is a Community rule and Community law prevails. But the Community is an evolving system. What of the instances where the Community has powers but has not exercised them or has only partially exercised them? The issue is relatively simple in matters affecting the internal operation of the Community where the transfer of powers is usually fairly clear-cut. Thus in Case 40/69 *Bollmann*[24]:

> "To the extent to which Member States have transferred legislative power in tariff matters with the object of ensuring the satisfactory operation of a common market in agriculture, they no longer have the powers to adopt legislative provisions in this field."[25]

[21] 11/70 *Internationale Handelsgesellschaft* v. *Evst-G* [1970] E.C.R. 1125.
[22] *Supra*, paras. 6–31 *et seq.*
[23] Cases 93/71 *Leonesio* v. *Ministry for Agriculture* [1972] E.C.R. 287, and 34/73 *Variola* [1973] E.C.R. 981 and 94/77 *Zerbone* [1978] E.C.R. 99.
[24] [1970] E.C.R. 69.
[25] *Ibid.* p.79.

7—09   Further, the position is fairly clear-cut where the Community has a power to legislate but has not exercised it: Member States are free to act providing they do not jeopardise the objectives or the functioning of the Community system: Case 3/76 *Kramer.*[26]

But what of the position where the Member States purport to confer exclusive power to act but the power has not in fact been exercised? *Kramer* indicates that the Member States no longer have the power to legislate in the now reserved area.[27]

The relationship between Community law and national measures in the external relations field is considered *infra* under the heading "Implied Powers and Competence." The considerations are arguably a little different and the discussions are therefore kept separate. In the view of the Court, however, the internal and external aspects have as their common point of origin Article 5 of the Treaty, according to which Member States "shall take all appropriate measures . . . to ensure fulfilment of" obligations of Community law and "shall facilitate the achievement of the Community's tasks" and "abstain from any measure which could jeopardise the attainment of the objectives of" the Treaty, described by the Court as "duties of co-operation."[28]

Direct applicability and direct effect of Community law

7—10   There is only one reference to direct applicability of Community law in the Treaties themselves; Article 189 refers to regulations as being directly applicable in all Member States. The notions of direct applicability or direct effect of Community law more generally have been developed by the Court of Justice. In Case 26/62 *Van Gend en Loos* v. *Nederlandse Administratie der Belastingen*[29] the Netherlands Tariefcommissie in referring the case to the European Court asked:

> "Whether Article 12 of the Treaty has direct application in national law in the sense that nationals of Member States may on the basis of this Article lay claim to rights which the national court must protect."[30]

In the event the European Court affirmed that:

> "Article 12 must be interpreted as producing direct effects and creating individual rights which Courts must protect."[31]

A question couched in terms of direct applicability (the language of Article 189) was thus answered by reference to a concept of

[26] [1976] E.C.R. 1279. See also Case 22/70 *AETR* [1971] E.C.R. 263.
[27] Apparently confirmed by Case 141/78 *France* v. *UK* [1979] E.C.R. 2923. See also Opinion 1/75 *Export Credits* [1975] E.C.R. 1355.
[28] Case 141/78 *supra*, note 27, p.2924.
[29] [1963] E.C.R. 1.
[30] *Ibid.* p.11.
[31] *Ibid.* p.13.

direct effects. In relation to regulations and Treaty provisions the meaning is nevertheless reasonably clear: directly applicable provisions have legal effect in the Member States without further enactment.[32]

7—11   It only becomes apparent that there may be more than one aspect to direct applicability or direct effect when decisions and directives within the meaning of Article 189 are considered. Article 189 is quite explicit that

> "a directive shall be binding, as to the result to be achieved, upon each Member State to which it is addressed, but shall leave to the national authorities the choice of form and method.
>
> A decision shall be binding in its entirety upon those to whom it is addressed."

The juxtaposition in Article 189 of statements as to the effect of regulations, and directives and decisions respectively appears to show that directives and decisions are not directly applicable in the same way as regulations. The Court has held, however, that provisions of decisions and directives can

> "produce direct effects and create individual rights which courts must protect."

The relevant cases are discussed below.

7—12   There is a literature based on these cases[33] which argues that "direct applicability" goes to the proposition that directly applicable provisions apply without further enactment, while "direct effect" goes to any remedies which may be available in national law in reliance on a provision of Community law. While this distinction is helpful particularly as an aid to understanding the cases on directives, the writers themselves acknowledge[34] that the Court has not been consistent in its own use of terminology.

Any distinction between direct applicability and direct effects is therefore best seen as two aspects of a single basic concept, which is that litigants are able to rely on Community law before national courts in more or less precisely defined circumstances. It will be apparent that the doctrine or doctrines are peculiarly a creature of the Article 177 procedure by which national courts can obtain preliminary rulings from the European Court. Their practical application therefore lies in litigation before national courts.[35]

[32] Cases 84/71 *Marimex* v. *Ministry of Finance* [1972] E.C.R. 89 and 93/71 *Leonesio* v. *Ministry for Agriculture* [1972] E.C.R. 287.
[33] See in particular J. A. Winter, [1972] 9 C.M.L. Rev. 425 and A. J. Easson, "The 'Direct Effect' of EEC Directives," [1979] 28 I.C.L.Q. 319.
[34] *Ibid.* and see D. Wyatt and A. Dashwood, *The Substantive Law of the EEC*, p.26.
[35] See Case 68/79 *Just* v. *Ministry for Fiscal Affairs* [1980] E.C.R. 501.

There is some ground for seeing in directly applicable provisions of Community law an analogy with so-called self-executing provisions of treaties. There is little doubt, however, that the notion of directly applicable Community law is to be construed purely in relation to the structure of the European Communities. It is better to speak of directly applicable Community law, as does the Court, rather than to refer to a notion drawn from monist theories of international law.

Direct applicability of treaty provisions

7—13 / It is not, perhaps, self-evident that any provisions of the Community Treaties should be regarded as being directly applicable in the Member States. On the one hand it is asserted that it is through the device of direct applicability alone that the supremacy of Community law can be, and is in fact, assured. On the other hand, it is asserted that Community law is only directly applicable because it is superior to, or has supremacy over, national law, direct applicability being only a particular manifestation of this supremacy. On the whole, the best view would appear to be that supremacy of Community law and direct applicability are both children of the doctrine that Community law constitutes a new legal order in international law; both are necessary appurtenances of the new legal order if it is to be effective.

If the Treaty itself refers to direct applicability of Community law only in relation to regulations, how is the attribution of direct applicability to Treaty articles to be justified? In the *Van Gend en Loos*/case the Court referred to the considerations regarding the creation of a new legal order, already touched on at the beginning of this chapter. The Court's argument runs that the EEC Treaty is more than an ordinary international agreement creating mutual rights and obligations for states. It creates a Common Market which is of direct concern to individuals. This concern is brought out notably in the creation of the democratic institutions of the European Parliament and the Economic and Social Committee. In addition the Article 177 machinery (discussed *infra*, Chapter 10) shows, so runs the Court's argument, that Community law is to have an authority which can be invoked by individuals before national courts.

> "The conclusion to be drawn from this is that the Community constitutes a new legal order of international law for the benefit of which the states have limited their sovereign rights, albeit within limited fields, and the subjects of which comprise not only Member States, but also their nationals. Independently of the legislation of Member States, Community law therefore not only imposes obligations on individuals but is also intended to confer upon them rights which become part of their legal heritage. These rights arise not only where they are expressly granted by the Treaty,

94

but also by reason of obligations which the Treaty imposes in a clearly defined way upon individuals as well as upon the Member States and upon the institutions of the Community."[36]

7—14 / The Court's decision is not entirely lucid but perhaps one may take the above passage as distilling the thinking of the Court: given that the Member States have limited their sovereign rights in favour of a new legal order which also has individuals as its subjects, it is only right that the same legal order should confer on individuals rights as well as obligations. The Court went on to consider expressly whether or not the procedures provided by Article 169 and 170 (actions against Member States for infringement of the Treaty) constituted a sufficient guarantee. It concluded that a restriction of guarantees against infringement to those provisions would remove all direct legal protection of the rights of individuals. The same views were expressed in later cases in which the very basis for direct applicability has been questioned.[37]

A directly applicable provision of Community law thus confers rights on individuals which national courts must protect. In cases of doubt resort may be had to the Article 177 mechanism for obtaining a ruling on the interpretation of Community law (*infra*, Chapter 10). The conditions under which effect is given to these rights are largely a matter for national law. Thus recovery of sums unduly paid in contravention of a provision subsequently held directly applicable is governed by national rules, including those on limitation periods and interest, subject only to the Community principles that the procedures should be no less favourable than for similar applications of a domestic nature and that they should not "make it impossible in practice to exercise the rights conferred by the Community legal order."[38] In principle a ruling that a provision is directly applicable takes effect from the date of coming into operation of the obligation in question, not merely prospectively.[39] Any exception to this principle will be rare.[40]

Conditions for direct applicability

Clarity

7—15   The provisions of the Treaty must be "clear"[41] or "clear and precise"[42] so as to be susceptible of direct application. The

---

[36] [1963] E.C.R. 1, 12.
[37] *e.g.* Case 28/67 *Molkerei-Zentrale* v. *HZA Paderborn* [1968] E.C.R. 143.
[38] Case 61/79 *Ammin, delle Finanze* v. *Denkavit Italiana* [1980] E.C.R. 1205.
[39] *Ibid.* and Cases 66, 127 & 128/79 *Ammin. delle Finanze* v. *Meridionale Industria Salumi S.r.l.* [1980] E.C.R. 1237.
[40] *Ibid.* see Case 43/75 *Defrenne* v. *Sabena* [1976] E.C.R. 455 and case 145/79.
[41] *Van Gend en Loos, supra,* note 1.
[42] 18/71 *Eunomia* [1971] E.C.R. 811.

clarity required relates not merely to the straightforwardness of the wording, but in particular to an obligation which is identifiable and recognisable. Thus, an obligation not to increase existing cutoms duties under Article 12[43] is readily recognisable, but the method for assessing the "total value" of quotas under Article 33 (1) is not.[44]

Unconditional Nature

7—16   The obligation imposed must be unconditional.[45] The Court has not given any specific meaning to the term "unconditional," but it seems to refer *inter alia* to an obligation which is effective at the time of the reference to the Court, and not subject to a transitional period or an implementing period which has not yet expired.[46]

There was some suggestion that it is a particular aspect of a more general rule that the obligation must consist in a duty to refrain from acting.[47] However, this cannot be correct because some articles which impose duties to take action have been held directly applicable.[48] The duty in such cases has consisted of the abolition of provisions of national law, which whilst involving action by Member States, does not usually require the enactment of *new* legislation. In other words, the Court seems to hold Treaty provisions imposing duties to act to be directly applicable where the Member States have no latitude of action. This approach is considerably reinforced in the judgment in *Salgoil*,[49] where the Court discusses the nature of Article 33.

The Court held that the uncertainty as to the concept of "total value" deprived that article of the possibility of being directly applicable. Before reaching this conclusion, however, the Court said that:

> "Since [the provisions of Article 33] consist of positive obligations, consideration should be given to the question whether the Member States may in performing them exercise any discretion such as to exclude the above mentioned effects wholly or in part."[50]

7—17   The problem with the approach that an unconditional obligation may be directly applicable, which may not immediately appear at the Community level, is that the simple abolition of national laws may lead to a vacuum in the national legal system and confusion as

[43] *Van Gend en Loos, supra,* note 1.
[44] 13/68 *Salgoil* [1968] E.C.R. 453.
[45] *Van Gend en Loos, supra,* note 1.
[46] 33/70 *SACE* v. *Ministry of Finance* [1970] E.C.R. 1213.
[47] 28/67 *Molkerei-Zentrale* v. *HZA Paderborn* [1968] E.C.R. 143; 27/67 *Fink-Frucht* v. *HZA München Landsbergerstrasse* [1968] E.C.R. 223.
[48] 57/65 *Lütticke* [1966] E.C.R. 205; 13/68 *Salgoil* [1968] E.C.R. 453.
[49] Note 44, *supra.*
[50] *Ibid.* p.461.

to how much of the law in question is actually abolished. For instance, Article 95 forbids discriminatory direct taxation. This article was directly applicable[51] from the end of the second stage of transition. But how much of the national law is abolished? It may be impossible to point to particular provisions of the law in question - only its effects are mitigated. This can mean that the scope of continuing validity is a matter of controversy. The difficulties have been evident in relation to the application of Articles 30 and 36 in determining the scope of national law relating to intellectual property, discussed *infra*, 14-05, but were particularly highlighted in the *French Merchant Seamen* case.[52] French law provided that certain jobs on French ships were to be reserved for French nationals only. The French government argued that because Article 48 prohibited discrimination against EEC nationals, the law was *pro tanto* of no effect (which meant that France was not in breach of its Treaty obligations). The Court however took the view that the mere existence of the provision constituted an infringement of the Treaty in that EEC nationals were faced with doubt as to how the law would be applied.[53] If the French Government were to comply with the Court's findings of an infringement it would therefore in fact be obliged to change its law and not merely to abolish the offending parts.

7–18 Even more problematic is the situation created by a declaration that a provision is directly applicable where previously the matter had been unresolved. In *Defrenne*[54] the Court declared that Article 119 (first para.) had been directly applicable since the end of the first stage of the transitional period. If carried through, this judgment would have created chaos in the legal systems of the Member States, with many people becoming theoretically entitled to back payments of wages retrospectively to 1962. Recognising this difficulty, the Court declared that its judgment was to have effect only as to the future. In making this declaration it relied on the principle of "legal certainty," one of the interpretative "general principles of law" constituting a source of Community law.[55] If it was able to do so in this case, it is arguable that it should also be called upon in other cases to discuss more fully the effects of its judgments. In subsequent cases, however, the Court has indicated that the *Defrenne* approach is of limited application.[56]

---

[51] Case 57/65 *Lütticke* [1966] E.C.R. 205.
[52] Case 167/73 *Commission* v. *France* [1973] E.C.R. 359.
[53] See also Case 33/76 *Rewe-Zentral finanz* [1976] E.C.R. 1989, where the Court indicated that procedural discrimination against persons wishing to assert Community rights might also constitute an infringement of the Treaty.
[54] 43/75 *Defrenne* v. *Sabena* [1976] E.C.R. 455.
[55] *Supra,* para. 6–30.
[56] Cases 61 and 66/79, *supra,* notes 38 & 39. But see *infra,* para. 9–09.

A table of treaty provisions so far held directly applicable is at Appendix 1.

Direct Applicability/Direct Effect of Community Acts

Regulations

7—19   Under Article 189, a regulation "shall have general application" and "shall be . . . directly applicable in all Member States." The direct applicability of regulations implies that regulations apply as law in all Member States without the necessity for an intervening act by the legislative authorities of the Member States. Any national requirement that regulations must be subject to national legislative procedures or adaptation is contrary to Community law.[57]

No doubt the implication that a regulation has direct effects by virtue of its direct applicability[58] could be avoided by the finding that it was not in fact a regulation at all. But it is clear that a provision of a regulation may not invariably have direct effects even if it is directly applicable. In Case 31/64 *Sociale Voorzorg* v. *Bertholet*[59] the Court examined Article 52 (1) of Regulation 3 to determine whether it was applicable in advance of the conclusion of bilateral agreements called for in the second paragraph of the same provision. It concluded that Article 52 (1) was worded in peremptory terms and that the provisions of the paragraph were clear and capable of direct application without difficulty.

In subsequent cases the Court has nevertheless adopted a more mechanical approach, holding that in consequence of its direct applicability a regulation

> "produces direct effects and, as such, is capable of conferring rights on individuals which national Courts have a duty to protect."[60]

Decisions

7—20   Decisions are binding in their entirety upon those to whom they are addressed. They too apply without any need for national legislative intervention and in this sense may be regarded as "directly applicable" although Article 189 does not describe their effect in these terms. The question arises, however, whether decisions cannot give rise to wider rights and obligations. The key pronouncement here is contained in paragraphs 5 and 6 of the judgment in Case 9/70 *Grad* v. *Finanzamt Traunstein*:[61]

---

[57] Case 8/70 *Commission* v. *Italy* [1970] E.C.R. 961 and *supra,* note 23. Although see Case 267/78 *Commission* v. *Italy* [1980] E.C.R. 31, as to possible limitations imposed by national criminal law.

[58] *Supra,* para. 7–12 as to the distinction between these concepts.

[59] [1965] E.C.R. 81.

[60] Case 84/71 *Marimex* v. *Italian Ministry for Finance* [1972] E.C.R. 91 and note 23, *supra.*

[61] [1970] E.C.R. 825.

"However, although it is true that by virtue of Article 189, regulations are directly applicable and therefore by virtue of their nature capable of producing direct effects, it does not follow from this that other categories of legal measures mentioned in that article can never produce similar effects. In particular, the provision according to which decisions are binding in their entirety on those to whom they are addressed enables the question to be put whether the obligation created by the decision can only be invoked by the Community institutions against the addressee or whether such a right may possibly be exercised by all those who have an interest in the fulfilment of this obligation. It would be incompatible with the binding effect attributed to decisions by Article 189 to exclude in principle the possibility that persons affected may invoke the obligation imposed by a decision. Particularly in cases where, for example, the Community authorities by means of a decision have imposed an obligation on a Member State or all the Member States to act in a certain way, the effectiveness ('l'effet utile') of such a measure would be weakened if the nationals of that State could not invoke it in the courts and the national courts could not take it into consideration as part of Community law. Although the effects of a decision may not be identical with those of a provision contained in a regulation, this difference does not exclude the possibility that the end result, namely the right of the individual to invoke the measure before the courts, may be the same as that of a directly applicable provision of a regulation.

Article 177, whereby the national courts are empowered to refer to the Court all questions regarding the validity and interpretation of all acts of the institutions without distinction, also implies that individuals may invoke such acts before the national courts. Therefore, in each particular case, it must be ascertained whether the nature, background and wording of the provision in question are capable of producing direct effects in the legal relationships between the addressee of the act and third parties."

In summary, the Court holds that there is no *a contrario* argument that legally binding instruments other than regulations can never produce effects similar to the direct effect of regulations; because these other instruments are described as binding the question arises as to whether they may not be invoked by all those affected or having an interest; the doctrine of effectiveness (*effet utile*) requires that it should be possible to rely on a binding instrument before national courts; and moreover Article 177 draws no distinction between types of binding Community acts. The decisions of the Court in all the subsequent cases are rooted in this passage in *Grad*.

In *Grad* the Court found that the decision in question contained an obligation which was unconditional and sufficiently clear and precise to be capable of producing direct effects in the legal relationships between the Member States and those subject to their jurisdiction.

Directives

7—21   What then of directives, which, in terms of Article 189 are only "binding, as to the result to be achieved, upon each Member State to which it is addressed"?

In *Grad* an obligation arising under a decision was said to be "perfected" by a directive fixing the date on which the obligation was to become effective.[62] The ruling in *SACE*[63] is to similar effect. In subsequent cases, however, the Court has ruled that provisions of directives may have direct effect on a more general level. In Case 41/74 *Van Duyn*[64] the Court held directly effective Article 3 (1) of Directive 64/221 which provides that "measures taken [on the movement and residence of foreign nationals] on grounds of public policy or public security shall be based exclusively on the personal conduct of the individual concerned." The Court's statement of the relevant principles is directly based on that in *Grad*.

Direct effect in these cases is predicated upon the usual criteria that the obligation is unconditional and sufficiently clear and precise. But how does this overcome the basic point that a regulation alone is described as being directly applicable, while a directive is only "binding, as to the result to be achieved. . . but shall leave to the national authorities the choice of form and methods"?

7—22   *Van Duyn* cites legal certainty and useful effect (*effet utile*). However, Case 51/76 *Nederlandse Ondernemingen*[65] throws further light on an additional reason given in *Van Duyn*. The Court held there that direct effect is especially appropriate where

"the individual invokes a provision of a directive before a national court in order that the competent national authorities, in exercising the choice which is left to them as to the form and the methods for implementing the directive, have kept within the limits as to their discretion set out in the directive."[66]

In other words, the Court does not deny the Member States'

[62] *Ibid.* p.837.
[63] Case 33/70 *SACE* v. *Italian Ministry of Finance* [1970] E.C.R. 1213.
[64] Case 41/74 *Van Duyn* v. *Home Office* [1976] E.C.R. 1337, confirmed by Cases 36/75 *Rutili* v. *Minister for the Interior* [1975] E.C.R. 1219 and 48/75 *Royer* [1976] E.C.R. 497.
[65] 51/76 *Verbond der Nederlandse Ondernemingen* v. *Inspecteur der Invoerrechten en Accijnzen* [1977] E.C.R. 113.
[66] *Ibid.* p.127.

discretion as to "choice of form and methods," but confers on individuals the right to seek judicial confirmation that this discretion has been properly exercised. In fact, in executing a directive a Member State must not adopt administrative or judicial measures which would have the effect of limiting the full exercise of the rights which the Community rule guarantees.[67] That is not to say, however, that penalties may not be fixed by Member States for breaches of provisions adopted in implementation of a directive.[68]

In some instances the rule laid down by the directive may in fact leave no discretion at all. The case for direct effect there is particularly clear.[69] In the converse case of wide discretion the Court has been able to rule that the discretion has not been exceeded so that direct effect is not strictly relevant.[70] The dividing line seems to be well illustrated by *Ratti*.[71] There the national court was directed not to apply a national provision incompatible with a directive which was already binding and in force but had not been incorporated into national law, but with which the defendant had nevertheless complied.[72]

Other Community acts

7—23   Of course, just as other Community acts, not apparently within the four corners of Article 189, may be assimilated to regulations or decisions,[73] so too such acts may be held to be directly applicable provided they fulfil the ordinary criteria for direct applicability.[74]

Conclusions

7—24   Arguments have been advanced as tending to show that direct effect in relation to directives and possibly decisions is something different from direct effect of regulations.[74a] The view has already been expressed that direct applicability and direct effect are aspects of the same question. In relation to directives the cases seem to show that direct effect confers a right to secure proper implementation. The Court does not seem to have been presented with the question whether a directive can be constitutive of rights, for instance as between private parties. In *Ratti* the Court said that "a directive by its nature imposes obligations only on Member States," but that would not seem to dispose of the point. Perhaps

[67] Case 8/77 *Sagulo, Brenca and Bakhouche* [1977] E.C.R. 1495.
[68] *Ibid.*
[69] Case 38/77 *Enka* v. *Inspecteur der Invoerrechten en Accijnzen* [1977] E.C.R. 2203, confirming Case 51/76 *supra*, note 65.
[70] *Cf.* Case 21/78 *Delkvist* v. *Anklagemyndigheden* [1978] E.C.R. 2327.
[71] Case 148/78 *Publico Ministero* v. *Ratti* [1979] E.C.R. 1629.
[72] Contrast Case 88/79 *Minstère Public* v. *Grunert* [1980] E.C.R. 1827.
[73] *Supra*, para. 6–18.
[74] *e.g.* Case 87/75 *Bresciani* v. *Amministrazione Italiana delle Finanze* [1976] E.C.R. 129.
[74a] See Case 131/79 *Santillo* [1980] E.C.R. 1585.

the only limitations on direct effect are those imposed by the form and addressees of the relevant instruments. Certainly the Court has rejected the view that Treaty provisions are constitutive of rights only *vis-a-vis* the State and not as between individuals.[75]

---

[75] Cases 127/73 *BRT* v. *SABAM* [1974] E.C.R. 51; 36/74 *Walrave & Koch* v. *Association Union Cycliste Internationale* [1974] E.C.R. 1405; and 43/75 *Defrenne* v. *Sabena* [1976] E.C.R. 455.

Chapter 8

STRUCTURE AND PROCEDURE OF THE EUROPEAN COURT

8—01   The Courts of Justice provided for in the Treaties establishing the three Communities[1] are constituted by a single Court of Justice,[2] which exercises the jurisdiction of the EEC and Euratom Courts of Justice, and that of the ECSC Court of Justice which it replaces. In recognition of the fact that the Court of Justice is the judicial arm for all three Communities, it describes itself as the Court of Justice of the European Communities. The existence of a single Court of Justice rather than of three separate such institutions is conducive to the achievement of a unity of jurisprudence and the easy resolution of any jurisdictional conflicts between the Treaties.

Besides those provisions on the composition and working of the Court in the Treaties establishing the Communities, more detailed provision is made in the Statute on the Court of Justice, annexed in slightly differing form to each of the Treaties. The Statutes are themselves elaborated upon in the Rules of Procedure of the Court.[3]

Composition of the Court of Justice

8—02   Article 165 EEC[4] provides for a Court of Justice of nine judges, assisted by four Advocates-General (Art. 166 EEC)[5], increased by one with the accession of Greece. Certain consequential amendments were effected upon accession.[6] Article 167 EEC provides that the judges and Advocates-General shall be chosen from persons whose independence is beyond doubt, and who possess the qualifications required for appointment to the highest judicial office in their respective countries, or who are jurisconsults of recognised competence. They are appointed by common accord of the Governments of the Member States in the same way that the Members of the Commission are chosen,[7] the independence of the Court from the

---

[1] *Supra*, para. 2–01, Arts. 7 and 31 *et seq.* ECSC: Arts. 4 and 164 *et seq.* EEC: Arts. 3 and 136 *et seq.* EAEC.

[2] By the Convention on Certain Institutions common to the European Communities signed with the Rome Treaties on March 25, 1957.

[3] O.J. 1974, L350/1, amended O.J. 1979, L238/1 with effect from October 6 1979 and see generally Jacobs and Durand, *References to the European Court* (1975).

[4] See also Article 32 ECSC and 137 EAEC, as amended by the 1972 Act of Accession.

[5] See also Articles 32a ECSC and 138 EAEC as amended by the 1972 Act of Accession.

[6] Article 16. This provision does not itself amend the Treaties establishing the Communities. No change is to be made in the number of Advocates General.

[7] *Supra*, para. 3–27.

Council, which might otherwise be expected to appoint its members, being thereby underlined.

One of the most notable features of the composition of the Court is that in contrast to the position under the provisions relating to the Commission[8] there is no requirement (a) that all Member States be represented on the Court, or (b) that the nominees of the Member States should all be nationals of Community countries. This formal omission has not, however, affected practice in the matter; all the Member States are represented upon the Court, and in fact by their own nationals. Similarly, the posts of Advocates-General have been occupied by nationals of the largest States, *i.e.* originally France and Germany, and now in addition, with the accession of new Member States in 1973, Italy and the United Kingdom.

8—03   The judges and Advocates-General are each appointed for a term of six years, but to ensure a continuity of composition, five judges are to be replaced alternately every three years.[9] The terms of office of the Advocates-General are also staggered.[10] Retiring judges and Advocates-General are, however, eligible for reappointment and there is no upper age limit for appointment.

The relatively short term of office provided for has been criticised as not safeguarding judicial independence sufficiently. There is some force in the criticism, which is not fully met by the reply that independence is inherent, and that the judges and Advocates-General are themselves required to be independent. Before taking up their duties, the judges and Advocates-General are required to take an oath in open court to perform their duties impartially and conscientiously, and to preserve the secrecy of the deliberations of the Court.[11] Judges and Advocates-General are debarred from holding any political or administrative office and they are disabled from engaging in any occupation, whether gainful or not, unless exemption is exceptionally granted by the Council.[12] But they are permitted to engage in teaching. The restrictions placed upon outside activities are similar to those placed on Members of the Commission.[13]

8—04   Upon taking up their duties, the judges and Advocates-General are required to give a solemn undertaking (in addition to the oath above, and immediately after having taken it[14]), that, both during and after their term of office, they will respect the obligations arising therefrom, in particular the duty to behave with integrity

---

[8] *Cf.* Art. 10 of the Merger Treaty.
[9] Anticipating the changes to be made pursuant to Art. 16 of the Greek Act of Accession.
[10] Art. 167 as amended and Dec. 81/209, O.J. 1981; L 100/21.
[11] Art. 2, EEC Statute. The form of the oath is set out in Article 3 of the Rules of Procedure.
[12] Art. 4, EEC Statute.
[13] *Supra,* para.3–28.
[14] Art. 3, para. 3, Rules of Procedure.

and discretion as regards acceptance, after they have ceased to hold office, of certain appointments or benefits. The ECSC Statute is more specific, prohibiting acceptance for a minimum period of three years after relinquishing office of any appointment in the coal and steel industries. In all cases the Court of Justice is the final arbiter of what is or is not permissible.

A judge or Advocate-General may be deprived of his office or of his right to a pension or other benefits in its stead only if, in the unanimous opinion of his fellow judges and Advocates-General of the Court, he no longer fulfils the requisite conditions or meets the obligations arising from his office.[15] This provision for discipline by internal means is itself a guarantee of independence, although the member affected has no right to vindicate himself in public, but only to present his comments at a private hearing.[16]

The provisions discussed above do, therefore, go some way towards mitigating the lack of security of tenure, and further, provisions relating to privileges and immunities afford some additional protection.[17] The judges also receive some measure of protection from the fact that no dissenting judgments are pronounced, so that no individual judge can be singled out for his views. Curiously enough, the Treaty contains no provision that the judges and Advocates-General shall neither seek nor take instructions from any Government or from any other body (*cf.* Art. 10 (2), second sub-para., of the Merger Treaty in relation to the Commission) but the seeking or taking of such instructions would manifestly be incompatible with the judicial function, and would bring into operation the disciplinary provisions of the Statutes.[18]

The President

8—05   Pursuant to Article 167 EEC, final paragraph, the judges elect the President of the Court of Justice from among their number for a term of three years. He may be re-elected. The election takes place after the appointment of the judges themselves, and is valid for the period until the next partial election.[19]

The President directs the work and the running of the Court,[20] and in particular decides upon matters of distribution, timetable and so forth. He presides over the sittings of the Court whether in open court or in private session, and the ancillary services of the Court are under his authority. The President has in addition a certain jurisdiction which is exclusive to himself. Thus he adjudicates alone on applications by way of summary procedure to suspend execution[21] and it is to him that applications are made

---

[15] Art. 6, EEC Statute.
[16] Art. 4, Rules of Procedure.
[17] Art. 3, EEC Statute and *supra,* paras. 5–12 *et seq.*
[18] Art. 6, EEC Statute.
[19] Art. 7, Rules of Procedure.
[20] Art. 8, Rules of Procedure.
[21] Art. 84, 85, Rules of Procedure.

for orders to ensure that inspections pursuant to Article 81 of the Euratom Treaty are carried out compulsorily.

The Advocates-General

8—06   As will have emerged from the above discussion, the status of the Advocates-General is for virtually all practical purposes identical with that of the judges. It is the duty of the Advocates-General, acting with complete impartiality and independence, to make, in open court, reasoned submissions on cases brought before the Court of Justice, in order to assist the Court in the performance of its task of ensuring that the law is observed in the interpretation and application of the Treaties.[22] The Advocates-General are also called upon to give opinions on the various steps the Court may take, but their primary function is to provide submissions for the guidance of the Court (whether sitting in chambers or in plenary session) in making its judgments. As a matter of procedure, the submissions of the Advocates-General are given orally, after the close of the oral hearing of the parties, and before judgment is given. They are reproduced after the judgments of the Court in the European Court Reports.

The system of submissions of Advocates-General is unknown to the English legal system. It derives from the practice of the French Conseil d'Etat, where the officer involved is the *Commissaire du Gouvernement*. His function is essentially to set out the matter under examination and to discuss the law applicable to the case and the implications of the various alternatives, finally suggesting what should be the outcome. The detail into which he will go into any question will depend upon the importance and difficulty of the case. The broad-ranging nature of his submissions serves as an invaluable background to the facts and implications of the judgment of the Conseil d'Etat, which is often extremely short and rather oracular. The submissions of the European Advocates-General are similarly elucidatory, but the tendency for the European Court to give more fully argued judgments dealing with facts and law has rather blurred the clear-cut roles as they may originally have been conceived.

The Registrar of the Court

8—07   Provision is made for the appointment of a Registrar in Article 168 of the EEC Treaty, and the existence of the office is confirmed, rather than provided for, in Articles 9 to 11 of the EEC Statute. The Registrar is required to take an oath identical to that of the judges and Advocates-General. It is to the Registrar that the officials and other servants attached to the Court are responsible under the authority of the President of the Court, but his most obvious public function is to handle the paper work of the Court.[23]

[22] Art. 166, EEC.

[23] Instructions to the Registrar, O.J. 1974, L 350/33 provided for in Art. 15 of the Rules of Procedure.

The Hearing of the Case

Chambers

8—08   Article 165 EEC, second para., sets out the general proposition that the Court of Justice sits in plenary session. It goes on to provide, however, that it may form chambers, each consisting of three or five judges, either to undertake certain preparatory inquiries or to adjudicate on particular categories of cases in accordance with rules laid down for this purpose.

In the early years this facility was used principally for consideration of staff cases. In 1979, however, Article 9 was revised so as to permit the dividing up of the Court into Chambers quite generally as well as for preparatory enquiries. Article 95 as revised now provides for assignment to Chambers (really a hearing of a divisional court rather than an application to a judge in chambers) of any reference for a preliminary ruling as well as any action instituted by a natural or legal person "insofar as the difficulty or the importance of the case or particular circumstances are not such as to require that the Court decide it in plenary session." The decision to assign is taken after consideration of the preliminary report represented by the judge-rapporteur (*infra*) and after hearing the Advocate-General. However, any Member State or institution of the Communities being a party to or intervening in or submitting written observations may request that the case be decided in plenary session. Staff cases are now assigned to a particular Chamber designated annually (Art. 95 (3)). A chamber can at any stage refer to the full court any case assigned to it or devolving upon it (Art. 95 (4)).

It will be noticed that assignment to Chambers of references for preliminary ruling is nevertheless at variance with Article 165 (3) of the Treaty, which requires such cases to be heard in plenary session. However, the volume of such references forced this change in the Court.

The judge-rapporteur

8—09   With the assignment of the case to one of the Chambers a judge-rapporteur is appointed from the Chamber. It is he who in effect guides the case through the Court. He presents a report at the end of the written procedure on whether preparatory inquiries are needed (Art. 44, *infra*). He drafts both the summary of the proceedings which appears first as the report for the hearing (and served on the parties) and then, amended as appropriate and expanded to take account of the oral procedure, prefixed to the judgment, as well as the judgment itself.

The Deliberations of the Court

8—10   The deliberations of the Court are, and remain secret.[24] Each

[24] Art. 32, EEC Statute.

judge taking part is nevertheless required to give his view and the reasons for it.[25] The opinion reached by the majority determines the decision of the Court.[25] Provision is made for voting.[25] There is nevertheless some indication that the views of the judge-rapporteur are usually decisive.

Quorums and Challenges

8—11   Decisions of the Court are only valid when an uneven number of its members is sitting in deliberation.[26] A quorum of seven judges is necessary for plenary sessions and three judges constitute a quorum for decisions of Chambers. Article 16 of the EEC Statute provides that "no judge or Advocate-General may take part in the disposal of any case in which he has previously taken part. . ." in any capacity whatsoever. The Court is itself the final arbiter in case of doubt on this point, but a judge or Advocate-General may disqualify himself for a particular case on his own motion, or else the President may notify him that he should not take part. The fact that a judge or Advocate-General has previously heard a case before the Court of Justice, involving the same parties and same subject-matter will not of course automatically disqualify him.

Although an individual could conceivably challenge a judge on grounds of partiality, Article 16 of the EEC Statute provides that "a party may not apply for a change in the composition of the Court or of one of its chambers on the grounds of either the nationality of a judge or the absence from the Court or from the Chamber of a judge of the nationality of that party" (last paragraph). This is in keeping with the Community spirit, and is in contrast to the system of ad hoc judges provided for by Article 31 of the Statute of the International Court of Justice. (The Statute of the latter court is in fact otherwise followed quite closely where appropriate).

Languages

8—12   A language of the case is designated for each case (Art. 29 of the Rules of Procedure). The proceedings take place and judgment is given in this language (para. 3) and the text in that language is authentic (Art. 31 of the Rules). The language of the case is chosen by the applicant subject to the rule that if the application is against a Member State or a natural or legal person having the nationality of a Member State the language of the case shall be the language of that Member State - or one of them, at the choice of the applicant, if there is more than one. The language of the case is the language of the referring court in references for

---

[25] Art. 27 of the Rules.
[26] Article 15 of the EEC Statute as amended by Article 20 of the 1972 Act of Accession.

preliminary rulings. Subject to these basic rules (in Art. 29) there is a good deal of flexibility. Another language of the case can be agreed upon or designated by the Court. Members of the Court and Member States may use their own language. In both cases the Registrar will arrange for appropriate translations. Otherwise documents may be submitted with a translation into the language of the case. The working language of the Court is in any event French, so all documents are likely to be translated into that language for the purposes of the Court.

Representation

8—13   A State or an institution of the Community is represented by an agent appointed for each case, who may be assisted by an adviser or by a lawyer entitled to practise before a court of a Member State.[27] In the practice of the institutions it is usually the legal service which conducts a case from beginning to end, and a member of this service who appears before the Court.

In the practice of the United Kingdom the agent is usually a member of the Treasury Solicitor's staff. Usually the case is conducted by counsel, although this is occasionally done by the Treasury Solicitors themselves or, more rarely, by a legal adviser to a government department responsible for the subject-matter.

Other parties, *i.e.* individuals, corporations, etc., must be represented by a lawyer entitled to practise before a court of a Member State.

The EEC Statute (Art. 17, fifth para.) makes it clear that university teachers having a right of audience at home will have a right of audience to the same extent before the Court of Justice.

The Court of Justice itself has disciplinary jurisdiction over agents, advisers and lawyers appearing before it, and may waive the rights and immunities which they otherwise enjoy for the independent exercise of their duties before the Court.[28]

Procedure

8—14   Title 2 of the Rules of Procedure,[29] itself entitled "Procedure" deals with the conduct of an action. It is divided into nine chapters of varying length, successively entitled:

(1) Written Procedure, (2) Preparatory Inquiries, (3) Oral Procedure, (4) Judgments, (5) Costs, (6) Legal Aid, (7) Discontinuance, (8) Service and (9) Time-Limits.

These provisions apply principally to direct actions, *i.e.* cases which originate before the European Court. Elements of them are applied to references for preliminary rulings (*infra*, Chapter 10). Pro-

---

[27] Art. 17, EEC Statute.
[28] *Ibid.* On procedural privilege see Case 155/79 *AM & S Europe* v. *Commission* (not yet decided).
[29] Note 3, *supra.*

vision is made for joinder of related cases of any type concerning the same subject-matter. This may occur at any stage of the proceedings (Art. 43).

Written procedure, preparatory enquiries and oral procedure

8—15   The written procedure (Arts. 37-44) bears comparison with an English civil action, with exchanges of application, defence, reply and rejoinder as appropriate. In requests for preliminary rulings this stage of course consists of the communication of the request.

Normally time-limits are fairly short: one month for lodging a defence (although this can be extended)[30] and similarly short periods fixed by the Court for other pleadings.

There is a limitation on introducing further evidence in reply or rejoinder and on raising fresh issues unless based on matters of law or of fact which come to light in the course of the written procedure.[31] This has proved a wide exception.[32] After the last written pleading has been lodged or the relevant time-limit has expired, the judge rapporteur presents his preliminary report to the Court, containing recommendations as to whether "a preparatory enquiry or any other preparatory step should be undertaken" and whether this should be done by referring the case to a Chamber.[33]

Preparatory enquiries (Arts. 45-54)

8—16   The Court has power to call for the personal appearance of the parties, to request information and documents, to call for oral testimony by witnesses, to seek experts' reports, or to hold a view. In practice the commonest forms of inquiry are requests to the institutions for particular instruments or questions to parties, the institutions or the Member States.

Oral procedure (Arts. 55 to 62)

8—17   Cases are normally heard in the order in which the preparatory inquiries has been completed.[34] The President conducts the proceedings.[35] He and the other judges and the Advocates-General may address questions to agents and lawyers.[36] The Court may at any time order a (further) measure of inquiry[37] or reopen the oral

---

[30] Art. 40.
[31] Art. 42.
[32] Cases 51, 86 and 96/75 *EMI.* v. *CBS.* [1976] E.C.R. 811, 871, 913; Reg. 1439/74 was first referred to in support of the defendant's case at the oral procedure. But see also Case 232/78 *Commission* v. *France* [1979] E.C.R. 2729.
[33] Art. 44.
[34] Art. 55.
[35] Art. 56.
[36] Art. 57.
[37] Art. 60.

procedure.[38] The oral procedure tends not to be the occasion for great oratory, since most of the arguments will have been gone into extensively during the written stage. It is, however, the occasion upon which questions of doubt and detail may be cleared up or to meet points which there was no opportunity to answer in the written procedure.[39] Technically part of the oral procedure, the Advocate-General's opinion is usually delivered a couple of weeks later, in open court. The Court gives a reserved judgment at a later stage, again in open court. It will be noted that this procedure is not strictly adversary as in Common law jurisdictions but, on the contrary, the Court may itself step in to direct the case, and in practice does so.

Judgments[40]

8–18   Article 63 sets out certain formal requirements for judgments. The judgment is delivered in open court.[41] There are provisions for publication of the judgment, for its revision for clerical errors and the like, and also for failure to rule on a given count or on costs.

Costs[42]

8–19   The normal rule in contentious action is that costs follow the event,[43] but a successful party may be ordered to pay the costs, if it has been guilty of vexatious behaviour, *e.g.* where the Commission as defendant was successful in the action but was largely responsible for the action being brought.[44] In awarding costs where an intervention has occurred the Court will have regard to the subject-matter and nature of the action, its importance from the stand point of Community law and the difficulties of the case.[45]

Article 104 of the Rules provides that in proceedings for a preliminary ruling it shall be for the national court or tribunal to decide as to the costs of the reference. The Court makes a standard-form order that "as these proceedings are, in so far as the parties to the main action are concerned, in the nature of a step in the action pending before the national court, the decision on costs is a matter for that court."[46] The proceedings before the Court are

---

[38] Art. 61.
[39] And see note 32, *supra.*
[40] Arts. 63 to 68.
[41] Art. 34, EEC Statute and Art. 64, Rules of Procedure.
[42] Arts. 69 to 75.
[43] Art. 69. The Commission now bears its own costs in staff cases: Art. 70.
[44] *Ibid.* and Cases 88/76 *Exportation des Sucres* v. *Commission* [1977] E.C.R. 709; 74/72 *Di Blasi* v. *Commission* [1973] E.C.R. 847 and 61/74 *Santopietro* v. *Commission* [1975] E.C.R. 483. "Official time is not chargeable": Case 126/76 *Dietz* v. *Commission* [1979] E.C.R. 2131.
[45] Cases 40/73 *Suikerunie* v. *Commission* [1975] E.C.R. 1663 and 4/73 *Nold* v. *Commission* [1975] E.C.R. 985.
[46] Case 62/72 *Bollmann* v. *HZA Hamburg Waltershof* [1973] E.C.R. 269.

in principle free, but the Court may require the amount of costs needlessly incurred to be refunded.[47]

Legal Aid[48]

8—20   Eligibility for legal aid is decided by the chamber to which the judge acting as rapporteur appointed to the case belongs, having regard to means and likelihood of success. The sums advanced by way of legal aid are deducted from the costs ordered by the Court.

Discontinuance[49]

8—21   Provision is made here for the striking-out of actions in the event of settlement or abandonment. Article 173 and 175 actions cannot be settled. Other grounds for striking out are dealt with as issues of admissibility under Article 92 of the Rules.

Service[50]

8—22   Parties are obliged to designate an address for service in Luxembourg. It is at this address that documents are served on the parties.

Time-limits[51]

8—23   Rules are laid down here for the computation of time-limits laid down in Annexes to the Rules of Procedure.

Title 3 : Special Forms of Procedure

8—24   Title 3 of the Rules of Procedure, entitled "Special Forms of Procedure" is divided into eleven Chapters successively entitled:

(1) Suspension of operation or enforcement and other interim measures, (2) Procedural Issues, (3) Intervention, (4) Judgments by default and applications to set them aside, (5) Cases assigned to chambers, (6) Exceptional review proceedings (1. Third party proceedings, 2. Revision), (7) Appeals against decisions of the (Euratom) Arbitration Committee, (8) Interpretation of judgments, (9) Preliminary rulings and other references for interpretation, (10) Special procedures under Articles 103 to 105 of the Euratom Treaty, (11) Opinions.

Most of the Chapter headings are self-explanatory. On others some elaboration is called for:

---

[47] Art. 72.
[48] Art. 76.
[49] Arts. 77 and 78.
[50] Art. 79.
[51] Arts. 80 to 82.

Procedural issues: Admissibility

8—25   Article 91 provides for hearing of procedural motions. Under Article 92 (1) actions can be struck out by reasoned order declaring the application inadmissible. Under paragraph 2 the Court may at any time consider *ex proprio motu* whether there is any absolute bar to proceeding with a case (*e.g. lis pendens*).[52] Often under Article 91 the decision on admissibility will be given in the judgment, possibly invalidating some but not all grounds of action.

Interim measures (Chapter 1)[53]

8—26   Article 185 of the Treaty envisages that Court actions shall not normally have suspensory effect on Community acts but the Court may order suspension "if it considers that circumstances so require." Article 83 (1) of the Rules makes it clear that an application for suspension will only be admissible if the applicant is challenging the measure in proceedings under Article 173. This "presupposes that the applicant must prove in a particularly clear fashion that he is concerned directly and individually."[54]

The application must in any event demonstrate urgency[55] and a prima facie case.[56] The Court will be reluctant to suspend a regulatory act where to do so would have an adverse effect upon others.[57] It is necessary to show that the measures are required in order to avoid irreparable damage or considerable expense.[58]

Article 186 of the Treaty provides that the Court may in any

---

[52] Cases 58 and 75/72 *Perinciolo* v. *Council* [1973] E.C.R. 511.

[53] Arts. 82 to 90.

[54] Case 44/75R *Könecke* v. *Commission* [1975] E.C.R. 637.

[55] 6/72 *Europemballage* v. *Commission* [1972] E.C.R. 157; 61/76 RII *Geist* v. *Commission* [1976] E.C.R. 2075; 31/79 R *Aciéries de Montereau* v. *Commission* [1979] E.C.R. 1077.

[56] 75/72 R *Perinciolo* v. *Council* [1972] E.C.R. 1201; 23/74 R *Küster* v. *Parliament* [1974] E.C.R. 331; 22/75 R *Küster* v. *Parliament* [1975] E.C.R. 277; 61/76 R *Geist* v. *Commission* [1976] E.C.R. 1349; 91/76 R *de Lacroix* v. *Court of Justice* [1976] E.C.R. 1563.

[57] 3/75 R *Johnson & Firth Brown* v. *Commission* [1975] E.C.R. 1; 54/75 R *De Dapper* v. *Parliament* [1975] E.C.R. 839; 26/76 R *Metro* v. *Commission* [1976] E.C.R. 1353; 91/76 R *de Lacroix* v. *Court of Justice* [1976] E.C.R. 1563; 243/78 R *Simmenthal* v. *Commission* [1978] E.C.R. 2391; 92/78 R *Simmenthal* v. *Commission* [1978] E.C.R. 1129.

[58] 6/72 R *Europemballage* v. *Commission* [1972] E.C.R. 157; 6 & 7/73 R *ICI* v. *Commission* [1973] E.C.R. 357; 20/74 R *Kali-Chemie* v. *Commission* [1974] E.C.R. 337; 62/74 R *Vellozzi* v. *Commission* [1974] E.C.R. 895; 71/74 R. &' RR *Frubo* v. *Commission* [1974] E.C.R. 1031; 3/75 R *Johnson & Firth Brown* v. *Commission* [1978] E.C.R. 1; 26/76 *Metro* v. *Commission* [1976] E.C.R. 1353; 88/76 *Exportation de Sucres* v. *Commission* [1976] E.C.R. 1585; 113/77 R & 113/79 R, INT *NTN Toyo* v. *Council* [1977] E.C.R. 1721 and 119/77 R & 121/77 R—[1977] E.C.R. 1867, 2107; 19/78 R *Authié* v. *Commission* [1978] E.C.R. 679; 4/78 R *Salerno* v. *Commission* [1978] E.C.R. 1; 48/79 R *Ooms* v. *Commission* [1979] E.C.R. 1703; 51/79 R *Buttner* v. *Commission* [1979] E.C.R. 1727; 51/79 R II *Buttner* v. *Commission* [1979] E.C.R. 2387; 809/79 R *Pardini* v. *Commission* [1980] E.C.R. 139.

cases before it prescribe any necessary interim measures. This is again covered by Article 83 (1) of the Rules. Here the considerations are similar to those under Article 185. The Court will not normally exercise its powers where the Commission could more properly take a decision.[59] The power has, however, been used to prevent a further deterioration before Articles 169 or 173 proceedings can be completed.[60]

Intervention[61]

8—27   Any person or body[62] establishing an interest in the result of any case[63] may apply to intervene.[64] Member States and institutions intervene as of right.[65] All interveners are, however, limited to supporting the submissions of one of the parties.[66] This does not mean that the intervener must adduce the same or similar arguments, but that he should have the same interest in the outcome.[67] In other words, general observations are not encouraged. An application to intervene must be made within three months of the publication of the notice of the case in the *Official Journal.*[68] The intervener must accept the case as he finds it at the time of intervention. He receives all the papers and is given a time-limit within which to make his written submissions.

Exceptional Review Proceedings[69]

8—28   The exceptional proceedings referred to are applications to have a judgment retried and modified, or to have it revised.

Interpretation of Judgments[70]

---

[59] 160/73R—161/73R *Miles Druce* v. *Commission* [1973] E.C.R. 1049; 160, 161—170/73R II, *ibid.* [1974] E.C.R. 281; 109/75R *National Carbonising Company* v. *Commission* [1975] E.C.R. 1193, [1977] E.C.R. 381; 792/79 R *Camera Care* v. *Commission* [1980] E.C.R. 119; 24 & 97/80 R *Commission* v. *France* [1980] E.C.R. 1319.

[60] 31/77R & 53/77R *Commission* v. *UK* [1977] E.C.R. 921; 61/77R *Commission* v. *Ireland* [1977] E.C.R. 937, 1411; 24 & 97/80 R *Supra*, note 59.

[61] Art. 93.

[62] Cases 41/73 *SA Générale Sucrière* v. *Commission* [1973] E.C.R. 1465 and 72/74 *Union Syndicale* v. *Council* [1975] E.C.R. 401.

[63] Cases 71/74 *Nederlandse Vereniging* v. *Commission* [1974] E.C.R. 1095; 116/77 *Amylum* v. *Council & Commission* [1978] E.C.R. 893; 113/77R, Int & RR *NTN TOYO* v. *Council* [1977] E.C.R. 1721.

[64] Art. 37, EEC Statute. This includes the Assembly: Cases 138 & 139/79 *Roquette,* and *Maizena* v. *Council* (October 29, 1980).

[65] *Ibid.*

[66] *Ibid.* and note 63, *supra.*

[67] Note 63, *supra.*

[68] Art. 93 (1) of the Rules.

[69] Article 41, EEC Statute, Arts. 97 to 100 Rules. See Case 116/78 Rev. *Bellintani* v. *Commission* [1980] E.C.R. 23.

[70] Art. 40, EEC Statute and Art. 102 of the Rules. See, *e.g.* Cases 24/66 Bis *Getreidehandel* v. *Commission* [1973] E.C.R. 1599 and 41/73 Interp. *Générale Sucrière* v. *Commission* [1977] E.C.R. 445.

8—29 In giving its ruling on a request for interpretation, the Court is required to act by way of judgment. The record of the interpretative judgment is annexed to the record of judgment so interpreted.

Preliminary rulings

8—30 Articles 103 and 104 attract to requests for preliminary rulings all the Rules of Procedure in Title 2 and following, other than those relating to exchanges of written pleadings. The written stage consists of the order of reference and any supporting document plus any statements of case or written observations lodged as of right[71] within a two-month time limit by any of the Member States, the Commission and the Council where appropriate (*i.e.* if a Council act is impugned). The Commission invariably submits written observations. Member States have done so increasingly.

The same rules apply to references under the Protocols concerning the interpretation of the Article 220 Conventions.[72]

Opinions[73]

8—31 This Chapter of the Rules of Procedure makes provision for the giving of opinions under Article 228 EEC (request for opinion as to compatibility of Treaties with Third States, etc.) and under Article 95 ECSC (*petite révision*).

---

[71] Art. 37, EEC Statute.
[72] *Infra.* Chapter 23 and see Case 12/73 *Tessili* v. *Dunlop* [1976] E.C.R. 1473.
[73] Arts. 107 to 109.

Chapter 9

SCOPE OF JURISDICTION, THE ROLE OF THE COURT AND EFFECT OF JUDGMENTS

Scope of Jurisdiction

9—01   Article 219 EEC states that Member States undertake not to submit disputes concerning the interpretation or application of the Treaty to any method of settlement other than those provided therein. (Article 193 Euratom is identical. Article 87 ECSC is to similar effect.) This provision creates a jurisdictional closed circuit, in that such questions of interpretation and application can only be decided in certain defined ways. In the vast majority of cases it is the Court of Justice which has jurisdiction, and generally exclusive jurisdiction, to decide the question, although Article 183 states that, save where jurisdiction is conferred on the Court by the EEC Treaty, disputes to which the Community is a party shall not on that ground be excluded from the jurisdiction of the courts or tribunals of the Member States. However, Article 4 EEC, which states that each institution of the Communities shall act within the limits of the powers conferred on it by the Treaties, makes it clear that the jurisdiction of the Court of Justice is one of attribution, *i.e.* that its jurisdiction is limited to that conferred.[1]

Whether the Court of Justice has jurisdiction in any particular circumstance cannot therefore be ascertained by a reference to general principles, but only by inspection of the relevant Treaty provisions (see schematic list of types of jurisdiction under the EEC, ECSC and Euratom Treaties in Appendix 2).

9—02   Admittedly, Article 164 states that the Court of Justice shall ensure that in the interpretation and application of the Treaty the law is observed, but this is not the same as conferring jurisdiction to decide such questions; it defines the Court's role without specifying when and how it is to be implemented. The main provisions on the jurisdiction of the Court (listed schematically in Appendix 2) are contained in Part Five of the Treaty - Institutions of the Community, Title 1, Chapter 1. Section 4, Articles 164 to 188, entitled The Court of Justice. In addition specialised jurisdictional provisions are contained in Article 93, in the Merger Treaty replacing Articles 157 and 160 of the Treaty of Rome, and in Articles 225 and 228. The generally applicable jurisdictional provisions of Articles 164 to 188 and 215 are considered in turn in the next Chapters as follows:

[1] Cases 12/63 *Schlieker* v. *H.A.* [1963] E.C.R. 85; 44/65 *Hessische knappschaft* v. *Singer* [1965] E.C.R. 965.

116

Chapter 10:
References from National Courts; Requests for Preliminary Rulings (Article 177).

Chapter 11:
Direct Actions before the European Court; Action against Member States for failure to fulfil an obligation (Articles 169 to 171); Action relating to penalties (Articles 172); Review of legality of Council and Commissions Acts: Action for annulment (Article 173); Action against the Council or Commission for failure to act (Article 175); Plea (Exception) of illegality (Article 184); Action for compensation (Article 215).

The Role of the Court of Justice

9—03 Article 164 EEC states that the role of the Court is to ensure that in the interpretation and application of the Treaties the law is observed. The formula of Article 31 ECSC is rather wider in that the Court is, additionally, under that Treaty, to fulfil the same functions in relation to the rules laid down for the implementation thereof. Nevertheless, it is clear that the Court has the same functions under the Paris and Rome Treaties, for Article 173 EEC provides for review by the Court of Justice of the legality of binding acts of the Council and the Commission, or, in other words, the rules laid down for the implementation of the Treaties. Despite the broad similarity of the general rule laid down, however, the actual scope of the jurisdiction of the Court varies as between the Treaties.[2]

Under the jurisdictional provisions contained in the Community Treaties the Court is variously called upon to deliver judgments, opinions and decisions. The vast majority of these provisions call for a judgment, and indeed applications resulting in a formal judgment make up the bulk of the work of the Court. In no circumstances, however, may the Court act without first having been seised of the question. Once seised, the Court must in fact give a judgment (or opinion or decision, where applicable), assuming the case is not withdrawn or struck out but in general only within the limits of the submissions of the parties in the case. The judgments of the Court are not subject to appeal.

Actions brought before the Court of Justice do not *ipso facto* suspend application of any act attacked, but the Court of Justice may in fact order such suspension if it considers that the circumstances so require. The Court may also prescribe any necessary interim measures.[3]

---

[2] 27/58 *Hauts Fourneaux de Givors* v. *H.A.* [1960] E.C.R. 241, 255—inapplicability of the rules of regional policy contained in Article 80 (2) EEC (Transport) to transport of ores coming under the ECSC Treaty.

[3] *Supra,* para. 8–26.

Effects of Judgments of the Court of Justice in General

9—04   Judgments of the Court of Justice are in terms only enforceable within the fairly narrow limits laid down in the Treaty. Thus under Article 192 the decisions of the Court are only enforceable where they impose a pecuniary obligation on persons other than States.[4] In such cases enforcement is governed by the rules of civil procedure in force in the state in the territory of which it is carried out. Enforcement is carried out at the national level without any formality other than that of verifying the authenticity of the decisions of the Court of Justice, to which is appended the order for its enforcement.

Where the judgment of the Court of Justice is not in terms enforceable, there is nonetheless generally an obligation to comply with it. Thus Member States found guilty of a failure to fulfil an obligation under the Treaty are required to take the necessary measures to comply with the judgment of the Court[5] and similarly, an institution whose act has been declared void or whose failure to act has been declared contrary to the Treaty is required to take the necessary measures to comply with the judgment.[6] The jurisdiction to give preliminary rulings does not give rise to a judgment susceptible of enforcement, and there is accordingly no similar requirement for the purposes of Article 177. Article 5 imposes the obligation on Member States to "take all appropriate measures . . . to ensure fulfilment of the obligations . . . resulting from action taken by the institutions of the Community."[7]

Particular Cases

Action for failure to fulfil an obligation

9—05   A judgment of the Court of Justice takes the form, under Articles 169 and 170, of a finding that a Member State has failed to fulfil an obligation, the judgment specifying the nature of the failure. The Member State is required to take the necessary measures to comply with the judgment (Art. 171) but a further failure to fulfil this obligation does not open the way for sanctions, as it does under the equivalent provision of the ECSC Treaty.[8] In terms of express Treaty provisions, redress for failure to fulfil an obligation under Article 171 of the EEC Treaty may therefore only be obtained by way of a further application under Article 169 or 170.

Review of legality of Community acts

9—06   If the Court of Justice finds an action seeking review of the

---

[4] See on currencies Cases 41, 43, 44/73 *SA Générale Sucrière* v. *Commission* [1977] E.C.R. 445.
[5] Article 171 EEC. Cases 24 & 97/80R *Commission* v. *France* [1970] E.C.R.1319.
[6] Article 176 EEC. Case 76/79, *Könecke* v. *Commission* [1980] E.C.R. 665.
[7] *Infra.*
[8] Article 88, ECSC.

legality of Community acts to be well founded, it is required, by Article 174 EEC, to declare "the act concerned" void. "In the case of a regulation, however, the Court of Justice shall if it considers this necessary, state which of the effects of the regulation which it has declared void shall be considered as definitive." Under Article 176 EEC the institution whose act has been declared void is required to take the necessary measures to comply with the judgment of the Court of Justice.

It is settled that the judgment of the Court declaring a Community act to be void has effect *erga omnes,* and not simply as between the parties. Since as a general rule invalidity runs from time of issue of the Community act, it was necessary to make provision for declaring certain effects of regulations definitive as otherwise undue hardship might result for those who reasonably relied upon the Community act. A distinction has nevertheless to be drawn between a judgment that a regulation is void and a judgment that an individual decision should be annulled, with an incidental finding that the rule in the regulation on which it is based is unlawful. In the latter instance the judgment applies only *inter partes,* so other individuals similarly affected are not relieved of the necessity to seek their own remedies.[9] Where the Community act has been held void it will generally be necessary for the Community Institution concerned to withdraw and replace it. Damages may also be payable.[10]

Actions for failure to act

9–07   Where the Court of Justice declares a failure to act on the part of a Community institution to be contrary to the Treaty, the institution concerned is required to take the necessary measures to comply with the judgment.[11] It may be asked how far, for example, the Commission could be held responsible for failure to take the necessary measures where the original failure concerns an obligation imposed on the Community as a whole, and action by the Commission is dependent upon action taken by the Council. It seems that the Court would be unlikely to entertain such an excuse sympathetically,[12] but such an excuse might be acceptable in respect of an obligation placed upon the Commission alone. Either way, a further Article 175 action is the only method of enforcing compliance with Article 176.

Preliminary rulings

9–08   Article 177 EEC, giving the Court of Justice jurisdiction to give preliminary rulings on questions referred to it by national courts,

[9] Case 15/73 *Schots-Kortner* v. *Council and Commission* [1974] E.C.R. 177.
[10] Case 116/77 *Amylum* v. *Council and Commission* [1979] E.C.R. 3497.
[11] Article 176.
[12] *Cf.* Case 45/64 *Commission* v. *Italy* [1965] E.C.R. 867.

offers no guidance as to the nature and effect of its judgment - for judgment it is, not a mere opinion - with the result that there is a certain amount of controversy particularly as to the scope of the judgment.

The judgment of the Court of Justice is binding on the Court that refers the question,[13] but the judgment is confined to an interpretation of Community law. It remains for the national court to apply that interpretation. It is therefore certainly not beyond the bounds of possibility that the outcome of two similar cases could be different although the courts deciding them claimed to be following the same interpretative ruling.

The interpretation by the Court of course relates only to the particular questions posed and in that sense cannot be said to have an effect *erga omnes*. However, if the same issue is raised again the Court may be expected to give an identical ruling and thus the decision can be said to have a universal effect. This phenomenon is highlighted by the procedure now adopted for assigning to a Chamber rather than requiring a decision of the full court.[14] It is not therefore necessary for a court, even a court of final appeal, to refer a question of interpretation if that question has already been ruled on by the Court.[15]

Temporal effects of Judgments

9-09 In *Defrenne*[16] the Court indicated that legal certainty required occasionally that in the case of judgments having retroactive effect, only persons who had already commenced proceedings could take advantage of the retroactive effect of the ruling.

It now seems that where the validty of a Community act is question under Article 173, the Court may be prepared to declare that any invalidity shall take effect only from the date of its judgment. This approach is apparently based on a broad interpretation of Article 174 and on legal certainty.[17]

---

[13] *Cf.* Cases 29/68 *Milch, Fett und Eierkontor* v. *HZA Saarbrüken* [1969] E.C.R. 165; 20/64 *Albatros* v. *Sopéco* [1965] E.C.R. 29.

[14] *Supra*, para. 8.08.

[15] Case 28/62 *Da Costa en Schaake* [1963] E.C.R. 31; 28/67 *Molkerei-Zentrale* v. *HZA Paderborn* [1968] E.C.R. 143.

[16] *Infra*, para. 25–05. Request for interpretation of Article 119 pursuant to Article 177.

[17] Cases 4/79 *Providence agricole de la Champagne* v. *ONIC*; 145/79 *Roquette* v. *Admin. des Douanes*; 109/79 *Maiseries de Beauce* v. *ONIC* (October 15, 1980).

Chapter 10

REFERENCES FROM NATIONAL COURTS: REQUESTS FOR PRELIMINARY RULINGS: ARTICLE 177

10—01 The Community possesses no administrative machinery or system of federal courts in each of the Member States to secure the application of Community law. Responsibility for implementation lies with the Member States and the national courts. Uniformity in interpretation and application is secured through the Article 177 procedure whereby national courts and tribunals may obtain rulings on the interpretation of Community law from the European Court. Proper application of Community law by the national administrations is further secured by the Article 169 procedure (action for infringement of the Treaty), discussed *infra*, Chapter 11.

Article 177 of the Treaty gives the Court of Justice jurisdiction to give preliminary rulings concerning:

(a) the interpretation of the Treaty;

(b) the validity and interpretation of acts of the institutions of the Community; and

(c) the interpretation of the statutes of bodies established by an act of the Council, where those statutes so provide.

10—02 The expression "preliminary rulings," which had currency before the definitive English text of the EEC Treaty was adopted, is not an entirely happy one, if only because it is rather opaque. The French *à titre préjudiciel* gives a much better idea of what is entailed; namely, that the domestic court seised of a question should be able to stay proceedings before and pending an interpretative decision from the Court of Justice on the point on which the case turns. The reference to the Court of Justice is thus not chronologically prior to the domestic action, but only to the judgment in the case. The jurisdiction to give preliminary rulings gives the Court of Justice exclusive power to pass upon matters referred to it under any of the heads of Article 177 EEC, under the substantially identical provisions of Article 150 Euratom, and under Article 41 ECSC, which enables the Court to give such rulings on the validity of Council or High Authority (*i.e.* Commission) acts, but on a somewhat different basis.

Article 177 EEC, Article 150 Euratom and Article 41 ECSC between them confer jurisdiction on the Court to give preliminary rulings on matters falling into four categories. The practice in relation to each category nevertheless shows a considerable unity, so that it is not for instance particularly useful to examine the power of the Court to interpret the Treaty in isolation from its power to interpret acts of the institutions. Essentially the jurisdiction of Court involves two powers: a power to give interpretations of Community law; and a power to rule on the validity of acts of the institutions.

Interpretation

10—03   Under sub-paragraph (*a*) of Article 177 the Court has jurisdiction to give preliminary rulings on the interpretation of the Treaty. This power extends only to the EEC and Euratom Treaties. The power to act under Article 41 ECSC is limited to ruling on the validity of Council and Commission acts.

Under sub-paragraph (*b*) of Article 177 EEC the Court of Justice has jurisdiction to give preliminary rulings on the interpretation of acts of the institutions of the Community.

"Act" implies an act with binding legal force even though the French text uses the term *délibérations* in the Paris Treaty. These notions are, however, probably co-extensive. Any action by a Community institution which alters the legal position of a party may be the subject of a preliminary ruling. The notion is almost certainly wider than "decision, regulation or directive" as described in Article 189. The cases in which the Court has been called upon to consider non-binding instruments suggest that limitations are to be found in the absence in such instruments of direct effects: but the Court is free to refer to non-binding instruments in interpreting the binding rules of Community law.[1]

10—04   Some difficulty arises over the term "institution" used in the Rome Treaties (Art. 41 ECSC refers expressly to the High Authority and the Council). The term must, it seems, be given its narrow meaning in Article 4 EEC. But a request for a preliminary ruling could not be made in relation to a decision of the Court of Justice, if only because there is a special revision or interpretation procedure. The argument that a judgment of the Court is binding and cannot therefore be put in question is not convincing without more. Acts of the Assembly are not binding and probably do not come within Article 177.

Sub-paragraph (*c*) gives the Court jurisdiction to interpret the statutes of bodies established by an act of the Council, where those statutes so provide. The phrase "statutes of bodies established by an act of the Council" is itself open to difficulties of interpretation. The argument that the Treaty does not give the Council power to establish such bodies must be rejected; the residual powers in Article 235, if nothing else, enable the Council to set up such bodies. But since such a setting-up must inevitably be by an act of the Council, surely this is in itself subject to interpretation

---

[1] Cases 9/73 *Schlüter* v. *HZA Lörrach* [1973] E.C.R. 1135; 59/75 *Pubblico Ministero* v. *Manghera* [1976] E.C.R. 91; 113/75 *Frecassetti* v. *Ammin. delle Finanze* [1976] E.C.R. 983.

under the previous head. The restrictive phrase "where those statutes provide" seems therefore to be without effect. It is in any case difficult to see how the matter could come before a domestic court in the first place so as to admit of an application to the Court of Justice, except perhaps, *e.g.* in relation to privileges and immunities.

The Concept of Interpretation

10—05 The first case to come before the Court of Justice under Article 177, *De Geus* v. *Bosch*[2] raised the question whether a territorially restricted agency agreement fell within the categories of agreements prohibited by Article 85 EEC, as of the entry into force of the Treaty. The defendants in the domestic action argued with some force that such a question involved not merely the interpretation of Article 85 but also its *application.* The Court held that the question of application was not one which it could decide under Article 177, and therefore confined itself to interpreting Article 85. There was, it held, no particular form in which questions had to be asked, and therefore it could sever those parts of the question over which it had jurisdiction, to give an interpretative ruling.

It was also argued that at the time of the application the interpretation of Article 85 was a matter for the Member States, because, under Article 88, it was for them to apply the rules of competition, not the Community, until the entry into force of regulations implementing Article 87 (in the event, Reg. 17/62). The Court agreed that it was for the Member States to apply the article, but rejected the corollary that it was therefore for them to interpret it.

In subsequent cases the essence of the Court's acceptance of jurisdiction has been that the Court is entitled only to pronounce on the interpretation of the Treaty and of acts of the institutions of the Community, but can neither apply them to a particular case[3] nor give judgment by means of this article on the interpretation or propriety of a measure of a domestic character.[4] Where the reference does not comply with these requirements the Court will reformulate the questions accordingly.[5] It will also do this where the reference does not disclose a question.[6] On the other hand, it will not consider issues not referred to it.[7] Nor will it consider the relevance of the question to the issues before the

---

[2] Case 13/61 [1962] E.C.R. 45.
[3] For a particularly clear example see Case 61/79 *Ammin. delle Finanze* v. *Denkavit Italiana* [1980] E.C.R. 1205.
[4] Case 26/62 *Van Gend En Loos* [1963] E.C.R. 1.
[5] *e.g.* case 6/64 *Costa* v. *ENEL* [1964] E.C.R. 585.
[6] *e.g.* Cases 83/78 *Pigs Marketing Board* v. *Redmond* [1978] E.C.R. 2347 and 253/78 & 1–3/79 *Guerlain et al* [1981] 2 C.M.L.R. 99.
[7] Case 44/65 *Hessische Knappschaft* v. *Singer* [1965] E.C.R. 965.

national courts[8] or the correctness of factual assumptions.[9] The court will not, however, entertain a collusive action, the effect of which is to attack the law of another Member State, Article 177 being designed for the settlement of genuine disputes.[9a]

Validity of acts of institutions

10—06 Although direct actions under Article 173 challenging the validity of acts of institutions must be brought within two months, this does not mean that the procedure under Article 177 is subject to the same limitations. It is "subject to objectives and rules different from those which govern the applications referred to in Article 173 of the Treaty."[10] Probably the principal objective of this aspect of Article 177 is similar to that of the interpretation aspect, namely, uniformity. Thus in the absence of a ruling on validity by the European Court, one national court might well be tempted to declare a Community act invalid whilst another would regard it as valid.[11] Conversely, there would be no guarantee that the provisons of Community acts which have been declared *ultra vires* by the European Court would have been found invalid by national courts.[12] The considerations which bear on the validity or otherwise of the legislation are the same as those which apply to Article 173 cases. Moreover, the Court, if it finds the legislation invalid, does not thereby *annul* it, so that past decisions adopted pursuant to the legislation are not invalid. However, the Community institution involved will be obliged to withdraw the act and replace it if necessary.[13]

What Bodies May or Must Refer Questions

10—07 The last two paragraphs of Article 177 indicate that any Court or tribunal (*juridiction*) may, if it considers that a decision on a question coming under any one of the heads listed is necessary to enable it to give judgment, request the Court to give a ruling thereon. The permissive facility becomes compulsory in the case of matters before courts "against whose decisions there is no judicial remedy under national law."

"Any court or tribunal"

10—08 References may be made by a Court acting in interlocutory

---

[8] *Infra,* note 23 and Case 53/79 *ONPTS* v. *Damiani* [1980] E.C.R. 273.

[9] *e.g.* Case 36/79 *Denkavit Futtermittel* v. *FA Warendorf* [1979] E.C.R. 3439.

[9a] Case 104/79 *Foglia* v. *Novello* [1980] E.C.R. 745.

[10] Case 156/77 *Commission* v. *Belgium* [1978] E.C.R. 1881.

[11] But contrast Article 41 ECSC where the Court has sole jurisdiction to pronounce on validity.

[12] See in particular cases on social security, *e.g.* 24/75, *Petroni* v. *ONPTS* [1975] E.C.R. 1149.

[13] *Supra,* para. 9–06.

124

proceedings, and it does not matter that the defendant did not appear or put in a defence.[14]

A premature referral is none the less valid.[15] The decision to refer will not constitute *res judicata*[16] but if it is in fact under appeal the European Court may stay the reference.[17] But the fact that the judge is bound on points of law by decisions of superior courts will not deprive him of his discretion to refer.[18] The fact that the Community rule queried is not directly applicable does not affect the Court's jurisdiction.[19]

Whether "arbitration bodies" in general have the right to refer questions is more difficult. It is suggested that any body, ad hoc or otherwise, established to decide questions according to legal principles probably will have that right.[20] In the United Kingdom this would seem to embrace all bodies to which the Arbitration Acts and the Tribunals and Inquiries legislation apply. It would seem that the right ought to extend to all types of tribunal whose decisions have legal or professional consequences for parties before it.[21] The decision to refer is entirely a matter for the judge,[22] although in English courts it is common practice to obtain the agreement of counsel to the referral and to the questions to be raised.

The question whether the ruling is "necessary" to enable the national court to give judgment is not a matter which concerns the European Court.[23] In England the Court of Appeal in *Bulmer* v. *Bollinger*[24] laid down certain guidelines, but the restrictive view of "necessary" there taken, together with the concept of "guidelines" has been the subject of criticism.[25] The Court of Appeal took the view that a ruling would only be "necessary" if the outcome of the case depended exclusively on it. The guidelines seem to have been largely disregarded in practice. Although

---

[14] Case 162/73 *Birra Dreher* [1974] E.C.R. 201.
[15] Case 70/77 *Simmenthal* [1978] E.C.R. 1453.
[16] *Bosch, supra,* note 2.
[17] Case 31/68 *Chanel* v. *Cepeha* [1970] E.C.R. 403.
[18] *Rheinmühlen* Cases 166 and 146/73 [1974] E.C.R. 33 and 139.
[19] Case 111/75 *Mazzalai* v. *Ferrovia del Renon* [1976] E.C.R. 657.
[20] Case 61/65 *Vaassen-Göbbels* v. *Beambtenfonds* [1966] E.C.R. 261.
[21] But see Case 65/77 *Razanatsimba* [1977] E.C.R. 2229 where the Cour d'Appel de Douai declared the Conseil de l'Ordre des Avocats de Lille was not a tribunal which could refer questions to the Court. Similarly 138/80, *Borker* [1980] E.C.R. 1975.
[22] See, *e.g.* Cases 127/73 *BRT* v. *SABAM,* [1974] E.C.R. 51; 93/78 *Mattheus* v. *Doego* [1978] E.C.R. 2203 and Case 44/65 *Hessische Knappschaft* v. *Singer* [1965] E.C.R. 965.
[23] Cases 19/68 *De Cicco* [1968] E.C.R. 473; 26/62 *Van Gend en Loos* [1963] E.C.R. 1; 6/64 *supra,* note 5 and *cf. Rheinmühlen* cases *supra,* note 18.
[24] [1974] Ch. 401; [1974] 2 C.M.L.R. 91.
[25] See generally D. Wyatt & A. Dashwood, *The Substantive Law of the EEC,* pp.68–69.

expense to the parties and delay to the case may be factors in weighing up whether to refer, waiting until the case is before an appeal court, supposedly better equipped to determine whether a reference is necessary, may be quite as conducive of expense and delay.

Courts of last instance

10—09   The third paragraph of Article 177 states that where any question falling within one of the listed heads is raised in a case pending before a court or tribunal against whose decisions there is no judicial remedy under national law, that court or tribunal must bring the matter before the Court of Justice. It is clear that "no judicial remedy" refers not only to full appeals to courts with power to decide on the merits but also to appeals to courts of cassation. Judicial review of administrative action would therefore prima facie come within the ambit of the phrase. It seems that courts whose decisions are not subject to review of any kind are obliged to refer questions, although they may only be courts equivalent to magistrates' courts. Where an interlocutory decision is "final" there will still be no duty to refer since in most cases the decision may be reversed or negated by the decision in the main action.[26] It appears that only the House of Lords in the United Kingdom may be regarded as the court of final instance even though appeal is subject to leave.

"Question of Community law"

10—10   The absolute terms of the final paragraph of Article 177 would appear to suggest that even an irrelevant issue should be referred, but this is unlikely to be the intention, and is certainly not the practice. On the other hand, what amounts to a "question" of Community law, or in other words what amounts to a controverted aspect of Community law, on which the Court of Justice ought to give a ruling, is itself a question of interpretation. There has been a tendency at times for courts to take the matter into their own hands, and to decide whether or not there is a question for interpretation. This approach has frequently been based on the *acte clair* doctrine of French administrative law under which courts refuse a reference on the ground that the point is so clear as not to require elucidation.[27] It has some justification where a question has previously been decided by the European Court.[28] Its applica-

---

[26] Case 107/76 *Hoffman La Roche* v. *Centrafarm* [1977] E.C.R. 957.

[27] *Shell-Berre* [1964] C.M.L.R. 462 (Conseil d'Etat); *French Republic* v. *Cornet* [1967] C.M.L.R. 351; *Administration des contributions indirectes* v. *Ramel* [1971] C.M.L.R. 315.

[28] Case 28/62 *Da Costa* [1963] E.C.R. 31: no need to refer again a question already decided by the Court. The Court will not, however, decline jurisdiction in a duplicate reference, but point to the earlier decision. See similarly Case 28/67 *Molkerei-Zentrale*

tion to other circumstances can lead to erroneous interpretations by national courts.

Conclusions

10—11   While Article 177 makes a valuable contribution to uniform interpretation and application of Community law, it plainly has certain shortcomings. In particular the absence of compulsion on lower courts to refer may mean that Community law is frequently applied without regard to a proper "centralised" jurisprudence. Moreover, the European Court can only interpret, or rule on validity: it cannot guarantee uniformity in the way its ruling is actually applied. Furthermore, the dependence of Community law on the authorities of the Member States for its application in detail, even in the case of regulations, means that significant divergences may result between the various Member States.

Chapter 11

DIRECT ACTIONS BEFORE THE EUROPEAN COURT
Action against Member States for Failure to Fulfil an Obligation: Arts 169 & 170

11—01 Article 169 states that:

> "If the Commission considers that a Member State has failed to fulfil an obligation under this Treaty, it shall deliver a reasoned opinion on the matter after giving the State concerned the opportunity to submit its observations.

> "If the State concerned does not comply with the opinion within the period laid down by the Commission, the latter may bring the matter before the Court of Justice."

Article 170 enables other Member States equally to bring such matters before the Court of Justice, subject to bringing the matter to the attention of the Commission.

This procedure is best described in English as the action against Member States for failure to fulfil an obligation. A similar procedure exists under Article 88 of the ECSC Treaty.

The procedure is not necessarily a contentious procedure, and may be set in motion with a view to obtaining an interpretation on a point not otherwise entirely clear.

11—02 Articles 169 and 170 set out the basic principles of the action, but it is subject to certain special procedures under various articles of the Treaties; thus Article 180 (a) enables the procedure to be operated by the Board of Directors of the European Investment Bank, and Articles 93 (2), 225 EEC and 38 and 82 Euratom provide for direct references to the Court without the administrative procedure provided in Article 169 first para. being required, since these articles contain comparable safeguards of their own. These articles do not, however, preclude use of Article 169 even where they apply.

The failure to fulfil an obligation may of course take the form of a failure on the part of a Member State to take implementing action.[1] Indeed the majority of cases under Article 169 have involved a failure of this kind. A Member State may also be brought before the Court under this article for introducing legislation which conflicts with Community law. Thus in Case 232/78 *Commission* v. *France*,[2] the French Government was held to have

---

[1] *e.g.* Case 31/69 *Commission* v. *Italy* [1970] E.C.R. 25 (regulation); 79/72 *Commission* v. *Italy* [1973] E.C.R. 667 (directive).
[2] [1979] E.C.R. 2729.

128

infringed the Community rules relating to free trade in agricultural goods by maintaining quotas on the import of lamb from other Member States.

11—03 For practical reasons the Commission cannot act on every failure which comes to its notice. An isolated failure by a national official is unlikely to provoke the Article 169 procedure. Indeed in many such instances the Member State would not have condoned the action by its official had it been aware of it at the time. It seems that only a consistent pattern of failure to comply with Community law would trigger the procedure. There is no special time-limit within which the Commission must initiate the Article 169 procedure. In some instances negotiations have gone on over a period of years over the breach of Community law.[3] In others a continuing breach has only been arrested after a period of years.[4] Furthermore, the fact that the breach has ended may not deprive the Article 169 procedure of its object.[5]

The Article 169 procedure is the Commission's principal way of discharging its watchdog functions under Article 155 in cases of failure to fulfil an obligation. Nevertheless the Commission is only obliged to issue the reasoned opinion which starts the procedure if, in the exercise of its discretion, the Commission considers that a Member State has failed to fulfil an obligation.

11—04 Failure to issue an opinion cannot be considered to be an actionable failure (except in the case where the failure results from a failure of the Commission to carry out its duty to guard against breaches of the Treaty). This emerges from Case 48/65 *Lütticke* v. *Commission.*[6] Lütticke had asked the Commission to initiate Article 169 proceedings against Germany, claiming that the compensatory turnover tax on imported diary products levied by the Federal Republic was incompatible with EEC Article 95. The Commission did not agree that Germany was in breach of the Treaty, and it was against this reply that Lütticke directed an action, alleging that the reply constituted a decision susceptible of annulment under Article 173 and complaining of the Commission's failure to act, under Article 175. The plaintiff failed on both counts, the Court holding that neither the reply nor any other act adopted by the Commission constituted a binding act capable of annulment, and that for the purposes of Article 175 the Commission could not be held to have failed to act since it had in fact replied.

11—05 It is generally agreed, however, that the Court could have rejected the action for failure to act on the narrower ground that

[3] Art. treasures cases *infra,* note 23.
[4] Case 7/71 *Commission* v. *France* [1971] E.C.R. 1003.
[5] *Infra,* para. 11–11.
[6] [1966] E.C.R. 19.

since the act requested was a non-binding act, it did not come within the category of acts mentioned by Article 175 EEC, or alternatively that the act in question was not one in which the plaintiff had a sufficient interest to request its issue.

Although an individual cannot therefore compel the opening of the Article 169 procedure, he may be able to obtain the same result by bringing a domestic action followed by a question under Article 177.[7] This impossibility of forcing the Commission to act is one of the chief differences between the EEC and the ECSC procedure under Article 88.[8] But an indirect attack under Article 177 EEC (preliminary ruling on the validity and interpretation of acts of the institutions) is permissible.[9] Since the Article 169 opinion is not a binding act, it is doubtful whether it could be annulled under Article 173, once given.

The procedure

11—06   The Article 169 procedure falls into two parts; what may be described as the pre-contentious procedure under the first paragraph, and the reference to the Court under the second paragraph.

Pre-contentious procedure

11—07   "If the Commission considers that a Member State has failed to fulfil an obligation under this Treaty, it shall deliver a reasoned opinion on the matter after giving the State concerned the opportunity to submit its observations."

The giving of at least the opportunity to be heard is fundamental to the procedure and cannot be dispensed with, although certain articles, which contain their own safeguards,[10] provide for direct reference to the Court.

The Member State is informed of the opening of the Article 169 procedure by letter, which must clearly state the grounds of complaint, but usually does not contain the full reasoning of the opinion, which may be required later. The Member State is usually given one month in which to reply, but this period can be extended with a degree of flexibility. If the State fails to reply, the Commission may issue its opinion without further delay. In fact, however, a reply is the rule rather than the exception, and indeed many cases have been settled at this stage without the necessity for an opinion.

The reasoned opinion

11—08   Again, the reasoned opinion is essential to the procedure. It

[7] Case 57/65 *Lütticke* v. *HZA Saarlouis* [1966] E.C.R. 205.
[8] *Infra*, para. 11–15.
[9] Case 26/62 *Van Gend en Loos* v. *Nederlandse administratie der Belastingen* [1963] E.C.R. 1.
[10] *Supra*, para. 9–02.

states the Commission's position as to the failure, and requests the Member State to put itself in order. The opinion does not itself have any legal force, nor does it make a determination that there has been a failure as does the decision taken in similar circumstances under Article 88 ECSC. This is a function of the Court.[11] But the difference is one of form, not of substance, for while the Commission's act is here non-binding, the Commission must seise the Court. Under the ECSC Treaty, its decision is binding, and the Member State may seise the Court if aggrieved.

As a matter of general practice, the Commission takes some care to provide exhaustive reasoning in its opinion. The reasoning is an essential element of legal security, and is required even though the facts of the case will be well known to all parties by this stage. On the other hand, the opinion need not as a matter of law contain more than a certain minimum of information. In Case 7/61 *Commission* v. *Italy*[12] the Italian Government claimed *inter alia* that the letter sent by the Commission as a reasoned opinion did not conform to the requirements of Article 169, first para., since it did not examine the relevance of the arguments advanced by the Italian Government. The Court held that:

11—09
>"The opinion referred to in Article 169 of the Treaty must be considered to contain a sufficient statement of reasons to satisfy the law when it contains - as it does in this case - a coherent statement of the reasons which lead the Commission to believe that the State in question has failed to fulfil an obligation under the Treaty.
>
>The letter of 21 December 1960 cited above, although not drawn up in due form, fulfils this requirement."[13]

Further, it is clear that the Commission is in no sense prevented from altering its reasons between the time of the initial complaint and the issue of the reasoned opinion.[14] The whole object of giving the Member State an opportunity to comment is to define issues.

The question remains what effect a lack of reasoning would have on a case brought under Article 169, second para. As emerges from Case 7/61 *Commission* v. *Italy*[15] it is probable that the Court would, in such circumstances, hold the reference to be inadmissible.

All this assumes, however, that the Member State fails to comply with the opinion. The Commission must give the State concerned time to comply with its opinion, and should give indications of what will constitute compliance, unless this is obvious from the context. These indications cannot constitute a decision as to the

[11] Cases 48/65 *Lütticke* v. *Commission, supra,* note 6 and 6 & 11/69 *Commission* v. *France* [1969] E.C.R. 523.
[12] [1961] E.C.R. 317.
[13] *Ibid.* p.327.
[14] *Ibid.*
[15] *Supra,* note 12.

method of compliance.[16]

If the Member State takes action designed to achieve compliance, but which does not in fact do so, the Commission may well be obliged to start an entirely fresh Article 169 procedure.[17]

Reference to the Court

11–10   If the Member State fails to comply, the Commission may seise the Court. It has a discretion in this matter, limited only by its duty under Article 155 to secure observance of the Treaty. There is no time-limit on making the reference - although the Court frowns on interminable delay in bringing any action. On the other hand, the Member State cannot engage in delaying tactics, *e.g.* by introducing a request for safeguards under Article 226 EEC (now expired), as happened in Case 7/61 *Commission* v. *Italy*[18] since this is part of an entirely separate procedure. Such attempts were specifically rejected in Cases 2 & 3/62 *Commission* v. *Belgium and Luxembourg*[19] and Case 7/61 *Commission* v. *Italy*.[20] Belgium and Luxembourg also argued in Cases 2 & 3/62[21] that since the Commission was itself allegedly at fault, there was no need to comply until the Commission had regularised its own position. This was rejected by the Court, as was a rather similar argument in 48/65 *Lütticke* v. *Commission*.[22] Nor, for that matter, may a Member State excuse its failure to act by pointing to a failure to act on the part of one of its constitutionally independent institutions, such as the legislature.[23]

11–11   A further issue raised by Case 7/61 *Commission* v. *Italy*[24] was whether the Commission could justifiably pursue its complaint although, between the reference to the Court and the hearing, Italy had in fact complied with the opinion. The Court held that the Commission had a valid interest in the proceedings, which, as it pointed out, were not designed to condemn the failure, but rather to obtain "a decision on the issue whether the failure occurred." The Court has consistently adopted this approach on "old" infringements,[25] but it has in some instances continued to

---

[16] Case 70/72 *Commission* v. *Germany* [1973] E.C.R. 813 and note 36, *infra*.
[17] Case 7/69 *Commission* v. *Italy* [1970] E.C.R. 111. See also Case 45/64 *Commission* v. *Italy* [1965] E.C.R. 857.
[18] *Supra,* note 12.
[19] [1962] E.C.R. 425.
[20] *Supra* note 12.
[21] See similarly Cases 90 & 91/63 [1964] E.C.R. 625.
[22] *Supra,* note 6.
[23] The first and second art treasures cases and the tachographs case are particularly striking examples: Cases 7/68 and 48/71 *Commission* v. *Italy* [1968] E.C.R. 423 and [1972] E.C.R. 527, and Case 128/78 *Commission* v. *United Kingdom* [1979] E.C.R. 419. Italy, the most frequent offender, has variously pleaded administrative, budgetary, parliamentary, political and constitutional difficulties, all to no avail.
[24] *Supra,* note 12.
[25] *e.g.* Case 39/72 *Commission* v. *Italy* [1973] E.C.R. 101.

take the point on whether the Commission had a sufficient legal interest.[26]

In one case the Commission discontinued its action after the Court had been seised on the basis of a clear statement of recognition of breach and of measures taken to comply.[27] However, discontinuance at any stage in the Article 169 procedure is not a finding of legality of the measure in question.[28] It is irrelevant that the failure allegedly had no adverse effect on the functioning of the common market.[29]

11—12   A question of considerable interest was whether the mere existence of a national law conflicting with Community law could give rise to Article 169 proceedings, or whether the doctrine of supremacy of Community law in effect removed the cause of action by curing the breach. This question was raised in relation to the legal interest of the Commission in Case 167/73 *Commission* v. *France*[30] where the French Government argued that the Community rules did not apply to the merchant navy and even if they did, French rules on the nationality of crews were not being applied in a manner discriminating against Community nationals. The Court was able to hold that the Commission need show no specific legal interest since in the general interest of the Community, its function is to ensure that the provisions of the Treaty are applied by the Member States. On the substantive point the Court found that the uncertainty created by the existence of a law on the statute books creating an apparent conflict with Community law was enough to justify a finding of failure under Article 169.

If a Member State introduces new legislation this may change the nature of the breach and a new procedure may have to be initiated.[31]

Procedure under Article 170

11—13   "A Member State which considers that another State has failed to fulfil an obligation under this Treaty may bring the matter before the Court of Justice" (Article 170, first para.). But before it takes such action, it must bring the matter before the Commission for a reasoned opinion, delivered after hearing the parties. Here again, the same exceptions to the obligation to submit to the pre-contentious procedure apply. In this case, the pre-contentious procedure involves two or more States rather than one.

The opinion given by the Commission will now be rather different from that given under Article 169; in the first place, the

[26] *e.g.* Cases 26/69 *Commission* v. *France* [1970] E.C.R. 565.
[27] Case 172/73 *Commission* v. *Italy* [1974] E.C.R. 475.
[28] Cases 15 & 16/76 *France* v. *Commission* [1979] E.C.R. 321.
[29] Case 95/77 *Commission* v. *Netherlands* [1978] E.C.R. 863.
[30] [1974] E.C.R. 359.
[31] *Supra,* note 17.

Commission can find that there is, in its opinion, no failure, and secondly, if it does find that there is a failure, it confines itself to that and little more. It seems likely, however, that if it does find a failure, the Commission will have to initiate an Article 169 procedure in addition, for the first paragraph of Article 169 then leaves it no discretion in the matter. Alternatively, Commission intervention seems to be enough.[32]

The introduction of a case under Article 170 is not dependent on an opinion of the Commission; the fourth paragraph makes it clear that its absence is not a bar to the action, but it must at least be asked for, and assuming that an opinion is given, there is similarly no bar on introducing an action, whether the opinion is positive or negative.

Article 171: effect of judgments under Arts. 169 and 170

11—14 If the Court finds that a Member State has failed to fulfil an obligation under the Treaty, the Member State is required to take the necessary measures to comply with the judgment. In contrast to the ECSC Treaty, no penalties exist under the Rome Treaties to compel compliance. The only remedy for non-compliance (apart, presumably, from political sanctions) is therefore a further round of proceedings under Article 169,[33] with a finding of failure to comply with Article 171. The order of the Court under Articles 169, 170 and 171 is not confined to a simple finding of failure to fulfil an obligation under the Treaty: it may, to be of practical effect, entail an obligation to require repayment of monies paid in breach of the Treaty.[34]

Procedure under the ECSC Treaty

11—15 Article 88 of the ECSC Treaty provides for a procedure somewhat similar to that under Article 169, the first paragraphs of both articles being to largely similar effect, with the difference that the Commission's opinion is here a decision. Under the second paragraph of Article 88 ECSC, however, it is for the Member State to institute proceedings before the Court, effectively to attack the decision concluding that there is a failure, for it is here the Commission that establishes the failure and not the Court. (It is clear that the decision can only record a failure, and is not used to state that there is no failure.)

If the Commission fails to take a decision, it can under this Treaty, in contrast to the EEC and Euratom procedure, be attacked for failure to act under Article 35 (1) ECSC.[35] The decision that

---

[32] Case 141/78 *France* v. *United Kingdom* [1979] E.C.R. 2923, Commission intervening.
[33] *Cf.* art treasures cases, *supra,* note 23 and Cases 24 & 97/80 R *Commission* v. *France* [1980] E.C.R. 1319.
[34] *Cf.* Case 70/72 *Commission* v. *Germany* [1973] E.C.R. 813.
[35] Cases 7 & 9/54 *Groupement des industries sidérurgiques Luxembourgeoises* v. *High Authority* [1954–56] E.C.R. 175.

is taken is only declaratory, and may not impose new obligations, although it can suggest how the situation can be corrected.[36] Here again, Member States cannot excuse their failure by pointing to a failure of the Commission.

Unlike Article 169, Article 88 ECSC provides for the application of sanctions against the Member State if it has not fulfilled its obligation within the time-limit, or if it brings an action which is dismissed, and the Council acting by a two-thirds majority assents. The Member State affected may appeal against the sanctions, but not against the original decision.

Article 182

11—16 Article 182 provides that:

> "The Court of Justice shall have jurisdiction in any dispute between Member States which relates to the subject-matter of this Treaty if the dispute is submitted to it under a special agreement between the parties."

Article 154 Euratom is identical. Article 89, second para., ECSC is *mutatis mutandis* identical.

Article 182 EEC is in some sense an extension of Article 170, for it includes within its ambit not only disputes relating to fulfilment of Treaty obligations, but the undefined area of disputes relating to the subject-matter of the Treaty. Article 170 in effect provides for compulsory jurisdiction, however, while Article 182 provides only for submission of disputes by both parties on an agreed basis. Article 182 offers a type of jurisdiction not unlike that of a more conventional international tribunal.

11—17 There is no case law on the application of Article 182. One question concerning Article 182 is whether it covers disputes concerning the *application* of the Treaty, given that by contrast Article 89, first para., ECSC established a separate head of jurisdiction in respect of disputes relating to the *subject-matter* of the ECSC Treaty in the second paragraph of the same article. Member States undertake by Article 219 EEC not to submit disputes concening the *interpretation* or *application* of the Treaty to any method of settlement other than those provided for therein, and it must be considered that the term "subject-matter" (French *objet*, German *Gegenstand*) used in Article 182 is to have a wide meaning, which would include disputes as to the *application* of the Treaty, although there is conceivably an area of disputes outside *interpretation* and *application* which are still within *subject-matter*.

Essentially, however, Article 182 is never likely to be a primary method for the settlement of disputes in the Community context, for actions between the Member States and the Commission are

---

[36] Cases 20 & 25/59 *Italy,* and *Netherlands* v. *High Authority* [1960] E.C.R. 325 & 355.

likely to resolve most questions, and Article 170 is perhaps likely
to be resorted to before Article 182. The type of dispute which
might result in a special agreement under Article 182 is probably
more readily settled at the political level, given the close ties
between the Member States within the Community. Part of the
difficulty is that a genuine dispute is unlikely to be referred to the
Court under this provision, while there is a danger that an attempted
collusive reference might be struck out.

Action Relating to Penalties: Article 172

11—18 Article 172 EEC provides that regulations made by the Council
pursuant to the provisions of that Treaty may give the Court of
Justice unlimited jurisdiction in regard to the penalties provided
for in such regulations. The Council is given a specific power to
issue regulations under four articles only: Article 43 (2), third
sub-para. (agricultural policy); Article 49 (free movement of
workers); Article 87 (1) (rules on competition); Article 94
(authorisation of state aids) (*cf.* also Art. 209); but this certainly
does not exhaust its power to make regulations, for a fairly large
number of articles enable the Council to "lay down provisions" or
otherwise to act, without the mode of action being limited.
Pursuant to Article 189, the Council can, where it has a power to
act, adopt any one of the types of acts referred to in that article
(and in practice other types besides) subject only to limitations
contained in the enabling power. The most general of the enabling
provisions is Article 235, which enables the Council to adopt
"the appropriate measures" where the Treaty has not provided the
necessary powers.

11—19 Only three regulations imposing penalties and conferring jurisdiction upon the Court have been adopted, namely Regulation
17/62[37] on competition, Regulation 11/60[38] on transport and
Regulation 1017/68[39] on competition in transport. Regulation
11 is based upon Article 79 of the EEC Treaty, Regulation 17
upon Article 87 and Regulation 1017/68 upon Articles 75 and 87.
Article 17 of Regulation 17 and Article 24 of Regulation 1017/68
provide that:

> "The Court of Justice shall have unlimited jurisdiction within
> the meaning of Article 172 of the Treaty to review decisions
> whereby the Commission has fixed a fine or periodic penalty
> payment; it may cancel, reduce or increase the fine or periodic
> penalty payment imposed."

Article 25 (2) of Regulation 11 provides that:

> "Pursuant to Article 172 of the Treaty, the Court of Justice

[37] J.O. 1962, 204.
[38] J.O. 1960, 1121.
[39] J.O. 1968, 175/1.

shall have unlimited jurisdiction in regard to any penalty imposed under Articles 17 and 18 [of the Regulation]. The Commission may not proceed with the enforcement of a penalty until the period allowed for appeal has expired."

11—20   It is to be noted that Article 172 to some extent duplicates the provisions of Article 173, second para., which enables a natural or legal person to institute proceedings against a decision addressed to himself or of direct and individual concern to him within a period of two months. Article 172 is not so limited by time, but it is difficult to avoid the conclusion that the plaintiff under the latter provision would equally have to show an interest to be able to sue, and would have to sue within a reasonable time.

The phrase "unlimited jurisdiction" is a translation of the French term *pleine juridiction*, which is to be contrasted with a limited type of jurisdiction, *e.g.* merely to annul. It is clear that by the reference to unlimited jurisdiction it was intended that the Court should be able to decide not only upon the validity of a penalty or its amount, but also upon the validity of the decision imposing the penalty, and that the applicant should be able to rely upon any of the four grounds of illegality mentioned in Article 173, if the action is brought in time. Alternatively, he might be able to rely upon the exception of illegality. Furthermore, the Court has power to investigate the functional basis of the act challenged. Under the EEC Treaty challenges to penalties imposed arise almost solely under the competition rules applicable to individuals. On several occasions the Court has significantly reduced a fine because it was excessive in relation to the conduct complained of.

Review of Legality of Council and Commission Acts:
Action for Annulment Art. 173

11—21 Article 173 of the EEC Treaty confers jurisdiction on the Court to review the legality of acts of the Council and the Commission[40] other than recommendations or opinions.

Acts other than recommendations or opinions

11—22   The clear intention here was to limit the right of action to challenges to binding acts within the meaning of Article 189. The Court has held, however, that the availability of the Article 173 procedure cannot be limited merely to the categories of measures referred to in Article 189:

"An action for annulment must therefore be available in the case of all measures adopted by institutions, whatever their nature or form, whic'a are intended to have legal effects"[41]

[40] The right cannot be extended to apply against other institutions: Case 91/76 *De Lacroix* v. *Court of Justice* [1977] E.C.R. 225.
[41] Case 22/70 *Commission* v. *Council* [1971] E.C.R. 263.

In the case in point,[42] "conclusions" of the Council were, the Court held, designed to lay down a course of action binding on both the institutions and the Member States and hence had definite legal effects. Similarly, a measure, asserted by the Commission to be a mere opinion, constitutes a decision if it affects the interests of the parties by bringing about a change in their legal position.[43]

Who may challenge?

11—23   Member States and the Commission and the Council can bring actions under Article 173 on any of the four grounds discussed below. This right is quite unfettered.[44] The same right is open to any natural or legal person, in respect of challenges against

> "a decision addressed to that person or against a decision which, although in the form of a regulation or a decision addressed to another person, is of direct and individual concern to the former."

11—24   Obviously there is no difficulty where the act contested is in fact a decision addressed to the plaintiff, although it may be a matter for argument as to whether it should be so categorised.[45] Where it cannot be so categorised the second limb of the quoted paragraph comes into play. The objective of this provision is, in the words of the Court, in particular to prevent the Community institutions from being in a position, merely by choosing the form of a regulation, to exclude an application by an individual against a decision which concerns him directly and individually.[46] The choice of form cannot change the nature of the measure.[47] By virtue of the second paragraph of Article 189 of the Treaty the criterion for distinguishing between a regulation and a decision is whether the measure is of general application or not. In particular a regulation applies to objectively determined situations and produces legal effects with regard to categories of persons regarded generally and in the abstract.[48] A decision by contrast is characterised by the limitation of persons to whom it is addressed.[49]

---

[42] *Ibid.*

[43] Cases 8 to 11/66 *Cimenteries CBR* v. *Commission* [1967] E.C.R. 75.

[44] *Cf.* Case 166/78 *Italy* v. *Council* [1979] E.C.R. 2575.

[45] Case 26/76 *Metro* v. *Commission* [1977] E.C.R. 1875.

[46] Case 101/76 *Koninklijke Scholten Honig* v. *Council and Commission* [1977] E.C.R. 797. This case in effect summarises the earlier authorities. Similarly Case 162/78 *Wagner* v. *Commission* [1979] E.C.R. 3467.

[47] *Ibid.* deriving from Cases 16 & 17/62 *Confédération Nationale des Producteurs de Fruits et Legumes* v. *Council* [1963] E.C.R. 471.

[48] *Ibid.*

[49] Cases 16 & 17/72 *supra*, note 47.

11—25   The nature of a measure as a regulation is not called in question by the possibility of determining more or less precisely the number or even the identity of the persons to whom it applies at a given moment as long as it is established that it is applied by virtue of an objective legal or factual situation defined by the measure in relation to its objectives.[50] Moreover, the fact that a legal provision may have different actual effects for the various persons to whom it applies is not inconsistent with its nature as a regulation when the situation is objectively defined.[51]

If, then, in accordance with the above criteria the act impugned is a purely regulatory act it cannot be impugned. It may be, however, that the act does not meet these criteria. If it does not, the plaintiff next has to demonstrate that the decision is of direct and individual concern to him. These requirements are not alternative but cumulative if an individual is successfully to invoke Article 173 against a decision addressed to someone other than himself.[52]

11—26   The article speaks of decisions addressed to "another person." But the fact that the decision is addressed to a Member State rather than an individual does not appear to affect the matter.[53] Various actions against instruments addressed to Member States have been decided on quite other grounds.[54]

The first cases[55] suggested that it was necessary first to show that the plaintiff was individually concerned, the question of direct concern arising only thereafter. In subsequent cases, however, the order of consideration has been reversed.[56] The order chosen seems to be principally a matter of the presentation of the pleadings, or else of expediency.[57]

11—27   The requirements of direct and individual concern have proved particularly difficult to meet, difficulties compounded by a number of inconsistencies in the rulings of the Court.[58]

The Court has consistently held that a measure is of individual concern to natural or legal persons only if it affects them by reason of certain attributes which are peculiar to them, or by

[50] Case 101/76 *supra*, note 46, deriving from Case 6/68 *Zuckerfabrik Watenstedt* v. *Council* [1968] E.C.R. 409.
[51] *Ibid.*
[52] Cases 38/74 *Getreide-Import Gesellschaft* v. *Commission* [1965] E.C.R. 203 and 25/62 *Plaumann* v. *Commission* [1963] E.C.R. 95.
[53] Case 25/62 *supra*, note 52, although see Case 69/69 *Alcan* v. *Commission* [1970] E.C.R. 385.
[54] See, *e.g.* cases cited in notes 47, 50 and 51, *supra*.
[55] Note 52, *supra*.
[56] Cases 106 & 107/63 *Toepfer* v. *Commission* [1965] E.C.R. 405; 62/70 *Bock* v. *Commission* [1971] E.C.R. 897.
[57] In, *e.g.* Case 72/74 *Union Syndicale* v. *Council* [1975] E.C.R. 401, direct concern does not seem to have been considered.
[58] For criticism see H. Rasmussen, "Why is Article 173 Interpreted Against Private Plaintiffs?" 1980 E.L.R. 112, and J. Dinnage, "Locus Standi and Article 173," 1979 E.L.R. 15.

reason of circumstances in which they are differentiated from all other persons, and by virtue of these factors distinguishes them individually just as in the case of the actual addressee of the instrument.[59] In this context, an organisation formed for the protection of the collective interests of a category of persons cannot be considered as directly and individually concerned by a measure affecting the general interests of the category.[60] In practice the requirement of individual concern seems only to have been satisfied where the identities of all those affected were already discoverable with complete certainty before the decision was taken. The fact that members of the class *in abstracto* may be affected puts the instrument back into the general regulatory category.[61]

11—28   It becomes clear at this point that there is no real distinction between the notion of "individual concern" and the definition of a decision as opposed to a regulation. Thus it becomes a matter of chance whether the court chooses to decide whether or not to assume jurisdiction on the basis of "no individual concern" as opposed to "no decision". The clearest cases are those in which the measure was taken either in full knowledge of who those affected might be (those who had already applied for import licenses, for instance,[62]) or of who those affected actually were, as in the *Ball Bearings* Cases.[63] It will be apparent that the absence of individual concern, its antithesis in fact, is demonstrated by the generality of the act impugned, thus:

> "In the present case the applicant is affected by the disputed decisions as an importer of clementines, that is to say, by reason of a commercial activity which may at any time be practiced by any person and is not therefore such as to distinguish the applicant in relation to the contested decision as in the case of the addressee."[64]

Even Case 26/76 *Metro* v. *Commission,*[65] the only one of the cases successful on admissibility, which concerned a decision in terms addressed to a natural or legal person not being a Member State, again seems to have turned on the "closed category" point,

[59] Case 72/74 *supra,* note 57, deriving from *Plaumann, supra,* note 52.
[60] Case 72/74 *supra,* note 57, deriving from Cases 16 & 17/62 *supra,* note 47.
[61] *Cf. supra.*
[62] Case 138/79 *Roquette* v. *Council* (October 29, 1980); 92/78 *Simmenthal* v. *Commission* [1979] E.C.R. 777; 112/77 *Töpfer* v. *Commission* [1978] E.C.R. 1019; 88/76 *Exportation des Sucres* v. *Commission* [1977] E.C.R. 709; 100/74 *CAM* v. *Council* [1975] E.C.R. 1393; 62/70 *Bock* v. *Commission* [1971] E.C.R. 897; 41–44/70 *International Fruit Company* v. *Commission* [1971] E.C.R. 411; 106–107/63 *Toepfer* v. *Commission* [1965] E.C.R. 405. All of these cases concerned tenders or applications for licences.
[63] In particular Cases 113/77 *NTN Toyo Bearing Co.* v. *Council* [1979] E.C.R. 1185 and 118/77 *ISO* v. *Council* [1979] E.C.R. 1277.
[64] Case 25/62 *supra,* note 52.
[65] *Supra,* note 45 and Dinnage, *op. cit., supra,* note 58.

or at least on a slightly broader application of it, since Metro sought to challenge a decision under Reg. 17/62 addressed to SABA on the basis that it did not meet Metro's complaint, which had triggered the Commission investigations leading to the decision in the first place.

Where direct concern has been specifically in issue the Court seems to have regarded the criterion as being whether the instrument could be regarded as having direct effects *vis-à-vis* the applicant,[66] without its being at the same time an instrument of a general regulatory character[67] or without the interposition of the powers and discretion of the Member States.[68] Where the interposition of national powers is so extensive any legal proceedings are properly to be brought before national courts.[69]

Despite the above cases, the Court has avoided laying down any concrete criteria for ascertaining whether or not an individual is "concerned," which is in keeping with its flexible approach under the ECSC Treaty. It is unlikely, however, that the Court would uphold a future interest; the individual must be concerned at the time,[70] not merely sometime in the future.

Article 173 is not the only article concerned with review of legality of acts of Community bodies; Article 180 (*c*) gives Member States, the Commission and the Board of Directors of the European Investment Bank, a right to bring Article 173 -type proceedings against measures adopted by the Board of Governors of the Bank on the conditions laid down in Article 173. A further limited right of action is given against measures adopted by the Board of Directors of the Bank. Actions may only be brought by Member States or the Commission under the conditions laid down in Article 173; and solely on grounds of non-compliance with the procedure provided for in Article 21 (2), (5), (6) and (7) of the statute of the Bank.

Grounds of Review

11—29 The first paragraph of Article 173 enables parties to attack a Community act on any of four grounds: lack of competence;

---

[66] Cases 16/62 *supra,* note 52 and 62/70, 88/76 and 92/78 *supra,* note 62.

[67] Case 1/64 *Glucoseries Réunies* v. *Commission* [1964] E.C.R. 413 and 42/71 *Nordgetreide* v. *Commission* [1972] E.C.R. 105.

[68] Cases 69/69 *supra,* note 53, 96/71 *Haegeman* v. *Commission* [1972] E.C.R. 1005 and 132/77 *Exportation des Sucres* v. *Commission* [1978] E.C.R. 1061. The Council defence on these lines was rejected in the *Ball Bearing* cases, *supra,* note 63, since national implementation was "purely automatic."

[69] *Ibid.* and Cases 103–109/78 *Usines de Beauport* v. *Council* [1979] E.C.R. 17.

[70] This may of course include a present interest in contesting a decision which has been fully implemented for the benefit of others either with a view to the applicant being restored to its original position or to inducing the Commission to make suitable amendments in its arrangements as to the future: Case 92/78, note 62, *supra.*

infringement of an essential procedural requirement; infringement of the Treaty or of any rule of law relating to its application; or misuse of powers.

The four terms used are taken from French administrative law and thus were already known as terms of art with definite meanings, which are only imperfectly conveyed by their literal translation. It is not, however, the case that these terms should only be understood in relation to French law. Whatever their origin, they are now terms of Community law and must be taken in that context alone.[71] The same terms are used in the comparable article of the ECSC Treaty (Art. 33) and a considerable jurispruden ·e has been built up which is probably applicable to Article 173 EEC.

1. Lack of competence

11–30   Probably the nearest English analogy to this ground of appeal is a complaint that the defendant institution has acted *ultra vires*. The ground appears rarely to have been invoked, but there are three discernible areas where a question of extent of competence arises:

(a) where there has been an invalid delegation of powers, *e.g.* Case 9/56 *Meroni* v. *HA*[72] where the Court held that a delegation of powers of the High Authority to another body was invalid, the delegation provided for relating only to powers of execution.

(b) where an institution has purported to exercise implied powers. Under the ECSC Treaty the powers of the institutions were regarded as limited to those expressly provided for.[73] However, under the EEC Treaty it is clear that the institutions do possess some implied powers. The legal basis for such powers is discussed elsewhere.[74]

(c) where an institution purports to extend its jurisdiction beyond EEC territory. This issue has arisen chiefly in the context of the competition policy, where parties to condemned practices or agreements have complained that the Commission has exceeded its own powers in either attacking the substance of such a practice or in seeking to levy execution of fines.[75] However in no case have these allegations resulted in a finding of excess of jurisdiction.

---

[71] Case 49/71 *Hagen OHG* v. *EVSt* [1972] E.C.R. 23.
[72] [1957–58] E.C.R. 133.
[73] See, *e.g.* Cases 8/55 *Fédéchar* v. *HA* [1954–56] E.C.R. 245 and Cases 20 & 25/59 *Italy, and Netherlands* v. *HA* [1960] E.C.R. 325 and 355.
[74] *Supra*, para. 3–43.
[75] See, *e.g.* Case 48/69 *ICI* v. *Commission* [1972] E.C.R. 619; Cases 6 & 7/73 *Commercial Solvents* v. *Commission* [1974] E.C.R. 223.

2. Infringement of an essential procedural requirement

11—31   Only the procedural rules laid down by the Treaty or by decisions or regulations are relevant here. Procedural practices of an internal nature are not legally binding. Three particular requirements have been the subject of litigation or controversy:

11—32 *The requirement to consult other institutions.* It is generally agreed in this respect that the requirement entails putting all the essential uses of the provisions proposed before the relevant body. However, provided this is done, there is no prohibition on a change in the final proposal which becomes the law.[76]

The requirement to state reasons. Under Article 190 of the EEC Treaty the Council and the Commission are required to state the reasons on which their decisions are based. The Court has held that Article 190 seeks to give an opportunity to the parties of defending their rights, to the Court of exercising its supervisory functions and to Member States and to all interested nationals of ascertaining the circumstances under which the institution has applied the Treaty. To attain these objectives, it is sufficient for the decision to set out, in a concise but clear and relevant manner, the principal issues of law and of fact upon which it is based and which are necessary in order that the reasoning which has led the institution to its decisions may be understood.[77] There seems to be a possibility that a non-reasoned act might be regarded as non-existent.[78] The degree of reasoning depends upon the circumstances.[79] Although a decision which fits into a well-established line of decisions may be reasoned in a summary manner, for example by reference to those decisions, if it goes appreciably

---

[76] Case 41/69 *ACF Chemiefarma* v. *Commission* [1970] E.C.R. 661. Where required, consultation of the Assembly is a formality which cannot be foregone: Cases 138 & 139/79 *Roquette,* and *Maizena* v. *Council* (October 29, 1980).

[77] Cases 24/62 *Commission* v. *Germany* [1963] E.C.R. 63; 8–11/66 *Cimenteries CBR* v. *Commission* [1967] E.C.R. 75.

[78] Cases 1 and 14/57 *Societé des Usines à Tubes de la Sarre* v. *HA* [1957–58] E.C.R. 105. Contra: Case 15 etc/73 *Schots-Kortner* v. *Council & Commission* [1974] E.C.R. 177, although see para. 6–13, *supra.* In any event an act which is not a regulation, directive or decision, is not subject to the requirements of Article 190 regarding reasons although such an act is subject to judicial review: Case 22/70 *Commission* v. *Council* [1971] E.C.R. 263 *(AETR).*

[79] See, *e.g.* Cases 73/74 *Groupement des Fabricants de Papiers Peints de Belgique et al* v. *Commission* [1975] E.C.R. 1491; 5/67 *Beus* v. *HZA München* [1968] E.C.R. 83. The reasons on which a piece of legislation is based may appear not only from its own wording, but also from the whole body of the legal rules governing the field under consideration: Case 92/77 *An Bord Bainne* v. *Minister for Agriculture* [1978] E.C.R. 497. As far as concerns general acts the requirements of Article 190 are satisfied if the statement of reasons explains in essence the measures taken by the institutions: Case 166/78 *Italy* v. *Council* [1979] E.C.R. 2575. See especially the Advocate General at p.2609.

further than the previous decisions, the institution must give an account of its reasoning.[80] Abbreviated reasoning will be acceptable where an urgent act is required.[81] In the case of decisions affecting individuals such as those under the competition policy the Court has held that the Commission is not obliged to deal with every argument adduced by the parties, let alone refute them.[82] In all cases, however, the essential reasoning must be substantiated, even if peripheral elements cannot be.[83]

11—33 *The requirement to publish.*[84] A regulation which has not been published in the *Official Journal, e.g.* as a result of a strike, would probably be invalid.[85] However, the Member States may not subject Community legislation to additional publication requirements.[86] Decisions must be notified to the parties, but this is not an essential procedural requirement going to the validity of the instrument. Failure to notify will at most have effects on coming into operation, time limits, etc.[87] But the operation of the decision will not be affected if all reasonable efforts have been made to notify the parties or if the addressee was in fact fully cognisant of the decision.[88]

3. Infringement of the Treaty or of any rule relating to its application

11—34 This head of jurisdiction has assumed a greater importance than the three others. The rather broad formulation has been the basis for the development of the Court's jurisprudence relating to the general principles of law, especially human rights.[89] It has also permitted the Court on occasions to come very close to an evaluation of the factual evidence of, rather than legal basis for, a decision. It allows the Court to evaluate the legal conclusions to be drawn from the facts. The line between what constitutes a legal as opposed to a factual conclusion is not easily drawn. For instance, in Cases 19 & 20/74 *Kali und Salz AG & Kali-Chemie v. Commission*[90] the Court struck down a decision refusing exemption under Article 85 (3) on the grounds that the wrong market had been taken into account in assessing whether there was likely to be an elimination of competition. The facts set out in the Commission's reasoning were found to be insufficient to support its conclusions as to the relevant market.

[80] *Ibid.* and Case 1/63 *Macchiorlati Dalmas* v. *HA* [1963] E.C.R. 303.
[81] Case 16/65 *Schwarze* v. *EVSt* [1965] E.C.R. 877.
[82] Case 41/69 *ACF Chemiefarma* v. *Commission* [1970] E.C.R. 661.
[83] Case 34/62 *Germany* v. *Commission* [1963] E.C.R. 134.
[84] See also *supra,* para. 6–20.
[85] Case 49/72 *Drescig* v. *Commission* [1973] E.C.R. 565.
[86] Case 39/72 *Commission* v. *Italy* [1973] E.C.R. 101.
[87] Case 76/79 *Könecke* v. *Commission* [1980] E.C.R. 665.
[88] Cases 6/72 *Europemballage Corporation and Continental Can* v. *Commission* [1973] E.C.R. 215 and 48/69 *supra,* note 75.
[89] *Supra,* para. 6–31.
[90] [1975] E.C.R. 499.

4. Misuse of powers

11—35   The invocation of this ground of review was much more common under the ECSC Treaty, not least because, if successful, it allowed an individual to challenge even a general decision. "Misuse of Powers" has been defined as involving that "the decision itself was in fact pursuing an objective other than that for the purposes of which the High Authority was entitled to act,"[91] or "for other than those stated."[92] It appears that a decision which incidentally does something for which powers were not provided will not be struck down provided the essential purpose for which the powers were provided underlies the act challenged.[93]

The standard of proof of misuse of powers is clearly very high.[94] But the plaintiff need not necessarily produce evidence of a motive, wrongful in itself, although the test of misuse depends on motive, if misuse be a reasonable implication from the facts. This has permitted a number of plaintiffs to allege misuse of powers where matters appear merely marginally out of the ordinary, or, to the plaintiff at least, obscure. But this is to put the hurdle of admissibility too low; there must be at least some evidence that the Community was acting illicitly: a *prima facie* case in fact.[95]

The relevance of misuse of powers to actions for annulment is clear; the ground of action is used to impugn the act complained of because its foundations are illegal. The ground of action is not therefore strictly relevant to the act itself, but rather to the motives for which it was done.

Review of Legality under the ECSC Treaty

11—36   Article 33 of the ECSC Treaty likewise provides for the review of legality of Community acts, and many of the rules developed under the ECSC Treaty have been transferred in practice to the EEC. There are, however, certain specific differences between the two procedures.

In the first place, undertakings and associations may under the ECSC Treaty only attack decisions (which may be of general or individual application) or recommendations (EEC directives) on all four grounds if they are individual in character. The Court has developed an extensive jurisprudence on the difference between an individual and a general decision, which, whilst appearing to follow the distinctions drawn in the EEC Treaty between regulations and decisions, actually diverges to some extent. It is not

---

[91] Case 2/57 *Compagnie des Hauts Fourneaux de Chasse* v. *HA* [1957–58] E.C.R. 199.
[92] Cases 18 & 35/65 *Gutmann* v. *Commission* [1966] E.C.R. 103.
[93] *Ibid.* and Cases 8/55 *supra*, note 73 and 1/54 *France* v. *HA* [1954–56] E.C.R.1.
[94] Case 10/55 *Mirossevich* v. *HA* [1954–56] E.C.R. 333.
[95] Cases 55–59/63 & 61–63/63 *Modena* v. *HA* [1964] E.C.R. 211. See also Cases 8/57 *Groupement des Hauts Fourneaux et Acieries Belges* v. *HA* [1957–58] E.C.R. 245 and 8/55 *supra*, note 73.

entirely clear that the existence of an individual concern under the ECSC Treaty depends upon the applicant showing that the act challenged was really a decision addressed to him. Once it has been established that the decision *is* an individual one, it is not apparently necessary that the applicant should show an effect on him in his legal position which differentiates him from all others.[96] Indeed, on occasion, the Court has decided that the applicant was individually concerned without giving any reasons at all.[97]

11—37   Secondly, undertakings or associations may attack even a general decision, where it is considered that it involves a misuse of powers affecting them, the Court holding that this is just a further aspect of the criterion of individual concern.[98]

Thirdly, Article 33 enables the Court of Justice to review economic facts or circumstances where the Commission is alleged to have misused its powers or to have manifestly failed to observe the provisions of the Treaty, or any rule relating to its application. This may be contrasted with the EEC Treaty, where the Court strictly speaking has no power to review facts at all, although the power to question the reasoning behind decisions means that the difference is not very great in practice.

Actions against the Council or the Commission for failure to Act: Article 175

11—38   It is clear that a failure by the authorities to take required action can be as serious in its consequences as the adoption of the wrong measures when action has been taken. The Paris and Rome Treaties therefore all provide for compelling Community institutions to take action. Under the ECSC Treaty the remedy for failure to act lies in regarding inaction beyond a specified deadline as an implied decision of refusal which can be challenged and annulled in the same way as any other decision.

11—39   The EEC Treaty, Article 175, goes about the matter somewhat differently. Member States and other institutions (including the Assembly, in contrast to Article 173) may call upon the Council or the Commission to take action where not to do so would amount to an infringement of the Treaty. The institution then has two months in which to "define its position," Article 175 therefore appears broader in its scope than Article 35 ECSC for it could be said to envisage the possibility of requiring the adoption of a non-binding act, in particular an opinion under Article 169.[99] In practice it seems that the difference is largely illusory and that a provision similar to Article 35 ECSC would have been quite

[96] Case 8/55 *Fédéchar supra,* note 73.
[97] Case 1/58 *Stork* v. *HA* [1959] E.C.R. 17.
[98] Case 8/55 *supra,* note 73.
[99] *Supra,* para. 11–03.

sufficient. This is because Article 175 only requires the institution to define its position, *not* to take the action requested. Thus, if the Commission, for instance, indicates that it is not going to adopt an opinion under Article 169, it has "defined its position" and there is no further remedy available under Article 175.[1] The communication from the Commission could not be challenged as an implied decision of refusal either because it would not be a binding act.[2] On the other hand, where a binding act is requested, the refusal would constitute an implied decision and hence be susceptible of challenge under Article 173.

11—40   Article 175, third paragraph, limits the right of an individual to a complaint that an institution has failed to address to him any act other than a recommendation or an opinion. This clearly envisages a challenge only where the omission amounts to a failure to adopt a binding act. The wording does, however, leave a measure of doubt as to whether the individual is in fact limited to the right to have a decision addressed to him, or whether he would have the right to a reply addressed to him in the form of a decision addressed to another but of direct and individual concern to him, or even of a regulation. Although in at least one case the Court appears to have taken the view that the individual must have been seeking a decision addressed to himself,[3] in later cases the Court has referred to the need for direct and individual concern[4] - not pehaps in itself a very substantial widening.

11—41   In practice therefore it seems that Article 175 is of limited importance. The individual or a Member State or institution could as well attack the implied decision of refusal under Article 173 as bringing an action under Article 175, because an annulment under Article 173 would result in a decision of the kind desired. The only important difference would be in the time limit, in that an Article 173 action would have to be brought within two months of the implied decision, the date of which might be uncertain if the nature of the act is questionable, whilst in Article 175

---

[1] Cases 48/65 *Lütticke* v. *Commission* [1966] E.C.R. 19; 15/71 *Mackprang* v. *Commission* [1971] E.C.R. 797.

[2] Case 125/78 *GEMA* v. *Commission* [1979] E.C.R. 3173.

[3] Case 15/71 *supra,* note 1.

[4] Case 42/71 *Nordgetreide* v. *Commission* [1972] E.C.R. 105 and *cf.* Case 134/73, *Holtz* v. *Council* [1974] E.C.R. 1:
"...the applicant has the object of procuring a provision of a general regulatory character...and not an act concerning it directly and individually. Such an act cannot be described, by reason either of its form or of its nature, as an act addressed to the applicant within the meaning of the third paragraph of Article 175."
In Case 153/73 *Holtz & Willemsen* v. *Council* [1974] E.C.R. 675, the Court said that this provision "gives individuals no right to bring an action for failure to issue a regulation."

the individual would have two months from the date that the institution has "defined its position" - a much broader notion.[5] Article 175 may not be used to circumvent the time limits of Article 173, *e.g.* by requesting the Commission to revoke a decision and challenging its refusal.[6]

The Plea (Exception) of Illegality: Article 184

11—42   Article 184 provides that:

> "Not withstanding the expiry of the period laid down in the third paragraph of Article 173, any party may, in proceedings in which a regulation of the Council or of the Commission is in issue, plead the grounds specified in the first paragraph of Article 173, in order to invoke before the Court of Justice the inapplicability of that regulation."

This article does not create a fresh ground of action.
  In the words of the Court:

> "Article 184 of the EEC Treaty gives expression to a general principle conferring upon any party to proceedings the right to challenge, for the purpose of obtaining the annulment of a decision of direct and individual concern to that party, the validity of previous acts of the institutions which form the legal basis of the decision which is being attacked, if that party was not entitled under Article 173 of the Treaty to bring a direct action challenging those acts by which it was thus affected without having been in a position to ask that they be declared void."[7]

11—43   In short, Article 184 is available where the act challenged was adopted pursuant to, and derived from,[8] an invalid regulation or a measure having similar effects.[9] The wording of Article 184 is not altogether clear so that in early cases it was sought to challenge regulations directly. The plea of illegality is available solely before the European Court[10]; it does not provide a direct avenue of recourse from a national court, thus bypassing the power to refer a request for a preliminary ruling to the European Court, a discretion purely of the national court.[11]

---

[5] A mere acknowledgement of the demand does not constitute definition of position: *cf.* Case 40/71 *Richez-Parise* v. *Commission* [1972] E.C.R. 73.

[6] Cases 10 & 18/68 *Eridania* v. *Commission* [1969] E.C.R. 459.

[7] Case 92/78 *Simmenthal* v. *Commission* [1979] E.C.R. 777, 800.

[8] See Case 32/65 *Italy* v. *Council and Commission* [1966] E.C.R. 389: "The regulation of which the legality is called in question must be applicable, directly or indirectly, to the issue with which the application is concerned."

[9] Case 92/78 *supra,* note 7.

[10] Cases 31 & 33/62 *Milchwerke Wöhrman* v. *Commission* [1962] E.C.R. 501 and 156/77 *Commission* v. *Belgium* [1978] E.C.R. 1881.

[11] *Ibid.* and see Case 44/65 *Hessische Knappschaft* v. *Singer* [1965] E.C.R. 965.

The effect of a ruling under Article 184 is that the act complained of is annulled because the underlying regulation is "inapplicable" to the case. This does not, therefore, entail the invalidity of the regulation *erga omnes*, so that persons who have lost the right to challenge the decision addressed to themselves will not be affected - clearly it could not be desirable that a regulation, enacted perhaps many years before, should be totally annulled with a consequent effect on all those who in the meantime had acquired rights or duties under it.

11—44 There is no exact parallel to Article 184 EEC in the ECSC Treaty but the Court has held that Article 36, last paragraph, will permit a party to challenge the underlying recommendations or decision, through the action against the penalty which it is contesting under the second paragraph of that article.[12] The Court referred expressly to its case law under Article 36 ECSC in explaining the rationale for Article 184 EEC.[13]

Action for Damages : Article 215

11—45 Non-contractual liability of the Community is governed primarily by Article 215 EEC, second paragraph, which provides that:

> "In the case of non-contractual liability, the Community shall, in accordance with the general principles common to the laws of the Member States, make good any damage caused by its institutions or by its servants in the performance of their duties."

The Court of Justice has jurisdiction in disputes relating to the compensation for damage provided for in Article 215, second para. (Art. 178 EEC).

Article 40 ECSC, first paragraph provides that:

> "Without prejudice to the first paragraph of Article 34, the Court shall have jurisdiction to order pecuniary reparation from the Community, on application by the injured party, to make good any injury caused in carrying out [the ECSC] Treaty by a wrongful act or omission on the part of the Community in the performance of its functions."

11—46 Further, Article 40, second paragraph, first sentence ECSC as amended by Article 26 of the Merger Treaty, stipulates: "The Court shall also have jurisdiction to order the Community to make good any injury caused by a personal wrong by a servant of the Community in the performance of his duties."

Article 34 ECSC referred to in Article 40 provides that the High Authority is to make good any direct and special harm suffered by

[12] 9/56 *Meroni* v. *HA* [1957–58] E.C.R. 133.
[13] Case 92/78 *supra,* note 7.

reason of a decision or recommendation held by the Court to be void and to involve a fault of such a nature as to render the Community liable.

The above provisions therefore render the Communities liable (under the conditions set out) for their or their servants acts (in the performance of their duties). Actions against Community employees personally remain subject to national law, although if the action was in fact a claim in the nature of official action the employee would have immunity.[14] The jurisdiction of the Court is compulsory in respect of these liabilities.

11—47   In Case 4/69 *Lütticke* v. *Commission*[15] the Court set out the principles of Community liability, subsequently restated as follows in Case 153/73 *Holtz & Willemsen* v. *Council*:

> "Under the second paragraph of Article 215 of the Treaty and the general principles to which this provision refers, Community responsibility depends on the coincidence of a set of conditions as regards the unlawfulness of the act alleged against the institutions, the fact of damage, and the existence of a direct link in the chain of causality between the wrongful act and the damage complained of."[16]

The unlawfulness is considered first, then the causal link, and thirdly the damage.

11—48   (a) **The unlawfulness of the act**

The principal issues have been whether:

(1)   Some kind of "fault" must be shown, and if so how blameworthy should the fault be?
(2)   Should the act in question be capable of annullment?

11—49   *Necessity to prove fault*

Although the effect of the Rome Treaty provisions as to non-contractual damage is broadly similar to those of the Paris Treaty as amended, Article 40 ECSC is somewhat deceptive, for it emerges from the French text that the injury for which reparation may be had must have been caused in the execution of the ECSC Treaty by a *"faute de service de la Communauté,"* or by a *"faute personnelle"* on the part of a Community servant in the performance of his duties, while the equivalent phrase in Article 215 EEC, second paragraph, is *"dommages causés par ses institutions ou par ses agents dans l'exercice de leurs fonctions."* Nevertheless, it would seem that similar principles are applicable, even though the EEC Treaty does not specify fault, because it refers instead to the

[14] *Supra,* para. 5–14.
[15] [1971] E.C.R. 325.
[16] [1974] E.C.R. 675 at 693.

"general principles common to the laws of the Member States," which are generally based on fault liability. and in countries with a distinct structure of administrative courts a refinement of the notion on the lines set out above is usually found. Certainly the Court has never awarded damages in the absence of some kind of fault, although it has been argued that it might be moving towards the idea that the institutions could be liable where damage results to an individual from a legislative act even though the act itself is not illegal,[17] but merely affects parties in an uneven manner.

The notion of fault

11–50   The fault which *must* be proved under the ECSC and which to date appears necessary also in the EEC Treaty is the so called *"faute de service"* as distinguished from *"faute personelle."* The terms are not readily translatable into English, but a *"faute de service"* may perhaps best be described as a malfunctioning of the system, whilst a *"faute personelle"* is a fault for which the system cannot be blamed. For instance, a series of bad decisions by officials might point to a serious deficiency in the method of appointing responsible people and controlling their activities. Therein would lie a *"faute de service."* On the other hand, negligent driving by an employee of the Community whilst on official business would normally not be a *"faute de service"* because the negligence cannot be laid at the door of any aspect of malfunctioning of the system.[18] Thus in the *Sayag* case[19] the Court ruled that:

> "driving a motor car is not in the nature of an act performed in an official capacity. . . ."[20]

It must however be emphasised that exceptionally such an act could be a *"faute de service,"* e.g. where "this activity cannot be carried out otherwise than under the authority of the Community and by its very own employees."[21]

It is clear, therefore, that it is not accurate to describe a *"faute*

---

[17] Cases 9 & 11/71 *Compagnie d'Approvisionnement* v. *Commission* [1972] E.C.R. 391 and see Lord Mackenzie Stuart, Maccabean Lecture on Jurisprudence 1975, 20.

[18] Case 5/68 *Sayag* v. *Leduc* [1968] E.C.R. 395 and similarly Case 9/69 *Sayag* v. *Leduc* [1969] E.C.R. 329.

[19] *Ibid.*

[20] *Ibid.* [1968] E.C.R. 402.

[21] *Ibid.*

de service" as "vicarious liability" in the sense of the English law of tort.[22]

The degree of fault

11—51   A malfunctioning of the system will often involve a degree of negligence on the part of the officials responsible, for instance where a system has been set up without proper supervision[23] or where there has been a failure to rectify a mistaken interpretation of facts.[24] In the early ECSC cases the Court repeatedly made mention of terms such as *"dol"* or *"negligence coupable",*[25] *"gravement negligé"*[26] or *"faute lourde."*[27] However, in the more recent past many applicants have claimed for what is sometimes called "normative injustice"; here, compensation is sought for damages resulting from the exercise of a legislative power involving a choice of economic policy as opposed to individual decisions.

11—52   The Court has recently restated the principles applicable to Community non-contractual liability under Community legislative acts in a series of cases dealing with production levies and refunds:

> " A finding that a legal situation resulting from legislative measures by the Community is illegal is insufficient by itself to involve it in liability. The Court has already stated this in its judgment of 25 May 1978 in Joined Cases 83/76 and Others, *Bayerische HNL & Others* v. *Council and Commission*[28] In this connection the Court referred to its consistent case-law in accordance with which the Community does not incur liability on account of a legislative measure which involves choices of economic policy unless a sufficiently serious breach of a superior rule of law for the protection of the individual has occurred.[29] Having regard to the principles in the legal systems of the Member States, governing the liability of public authorities for damage caused to individuals by legislative measures, the Court has

---

[22] Laferriére, cited by Vedel and quoted by Dumon in "La responsabilité extracontractuelle des Communautés," 1969, *Cahiers de Droit Européen,* 1 at p.14, differentiates *"faute de service"* from *"faute personnelle"* in the following terms:
"il y a faute de service si l'acte dommageable administratif est impersonnel et révèle l'administrateur plus ou moins sujet à erreur. La faute personnelle, au contraire, est celle qui révèle l'homme avec ses faiblesses, ses passions, son imprudence."
[23] Cases 19–21/60 and 2,3/61 *Fives Lille Cail* v. *High Authority* [1961] E.C.R. 281. *Cf.* also Case 23/59 *FERAM* v. *HA* [1959] E.C.R. 245.
[24] Cases 19, etc/69 *Richez-Parise* v. *Commission* [1970] E.C.R. 325.
[25] See Cases 7/56 and 3–7/57 *Algera* v. *Assembly* [1957–58] E.C.R. 39.
[26] Case 3/61 *Fives Lille Cail supra,* note 23.
[27] Case 30/66 *Becher* v. *Commission* [1967] E.C.R. 285.
[28] [1978] E.C.R. 1209.
[29] First stated in Case 5/71 *Aktien-Zuckerfabrik Schöppenstedt* v. *Council* [1971] E.C.R. 975.

stated[30] that in the context of Community legislation in which one of the chief features is the exercise of a wide discretion essential for the implementation of the common agricultural policy, the liability of the Community can arise only exceptionally in cases in which the institution concerned has manifestly and gravely disregarded the limits on the exercise of its powers."[31]

It is therefore insufficient for the applicant to allege only that the act is illegal. He must be able to demonstrate in cases involving choices of economic policy that there is a flagrant breach of a superior rule of law for the protection of the individual[32] and futhermore in cases of wide Community discretion that the institution concerned has manifestly and gravely disregarded the limits of the exercise of its powers. Does this mean, then, that it is *only* where the Community act can be annulled that Community liability arises?

Must the act be capable of annulment?

11—53   Although arguments have been made that the illegality of the act is not a necessary pre-requisite of liability,[33] the grounds for annulling an act are probably wide enough to encompass any case where liability is found under Article 215. Thus, although it has been claimed that the Court should recognise the French principle of "equality in the face of public burdens" and give compensation to those bearing an excessive portion of the burden,[34] there seems to be no reason why legislation which imposed such a burden should not in fact be regarded as illegal under the criteria in Article 173. The same argument applies to the principle of "legitimate expectation," often invoked in the context of MCAs. To the extent that such principles are recognised they are "superior rules of law" to which all Community legislation is subject. It seems in fact that in the cases in which damages have been awarded the underlying act had either already been annulled or was of a character which would have resulted in its annulment.

11—54   A separate but related question is whether the act which is the object of the action for damages must actually have been annulled before an action will lie under Article 215. In Case 25/62 *Plaumann* v. *Commission*[35] the Court held that it

"cannot by way of an action for compensation take steps

---

[30] In 83/76 itself.
[31] Cases 116 & 124/77 *Amylum* v. *Council & Commission* [1979] E.C.R. 3497, 3560; first appears in 238/78 *Ireks-Arkady* v. *Council & Commission* [1979] E.C.R. 2955.
[32] The terminology of Case 5/71 *supra*, note 29 and most later cases.
[33] Cases 9 and 11/71 *supra*, note 17 and see cases cited in note 40, *infra*. Case 169/73 *Compagnie Continentale France* v. *Council* [1975] E.C.R. 117.
[34] Cases 9 & 11/71. *Supra*, note 17.
[35] [1963] E.C.R. 95.

which would nullify the legal effects of a decision which . . . has not been annulled."[36]

In other cases, however, both before and since, the Court has emphasised that:

> "the action for damages . . . was included as an autonomous form of action, with a particular purpose to fulfil within the system of actions, and subject to conditions on its use by its specific nature.
>
> Such an action differs from an action for annulment in that its end is not the cancellation of a particular measure but compensation for damage caused by an institution in the performance of its duties.
>
> The action for damages seeks only recognition that a right to compensation exists and, therefore, satisfaction solely for the benefit of the applicant."[37]

It seems, therefore, that it is only where the Article 215 action seeks to attain a result which can only be attained under another head of jurisdiction that the *Plaumann* approach comes into play.[38] Nevertheless, the amount of damages may be affected by failure to seek annulment.[39]

(b) The causal link

11—55   Rules on remoteness have not been elaborated to any great degree although the Court uses the test of a prudent person to determine whether the applicant's actions in reliance on Community action show a close enough link.[40] Foreseeability of the Community action will also be relevant to the success of the claim.[41] Where the applicant justifiably relies on "legitimate expectation," involving reliance on a continuing state of affairs which is abruptly changed, the necessary link will be supplied if the applicant has entered into binding contracts, the breach of which is necessitated by the change.[42] But random profit is not

[36] *Ibid.* p.108.

[37] Cases 43/72 *Merkur* v. *Commission* [1973] E.C.R. 1055 and 5/71 *supra*, note 28. There are similar statements in relation to: Article 40 ECSC: Cases 9 & 12/60 *Vloeberghs* v. *HA* [1961] E.C.R. 197; Article 175 EEC: Case 4/69 *Supra*, note 15; Article 177 EEC: in *Merkur* itself.

[38] Cases 153/73 *Holtz & Willemsen* v. *Council & Commission* [1974] E.C.R. 675 and 15–33, etc/73 *Schots-Kortner* v. *Commission* [1974] E.C.R. 177.

[39] Case 4/67 *Muller-Collignon* v. *Commission* [1967] E.C.R. 365.

[40] Cases 169/73 *supra*, note 33; 97/76 *Merkur* v. *Commission* [1977] E.C.R. 1063. *Cf.* also Cases 5, 7 and 13–24/66 *Kampffmeyer* v. *Commission* [1967] E.C.R. 245 ("diligent importer").

[41] See, *e.g.* Cases 44–51/77 *Union Malt* v. *Commission* [1978] E.C.R. 57.

[42] Cases 97/76 *supra*, note 40 and 74/74 *CNTA* v. *Council & Commission* [1975] E.C.R. 533. See, *e.g.* 40/75 *Société des Produits Bertrand SA* v. *Commission* [1976] E.C.R. 1, where the applicant failed to establish the causal link.

guaranteed.[43]

The act or omission complained of must be a legally binding act of a Community institution:[44] the Treaties themselves cannot be a source of Community liability.[45]

The Court has held, however, that where the loss complained of arose in the first instance out of action by a Member State, the applicant must bring suit there first. The causal link with the Community action only arises when the Member State fails to make, or is held not liable to make, reparation,[46] unless, perhaps the remedies before national courts would be illusory or inadequate.[47]

(c) The resulting damage

11–56   It appears that the individual applicant need not show that the damage he has suffered is peculiar to him in the sense of "direct and individual concern" under Article 173,[48] but he must show "special circumstances."[49] The damage must be certain and ascertainable[50] rather than speculative and future,[51] but need not be quantifiable at the time of the action. The Court may postpone an award until the damage is known, and if none can be established, the applicant will receive nothing.[52] The damage suffered may be non-material as well as material.[53] Interest may be awarded.[54]

Limitation of actions

11–57   Article 43 of the EEC Statute on the Court of Justice, with which Article 40 of the ECSC Statute is, *mutatis mutandis*, identical, provides that proceedings against the Community in matters arising from non-contractual liability (*i.e.* under Art. 215 EEC, second para., and Art. 40 ECSC, but not Art. 34 ECSC) shall be barred after a period of five years from the occurrence of the event giving rise thereto. The second sentence of these articles

---

[43] Case 60/75 *Russo* v. *AIMA* [1976] E.C.R. 45. *Cf.* also *Kampffmeyer, supra,* note 40.

[44] Case 132/77 *Société pour l'Exportation des Sucres* v. *Commission* [1978] E.C.R. 1061.

[45] Case 169/73 *supra,* note 33.

[46] *Kampffmeyer, supra,* note 40 and Case 99/74 *Grands Moulins des Antilles* v. *Commission* [1975] E.C.R. 1531. Art. 215 has no relevance to liability of national authorities: Case 101/78 *Granaria* v. *Hoofdproduktschap* [1979] E.C.R. 623.

[47] *Dietz* v. *Commission* [1977] E.C.R. 2431.

[48] *Kampffmeyer, supra,* note 40. See note 28, *supra,* on degree of fault.

[49] Cases 83 & 94/76, 4, 15 & 40/77 *Bayerische HNL Vermehrungsbetriebe, supra,* note 28.

[50] *Kampffmeyer, supra,* note 40 but *cf.* Cases 14, etc/60 and 1/61, *Meroni* v. *HA* [1961] E.C.R. 161 and 29, etc/63 *Usines de la Providence* v. *HA* [1965] E.C.R. 911.

[51] *Kampffmeyer, supra,* note 40. Unless clearly foreseeable: Cases 56–60/74 *Kampffmeyer* v. *Commission & Council* [1976] E.C.R. 711.

[52] Cases 74/74 *Supra,* note 42 and 67–85/75 *Lesieur* v. *Commission* [1975] E.C.R. 391.

[53] Cases 7/56 & 3–7/57 *Algera* v. *Common Assembly* [1957–58] E.C.R. 39.

[54] Case 238/78 *Ireks-Arkady* v. *Council & Commission* [1979] E.C.R. 2955 (6% ordered).

provides for the "interruption" of time running by introducing an action before the Court, or by application to the relevant institution, followed by introduction of an action within two months (one month ECSC), the provisions of the second paragraph of Article 17 of the EEC and Euratom Statutes (Art. 35 ECSC) applying "where appropriate."

This is a decidedly obscure provision but it is clear that the application made to the relevant institution does not turn the action into something other than an action for indemnity under Article 215 EEC, second para., or Article 40 ECSC. Cases 5, 7, 13-24/66, *Kampffmeyer* v. *Commission*,[55] suggest that:

(1) an action brought on the last day of the five years from the date of the injury (not of the wrongful act) will be in time whenever the judgment is given, and

(2) a preliminary application made within five years, followed by an action, will be in time if the action is brought within two months if the act complained of is an illegal act, or within four months if a failure to act was complained of, for the institutions are normally given no time to remedy the illegal act, but two months to fill a lacuna. In either case the plaintiff has two months for his own benefit. If he in fact fails to set down an action time is not interrupted.[56]

General provision as to limitation of actions

11—58   It is to be noted that Article 43 of the EEC Statute on the Court of Justice and Article 40 of the ECSC Statute are the only provisions on limitation of actions contained in the Treaties. In the *Quinine Cartel* and *Dyestuffs* cases,[57] the Court refused to refer to general principles of law in order to fix a general period of prescription, leaving it to the Community legislator to do so. Regulation 2988/74[58] introduces a limitation period in proceedings for the enforcement of sanctions under the transport and competition rules.

It appears, however, that the Court may be developing a rule of limitation for more general purposes, notably to prevent Community institutions bringing actions long after the event complained of having occured.[59]

---

[55] *Supra*, note 40. Apparently confirmed by Case 11/72 *Giordano* v. *Commission* [1973] E.C.R. 417.

[56] Case 11/72 *supra*, note 55.

[57] Cases 41/69 *ACF Chemiefarma* v. *Commission* [1970] E.C.R. 661 and related cases and 48/69 *ICI* [1972] E.C.R. 619 and related cases. Similarly cases 119 & 126/79.

[58] O.J. 1974, L319/1.

[59] See, *e.g.* Cases 59/70 *Netherlands* v. *Commission* [1971] E.C.R. 639 and 48/69 *supra*, note 57.

Contractual liability of the Community: actions brought by Community servants, and other contractual actions

11—59   Article 181 EEC, with which Article 42 ECSC is identical, gives the Court of Justice—

> ". . . jurisdiction to give judgment pursuant to any arbitration clause contained in a contract concluded by or on behalf of the Community, whether that contract be governed by public or private law."

Article 179 EEC gives the Court of Justice—

> ". . . jurisdiction in any dispute between the Community and its servants within the limits and under the conditions laid down in the Staff Regulations or the Conditions of Employment."

Article 215, first para., amplifies the above-mentioned provisions, stating that: "The contractual liability of the Community shall be governed by the law applicable to the contract in question."

Article 179 is a specific application of Article 181, at least in so far as contractual matters are concerned. There is no equivalent in the ECSC Treaty, such actions being brought pursuant to Article 42 ECSC, which is identical with Article 181 EEC.

So far as Community employees are concerned, their contracts of employment have been held to be contracts under public law.[60] As such they are governed by Community regulations, rather than by contracts of employment[61] and are outside the scope of Articles 178 and 215 EEC.[62]

11—60   The conditions of employment of Community servants are governed by Regulation 31 of 1962, and Regulations 259/68.[63] Article 91 (1), which picks up Article 179 EEC, provides that the Court of Justice is to have jurisdiction over disputes between the Community and its servants regarding the legality of any act complained of by such persons.[64] It is accepted that this jurisdiction embraces the four grounds of illegality provided for in Article 173, and also failure to act (*cf.* Article 175).

The second limb of Article 91 (1) provides for unlimited jurisdiction (*cf.* Art. 172) (a) in the cases mentioned in Regulation 31 itself, and (b) in disputes of a financial character.

Article 91 (2) lays down a three-month time-limit from publication or notification for actions against acts, and a two-month

---

[60] *e.g.* Case 1/55 *Kergall* v. *Assembly* [1954–56] E.C.R. 151.
[61] Case 28/74 *Gillet* v. *Commission* [1975] E.C.R. 463.
[62] Cases 9/75 *Meyer-Burckhardt* v. *Commission* [1975] E.C.R. 1171; 48/76 *Reinarz* v. *Commission & Council* [1977] E.C.R. 291.
[63] J.O. 1962, 1385 and J.O. 1968, L56/1; numerous amendments.
[64] As to meaning of "person" see Cases 175/73 *Union Syndicale* v. *Council* [1974] E.C.R. 917, and 18/74 *Syndicat Général* v. *Commission* [1974] E.C.R. 933.

time-limit from the expiry of a two-month period of silence in the case of failure to react to a complaint. There appear to be no grounds for thinking that the "unlimited jurisdiction" provision of Article 99 (1) would enable the Court to hear a case time-barred by Article 91 (2).

As already mentioned above, Article 215, first para., leaves the contractual liability of the Community to be governed by the law applicable to the contract in question. In relation to service contracts with Community servants the applicable law is Regulation 31 itself, although the regulation will not necessarily provide all the answers. Where a "gap" is evident, the Court may have recourse to the general principles of law of the Member States.[65] Probably the regulations apply to persons who claim that they have the status of Community employees.[66]

11—61   The Court is required in "ordinary" contract actions brought pursuant to Article 181 to apply the proper law of the contract, this being laid down in the first paragraph of Article 215. This is a somewhat unusual provision for a Court with international jurisdiction, and is suggestive of the jurisdiction of United States Federal Courts, conferred by the United States Constitution, where the law of the state governing the contract is normally applied.

---

[65] Case 44/74 *Acton* v. *Commission* [1975] E.C.R. 383.
[66] Case 65/74 *Porrini* v. *EAEC* [1975] E.C.R. 319.

Part 4

THE FOUNDATIONS OF THE COMMUNITY: THE FOUR FREEDOMS

Chapter 12

THE SETTING UP OF THE EUROPEAN ECONOMIC COMMUNITY

The Treaty setting up the EEC

Preamble and Introductory Articles of the Treaty

Preamble

12—01   The preamble to the EEC Treaty consists of a list of principles relating to the Economic Community. The list neither describes the principles exhaustively, nor lists all the applicable principles, and cannot as a result be said to contain clauses which have substantive legal effect. The preamble to any Treaty is nevertheless of some importance for its interpretation, and clearly constitutes an integral part of it. The preamble to the EEC Treaty is no different from others in this respect. The Court of Justice has used the preamble extensively in interpreting the Treaty.[1]

Perhaps the most notable feature of the preamble lies in its omissions. Apart from the expressed determination to lay the foundations of an ever closer union among the peoples of Europe, confirmed by the preambles to the Merger Treaty and the various Treaties of Accession, there is no mention in the Treaty of Rome of European integration or of supranationality. It is clear, nevertheless, that the Treaty lays the foundations for progress towards at least some kind of political integration.

12—02   Any treaty is of course a product of its times and it is therefore perhaps natural that the preamble to the Treaty of Rome contains no mention of human rights or fundamental rights. These matters have been a preoccupation more of the late 1960s and the 1970s rather than of the 1950s, when the Treaty was signed. This omission is partially compensated for by the case-law of the Court and by the Joint Declaration on Fundamental Rights of April 5, 1977.[2]

One of the most important aspects of the preamble is that it provides some guide to the interpretation and application of the substantive provisions of the Treaty. No real *travaux préparatoires* exist for the Treaty of Rome apart from the Spaak Report to the Foreign Ministers on the Unification of Europe,[3] which formed

[1] See, *e.g.* Case 26/62 *Van Gend en Loos* v. *Nederlandse Administratie der Belastingen* [1963] E.C.R. 1, 12.
[2] *Supra*, para. 6–31.
[3] *Rapport des chefs de délégations aux ministres des affaires étrangères concernant l'unification de l'Europe dans le domaine économique,* Brussels, 1956.

the basis for the negotiations leading to the creation of the EEC, and the reports of the national delegations to their respective Parliaments. The preamble has been relied upon to justify Community action under Article 235 of the Treaty (action necessary to achieve an objective of the Community, but where no power is provided in the Treaty), but cannot be considered to form a substantive basis for Community action on its own.

There is some question as to whether the preamble can be said to have obligatory force. The better view would appear to be that the answer must be in the negative, but the point is of little importance in view of the breadth and vagueness of the language. It can at best be used in appraising the legitimacy of particular acts, and cannot easily be relied upon to support a line of legal argument except in the sense that it has evidentiary value.

Part One of the EEC Treaty - "principles" - Articles 1 to 8

12—03   Article 1 gives substantive effect to the preamble, in setting up a European Economic Community between the High Contracting Parties, namely, Belgium, Germany, France, Italy, Luxembourg and the Netherlands. The Treaty of Accession of January 22, 1972,[4] and the decision of the Council of the same date provided for the accession of Denmark, Ireland, Norway and the United Kingdom to all three European Communities. Following the negative result of a referendum, Norway did not join the Community. Greece acceded to the Community on January 1, 1981, by a similar Treaty of Accession of May 28, 1979.[5]

Article 2 sets out a number of objectives to be achieved by the Community: harmonious development of economic activities, continuous and balanced expansion, an increase in stability, an accelerated raising of the standard of living and closer relations between Member States. These objectives largely reiterate the preamble, and are, with the exception of the last, normal objectives of economic policy. They are to be achieved through the establishment of a common market and the approximation of national economic policies.

12—04   Article 3 sets out a non-exhaustive list of activities of the Community for the purposes of Article 2. The list must be considered non-exhaustive since the activities "shall include" those listed, and since other, unlisted activities are provided for in the body of the Treaty, *e.g.* the tax provisions of Articles 95 to 99. Article 235 provides for the Council, acting unanimously on a proposal from the Commission and after consulting the Assembly, to take the appropriate measures if action by the Community should prove necessary to attain, in the course of the operation of the Common Market, one of the objectives of the Community,

[4] T S No 1 (1973), Cmnd. 5179.
[5] E C No 18 (1979), Cmnd. 7650.

and if the Treaty has not provided the necessary powers. The view had been taken however that this Article is not to be an instrument for licencing completely new activities not already envisaged by the Treaty structures.

It emerges clearly from the enumeration of the Community activities in Article 3, and from their description elsewhere in the Treaty, that by "Common Market" is meant a single economic area in which conditions similar to those existing in a national market will prevail. This aim is a reflection of the neo-liberal economic theory inspiring the Treaty. As emerges from Article 3 and from the rest of the Treaty, the conditions referred to imply at least free movement of goods, and free movement of persons, services and capital ("the four freedoms" - Art. 3 (*a*) and (*c*) and Arts. 9 to 17 and 30 to 37, and 48 to 73), plus a common customs tariff and a common commercial policy towards third countries (Art. 3 (*b*) and Arts. 18 to 29 and 110 to 116), a common agricultural policy (Art. 3 (*d*) and Arts. 38 to 47) and a common transport policy (Art. 3 (*e*) and Arts. 74 to 84). In order to ensure that the conditions to be attained do not vary from one Member State to another, rules to ensure that competition is not distorted are required (Art. 3 (*f*) and Arts. 85 to 94); rules on economic policies (Art. 3 (*g*) and Arts. 103 to 116) rules on the approximation of laws (Art. 3 (*h*) and Arts. 100 to 102), and provisions on social and regional policies (Art. 3 (*i*) and (*j*) and Arts. 117 to 128 and 129 to 130). Finally Article 3 (*k*) makes mention of association of the overseas countries and territories still under the jurisdiction of Member States, the purpose of which is "to increase trade and to promote jointly economic and social development." The substantive provisions on the association of those countries and territories are contained in Articles 131 to 136.

12–05   At first sight there would seem to be some conflict between the two tools provided in Article 2, the establishing of a common market and the approximation of economic policies, but it seems clear that the approximation of economic policies is only in question in matters outside the immediate ambit of the activities of the Common Market. To the extent that these activities may be expanded, opportunity for Member States to engage in their own distinctive economic policies may be affected.[6] Such expansion is clearly envisaged, for Article 3 ("in accordance with the timetable set out" for the Treaty) provides for the development of Community action in specific matters.

Article 4 relates back to Article 2, in that it stipulates that the tasks entrusted to the Community are to be carried out by an Assembly, a Council, a Commission and a Court of Justice.[7]

---

[6] Case 22/70 *Commission* v. *Council* [1971] E.C.R. 263.
[7] See generally part 2, *supra*.

Apart from listing the institutions, it is to be noticed that Article 4 requires each institution to act within the limits of the powers conferred upon it by the Treaty. This phrase makes it clear that the powers of the institutions are powers of attribution; they extend only so far as the Treaty confers them, and no institution may arrogate powers or competences to itself, although it may have certain implied powers. (See also para. 3-43, *supra*.)

12—06   By Article 5, first para., the Member States are to "take all appropriate measures, whether general or particular, to ensure the fulfilment of the obligations arising out of this Treaty or resulting from action taken by the institutions," *i.e.* from secondary legislation in the sense of Article 189. The obligation is one requiring action (or restraint) in execution of obligations. The second sentence of the first paragraph requires Member States to "facilitate the achievement of the Community's tasks." This is a more active obligation, requiring Member States to give the Community all assistance possible.

The duty laid down in the first paragraph of this Article is reinforced in negative form in the second paragraph, which requires the State to refrain from prejudicial behaviour. In view of the scope of discretion left to both the Member States and Community institutions to determine the concrete application of this Article, it cannot be, and has not been regarded as directly applicable.[8]

12—07   The Member States are required by Article 6 to co-ordinate their economic policies to the extent necessary to attain the objectives of the Treaty. This co-ordination is to take place in close co-operation with the institutions of the Community. These latter are required to take care not to prejudice the internal and external financial stability of the Member States.

Article 145, requiring the Council to ensure co-ordination of the general economic policies of the Member States, makes it clear that the institution bears a primary responsibility in economic matters although national interest is predominant here.[9] The various committees with economic responsibility are concerned here also, notably the Monetary Committee, Budgetary Policy Committee, and Committee of the Governors of the Central Banks. This is discussed in Chapter 24.

The Treaty contains additional provisions on economic policies in Article 103 (conjunctural policy) and Articles 104 to 109 (balance of payments). These dispositions are, however, much more specific, while the ambit of Article 6 (1) grows with the expansion of Community activities in general (see generally Chapter 24, on ecomonic policy).

[8] Case 78/80 *Deutsche Grammophon Gesellschaft* v. *Metro—SB—Grossmärkte GmbH* [1971] E.C.R. 487.
[9] Opinion 1/78 *IANR* [1979] E.C.R. 2871.

12–08   The rule contained in Article 7 is one of the fundamental rules of the Community.[10] By Article 7, first paragraph,

> "within the scope of application of this Treaty, and without prejudice to any special provisions contained therein, any discrimination on grounds of nationality shall be prohibited."

The second paragraph provides for the adoption of Council rules designed to prohibit such discrimination. Whether due to the implication to be drawn from the second paragraph (which has not been used) or from the reference in the first paragraph to special provisions regarding non-discrimination contained in the Treaty itself, (see, *e.g.* Articles, 31, 40, 44, 45, 48, 59, 132, etc.), the Court has never held the first paragraph on its own to be directly applicable. The reference is always, *e.g.* to Article 7 "as implemented" by other provisions of Community law.[11] Article 7 could form the basis for an Article 169 proceeding. It could justify annulment of secondary legislation which infringes it. It is also applicable to discrimination exercised by individuals or associations,[12] with the proviso that because of the limitation of the article to the scope of application of the Treaty, it does not apply to matters having nothing to do with an economic activity, *e.g.* "a question of purely sporting interest."[12]

12–09   Discrimination within the meaning of Article 7 may be overt, but it may also be indirect or covert.[13] The Court has defined discrimination as involving the different treatment of similar situations and the similar treatment of dissimilar situations.[14] But difference in treatment cannot be regarded as constituting discrimination which is prohibited unless it is arbitrary.[15]

Article 7 does not regulate the effect of differences between the laws of the Member States which may cause nationals of one State to bear a greater burden than those of other Member States. This is due to the characteristic effects of territorial jurisdiction.[16] A remedy for disparities in the impact of legislation in different

---

[10] Case 2/74 *Reyners* v. *Belgium* [1974] E.C.R. 631, 651.
[11] Case 1/78 *Kenny* v. *Insurance Officer* [1978] E.C.R. 1489, 1497, para. 12 and 8/77 *Sagulo, Brenca and Bakhouche* [1977] E.C.R. 1495, 1505, para. 11.
[12] Cases 36/74 *Walrave* v.*Union Cycliste* [1974] E.C.R. 1405; 13/76 *Dona* v. *Mantero* [1976] E.C.R. 1333.
[13] Cases 152/73 *Sotgiu* v. *Deutsche Bundespost* [1974] E.C.R. 153; 61/77 *Commission* v. *Ireland* [1978] E.C.R. 417; 237/78 *CRAM* v. *Toia* [1979] E.C.R. 2645.
[14] Case 13/63 *Government of Italy* v. *Commission* [1963] E.C.R. 165. See also Case 79/77 *Kühlhaus Zentrum* v. *HZA* [1979] E.C.R. 611, 620: " ... discrimination consists above all in treating comparable situations differently. ... "
[15] Case 11/74 *Minotiers de la Champagne* v. *France* [1974] E.C.R. 877. It does not therefore prohibit control of aliens *per se*—Case 118/75 *Watson and Belmann* [1976] E.C.R. 1185.
[16] Case 185 to 204/78 *Van Dam* [1979] E.C.R. 2345; 31/78 *Bussone* [1978] E.C.R. 2429; 86/78 *Peureux* v. *Directeur des Services Fiscaux de la Haute Saône* [1979] E.C.R. 897; and 175/78 *R.* v. *Saunders* [1979] E.C.R. 1129.

Member States has to be sought outside Article 7, *e.g.* under Articles 5 or 100 and 101. The question whether Article 7 (in conjunction with other Articles concerning discrimination) could be invoked where a Member State discriminates against its own nationals is discussed *infra*, Chapter 16.

12—10   Article 8 is now largely spent. The article states the principle that the Community was to be progressively established during a transitional period of 12 years, divided into three equal stages of four years. It provided for modification of this timetable, but none of significance was in fact effected, although the setting up of the customs union was accelerated.[17]

Article 8 (7) states that the expiry of the transitional period which occurred on December 31, 1969, constituted the latest date by which all the rules laid down must enter into force. This is subject to any exceptions or derogations provided for in the Treaty (*e.g.* Art. 26; postponement of alignment with the CCT of specific items).[18] The expiry of the period of transition clearly did not affect provisions intended to be of application throughout the existence of the Community, but as of that date certain provisions ceased to be of application (*e.g.* the transitional safeguards in Art. 226), while others came into operation for the first time (*e.g.* tariff negotiation provisions in Art. 113). Irrespective of the state of implementation at that date, many of these provisions have been held directly applicable by the Court in the years since the end of the transitional period.

[17] This acceleration did not affect the length of the transitional period Case 27/78 *Rasham* [1978] E.C.R. 1761.
[18] See Case 231/78 *Commission* v. *UK* [1979] E.C.R. 1447.

Chapter 13

FREE MOVEMENT OF GOODS

Free Movement of Goods - Articles 9 to 11

3—01   Articles 9 to 11 of the Treaty set out the general principles of the customs union. Article 9 refers to the Community as being based upon a customs union covering all trade in goods and the term "goods" includes all such items as are listed in the Community customs tariff described below. Coins are generally not "goods" but fall within the notion of capital[1] or "means of payment" for which the Treaty makes express provision elsewhere. A customs union is more comprehensive than a free trade area; as stated in Article 9 it entails, in addition to free trade between Member States ensured by prohibition of customs duties on imports and exports, and of all charges having equivalent effect, the adoption of a common customs tariff *vis-à-vis* non-Member States.[2] Community action is not limited to this, for the customs union is only one element in the creation of a common market in goods and services (*i.e.* comprising the so-called four freedoms) and does not exhaust the potential of the Community: the plans for economic and monetary union described in the Chapter on Economic Policy later in this book were based upon the existing structure of the Community, and involved its amplification; they did not constitute a separate movement.[3] Economic and monetary union did not, however, envisage integration to the degree obtaining in a federal state.

3—02   The EEC Treaty also calls for the suppression of quantitative restrictions under Articles 30 to 37. As the structuring of Title 1 - "Free Movement of Goods" - of Part Two of the Treaty - "Foundations of the Community" - itself indicates, elimination of such restrictions was not apparently considered to be part and parcel of the customs union *stricto sensu*: Chapter 1 is entitled the "Customs Union," while the "Elimination of Quantitative Restrictions" forms a separate Chapter 2.

Furthermore, the Customs Union did not entail the common administration of quotas until the end of the transitional period, and in fact it was only in May 1979 that this responsibility was transferred to the Commission.[4]

[1] Case 7/78 *Thompson* v. *Johnson and Woodiwiss* [1978] E.C.R. 2247.
[2] See Swann D, "Economics of the Common Market" (Penguin, 3rd ed., 1975).
[3] Werner Plan: Report to the Council and the Commission on the realisation by stages of Economic and Monetary Union in the Community: Bulletin Suppt. 11, 1970.
[4] See *infra*.

The abolition of custom duties between Member States does not eliminate all controls at frontiers at a stroke. In the first place, important restrictions are still permitted on grounds of public policy (*e.g.* Article 36, discussed below) and in the second place, customs controls are in many cases replaced by revenue controls operating as internal taxes. For although Member States may not tax goods imported from other Member States at a higher rate than the domestic product, they may nevertheless impose the same rate, and this will be done at the frontier (Arts. 95 and 96). Among the chief objects of the harmonisation of the national system of turnover taxes and institution of a common value added tax system was the elimination on the one hand of instances of double taxation by enabling goods to be exported tax-free to other Member States, and on the other hand, the securing of an even level of taxation (as yet still far from being achieved).

"Customs duty" and "charges equivalent to customs duties"

13—03   With the expiry of the original transitional period, the Court has taken the view that any charge levied by reason of goods crossing an internal frontier is prohibited, whatever its purpose might be (*i.e.* whether protective, fiscal or to cover administrative costs).[5] Furthermore, it is not necessary that the charge actually be levied at the frontier or at the time of crossing the frontier, for it to be prohibited. If it is levied exclusively on imports or in a manner differentiating imported goods from home produced goods it is clearly caught.[6] It is also sufficient that it falls more heavily on the imported or exported product than on domestic products.[7] The prohibition in Article 9 only applies, as regards trade with third countries, to goods in free circulation in a Member State under Article 10 (2).[8] It is irrelevant that the charge is made at any particular stage, *e.g.* at the stage of marketing or the stage of processing. If they are not part of a system covering also home produced goods,[9] even charges imposed in the course of admini-

[5] See, *e.g.* Cases 2 and 3/62 *Commission* v. *Luxembourg and Belgium* [1962] E.C.R. 425; Case 77/72 *Capolongo* v. *Maya* [1973] E.C.R. 611; 39/73 *Rewe—Zentralfinanz* v. *Landwirtschaftkammer Westfalen-Lippe* [1973] E.C.R. 1039; Case 63/74 *W Cadsky SpA* v. *Instituto nazionale per il commercio estero* [1975] E.C.R. 281.

[6] Cases 29/72 *Marimex* v. *Amministrazione Finanziaria* [1972] E.C.R. 1309; Case 94/74 *IGAV* v. *ENCC* [1975] E.C.R. 281; 21/75 *Schroeder* v. *Stadt Köln* [1975] E.C.R. 905; 87/75 *Bresciani* v. *Amministrazione Italiana delle Finanze* [1976] E.C.R. 129; 35/76 *Simmenthal* v. *Italian Minister for Finance* [1976] E.C.R. 1871.

[7] Case 78/76 *Firma Steinicke & Weinlig* v. *Federal Republic of Germany* [19] E.C.R. 595.

[8] Case 148/77 *Hansen* v. *HZA Flensburg* [1978] E.C.R. 1787; 70/77 *Simmenthal* v. *Ammin. delle Finanze* [1978] E.C.R. 1453; Case 119/78 *Peureux* v. *Services Fiscaux de la Haute Saône* [1979] E.C.R. 975.

[9] *i.e.* notably a system of internal taxation under Art. 95. See Cases 77/72 *Capolongo* v. *Maya* [1973] E.C.R. 611; 39/73 *Rewe-Zentralfinanz* v. *Landwirtschaftskammer Westfalen-Lippe* [1973] E.C.R. 1039; 94/74 *IGAV* v. *ENCC* [1975] E.C.R. 699; 77/76 *Cucchi* v. *Avez* [1977] E.C.R. 987; 105/76 *Interzuccheri* v. *Ditta Rezzano e Cavassa* [1977] E.C.R. 1029; 78/76 *Steinike and Weinlig* v. *Commission* [1977] E.C.R. 595; 222/78 *ICAP* v. *Beneventi* [1979] E.C.R. 1163; 132/78 *Denkavit* v. *France* [1979] E.C.R. 1923.

strative controls permitted by Article 36, discussed below, are forbidden.[10]

It should be noted that the questions discussed in this paragraph and the interpretations given by the Court equally apply to Articles 12, 13 and 16 and also to regulations using the same terminology.[11]

13—04   There are two established exceptions to this rule. First, such charges may be permissible if expressly authorised by Community rules[12] and/or are in furtherance of an international Convention to which all Member States are parties,[13] at any rate if the effect is to eliminate duplication of frontier controls by charging for inspections on exports rather than imports or if the charge does not exceed the cost of providing the check.[14] However, if the Community has laid down its own rules on such checks (especially in the context of the agricultural policy where, in respect of particular goods, internal checks are mutually recognised by all Member States) a Member State will no longer be justified in making charges for inspections on importation of the goods or indeed in carrying out the check at all on a separate basis at the frontier.[15] Secondly, if the charges are levied exclusively in respect of services rendered to the importer and are proportionate to the services, they may be permissible.[16] Quality controls do not constitute a relevant benefit, and benefits of a general kind, such as a statistical service, are insufficient to justify the charge.[17]

Goods "in free circulation"

13—05   Under Article 9 (2), the provisions for free circulation of goods apply of course to all goods produced in the Community but additionally they apply to goods obtained outside the Community, and in free circulation in the Member States. Article 10 defines these latter as being goods which have complied with the import formalities of the relevant Member State, and on which any customs duties or equivalent charges which are payable have been levied in that Member State, and which have not benefited from a total or partial drawback of such duties or charges. However, compliance with these formalities will not by-pass import pro-

---

[10] Case 29/72 *Marimex SpA* v. *Minister of Finance* [1972] E.C.R. 1309.
[11] Case 84/71 *Marimex* [1972] E.C.R. 1309.
[12] Cases 46/76 *WJG Bauhuis* v. *the Netherlands* [1977] E.C.R. 5; 70/77 *Simmenthal* v. *Ammin delle Finanze* [1978] E.C.R. 1453.
[13] Case 89/76 *Commission* v. *Netherlands* [1977] E.C.R. 1355.
[14] Case 46/76 *Bauhuis, supra,* note 12.
[15] Case 35/76 *Simmenthal SpA* v. *Italian Minister for Finance* [1976] E.C.R. 1871.
[16] Case 52 and 55/65 *Germany* v. *Commission* [1966] E.C.R. 159; 63/74 *Cadsky supra,* note 5; Case 132/78 *Denkavit* v. *France supra,* note 9.
[17] Case 24/68 *Commission* v. *Italy* [1969] E.C.R. 193.

hibitions based on other grounds, *e.g.* violation of industrial property rights.[18]

The Protocol to the Treaty of Rome on German Internal Trade makes it clear that goods originating in the German Democratic Republic are to be considered as in free circulation, subject to limitations and to particular safeguards.[19]

13—06   Article 10 (2) is the legal basis for decisions of the Commission determining the methods of administrative co-operation to be adopted for the purpose of applying Article 9 (2), *i.e.* for keeping a check on goods entitled to free movement. Control was at first largely effected through the use of movement certificates, but now that there is a unified régime for goods in transit in the Community[20] the internal movement certificates have been suppressed, since goods in fact within the Community are by and large assumed to be entitled to benefit from the free movement provisions. Subject to this, Article 9 (2) ensures that goods originating in third countries and in free circulation should not be subject to different administrative procedures from goods originating in the Community.[21] Both are subject to a uniform system of transit documentation, based on the use of a "T2" document.[22]

The second sub-paragraph of paragraph 2 of Article 10 requires that rules be laid down the control of inward processing trade between Member States, where customs duty has been paid on only a part of the material imcorporated into a finished product. The principle to be aimed at here was clearly that all goods should bear the requisite charges in conformity with Article 10 (1) by the expiry of the period of transition, and Decision 68/284[23] gave effect to this, replacing earlier partial solutions.

13—07   Article 11, requiring Member States to take all appropriate measures to enable governments to carry out, within the periods of time laid down, the obligations with regard to customs duties which devolve on them pursuant to the Treaty, applies the principles of Article 5 to the specific case of Articles 9 to 17 on customs matters. But it has been suggested that the obligation is slightly wider than this, in that there is here in effect a duty on the Member States to see that legislation is passed or administrative measures are taken empowering the governments to act.

---

[18] See Cases 51, 86, 96/75 *EMI* v. *CBS* [1976] E.C.R. 811, 871, 913; 41/76 *Donckerwolcke* v. *Procureur de la République, infra,* note 21, on the scope of "in free circulation."
[19] And see Case 14/74 *Fleischkontor* v. *HZA Hamburg-Jonas* [1974] E.C.R. 899.
[20] Currently Regulations 222/77, O.J. 1977, L38/1 and 223/77, O.J. 1977, L38/20, amended by Reg. 1601/77, O.J. 1977, L182/1 and by Reg. 526/79 O.J. 1979, L74/1.
[21] Case 42/76 *Suzanne Criel, née Donckerwolke & Henri Schon* v. *Procureur de la République au Tribunal de Grande Instance, Lille and Director General of Customs* [1976] E.C.R. 1921.
[22] Provided for by the regulations mentioned *supra,* note 20.
[23] J.O. 1968, L 167/10.

As already mentioned, Articles 9 to 11 set out the general principles of the customs union. The succeeding articles are more specific; new duties and equivalent charges on imports and exports are prohibited (Art. 12): existing ones are abolished (Arts. 13 to 17): and the common customs tariff is set up (Arts. 17 to 29);[24] All these provisions are of quite general application. In principle therefore, they apply equally to agriculture, save as otherwise provided in Articles 39 to 46 or by provisions of the common agricultural policy. It is now clear that from the end of the transitional period and (where appropriate) the end of the various Accession transitional periods, it is no longer permissible to levy customs duties or charges having equivalent effect on agricultural goods even if no common policy exists for the goods in question.[25]

The Customs Union - Articles 12 to 29

13—08 The elimination of customs duties between Member States - Articles 12 to 17

By Article 12 Member States are bound to refrain from introducing between themselves any new customs duties on imports or exports, or any equivalent charges, and from increasing those already extant. Articles 9 to 12 together constitute a basic rule so that derogations must be clearly and explicitly provided for.[26] Article 12 is directly applicable.[27] The provisions for the abolition of customs duties as between Member States are now largely of academic interest, since all such duties and equivalent charges were to be abolished by the end of the transitional period. It is sufficient to note that under Article 13 (1) customs duties on imports were to be abolished during the transitional period in accordance with the time-table laid down in Articles 14 and 15. In fact, however, the Member States abolished all duties on industrial goods as of July 1, 1968.[28]

Under Article 13 (2) equivalent charges were to be abolished during the transitional period on the basis of a time-table laid down by Commission directives.[29] Despite the provision for directives, the paragraph has been interpreted as creating directly applicable obligations to abolish all equivalent charges between Member States by the end of the transitional period.[30] The nature and scope of charges equivalent to customs duties are discussed

[24] The cases are conveniently summarised in Case 61/79 *Ammin. delle Finanze* v. *Denkavit Italiana*, [1980] E.C.R. 1205.
[25] Cases 48/74 *Charmasson* v. *Minister for Economic Affairs and Finance* [1974] E.C.R. 1383; 63/74 *Cadsky* v. *Istituto Nazionale Per il Commercio Estero* [1975] E.C.R. 281; 80 & 81/77 *Commissionaires Réunis* v. *Receveur des Douanes* [1978] E.C.R. 927.
[26] Cases 2 and 3/72 *Commission* v. *Luxembourg and Belgium*, note 5, *supra*.
[27] Case 26/62 *Van Gend en Loos* [1963] E.C.R. 1.
[28] Decision 66/532 J.O. 1966, 2971.
[29] See *supra* on charges having equivalent effect.
[30] Case 33/70 *SACE* v. *Italian Ministry of Finance* [1970] E.C.R. 1213; 77/72 *Capolongo* v. *Maya* [1973] E.C.R. 611; 94/74 *IGAV* v. *ENCC* [1975] E.C.R. 699.

above. If a charge is made and subsequently found to be illegitimate then duties paid under protest or without full appreciation of the scope of this provision are recoverable within the terms of the national legislation on the subject. Community law does not control the conditions for such recovery provided only that procedural obstacles do not make it impossible.[31]

Article 16 provided for the abolition between Member States of export duties and charges having equivalent effect[32] by the end of the first stage of the transitional period. It is directly applicable.[33]

Article 17 deals specifically with the abolition of customs duties of a fiscal nature, *i.e.* those intended to produce revenue and not primarily designed to protect. These were to be abolished, since the difference between protective and revenue producing duties is not in practice entirely clear-cut. Article 17 (3) permits the replacement of fiscal duties by internal taxes complying with Article 95.

Setting up of the Common Customs Tariff (CCT) - Articles 18 to 29

13—09   The section of the Treaty on the setting up of the CCT opens with a declaration that the Member States are ready to enter into agreements "designed . . . to reduce duties below the general level of which they could avail themselves as a result of the establishment of a customs union between them," for the purposes of contributing to the development of international trade and the lowering of barriers to trade (Art. 18). It may be questioned whether this provision imposes any obligation at all. The better view appears to be that it enunciates a principle to be acted upon, but not an obligation. There have been two significant general reductions in tariffs since the formation of the Common Market in the framework of the GATT - The Kennedy and Tokyo Rounds.

However, amidst complaints of dumping and cheap goods overseas "subsidised" by cheap labour or cheaper fuel costs, protective measures have frequently been called for. In 1979 the Council responded to these calls in a general way by strengthening the anti-dumping mechanisms.

13—10   In carrying out the tasks entrusted to it under this section of the Treaty on the setting up of the CCT, the Commission is to be guided by a series of principles set out in Article 29, namely:

"(a) the need to promote trade between Member States and third countries;

(b) developments in conditions of competition within the Community in so far as they lead to an improvement in the competitive capacity of undertakings;

[31] Case 61/69, *Denkavit Italiana, supra,* note 24.
[32] See Cases 51/74 *Van der Hulst's Zonen* v. *Produktschap voor Siergewassen* [1978] E.C.R. 79; 63/74 *Cadsky, supra,* note 5 and 45/76 *Comet* v. *Produktschap voor Siergewassen* [1976] E.C.R. 2043 and see *supra,* para. 13–03.
[33] Case 18/71 *Eunomia* v. *Italian Ministry of Education* [1971] E.C.R. 811.

(c) the requirements of the Community as regards the supply of raw materials and semi-finished goods; in this connection the Commission shall take care to avoid distorting conditions of competition between Member States in respect of finished goods;

(d) the need to avoid serious disturbances in the economies of Member States and to ensure rational development of production and an expansion of consumption within the Community."

These principles are binding on the Commission only, but in so far as they must necessarily appear in Commission proposals, they affect the entire Community. The Court has referred to the necessity to have regard to these principles in granting tariff quotas under Article 25.[34]

The fixing of duties

13—11   The basic level of the CCT was originally fixed at the arithmetical average of the duties applied in the four customs territories (Benelux, France, Germany and Italy) comprised in the Community on January 1, 1957 (Art. 19). This basic rule was, however, subject to a number of exceptions and restrictions, governed by Article 19 itself, and Articles 20 and 22. Article 23 (3) provides that the CCT was to be applied in its entirety by the end of the transitional period at the latest. Article XXIV of the GATT placed certain restrictions upon the fixing of a CCT by "customs unions," but the GATT never in fact gave a final ruling on the compatibility of the EEC Treaty with its rules. This is not to say, however, that the Community is to be considered to exist in any way in violation of GATT.[35]

The Tariff

13—12   The implementation of the CCT did not follow the timetable set out in Article 23; rather it was speeded up by the same two acceleration decisions referred to in connection with elimination of duties between Member States and finally set in place for industrial products by the same final decision as for customs duties as of July 1, 1968, the tariff being set out in Regulation 950/68[36] and subsequent amendments to its annex. The legal basis for this alignment is to be found in Article 24, echoing Article 15 (2), and in Article 235. The level of customs duties for any given year is now governed by an annual consolidating tariff regulation amending the annex to Regulation 950/68.

---

[34] Cases 24 & 34/62 *Germany* v. *Commission* [1963] E.C.R. 63 & 131.
[35] See, *e.g.* Written Question 456/71; J.O. 1972, C23/11.
[36] J.O. 1968, L 172/1; O.J. 1968, (1), 275, Version for 1981 Reg. 3000/80, O.J. 1980. L 315/1.

13—13   The common customs tariff sets out the tariff headings, divisions
and sub-divisions, and beside them the applicable duties are set
out, listed in two columns: autonomous duties in the sense of
Article 28 (*i.e.* those fixed by the Community without particular
reference to third states) in the first column, and duties arrived at
under Article 113 by international convention. The tariff regulation contains rules as to its interpretation. Most notable is the
provision that the CCT is completely closed; no goods are outside
it. The Commission, assisted by the nomenclature committee[37]
issues explanatory notes on the sub-divisions of the CCT, themselves based upon the Brussels Convention on Customs Nomenclature of December 15, 1950, as amended[38] to which all Member
States are party, and which is accepted by the Community. The
explanatory notes cannot however modify the CCT, so the latter
must always prevail,[39] but in the absence of explicit Community
provisions the notes are an authoritative guide.[40] The interpretation of the tariff is entirely a matter of Community rather
than national law,[41] although the classification opinions collected
by the Customs Co-operation Council (set up in conjunction with
the Brussels Nomenclature) have *persuasive* force, so that if a
particular classification reflects general practice it can only be set
aside if it appears incompatible with the particular heading.[42]
     The CCT must be used not only for imposition of duties but
also of levies within the framework of the CAP (post) and of
monetary compensatory amounts; the same is true of the criteria
used for its interpretation.[43]

Derogations from the CCT

13—14 Article 25 provides for the granting of tariff quotas to Member
States, paragraph 1 directs that if the Commission finds that the
Community production of particular products contained in lists
B, C and D falls short of the requirements of one of the Member
States, and that such supply traditionally depends to a considerable
extent on imports from third countries, the Council is to grant the
Member State concerned tariff quotas at a reduced rate of duty or
duty free, acting by a qualified majority on a proposal from the
Commission. Under paragraph 2 of the Commission is itself to
grant such quotas for particular products contained in lists E and
G where difficulties with supplies are such as to entail harmful
consequences for the processing industries of a Member State.

[37] Regulation 97/69, J.O. 1969 114/1, setting up the Committee.
[38] Cmnd. 4870; TS No 11 (1972).
[39] Case 183/73 *Osram GmbH* v. *Oberfinanzdirektion Frankfurt* [1974] E.C.R. 477.
[40] See, *e.g.* Cases 14/70 *Bakels* v. *Oberfinanzdirektion München* [1970] E.C.R. 1001 and
35/75 *Matisa—Maschinen GmbH* v. *HZA Berlin—Packhof* [1975] E.C.R. 1205.
[41] Case 38/75 *Douanagent der NV Nederlandse Spoorwegen* v. *Inspecteur der
invoerrechten en accijnzen* [1975] E.C.R. 1439.
[42] *Ibid.*
[43] Case 158/78 *P Biegi* v. *HZA Bochum* [1979] E.C.R. 1103.

These quotas are granted on request from the Member State concerned. Under paragraph 3 the Commission may authorise a Member State to suspend collection of applicable duties on Annex II (*i.e.* agricultural) products or may grant tariff quotas. Action under any of the three paragraphs must be taken in such a way as to avoid harmful effects on other Member States or on the agricultural markets. Since variable levies rather than customs duties are applied in respect of many agricultural products subject to a common organisation, this particular power is only of limited significance. Where the conditions for granting the quota exist, it must, under the first two of the three paragraphs, be granted. But the granting of a quota is never automatic, for all the elements must be taken into account, and in particular the Commission must have regard to the guiding principles set out in Article 29.

13—15   Article 28 refers to "autonomous alteration or suspension of duties" in the CCT. An autonomous duty is a duty fixed by the Community, without particular reference to third States. Such a duty is to be contrasted with a duty fixed in the first place by international convention, and subsequently incorporated into the Community tariff. Conventional duties, so called, are arrived at under powers formerly based on Article 111, now based on 113 and 114 (discussed below). The decision to alter or suspend duties under Article 28 is taken by the Council acting unanimously. No Commission proposal, of the type provided for in Article 148, is here in question, although the Council may in fact act at the instigation of the Commission. Temporary derogations from the CCT are fixed by the Council acting by a qualified majority on a proposal from the Commission. The alterations or suspensions carried out by way of derogation are not to exceed 20 per cent. of the rate in the case of any one duty, and may last for a period of six months maximum. A single extension for a further period of six months may subsequently be granted under the same condition. It is in exercise of this latter power that tariff quotas (*e.g.* 100 tons of a given product at 5 per cent. or 0 per cent. instead of 10 per cent. import duty) are granted. Unlike the suspension under Article 25, these are of general application, and do not concern one State alone.

13—16   It would appear that although the Community has sole power to determine the use to which quotas will be put it may expressly or impliedly permit the exercise of a discretion by Member States or their appointed agencies to allocate the quota on any basis including any preferential basis that they think fit.[44] However, such allocation must not exceed or depart from the governing

---

[44] Case 124/79 *J A van Walsum RV* v. *Produktschap voor Vee en Vlees* [1980] E.C.R. 813 (by analogy with the quotas opened in the context of the common commercial policy under Article 113).

Community objectives if such are set.[45]

Harmonisation of Customs legislation

13—17   The adoption of a common customs tariff would be virtually meaningless if it were not accompanied by harmonisation of the rules by which it is administered, *i.e.* rules covering such matters as valuation, origin of goods, personal luggage allowances and so on. Surprisingly however no specific provision was inserted which would have given the Community harmonising powers over and above those set out in Articles 100 - 102. These powers were found not to be sufficient because the necessary degree of uniformity called for the adoption of regulations in some areas, rather than directives. A great many regulations and directives have been adopted although the Commission considers that many important aspects are still not covered.[46]

Article 235 has been used extensively as the legal basis for these measures.[47] A regulation of particular importance is that laying down the régime on the valuation of goods the primary purpose of which is to secure uniform treatment of valuation throughout the EEC. The original regulation applicable since the transitional period has recently been repealed and replaced by a new régime (Regulation 1224/80[48]) intended to implement the arrangements agreed in the context of the Tokyo round. The new valuation basis provides that the value of goods should normally be assessed on the invoice price, *i.e.* "the transaction value" and does away therefore with the previous "normal value" concept. If the Customs authorities are able to establish that the invoice price does not reflect the true value of the goods, they may proceed to assess the value on a number of different bases which must be applied in a strict order until a satisfactory basis is found. Measures based on the former Regulation 803/68 are validated by Regulation 1493/80.[49] Further regulations set out interpretative notes and generally accepted accounting principles for the purposes of customs value,[50] amplify the provisions of Regulation 1224/80,[51] and provide forms for declarations of duty.[52]

13—18   Although this harmonisation has been achieved through the use of a regulation, a good deal of discretion is left to national authorities, such as, for instance the determination of sufficient proof of value.[53]

[45] Case 35/79 *Spa Grosoli* v. *Italian Ministry for Foreign Trade* [1980] E.C.R. 177.
[46] See, *e.g.* the Multiannual programmes for the attainment of the Customs Union, O.J. 1979, C 84/2; 1981 Programme, O.J. 1981, C 106/2.
[47] Case 8/73 *HZA Bremerhaven* v. *Massey Ferguson* [1973] E.C.R. 897.
[48] O.J. 1980, L134/1.
[49] O.J. 1980, L154/1.
[50] Regulation 1494/80, O.J. 1980, L154/3.
[51] Regulation 1495/80, O.J. 1980, L154/14.
[52] Regulation 1496/80, O.J. 1980, L154/16.
[53] See Case 84/79 *Meyer—Uetze* v. *HZA Bad Reichenhall* [1980] E.C.R. 291.

A number of general principles were elaborated by the Court under the former Regulation 803/68 tending to emphasise that the purpose of the valuation regulations is to establish the correct value of goods for the purposes of levying customs duty on goods and that therefore it is impermissible to use the rules for another purpose under the cloak of valuation[54] or to seek to apply the duties to incorporeal items such as the value of trademarks or patents.[55] These interpretations will almost certainly be valid also for the new Regulation.

Another Regulation of particular general significance is that relating to the determination of the origin of goods for the purposes of applying preferential treatment or selective import controls, *e.g.* against a particular country. Article 5 of Regulation 802/68[56] indicates that a product is regarded as originating;

> "in the country in which the last substantial process or operation that is economically justified was performed, having been carried out in an undertaking equipped for the purpose, and resulting in the manufacture of a new product or representing an important stage of manufacture."

This broad definition has been supplemented on a number of occasions by more specific regulations dealing with particular products such as Regulation 749/78.[57]

The role of the Member States

13—19   In all the areas where the Community has been given the power to legislate or has acted, Community law rules out any national legislation conflicting or even co-existing with Community legislation.[58] In particular, the Member States may not introduce new charges on goods imported directly from third countries or raise the level of those in existence.[59]

---

[54] Case 65/79 *Procureur de la République Française* v. *Réne Châtain ("Sandoz")* [1980] E.C.R. 1345.
[55] Case 1/77 *Robert Bosch* v. *HZA Hildesheim* [1977] E.C.R. 1473.
[56] J.O. 1968, L148/1.
[57] O.J. 1978, L101/7. And see generally Ian S. Forrester, *EEC Customs Law: Rules of Origin and Preferential Duty Treatment*, (1980) 5 E.L.Rev. 167.
[58] See especially 40/69 *HZA Hamburg-Oberelbe* v. *Bollmann* [1970] E.C.R. 69; 74/69 *HZA Bremen-Freihafen* v. *Krohn* [1970] E.C.R. 451; 39/70 *Fleischkontor* v. *HZA Hamburg-St. Annen* [1971] E.C.R. 49; 51–54/71 *International Fruit Company* v. *Produktschap voor Groenten en Fruit* [1971] E.C.R. 1107; 94/71 *Schlüter & Maack* v. *HZA Hamburg-Jonas* [1972] E.C.R. 307; 223/78 *Grosoli* [1979] E.C.R. 2621 and other price control cases discussed *infra*, para. 13–32 and Case 177/78 *Pigs and Bacon Commission* v. *McCarren* [1979] E.C.R. 2161.
[59] Cases 37 and 38/73 *Sociaal Fonds voor de Diamantarbeiders* v. *NV Indiamex and Association de fait de Belder* [1973] E.C.R. 1609; 46/76 *Bauhuis* [1977] E.C.R. 5; 70/77 *Simmenthal* v. *Ammin. Delle Finanze* [1978] E.C.R. 1453.

The Elimination of Quantitative Restrictions between Member States

13—20   "Quantitative restrictions on imports and all measures having equivalent effect [are], without prejudice to [Articles 31 to 37], prohibited between Member States" (Art. 30), and new restrictions of the same kind are prohibited (Art. 31, first para.), but the latter obligation relates only to the degree of liberalisation attained in pursuance of the decisions of the Council of the OEEC (now OECD) of January 14, 1955, (Art. 31, second para.). The OEEC had achieved the suppression of quantitative restrictions on 90 per cent. of goods imported by OEEC Members from other OEEC Member States. Despite this liberalisation, however, it was considered that quantitative restrictions would, if not abolished, hinder the creation of the Common Market; hence the provisions for their elimination in the EEC Treaty. Article 31 must now be regarded as applying to all new measures having equivalent effect.[60] Article 34 contains a parallel provision forbidding the maintenance of export restrictions. Article 32 contains a general standstill clause and Article 33 lays down a timetable for the abolition of restrictions, which could be accelerated under Article 35, a provision similar to Articles 15 and 24, *supra*, Article 36 sets out certain general exceptions to the general principles of Articles 30, 31 and 34 and is dealt with below. Articles 30, 31 (first para.), 32 (1), 34 and possibly Article 33 have been declared directly applicable.[61]

The notions of "quantitative restriction" and "measure having equivalent effect"

13—21   Quantitative restrictions have the effect of limiting imports (or exports) of products by number, weight or value. These restrictions are more familiarly known as quotas, but the term "quantitative restriction" (of which quotas are but one type) is more accurate. According to the Court's judgment in *Dassonville*[62], "all trading rules enacted by Member States which are capable of hindering, directly or indirectly, actually or potentially, intra-Community trade, are to be considered as measures having an effect equivalent to quantitative restrictions." Thus the prohibition applies even where the restriction limits imports through one channel of trade as opposed to another. The number of restrictions as so defined is

---

[60] See also Decision of May 12, 1960, J.O. 1960, 1217, Decision 66/532 J.O. 1966, 2971, Cases 51–54/71 *International Fruit Company* v. *Produktschap voor Groenten en Fruit* [1971] E.C.R. 1107.

[61] Case 74/76 *Iannelli* v. *Meroni* [1977] E.C.R. 557 (Article 30); Case 13/68 *Salgoil* v. *Italian Ministry for Foreign Trade* [1968] E.C.R. 453, (Article 31 and 32 (1)); Case 83/79 *Pigs Marketing Board* v. *Redmond* [1978] E.C.R. 2347 (Articles 30 and 34), Case 48/74 *Charmasson* v. *Minister for Economic Affairs* [1974] E.C.R. 1383 (Article 33).

[62] Case 8/74 *Procureur du Roi* v. *Benoit de Gustave Dassonville* [1974] E.C.R. 837; and see also Case 2/78 *Commission* v. *Belgium* [1979] E.C.R. 1761.

theoretically very great. The Commission had, in particular in Directive 70/50,[63] attempted to spell out many of them, instructing the Member States to take action to make sure they were abolished, but the list was not complete and many more have come to light through litigation or Commission investigation. A number of principles may be deduced from the Court's decisions as follows.

13—22   A national measure may be prohibited as a measure equivalent to a quantitative restriction if -

1.   It applies only to imported goods or in a manner differentiating against imports, and is more difficult to satisfy in respect of imported products.[64]

2.   It applies to both domestic and imported goods but affects the latter more severely, *e.g.* a maximum price for the product which is fixed at a level which makes it unprofitable to import the product from abroad;[65] or a form of price control which results from administrative difficulties in notifying and getting approval for price increases[66]: or a minimum alcohol content for certain types of drink which tends to exclude products from other Member States because they have a lower content.[67]

3.   It provides for controls or checks at the frontier not otherwise justified by Article 36 or other Community rules.[68]

4.   It applies to both domestic and imported goods but prevents importers from gaining a greater share of the market, *e.g.* a *minimum* price system which does not permit lower production costs to be used to reduce the retail selling price.[69]

5.   It has the effect of facilitating an abuse of a dominant position (under Article 86),[70]

6.   It requires the importer to provide information relating, *e.g.* to the origin of the goods, which is obtainable only with

[63] Article 33 (7) provided for the issue of directives during the original transitional period for the abolition of equivalent measures: five were issued: 64/486, J.O. 1964, 2253; 66/682, J.O. 1966, 3745; 66/683, J.O. 1966, 3748; 70/32, J.O. 1970, L 13/1; 70/50, J.O. 1970, L 13/29. (And see Written Question 118/66–67, J.O. 1967, 122 and 90).

[64] Case 4/75 *Rewe Zentralfinanz* v. *Landwirtschaftskammer* [1975] E.C.R. 843.

[65] Cases 88–90/75 *Società SADAM and others* v. *Comitato Interministeriale dei Prezzi and others* [1976] E.C.R. 323; 5/79 *Procureur Général at the Cour d'Appel, Rouen* v. *Buys & Denkavit* [1979] E.C.R. 3203.

[66] Cases 16–20/79 *Openbaar Ministerie* v. *Danis and others* [1979] E.C.R. 3327.

[67] Case 120/78 *Rewe Zentral* v. *Bundesmonopolverwaltung* [1979] E.C.R. 649. See also important Commission Communications on this case; O.J. 1980, C256/2, and Case 788/79 *Gilli* [1980] E.C.R. 2071.

[68] Case 35/76 *Simmenthal* v. *Italian Minister for Finance* [1976] E.C.R. 1871; 251/78, *Denkavit Futtesmittel*, [1979] E.C.R. 3369.

[69] Case 82/77 *Openbaar Ministerie of the Netherlands* v. *Van Tiggele* [1978] E.C.R. 25.

[70] Case 13/77 *GB—INNO—BM* v. *A.T.A.B.* [1977] E.C.R. 2115.

great difficulty, and the penalties for failure to supply it are disproportionate.[71]

7. It makes the marketing of the product more difficult, *e.g.* by restricting advertising through control of television stations,[72] or making it difficult to obtain certificates of authenticity.[73]

8. It confines the use of names which are not indicative of origin or source or designation of quality to domestic products only;[74]

9. It is designed to ration production or control sales outlets in circumstances when Community rules provide for freedom of commercial transactions.[75]

10. It channels imports only to certain traders[76] or through a marketing board.[77]

11. It limits state monopoly purchasing to goods produced from home products.[78]

13—23   The above list is not exhaustive. Examples of quantitative restrictions will continue to appear.

It is open to question, looking at the above principles, whether the term might be said to apply to general measures of national economic policy, for the methods of control of the economy clearly do have an effect on the volume of imports or exports between Member States. The Court has indicated that, at the present state of development, general price controls are not prohibited *per se* by Articles 30 *et seq.*[79] and that other areas of the Treaty may either expressly or tacitly have reserved to the Member States the right to continue such measures.[80] As soon as it is recognised that measures may be prohibited under these articles even though they treat domestic and imported goods alike, simply because there is a resultant disadvantage to imported goods, a question of balancing arises: the implicit right of Member States to continue with national legislation on such matters as tax

[71] Cases 179/78 *Procureur* v. *Rivoira* [1979] E.C.R. 1147; 52/77 *Leone Cayrol* v. *Giovanni Rivoira e Figli* [1977] E.C.R. 2261; Case 41/76 *Suzanne Criel, née Donckerwolke & Henri Schon* v. *Procureur de la République au Tribunal de Grande Instance Lille and Director General of Customs* [1976] E.C.R. 1921.
[72] Case 155/73 *Giuseppe Sacchi* [1974] E.C.R. 409.
[73] Case 8/74 *Procureur du Roi* v. *Benôit and Gustave Dassonville* [1974] E.C.R. 837. See also 2/78 *Commission* v. *Belgium* [1979] E.C.R. 1761.
[74] Case 12/74 *Commission* v. *Federal Republic of Germany* [1975] E.C.R. 181; Case 13/78 *Eggers* v. *HZA Bremen* [1978] E.C.R. 1935.
[75] Cases 94/79 *Pieter Vriend* [1980] E.C.R. 327; 190/73 *Officier van Justitie* v. *Van Haaster* [1974] E.C.R. 1123; Contrast Cases 3, 4 & 6/76 *Kramer* [1976] E.C.R. 1279 (conservation measures not prohibited).
[76] 104/75 *De Peijper* [1976] E.C.R. 613.
[77] 83/79 *Pigs Marketing Board* v. *Redmond* [1978] E.C.R. 2347.
[78] 119/79 *Peureux* v. *Directeur des Services Fiscaux de la Haute Saône* [1979] E.C.R. 975.   [79] Case 82/77 *Van Tiggele, supra,* note 69.
[80] Case 13/77 *GB supra,* note 70. See also case 113/80 *Commission* v. *Ireland* (June 17, 1981). *Cf.* cases in note 67, *supra.*

recovery, consumer protection and economic policy must be carefully considered before a measure is regarded as prohibited.[81]

The products covered

13—24   Although Article 30, read together with Article 31, might suggest that products not liberalised under the OEEC were exempt from the general prohibition, there seems little doubt now that all products are covered.[82]

Agricultural products created more of a problem. During the transitional period quantitative restrictions were progressively abolished with the setting up of market organisations. However not all products were so organised, and in such cases national market organisations, in order to carry out their functions, may have operated direct or indirect restrictions on imports or exports. It is now clear that such restrictions were illegal, from the end of the relevant transitional period.[83]

The exceptions - Article 36

13—25   Article 36 reads as follows:

> "The provisions of Articles 30 to 34 shall not preclude prohibitions or restrictions on imports, exports or goods in transit justified on grounds of public morality, public policy or public security; the protection of health and life of humans, animals or plants; the protection of national treasures possessing artistic, historic or archaeological value; or the protection of industrial and commercial property. Such prohibitions or restrictions shall not, however, constitute a means of arbitrary discrimination or a disguised restriction on trade between Member States."

This Article, as an exception to the general principle of free movement must be interpreted strictly[84] and thus cannot be understood as authorising measures of a different nature from those referred to in Articles 30-34, *i.e.* it does not authorise *charges* having an equivalent effect to customs duties even though those charges may be levied in furtherance of legitimate "quantitative restrictions."[85] It is not capable of extension into a general "public policy" exception based on any kind of alleged beneficial effect of a

---

[81] Case 180/78 *Rewe—Zentral infra,* note 87 and Case 2/78 *Commission* v. *Belgium* [1979] E.C.R. 1761 and see note 67 *supra.* See also Case 15/79, *Groenvel* v. *Produktschap,* [1979] E.C.R. 3609 (prohibition on manufacture of meat products based on horsemeat not *per se* a measure having equivalent effect).

[82] See note 60.

[83] Cases 48/74 *Charmasson* [1974] E.C.R. 1383; 68/76 *Re the Export of potatoes: Commission* v. *France* [1977] E.C.R. 515; 118/79 *Meijer* v. *DOT* [1979] E.C.R. 1387; 231/78 *Commission* v. *UK* [1979] E.C.R. 1447; *Danis, supra* note 65.

[84] Case 29/72 *Marimex, supra,* note 11; Case 24/62 *Germany* v. *Commission* [1963] E.C.R. 63.

[85] Case 7/68 *Italy* v. *Commission* [1968] E.C.R. 423.

181

national law.[86] It should nevertheless be borne in mind that in assessing whether a restriction falls within Articles 30-34, it may be necessary to determine the purpose of national legislation, at any rate where the measure applies to both imported and domestically produced goods but may or may not be excessively burdensome to imported goods and could be replaced by a less "discriminating" measure.[87] In view of the last sentence of Article 36 it is clear that even measures which are adopted for one of the specified purposes must be carefully examined to see whether they are in fact justified.[88] Again, if other less restrictive methods could be adjusted for the same ends, Article 36 cannot be relied on.[89]

Where the measure adopted covers the same ground, or conflicts with, measures adopted by the Community, the latter must prevail.[90] This is particularly the case as regards agriculture where Community legislation is most developed. The cases here turned on the provisions of legislation similar in purpose to Article 36 EEC.

13—26   The problems here are well illustrated by two contrasting cases. In Case 148/78 *Pubblico Ministero* v. *Ratti*[91] the Court held:

"When, pursuant to Article 100 of the Treaty, Community directives provide for the harmonization of measures necessary to ensure the protection of the health of humans and animals and establish Community procedures to supervise compliance therewith, recourse to Article 36 ceases to be justified and the appropriate controls must henceforth be carried out and the protective measures taken in accordance with the scheme laid down in the harmonizing directive."[92]

In Case 88/79 *Ministère Public* v. *Grunert*[93] on the other hand, one of the directives in question was described as being only a first stage of harmonisation. The Community rules were held to leave to Member States a large measure of freedom as to whether or

[86] Cases 7/61 *Commission* v. *Italy* [1961] E.C.R. 317; 12/74 *Commission* v. *Germany* [1975] E.C.R. 181; 251/78, *Denkavit Futtermittel, supra* note 68.
[87] Case 120/78 *Rewe Zentrale AG* v. *Bundesmonopolverwaltung für Branntwein* [1979] E.C.R. 649.
[88] Case 13/63 *Italy* v. *Commission* [1963] E.C.R. 165; 7/68 *Italy* v. *Commission* [1968] E.C.R. 423; 4/75 *Rewe-Zentralfinanz* v. *Landwirtschaftskammer* [1975] E.C.R. 843; 35/76 *Simmenthal SpA* v. *Italian Minister for Finance* [1976] E.C.R. 1871; 34/79 *R.* v. *Henn and Darby* [1979] E.C.R. 3795; 251/78, *Denkavit, supra,* note 86.
[89] Cases 29/72 *Marimex supra,* note 11; 104/75 *de Peijper* [1976] E.C.R. 613; 46/76 *Bauhuis, supra* note 12; 5/77 *Tedeschi* v. *Denkavit* [1977] E.C.R. 1555; 251/78 *Denkavit Futtermittel* v. *Minister for Food, Agriculture and Fisheries* [1979] E.C.R. 3369.
[90] Case 35/76 *Simmenthal, supra,* note 6.
[91] [1979] E.C.R. 1629.
[92] *Ibid,* p. 1644.
[93] [1980] E.C.R. 1827.

not to authorise the use in foodstuffs of certain preservatives and additives, subject only to the basic rule that Member States might no longer prohibit altogether their use or prevent all marketing, since the directives so provided. The Court was able to hold this rule directly applicable, although it must be admitted that the case will be rare in which a permissible selective ban can positively be identified as an illegal total ban. A great deal of importance is nevertheless attached at Community level to the safety aspects and delays in permitting uses of substances are unlikely to be actionable.[94]

The principal subject-matter of litigation involving Article 36 has been intellectual property. The cases are considered in Chapter 14 on this subject.

13—27   **State monopolies of a commercial character: Article 37**

Article 37 (1) requires Member States to "adjust any state monopolies of a commercial character . . . so as to ensure that . . . no discrimination regarding the conditions under which goods are procured and marketed exists between nationals of Member States." Article 37 (2) gives focus to this stipulation, requiring Member States to refrain from introducing new discriminatory measures *or* from introducing any measure which "restricts the scope of the articles dealing with the abolition of customs duties and quantitative restrictions" between Member States. The obligation in paragraph 2 was to take effect at once; that in paragraph 1 was to be met by the end of the original period of transition or by the end of transitional periods provided for in the Acts of Accession. Both paragraphs have been held directly applicable.[95]

State monopoly of a commercial character

13—28   Article 37 (1), second sub-paragraph, states that:

> "the provisions of this article shall apply to any body through which a Member State, in law or in fact, either directly or indirectly supervises, determines or appreciably influences imports or exports between Member States. These provisions shall likewise apply to monopolies delegated by the state to others."

The more common view is that the second sub-para. set out above offers a definition of "monopoly" in the sense that the organisation in question need not necessarily be an arm of the government or even under its strict legal control. It is potentially capable of a very wide interpretation in that sense. It might also suggest that the term "monopoly" does not refer to absolute monopoly,

---

[94] *Ibid.*
[95] Case 59/75 *Pubblico Ministero* v. *Manghera* [1976] E.C.R. 91 (para. 1); Case 6/64 *Costa* v. *ENEL* [1964] E.C.R. 585 (para. 2).

provided that the organisation in question does have power to influence imports or exports. In other words, any organisation which possesses a "dominant position" might be caught, especially a public sector enterprise. It appears that there must, however, be an "organisation" or entity as opposed to a mere system (*e.g.* of licensing private firms).

In *Costa* v. *ENEL*[96] the Court ruled that:

13—29
"To fall under this prohibition the State monopolies and bodies in question must, first, have as their object transactions regarding a commercial product capable of being the subject of competition and trade between Member States, and secondly must play an effective part in such trade."

This would seem to suggest that "monopolies" (in the broad sense) not having such purposes were outside the scope of Article 37 even if their existence and activities might otherwise affect trade between Member States. The Court has since indicated, however, that even after the adjustment called for by the article, any activity by a monopoly which contravenes the prohibitions on discrimination and quantitative restrictions in paragraphs 1 and 2 will be caught by the article.[97] Specifically:

"It follows that its application is not limited to imports or exports which are directly subject to the monopoly but covers all measures which are connected with its existence and affect trade betwen Member States in certain products, whether or not subject to the monopoly, and thus covers charges which would result in discrimination against imported products as compared with national products coming under the monopoly."[98]

A national system established to give effect to rules on an agricultural market organisation is not to be regarded as a "monopoly" falling within Article 37 since it is formed by virtue of Community rules adopted under different provisions of the Treaty.[99]

The measures prohibited

13—30
Article 37 does not prohibit the existence of commercial monopolies after the end of the periods of transition laid down in the Treaties. Article 90 (in so far as it overlaps with Article 37) presupposes their continued existence following adjustment so as to eliminate discrimination (para. 1) or measures impinging on the

[96] Case 6/64 [1964] E.C.R. 585, 598.
[97] Case 91/78 *Hansen* v. *HZA Flensburg* [1979] E.C.R. 935 and Case 119/78 *Peureux* v. *Services Fiscaux* [1979] E.C.R. 975. See, *e.g.* Recommendations 74/430, O.J. 1974, L 237/2 on the adjustment of the French match monopoly and Recommendations 74/501, O.J. 1974, L27/16 on spirits.
[98] Case 45/75 *Rewe-Zentrale* v. *HZA Landau* [1976] E.C.R. 181, 198.
[99] Case 177/78 *Pigs & Bacon Commission* v. *McCarren* [1979] E.C.R. 2161.

abolition of customs duties, quantitative restrictions and charges and measures having equivalent effect (para. 2).

The Court has held that every national monopoly of a commercial character must be adjusted as from the end of the relevant periods of transition so as to eliminate the exclusive right to import from other Member States.[1] The same principle no doubt applies to exports. The rules contained in Article 37 (1) and (2) concern only activities intrinsically connected with the specific business of the monopoly and are irrelevant to national provisions which have no connection with its specific business.[2] The Court has held that Article 37 is therefore irrelevant to national provisions not concerning the monopoly's exclusive rights but governing generally the production and marketing of goods, whether or not they are covered by the monopoly in question.[3] Furthermore a monopoly of purely national scope is not caught by Article 37 because an exclusive right for example to buy all nationally produced alcohol[4] or all spirits imported from third countries[5] neither discriminates as between Community nationals nor yet constitutes a measure having equivalent effect to a quantitative restriction. Similarly a measure of general taxation which happens to fall more heavily on national products than on imported products is not caught by Article 37.[6]

13—31   Article 37 does not cover the supply of services, though if restrictions on the latter affect the free movement of goods, Articles 30-37 may apply. For instance, exclusive rights granted to an undertaking to transmit advertisements may fall under Article 37 if the exclusive right were used to favour particular trade channels or particular economic concerns in preference to others.[7] It seems that the supply of electricity could be considered to fall under Article 37.[8]

The article does not apply to measures affecting trade with third countries,[9] but does apply to goods in free circulation.[10]

The relationship of Article 37 to other Articles of the Treaty

13—32   It was thought initially that Article 37 constituted a *lex specialis* or specific rule which in effect exempted a monopoly from other provisions of the Treaty provided only that the monopoly was

---

[1] Case 59/75 *supra*, note 95.
[2] Case 119/78 *supra*, note 97.
[3] Case 120/78 *Rewe Zentrale* v. *Bundesmonopolverwaltung für Branntwein* [1979] E.C.R. 649.
[4] Case 119/78 *Supra*, note 97.
[5] Case 91/78 *supra*, note 97.
[6] Case 86/78 *Peureux* v. *Services Fiscaux* [1979] E.C.R. 897.
[7] Case 155/73 *Sacchi* [1974] E.C.R. 409.
[8] Case 6/64 *supra*, note 95.
[9] Case 91/78 *supra*, note 97.
[10] Case 119/78 *supra*, note 97.

compatible with Article 37 itself. This point was argued in *Miritz*[11] and seems at first sight to receive some support in the judgment. In subsequent cases the Court has held that Article 37 constitutes a *lex specialis* in the diametrically opposed sense that compatibility of the monopoly has in any event to be considered in relation to Article 37, but that the requirements of other provisions of the Treaty must be met at the same time. In three judgments given on March 13, 1979, the Court adopted this approach in relation to Articles 95,[12] 92-94,[13] and 30.[14]

Article 37 (4) provided that "equivalent safeguards for the employment and standard of living of the producers concerned" were to be secured when agricultural monopolies were adjusted. It was thought for some considerable time after the end of the original transitional period that this legitimised the continued existence of national market organisations where no common organisation of a market had been achieved, in that without it there would be no "shield" from the application of the general rules on the free movement of goods (despite Articles 43 (3) and 45). The Court in *Charmasson*[15] dismissed this argument by indicating that Article 37 (4) was not an authorisation to derogate from Article 37 (1) and (2). Still less will Article 37 justify monopoly buying arrangements in conflict with the rules of an agricultural market organisation.[16]

13—33   Article 90 also deals with monopolies. It provides that:

> "undertakings entrusted with the operation of services of general economic interest or having the character of a revenue-producing monopoly shall be subject to the rules of the Treaty, in particular to the rules on competition, in so far as the application of such rules does not obstruct the performance, in law or in fact, of the particular tasks assigned to them. The development of trade must not be affected to such an extent as would be contrary to the interests of the Community."

The term "particular tasks" relates of course to the task of operating a commercial monopoly, and protecting the revenue therefrom, and does not include, *e.g.* any protective mission. This being so, it is generally agreed that such undertakings are subject to the adjustment procedures of Article 37.

---

[11] Case 91/75 *HZA Göttingen* v. *Miritz* [1976] E.C.R. 217.
[12] Case 86/78 *supra*, note 6. Perhaps foreshadowed by Cases 45/75 *supra* note 98, and 148/77 *Hansen* v. *HZA Flensburg* [1978] E.C.R. 1787.
[13] Case 91/78 *supra*, note 97.
[14] Case 199/78 *supra*, note 97.
[15] Case 48/74 *Charmasson* v. *Minister for Economic Affairs* [1974] E.C.R. 1383.
[16] Case 83/78 *Pigs Marketing Board* v. *Redmond* [1978] E.C.R. 2347.

Note on the free movement of goods covered by the ECSC and EAEC Treaties

13—34   Article 232 of the EEC Treaty states that the provisions of that Treaty "shall not affect the provisions of the [ECSC Treaty]" (para. 1) and "shall not derogate from those of the [Euratom Treaty]." The ECSC Treaty leaves matters of external policy in the hands of the Member States, and provides only for a maximum and minimum tariff level (Art. 72). There is a unified (but not common) ECSC Tariff. Import and export duties and quantitative restrictions are illegal (Art. 4). The Euratom Treaty provides for the elimination of the same measures (Art. 93). Where, however, there is no specific provision for dealing with a particular matter (*e.g.* harmonisation of legislation in the ECSC and Euratom Treaties) the EEC rules will be of application, since they apply to the other two Communities wherever there is no specific rule.

Greek accession and the free movement of goods

13—35   The accession arrangements follow the basic pattern laid down by the 1972 Accession arrangements here as elsewhere.

The basic principle, enunciated in Article 25 of the 1979 Act of Accession, is of tariff disarmament between Greece and the Community in six annual tranches, the first two of 10 per cent., the remainder of 20 per cent. of the duties actually applied on July 1, 1980, starting on January 1, 1981, and finishing on January 1, 1986. Existing Community exemptions on goods in personal luggage and small consignments are to apply from the date of accession (Article 25 (2)), and export duties are abolished on the same date (Article 30). Article 25 is subject to an upper ceiling: the duties applied are in no instance to be higher than the Community m.f.n. rate (Article 26). Suspension is also possible: Article 27.

A parallel timetable is applied to charges having equivalent effect to customs duties applied on December 31, 1980 (Article 29) but charges introduced from January 1, 1979, onwards are abolished on January 1, 1981, in their entirety (Article 28).

At the same time, Greece is to align with the CCT for the purposes of external tariff in step with the timetable for internal disarmament under Article 29 (Article 31). Where, however, the basic duties do not differ by more than 15 per cent. on January 1, 1982, (the date for application of the second tranche) the CCT is to be applied from that date for those tariff headings.

13—36   Since Greece currently also operates certain duties "different in nature" from CCT duties (*e.g.* duties by weight, not on an *ad valorem* basis) Article 33 makes provision for their reduction by adding them to the CCT corresponding elements and then reducing them whilst at the same time starting the CCT duty at zero and increasing it progressively, both operations to be in

Free Movement of Goods

accordance with the above timetable (Article 33). In all cases there is provision for accelerated alignment by Greece.

Article 35 provides for the abolition of all quantitative restrictions by both parties on accession. However, Greece is permitted a staggered timetable for the progressive extension of quotas on goods listed in Annex III of the Act of Accession, both in terms of volume and value. These quotas are finally to be abolished by December 31, 1985 (the end of the transitional period). A modified progressive enlargement of the quota is provided for coaches, buses and motor vehicles (Article 36 (3), third sub-paragraph).

Article 38 additionally sets out a timetable for the elimination of import deposits and requirements for cash payments in force in Greece on December 31, 1980. These are to be reduced in four tranches of 25 per cent. per year ending on January 1, 1984.

Article 39 requires the progressive abolition of preferences for public contracts whilst Article 40 introduces the progressive adjustment of state monopolies pursuant to Article 37 of the EEC Treaty, to be completed by December 31, 1985.

Articles 41 to 43 make administrative provision for operating the arrangements, notably the calculation of compensatory amounts (Article 43).

Chapter 14

INTELLECTUAL PROPERTY

—01 Although the Treaty of Rome contains passing references to intellectual property[1] it does not in any way purport to set up a system of intellectual property law of its own to replace that already existing in the Member States. In terms therefore of the Treaty EEC law is not concerned with the *substance* of any system of intellectual property law. On the other hand, the discussion which follows will show that the EEC Treaty has had a considerable influence on the exercise of intellectual property rights which derive from national law. This has given an impetus to the elaboration of intellectual property rules at Community level and indeed in a wider European context,[2] in parallel with international arrangements already extant, notably under the aegis of the World Intellectual Property Organization (WIPO) in Geneva.[3] Reference must be made to national legislation for precise legal definitions of the various forms of intellectual property. It is nevertheless broadly understood as embracing the following: patents, trademarks and tradenames, copyright and neighbouring rights, breeders' rights and "know-how."

—02 Patents are entirely the creatures of specific legislation and afford to their holders, "patentees," the right to prevent anyone other than themselves from manufacturing or selling the patented products during the lifetime of the patents.[4] The patent has been described as a contract between the patentee and the grantor state,[5] from which both derive a benefit, the former getting a proper reward for his inventiveness and effort, the latter, on behalf of the population at large, enjoying those benefits and, through publication to the world at large, seeing possible further developments based on the published ideas.

A trademark on the other hand serves to indicate the origin of goods, expressed as indicating a "connection in trade." Its owner has the exclusive right to use it in relation to his products, and infringements of that right are protected in most countries both

[1] Article 36 mentions "industrial and commercial property"; Article 222, at a more general level makes mention of "property law" in the member states; see *infra*, para. 14–04.
[2] See *infra*, para. 14–22.
[3] Convention Establishing the World Intellectual Property Organisation, Signed at Stockholm, July 14, 1967, Cmnd. 4408, T.S. No. 52 (1970).
[4] This description is subject to the qualifications introduced by the Court of Justice, discussed *infra* paras. 14–05 *et seq*. In the United Kingdom the applicable legislation is the Patents Act 1977.
[5] See, *e.g.* Röttger, "The Problem of Parallel Patents" (1974) C.M.L. Rev. 273.

by specific trademark legislation[6] and by more general law relating to "unfair competition."[7] The mark protects both the owner in his trade and consumers who, through the indication of origin, derive an assurance of quality.[8]

Copyright secures for its owner the right to prevent others from imitating his literary, dramatic, musical or artistic works, whilst "neighbouring rights" protect, in much the same way, more "economic" works, such as sound recording rights or films. Both are generally protected by specific legislation in Member States.[9]

Plant breeders' rights, which are now recognised in a growing number of countries,[10] give to their holders protection for new plant varieties which they have developed. These rights are similar in purpose to patents and indeed some countries (notably the United States) actually have plant patents.

Finally "know-how" consists of information relating to industrial or commercial processes which may or may not in fact be patentable, and which is often ancillary to published patent information. It is generally not protected by specific legislation, but its value, which of course lies in its remaining secret, may be protected by the law of contract and by the law of trusts.[11]

The common feature of all these various rights is the exclusivity conferred on their holders. But the latter may if they wish transfer that exclusivity to another[12] either by way of outright assignment or through a licence. In the case of patents a licence granted to another may have conditions attached, which may bind persons, not parties to the licence agreement, in a way similar to the operation of restrictive covenants over land.[13]

Relationship of intellectual property law with the Treaty in general

14—03   Conflicts between the Treaty and intellectual property laws fall into two categories. First, there are those which derive from the fact that at present there are now 10 separate systems of intellectual property law. Secondly, there is the conflict which arises from the

---

[6] In the UK, the Trademarks Act 1938 and the tort of "passing off," which also protects the trade name.

[7] Again this description must be read subject to the discussion below, paras. 14–05 *et seq.*

[8] Although the *effect* may be to guarantee quality, the law does not recognise that function, at any rate in England: *Champagne Heidsieck* v. *Buxton* [1930] 1 Ch. 330.

[9] In the UK, by the Copyright Act 1956.

[10] In the UK, under the Plant Varieties and Seeds Act 1964. Much of the work in developing the legal concept of this right has been done under the Paris Union for the Protection of New Varieties of Plants (Convention and Additional Act of November 10, 1972, TS No. 79 (1980); Cmnd. 8036; Revised October 23, 1978, Misc. No. 12 (1979); Cmnd 7571).

[11] See in particular *Seager* v. *Copydex* [1967] 1 W.L.R. 923.

[12] In England, the Trade Marks Act of 1875 did not allow the assignment of a trade mark without the goodwill of the business, but this rule has been relaxed by section 22 of the Trade Marks Act 1938.

[13] See, *e.g. National Phonograph Co. of Australia* v. *Menck* (1911) 28 R.P.C. 229; *Gillette Industries Ltd.* v. *Bernstein* 58 R.P.C. 271.

nature of intellectual property law, whether it be national or "European."

Turning to the first category it is possible to discern three particular areas of conflict. First, the Treaty proclaims the creation of a common market based *inter alia* on the free movement of goods; but so long as national laws which grant exclusive rights to deal in goods continue to exist, this objective cannot be entirely achieved, in so far as those laws extend the protection of that exclusivity to prevent goods being imported from another Member State.[14] Such restrictions would be in the nature of "measures equivalent to quantitative restrictions" under Article 30 of the Treaty. It will be recalled, however, that Article 36 makes a special derogation *inter alia* for the protection of "industrial and commercial property":

> "The provisions of Articles 30 to 34 shall not preclude prohibitions or restrictions on imports . . . justified on grounds of . . . the protection of industrial and commercial property."

The use of the terms "industrial and commercial property" at first sight might appear to be narrower than the term "intellectual property," for, at any rate, copyright does not primarily protect economic rights (although neighbouring rights *do*). However, artistic and literary works are, if they become the subject of inter state trade, probably best regarded as at least "commercial property."[15]

Article 36, however, goes on to provide:

> "Such prohibitions or restrictions shall not, however, constitute a means of arbitrary discrimination or a disguised restriction on trade between Member States."

4—04   Secondly, the Treaty provides for the creation of a competition policy at the Community level.[16] In implementation of this, Article 85 of the Treaty prohibits agreements, and concerted practices between undertakings which harm competition and which may affect the trade between Member States.[17] A licence agreement might, for example, purport to confer exclusive territorial rights in a Member State, to be exercised so as to prevent products which are the subject of the licence from entering that Member State where they have been placed on the market in

---

[14] Of course, it may also be said that enforcement of exclusive rights even against "domestic" infringers have an adverse effect on the free movement of goods. Conceivably such enforcement may, on the basis of the case law below, itself be incompatible with the Treaty.

[15] See Harris, [1976] 1 E.L.Rev. 515. But see Case 78/80 *DGG* v. *Metro* [1971] E.C.R. 487, where the court failed clearly to indicate that even neighbouring rights were within the meaning of the term

[16] This is an objective proclaimed by Article 3 (*f*). And see Chapter 20.

[17] See generally, Chapter 20.

another Member State. Such an arrangement would impair competition so far as concerned any third party who had legally
obtained the products in a Member State and then wished to
export them to the Member State covered by the exclusive territorial rights. The arrangement, designed to prevent what are known
as "parallel imports," would therefore infringe Article 85 of the
Treaty. Article 85 contains no reservation akin to Article 36, but
must be read subject to Article 222:

> "This Treaty shall in no way prejudice the rules in Member
> States governing the system of property ownership."

This is a less specific safeguard than that in Article 36 but no
material differences in application emerge from the case-law of the
Court.

Finally, the continued existence of national intellectual property
laws may come into conflict with the objectives of the Treaty
simply because their provisions are different, in the same way, say,
that although every Member State has a system of company law,
the differences between those laws may impede the effective
exercise of the right of establishment and the freedom to provide
services.[17a]

The free movement of goods, Article 36, and Article 85

14—05   Because of the similarity between the first two types of conflict mentioned above, it is possible to consider the developments
in those fields together. This coincides with the approach of the
European Court which has tended to treat them as two aspects of
the same problem.[18] Furthermore, as with any case law, the
development has been piecemeal, sometimes concerning the
competition provisions, sometimes the provisions on the free
movement of goods, sometimes both.

The problem of "parallel imports" first fell to be considered
in the *Grundig* case.[19] Grundig had granted to Consten the
exclusive right to sell Grundig products in France. In furtherance
of that arrangement it had permitted Consten to register in the
latter's name a trademark "GINT." It seems reasonably clear that
the sole object in registering this mark in Consten's name was
to secure absolute territorial protection, for it appears that at a
time when it did not have this mark, Consten had failed, in a
previous Court action, to prevent the sale of imported Grundig
goods.[20] Furthermore, the trademark manifestly did not serve
to indicate the origin of the goods, which as we have seen, is
supposed to be its principal function because all Grundig products

---

[17a] Case 62/79, *Codilel* v. *Ciné Vog Films* [1980] E.C.R. 881 (freedom to provide services
does not preclude exercise of intellectual property rights).
[18] See, *e.g. DGG* v. *Metro supra*, note 15.
[19] Cases 56 & 58/64 *Ets Consten SARL and Grundig-Verkaufs-GmbH* v. *Commission*
[1966] E.C.R. 299.
[20] See Megret, Waelbroeck, *Droit de la CEE*, Vol. 4, Concurrence, pp. 212–3.

were clearly indicated to be made by Grundig, and so far as the consumer was concerned, that would have been the sole consideration, the quality of the goods thereby being assured. It was not therefore surprising that the Commission, when examining the agreement, attempted to attack also that part of it which had allowed Consten to register the GINT trademark. It was also hardly surprising that Grundig and Consten, in appealing to the Court, objected *inter alia* to this aspect of the Commission's decision on two related grounds: first, that the power to exercise the rights derived in reality not from the agreement but from the existence of the national law on trademarks. Hence the resulting restriction on competition was not the "object or effect" of the agreement. The Court brushed this argument aside by declaring that it was by virtue of an agreement with Grundig that Consten was able to effect the registration.[21]

4—06   The second argument made was to the effect that even if the agreement did have the necessary restrictive effect, this effect could not be challenged because such a challenge would endanger the intellectual property law whose preservation was guaranteed by the Treaty.
The Court upheld the Commission's decision on these points. It declared:

> "The injunction contained in Article 3 of the operative part of the contested decision to refrain from using rights under national trade-mark law in order to set an obstacle in the way of parallel imports does not affect the grant of those rights, but only limits their exercise to the extent necessary to give effect to the prohibition under Article 85 (1)."

The Court went on to say that the competition system

> "by reason of its nature described above and its function, does not allow the improper use of rights under any national trade-mark law in order to frustrate the Community's law on cartels."[22]

The Court did not elaborate further on the concept of an "abusive use of rights," and in particular did not explain how that abuse[23] was to be ascertained beyond indicating that the competition provisions were not to be impaired by the exercise of those rights so as to obstruct "parallel imports." The formula is

[21] *Ibid*, p. 345. In Case 40/70 *Sirena* v. *Eda* [1971] E.C.R. 69, the Court considered that an outright assignment of a mark for a particular territory could infringe Article 85 (1) if it permitted the assignee or his successors in title to invoke national trademark law at some time in the future so as to partition the common market. This extreme view has been modified by Cases 51, 86 & 96/75 *EMI* v. *CBS infra*, note 48 where the Court ruled that the partitioning of the market must at least result from a *continuing* concerted practice or agreement.
[22] [1966] E.C.R. 299, 345–6.
[23] Not to be confused with an abuse of a dominant position under Art. 86.

clearly too vague to form the basis of any general rule which could conveniently draw a dividing line between the competition provisions on the one hand and intellectual property law on the other.[24]

14—07   Some elucidation was, however, forthcoming in Case 78/70, *DGG* v. *Metro*.[25] Metro, a German wholsale supermarket, had imported into Germany for sale there a quantity of records bearing DGG's label "Polydor," these records having previously been marketed in France with DGG's consent. DGG brought an action for the infringement of its sound recording rights, and Metro argued in defence that the action could not succeed in this case *inter alia* because it amounted to a "disguised restriction on trade" within the meaning of Article 36. The European Court, on reference from the German court, ruled:

> "Amongst the prohibitions or restrictions on the free movement of goods which it concedes Article 36 refers to industrial and commercial property. On the assumption that those provisions may be relevant to a right related to copyright, it is nevertheless clear from that article that, although the Treaty does not affect the existence of rights recognised by the legislation of a Member State with regard to industrial and commercial property, the exercise of such rights may nevertheless fall within the prohibitions laid down by the Treaty. Although it permits prohibitions or restrictions on the free movement of products, which are justified for the purpose of protecting industrial and commercial property, Article 36 only admits derogations from that freedom to the extent to which they are justified for the purpose of safeguarding rights which constitute the specific subject-matter of such property."[26]

Here the Court begins by repeating the formula it had adopted in the *Grundig* case, but goes on to make reference to the specific subject matter of this property. From this it follows that the Court was of the opinion that there was some general concept applicable to intellectual property which would enable a dividing line to be drawn between proper and abusive exercise of rights. This concept, it was widely suggested, might be the so-called "exhaustion of rights" doctrine. This has been defined as follows:

> "Where a patented article is put on the market in the ordinary course of business by the proprietor of the patent, or by an appointed licensee, that article may freely circulate throughout the jurisdiction where the first sale took place

[24] See Johannes, *Industrial Property and Copyright in European Community Law*, p. 20.
[25] *Supra*, note 15.
[26] [1971] E.C.R. 487, pp. 499–500.

without further control by the proprietor of the patent."[27]

There are several points to be noted in this definition.

—08   First, in common law jurisdictions at any rate, the doctrine had, if at all, been considered as applying to patents. The theory was that the object of a patent grant was not to secure the patentee a monopoly in *trade* in his product, although he would be entitled to attach various conditions as to the manner in which it is traded.

Secondly, it is not specifically a doctrine relating to importations. It is equally applicable where the goods were first marketed in the same jurisdiction. It seems that it had been to some extent recognised in English law as extending to the case where the patentee held a patent in two or more countries and marketed the goods in one of them. He could not then prevent the goods being imported from that territory into the other.[28]

In Germany the doctrine seems to have been recognised also in relation to trademarks.[29] The reference to the doctrine by the Bundesgerichtshof appears to indicate that the doctrine was not a rule of law, or term of art, in itself, but a particular manifestation of an abuse of the rights of a trademark within the meaning of Article 24 of the German Trademark Law.[30]

1—09   The doctrine as applied to trademarks appears to have been recognised in England in the case of *Champagne Heidsieck* v. *Buxton*.[31] In this case champagne bearing the Heidsieck mark was made and sold on the continent and in England under that mark, although the English champagne was made slightly drier for English taste. An agent in Germany sold a quantity to an English importer, and the proprietors of the mark attempted to prevent the importation by claiming that the goods were being passed off by the importer as his own. The Court disagreed, stating that the goods as marketed did not misrepresent their origin. By implication therefore, once the goods had been put into circulation, they were no longer within the control of the proprietor of the mark.

More recent cases arguably have confirmed that the spirit of the principle is followed at least in trademark law, although English law is probably based on the principle that the owner of the mark has impliedly consented to the importation of goods bearing that mark where he is the owner of the trademark in the exporting

[27] Melville, "The Basis of the Exhaustion Principle in Intellectual Property," Law Society Gazette of 1/1/78, p. 1085. The author suggests that it first made its appearance in 1789 at the Constitutional Conference of the United States of America.
[28] *Betts* v. *Willmot* LR 6 Ch. App. 239 (CA). But *cf. Minnesota Mining and Manufacturing Co.* v. *Geerpress Europe Ltd.* [1973] C.M.L.R. 259.
[29] BGH 1964 GRUR 373—*MAJA*.
[30] See Röttger, op. cit. at p. 278.
[31] *Supra*, note 8.

country and the United Kingdom and has himself imported goods even if through a subsidiary.[32] This may well apply also to copyright law.[33]

14—10   The European Court subsequently appeared to encourage the view that the exhaustion of rights doctrine was at least partly what it had in mind when referring to the "specific subject matter" of the property, when it gave a ruling in the 1974 *Centrafarm* cases.[34] Here, the patentee was the Sterling Drug Inc. It held patents in both the Netherlands and the United Kingdom relating to a drug sold under the trade name "Negram." Sterling had licensed its subsidiary, Winthrop, to use the patent and trade name. Centrafarm purchased a quantity of "Negram" in the United Kingdom and imported it into the Netherlands. Sterling and Winthrop attempted to prevent the sale in the Netherlands by bringing infringement actions against Centrafarm. On reference under Article 177 the European Court ruled:

> "In relation to patents, the specific subject matter of the industrial property is the guarantee that the patentee, to reward the creative effort of the inventor, has the exclusive right to use an invention with a view to manufacturing industrial products and putting them into circulation for the first time, either directly or by the grant of licenses to third parties, as well as the right to oppose infringements."[35]

The reference to the placing of the goods on the market for the first time seems to be an allusion to the exhaustion of rights doctrine although in considering that the right might be exhausted where the owner *indirectly* places the goods on the market, *i.e.* through a licensee, the Court may have gone beyond the scope of the doctrine, at least so far as it could be said to have manifested itself in English law. German law, however, appeared by that time to coincide with the view.[36]

14—11   Subsequent cases may also, on their facts, be reconciled with the doctrine. In Case 119/75 *Terrapin* v. *Terranova*[37] a German company using the name "Terranova" sought to prevent the sale of goods, similar to those in relation to which it used the name,

[32] *Revlon Inc.* v. *Cripps and Lee Ltd.* [1980] F.S.R. 85.
[33] *Polydor Ltd. & RSO Records* v. *Harlequin Record Shops Ltd.* [1980] 2 C.M.L.R. 413 where section 16 (2) of the 1956 Copyright Act was considered possibly incompatible with Article 30 EEC. This case has now been referred to the European Court (Case 270/80). See also *CBS UK Ltd.* v. *Charmdale Record Distributors Ltd.* [1980] 3 W.L.R. 476.
[34] Cases 15/74 *Centrafarm BV* v. *Sterling Drug Co. Inc* [1974] E.C.R. 1147; and 16/74 *Centrafarm* v. *Winthrop* [1974] E.C.R. 1183.
[35] [1974] E.C.R. 1147, 1162. The ruling is *mutatis mutandis* very similar in *Winthrop* in relation to trademarks.
[36] BGH 1973 11C 435, *Cinzano*. Translated in [1974] 2 C.M.L.R. 21.
[37] [1976] E.C.R. 1039.

which had been imported from England bearing the mark "Terrapin." The European Court ruled that the infringement action could be permitted. Although the effect would be to preclude imports from the United Kingdom, to decide otherwise would be to undermine the specific subject-matter of the property. Clearly the ruling could be explained on the ground that here there was no question of the owner of the Terranova name having "exhausted his rights" because he had never had anything to do with the marketing of "Terrapin" goods. In Case 102/77 *Hoffman La Roche* v. *Centrafarm*[38] the plaintiff marketed a drug, "Valium" in both the United Kingdom and Germany, though in different quantities and packaging. The defendant imported a quantity of this drug into Germany after it had been purchased in the United Kingdom and repackaged in the Netherlands by the defendant's parent company. The Court indicated that it would not be contrary to the Treaty to prevent the imports if the goods had been altered in their condition in some way as a result of the repackaging. This would appear to be in harmony with national trademark law, even if the "exhaustion of rights doctrine" were fully recognised, because the owner of the mark is, in some cases, allowed to intervene when there is a danger that the alteration in the condition of the goods may injure the reputation of the mark.[39] Finally, in Case 3/78 *Centrafarm* v. *American Home Products Corporation*[40] the Court ruled that generally where a product had been marketed under different marks in different states, it would be permissible to stop imports bearing the mark used in the importing state where that had been affixed by the importer.

The exhausation of rights doctrine is unfortunately not able to explain a number of other cases.

14—12   *Van Zuylen Frères v. Hag*[41]

Before the Second World War, the German Hag company owned the "Hag" trademark for Germany, Luxembourg and Belgium. At the end of the war, it was, like all German property, confiscated by the authorities. The mark was transferred by the Belgian and Luxembourg authorities to a Belgian national, and subsequently came into the hands of another Belgian firm, Van Zuylen. In the early 1970s, encouraged no doubt by the previous rulings of the European Court, the German Hag Company, which still owned the mark for Germany, started selling its coffee under the Hag mark directly into Luxembourg. Van Zuylen brought proceedings for infringement of its mark, but on reference to the European Court, it became apparent that EEC law would not permit the action:

[38] [1978] E.C.R. 1139.
[39] Trade Marks Act 1938, s. 6.
[40] [1978] E.C.R. 1823.
[41] Case 192/73 [1973] E.C.R. 731.

". . . one cannot allow the holder of a trade mark to rely upon the exclusiveness of a trade mark right - which may be the consequence of the territorial limitation of national legislations - with a view to prohibiting the marketing in a Member State of goods legally produced in another Member State under an identical trade mark having the same origin. Such a prohibition, which would legitimise the isolation of national markets, would collide with one of the essential objects of the Treaty, which is to unite national markets in a single market."[42]

The distinguishing feature of this case, and the reason for holding that no infringement action could be justified here, was that the mark had had a common origin. The parties had argued that this would lead to confusion of the public, but the Court said there were ways of avoiding this - for instance, by indicating the geographical origin of the goods. This may seem rather odd, bearing in mind that the trademark itself is supposed to fulfil this, or a closely related function.[43]

The exhaustion of rights principle did not apply here because of course, the trademark owner had not at any time marketed the goods in question. Moreover, it is not immediately clear that the existence/exercise distinction with its emphasis on the abusive use of a right, can explain the case either.

It was possible to suppose from *Hag* that the Court would take the view that intellectual property rights could never be invoked against goods imported from another Member State. The *Terrapin* case[44] indicates that this is not so. Where the mark has no common origin, an infringement action may be permitted even if it does have the effect of preventing imports of goods. (The fact that the marks in *Terrapin* were only confusingly similar, not identical, appears to be immaterial for this purpose).

Terrapin,[45] *Hoffman La Roche*[46] *and American Home Products*[47]

14–13   The exhaustion of rights theory is also unable to explain the provisos to be found in all the above mentioned cases, to the effect that even though generally actions such as were in issue there were permissible, national courts should examine whether nevertheless the result of their decisions would be to create a disguised restriction on trade, and to that extent it would be necessary to see whether the property rights were being abused.

[42] [1974] E.C.R. 731, 744.
[43] *Supra*, para. 14–02.
[44] *Supra*, note 37.
[45] *Supra*, note 37.
[46] *Supra*, note 38.
[47] *Supra*, note 40.

EMI v. CBS[48]

4—14   Finally, the |Court in the *EMI* v. *CBS* cases[48] indicated that there could be no objection to the prevention of "parallel imports" from countries outside the EEC.| This also indicates possibly that /the exhaustion of rights doctrine cannot really explain the Court's decisions./ If it were the explanation, then why should it be limited to cases involving imports only from EEC countries? It was not, as we have seen, a doctrine especially developed for "EEC cases." If it is an integral part of the concept of intellectual property, (limiting the "specific subject matter of the property") then it should apply in *any* case regardless of the origin of the goods. In Case 270/80 *Polydor* v. *Harlequin*, not yet decided, the Court is directly faced with the issue of imports from a third state (Portugal). There it is argued that the close similarity of language of Articles 14 and 23 of the EEC/Portugal agreement with Articles 30 and 36 of the EEC Treaty means that the same rules apply. This argument seems to overlook that the objects of the EEC/Portugal agreement are more limited than those of the EEC Treaty. Certainly it appears that Portugal would be in no position to offer reciprocal "Community treatment" in the field of copyright to which the case relates.

The conclusion to be drawn from the decided cases must be that there is no immediately apparent general rule which can be used to explain them. There appear in fact to be at least three rules applicable in the appropriate circumstances. Where an infringement action seeks to prevent the importation of goods from another Member State that action will fail:

1. where those goods were previously marketed by or with the consent of the person bringing the action;[49]
2. where the right (at least if it is a trademark) had a "common origin";[50]
3. where the action is an abusive exercise of the property right.[51]

The third rule above could be used as the basis for a single rule, albeit at a level of abstraction which might be considered to render it of little practical use.

14—15   The common element in all the cases was that the party seeking relief was doing so not only because an infringement had taken place, but also because he was seeking, whether intentionally or incidentally, to prevent goods being imported from another Member State. The third rule would hold that if after examination of the facts it became clear that the plaintiff was deliberately taking advantage of the partitioning of the common market caused by the existence of national intellectual property law, then that

[48] Cases 51, 86 and 96/75 [1976] E.C.R. 811, 871 & 913.
[49] As in *Grundig Supra*, note 19; *DGG supra*, note 15.
[50] As in *Hag, supra*, note 41.
[51] As in *American Home Products Corporation, supra*, note 40.

would amount to an abusive exercise of his rights. In the words of the Court:

> "If a right related to copyright is relied upon to prevent the marketing in a Member State of products distributed by the holder of the right or with his consent on the territory of another Member State on the sole ground that such distribution did not take place on the national territory, such a prohibition, which would legitimize the isolation of national markets, would be repugnant to the essential purpose of the Treaty, which is to unite national markets into a single market."[52]

For instance, Terranova's action would be permissible because that action was instigated simply to prevent an infringement, in the same way that it would have instigated an action against a "domestic" infringement. If there were evidence that domestic infringements are not pursued with the same vigour, this might lead to the conclusion that Terranova was taking advantage of the existence of different laws.[53] Hoffman La Roche would be permitted to succeed providing it could show that its object in preventing parallel imports was to preserve the reputation of its mark[54] and not simply to prevent goods coming in which bore its trademark. The plaintiff in *American Home Products*[55] would be permitted to succeed provided it could show that its use of different trademarks in different states in relation to the same product was not part of an overall scheme for dividing up the common market by taking advantage of the various national laws. Even *Hag* can just about be made to fit into this scheme, although in a rather unusual way: although it is in the nature of things that identical or similar marks may arise independently of each other in various territories, the mark in this case was split artificially by the legislation of one of the states involved. Van Zuylen was therefore taking advantage of that special circumstance, and could not claim that the prevention of parallel imports was simply a consequence of the territoriality of the law. Indeed, presumably but for the split, he would have had no mark at all. It must be conceded that it is perhaps rather harsh to characterise this as an abuse, however.

14—16   If this principle is correct, there is no reason why it should not apply to all types of intellectual property where relevant. The Commission has recently indicated that the "specific subject matter" doctrine (on which the principle is based) applies to breeding rights[56] and it may also apply to copyright. There has

---

[52] Case 78/70 *DGG* v. *Metro* [1971] E.C.R. 487, 500.

[53] Example given by the Court in *Terrapin* [1976] E.C.R. 1039, 1060.

[54] Example given by the Court in the *Hoffman La Roche* case *supra*, note 38, where the right to prevent imports was contingent upon a showing *inter alia* that repackaging of the goods would alter the condition of the goods.

[55] *Supra*, note 40.

[56] *Eisele*. O.J. 1978, 1286/23; [1978] 3 C.M.L.R. 434; see also Case 258/78 *Nungesser & Eisele* v. *Commission* (not yet decided).

been no application to know-how yet.

Problems arising from the differing content of the various national laws

14—17   The content of different intellectual property rules might in itself affect the attainment of the common market. This may happen perhaps because it is more difficult to obtain a patent in one country than in another, thus discouraging the setting up of facilities in that country for the manufacture of the product involved; or distortions of trade may result from the fact that a product is protected in one country but not in another. This is obviously important but has not received much attention in the form of harmonisation because as we have seen, it is the mere existence of different laws which lies at the root of the problems which have chiefly preoccupied EEC lawyers. Moreover for many years negotiations have been in progress to achieve a single Community patent and trademark system.[57]

The second category of conflicts - the reconciliation of intellectual property law in general with the Treaty

14—18   There is a general irreconcilability between the intellectual property law of a country and its laws designed to ensure the preservation of competition. This conflict arises, as one might expect, from the exclusive nature of the rights granted by the former, and the general bias against monopolistic power on the part of the latter. Since the exclusivity granted to the holder of a right is in the very nature of that right, this at least must co-exist with the competition rules. On the other hand, the licensing of others to use that right, and the conditions which may be attached to such licences may fall foul of the competition law. The United States, which has at the Federal level both a patent law and a law to regulate competition, has experienced this problem. It is not therefore a problem which is peculiar to the EEC. On the other hand, the EEC has certainly had to face up to this question, because it has its own competition policy in the form of Article 85 and the problem is rendered more acute because there is at present no Community intellectual property law. Furthermore, the possession of an exclusive right may suggest that the holder is in a dominant position in the market place. Hence, the role of Article 86 may fall to be considered.

Article 85 - Licensing

14—19   A number of different theories have been advanced as to how the "dividing line" might be drawn between legitimate and illegitimate licensing practices.[58] One such theory, which now appears

---

[57] *Infra*, paras. 14–22 *et seq*.
[58] Waelbroeck, *op. cit.* note 20 suggests four such approaches.

to have fallen into disfavour, held that there could be no infringement of the competition provisions if the patentee grants some of the rights which he derives from the patent whilst refusing the grant of other rights, for he has not thereby imposed a restriction, but merely kept back those rights not licensed.[59] The Commission's decisions in this field cannot really be reconciled with this theory.

The second theory resorts to the notion of the "specific subject matter" of the property. We saw earlier that this notion was used by the Court to prevent the holders of intellectual property rights from using those rights to partition the common market. From this, a common principle was derived couched in terms of an abusive exercise of intellectual property rights. If the concept of "the specific subject matter of the property" applies in the context of patent and trademark licensing generally, then the exercise of property rights going beyond that might turn out to be other examples of "abusive exercise." The Commission has increasingly used the "specific subject matter" approach in relation to licensing.[60] In the field of licensing generally, however, that type of abuse turns out to be only one of many different "abuses," or actions which go beyond the "specific subject matter."

Perhaps the most significant type of clause in a licence which has been found to infringe Article 85 (1) is that conferring exclusivity on the licensee. Contrary to earlier indications[61] the Commission has now established that an exclusive manufacturing licence may infringe Article 85 (1). In *Burroughs/Delplanque*[62] it stated:

> "A patent confers on its holder the exclusive right to manufacture the products which are the subject of the invention. The holder may cede, by licenses, for a given territory, the use of the rights derived from its patent. However, if it undertakes to limit the exploitation of its exclusive right to a single undertaking in a territory and thus confers on that single undertaking the right to exploit the invention and to prevent other undertakings from using it, it thus loses the power to contract with other applicants for a license. In certain cases such exclusive character of a manufacturing license may restrict competition and be covered by the prohibition set out in Article 85 (1)."

14—20   Subsequent decisions have shown that it is probably the normal rule that exclusive licences will be found to infringe the prohibition of Article 85.[63] The Commission's view has been heavily

[59] See article 20 of the German "Gesetz gegen Wettbewerbabeschänkungen."
[60] See the Decisions cited below.
[61] See Notice on Patent Licences of December 24, 1962, J.O. 1962, 2922.
[62] J.O. 1972, L13/50; [1972] C.M.L.R. D67, D70.
[63] See *Kabelmetal/Luchaire* O.J. 1975, L222/34; [1975] 2 C.M.LR. D40; also *AOIP/Beyrard* O.J. 1976, L6/8; [1976] 1 C.M.L.R. D14.

criticised; it is argued that the right to grant exclusivity necessarily forms part of the specific subject matter of the right, at least in the case of patents, if only because the legislation of most countries make a special provision for the exclusive licensee's protection. A draft regulation[64] which would grant block exemptions to such licences in certain cases has met strong opposition *inter alia* because of its assumption that such licences do fall within Article 85.

Many other clauses in licences of patents and know-how have fallen to be considered under Article 85; some have been granted exemption under Article 85 (3). More generally, where the know-how is granted in the context of a sub-contracting arrangement, the Commission has indicated that some restrictions on its use and of the use of further know-how developed by the sub-contractor will not infringe Article 85 (1).[65]

Article 86

14–21   Article 86 prohibits undertakings from abusing their dominant position in the market place. At first sight, the existence of a "monopoly" in the manufacture and sale of goods might itself appear to amount to a dominant position. The better view, however, already suggested in Case 24/67 *Parke Davis* v. *Probel*[66] and confirmed in Case 27/76 *United Brands*[67] is that intellectual property rights do not of themselves create a dominant position. It is necessary to look at the relevant market to ascertain the importance of the patented product; the same appears to be true for trademarks.[68] Intellectual property rights may, however, be an instrument used by a dominant undertaking in the course of abusing its position.[69]

Action at the European level

14–22   Reference has already been made to developments at the "European level" aimed at resolving at least some of the difficulties outlined above. As early as 1959[70] work was started on a "Community Patent Convention" which was intended to set up machinery for the granting of patents which would be valid for the entire common market. Eventually, the solution settled on was to provide for two patent conventions.

The first Convention, the so-called European Patent Convention,[71] embraces all the Member States of the Community. In

---

[64] In its final form: O.J. 1979, C58/12; [1979] 1 C.M.L.R. 478.
[65] Notice of December 18, 1978. O.J. 1979, C1/2; [1979] 1 C.M.L.R. L64.
[66] [1968] E.C.R. 55, 72.
[67] [1978] E.C.R. 207.
[68] Case 51/75 *EMI* v. *CBS* [1976] E.C.R. 811, 849.
[69] Case 27/76 *supra*, note 67.
[70] see, *e.g.* Van Empel (1973) 9 C.M.L.Rev. 13, 456.
[71] Convention on the Grant of European Patents (European Patent Convention), Signed at Munich on October 5, 1973. Entered into force October 7, 1977. All Community Member States are parties. TS No 20 (1978); Cmnd. 7090.

addition most other Western European States including Yugoslavia and Turkey may become or are already parties. The Convention establishes a European Patent Organisation. The tasks of the Organisation are carried out by the European Patent Office. The convention establishes a system of law, common to the Contracting Parties, for the grant of patents.[72] A patent granted by virtue of the convention has the effect of a national patent in each of the countries for which it is granted.[73] A European Patent granted by the European Patent Office is therefore a bundle of national patents. The system, designed to key in with that of the Patent Co-operation Treaty, is expected to provide substantial savings in fees and time and effort and gains in terms of uniformity. It was anticipated that a prospective patentee hoping to obtain protection in at least three Contracting States would normally wish to opt for a European Patent designating those three countries, rather than for three national patents.

14—23   The Member States of the European Communities concluded among themselves and in parallel a second convention, the Convention for the European Patent for the Common Market,[74] or Community Patent Convention, intended, as its name implies, to lay down special rules, procedures and machinery for European Patents for Member States of the Community. The intention is that the Community Patent should be administered from a special section of the European Patent Office. It will go much further than the European Patent system in requiring that in principle[75] a designation of one Member State of the Community constitutes designation of all of them. Further, the Community Patent, instead of being a bundle of national patents, will be governed by its own system of law.[76] In particular it incorporates the "exhaustion of rights" principle.[77] There are provisions dealing with the scope of licensing; exclusive licences are permitted for part of the EEC territory.[78] In principle the Community patent system is to be administered by national courts.[79] Provision is made for references to the European Court for preliminary rulings concerning the interpretation of the Community Convention and its implementing rules and of those parts of the European Patent Convention which are binding on every Com-

[72] *Ibid*, Art. 1.
[73] *Ibid*. Art. 2 (2).
[74] Convention for the European Patent for the Common Market (Community Patent Convention) Signed at Luxembourg December 15, 1975. Not yet in force. EC No. 18 (1976); Cmnd. 6553. Also in O.J. 1976, L17 (some typographical errors).
[75] Art. 3, subject to a transitional period of indefinite duration: Art. 86.
[76] Art. 1 (2) and 2 (3).
[77] Art. 32.
[78] Art. 43.
[79] Arts. 68 to 72. Some centralisation of jurisdiction is envisaged by annexed resolutions on centralisation and on litigation of Community patents.

munity patent.[80] The precise relationship with the main body of Community law will no doubt have to be worked out having regard both to the proposition that the EEC Treaty is to prevail in case of conflict,[81] while at the same time the Community patent system is not part of, but only linked to the Community legal order.[82]

14—24   The Convention also lays down provisions relating to national patents, which are to continue to exist, in parallel with the Community patent.[83] National patent law is to be subject to the doctrine of "exhaustion of rights" and to the rule that no infringement action may be brought to prevent the marketing of a patented product, where there are "economic connections" between the plaintiff's patent and the defendant's patent.[84] In the field of Trademark law the Commission proposes a Council Regulation, to establish a Community Trademark along the lines of the Community Patent together with a draft directive on approximation of national trademark laws.[85] Discussions are still at a preliminary stage.

[80] Art. 73. Modelled on Art. 177 EEC.
[81] Art. 93.
[82] Preambular para. six.
[83] Arts. 80 to 84.
[84] Art. 81.
[85] Latest versions in O.J. 1980, C 351.

Chapter 15

AGRICULTURE

I Treaty Provisions

15—01   Article 2 (*d*) of the EEC Treaty refers to the adoption of a common policy in the sphere of agriculture. Substantive provisions are contained in Articles 38 to 47.

Objectives of the Agricultural Policy

15—02   The form of the Community in its agricultural sector is largely governed by Article 39, which sets out the objectives of the common agricultural policy. Given that Articles 40 (2) and (3), and 41 provide for the establishment of common organisations of agricultural markets "in order to attain the objectives set out in Article 39," while under Article 40 (3), second sub-para. "the common organisation shall be limited to pursuit" of those objectives, this enumeration must be considered by and large to be exhaustive.

Article 39 states that the objectives of the common agricultural policy (or CAP) shall be to increase productivity, to ensure a fair standard of living for the agricultural community in particular by raising farm wages; to stabilise the markets; and to ensure the availability of supplies, and reasonable prices for consumers.

The social structure, is, however, to be taken into account, and is to be safeguarded, or at least not abruptly altered, and disparities between regions are not to be aggravated (Art. 39 (2)). In particular, account is to be taken of the fact that in the Member States agriculture constitutes a sector closely linked with the economy as a whole (Art. 39 (2) (*c*)). Clearly, therefore, an equilibrium has to be achieved between conflicting objectives.[1]

Content

15—03   Article 38 (1) states that "the common market shall extend to agriculture and agricultural products." "Agricultural products" means the "products of the soil, of stockfarming and of fisheries and products of first-stage processing directly related to these products." These products are listed in Annex II. Article 38 (3) allowed for additions to Annex II within two years of the entry into force of the Treaty. Additions were in fact made by Regulation 7 *bis*.[2] It has been suggested that Article 235 (the general

---

[1] Case 5/67 *Beus* v. *HZA München-Landsbergerstrasse* [1968] E.C.R. 83.
[2] J.O. 1961, 71.

206

power clause) could be used to add to the list, and a proposal was in fact made on this basis by the Commission, but no action was taken, and the view was expressed that such action would clash with the clear intention of Article 38 (3), and the need for legal certainty. The list is thus now considered to be exhaustive, in that the products falling outside it are not agricultural products for the purposes of the Common Market, *e.g.* timber.[3]

15—04   On the other hand the Court has held that the definition of "agricultural products" would be devoid of practical meaning if it were not to be interpreted in the light of the aims of the CAP and with reference to the products with which the authors of the Treaty considered that policy to be concerned.[3]

Although the Court has also been called upon to consider terms such as "agricultural producers" and "agricultural holding," it concluded in both cases that the terms were not susceptible of definition outside their respective regulations. So it would be unwise to draw general conclusions from such decisions.[4]

Article 38 (4) states that "the operation and development of the common market for agricultural products must *be accompanied* by the establishment of a common agricultural policy among the Member States." Article 38 (2) applies the general rules of the Treaty outside the Title on Agriculture to agricultural products, save as otherwise provided in Articles 39 to 46, *e.g.* Article 42, suspending the competition rules.[5]

Establishment of the Common Agricultural Policy (CAP)

15—05   The CAP is established pursuant to Articles 40 *et seq.* having regard to the objectives set out in Article 39. Article 40 (2) requires the establishment of a "common organisation of agricultural markets" in order to attain those objectives, and goes on to state that

> "this organisation shall take one of the following forms, depending on the product concerned;
>
> (a) common rules on competition;
> (b) compulsory co-ordination of the various national market organisations;
> (c) a European market organisation."

Although the expression "common organisation of markets" is in the singular, it is clear from the phrase "depending on the product concerned," and its surrounding context, that individual

---

[3] See Case 185/73 *HZA Bielefeld* v. *König* [1974] E.C.R. 607 on the scope and possibility of extension.
[4] Case 139/77 *Denkavit Futtermittel GmbH* v. *FA Warendorf* [1978] E.C.R. 1317; Case 85/77 *Societa Sant' Anna Azienda Avicola* v. *INPS* [1978] E.C.R. 527.
[5] For a discussion of this subject see *infra*, para. 15–10.

market organisations for each product were envisaged.

It became immediately apparent that for most if not all agricultural sectors, the only really practicable alternative specified was the third, since the first touches only one aspect of the agricultural markets, while the second would have been very difficult to introduce at the outset.

15--06   Article 40 (3) is the "powers" clause for the market organisations; providing that the market organisations may include all measures required to attain the objectives set out in Article 39, in particular regulation of prices, aids for the production and marketing of the various products, storage and carry-over arrangements and common machinery for stabilising imports or exports. These powers are to be exercised in the light of Article 39, but with the additional condition of non-discrimination between producers or consumers within the Community (Art. 40 (3), third sub-para.). The fact that prices vary from Member State to Member State does not violate this principle, so long as the prices are "based on common criteria and uniform methods of calculation" (Art. 40 (3), third sub-para.) where a common price policy has been worked out, as it has impliedly or expressly for most products subject to market organisations. The principle of non-discrimination is to be contrasted with that contained in Article 7, which deals only with discrimination based on nationality. Price control practised at the national level is not in itself incompatible with this principle, but may become so if it has the effect of depressing prices below the intervention price or the target price.[6]

15—07   Article 40 (1) required in principle the setting-up of a CAP by the end of the transitional period, but Article 40 deals only with one aspect of it - the form that market organisations are to take (apart from Art. 40 (4), upon which the European Agricultural Guidance and Guarantee Fund is based - see further below). Article 41 supplies limited additional powers to supplement those given in Article 40, providing notably for dispositions on training, research, etc., in the context of a given market organisation.

Article 42 suspends the application to the agricultural sector of the competition rules pending a decision of the Council. The rules of competition were in fact applied to agriculture by Regulation 26 of 1962.[7]

Article 43 provides the legal basis for the regulations setting up the CAP and for subsequent rules governing it. The Council, acting on the basis of proposals from the Commission and after consulting the Assembly, has the power to make regulations, issue directives and to take decisions without prejudice to any recom-

---

[6] See, *e.g.* Case 65/76 *Riccardo Tasca* [1976] E.C.R. 291; Case 60/75 *Russo* v. *AIMA* [1976] E.C.R. 45.
[7] J.O. 1962, 993. See *infra*, para. 15–10.

mendations which it may make (para. 2, third sub-para.). The Council acts by a qualified majority vote - unanimity being required during the first two stages of the original transitional period. Most of the common organisations relating to agricultural products have now been set up, replacing the national organisations, subject to the limited safeguards of Article 43 (3) though there are still no market organisations for wool, alcohol or potatoes.[8] As a source of new initiatives in setting up the CAP or revision of market organisations, the article is still important.

15—08   Where national market organisations still exist (as permitted by Articles 43 and 46, and including those mentioned above), Article 45 nevertheless provides that trade should be developed during the first stage, and it was envisaged that all national organisations would be abolished by the end of the transitional period. Hence in so far as markets are still organised on a national basis,

> "the derogations which a national organisation may effect from the general rules of the Treaty are only permissible provisionally, to the extent necessary to ensure its functioning, without however impeding the adaptations which are involved in the establishment of the common agricultural policy."[9]

The range of tools available for setting up the CAP is completed by special mention (Art. 47) of the agricultural section of the Economic and Social Committee, which is to hold itself at the disposal of the Commission to prepare the deliberations of the full Committee.

II The Common Agricultural Policy

A. *Achievement of a Common Market in Agricultural Goods*

1. Free movement of goods

15—09   From the end of the transitional period, or earlier where a common market organisation had already been established for a particular product, agricultural goods were to be permitted the same freedom of movement as any other goods. Thus each regulation which sets up a market organisation provides in essence for the abolition of customs duties and quantitative restrictions (together with charges and measures having equivalent effect). The references in the regulation to such duties, restrictions, etc., have generally the same scope and meaning as in the corresponding Treaty provisions,[10] and they apply equally to imports and

---

[8] A proposal of 1975 (O.J. 1976, C309) for the common organisation of the market in ethyl alcohol was amended in 1979 (O.J. 1979, C193).

[9] Case 48/74 *Charmasson* v. *Minister for Economic Affairs and Finance* [1974] E.C.R. 1383.

[10] Case 34/73 *Variola* v. *Amministrazione Italiana delle Finanze* [1973] E.C.R. 981.

exports.[11] These are supplemented by directives setting up common standards and procedures regarding health checks and other matters particularly in the field of animal products (*e.g.* control of swine fever) and vegetables (*e.g.* the common catalogue of seed varieties, and rules on the use of additives, preservatives and colouring matters). In fact, the measures to facilitate free movement frequently go beyond simple parallels with the provisions of the Treaty. Thus, for example, national health checks at the internal frontiers of the Community may no longer be permitted where Community arrangements make these unnecessary.[12] Again, although Member States may continue to impose price controls on the retail and consumption stage these controls must not influence the formation of prices at the wholesale stage nor act as quantitative restrictions on imports or exports.[13] Where *no* common organisation of a market has yet been established, the national organisations may continue to exist, but it is now clear that from the end of the original transitional period these may only function subject to the general Treaty rules.[14] Similarly, the derogations in the 1972 Act of Accession did not have the effect of creating permanent exceptions to the CAP but only lasted until the end of the transitional period in that Act.[15]

2. Competition

15—10   In view of the special derogation contained in Article 42,[16] Regulation 17/62[17] did not initially apply to argicultural goods. Regulation 26[18] subsequently provided for the application of the competition rules subject to the exceptions in its Article 2. These are that Article 85 (1) shall not apply where an otherwise prohibited agreement, etc., forms an integral part of a market organisation or is necessary for the attainment of the objectives set out in Article 39, and in particular provided that Article 85 (1) should not apply to "agreements, decisions and practices of farmers, farmers' associations, or associations of such associations, belonging to a single Member State which concern the production or sale of agricultural products or the use of joint facilities for the storage, treatment or processing of agricultural products, and under which there is no obligation to charge identical prices, unless the Commission finds that competition is thereby excluded or that the

---

[11] Case 51/74 *P.J. Van der Hulst's Zonen* v. *Produktschap voor Siergewassen* [1975] E.C.R. 79.
[12] *Ibid.*; Case 46/76 *WJG Bauhuis* v. *The Netherlands State* [1977] E.C.R. 5; Case 89/76 *Commission* v. *Netherlands* [1977] E.C.R. 1355.
[13] Case 223/78 *Grosoli* [1979] E.C.R. 2621.
[14] Case 48/74 *Charmasson* v. *Minister for Economic Affairs and Finance, supra,* note 9.
[15] Case 231/78 *Commission* v. *UK* [1979] E.C.R. 1447.
[16] *Supra.*
[17] *Infra,* Chapter 20.
[18] J.O. 1962, 993.

objectives of Article 39 of the Treaty are jeopardised." Scope for application of the exceptions in Article 2 seems limited in view of the few national market organisations remaining.

It appears that once a common organisation has been established for given products, additional separate national rules or arrangements are not likely to be justified in terms of fulfilling the objectives of Article 39 because the common organisation is deemed exclusively to do so, so that, effectively, the sector becomes fully subject to Article 85.[19] Furthermore, they would have to fulfill all the objectives of Article 39.

3. Other provisions

15—11   While Article 43 provides a quite general power of decision-making to give effect to the agricultural policy, other Treaty provisions of general application may be invoked either separately or in conjunction with Article 43 as envisaged by Article 38 (2).[20]

Thus the adoption of Regulation 120/67 completing the common organisation of the market in the cereals sector was held not to exclude the application of general provisions of the Treaty and in particular Article 226.[21]

B. Agricultural Policy

1. Market organisations

The establishment and management of the organisations

15—12   Under Article 43 of the Treaty the Council has a power of decision of the widest kind acting on proposals of the Commission and after consulting the Assembly. Under this power the basic principles of each market organisation are laid down by regulations; they may of course subsequently be amended or varied. Power to legislate in detailed day-to-day matters is shared between Council and Commission, the Commission receiving delegated powers from the Council, which is the only institution here given decision-making powers directly (*cf.* Article 155, last hyphen). In practice, however, it was soon felt that there was a need for close co-operation between the Community and Member States. In order to provide for this co-operation, management or advisory committees were set up for each product or group of products for the period of transition, it being left to be decided subsequently what permanent arrangement should be made. These committees are composed of representatives of each Member State, voting in accordance with the rules set out in Article 148 (2) as amended by the Acts of Accession.[22] They are presided over by a rep-

[19] Case 71/74 *Frubo* v. *Commission* [1975] E.C.R. 563.
[20] See Case 5/73 *Balkan-Import-Export* v. *HZA Berlin Packhof* [1973] E.C.R. 1091.
[21] Case 72/72 *EVSt Getreide* v. *Baer-Getreide GmbH* [1973] E.C.R. 377.
[22] *Supra*, para. 3–36.

resentative of the Commission. The establishment of such bodies has no direct basis in the Treaty, but their legality was upheld by the Court in Case 25/70 *EVSt.* v. *Köster, Berodt*[23] and their importance is such that their existence has been maintained beyond the end of the transitional period.[24]

15—13   The division of the power of decision, discussed in detail in *Köster*, is now as follows:

1. The Council sets up the market organisations and lays down other rules of the CAP under Article 43 (2). The Council also lays down the more important supplementary regulations, including, for example, those fixing annually the price levels. Implementing regulations need not necessarily be made by the Council under Article 43 (2).

2. The Commission acts on its own responsibility in routine and in emergency matters, acting under delegated authority pursuant to Article 155, unless it has autonomous powers derived from other parts of the Treaty, *e.g.* Article 115.

3. On other matters, the Commission consults the relevant management committee if there is one, and then takes its own decision. It is not obliged to take its decision in conformity with the opinion of the management committee, but if it does not do so, it must at once inform the Council. The Council may, generally within one month, amend the decision of the Commission; in the interim the Commission is not obliged to suspend application of its decision.

15—14   In accordance with Article 43 (1) a conference was held in 1958 at Stresa, Italy, with a view to ascertaining the requirements of the Common Agricultural Policy. It was not until the end of the first stage, however, that the first part of the CAP was set up by the Council in a series of regulations after a marathon session in December 1961 and January 1962. The first such regulations dealt with the cereals sector, since the price of cereals, a major input cost factor in the production of animal protein, is of fundamental importance to the rest of the economy. Other products were dealt with in turn although not without the intervention of a severe crisis in 1966, which led to the Luxembourg Accords.[25] By the end of the transitional period the main agricultural products were covered - cereals, beef and veal, pigmeat, eggs and poultrymeat, dairy products, tobacco, fruit and vegetables, wine, hops, oils and fats, sugar, seeds, live plants and flowers, processed vegetables,

[23] [1970] E.C.R. 1161; on the role of management committees see also Case 57/72 *Westzucker* v. *EVSt für Zucker* [1973] E.C.R. 321.
[24] Regulation 2602/69, J.O. 1969, L 324/23, O.J. 1969, 588.
[25] *Supra*, para. 3–37.

flax and hemp, and fisheries. In 1973 the Commission put forward proposals for making many of these organisations more flexible with the purpose *inter alia* of reducing surpluses and eliminating fraud. In many cases this led to new basic regulations, and it is these which are described below. The sudden reversal in grain prices in 1973 (when the world market price rose above the Community price), together with the energy crisis, led to a demand for fodder which required a common organisation of that product. As already mentioned the main products still not covered are potatoes, wool and alcohol. In 1976 approximately 96 per cent. of Community products were subject to common organisation,[26] and the percentage is now higher with the advent of the common organisation of the sheepmeat and goatmeat market.

Common organisation of markets for goods produced within the Community

15—15   There is no single overall system in the common organisation of the markets. Some, *e.g.* cereals, are based on a price support mechanism (buying-in to keep the price up to a guaranteed level coupled with a variable levy on imported goods and export refunds); some on external protection only (application of the common customs tariff); some, *e.g.* olive oil on production aid (not unlike the former British deficiency payments scheme under which the government made up the difference between an agreed price and the actual market price); and some on flat-rate aid per hectare, *e.g.* flax and hemp.

Where a system of price support has been adopted, it will rely on a number of prices basically fixed annually by the Council. For the purposes of directing the internal market a price is fixed at which it is intended that transactions take place within the Community. This price is usually called a *target* price. The level of the target price is set having regard to the objectives of Article 39. To supplement this, a second price is fixed, generally expressed as a percentage of the first, at which national intervention bodies will intervene (by buying on the market) to maintain the price level. This is called the *intervention* price. Generally the prices in a sector, or part of a sector, will be fixed for a particular product of a standard type and quality in a particular place, and prices for other products in the same sector or at other places will be derived from that price (*derived intervention price*).

15—16   Where there is a price support system operating within the Community, full protection against imports is provided for by a system of variable levies on the commodity, the amount of the levy being expressed to be equal to the difference between the c.i.f. or the free-at-frontier price of the product on arrival in the importing

---

[26] See "The agricultural policy of the European Community," European Documentation, 1976/6.

State and the *threshold* price at a particular entry point fixed for the Community. The *threshold* price is calculated in such a way that it amounts to the *target* price less the cost of transportation to the centre of greatest shortfall of the product covered. If goods are purchased on the world market below that price they will be subject to a levy on importation into the Community so as to bring them to the threshold price level. In some cases the levy contains an additional element of protection, taking the price above the target price. The levy system is considered to be regulatory in character and not merely protective, and does not amount to a tax or customs duty.[27]

In many sectors quality standards have been established which effectively limit circulation of goods not complying with such standards and prevent both their export and import. These standards thus constitute a further protective element.

15—17   Surpluses on the market, generally priced well above world-market prices because of the intervention system, are disposed of in part by export refunds. These are fixed by the Community at a common level for each product for the whole territory of the Community, generally under a regulation separate from that setting up the market organisation. A common system for exports is set up by Regulation 2603/69.[28] In addition to the refund system, there are mechanisms allowing for the denaturing of products (quality butter into lower quality - good wheat into cattle fodder, etc.), and for the distribution of products at reduced prices, or in the case of perishables, even free to certain organisations, including the armed forces, and charitable or educational institutions.

The protective and support mechanisms are reinforced by certification systems designed to keep track of transactions and movements, and to eliminate fraud.[29]

Finally, the market structures are backed up by safeguard clauses, contained in the regulations setting them up, generally of two kinds: Type (1) apply where serious disturbances are present or are to be feared in the market and are liable to imperil the objectives of Article 39. The Commission has a power of decision here,

---

[27] Case 17/67 *Neumann* v. *HZA Hof/Saale* [1967] E.C.R. 441.
[28] J.O. 1969, L 324/25; Detailed rules are contined in Regulation 2730/79, O.J. 1979, L 317/1 and Regulation 565/80, O.J. 1980, L 62/5 on the advance payment of export refunds.
[29] Regulation 283/72, J.O. 1972, L 36/1, O.J. 1972, 90; see also Directive 77/435, O.J. 1977, L 172/17 on the scrutiny of accounts and commercial documents of undertakings in receipt of Guarantee section funds. Under tth directive, Member States are obliged to carry out systematic selective scrutiny of commercial documents and should ensure that provisions relating to the seizure of documents apply in any case which may constitute an irregularity. There is provision for mutual assistance between Member States. The earlier regulation provides for the supply periodically to the Commission of information concerning prosecutions, and requires national authorities to take prompt action to prosecute in the case of fraud.

subject to annulment or modification by the Council. Type (2) applies where it is necessary to neutralise price rises in the Community market.

The rules as to market organisations are to be interpreted at the Community level, and cannot be subject to national variations.[30]

The Individual Organisations

Cereals

15—18 The common organisation of the market in cereals is provided for by Regulation 2727/75.[31] Most cereals and derived flours are covered by these regulations,[32] and processed products are covered for some purposes.[33]

Products produced and marketed within the Community

15—19   There is a *common single intervention* price[34] for common wheat, barley and maize, and *single intervention* price[35] for rye and durum wheat. Intervention prices are fixed for the Ormes intervention centre, being the centre with the greatest production surplus.[36] A *reference*[37] price is fixed for common wheat of breadmaking quality; this is calculated by adding to the *common single intervention* price for this product an amount reflecting the difference in return between the price of this product and that of common wheat of non-breadmaking quality.[38] The intervention bodies can dispose of products held by them on the home market or by way of export.[39] They may also be disposed of as food aid.[40] A *target* price is fixed for common wheat, durum wheat and rye and a *common target* price exists for barley and maize. The *target* prices are calculated by including the addition of a market element and an element reflecting the cost of transport between the Ormes area and the Duisburg area (the area of greatest shortfall) to the intervention and reference prices where applicable. For rye, durum and common wheat, the market element is arrived at by calculating the difference between the relevant fixed prices for each of the cereals and the level of market prices to be expected in a normal harvest and under natural conditions of price formation on the Community market in the area having the greatest surplus.

[30] Case 74/69 *HZA Bremen-Freihafen* v. *Krohn* [1970] E.C.R. 467.
[31] O.J. 1975 L 281/1. Significant changes were made in particular by Regulations 1143/76, O.J. 1976, L 130/1.
[32] Regulation 2727/75, Article 1.
[33] *Ibid*. Article 1 (d).
[34] See paras 15–15 to 15–17 on terminology.
[35] *Ibid*.
[36] Regulation 2727/75, Article 3 as amended by Regulation 1143/76, Article 1.
[37] See paras 15–15 to 15–17 on terminology.
[38] Regulation 2727/75, Article 3 as amended by Regulation 1143/76, Article 1.
[39] Regulation 2727/75, Article 7.
[40] *Ibid*. Article 28.

For barley and maize, the market element is the difference between the normal market price and single intervention price *plus* the difference in market prices reflecting the ratio between the average relative values of the two cereals concerned for use in animal feed. The transport element in both cases is calculated on the basis of the most favourable means of transport.[41]

15—20   All these prices are fixed for the marketing year,[42] but for cereals harvested in the Community, and for malt, a "carry-over payment" may be made for stocks existing at the end of the marketing year.[43] The prices must in practice be fixed by the Council before March 15[44] since the prices apply as from June 1 of each year to the products of the following marketing year, where such products are available before its commencement.[45]

Special intervention measures may be taken as regards common wheat of breadmaking quality to avoid substantial purchases at particular centres.[46] Furthermore, aid is granted for the production of durum wheat (replacing a minimum price system),[47] and production refunds are available for maize and common wheat used in the manufacture of starch (this also applies to *potato* starch) and for maize groats and meal used in the manufacture of glucose.[48]

Trade with third countries

15—21   A *threshold*[49] price is fixed in respect of common wheat, durum wheat, barley, maize and rye.[50]

Imports of all products listed in Article 1 of Regulation 2727/75 are subject to a licensing system, licences being obtained from the authorities on payment of a deposit.[51] Imports of the primary cereals and resulting flours are subject to a levy.[52] The importer, when applying for a licence, may request a fixed levy for the duration of the licence, in which case a premium is added.[53] For processed products covered by Article 1 (*d*) of Regulation 2727/75, a levy is imposed which contains a variable component (based on the amount of the primary product contained in the

---

[41] Regulation 2727/75, Article 3, as amended by Regulation 1143/76, Article 1.
[42] August 1 to July 31; Regulation 2727/75, Article 3 as amended by Regulation 1143/76, Article 1. However, monthly increases are built in to the fixed prices, *ibid*. Article 6.
[43] *Ibid*. Article 9.
[44] *Ibid*. Article 5.
[45] *Ibid*. Article 6. This provides that monthly increases of the initial amount are to be fixed but does not appear to *require* the initial amount to be so fixed.
[46] *Ibid*. Article 8.
[47] *Ibid*. Article 10, as amended by Regulation 1143/75, Article 5.
[48] *Ibid*. Article 11.
[49] See paras 15–15 to 15–17 on terminology.
[50] Regulation 2727/75, Article 5.
[51] *Ibid*. Article 12.
[52] *Ibid*. Article 13. The levy is calculated as indicated *supra*.
[53] Regulation 2727/75, Article 15.

manufactured goods) and a fixed component designed to protect the processing industry.[54]

Exports are also subject to the licensing system and are eligible for export refunds.[55] These refunds may also be fixed in advance, on request, as regards the primary cereals and resulting flours.[56]

The organisation of the cereals market has undergone considerable changes since the first regulations. The present system appears to allow greater market fluidity and a sounder balance between the various kinds of cereals,[57] gives incentives for the production of better quality wheats, in particular[58] and subjects the various cereals more closely to market forces.[59] The basic regulation contains more or less standard form provisions on safeguards[60] inward processing, customs matters, state aids and management committee procedures.

Pigmeat, Eggs and Poultrymeat

15–22   Since these sectors depend to a large extent upon the price of cereals used as feedingstuffs it is natural that the organisations of each should be very similar. In all three cases the basic regulations indicate that measures may be taken to improve organisation and quality.

Products produced and marketed within the Community

15–23   Only Regulation 2759/75,[61] concerning *pigmeat*, provides for price support for the domestic product. A *basic*[62] price must be fixed for pig carcasses before August 1 each year valid from November 1 of the same year. Intervention may take place when the Community market price is likely to remain at less than 103 per cent. of the basic price;[63] the buying-in price, at least for carcasses of a standard quality may not be more than 92 per cent. nor less than 78 per cent. of the basic price.[64] As an alternative to direct intervention, aid may be granted towards the cost of private storage.[65]

---

[54] *Ibid.* Article 14.
[55] *Ibid.* Article 16.
[56] *Ibid.* Article 16.
[57] Eleventh General Report 1977, p. 159 and see also Parliament's opinion on the reforms: O.J. 1977, C93.
[58] *Ibid.*
[59] Tenth general report, point 326, (p. 174).
[60] Articles 19 and 20.
[61] Regulation 2759/75, O.J. 1975, L 282/1 as amended by Regulation 1432/78, O.J. 1978, L 179/19.
[62] See *Supra* paras. 15–15 to 15–17 on terminology.
[63] Regulation 2759/75, Article 4.
[64] *Ibid.* Article 5 as amended by Regulation 1423/78.
[65] *Ibid.* Article 3.

Trade with third countries

15—24   All three regulations[66] provide for levies on the *imported* product. A basic levy is calculated principally with reference to the cost of feedingstuffs. In addition, a *sluice-gate*[67] price is fixed, again largely based on the cost of feedingstuffs, and the levy is normally to be increased by the difference between that price and the free at frontier price if prices fall below the level of the former.[68] This mechanism is not applied where the exporting country agrees to voluntary restraint. For derived pigmeat products the sluice-gate price is calculated from the basic sluice-gate price for carcasses, and licences may be required for imports.[69] In the eggs sector sluice-gate prices are also fixed for certain processed products depending on their egg content.[70] All three regulations contain both the usual safeguard clauses and special provisions for supporting the market both in the event of restrictions on free circulation imposed for the purposes of preventing disease, and in the event of shortages.

Exports may benefit from export refunds where necessary, such refunds amounting to the difference between the prices ruling on the world market and Community prices.

Rice

15—25   Regulation 1418/76,[71] as amended by Regulations 1158/77,[72] 1126/78,[73] and 113/80[74] covers most types of rice and resulting flours, meal, pellets and starch. It bears a close similarity to the organisation of the cereals market.

Rice produced and marketed within the Community

15—26   A *single intervention*[75] price must be fixed for paddy rice before August 1 of each year for Vercelli,[76] the centre with the largest rice surplus. A *target*[77] price is fixed for Duisburg for husked rice, calculated by adding to the intervention price the cost of processing paddy rice and adding various other costs. As with cereals, intervention depends upon the fixing of standard qualities; the prices are to be subject to phased increases and a carry-over payment scheme[78] exists. Production refunds are available for

---

[66] *Viz.* Regulations 2759/75, *supra*, (pigmeat); 2771/75, O.J. 1975, L 282/49 (eggs); 2777/75, O.J. 1975, L282/77 (poultrymeat).
[67] A variation of the threshold price.
[68] *e.g.* Regulation 2759/75, Article 13.
[69] *Ibid.* Article 14.
[70] Regulation 2771/75, Article 7.
[71] O.J. 1976, L166/1.
[72] O.J. 1977, L136/13.
[73] O.J. 1978, L142/23.
[74] O.J. 1980, L16/1.
[75] See paras. 15–15 to 15–17 on terminology.
[76] Regulation 1418/76 (as amended), Article 4.
[77] See paras 15–15 to 15–17 on terminology.
[78] *Ibid.*

broken rice used in the manufacture of starch or by the brewing industry for the production of beer.[79]

Trade with third countries

5—27   Again as with cereals, *imports* are subject to a levy, the submission of licences and payment of deposits. A *threshold* price is fixed for some types of rice according to differing criteria[80] and in those cases the levy is the difference between that price and c.i.f. price Rotterdam.[81] For other types of rice the levy is based on that for the types for which there is a threshold price, adjusted by a conversion rate.[82] There are the usual safeguard provisions.
        Exports are entitled to refunds calculated in the usual way.

Sugar

5--28   The sugar market is organised principally by Regulation 3330/74[83] as amended or supplemented by subsequent regulations,[84] and covers beet and cane sugar, sugar beet, other sugars (except lactose, glucose or isoglucose[85]), sugar syrups, molasses and sugar wastes.[86]

Products produced and marketed within the Community

5—29   Before August 1 of each year a *target* and *intervention* price is fixed for white sugar, for a standard quality and for the area having the largest surplus. *Derived intervention* prices are fixed for other centres as well as for French overseas departments. A *minimum* price, established on the basis of the *intervention* price, is fixed for beet, and sugar manufacturers are obliged to pay that price.[87] Conditions of trading are to be fixed by the Council.[88] Special provision is made for cane.[89] Where surpluses occur in either beet or cane, storage costs for Community produced sugar and preferential sugar[90] are reimbursed at uniform flat rates by the Member States but sugar manufacturers are subjected to a production levy according to quantity and type of sugar produced;[91] under intervention buying denaturing premiums may

[79] Regulation 1418/76 as amended.
[80] See Regulation 1418/76, Articles 14 and 15 (as amended).
[81] Calculated in accordance with Article 16, *ibid*.
[82] *Ibid*. Article 11.
[83] O.J. 1974, L359/1.
[84] *Viz*. Regulation 2623/75, O.J. 1975, L268/1; Regulation 1487/76, O.J. 1976, L167/9; Regulation 1110/77, O.J. 1977, L134/1; Regulation 705/78, O.J.1978, L94/1; Regulation 1396/78, O.J. 1978, L170/1.
[85] See also para. 15–77 on structural aspects.
[86] Regulation 3330/74, Article 1.
[87] *Ibid*. Articles 4 and 5.
[88] *Ibid*. Article 6.
[89] *Ibid*. Articles 7 and 36.
[90] *Infra*, para. 15–77.
[91] Regulation 3330/74 (as amended), Article 8.

also be paid;[92] and production refunds may be paid for sugar used in the chemical industry.[93]

Trade with third countries

15—30   *Imports* are subject to the levy and certification system. *Threshold* prices are fixed for white sugar, raw sugar and molasses and as a general rule the levy will be the difference between that price and c.i.f. price. For other products the levy is calculated as a flat rate on the basis of the amount of the sucrose content (*i.e.* derived from the products mentioned), and the levy on white sugar. The levy calculated as above on raw sugar may be replaced by the levy applicable to white sugar in some cases.[94] *Exports* may benefit from refunds in the usual manner. In the event of supply difficulties, levies may be imposed on *exports* and *imports* may benefit from subsidies. This is backed up by a system of minimum stocks.

In respect of sugar from certain countries parties to the Lomé Convention ("preferential sugar") a derogation from the import levy system is provided for by Articles 43 to 47 of Regulation 3330/74 and texts referred to therein.[95]

A new regulation has been proposed[96] covering the market in sugar and isoglucose but has not yet been adopted.

Milk and Milk Products

15—31   Regulation 804/68[97] on the common organisation of this sector extends to milk, cream, cheese, butter, lactose sugar and syrup, and derived animal forage.

Products produced and marketed within the Community

15—32   Before August 1 of each year a *target* price for milk, and *intervention* prices for butter, skimmed milk powder and Grana padano and Parmigiano Reggiano cheeses must be fixed. Intervention takes the form of buying-in and subsidies for private storage. There are detailed rules relating to the disposal of products subjected to intervention, but if large surpluses build up, special measures to facilitate disposal may be taken.[98] Aid is available for skimmed milk intended for use as feedingstuffs or casein.

---

[92] *Ibid.* Article 9.
[93] *Ibid.* Article 9 (4).
[94] *Ibid.* Article 15.
[95] Agreement with India, O.J. 1975, L190/36; Cmnd 6273, EC 1975/143.
[96] O.J. 1980, C60.
[97] J.O. 1968, L148/10; O.J. (SE) 1968, 176. Subsequent substantial amendments: Regulation 419/74, O.J. 1974, L49/2; Regulation 465/75, O.J. 1975, L 52/8; Regulation 740/75, O.J. 1975, L74/1; Regulation 559/76; O.J. 1976, L67/9; Regulation 1038/78, O.J. 1978, L134/4; Regulation 1421/78, O.J. 1978, L171/12; Regulation 176/78, O.J. 1978, L204/6.
[98] Regulation 804/68, Article 12 as amended.

Trade with third countries

5—33   For all products except fresh milk and cream a levy is imposed on *imports*, equal to the difference between a *threshold* price fixed for a pilot product from each of various groups as designated[99] and the *free-at-frontier price* for those products.[1] Imports and exports are subject to licences and export refunds of the usual kind are available. Protocol 18 to the United Kingdom Act of Accession provided for exceptional arrangements for butter imported from New Zealand in the form of reduced levy quotas, continuing beyond the end of the transitional period,[2] and this was affirmed by the Dublin summit in 1975. Those arrangements were destined to terminate in December 1980 the amounts decreasing each year until then.

There are the usual provisions on safeguards and management committee procedures. Non-tariff barriers were a feature of protection of the milk and milk products market and this was preserved by Regulation 804/68 until the end of the transitional period. The normal prohibitions now apply.

Effect of the Community regulations in the United Kingdom

15—34   The marketing of milk in the United Kingdom is largely carried out through the milk-marketing board. The preservation of this organisation was alluded to by a Declaration annexed to the Final Act to the Treaty of Accession, which refers also to pigmeat and eggs. In 1978 a move to abolish the board was made by the Council, although opposed by the Commission. A ballot of United Kingdom farmers was held and the overwhelming majority voted to retain it. The board therefore has continued in existence[3] despite the advantage which it undoubtedly affords to United Kingdom farmers in marketing their products through the system of home delivery, which would, it was alleged, have come to an end but for the existence of the board.

Oils and Fats

15—35   The common organisation of the market in oils and fats is provided for by Regulation 136/66[4] as amended[5] and covers oil seeds, oleaginous fruit, vegetable oils and fats, and oils and fats of fish or marine mammals.

---

[99] *Ibid.* Article 4.
[1] *Ibid.* Article 14.
[2] Protocol 18, Article 5. New Zealand cheese ceased however to be given special treatment from the end of 1977. Extending Regulation: 1655/76, O.J. 1976, L185/1.
[3] See Twelfth General Report, point 321; O.J. 1978, L171/12.
[4] J.O. 1966, 3025; O.J. (SE) 1965–1966, 221.
[5] Regulations 1707/73, O.J. 1973, L175/5; 1419/78, O.J. 1978, L171/8; 1562/78, O.J. 1978, L185/1; 590/79 O.J. 1979, L78/1.

(a) Olive Oil
Products produced and marketed within the Community

15—36 A *production target*[6] price, together with an *intervention*[7] price must be fixed before August 1. A system of aid to producers is set up by Article 5 of Regulation 136/66, as amended by Regulation 1562/78,[8] and the *intervention* price must be equal to the *production target* price *less* that aid *plus* an amount allowing for market fluctuations and for the cost of transporting olive oil from production to consumption areas.[9] In addition a *representative market* price is fixed before October 1. If the *production target* price *less* the production aid exceeds the latter price, a consumption aid must be granted.[10]

Trade with third countries

15—37 Before October 1 each year, a *threshold*[11] price must be fixed, and a levy is imposed on imports of untreated olive oil equal to the difference between that price and the c.i.f. price (if the latter is lower). For derived products, a levy is imposed calculated on the basis of the amount of olive oil content plus an element to protect the processing industry.

If an open market c.i.f. price is not determinable because the offer price is lower than the world price and the latter does not determine the offer price a price determined on the offer price may be substituted for the c.i.f. price.[12] If the world market price is not determinable the import levy may be fixed by a tendering procedure,[13] subject to a minimum levy. For olives and other similar products, a derived levy is imposed. Some levies may be subject to advance fixing. Import and export licences are required for olive oil.[14] Exports benefit from refunds in the usual way, and the normal safeguard clauses exist.

(b) Other Products

15—38 Apart from olive oil Regulation 136/66 itself deals specifically only with the markets in colza and rape seed, and sunflower seed, the others being subject only to the normal incidence of the common customs tariff.

Products produced and marketed within the Community

15—39 At present single *target* prices for these products must be fixed

[6] *Supra*, paras. 15–15 to 15–17 on terminology.
[7] *Ibid.*
[8] Administered by producer groups. Formed in accordance with Regulation 1360/78 and Regulation 136/66, Article 20 (c) (as amended).
[9] Regulation 136/66 as amended, Article 8.
[10] *Ibid.* Article 11.
[11] *Supra*, paras. 15–15 to 15–17 on terminology.
[12] Regulation 136/66 as amended, Article 14.
[13] *Ibid.* Article 16.
[14] *Ibid.* Article 19.

annually together with a *basic intervention* price on dates, and in the case of the latter, for a centre, agreed through the management committee process. *Derived intervention* prices must be fixed for other intervention centres.[15] Where the *target* price is higher than the world market price, a subsidy may be granted to make up the difference between the two.[16] From the marketing year 1982/3 onwards, a target and basic intervention price is to be fixed for each species of oil seed. There will be no derived intervention prices but the intervention price will be fixed by reducing the target price to allow for market fluctuations and for a component taking into account the cost of transporting the seed from the production areas to the areas where it is used.[17]

Trade with third countries

15–40   These products benefit from export refunds in the usual way, but no import levy system operates, imports being subject only to the CCT. However, for these products there is a safeguard clause applying compensatory amounts to imports which have been subsidised abroad.[18]
Soya bean,[19] castor seed[20] and flaxseed[21] (linseed) also benefit from support in the form of a *guide* price system, under which a subsidy or aid will be granted to producers to make up the difference between that price and the world price if the latter is lower.

Beef and Veal

15–41   The market organisation set up for beef and veal[22] is designed in the first place to ensure that structural improvements are made in this sector.[23]

Products produced and marketed within the Community

15–42   Before August 1 of each year a *guide* price for adult bovine animals must be fixed. There is no *intervention* price as such, but intervention occurs on a *selective regional* and *quality* basis when the price for adult bovine animals falls below 98 per cent. of the *guide* price *and* the price of imports[24] of a defined quality in a

[15] *Ibid.* Article 22.
[16] *Ibid.* Article 27.
[17] Regulation 1385/80 O.J. 1980, L160/2. There are provisions for a smooth transition to the new single intervention price system.
[18] Reg. 136/66, Article 3 (6).
[19] Regulation 1900/74, O.J. 1974, L201/5.
[20] Regulation 2874/77, O.J. 1977, L332/1.
[21] Regulation 569/76, O.J. 1976, L67/29.
[22] Regulation 805/68, J.O. 1968, L148/24; O.J. (SE) 1968, 187 as amended by Regulation 425/77, O.J. 1977, L61/1 and Regulation 2916/79, O.J. 1979, L329/75; also, Regulation 568/76, O.J. 1976, L67/28.
[23] Regulation 805/68, Article 1. See *infra*, paras. 15–71 *et seq.*
[24] Calculated in accordance with Article 10 (2). Regulation 805/68, as amended.

particular region or regions falls below 93 per cent. of the *guide* price adjusted in accordance with Article 6 (1) (*b*).[25] Intervention may take place *generally* if the price of the Community product falls below 93 per cent. of the *guide* price.[26]

Trade with third countries

15—43   Protection is accorded both by imposition of the CCT duty and a levy based on a basic levy, amounting to the difference between the c.i.f. price and the *guide* price.[27] Specific basic levies may be imposed in some cases according to average import prices.[28] For fresh, salted or prepared meats, the basic levy for bovine animals is multiplied by a flat-rate coefficient;[29] for frozen meat a basic levy is calculated, amounting to the difference between the *guide* price multiplied by a coefficient and the free at Community frontier offer price plus CCT duty.[30] From the basic levy are then derived reduced levies in the case where the price of the domestic product exceeds the *guide* price, and increased levies where the price of the domestic product is below the *guide* price.[31] There are some exceptions to this.[32] Imports and exports are in general subject to licences, and exports benefit from export refunds in the usual way.[33]

Fruit and Vegetables

15—44 The market organisation for fruit and vegetables[34] covers most types of fruit and vegetables with the notable exception of potatoes.[35] Common quality standards are of primary importance here.[36] Only those goods conforming to the established standards may be marketed, imported, or exported. Derogations and additional categories are permissible in case of shortage.[37]

Products produced and marketed within the Community

15—45   Regulation 1035/72 provides for the setting up of producers' organisations; these may sell their members' produce and promote

[25] *Ibid*. Article 6 (1) (*a*) and (*b*).
[26] *Ibid*. Article 6 (2).
[27] *Ibid*. Article 10 (2).
[28] *Ibid*. Article 10 (3).
[29] *Ibid*. Article 10 (4).
[30] *Ibid*. Article 11.
[31] *Ibid*. Article 12.
[32] *Ibid*. Articles 13 and 14.
[33] *Ibid*. Articles 15 and 18.
[34] Regulations 1035/72, J.O. 1972, L118/1; O.J. 1972, 437 as amended by Regulation 2454/72, J.O. 1972, L266/1; O.J. 1972, (Nov) 60. Regulation 793/76, O.J. 1976, L93/1, Regulation 1034/77, O.J. 1977, L125/1, Regulation 1154/78, O.J. 1978, L144/5; Regulation 1315/80 O.J. 1980, L134/20.
[35] The products covered are described in the Annexes.
[36] Regulation 1035/72, Articles 2–12.
[37] *Ibid*. Article 5.

a better relationship between supply and demand. These organisations are entitled to fix *withdrawal* prices. This system is financed by an intervention fund, maintained by contributions assessed on quantities offered for sale[38]; but Member States may provide financial compensation in most cases if the *withdrawal* price is fixed in accordance with Article 18 of Regulation 1035/72 (as amended).

In addition, a *basic* price and a buying-in price for a limited number of products listed in Annex II of the Treaty are fixed annually before August 1. Where the price of these products falls below the buying-in price for three consecutive days, Member States must normally buy-in the products at the price, with adjustments, until such time as the market price remains above that price for three consecutive days. There are special arrangements for disposing of the products withdrawn or bought-in.

Trade with third countries

5—46   All imports are subject to CCT duty. In addition, for each product a *reference* price must be fixed annually.[39] *Entry* prices are then calculated according to Article 24, and if the latter remains at least 0.6 ECU below the reference price for two consecutive days, a countervailing duty is applied to make up the difference. Provision is made for export refunds and safeguards in the event of serious disturbances.

Live Trees, Plants, Flowers, Bulbs etc.[40]

5—47   There is no domestic price support system in this sector, and imports are subject only to CCT duty (except where the safeguard clause operates). The regulation concentrates on minimum quality standards, production methods and marketing, which of course may have a "protective" effect in themselves. *Exports* of some products may be subject to minimum prices.[41]

Raw Tobacco

Raw Tobacco produced and marketed within the EEC

5—48   Before August 1 each year a *norm* price must be fixed, together with an *intervention* price at 90 per cent of the former.[42] In addition premiums may be paid to first purchasers of leaf tobacco, these being fixed so as to "secure" the norm price.[43] *Derived intervention* prices may be applied to baled tobacco, but these are only applicable where a premium has not been paid.

[38] *Ibid.* Article 15.
[39] *Ibid.* Article 23.
[40] Regulation 234/68, J.O. 1968, L55/1; O.J. 1968, 26.
[41] *Ibid.* Article 7.
[42] Regulation 727/70, J.O. 1970, L94/1, O.J. 1970.
[43] *Ibid.* Articles 2 and 3.

Trade with third countries

15—49   Imports are subject only to CCT duty, but the usual safeguard clause is present. Exports benefit from refunds in the usual way.

Wine

15—50   The common organisation of the wine market is now provided for by Regulation 337/79[44] and covers wine, grape juice and must, wine grapes, wine vinegar and residues.

Wine, etc., produced and marketed within the Community

15—51   (a) **Table wine**. A *guide* price must be fixed annually to be valid from December 16 of that year to December 15 of the following year, for each type of table wine representative of Community production with a minimum alcoholic content. An intervention system is provided for through the use of an *activating* price,[45] which may not exceed 95 per cent. of the *guide* price. A system of *producer* or *representative* prices is also provided for.[46] Intervention then takes the form principally of private storage aid[47] for table wine and grape must, but intervention agencies may be required to undertake the storage themselves.[48] If the amount of wine stored exceeds 7 million hectolitres, preventive distillation may take place, which entails that wine be bought in by distillers at a price of at least 55 per cent. of the *guide* price. If the *representative* price remains below the *activating* price for more than three weeks, additional long term storage aid and distillation may be invoked.[49]

15—52   (b) **All wines**. Wines of superior quality are not supported by an internal price support mechanism. However, *all* Community wine production is subject to stringent rules concerning: (1) prodution and control of planting; and oenological processes (increase in alcoholic strength and level of sulphur dioxide, blending, coupage, types of grapes, etc.);[50] (2) release on to the market (system of accompanying documents),[51] and detailed provisions on labelling.[52]

Trade with third countries

15—53   *Imports* of wines and grape musts are subject to a licensing

---

[44] O.J. 1979, L54/1 amended by Regulation 2961/79, O.J. 1979, L336/9 and Regulations 453 and 459/80, O.J. 1980, L59/1.
[45] Regulation 337/79, Articles 2 and 3.
[46] *Ibid*. Article 4.
[47] *Ibid*. Articles 7 *et seq*.
[48] *Ibid*. Article 9.
[49] *Ibid*. Article 12.
[50] *Ibid*. Articles 32 *et seq. Ibid*. Articles 27 to 31.
[51] *Ibid*. Article 53.

system. *Exports* of all products may also be subject to licensing. *Reference* prices must be fixed annually before December 16 for red and white wine (based on the *guide* prices for representative red and white table wines), and for other products covered by the common organisation. If the free-at-frontier offer prices and customs duties are lower than the reference prices, a counter-vailing duty must be charged. In addition, a levy is charged on the added sugar content of some products, the levy applying in the same way as for processed fruit and vegetables.[53] Finally, imports of wines must conform with the provisions laid down in the country of production, must have a specified alcoholic strength and, if intended for direct human consumption, be accompanied by an analysis report.[54] They must also be accompanied by the required documents.

Exports benefit from refunds in the usual way where necessary.

Seeds[55]

15—54   Where seed producers are not getting a fair income because of the market situation in the Community, production aid may be granted, such aid being fixed every two years normally before August 1.[56] *Imports* may be subject to licensing.[57] For imports of hybrid maize, a reference price must be fixed before July 1 and counter-vailing duties will be levied if the free-at-frontier offer price plus CCT duty is lower than the reference price.[58] Seed multiplication contracts between seed undertakings in the Community and third country producers are, for some species, subject to registration.[59] The usual safeguard provisions exist.

Flax and Hemp

15—55   The regulation[60] setting up a marketing organisation for flax and hemp affords mechanisms designed to promote rational marketing of flax (production of which exceeds Community needs) and improvement in production techniques and quality. Support is given in the form of standard aids, payable on each hectare of flax or hemp produced. Additionally, aids are payable for private storage, granted to holders of fibres concluding storage contracts with intervention agencies in time of surplus. Imports are subject to the CCT and safeguard clauses.

---

[52] *Ibid.* Article 54 and Regulation 355/79, O.J. 1979, L54/99.
[53] *Ibid.* Article 19.
[54] *Ibid.* Articles 50, 51.
[55] Regulation 2358/71, J.O. 1971, L246/1; O.J. 1971, 894, as amended by Regulation 346/78, O.J. 1978, L165/1.
[56] Regulation 2358/71, Article 3 (1) as amended.
[57] *Ibid.* Article 4.
[58] *Ibid.* Article 6.
[59] *Ibid.* Article 3a.
[60] Regulation 1308/70, J.O. 1970, L146/1 O.J. 1970 (II) 411.

Fisheries

Products produced and marketed within the Community

15—56   The market in fishery products provided for by Regulation
100/76[61] includes fresh, frozen, smoked and preserved fish,
shellfish, offals and fishmeat. It aims, first, at setting up common
marketing standards for such products.[62]

Secondly the regulation provides for the setting up of producers'
organisations: these are empowered to market the products of
their members and to adopt rules aimed at the regularisation of
prices. In the latter case, they are permitted to fix *withdrawal
prices*[63] for most products below which they will not sell. The
withdrawal price must be fixed by the method stipulated by
Article 11 (4), in relation to a *guide*[64] price fixed before the
beginning of the fishing year, the principal consideration in this
calculation being the need to avoid structural surpluses. In such
cases the members are indemnified by an intervention fund which
is principally financed either by contributions from members or
by an equalisation scheme, and financial compensation is in turn
payable by Member States to the producers' organisation to cover
a proportion of such intervention costs, provided the withdrawal
price has been fixed in the way stipulated. In addition, there is an
intervention mechanism for fresh or chilled sardines and anchovies,
such that if the prices for those products fall below the intervention prices fixed for them for three successive market days,
they must be bought in by the relevant bodies. For some frozen
products there is a *guide* price system accompanied by private
storage aid in the event of the market price falling below it.
Special compensation is available for tunny, based on a Community
producer price.[65]

Trade with third countries

15—57   For most products covered by the regulation, *reference* prices[66]
must be established such that imports of any product whose
entry price falls below the reference price may in some cases be
suspended and in others subject to a countervailing duty.[67] The
calculation of the entry price varies according to the product.
Suspension is not applicable where the exporting state adopts
voluntary restraints.[68] These arrangements are backed up by a
safeguard provision.[69] For certain types of fish the CCT is

[61] O.J. 1976, L20/1.
[62] Regulation 100/76, Articles 2–4.
[63] *Ibid*. Article 8.
[64] *Supra*, paras. 15–15 to 15–17 on terminology.
[65] Regulation 100/76, Article 16.
[66] Regulation 100/76, Article 19.
[67] *Ibid*. Article 19 (4).
[68] *Ibid*. Article 19 (5).
[69] *Ibid*. Article 22.

suspended altogether, or for part of the year.[70] In other cases normal CCT rules apply.

Export refunds are payable in respect of economically important exports of all the products subject to the market organisation.[71]

Hops[72]

Hops produced and marketed within the Community

5—58   All of the products covered must be accompanied by a certificate indicating the place of production, the year(s) of harvesting and the variety or varieties. Only those hops meeting required quality standards will receive a certificate. Contracts between producers and buyers must be registered. Producer groups consisting "mainly of hop producers" are provided for, and these may set up common rules for various objectives listed in Article 7 of the regulation (as amended). Member States may grant aid to these groups.[73]

Production aid may be granted to producers to ensure them a fair income for specified regions and per hectare. A report must be made each year and where this indicates a risk of structural surpluses or disturbances in the market, aid may be limited to part of the area under hop cultivation only; furthermore appropriate measures may be taken by the Council to prevent market imbalance.[74]

Trade with third countries

5—59   Imports must meet the standard of the Community equivalents, which they will be deemed to do if accompanied by a recognised attestation by the authorities of the country of origin. They are subject to the CCT and safeguard provisions.

Dried Fodder

5—60   A Regulation had been introduced in 1974[75] setting up a common organisation of the market in dehydrated fodder following the somewhat exceptional circumstances of that year when the price of grain feedstuffs on the world market rose due to the sudden increase in fuel costs. This led to a demand for dehydrated fodder. This was replaced in 1978 by an organisation of the market in dried fodder[76] covering a somewhat wider range of products but differentiating between "green fodder" (specially cultivated) and

[70] *Ibid.* Article 17.
[71] *Ibid.* Article 23.
[72] Regulation 1696/71, J.O. 1971, L175/1, O.J. 1971, 634 as amended by Regulation 1170/77 O.J. 1977, L137/7.
[73] *Ibid.* Article 8 (as amended).
[74] *Ibid.* Article 16a.
[75] Regulation 1067/74 O.J. L120/2.
[76] Regulation 1117/78 O.J. 1978, L142/1 as amended by Regulations 2285/79 O.J. L263/1 and 114/80 O.J. 1980, L16/3.

dehydrated fodder (potatoes, flour and meal unfit for human consumption). For all products covered there is a flat-rate aid system (differing in respect of the latter products). For the former products there is a system of supplementary aid if the *guide* price, fixed at the beginning of each marketing year, is higher than the average world price. Imports are subject to the CCT.

Processed Products

15–61 (a) Products processed from fruit and vegetables[77]

Products produced and marketed within the Community

For most products no "internal" price support system exists. However, in the case of prunes, and various forms of tomato and peaches, Articles 3 a-c and 36 of Regulation 516/77 provide for production aid. Minimum prices may be set for the "raw material," and contracts between processors and producers must be based on those prices. Production aid then makes up the difference between the prices of the processed product and imported products.[78]

Trade with third countries

15–62 For imports both CCT duty and import levies are applicable. The levy is calculated as the difference between average *threshold* and c.i.f. prices for sugar,[79] subject to adjustments in certain cases.[80] In the case of tomato concentrates there is provision for a *minimum* price, to be fixed before April 1 of each year.[81] Furthermore, a *floor* price may be fixed if necessary. Export refunds are available, both on the basis of sugar content and generally.

(b) Other processed products

15–63 These are now covered by the regulations setting up the market in the basic products, although more detailed general rules on export refunds are laid down for them by Regulation 204/69.[82]

Residual Annex II Products

15–64 Before the end of the transitional period it was recognised that there would still be a certain number of products listed in Annex II without a common organisation. Accordingly Regulation 827/68[83] set up safeguard mechanisms analogous to those found in other

---

[77] Regulation 516/77, O.J. 1977, L73/1 as amended by Regulations 1152/78 O.J. 1978, L144/1, and 1314/80 O.J. 1980, L134/18.

[78] Regulation 516/77, Articles 3 (a) and (b) incorporated by Regulation 1152/78.

[79] See *Supra*, paras. 15–28 *et seq.*

[80] Regulation 516/77, Article 2.

[81] *Ibid.* Article 3.

[82] J.O. 1969, L29/1; O.J. (SE) 1969, 35.

[83] J.O. 1968, L151/16; O.J. 1968, 209.

organisations (serious disturbance). The products covered include, tea, coffee and dates.

Sheepmeat and Goatmeat

5- 65 The wrangle over the United Kingdom's budgetary contribution in 1979/80 was finally settled by a package of measures including *inter alia* agreement to the establishment of a common organisation of the market in live sheep and goats, sheepmeat (mutton and lamb), goatmeat, offals and fats.[84]

Products produced and marketed within the Community

5—66 For sheepmeat, a *basic* price and a *reference* price are to be fixed for five different regions, Italy, France, Germany and Denmark, Benelux, Ireland and the United Kingdom, each year.[85] A *representative* price is ascertained and if it falls below 90 per cent. of the *basic* price and is likely to remain so, intervention measures in the form of private storage aid may be taken.[86] For the latter half of the year (July-December) *intervention* measures *may* be taken for a requesting Member State if the *representative* price falls below 85 per cent. of the seasonally adjusted *basic* price (such price being fixed as a *seasonally adjusted intervention price*).[87] A seasonally adjusted *derived intervention* price is also fixed for regions having a surplus which is "traditionally sent to other regions," and intervention measures may then be taken if the price falls below these latter prices.[88] A premium is also to be granted for sheepmeat producers to take into account the loss of income resulting from the establishment of the common organisation, to be calculated at the beginning of each marketing year but revised so as to reflect the actual loss of income.[89] Where intervention buying occurs, account should be taken of the effect of setting a ceiling to the premium equal to the difference between the *reference* price and the *seasonally adjusted intervention* price.[90] Under Article 9, for regions where intervention measures are *not* applied, the Member States may pay a *slaughter premium* for sheep when the prices recorded on the representative markets of the Member State(s) concerned fall below 85 per cent. of the basic price, but that premium is claimed back if the resultant sheepmeat leaves the territory of the Member State concerned.

5—67 It appears that this scheme thus allows two different support

[84] Regulation 1837/80, O.J. 1980, L183/1. Implementing rules are contained in a series of regulations in O.J. 1980, L275 and 276.
[85] *Ibid.* Article 3.
[86] Articles 7 (1) and 6.
[87] Article 7 (2).
[88] Article 7 (3).
[89] Article 5.
[90] Article 5 (3).

systems to coexist. On the one hand, an intervention scheme causing prices not to fall below a minimum. On the other hand, a subsidy system (the slaughter premium) which allows prices to find their natural level. The two systems coexist because the latter premium is repayable in the event of export from the "region" in question, having the effect of making it probably uneconomical to export except where the price is significantly above the intervention level throughout the regions concerned.

There are no intervention procedures for other products covered by the regulation but the latter does provide for general measures aimed at improving the structure and functioning of the market.[91]

Trade with third countries

15—68 The CCT applies to goatmeat and offals whilst a levy system is introduced for sheepmeat, with the levy being equal to the difference between the free-at-frontier offer price and the *basic price*,[92] except where a rate of duty has been bound under GATT.[92a] Export refunds are payable in the normal way, and both imports and exports are subject to licensing.

Since the regulation will affect existing schemes in Member States for support of sheep farmers, the Commission is empowered to adopt transitional measures to facilitate the introduction of the regulation scheme.[93] The Council is to review the system and make appropriate amendments in 1984, if necessary. If however expenditure in this sector exceeds the estimates, the examination must be brought forward.[94]

Monetary Compensatory Amounts

15—69 Agricultural prices were originally and still are fixed in an artificial unit of account, initially equal to 0.88 mgs. of fine gold (initially also equal to one U.S. Dollar). This system worked adequately until the end of the 1960s, when parity changes in national currencies affected the prices obtained whether by producers, or, ultimately, by importers or exporters.

In order to smooth out these currency fluctuations and ensure uniformity of prices, a system of Monetary Compensatory Amounts was introduced, financed out of the EAGGF. This was to have been a temporary system, but has now become institutionalised. However, the EMS[95] participants entered into a gentleman's agreement in March 1979 to try and reduce MCAs and avoid creating new ones. Some practical success has been recorded.[96]

---

[91] Article 2.   [92] Article 12.
[92a] See Appendix 3 for VRAs applicable in this sector.
[93] Article 33.
[94] Article 34.
[95] *Infra*, para. 22–24.
[96] W.Q. 693/79, O.J. 1979, C316/42 and W.Q. 694/79, O.J. 1980, C206/1.

MCAs are payable on import into and export from Member States. They apply to intra-Community trade as well as to trade with third countries.[97] MCAs have been recognised by the Court as necessary if the objectives of Article 39 of the Treaty are to be fulfilled.[98] Calculation of MCAs is now based on the European Currency Unit (ECU).[99]

5—70   Initially Regulation 974/71,[1] the basic regulation, was based on Article 103, though later regulations consolidating the system were adopted (legally, following the *Balkan* case) under Article 43 of the Treaty. Their validity depends on the need to counteract disturbances in intervention-based organisations[2] and for this reason they have legitimately been applied on occasion not only to the products covered by a common market organisation but also to the processed products derived from them where MCAs on the former product have an incidence on the price of the latter.[3] The various changes in methods of calculation, the frequent changes in the amounts themselves and the complication of applying them to specific products (some generalisations have to be made) have led to a great deal of litigation, particularly claims for damages under Articles 178 and 215. Although the actual scheme of MCAs has continually been upheld by the Court, occasional measures have been struck down,[4] and where traders have relied on the grant of MCAs as a means of avoiding loss on currency exchange, their sudden abolition in a given sector may permit the recovery of damages under Article 215.[5] However because they are designed to compensate for disturbances, it may be necessary on occasion to fix them retroactively.[6] The worst of these difficulties may prove to have been overcome by new arrangements for discretionary exemption by Member States from new MCAs where the new MCA is introduced as a result of currency movements and the trader can show he has a firmly concluded contract under the old basis.[7]

[97] The main instruments governing MCAs are Regulations 974/71, J.O. 1971, L 106/1, as amended, and Regulation 1013/71, J.O. 1971, L 110/8, as amended. Detailed rules for the calculation of MCAs are contained in Regulation 1380/75, O.J. 1975, L139/37. Advance fixing arrangements are provided for in Reg. 243/78, L37/5, and Reg. 1516/78, O.J. 1978, L178/63.
[98] Case 5/73 *Balkan Import—Export* v. *HZA Berlin—Packhof* [1973] E.C.R. 1091. See also Case 38/79 *Nordmark* v. *HZA Jonas* [1980] E.C.R. 643 on the relationship and relative characteristics of MCAs and export refunds.
[99] See Regs. 652/79, O.J. 1979, L84/1 and 706/79, O.J. 1979, L89/3, and Regulation 3308/80 O.J. 1980, L345/1.
[1] *Supra,* note 97.
[2] See Cases 67–85/75 *Lesieur Cotelle et Associés SA et al* v. *Commission* [1976] E.C.R. 391.
[3] See, *e.g.* Case 11/78 *Italian Republic* v. *Commission* [1979] E.C.R. 1527.
[4] Case 8/78 *Milac* v. *HZA Freiburg* [1978] E.C.R. 1721.
[5] Case 74/74 *CNTA* v. *Commission* [1975] E.C.R. 533.
[6] Case 98/78 *Racke* v. *HZA Mainz* [1979] E.C.R. 69.
[7] Reg. 926/80, O.J. 1980, L99/15.

Structural Policy

15--71   A policy to improve the structure of agriculture in the Community has always been an integral part of the common policy, although its achievements bear little comparison with the achievements in the organisation of the markets. Discussion of the policy may be arranged under three heads - general measures; measures related to particular products; and measures related to particular areas.

(a) General policy

15—72   Initially, positive Community action in this area was limited to the use of the guidance section of the European Agricultural Guidance and Guarantee Fund in reimbursing to national governments a proportion of the cost of projects of value to the Community (projects for adaptation and improvement of conditions of probation, of production itself and of marketing techniques and outlets).[8] Aid is still granted under the regulation, but the system was totally inadequate if any thoroughgoing reform of Community agriculture was to be undertaken, and its shortcomings prompted the Commissioner responsible for agriculture in 1968 - Sicco Mansholt - to propose a plan for the radical reform of agriculture which aimed at tackling the structural problems (chiefly too many small farms and the age of farmers). The most controversial aspects of the plan involved reorganising the markets to cut out surpluses, and reducing the surface area given over to farming by some 5 million hectares.

15--73   The plan led to the adoption in 1972 of three directives which implemented its less controversial aspects. Directive 72/159[9] aims at the modernisation of farms and its designed particularly to enable low-income farmers to achieve a reasonable income through a six year development programme. Assistance is provided for various kinds of improvements such as machinery co-operatives and irrigation schemes, the Community contributing 25 per cent. of the cost, the rest being provided by the Member States. This directive also gives the modernising farmer a priority on acquisition of land given up pursuant to the second directive, 72/160,[10] which provides an incentive to farmers aged between 55 and 65 to give up farming by permitting annual or lump sum payments. Again the Community will normally provide 25 per cent of the cost but up to 65 per cent. where the farming population is higher

---

[8] Regulation 17/64, J.O. 1964, 586.
[9] J.O, 1972, L96/1, O.J. 1972 (II) 324 as amended by Directive 78/1017, O.J. 1978, L349/32.
[10] J.O. 1972, L96/9, O.J. 1972, (II) 332 as amended by Directive 78/1017, O.J. 1978, L349/32.

and GDP lower than the Community average. Directive 72/161[11] attempts to create and improve information services for farmers and initially also created funds for vocational training, a function now largely taken over by the Social Fund.[12]

Directives have since been adopted to adapt the above to the regional policy[13] and (in that connection also) on farming in mountainous and less favoured areas.[14] This latter sets up a scheme for direct payments related to the size of the farm, again with a 25 per cent Community participation.

Other general measures have included a common measure in respect of forestry in Mediterranean zones, adopted in February 1979,[15] mechanisms for acquiring information about national policies, and on farming in the Community (the farm accountancy data base, now at 28,000 holdings). An advisory committee on agricultural structures was set up in 1962.[16] 1978 saw the adoption of a long-awaited regulation on producers' groups.[17]

(b) Structural measures in relation to particular products

15–75 The measures undertaken here were or are necessary corollaries to the organisations of the market, in particular where large structural surpluses have occurred due to the intervention mechanisms.

A general measure was adopted in 1977 to improve the conditions under which products are processed and marketed, which encourages Member States to propose plans for approval by the Commission.[18]

Furthermore the Commission has also made sweeping proposals for reducing structural surpluses in many areas which would entail transfer of the cost of disposing of such surpluses to the producers. It was estimated at the time of proposal that such measures could save 1000 million EUA per year.

Diary products

15–76 As early as 1964 the Community introduced incentives for the conversion of diary herds in order to try and reduce the number of cows producing milk and thereby a chronic surplus of production, particularly in small uneconomic farms.[19] This was varied in 1973

---

[11] J.O. 1972, L96/15 O.J. 1972, (II) 339 as amended by Directive 78/1017, O.J. 1978, L349/32.
[12] See generally Chapter 25, *infra*.
[13] Directive 73/440, O.J. 1973, L356/85.
[14] Directive 75/268–276, O.J. 1975, L728/1.
[15] O.J. 1979, L381.
[16] Decision of December 4, 1962, J.O. 1962, 2892.
[17] Reg. 1360/78, O.J. L166/1; implementing Regs. 2083 & 4/80, O.J. 1980, L203/5 and 9.
[18] Regulation L355/75, O.J. 1977, L51/1, 133.6 MECU appropriated in 1979.
[19] Regulation 17/64, J.O. 1964, 34.

with the adoption of a premium system, extended also to the non-marketing of milk.[20] A system of payments for slaughtered cows was created in 1969[21] but terminated in 1971.[22] In May 1977 a co-responsibility levy was introduced on milk production, initially for a period of two years but still in force in an amended form. Measures were also taken towards expanding the milk market[23] at the same time.

Sugar

15—77   The organisation of the sugar market in its final stage would, if introduced immediately, have caused great difficulties because of the regional disparities between producers. Furthermore, the importance of sugar for the developing world meant that politically there could not be a protective system as for instance for grain. A quota system was therefore introduced[24] which though intended to be temporary, has been renewed several times.

The system is founded on a basic quota ('A' quota), fixed by Member States for each factory (the Member States having received a block quota), together with a maximum quota ('B' quota) fixed at 35 per cent. of the basic quota. Sugar produced up to the basic quota qualifies for full market support. Any sugar produced beyond that and up to the maximum quota is subject to a production levy of 30 per cent. Sugar produced outside the quota ('C' quota) does not qualify for any support and indeed its sale may be forbidden. The object of course is to reduce surplus sugar within the Community. The measures apply to both white sugar and beet.

Protocol 17 to the 1972 Act of Accession made special provision for sugar imported under the Commonwealth Sugar Agreement but these arrangements were due to expire in 1975 and were replaced by the Lomé Convention, under which comprehensive arrangements govern the import of sugar from the ACP countries. These arrangements have beeen continued by the new Lomé Convention.[25]

Fruit and vegetables

15—78   Reorganisation measures were initially provided for in 1969[26] and were insufficient to reduce in particular a surplus of certain varieties of apples and pears. Thus, grubbing premiums were

[20] Regulation 1353/73, O.J. L141/18, Regulation 1078/77, O.J. 1977, L131/1 as amended by Regulation 1365/80, O.J. 1980 L140/18.
[21] Regulation 1975/69, J.O. 1969, L252/1.
[22] Regulation 1290/71, J.O. 1971, L137/1.
[23] Regulation 1079/77 O.J. 1977, L131/6; See also Regulation 1364/80, O.J. 1980, L140/16.
[24] Regulation 1009/67, J.O. 308/1, O.J. 1967, 304, renewed with the introduction of Regulation 3330/74, *supra*, para. 15–28.
[25] *Infra*, para. 31–21.
[26] See Regulation 2517/69, J.O. L318/15.

subsequently offered from time to time to owners of apple, pear and peach orchards. The last scheme relating to these premiums was laid down by Regulation 794/76[27] which provided for payment of lump-sum premiums on the grubbing of orchards together with an undertaking not to replant for five years.

Fisheries

15—79   The fishing industry in the original Member States had always been a weak one, and measures were adopted prior to the Accession of new Member States in 1973 regarding the co-ordination of national structural policy,[28] the formation of a Standing Committee for the Fishing Industry, and the formation of producer groups (which play an important role in the marketing of fish).[29] Common measures on restructuring the industry have so far been adopted only with regard to the salt-cod sector[30] where the aim is to convert the fleet to other uses. Other measures have been held up because of the difficulties encountered in reconciling the interests of the first three new Member States, notably with regard to the conservation of resources.[31]

15—80   Article 102 of the 1972 Act of Accession provided that a common policy for the conservation of resources should be adopted from the sixth year following Accession, *i.e.* from the end of 1978 onwards.[32] Although the need for conservation and the principle of common access to national fishing waters are both recognised in the basic regulation and in Articles 100 to 102 of the Act of Accession and have been reinforced by decisions of the Court,[33] it has not been possible to arrive at common rules except in limited areas. It has therefore been necessary to adopt interim measures allowing Member States to maintain or introduce controls applicablé to their own fishing waters.[34] The right to introduce national

[27] O.J. 1976, L93/3.
[28] Regulation 2141/70, J.O. 1970, L236/1, O.J. 1970, (III) 703 replaced by Regulation 100/76, O.J. 1976, L20/1.
[29] Regulation 2142/70, J.O. 1970 L236/5 O.J. 1970, (III) 707 replaced by Regulation 101/76, O.J. 1976, L20/9.
[30] Regulation 2722/72 J.O. 1972, L291/30 and Regulation 645/74, O.J. 1974, L78/19.
[31] Interim Aid Measures were however provided for: Regulation 1852/78, O.J. 1978, L211/30.
[32] As interpreted in Cases 185–204/78 *Van Dam* [1979] E.C.R. 2345.
[33] Notably Case 61/77 *Commission* v. *Ireland* [1978] E.C.R. 417; Interim measures ordered [1979] E.C.R. 937, 1411.
[34] Following on from Regulation 100/76, *supra,* note 28 and Articles 100 and 101 of the 1972 Act of Accession: Hague Resolution of October 30, 1976, Annex VI (set out and discussed in Cases 61/77 *Commission* v. *Ireland* [1978] E.C.R. 417, 444 and 141/78 *France* v. *UK* [1979] E.C.R. 2923. See also Commissioner Gundelach's statement of July 6, 1977, in the European Parliament explaining the Hague arrangements, *Debates,* pp. 251, 252). Pending the adoption of an overall common fisheries policy these temporary arrangements are maintained by so-called roll-forward decisions: see 80/993, O.J. 1980, L298/38 and Regulation 2527/80, O.J. 1980 L258/1, extended by Regulation 3458/80, O.J. 1980 L360/20.

measures in the absence of Community rules has been upheld by the Court.[35] Measures must, however, be notified to the Commission.[36]

15–81   The Hague Resolution of October 30, 1976,[37] whereby the Member States extended the limits of their fishing zones to 200 miles from January 1, 1977, focused attention on the international aspects of the fisheries policy; indeed the Court had already paved the way by holding that from the deadline set in Article 102 of the Act of Accession onwards there should be a common external policy in this field, even if no common internal measures had been taken.[38] In the interim Member States retain certain transitional powers.[39] At the Community level certain steps have already been taken. In 1978 the Community entered into the Convention on Future Multilateral Co-operation in the Northwest Atlantic Fisheries.[40] Agreements have been negotiated with several countries on reciprocal access to waters, but for the most part entry into force has been delayed for the reasons which have blocked the domestic policy. Interim unilateral arrangements have been introduced for some of these countries. Under Community regulations there are arrangements for non-reciprocal access for Community vessels to the waters of still other third countries.[41] Any applicable bilateral arrangements concluded by Member States continue until over-taken by Community arrangements.

The Council has recognised the importance of establishing a common fisheries policy, and of the need to proceed towards the setting of quotas in particular.[42]

(c) Structural measures in relation to particular regions

15–82   With the creation of the Regional Development Fund and the

---

[35] Cases 3, 4 and 6/76 *Kramer et al* [1976] E.C.R. 1279: 61/77 *supra,* note 34; 185–204/78, *supra,* note 32; 32/79 *Commission* v. *United Kingdom* [1981] 1 C.M.L.R. 219; 804/79 *Commission* v. *UK* (May 5, 1981); 812/79 *A.G* v. *Burgoa* (October 14, 1980).

[36] Under Annex VI of the Hague Resolution *supra* note 34 and see also Case 141/78 *France* v. *UK, supra* note 34, and 32/79 *Commission* v. *UK* (July 10, 1980).

[37] Text of this part in Bull EC 10–1976, point 1503. See also note 34, *supra.*

[38] Cases 3, 4 and 6/76 *Kramer et al supra,* note 35.

[39] *Ibid.* and Case 141/78 *supra,* note 36.

[40] Regulation 3179/78, O.J. 1978, L378/1, amended by Regulation 653/80, O.J. 1980, L74/1 and see Regulation 2622/79, O.J. 1979, L303/1 on certain technical measures (net sizes) concerning conservation within the area regulated by the North Atlantic Fisheries Organisation. Also Regulations 2165/80, O.J. 1980, L212/1 on catch quotas for Community vessels fishing in the Regulatory area defined by the Convention and 2166/80, O.J. 1980, L212/6 on conservation of the West Greenland coast.

[41] For a comprehensive survey of these and other aspects see R. Churchill "Revision of the EEC's Common Fisheries Policy," 1980 E.L.R. 1 and 95. See the survey of agreements *infra* and Appendix 3 for agreements.

[42] Declaration of May 30, 1980, C158/2. The overall policy was to have been in place by January 1, 1981—an objective not in fact attained: Statement on Fisheries Ministers' Meeting (Mr. Younger) HC Deb. 18 Dec. 1980, col. 857.

move towards a regional policy, the Council has felt able to begin adopting specific structural measures in agriculture for disadvantaged regions. These have included irrigation and drainage schemes in Ireland and Italy, flood protection in the Herault Valley (France) and an advisory service for farmers in Italy.[43] In particular the Council adopted the regulation on producer groups, which is designed to effect improvements in agriculture in France, Italy and southern Belgium.[44] In 1979 the Council adopted directives on drainage on both sides of the Ulster border and on the conversion of wine-growing areas in France and a regulation on forestry in certain Mediterranean zones of the Community.[45]

III The European Agricultural Guidance and Guarantee Fund

15—83 Article 40 (4) of the Treaty provides for the setting up of one or more agricultural guidance and guarantee funds; in fact only one - known as EAGGF - the European Agricultural Guidance and Guarantee Fund - was set up, covering all sectors subject to market organisation.[46] The Fund is not an organ or institution, but a part of the Community budget.[47] It was divided into a guarantee section (operating the support system) and a guidance system (operating the structural policy) by Regulation 17/64, which sets out many of the functions. At first, the Fund paid one-sixth of the CAP costs, but it now bears the whole cost of the interventions on the market under its guarantee section. Under the guidance section it bears a proportion of costs.[48] The final total Community expenditure in the agricultural sector alone in 1980 is expected to have exceeded 11,000 Million ECU; far and away the largest slice of the Community budget and a growing source of dissatisfaction.

Expenditure

15—84 The definitive regime governing the use of the EAGGF is set out in Regulation 729/70.[49] The main characteristic of this is that

---

[43] See 12th General Report (1978) Point 334.
[44] *Supra*, note 17.
[45] 13th Annual Report (1979) p. 146
[46] Regulations 25/62, J.O. 1962, 991; O.J. 1959–62, 126 and 17/64, J.O. 1964, 586; O.J. 1963–64, 103.
[47] Article 1 of Regulation 25/62 and Regulation 729/70 J.O. 1970, L94/13. On the budget see *supra*, paras. 3–69 *et seq.*
[48] Regulations 645/74, O.J. 1974, L78/19.
[49] J.O. 1970, L94/19, see also Regulation 380/78, O.J. 1978, L56/1 and Regulation 1883/78, O.J. 1978, L216/1 on general rules for the financing of intervention by the EAGGF. For rules on units of account, *etc.,* see generally *supra* para. 3–76 and Reg. 129/62, J.O. 1962, 2553; O.J.1958–62, 274; Reg. 653/68, J.O. 1968, L123/4, O.J. 1968, 121; Reg. 1134/68, J.O. 1968, L188/1, O.J. 1968, 34 (value of unit of account and adjustment mechanism); Reg. 878/77, O.J. 1977, L106/27 (exchange rates to be applied in agriculture); Reg. 129/78, O.J. 1978, L20/16 (exchange rates to be applied for the purposes of the structures policy); Reg. 652/79, O.J. 1979, L84/1 and Reg. 706/79, O.J. 1979, L89/3 (impact of the EMS on the CAP: *i.e.* application of the ECU).

the fund actually *advances* sums to Member States to cover their expenditure in carrying out the common policy, unlike the initial system which merely reimbursed them. Tight controls can thus be exercised over the way the money is employed, and the departments or agencies making payments must be designated to the Commission. Moreover, it means that the amount to be spent on agriculture is determined as part of the Community budget, in advance. This considerably strengthens the ability of the Community institutions, in particular the Assembly, to determine the direction of agricultural policy by fixing limits to expenditure and types of expenditure. However, the growing problem of surplus and of MCAs meant that over the years increasing amounts have had to be provided by supplementary budgets.

Responsibility for agricultural disbursements to the producer lies with the national authorities. If they are responsible for incorrect execution of the Community rules they bear the financial consequences.[50] By the same token it is to national authorities that traders must look for recovery of sums charged on the basis of Community regulations which have been declared invalid. Recovery is governed by national law, subject only to the Community principles of non-discrimination and that national measures must not impair the operation of Community rules.[51]

Community rules have been adopted on supply of information to keep a check on irregularities and to recover sums wrongly paid;[52] on scrutiny of transactions;[53] and on mutual assistance for the recovery of claims.[54] All these measures are designed to ease the workings of the EAGGF and combat fraud and irregularities.

Arrangements for Greek Accession

15–85   Title IV of the Act of Accession applies to agriculture.

Application of the common agricultural policy in Greece

15–86   *Article 57* provides that Greece should adopt the common agricultural policy from January 1, 1981. However, this general rule is subject to modifications set out in the ensuing articles.

Article 58 provides for the initial fixing of prices "at a level which allows producers . . . to obtain market prices equivalent to those obtained . . . under the previous national system applied in Greece." If those prices are different from Community prices,

[50] Case 11/76 *Netherlands* v. *Commission* [1979] E.C.R. 245; Cases 15 and 16/76 *France* v. *Commission* [1976] E.C.R. 321; 18/76 *Germany* v. *Commission* [1979] E.C.R. 343.
[51] Case 130/79 *Express Diary Foods* v. *Intervention Board for Agricultural Produce* [1980] E.C.R. 1887.
[52] Reg. 283/72, J.O. 1972, L36/1; O.J. 1972, 90.
[53] Dir. 77/435, O.J. 1977, L172/17.
[54] Dirs. 76/308, J.O. 1976, L73/18; 77/794, O.J. 1977, L333/11.

then they are to be progressively aligned with the latter in five stages.[5 5]

Article 60 allows for immediate application of common prices if the difference between these and Greek prices is minimal.

The prices are reduced or increased successively by a fifth, a quarter, a third and a half of the difference between the Greek price and the common price prevailing before each move before the next alignment. For tomatoes and peaches, and products processed therefrom, seven stages are envisaged before equalisation.

Articles 58 and 59 only apply where so specified by Chapter 2 of Title IV in respect of the individual markets. There is provision for derogation by Council decision in the interests of a smooth transition.

15—87   Under *Article 68* Community aids are to be introduced into Greece only where national aids had previously been applied and where so specified for the individual markets as set out in Chapter 2. Where aid is applicable it should match the level of national aid but cannot exceed the comparable Community level at the date of Accession. These aids are then progressively aligned in accordance with the timetable set out in paragraph 2 (*b*) of Article 68.

Article 69 provides for the continuation of *national* aids but requires the Council to adopt a timetable for their progressive abolition.

Article 70 lays down that for dried figs, dried grapes and olives other than for the production of oil, national income-support measures may be retained by Greece for varying periods not exceeding the transitional period.

15—88   Finally, *Article 73* provides that measures may in addition be adopted by the Council to apply until January 31, 1982, to facilitate the introduction of the common agricultural policy.

The sectors to which in general the complete "transitional package" applies, *i.e.* Articles 58, 59 and 61 are: oils and fats; milk and milk products; beef and veal; sugar; cereals; pigmeat; eggs and poultrymeat; rice; and wine.

Article 58 alone applies in respect of tobacco. Article 59 applies to fruit and vegetables (with special compensatory arrangements replacing those of Article 61[5 6]) and to dried fodder, but in both cases the initial price is calculated at variance with the provisions of Article 58. Article 68 applies to flax and hemp, hops and seeds.

---

[55] Arts. 59(1) and (3) of the Act.
[56] *Infra.*

Trade between Greece and the Community as constituted on Accession

15—89 The progressive reduction of customs duties provided for in Article 25[57] applies where duties under the CCT and under the Greek customs tariff have been charged.[58] For many agricultural products imported into the EEC and subject to a common organisation involving levies on goods from third countries, the progressive reductions will therefore not apply, any Greek duties previously applied being replaced immediately by compensatory amounts (MCAs) discussed below. Products falling within the common organisation of the market of beef and veal are subject to a 20 per cent. reduction for each of the five marketing years following Accession.[59] Both parties may reduce their duties more quickly.[60]

Levies on imports into the EEC from Greece and vice versa where applied at present will be replaced by monetary compensatory amounts. These MCAs are to be applied only where there is a difference in the price levels fixed for the Greek market and the common price[61] and therefore only where specifically implemented in respect of markets where there is to be a progressive alignment of prices as described above.

Greece is bound in other respects to observe the general rules on the free movement of goods where a common organisation of the market already exists (*i.e.* for most products). Where no organisation yet exists the above rules need not be applied if the measures in question form part of a national market organisation, but these measures must be abolished when a common organisation is formed and in any event not later than December 31, 1985.[62]

Trade between Greece and third countries

15—90 The CCT nomenclature is to be applied to products in Annex II of the EEC Treaty from January 1, 1981.

In respect of products which, when imported into the Community as constituted at Accession are subject to Customs duties, Greece is to reduce its duties to align with the CCT in accordance with Article 31[63] except for beef and veal, fruit and vegetables, fish, and wine where the CCT is to apply immediately as from January 1, 1981.[64]

In respect of products subject to the levy system Greece must also apply the levy applied by the rest of the Community in trade

[57] *Supra,* para. 13–35.
[58] Art. 64 of the Act.
[59] *Ibid.*
[60] *Ibid.*
[61] Art. 61 of the Act.
[62] Art. 65 (2).
[63] *Supra,* para. 13–35; by virtue of Articles 64 (2) (*a*).
[64] Art. 64 (2) (*b*).

with third countries, but increase or reduce it as the case may be by the MCA applicable to trade between Greece and the Community as constituted before Accession.[65] The same applies *mutatis mutandis* to export refunds.

[65] Art. 61.

Chapter 16

THE WORKER AND THE COMMUNITY

16–01 The Treaty of Rome deals with labour and related topics at two separate points: in Articles 48 to 51 in Part Two, Title III - "Free Movement of Persons, Services and Capital" under the chapter heading "Workers" and in Articles 117 to 128 in Part Three, Title III - "Social Policy." The division is somewhat arbitary, but broadly Articles 48 to 51 lay down the principles of free movement of workers and provisions for the social security of Community migrant workers, while Articles 117 to 128 implement or list various social policy or labour law objectives and provide for the establishment of a European Social Fund, and a European policy of vocational training and guidance. In this respect, the division between the achievement of a "common market" in labour, and the policy to be followed within that market is made clear by the Treaty itself. The "social policy" is dealt with at a later point.

16–02 The chapter "Workers" relates only to persons who are employed by others and in principle not to those who are self-employed, the latter being provided for under the chapter heading "Right of Establishment" (Articles 52 to 58). The free movement of persons, more specifically of workers, is one of the "four freedoms" of the European Economic Community. In an economic unit such as the Community and in an economically and technologically changing society, it is essential to maximise the use of labour, and thus workers must be able to move wherever they are most needed.

Although the economic considerations may originally have inspired the provisions on the free movement of workers, it is clear that these provisions now find a justification in the objective expressed in the preamble, of creating ever closer relations between the peoples of the Member States. The extension of the rights under social security legislation to holidaymakers illustrates this general tendency.

16–03 The general scope of Articles 48 to 51 is more comprehensive than the isolated provisions of Article 69 of the ECSC Treaty and Article 96 of the Euratom Treaty which deal only with specialised categories of workers from the relevant industries.

Thus, Article 69 of the ECSC Treaty provides for free movement of workers with "recognised qualifications in a coalmining or steel-making occupation." For its implementation, the Member States were to draw up common definitions of skilled trades and qualifications (Article 69 (2)). The list which was eventually drawn up did not embrace the majority of workers in these industries.

Article 96 of the Euratom Treaty lays down that the Member States shall abolish all restrictions based on nationality which affect the right of nationals of any Member State to take skilled employment in the field of nuclear energy. Like Article 69 of the ECSC Treaty, this article is of narrow application. The directive of March 5, 1962,[1] issued in application of Article 96, lists occupations requiring considerable qualifications as eligible for free movement. It would appear that for unqualified and unskilled workers in industries covered by the ECSC and Euratom Treaties, the general provisions of Articles 48 to 51 of the EEC Treaty apply.

Article 232 of the EEC Treaty states that the provisions of that Treaty shall not affect those of the ECSC Treaty, nor shall they derogate from those of the Euratom Treaty; however, the EEC provisions regarding free movement of workers are supplementary to the other Treaties and deal with persons not otherwise covered by the sectoral Treaties.[2]

Article 48

16–04   Article 48 (1) EEC provides that freedom of movement for workers was to be secured within the Community by the end of the original transitional period at the latest. The Article was declared directly applicable in Case 167/73 *Commission* v. *France.*[3] Article 48 (2) defines the freedom of movement as entailing the abolition of any kind of discrimination[4] based on nationality between workers of Member States as regards employment, renumeration and other conditions of employment.

"Workers"

16–05   No definition is given of this term by the Treaty. The Court has held that it must have a Community meaning and cannot be the subject of differing interpretations by the Member States.[5] Regulation 1612/68,[6] Article 1, set out below, para. 16-20, which may act at least as a guide to the meaning of the Treaty provision, purports to cover "nationals" of the Member States who are *"employed persons."* The definition contained in the basic social

---

[1] J.O. 1962, 1650.

[2] Regulations 1612/68, J.O. 1968, L251/2, O.J. 1968 475 Article 42.

[3] [1974] E.C.R. 359 (The *French Merchant Seamen* case). See also Case 41/74 *Van Duyn* v. *Home Office* [1974] E.C.R. 1337 (directly applicable in spite of public policy provision).

[4] See also Article 7, discussed *supra,* para. 12–08.

[5] Cases 75/63 *Hoekstra (née Unger)* v. *BBDA* [1964] E.C.R. 177; 17/76 *Brack* v. *Insurance Commissioner* [1976] E.C.R. 1429; 99/80, *Galinsky* v. *Insurance Officer.*

[6] *Supra,* note 2.

security regulation[7] adopted under Article 51 is much more detailed and is probably broader than the scope of Article 48 since it purports to cover *inter alia* certain non-nationals such as stateless persons and refugees; and although the Treaty does not specify "EEC" nationality it seems clear that Article 48 was intended only to protect nationals. Further there is a Declaration of the Representatives of the Member States on special treatment for refugees and stateless persons.[8] The question also arises as to whether unemployed persons, the handicapped, and retired persons are "workers" within Article 48. The implementing legislation in fact makes provision for all these cases. It also appears to cover the ambiguous case of the armed forces.

16—06   In *R. v. Secchi*[9] an English magistrate on being informed that the defendant had "lived the life of an itinerant vagrant . . . and that the only work he has done has been of the casual work of the washing-up-in-restaurants variety" held that the defendant was not a "worker" for the purposes of Article 48.

A person who plays for a professional sports team enjoys the benefits of Article 48[10] but an amateur player does not. However the Commission has recently made proposals for extending the rights granted under the implementing legislation to persons not carrying on any economic activity.[11]

The application of the Treaty between employed and self-employed is also unclear; in this connection the definitions used by the basic regulation on social security may be helpful because the status of a person as self-employed is normally resolved in terms of whether he has the duty to make social security contributions of a type normally paid by workers.

Non-nationals have increasingly become the subject of concern for both the Community and the Member States, particularly Yugoslavs, Turks and North Africans who flocked in great numbers into the Community, especially West Germany. However, no action has been taken at the Community level.[12] Paradoxically many non-EEC nationals, who do not benefit from the free movement provisions, were entitled to vote in the United Kingdom in the 1979 direct elections to the European Parliament.

The Discrimination prohibited by Article 48

16—07   All forms of action against workers from other Member States

[7] Regulation 1408/71, J.O. 1971, L149/2; O.J. 1971, 416, (Article 1). Codified in O.J. 1980 C138/1.
[8] J.O. 1964, 1225.
[9] [1975] I C.M.L.R. 383; see also *City of Wiesbaden* v. *Barulli* [1968] C.M.L.R. 239.
[10] Cases 36/74 *Walrave and Koch* v. *Union Cycliste* [1974] E.C.R. 1405; 13/76 *Dona* v. *Mantero* [1976] E.C.R. 1333.
[11] O.J. 1979, C207/14.
[12] But see Council Resolution of February 9, 1976, on an action programme for migrant workers and members of their families, O.J. 1976, C34/2.

are prohibited, even if indirect or covert, if the effect is to put the foreign worker at a disadvantage compared with national workers.[13] This may potentially extend, *e.g.* to national requirements on driving licences although such national rules are not in principle incompatible with Community Law.[14] Rules such as those relating to the taking of driving tests do raise fundamental problems as regards the degree of discrimination prohibited. Member States may well argue that no discrimination exists because it is open to all to take driving tests. The foreign national on the other hand has a different viewpoint: he has passed a driving test in his country of residence and may be an experienced driver. The taking of another test thus imposes a burden on him which usually stems from his non-national origin.

The real problem here lies in the fact that the Treaty has not made any provision for common rules or mutual recognition of such qualifications as regards workers. Without such rules the Member States must remain free to impose their own (differing) rules; in the absence of such a power, a legal vacuum would exist. The adoption of common rules on the mutual recognition of qualifications would make the ban on discrimination more effective in this area.

16—08 The taking into consideration of the fact that a worker has had his residence in another Member State may be forbidden unless it is based on objective differences between residence domestically or abroad.[15]

The prohibition extends to the situation where a Member State's legislation purports to discriminate, but is not enforced, against EEC nationals, because the uncertainty thereby created is itself a form of discrimination.[16] The "extension" of the prohibition by reference to residence would appear to have its origin in the assumption that foreign residence and foreign nationality are usually linked, so that discrimination "on grounds of residence" means discrimination on grounds of nationality. However, there is no reason why a national of the State in question may not suffer equally from the discrimination if he has lived or lives in another Member State. The Court appears to be coming to the view that in this respect a State's own nationals may have rights under the Treaty as well. In *Choquet*[17] a Dutch national invoked the Treaty against his own government when he was required to pass a Dutch driving test after having qualified to drive in another Member State.

---

[13] Cases 44/72 *Marsman* v. *Rosskamp* [1972] E.C.R. 1243; 152/73 *Giovanni Maria Sotgiu* v. *Deutsche Bundespost* [1974] E.C.R. 153; 112/75 *Directeur Régional* v. *Hiarédin* [1976] E.C.R. 553.
[14] Case 16/78 *Choquet* [1978] E.C.R. 2293.
[15] Case 152/73 *Sotigui, supra,* note 13.
[16] *French merchant seamen* case, *supra,* note 2.
[17] Case 16/78 *Choquet, supra,* note 14.

The protection for a State's own nationals in this type of case must however be distinguished from the general rule that own nationals are not protected *per se* from discrimination in areas outside the scope of the Treaty.[18]

16—09   Article 48 (3) states that free movement is further to entail the right, subject to limitations justified on ground of public policy, public security or public health[19]:

"(a) to accept offers of employment actually made;
(b) to move freely within the territory of Member States for this purpose;
(c) to stay in a Member State for the purpose of employment in accordance with the provisions governing the employment of nationals of that State laid down by law, regulation or administrative action,
(d) to remain in the territory of a Member State after having been employed in that State, subject to conditions which shall be embodied in implementing regulations to be drawn up by the Commission."

Directive 64/221

16—10   The exception to Article 48 (3): "subject to limitations justified on grounds of public policy, public security or public health," has been considered in some detail by the Court, both in relation to Article 48 (3) and in relation to Article 56 (1) in the chapter on establishment (*infra*, para. 17-25), which uses similar terminology, and in relation to Directive 64/221[20] on the co-ordination of special measures concerning the movement and residence of foreign nationals which are justified on these grounds, which implements both Treaty provisions and therefore covers free movement of workers, establishment and (by virtue of Article 66) services as well. The directive is in part based on the 1955 European Convention on Establishment.[21]

16—11   *Royer*[22] came to the Court in circumstances where it was unclear whether the provisions on free movement of workers or on establishment or services were at issue. The Court held that they were based on the same principles so far as concerned entry and residence and that substantially identical provisions of Community law apply.

16—12   The directive applies to beneficiaries of the various types of liberalisation and to spouses and members of the family benefiting under any regulations or directives adopted in these areas. The directive goes some way towards providing a limitative list of the

[18] Case 175/78 *R.* v. *Saunders* [1979] E.C.R. 1129 (domestic criminal law).
[19] These limitations are discussed *infra*. para. 16–10.
[20] J.O. 1964, 850, O.J. 1963–64, 117.
[21] December 13, 1955, TS No.1 (1971), Cmnd. 4573.
[22] Case 48/75 *Royer* [1976] E.C.R. 497.

situations in which the public policy exceptions may be invoked, and also places limitations on deportation and curtailment of stay.

No measures may be taken under the guise of public policy solely for economic ends (Article 2 (2)). Article 3 constitutes a condensed Community equivalent to the European Convention on Human Rights.[23]

> "1. Measures taken on grounds of public policy or of public security shall be based exclusively on the personal conduct of the individual concerned.
>
> 2. Previous criminal convictions shall not in themselves constitute grounds for the taking of such measures.
>
> 3. Expiry of the identity card or passport used by the person concerned to enter the host country and to obtain a residence permit shall not justify expulsion from the territory.
>
> 4. The State which issued the identity card of passport shall allow the holder of such document to re-enter its territory without any formality even if the document is no longer valid or the nationality of the holder is in dispute."

16—13   Article 3 (1) of the Directive was held directly applicable in *Van Duyn*.[24] In the context of that provision it was held that:

> "The concept of public policy in the context of the Community and where, in particular, it is used as a justification for derogating from the fundamental principle of freedom of movement for workers, must be interpreted strictly, so that its scope cannot be determined unilaterally by each Member State without being subject to control by the institutions of the Community. Nevertheless, the particular circumstances justifying recourse to the concept of public policy may vary from one country to another and from one period to another, and it is therefore necessary in this matter to allow the competent national authorities an area of discretion within the limits imposed by the Treaty."

16—14   On the substance of the case the Court held:

> "Article 48 of the EEC Treaty and Article 3 (1) of Directive No. 64/221 are to be interpreted as meaning that a Member

---

[23] *cf.* Case 36/75 *Rutili* v. *Minister for the Interior* [1975] 1219. See also Cases 131/79 *Ex p. Santillo* [1980] E.C.R. 1585 and 98/79 *Pecastaing* v. *Belgian State* [1980] E.C.R. 691.
[24] Case 41/74 *Van Duyn* v. *Home Office* [1974] E.C.R. 1337.

State, in imposing restrictions justified on grounds of public
policy, is entitled to take into account, as a matter of personal
conduct of the individual concerned, the fact that the
individual is associated with some body or organisation the
activities of which the Member State considers socially harmful but which are not unlawful in that State, despite the fact
that no restriction is placed upon nationals of the said Member
State who wish to take similar employment with these same
bodies or organisations."

The emphasis on "personal conduct," however, clearly prohibits
expulsion as a deterrent to others, *i.e.* no alien may be held up as
an example to others - his or her case must be treated on a purely
individual basis. As a natural extension, therefore, the Court has
also held that the public policy exception in Article 48 concerns
not only legislative provisions but also individual decisions taken
in application.[25] Furthermore, *"justified* on grounds of public
policy" means justified by reference to the law including Community rules on free movement. Thus for example the exception
does not allow a Member State to impose penalties or limitations
on a person's right to take part in trade union activities since
that right is guaranteed (as concerns workers) by Regulation
1612/68.[26]

16–15   In later cases the freedom of action of Member States seems to
have been reduced somewhat: in *Rutili*[27] the Court held that:

"Restrictions cannot be imposed on the right of a national of
any Member State to enter the territory of another Member
State, to stay there and to move within it unless his presence
or conduct constitutes a genuine and sufficiently serious
threat to public policy."

Residence prohibitions within a Member State which are
territorially limited may be imposed only in circumstances where
such prohibitions may be imposed on that Member State's own
nationals.
     The importance of individual circumstances was again stressed,
together with the importance of the procedural safeguards enshrined
in the directive.[28]

16–16   As regards expulsion, the Court has held that "the mere failure
by a national of a Member State to complete the legal formalities
concerning access, movement and residence of aliens does not
justify a decision ordering expulsion since it is a question of the

[25] *cf.* Case 36/75 *Rutili* v. *Minister for the Interior, supra,* note 23.
[26] *Ibid.*
[27] *Ibid.*
[28] Case 48/75 *Royer, supra,* note 22.

exercise of a right acquired under the Treaty itself. Such conduct cannot be regarded as constituting in itself a breach of public policy or public security."[29] Nevertheless, penalties falling short of imprisonment let alone expulsion may be appropriate.[30] In relation to a duty imposed on aliens to report their presence to the authorities the Court talks in *Watson & Belmann*[31] of "dispro-portionate" penalties, measured by reference to penalties attaching to infringement by nationals of provisions of equal importance and by reference to the gravity of the infringement. But aliens control is not as such contrary to the non-discrimination provisions of Article 7 of the Treaty. In *Bouchereau*[32] Article 3 (2) was interpreted to mean that previous criminal convictions are relevant only in so far as the circumstances which gave rise to them are *evidence* of personal conduct constituting a *present* threat to the requirements of public policy. Moreover, recourse to public policy presupposes the existence of a genuine and sufficiently serious threat affecting one of the fundamental interests of society.

16—17   Article 4 refers to an annexed list of diseases and disabilities which may be invoked for refusing entry to a Member State on health grounds. The list is expressed to be limitative. The diseases referred to are (a) diseases which might endanger public health, namely quarantinable diseases within the meaning of WHO Regulation 2 of May 25, 1951 and (b) diseases and disabilities which might threaten public policy or security, namely drug addiction and profound mental disturbance.

Articles 5 to 9 guarantee certain administrative and procedural safeguards to persons involved in a dispute regarding a refusal of entry, etc., on one the three grounds of public policy, security or health. A person must be notified of the result of his application for a first residence permit within six months.[33] If his application is refused, he must be informed of the grounds on which the decision was taken:[34] a person must be given at least 15 days' notice of refusal to grant or to renew a permit, or of expulsion[35] and will have the local legal remedies against such a decision.[36]

16—18   By virtue of Article 48 (4) the provisions of Article 48 and therefore the secondary legislation based on that article "shall not apply to employment in the public service."[37] In case 152/73 *Sotgiu* v. *Deutsche Bundespost*[37] the Court held that this exemp-

---

[29] *Ibid.*
[30] *Ibid.*
[31] Case 118/75 *Watson & Belmann* [1976] E.C.R. 1185.
[32] Case 30/77 *Bouchereau* [1977] E.C.R. 1999.
[33] Directive 64/221, Article 5.
[34] *Ibid.* Article 6. See Case 131/79, *supra*, note 23.
[35] *Ibid.* Article 7.
[36] *Ibid.* Articles 8 and 9. See Cases 98/79 and 131/79, *supra*, note 23.
[37] [1974] E.C.R. 153. See also Case 149/79 *Commission* v. *Belgium* (December 17, 1980).

tion must be strictly defined. If a Member State does in fact permit foreign nationals to exercise official functions Article 48 (4) does not allow it to operate any discrimination within that function. The exception therefore concerns only access to posts forming part of the public services. The nature of the legal relationship (*e.g.* private law contract or public law appointment) between employee and administration is irrelevant.

Article 49

16—19 Article 49 requries that the freedom of movement for workers should be achieved by progressive stages:

(a) by ensuring close co-operation between national employ- ment services;
(b) by abolishing administrative barriers in the shape of qualifying periods and of formalities for eligibility for available employment; or
(c) for free choice of employment; and
(d) by setting up a system for the communication of job opportunities and a balancing machinery to equalise supply and demand.

The Council is empowered to issue directives or regulations to this end acting on a proposal from the Commission after consulting the Economic and Social Committee.

Free movement for workers was secured in three discernible stages, each stage being governed by a regulation of general application. The first stage was inaugurated by the issue of Regulation 15 of August 16, 1961.[38] This regulation was super- seded by Regulation 38/64 of March 25, 1964,[39] which inau- gurated the second phase. This regulation was itself superseded by Regulation 1612/68 of October 15, 1968.[40] A directive on the abolition of restrictions on the movement and residence within the Community of workers of Member States and their families was adopted with each regulation, the current one being Directive 68/360.[41]

Regulation 1612/68

16—20 **Personal scope - "employed person"**

Article 1 (1) states that:

"Any national of a Member State, shall irrespective of his place of residence, have the right to take up an activity as an employed person, and to pursue such activity within the

---

[38] J.O. 1961, 1073.
[39] J.O. 1964, 965.
[40] J.O. 1968, L257/2. There have been numerous minor amendments.
[41] J.O. 1968, L257/15; O.J. 1968, 485.

territory of another Member State in accordance with the provisions laid down by law, regulation or administrative action governing the employment of nationals of that State."

The elimination of discrimination in employment and related benefits

16—21   Regulation 1612/68[42] seeks in its Articles 1-12 to proscribe the most common kinds of disadvantage which a foreign worker might encounter in trying to obtain work in another Member State together with discrimination in terms and conditions of employment. He must be treated as eligible for any employment vacancy on the same basis as nationals,[43] and be given the same assistance[44] and subjected to the same qualification requirements, as nationals.[45]

16—22   Article 7 ensures basic equality of treatment for Community workers in any Member State as regards terms and conditions of employment. Discrimination against Community nationals in social and tax matters, in eligibility for vocational training, and in the terms of collective or individual agreements on pay is prohibited. Social and tax advantages need not be linked to the contract of employment.[46] Article 8 gives Community nationals equal rights to become members of trade unions and to exercise associated rights, but they are excluded from certain workers' tribunals (*e.g. Conseils des Prud' hommes*). The Community worker is to enjoy all rights afforded to national workers in matters of housing, including eligibility to be entered on housing lists on equal terms (Article 9). Article 10 gives the worker the right to bring his spouse and children under 21 and dependent children and ascendant dependent relatives into the country in which he works, if he has available suitable accommodation for them (para. 3). Article 11 extends the right to work in the host State to the worker's spouse and children, and Article 12 grants the child the right to be educated and trained there. This includes associated rights, such as educational grants for higher education.[47] Although the worker's family enjoy rights by virtue of his status as a worker, it is not necessary that the benefits they receive be linked to the incidents of employment, any more than the worker's own benefits must be so linked, as indicated in the context of Article 7 of the regulation. Thus the mentally handicapped child of a foreign worker would be entitled to the benefit of a fund set up to assist persons whose chances of employment are diminished

---

[42] J.O. 1968, L257/2. O.J. 1968 455. There have been numerous minor amendments.
[43] *Ibid.* Article 1 (2).
[44] *Ibid.* Article 5.
[45] *Ibid.* Article 6.
[46] Case 63/76 *Vito Inzirillo* v. *Caisse d'Allocations Familiales de l'arrondisement de Lyon* [1976] E.C.R. 2057. Case 32/75 *Anita Cristini* v. *SNCF* [1975] E.C.R. 1085.
[47] Case 68/74 *Alaimo* v. *Préfet du Rhône* [1975] E.C.R. 109.

by reason of such a handicap.[48]

Article 12 is supplemented by Directive 77/486[49] on the education of the children of migrant workers, adopted within the context of the social action programme.[50] This directive provides for special free tuition to facilitate the initial reception of the children in the new Member State, including training in the official language. Continued education related to their own culture and mother tongue is also provided for.

The elimination of discrimination in entering residing and leaving the Member State

16—23   Clearly it is not enough to protect the worker from discrimination as regards work itself. Without corresponding provisions securing the right for workers to enter, reside and leave the Member States, Regulation 1612/68 would have been pointless. Hence, Directive 68/360[51] was adopted in parallel with the regulation to deal with these matters. In fact this directive goes beyond the scope of the regulation in that its provisions apply not only to workers who are taking up employment but also to those wishing to enter another Member State for the purpose of finding work. The right is granted for a stay of up to three months. Article 69 of Regulation 1408/71, (*infra*) complements this right by preserving the worker's right to unemployment benefit in the original State for up to three months from his date of departure.

The directive provides for a document called a "Residence Permit for a National of a Member State of the EEC" (Article 4). The receiving state must, on production by the worker of a valid identity card or passport (Article 3) and a declaration from the future employer, issue such a residence permit to the applicant, valid throughout the territory of that Member State for at least five years and automatically renewable (Article 6). It is available as of right.[52] The permit may not be withdrawn merely because the holder is no longer working (Article 7). It is not to be assimilated to a residence permit in the normal sense, so that an EEC national can not be expelled for not having it - it is purely a document declaratory of the worker's status. Any penalty imposed for not producing or possessing such a permit must take these facts into account.[53]

16—24   The only right mentioned in Article 48 (3) EEC which was not covered by Regulation 1612/68 is the right "(d) to remain in the

---

[48] Case 76/72 *Michel S* v. *FNRSH* [1973] E.C.R. 457.

[49] O.J. 1977, L199/32.

[50] Council Resolution of January 21, 1974, O.J. 1974, C13/1 and February 9, 1976, O.J. 1976, C34/2.

[51] J.O. 1968, L257/13; O.J. 1968, 485. Numerous minor amendments.

[52] Case 48/75 *Royer* [1976] E.C.R. 497.

[53] Cases 48/75 *Royer* [1976] E.C.R. 497; 118/75 *Watson & Belmann* [1976] E.C.R. 1185; Case 8/77 *Concetta Sagulo, Gennaro Brenca and Addelmadjid Bakhouche* [1977] E.C.R. 1495; Case 157/79 *R.* v. *Stanislaus Pieck* [1980] 3 C.M.L.R. 220.

territory of a Member State after having been employed in that State . . . ." Such a right is granted by Regulation 1251/70[54] to any migrant Community worker who:

(a) has reached the qualifying age for an old age pension and has been employed in the host state for at least the last 12 months, and resided there continuously for more than three years; or

(b) ceases work because of a permanent incapacity to work, provided he has resided there for more than two years (no such residence qualification is imposed if the incapacity arose from an industrial accident or occupational disease); or

(c) has been a frontier worker for at least three years.

The right to remain resident in the host country is extended to the worker's family originally qualifying for admission under Article 10 of Regulation 1612/68.

Co-operation between Member States

16—25 Regulation 1612/68 also attempts to secure administrative co-operation in exchange of information on job vacancies and the like.

Under Articles 13 and 14 of the regulation the Member States are to co-operate through the Commission in dealing with employment questions and problems, and are, through the mechanisms established under Articles 15 to 18, to exchange information on employment vacancies. Measures are being taken in conjunction with the Commission for controlling the balance of the labour market.[55] Overall responsibility for co-ordinating the balance of vacancies and applications for employment lies with the European Co-ordination Office, first set up under Regulation 15.[56] An Advisory Committee[57] is responsible for assisting the Commission in the examination of problems regarding the free movement of workers, in the study of the effects of the regulation, and in submitting proposals for revision of the regulation.[58] The Committee, whose members are appointed by the Council[59] is composed of six members from each Member State, two representing the government, two the trade unions and two the employers' associations.[60] It is chaired by a member of the Commission or his alternate.[61] A Technical Committee has as its task the preparation, promotion and following up of technical aspects

---

[54] J.O. 1970, L142/24, O.J. 1970, 402.
[55] Articles 19 and 20 of Regulation 1612/68.
[56] *Ibid.* Articles 21–23.
[57] *Ibid.* Articles 24–31.
[58] *Ibid.* Articles 24 and 25.
[59] *Ibid.* Article 27.
[60] *Ibid.* Article 26.
[61] *Ibid.* Article 28.

of implementing the regulation;[62] it is composed of representatives of the governments of the Member States[63] and is again chaired by a member of the Commission or his representative.[64] The Commission is currently engaged on the setting up of a Community wide vacancy clearance system known as SEDOC. Exchanges of employment ministry officials have also taken place.

Article 50

16—26 Article 50 provides that Member States shall encourage the exchange of young workers within the framework of a joint programme. In fact even before 1958 Member States had already made bilateral arrangements in this respect and a multilateral convention on the subject was drawn up in the context of the Brussels Treaty Organisation.[65] An initial programme of exchanges was set up by a declaration of the representatives of the Member States in May 1964.[66]

Article 51 Social Security and Regulation 1408/71

16—27 Article 51 forms the necessary complement to the principle of free movement of labour, providing for the adoption by the Council, acting unanimously on a proposal from the Commission, of

> "such measures as are necessary to provide freedom of movement for workers; to this end, it shall make arrangements to secure for workers and their dependents:
> (a) aggregation, for the purpose of acquiring and retaining the right to benefit and of calculating the amount of benefit, of all periods taken into account under the laws of the several countries;
> (b) payment of benefits to persons resident in the territories of Member States."

16—28   The effect of this is to require that migrant workers be guaranteed in the country to which they migrate equivalent social security benefits, based on an aggregation (*i.e.* totalisation) of social security credits and qualifications earned or paid by them wheresoever within the Community. No worker would be tempted to move to another country if as a result he automatically lost his right to social security and pension benefits.[67] And indeed the

[62] *Ibid.* Articles 32–37.
[63] *Ibid.* Article 34.
[64] *Ibid.* Article 35.
[65] Convention concerning student employees of April 17, 1950, T.S. 8 (1952); Cmnd. 8478.
[66] Decl. 64/307, J.O. 1964, 1226.
[67] See, *e.g.* Cases 1/67 *Ciechelski* v. *Caisse Régionale* [1967] E.C.R. 181; 24/75 *Petroni* v. *ONPTS* [1975] E.C.R. 1149, and 50/75 *Caisse De Pension* v. *Massonet* [1975] E.C.R. 1473; 19/76 *Triches* v. *Caisse Liégoise* [1976] E.C.R. 1243; 1/80 *FNROM* v. *Salmon* [1980] E.C.R. 1937, on scope of Art. 51.

implementing arrangements safeguard rights secured under the legislation of a single Member State. Prior to the creation of the Community, bilateral treaties between Member States had secured a degree of reciprocal recognition of such benefits but their operation was not uniform. Article 51 EEC, requiring the adoption of positive measures, goes further than the comparable article in the ECSC Treaty, Article 69 (4), which merely states that the Member States "shall endeavour to settle among themselves any matters remaining to be dealt with in order to ensure that social security arrangements do not inhibit labour mobility."

6–29   Article 51 is not the means for laying down a completely uniform Community rule, since the rules laid down under it only effect a co-ordination of national rules.[68] The article was originally implemented by Regulations 3[69] and 4/58[70] but these were replaced and modified in the light of experience by Regulations 1408/71[71] and 574/72.[72] The initial regulations excluded for certain purposes a number of categories of migrant workers, such as frontier workers, but the present regulations are comprehensive. Certain international conventions are nevertheless preserved and notably any ILO convention and the more favourable provisions of bilateral social security conventions between Member States.[73]

"Social security"

6–30   Article 51 does not define the scope of this term, but Regulation 1408/71, Article 4 (1), refers to all classical forms of social security benefit - sickness and maternity, disability, old-age, survivors', industrial accident and disease, death and unemployment and family benefits. Certain benefits are specifically excluded by Article 4 (4) of Regulation 1408, *viz.* social assistance and medical aid, war victims benefit schemes and special schemes for civil servants and assimilated persons. In defining the scope of the regulation, a distinction has been drawn by the Court of Justice between discretionary grants which are given to individuals on the basis of need and those to which an individual becomes entitled if he satisfies the conditions.[74] The Member States have made

---

[68] See, *e.g.* Case 44/65 *Hessische Knappschaft* v. *Singer* [1965] E.C.R. 965; Case 1/67 *Ciechelski* v. *Caisse Régionale* [1967] E.C.R. 181, and Case 2/67 *De Moor* v. *Caisse de Pension* [1967] E.C.R. 197; 100/78, *Rossi* v. *Caisse De Compensation* [1979] E.C.R. 831.

[69] J.O. 1958, 561.

[70] J.O. 1958, 597.

[71] J.O. 1971, L149/2, O.J. 1971, 416 amended by Regulations 1392/74, O.J. 1974, L152/1. Codified in O.J. 1980, C138/1 and O.J. 1980, C138/65.

[72] J.O. 1972, L74/1 amended by Regulation 878/73, O.J. 1973, L86/1.

[73] Regulation 1408/71, *supra*, Article 7.

[74] Cases 24/74 *Caisse régionale d'assurance maladie de Paris* v. *Biason* [1974] E.C.R. 99; 39/74 *Luciana Costa* v. *Belgian State* [1974] E.C.R. 1251. Since Article 51 only provides for adoption of rules on social security benefits other types of benefits need not be provided for by Community legislation—Case 144/78 *Tinelli* v. *Berufsgenossenschaft der Chemischen Industrie* [1979] E.C.R. 757.

The Worker and the Community

declarations[75] as to the benefits which they consider fall within
Article 4 (1); the fact that a benefit is not included in the declaration does not prevent it from falling within Article 4 (1), although
if it is included, that is sufficient proof that it does so fall.[76]
The scope of the term depends on *all* the factors relating to each
benefit, in particular its purposes and the conditions for its grant.[77]

Persons covered

16—31   The regulation applies to workers who are nationals of Member
States or who are refugees or stateless persons.[78] Article 1 (*a*)
defines "worker" by reference to insurance for

> "one or more of the contingencies covered by the branches
> of a social security scheme for employed persons."

Thus the person concerned may not necessarily be "employed."
Interpreting the regulation in the light of its spirit and of the objectives of the Treaty the Court has held that the Community rules
on social security "follow a general tendency of the social law of
the Member States to extend the benefits of social security in
favour of new categories of persons by reason of identical risks."[79]
In the case of compulsory insurance it is for the authorities of the
Member States to decide whether an obligation exists to be so
insured.[80] The fact that a person is not insured under a scheme
will not prevent him being a "worker" if he should have been so
insured.[81] It appears that a self-employed person will come within
the ambit of the regulation at any rate if he had at one time been
employed.[82] The legislation protects the dependants of a worker
whatever their nationality. Thus a dependant of an EEC national
who is a worker is entitled to all benefits which a national might
receive even if that dependant is not a worker,[83] and even if the
dependant is resident elsewhere.[84]

Regulation 1408/71 essentially sets out (1) to lay down the
rules regarding the applicable law with respect to social security

---

[75] See now O.J. 1980, C139/1 summarizing the status of declarations.
[76] Case 35/77 *Elizabeth Beerens* v. *Rijksdienst voor Arbeidsvoorzieming* [1977] E.C.R. 2249.
[77] Case 9/78 *Directeur régional de la sécurité sociale de Nancy* v. *Gillard* [1978] E.C.R. 1661.
[78] Article 2 of Regulation 1408/71.
[79] Cases 19/68 *De Cicco* [1968] E.C.R. 473; 23/71, *Janssen* [1971] E.C.R. 864; 17/76 *Brack* [1976] E.C.R. 1429.
[80] Case 84/77 *Caisse primaire d'assurance maladie d'Eure et Loire* v. *Tessier* [1978] E.C.R. 7.
[81] Case 39/76 *Bestuur der Bedrijfsvereniging voor de Metaalnijnerheid* v. *L J Mouthaan* [1976] E.C.R. 1901.
[82] Case 19/68 *de Cicco, supra,* note 79: 17/76 *Brack* [1976] E.C.R. 1429; 99/80 *Galinsky, supra,* note 5.
[83] Case 115/77 *Laumarin* v. *Landesversicherungsanstalt Rheinprovinz* [1978] E.C.R. 805.
[84] See Case 1/78 *Kenny* v. *Insurance Officer* [1978] E.C.R. 1489.

258

benefits and obligations and (2) to ensure that no worker is worse off by virtue of moving to another Member State and thereby becoming subjected to those rules.

Determination of applicable rules

16—32   The Regulation sets out the general rule that a worker is to be subject to the legislation of the State where he is employed, wherever he happens to reside.[85] More precisely this entails that

- the worker will pay contributions (where required) to the authorities of the employment state
- the authorities of that state will assume responsibility financially for payment of any benefits.

There are exceptions in the case of temporary postings, employment by an undertaking whose operations "straddle a common frontier," workers in international transport and seafarers. In particular a person who works for more than one firm, located in different Member States, is to be subject to the legislation of the state where he resides, unless residence is in a third state when the location of the registered office of the employing undertaking is the determining factor.[86]

The rule that the legislation of only one state may apply to the worker is appropriate for those types of benefit which are not variable according to the length of time of employment, but are clearly inappropriate where the benefits are so variable (*e.g.* retirement and invalidity pensions). Hence for these kinds of benefits the regulation makes provision for each Member State to assume financial responsibility for the share accumulated under its legislation.

Preserving the worker's rights

16—33   First, in so far as the scheme adopted by the regulation opts for the application of the legislation of one state only, there must be provision for the aggregation of periods or contributions under the laws of the various Member States where a worker may have worked so as to ensure that a move to another Member State will not prejudice his right to benefits. Thus, the worker may become unemployed in State A not having completed his qualifying periods there but having been continually employed previously in State B. Regulation 1408/71 deals with this situation by requiring the aggregation of periods of employment which would qualify under State B's legislation with the qualifying period (if any) in State A.

Secondly, the worker must not suffer any discrimination by the responsible state. Hence Article 3 [87] provides that qualifying

[85] Article 13, Regulation 1408/71.
[86] *Ibid.* Article 4.
[87] Read with Arts. 7 & 48 EEC, Art. 3 is directly applicable; *Kenny, supra*, note 84.

workers resident in another Member State of the EEC are entitled to the same treatment as nationals of that state. Once the applicable legislation is determined, the worker is entitled to all the benefits which nationals of the state in question may receive (provided of course that they also satisfy the conditions). The worker must of course also comply with the duties enforced by the legislation. The term "legislation" includes all implementing measures taken by the authorities.[88]

16–34   The regulation only seeks to ensure that the foreign worker is no worse off as a result of moving to another Member State. Where the application of the rules laid down results in his being better off than other comparable nationals, provision is made for reduction of benefits by the competent state. Thus, if the state from which the worker comes continues to allow payment of a benefit even though a full benefit may be obtained from the employment state, the latter may reduce the benefit by the amount of the surplus.[89] This is most likely to arise where the same qualifying period is taken into account by two or more Member States and thus gives rise to a double payment. This rule against the duplication of benefits does not, as one might expect, apply where it has been necessary to permit *pro rata* payments by two or more Member States.[90]

The rules preventing the overlapping of benefits only apply where the worker's rights *result from* the application by the Member States of Community legislation. It has often happened that the national legislation allows a benefit independently of EEC rules (*e.g.* the competent state allows payment of a benefit without a qualifying period). The Court has held that since the regulation is not applied in such cases, the rules on the overlapping of benefits do not apply.[91] Of course, where national rules do provide benefits but these are less than those under Community law, the worker can rely on the latter.[92]

16–35   The two objectives of Regulation 1408/71 may appear to come into conflict where the worker would, but for the rule on the application of one legislation only, be required to contribute to two or more schemes but would also receive benefits in respect of both giving rise to a total of benefits greater than the entitlement under Community law. The Court originally took the view that

[88] Article 1 (j); Case 97/76 *Walter Bozzone* v. *Office de sécurité sociale d'outre-mer* [1977] E.C.R. 687.
[89] Article 12.
[90] *Ibid.*
[91] Cases 34/69 *Caisse d'assurance viellesse des travailleurs salariés de Paris* v. *Duffy* [1969] E.C.R. 597; 98/77 *Schaap* v. *Bestuur van de Bedrijfsvereniging voor Bank-en Verzekerings-wesen, Groothandel en vrije Beroefen* [1978] E.C.R. 707; 49/75 *Camilla Borella* v. *Landesversicherungsanstalt Schwaben* [1975] E.C.R. 1461; Case 24/75 *Petroni* v. *ONPTS* [1975] E.C.R. 1149; 27/75 *Bonaffini* v. *INPS* [1975] E.C.R. 971.
[92] See, *e.g.* Case 37/77 *Fernando Greco* v. *Fonds national de retraite des ouvriers mineurs* [1977] E.C.R. 1711.

the regulation was incompatible with Article 51 of the Treaty in so far as it would be construed as prohibiting the worker from *benefiting* from the application of two or more legislations.[93] However, it may now be coming to the view that the "one legislation" rule must be applied regardless of whether the worker is worse off as a result.[94]

As a result of the adoption of this system it was necessary (again in relation to each form of benefit) to provide for the reimbursement of the paying authority in respect of the periods completed by the worker in other Member States. In addition, where the authorities of a Member State enjoy rights of subrogation under their national law, they are entitled under Article 93 to take advantage of those rights in other Member States. Thus a German institution would be entitled to be subrogated in a tort claim in the United Kingdom made by a beneficiary of German benefits.

Administration and co-operation between Member States

16--36   Articles 80 and 81 provide for an Administrative Commission for the Social Security of Workers, composed of representatives of the governments of Member States, advised by a representative of the Commission, and empowered to call upon the ILO for further technical advice. (A similar Commission had existed under Regulation 3.) The prime duty of the Administrative Commission is to "settle all administrative questions and questions of interpretation arising under this Regulation and subsequent Regulations, or under any consequential agreement or arrangement, without prejudice to the right of the authorities, institutions and persons concerned to have recourse to the procedures and legal remedies prescribed under the legislation of a Member State, in this Regulation or in the Treaty."[95] Some doubt arose as to whether the Administrative Commission could give definitive interpretative decisions under the identical Article 43 of Regulation 3. The Court of Justice held that these decisions have the value of opinions and that any other interpretation of Article 43 (*a*) of Regulation 3 would conflict with Article 177, setting up a system for the interpretation of Community law (which confers exclusive jurisdiction on the Court of Justice).[96]

The Administrative Commission's other tasks are essentially to foster and improve co-operation between Member States in the field of social security, in particular with a view to expediting payments of benefits.[97]

[93] Case 92/63 *Nonnenmacher, widow Moebs* v. *Bestuur der Soziale Verzekeringsbank* [1964] E.C.R. 281.
[94] Case 102/76 *Perenboom* v. *Inspecteur der directe Belastingen* [1977] E.C.R. 815.
[95] Regulation 1408/71, Art. 81 (*a*).
[96] Case 19/67 *Bestuur der Soziale Verzekeringsbank* v. *Van der Vecht* [1967] E.C.R. 345.
[97] Regulation 1408/71, Art. 81.

16—37   In addition to the Administrative Commission, the regulation provides for an Advisory Committee for the Social Security of Migrant Workers,[98] which is made up in tripartite fashion, with two representatives each from the government, trade unions and employers' organisations from each Member State, appointed by the Council, and chaired by a member from the Commission or his representative. The Committee is empowered:

> "(a) to examine general questions or questions of principle and the problems arising from the implementation of the Regulations adopted within the framework of the provisions of Article 51 of the Treaty;
> (b) to formulate opinions on the subject for the Administrative Commission and proposals for any revision of the Regulations."[99]

16—38   Effectively, however, responsibility for the operation of the Regulation lies with the national social security authorities and Article 84 recognises this by stating that:

> "1. the competent authorities of Member States shall communicate to each other all information regarding:
> (a) measures taken to implement this Regulation;
> (b) changes in their legislation which are likely to affect the implementation of this Regulation.
>
> 2. for the purposes of implementing this Regulation, the authorities and institutions of Member States shall lend their good offices and act as though implementing their own legislation."

[98] *Ibid.* Articles 82 and 83.
[99] *Ibid.* Article 83.

Chapter 17

THE RIGHT OF ESTABLISHMENT AND FREEDOM TO PROVIDE SERVICES

1. *The Right of Establishment*

7—01 The right of establishment (Arts. 52 to 58) is economically and legally speaking the right for a person or body, corporate or unincorporate, bearing the nationality of one State to cross into another State, and establish himself or itself there either by undertaking work from a permanent base, or by establishing an agency, branch, sudsidiary, etc. As such it does not extend to a right generally to establish a residence in another Member State if that residence is not connected with the pursuit of an economic activity.[1]

Article 52

7—02 Article 52, first para., states the basic principle that restrictions on the freedom of establishment of nationals of a Member State in the territory of another Member State were to be abolished by progressive stages in the course of the original transitional period. This progressive abolition was also to apply to restrictions on the setting up of agencies, branches or subsidiaries in one Member State by nationals of another Member State.

The second paragraph of Article 52 makes it clear that freedom of establishment includes the right to take up self-employed occupations and to set up and manage undertakings, subject to applicable laws of the host State, and to the provisions of the chapter relating to capital (*infra*, Chapter 18).

7—03 Until 1974 it was thought that Article 52 was not directly applicable, principally because of the problems associated with professional qualifications, dealt with by Article 57, below. Indeed, the argument was made that the content of the ensuing articles gave rise to a necessary implication that Article 52 was not intended to be directly applicable. The Commission appears also to have been of this view, since it had prior to 1974 drawn up a number of directives aimed at gradually reducing restrictions based purely on nationality. In Case 2/74 *Reyners*[2] the Court dispelled these doubts and declared Article 52 directly applicable. The practical effect of this judgment is that a person who carries on a trade or

---

[1] See, on the subject of economic activity, Case 36/74 *B. N. O. Walrave & L. G. N. Koch v. Association Union Cycliste Internationale* [1974] E.C.R. 1405.
[2] *Jean Reyners v. Belgian State* [1974] E.C.R. 631.

263

profession may not be prevented from exercising it by reason only of his nationality. This may even apply to a State's own nationals where the individual possesses a foreign qualification.[3] Subsequent judgments have substantially expanded this basic ruling, holding that Article 52 cannot be got round by the imposition of artifical and therefore discriminatory professional requirements. Thus in *Thieffry*[4] the Court was faced with the case of a Belgian advocate who had qualified in Belgium but desired to practise in France. The Belgian legal qualification had been accepted as equivalent to a French degree in law by the university authorities, but the rules of the Paris Bar prevented him from completing his training and qualifications *inter alia* because he did not have a French law degree. It was held that possession of a qualification recognised as equivalent by the competent French authority meant that the restriction on his completing his training was a restriction incompatible with Article 52 even in the absence of the directives provided for by Article 57. In *Patrick*[5] this was carried slightly further. An architect with a British qualification wished to establish himself in France, but he was not permitted to do so because, although the French authorities had agreed that the British qualification should be equivalent to the French one, the declaration of equivalence had been refused for want of an agreement on reciprocity with the United Kingdom. Again the Court ruled that the recognition of equivalence had the effect of rendering the refusal a discrimination on grounds of nationality.

The fact that the discrimination derives from rules of an international association located outside the Community is irrelevant if they apply to legal relationships which can be located within the territory of the Community.[6]

17–04   Identification of nationality is not usually a problem as regards individuals, but for legal persons it was deemed necessary to provide a rule for identification of potential beneficiaries. This is to be found in Article 58, which lays down a double criterion: undertakings which are incorporated in a Member State and have their registered office, central administration or principal place of business in a Member State are to be treated in the same way as natural persons who are nationals of Member States (see further *infra*, para. 13-34). The measures which restrict freedom of establishment and which are required to be abolished are those based on nationality, although a State may still maintain a State

[3] Cases 115/78 *Knoors* v. *Secretary of State for economic affairs* [1979] E.C.R. 399; 136/78 *Ministère Public* v. *Auer* [1979] E.C.R. 437.
[4] Case 71/76 *Jean Thieffry* v. *Conseil de l'ordre des avocats à la Cour de Paris* [1977] E.C.R. 765.
[5] Case 11/77 *Richard Hugh Patrick* v. *Ministre des Affaires Culturelles* [1977] E.C.R. 1199; similarly Case 159/78 *Commission* v. *Italy* [1979] E.C.R. 3247 (customs agents).
[6] Case 36/74 *Walrave, supra*, note 1 and Case 90/76 *Van Ameyde* v. *UCI* [1977] E.C.R. 1091.

monopoly for a particular industry or trade, by virtue of Article 37 EEC (*supra*, para. 13-27).

17—05   The principle of freedom of establishment is subjected by Article 52, second para., to the provisions relating to the free movement of capital, which is in theory an important restriction, since it is difficult to set up an establishment in another Member State without some transfer of capital. The restrictions on the movement of capital for investment purposes were, however, lifted before the adoption of measures on the freedom of establishment.[7]

Article 53

17—06   This is a standstill clause, prohibiting the introduction of any new restrictions on the right of establishment of Community nationals, save as otherwise provided in the Treaty. It was held directly applicable in *Costa* v. *ENEL*.[8] Liberalisation once introduced cannot be revoked.[9]

Article 54

17—07   Article 54 lays down the timetable and the means of implementation of the general principle of the right of establishment, outlined in Article 52. As such it constitutes the primary method of implementing the right of establishment, *viz.* by Community legislation aimed at abolishing restrictions based on nationality, which may or may not have to include provisions for the mutual recognition of diplomas.[10] By Article 54 (1) the Council, acting unanimously on a proposal from the Commission and after consulting the Economic and Social Committee and the Assembly, was to draw up a general programme for the abolition of restrictions on the freedom of establishment before the end of the first stage. This was done on December 18, 1961.[11] A general programme is not one of the instruments mentioned in Article 189 EEC as having binding force, and cannot of itself create obligations binding on the Member States or on individuals. However the Court has held that it provides useful guidance for the implementation of the relevant provisions of the Treaty[12] and it is generally considered that the Community institutions are constrained to adhere to its provisions. The programme has not, however, been executed according to its own timetable, and much remains to be done.

---

[7] Directive of May 11, 1960, J.O. 1960, 921; O.J. 1959–62 49.
[8] Case 6/64 [1964] E.C.R. 585.
[9] Case 48/75 *Procureur du Roi v. Royer* [1976] E.C.R. 497.
[10] See, *e.g.* Directives 68/363 and 68/364 on self employed persons in the retail trade, *infra*, notes 37 and 38.
[11] J.O. 1962, 36.
[12] Case 71/76 *Thieffry, supra,* note 4.

17—08   Article 54 (1), second sub-para. required the programme to set out the general conditions under which freedom of establishment was to be attained in the case of each type of activity and in particular the stages by which it was to be attained. The programme was drawn up having regard to those activities bearing most closely on the customs union - *cf.* Article 54 (3) (*a*). The remaining part of the transitional period was divided into portions of two years each, 1962-63, 1964-65, 1966-67, 1968 to the end of the transitional period on December 31, 1969 (Title IV). During each of these periods, certain activities were to be liberalised, the main ones in the first period being those activities relating to wholesaling and industry; in the second period, retailing and food; in the third and fourth periods, the liberal professions.

The Community was to implement the programme on the right of establishment by means of Council directives (Art. 54 (2) of the Treaty). Directives are the obvious tool here since the crux of the operation envisaged is a co-ordination of national rules on the particular subject, rather than the promulgation of directly applicable rules.

17—09   Article 54 (3) of the Treaty lists eight specific rules or priorities to be taken into account in adopting measures. The first three, (*a*) to (*c*), are mere elaborations upon the general principle in Article 52 of the elimination of restrictions on the freedom of establishment of Community nationals requiring:

(a) priority examination and treatment of activities contributing to the development of Community trade;
(b) the achievement of close co-operation between competent authorities;
(c) the abolition of obstacles to freedom of establishment.

Article 54 (3) (*d*) requires the Community to ensure that provision is made enabling workers of one Member State employed in the territory of another Member State to remain in that territory for the purpose of taking up a self-employed occupation.

Article 54 (3) (*e*) calls for action to facilitate acquisitions and use by nationals of one Member State of land or buildings situated in the territory of another Member State. Restrictions on land holding by aliens had related particularly to agricultural holdings, and it is to this type of restriction that the sub-paragraph is primarily directed, but action taken under the sub-paragraph is not to conflict with Article 39 (2) which requires account to be taken of the nature and structure of agriculture in working out the CAP.

17—10   In providing for the removal of restrictions in any given sector, the Council and the Commission are required by Article 54 (3) (*f*) to deal also with restrictions on the setting up of agencies, etc., and with restrictions on the entry of personnel from the main establishment into managerial or supervisory posts in such agencies, etc.,

Article 54 (3) (*g*), relating to the co-ordination of safeguards built into corporate structures for the protection of members and others, is the basis for co-ordinating measures taken in the field of company law.[13]

Article 54 (3) (*h*) requires the Council and the Commission to satisfy themselves that the conditions of establishment are not distorted by aids granted by Member States.

Although many trades were liberalised during the transitional period, not all those specified in the general programme were liberalised and progress on liberalising the professions was painfully slow. Much work still needs to be done in this area.

Articles 55 - 58 are dealt with below, para. 17-22, after the discussion of Services.

2. *Freedom to Provide Services*

Article 59

17—11   Article 59 provides for the progressive abolition of restrictions on freedom to provide services within the Community in respect of "nationals of Member States who are established in a State of the Community other than that of the person for whom the services are intended." This phrase makes clear the distinction between a right of establishment, which permits movement to the State where the service or activity is to be performed or carried out, and freedom to provide services, which generally involves retaining an establishment in one State, and effecting the service in another State. This may be undertaken in one of three ways:

(a) the person who provides the services lives in State A, but travels to State B and performs the service there, *e.g.* a doctor travels from England to France to treat a sick patient;

(b) the person giving the service supplies it from State A, where he lives, across the border to State B, without, however, going there, *e.g.* a doctor established in England sends a diagnosis and prescription to a patient in France, both parties remaining in their respective countries;

(c) the recipient of the services travels from State B to State A where the person furnishing the service performs the necessary task, *e.g.* the sick Frenchman goes to see his doctor in England.

17—12   Case (a) in fact resembles the right of establishment in all but the degree of permanence of residence in the second State, and

---

[13] *Infra,* paras. 17–34 *et seq.*

is the most important type of service dealt with by the chapter on services.

Case (b) may involve the transfer of processed goods and thus may involve also the provisions on free movement of goods[14] or on agriculture[15] and the remuneration for the services provided involves what is sometimes called the fifth freedom, or freedom of payments outlined in Article 106 EEC Treaty.

Cases (a) and (b) are clearly catered for by the Treaty. The terms of Article 59 appear to cover case (c) also, and it is noteworthy that the General Programme on Services[16] refers to indirect restrictions on services which relate to the recipient of the services or the type of service.[17] Directive 73/148[18] also deals with restrictions on the movement and residence of *inter alia* "nationals of Member States wishing to go to another Member State as recipients of services."

17—13   However, to admit that case (c) is covered by Article 59 would have an extremely wide-reaching effect on the rights of free movement discussed above, for as A.G. Trabucchi indicated in *Watson & Belmann*[19]:

> "the practical effect is to extend the right of freedom of movement to all nationals of the Member States because every one is actually or potentially a recipient of services."[20]

The Court did not pronounce upon the issue in the above case but left the question of the individuals' status to the national court to decide.

17—14   The Court held directly applicable the first paragraph of Article 59 together with the third paragraph of Article 60 (below) in Case 33/74 *Van Binsbergen*.[21] Again this entails that Member States may not discriminate against nationals of other Member States on the grounds of nationality, but it also prohibits indirect discrimination, on grounds of residence. As the Court ruled in *Royer*[22] the principles applicable under Article 59 are very similar to the principles applicable under Articles 48 and 52. The case law on those provisions (*supra*, paras. 16-04 *et seq.* and 17-02 *et seq*). is therefore relevant here also. Hence, Articles 59-60 might apply to negate a rule like that forming the subject of *Van Binsbergen*,

---

[14] Treaty Articles 9 to 37.
[15] Treaty Articles 38 to 47.
[16] J.O. 1962, 32.
[17] *Ibid.* Title III, first para. See also Article 1 of Directive 64/221, J.O. 1964, 850, O.J. 1963–67, 117.
[18] O.J. 1973, L172/14.
[19] Case 118/75 *Lynne Watson and Alessandro Belmann* [1976] E.C.R. 1185.
[20] *Ibid.* at p.1204.
[21] *Johannes Henricus Maria van Binsbergen* v. *Bestuur van de Bedrijfsvereniging voor de Metaalnijverheid* [1974] E.C.R. 1299.
[22] *Supra*, note 9.

requiring the representative of a party before a tribunal to reside in the same State as the tribunal. To maintain the requirement it would be necessary to show that it was objectively justified by the need to ensure observance of rules of professional conduct and that the Member State was unable to apply other, less restrictive, measures to ensure that result.[23] Articles 59 *et seq.* appear to prohibit discrimination even in respect of the State's own nationals[24] if they happen to be established in another State. For discrimination to fall under the prohibition contained in Article 59 it suffices that it results from rules of whatever kind which seek to govern the carrying on of the business in question. It is not relevant whether the discrimination originated in measures of a public authority, or, on the contrary, in measures attributable to an international association or private parties.[25]

17—15   The second paragraph of Article 59 enables the Council, acting unanimously on a proposal from the Commission, to extend the provisions of the chapter on services to nationals of third countries established within the Community. There is no parallel provision in the chapter on establishment. This apparent lacuna is explained upon analysis by the fact that Article 59, second para., grants only a secondary right; the prerequisite for its exercise is establishment within the Community. The existence of this secondary right is thus dependent upon the prior acceptance by another Member State of the potential beneficiary as an established person in its territory. Admission of nationals of third States to establishment, without more, would eliminate any element of prior selection, such as is inherent in the provisions of Article 59. The distinction is nevertheless as yet academic, for the power has not yet been used, possibly in part because corporations from third countries will usually incorporate a subsidiary which acquires the status of a Community national, thus largely alleviating any problems.

Article 60

17—16   Article 60 provides that services shall be considered to be "services" within the meaning of the Treaty where they are normally provided for remuneration in so far as they are not governed by any of the other freedoms of the Treaty, *i.e.* goods, persons and capital; thus the provisions on services will apply to a particular situation only if the provisions on free movement of workers or on the right of establishment in particular are inapplicable. Where the activity in question shows aspects of more than one freedom, the provisions of the Treaty relating to the

---

[23] See also Case 39/75 *Robert Geradus Coenen and others* v. *Sociaal Economische Raad* [1975] E.C.R. 1547 and Cases 110 and 111/78 *Ministère public* v. *van Wesemael* [1979] E.C.R. 85.
[24] See Cases cited, *supra,* note 3.
[25] Cases 36/74 *Walrave, supra,* note 1 and 90/76 *Van Ameyde supra,* note 6.

predominant aspect will apply. Thus television signals are services but trade in related material and products are subject to the rules relating to free movement of goods.[26] The execution of stock exchange orders and opening of a line of credit are also services.[27]

Article 61

17—17   Article 61 restricts the operation of the chapter on services in two distinct fields. Article 61 (1) excepts the provision of services in the field of transport from the chapter; these are dealt with in the chapter on transport (*infra*, Chapter 19). Article 61 (2) requires the freeing of banking and insurance services to be co-ordinated with the freeing of restrictions on capital, in so far as they relate to the movement of capital. The General Programme for Services[28] envisaged elimination of restrictions on banking services not linked to the movement of capital by the end of 1965 (a target which was not met). Since the elimination of restrictions on the movement of capital has also been slow, the freeing of the related banking and insurance services has yet to be accomplished although a number of limited directives have been introduced in the field of banking and insurance. Unlike many areas, the difficulties are to be found more in the provision of services than in the right of establishment here, because the limitations imposed by Member States emphasise the financial safeguards required - minimum reserves and liquidity margins in particular. Thus whilst it may not be too difficult to provide for the right of establishment according to local rules, the supply of services across national frontiers depends on the harmonisation of the minimum requirements. Work is in progress in this respect but there are many obstacles yet to overcome, including besides those mentioned, taxes on premiums.

Article 62

17—18   Article 62 is very similar to the standstill provisions of Article 53 in the chapter on establishment and is of the same legal effect.

Article 63

17—19   Article 63 is similar in import to Article 54 in the establishment chapter in that it indicates, for the field of services, the same series of Community measures to be taken for the freeing of the provision of services, and specifies some of the priorities to be taken into account. In common with Article 54, Article 63 makes provision for a general programme to be drawn up. This was done at the same time as the General Programme on Establishment and its

---

[26] Case 155/73 *Sacchi* [1974] E.C.R. 409. See also Cases 52/79 *Procureur* v. *Debauve* [1980] E.C.R. 833 and 62/79 *Coditel* v. *Ciné Vog* [1980] E.C.R. 881 (cable T.V.).
[27] Case 15/78 *Société Générale* v. *Koestler* [1978] E.C.R. 1971.
[28] *Supra,* note 16.

provisions are basically the same and, indeed, it refers to the time-table of abolition of restrictions contained in that programme.[29] The General Programme for Services was similarly to be implemented by Directives.[30]

As regards the proposals envisaged, Article 63 (3) requires priority to be given as a general rule to those services which directly affect production costs or the liberalisation of which helps to promote trade in goods.

Article 64

7—20   By Article 64, the Member States declare their readiness to undertake the liberalisation of services beyond the extent required by the directives issued pursuant to Article 63 (2), if their general economic situation and the situation of the economic sector concerned so permit. To this end the Commission is to make recommendations to the Member States concerned. No such declaration is contained in the chapter on establishment, evidently because such liberalisation was not considered realistic in respect of that chapter. In common with the similar Article 71, second para., and Article 106 (1), second sub-para. Article 64 has never been used.

Article 65

7—21   Article 65 supplements the standstill provision of Article 62. It provides for non-discriminatory application of national restrictions until full freedom of services is established. Thus Member States may not apply more restrictive conditions to the provision of services by nationals or residents of one Member State than they do to those of another. Conversely the application of more favourable conditions to nationals or residents of one Member State than to those of the others is similarly prohibited.

It is generally considered that Article 65 does not require the extension to the other Member States of any liberalisation granted in the framework of Benelux or the Belgium-Luxembourg Economic Union which goes beyond that effected by the Treaty or in the context of the Treaty.

3. *Provisions common to both the Right of Establishment and Freedom to Provide Services*

7—22   Article 66 EEC applies the provisions of Articles 55 - 58 inclusive to services as well as the right of establishment, and references in this section to the latter include the former.

Article 55

7—23   Article 55, first para. constitutes the first of two exceptions to

---

[29] *Ibid.*
[30] Treaty Article 63 (2).

the general provisions on the liberalisation of restrictions on establishment, stating that those provisions are not to apply to activities which are, in any given State, connected even occasionally with the exercise of official authority.

Article 55, second para. enables the Council, acting by a qualified majority on a proposal from the Commission, to except other activities from the chapter. This facility has not so far been used.

17—24   The first paragraph of Article 55 is similar to Article 48 (4) (*supra*, para. 16-18), excepting employment in the public service from the provisions on free movement of workers. While the latter is much more broadly based, apparently excepting whole activities where their exercise has even an occasional official flavour, the Court has by contrast given a very narrow interpretation to Article 55. In *Reyners*[31] it ruled that the exception must be restricted to "those activities which in themselves involve a direct and specific connection with the exercise of official authority." An entire profession could only be so exempted if activities involving the exercise of official authority were linked with the relevant profession (in this case that of *avocat*) "in such a way that freedom of establishment would result in imposing on the Member State concerned the obligation to allow the exercise, even occasionally, by non-nationals of functions appertaining to official authority." The difficulties of the practical application of this ruling are illustrated by the role performed by the solicitors' profession in the United Kingdom, where the solicitor is an officer of the Court for certain purposes. If a Member State does in fact permit foreign nationals to exercise official functions neither Article 48 (4) nor 55 allow it to operate any discrimination within that function.[32]

Article 56

17—25   Article 56 constitutes the second exception to the general principle of the right of establishment, but whereas Article 55 acts to exclude specific categories from the general principles of freedom of establishment, Article 56 permits national rules on the special treatment of aliens on grounds of public policy, public security or public health to prevail over the general Community rule providing for freedom of establishment. The Court has held this provision to be substantially identical to the corresponding provision in Article 48 (3) (see para. 16-10 *supra*).

Article 57

17—26   Article 57 constitutes a general second method of achieving the right of establishment within the Community. It provides for the

[31] Case 2/74 *Reyners supra*, note 2.
[32] Case 152/73 *Sotgiu* v. *Deutsche Bundespost* [1974] E.C.R. 153.

mutual recognition of qualifications as opposed to the elimination of national restrictions on establishment, or services as defined in Article 52. The two methods of attacking the problem are of course complementary, but it is generally considered that the more that can be achieved by co-ordination, the easier will be the task of eliminating national restrictions. Indeed this is recognised explicitly at least for the medical and allied and pharmaceutical professions, for Article 57 (3) states that for these professions "the progressive abolition of restrictions shall be dependent upon co-ordination of the conditions for their exercise in the various Member States."

7—27   Article 57 envisages the issue of directives by the Council, acting now by a qualified majority on a proposal from the Commission and after consulting the Assembly, first to ensure "the mutual recognition of diplomas, certificates and other evidence of formal qualifications,"[33] and secondly to co-ordinate the provisions in each Member State "concerning the taking up and pursuit of activities as self-employed persons."[34] The co-ordination referred to here is again to be effected by directives, issued by the Council acting on a proposal from the Commission and after consulting the Assembly. Where the subject-matter of the draft directive is the subject of legislation in at least one Member State, or relates to the protection of savings, in particular the granting of credit and the exercise of the banking profession or to the medical and allied, and pharmaceutical profession, the Council is to act unanimously. In other cases the Council was to act unanimously during the first stage of the original period of transition, and now by qualified majority.

7—28   Although it may thus be thought that the freedom to provide professional services in particular would be contingent upon mutual recognition of qualifications, it has proved possible, so far as concerns lawyers, to attain considerable freedom without any such mutual recognition.[35] It is conceivable that certain other liberal professions could also be liberalised in this way.

The two solutions for the problem of freeing establishment, that of Article 52 (elimination of restrictions) and Article 57 (co-ordination of measures regarding access to activities) were intermeshed by the General Programme, as well as by Article 57 (3) of the Treaty. Thus Title IV of the General Programme,[36] which set out the timetable for the elimination of restrictions, was in practice taken with the provisions of Title V, requiring the process of elimination of restrictions to be preceded, accompanied or followed by the co-ordination of qualifications for activities. Title V also made provision for a transitional regime before full

[33] Treaty Article 57 (1).
[34] Treaty Article 57 (2).
[35] See Directive 77/349, O.J. 1979, L78/17.
[36] *Supra,* note 16.

co-ordination of measures in order to facilitate access to activities. For some activities co-ordination alone, without simultaneous elimination of national restrictions, might have hindered the freeing of establishment too greatly, so that a transitional period was desirable. The directives on the freedom of establishment were normally issued two at a time, one on the achievement of freedom of establishment and the other on a transitional period for the co-ordination of qualifications, *e.g.* Directives 68/363[37] and 68/364[38], concerning self-employed persons in the retail trade.

17—29   Much of the importance of this whole process was nevertheless removed by the ruling in *Reyners*[39] that after the expiry of the transitional period the directives provided for by the chapter on the right of establishment have become superfluous with regard to implementing the rule on nationality, since this is henceforth sanctioned by Article 52 of the Treaty itself with direct effect. As the Court pointed out, however, the directives retain some importance in facilitating the exercise of the directly applicable right.[40]

Article 58

17—30   Article 58 amplifies the definition of the beneficiaries of freedom of establishment in Article 52 making it clear that companies and firms are included or on equal footing. This provision is discussed *infra*, para. 13-34.

4. *General Measures connected with the Right of Establishment and Freedom to provide Services*

17—31   A directive containing limited provisions relating to the abolition of restrictions on movement and residence within the Community of self employed persons[41] was replaced and extended by the present directive on this subject, Directive 73/148.[42] Its provisions are along the same lines as those for workers contained in Directive 68/360.[43] The right to remain in the territory of another Member State after having been self-employed there is guaranteed by Directive 75/34[44] and the application of Directive 64/221 on public policy, etc., is guaranteed by Directive 75/35.[45] These two directives resemble the measures adopted in respect of workers[46] a few years previously. A general right to stay in a Member State

[37] J.O. 1968, L260/1.
[38] J.O. 1968, L260/6.
[39] *Supra,* note 2.
[40] See also Case 136/78 *Auer supra,* note 3.
[41] Directive 64/220, J.O. 1964, 845.
[42] *Supra,* note 18.
[43] *Supra,* para. 16–23.
[44] O.J. 1975, L14/10.
[45] O.J. 1975, L14/14.
[46] *Supra,* Chapter 16.

even when not carrying on any economic activity has now been proposed.[47]

5. Two Special Problems - Public Contracts, and Companies

Public Contracts

17—32 Works on behalf of public authorities and purchases by those authorities form a very substantial part of the economy in any country. The reservation of the public works and public purchasing markets to nationals constitutes a non-tariff barrier to trade and a discrimination against establishment and the free provision of services. The problem in the case of public works was recognised by the Community early on; the first proposals on this subject were made in 1964[48] but it was only in 1971 that directives on the subject were issued. The first, 71/304,[49] relates to the abolition of restrictions on freedom to provide services in the field of public works contracts and the award of public works contracts through the intermediary of agencies and subsidiaries. The directive was adopted on the legal basis of Articles 54 (2) and 63 (2) - the general implementing provisions of the establishment and services chapters. Article 1 states the aim of general abolition of discrimination against non-nationals and Article 3 (1) (c) particularly emphasises that discriminatory technical specifications in contracts, though applicable irrespective of nationality, should be abolished. This would relate especially to the specification in a contract for the use of patented materials or devices.

17—33 The second Directive, 71/305,[50] aims at the co-ordination of procedures for the award of public contracts, and is based on Articles 57 (2), 66 and 100. It lays down elaborate provisions dependent on the size of the contract and the procedure to be adopted for publicising the contract, but the key provisions are that any governmental contract worth more than 1 million ECU[51] must be publicised in the Official Journal, and that any firm registered in a Member State of the Community is eligible to tender for it.

Directive 77/62[52] provides for similar treatment for public supply contracts. Here the rules on publication and technical specifications apply to contracts whose estimated value is not less than 200,000 ECU.

The Community is a party to the GATT Agreement on Govern-

---

[47] O.J. 1979, C207.
[48] Suppt 9/10, Bulletin EC, 1964.
[49] J.O. 1971, L185/1; O.J. 1971, 678.
[50] J.O. 1971, L185/5 O.J. 1971, 652 amended by Directive 78/669 O.J. 1978, L225/41. See also Directive 72/277, O.J. 1972, L176/12 on publication of notices.
[51] *Ibid.*
[52] O.J. 1977, L13/1. See also Directive 80/767, O.J. 1980, L215/1.

ment Procurement of April 12, 1979.[53] The Agreement applies to any governmental procurement contract of a value of 150,000 Special Drawing Rights or more, for products including incidental services (Art. I). The principal feature is national treatment and non-discrimination for the products and suppliers of other parties to the agreement in the procurement process, without prejudice to customs duties, etc., applicable (Art. II). The agreement provides for certain relaxations in favour of, and for technical assistance to, developing countries (Art. III). The practical effect of the Agreement once in force will be to enable prospective suppliers to respond to tenders advertised under the Community arrangements contained in Directive 77/62.

Companies

17—34   As has already been indicated, freedom of establishment in the context of the EEC Treaty (Arts. 52 to 58) relates to all Community nationals, whether these be natural or legal persons; thus a definition is included in the second paragraph of Article 52 of "freedom of establishment" as embracing "the right to set up and manage undertakings, in particular companies or firms within the meaning of the second paragraph of Article 58" upon the same terms as nationals of the country of establishment, subject, however, to the provisions of the chapter relating to capital.

By Article 58, second para., "companies or firms" are defined to mean companies or firms "constituted under civil or commercial law, including cooperative societies, and other legal persons governed by public or private law, save for those which are non-profit making."

By Article 58, first para., companies and firms coming within this definition formed in accordance with the law of any Member State and having their "registered office, central administration or principal place of business within the Community" are to be treated "in the same way as natural persons who are nationals of Member States."

17—35   The Treaty thus avoids the adoption of any single determinant of the national character of companies, as perhaps it was bound to do since even within the original six Member States the tests adopted varied from the place of registration or principal place of business in Italy, to place of registration in France, Germany and Luxembourg. But instead of simply referring the whole question to national law, Article 58 so far combines the tests of the place of registration and of actual or real head office as to provide for treatment on an equal footing with nationals of Member States of companies registered under the law of any Member State and having their registered offices or central administration or principal

---

[53] Annexed to Decision 80/271, O.J. 1980, L71/1 at p.44.

places of business anywhere within the Community.

It has been suggested that the apparent breadth of this provision is cut down so as to include within it only those companies having an effective link with the Community, for Article 52 confines freedom of establishment to the right to set up and manage under-takings "under the conditions laid down for its own nationals by the law of the country where such establishment is effected." But this limitation would appear to relate exclusively to the capacity of nationals of one Member State to incorporate companies under the law of another. The same result is, however, achieved by Title 1 of the General Programme on the Freedom of Establishment which states that where a company has only a registered office within the Community, its activities must have an effective and continuous link with the economy of the Member State if it is to benefit from the right of establishment. This provision is paralleled by similar provisions in various types of commercial treaties concluded by individual States, *e.g.* air service agreements and double taxation conventions.

17—36   Article 54 provides for the progressive abolition of existing restrictions upon freedom of establishment through action of the Council and Commission *inter alia* under paragraph 3 (*g*):

> "by co-ordinating to the necessary extent the safeguards which, for the protection of the interests of members and others, are required by Member States of companies or firms within the meaning of the second paragraph of Article 58 with a view to making such safeguards equivalent throughout the Community."

In addition, Article 220 stipulates that:

> "Member States shall, so far as is necessary, enter into negotiations with each other with a view to securing for the benefit of their nationals . . . the mutual recognition of com-panies or firms within the meaning of the second paragraph of Article 58, the retention of legal personality in the event of transfer of their seat from one country to another, and the possibility of mergers between companies or firms governed by the laws of different countries."

A convention has been adopted under this provision on the mutual recognition of companies, *infra*, para. 17-46.

Directives

17—37   Article 54 (3) (*g*) has formed the basis for a number of directives. A number of others are in draft.

Directive 68/151[54] applies only to companies limited by shares

---

[54] J.O. 1968, L65/8, O.J. 1968, 41.

and thus not to every type of concern within Article 58 (2). The directive is designed not only to effect the co-ordination of safeguards for third persons dealing with companies, but also to afford uniform protection to persons belonging to one Member State becoming members or shareholders of companies in other Member States, as they have tended increasingly to do as a result of the freeing of the movement of capital within the Community and of the achievement of national treatment for investors under Article 221 of the Treaty.

17—38   This directive lays down what information concerning its affairs a company must be required to disclose (Art. 2) and how this is to be made available to the public (Art. 3). The information required includes the memorandum and articles, the names of directors, the amount of paid-up capital, the balance sheet and profit and loss account, and any details of transfer of domicile, winding-up or liquidation.

The disclosure of *financial* information was not required of "private" companies within the six original Member States because national law had not required it. Article 2 (1) (*f*) indicated that such disclosure would be required within limits when a directive on accounts was adopted. Directive 78/660 (*infra*, para. 17-43) is the relevant instrument. Articles 11 and 47 (2) of that directive allow for abridged accounts in the case of small companies.

Article 3 (5) of the directive operates as a sanction by providing that documents or particulars required to be disclosed may be relied upon by the company against a third party, in the absence of proof that the latter had knowledge thereof, only after publication in the appropriate national gazette as required under Article 3 (4). The non-publication of financial provisions is left to be penalised expressly (Art. 6).

17—39   By Article 7 promoters of a company are to be made jointly and severally liable for any act performed during the promotion of a company, for which responsibility is not subsequently accepted by the company. Article 8 provides that where the formalities of disclosure of the names of persons authorised to represent the company have been completed, any actual irregularity in the appointment of those persons may not be relied upon by the company against third parties unless actual notice is proved. By Article 9 companies are to be made liable for acts going beyond the scope of their objects but which are within their capacity under domestic law. Member States may, however, legislate so as to negate liability to third parties having actual notice of the *ultra vires* quality of any act (Art. 9 (1)). The United Kingdom has made use of this facility in section 9 of the European Communities Act 1972. The intention of this section seems to have been to protect those who have dealt in good faith with a company or at any rate with its directors.

17—40   The third part of the directives refers to "nullity" of companies, a concept unknown to United Kingdom company law. In Article 11 (2) are listed six grounds upon which nullity may be ordered, including the illegal objects of the company and the absence of an instrument of constitution. Article 12 (3) lays down, consistently with the general aim of protection of persons dealing with companies, that notwithstanding that nullity results in the termination of a company's existence it shall not affect the validity of earlier transactions. The consequences of an order of nullity are not dealt with by the directive save in so far as they are remitted to the sphere of national law (Art. 12 (4)). The directive does not require Member States to introduce rules on nullity of companies where none existed before, and the United Kingdom did not adopt such a course in the European Communities Act 1972 because under the Companies Act 1948 the certificate of incorporation is conclusive evidence that the company has been duly formed (s. 15 (1)).

17—41   The second Directive, 77/91,[55] is designed to co-ordinate safeguards respecting the formation of public limited companies, and the maintenance and alteration of capital. Private companies and partnerships are not dealt with because they present separate problems. Protection of creditors is also dealt with. Companies are required to disclose details of capitalisation and management (Art. 2) and share structure (Art. 3). The minimum prescribed paid-up capital is fixed at 25,000 ECU. (Art. 6). Articles 7 to 14 provide safeguards against issue of shares at under-value. Corresponding safeguards are provided in Articles 26 to 29 on increases in capital. By Articles 15 and 16 companies are restrained from declaring dividends if at any time their assets, including reserves, fall below the amount of their paid-up capital. Articles 18 to 24 impose restrictions upon purchase of their own shares by companies more stringent than those prevailing under the municipal legislation of the original six Member States, though less severe than those applying in English law. Article 25, 30 and 31 permit capital increases or reductions only by resolution in general meeting and of meetings of each class of shareholders affected. Other safeguards on reduction are contained in Articles 34 to 39. Articles 32 and 33 institute a system for securing debts contracted before any reductions of capital. Article 42 institutes a fundamental concept of equal treatment for all shareholders within any class.

17—42   The third Directive, 78/855,[56] covers the merger of public limited companies, or more particularly, merger by the acquisition of one or more companies by another and merger by the forma-

[55] O.J. 1977, L26/1.
[56] O.J. 1978, L295/36.

tion of a new company. It requires Member States to make provision for rules governing such mergers (Art. 1) and lays down in particular requirements in respect of disclosure of the terms on which the merger is to be effected (Arts. 5 and 6), formalities with respect to approval by the general meeting (Arts. 7 and 8) and, perhaps most significantly, a rule that an independent body of experts is to examine the draft terms of the merger and draw up a written report to the shareholders (Art. 10). Shareholders and creditors are also to be given protection (Arts. 11 and 13-15). Articles 27 to 29 make allowance for the provisions of the Companies Act 1948, s. 209, *viz.* that a company holding at least 90 per cent of the share capital of another company may be able to acquire the remaining shares and so effect a merger without first obtaining the approval of the general meeting. Article 12 makes a specific saving in favour of employees' rights by reference to Directive 77/187.[57]

17—43   The fourth Directive, 78/660,[58] requires the harmonisation of guarantees required in respect of public and private limited companies to protect the interests both of shareholders and outsiders as regards the structure and contents of the annual accounts and annual return. It introduces common rules on the layout of accounts, stipulating minimum standards of disclosure. It does not require the use of inflation accounting techniques but does allow Member States to provide for it (Art. 33). Pending subsequent co-ordination, Member States are not required to apply the directive to banks and other financial institutions and insurance companies (Art. 1 (2)).

17—44   Due to come into force in 1981, Directive 79/279[59] co-ordinating the conditions for the admission of securities to official stock exchange listing is designed to provide protection for investors through guarantees and disclosure of information besides serving a long-term goal of allowing for interpenetration of national securities markets. It goes beyond the securities of companies covered by Article 58 and covers also securities issued by non-Member States or their regional or local authorities and international bodies. Member States may choose not to apply it to issues of their own public authorities (Art. 1). Co-ordination consists in laying down minimum conditions, but confers no right to listing, beyond ensuring non-discrimination. However there is a legal right to appeal against a refusal (Art. 15). Complementing Directive 79/279 is Directive 80/390,[60] co-ordinating the require-

[57] O.J. 1977, L61/26.
[58] O.J. 1978, L222/11.
[59] O.J. 1979, L66/21.
[60] O.J. 1980, L100/1. See also Commission Recommendation 77/534 of July 25, 1977, concerning a European Code of Conduct relating to transactions in transferable securities, O.J. 1977, L212/37.

ments for the drawing up, scrutiny and distribution of the listing particulars to be published for the admission of securities to official stock exchange listing.

17—45   Other proposals for directives concern:

- the structure of public limited companies;[61]
- group accounts;[62]
- the minimum qualifications for auditors.[63]

The first mentioned is the most controversial in that it would introduce a form of employee participation in management not unlike that existing now in West Germany.

The taxation of companies and capital is discussed in the chapter on taxation.[64]

Conventions

17—46   Although Article 58 EEC in effect extends "national treatment" to corporations, it neither defines the requisites for recognition of foreign companies nor indicates with any precision the consequences of such recognition. Accordingly, recourse was had to Article 220 pursuant to which the Convention on the Mutual Recognition of Companies and Bodies Corporate was drawn up.[65]

By Article 1 of the latter Convention:

"Companies under civil or commercial law, including co-operative societies, established in accordance with the law of a Contracting State which grants them the capacity of persons having rights and duties, and having their statutory registered office in the territories to which the present Convention applies, shall be recognised as of right."

Article 2 of the Convention provides:

"Bodies corporate under public or private law, other than the companies specified in Article 1, which fulfil the conditions stipulated in the said Article, which have as their main or accessory object an economic activity normally exercised for reward, and which, without infringing the law under which they were established, do in fact continuously exercise such activity, shall also be recognised as of right."

17—47   The Convention thus applies to companies established with capacity under civil or commercial law of a Member State and

---

[61] See Suppt. 8/75—Bulletin EC (a Community "green paper").
[62] See Suppt. 9/76—Bulletin EC.
[63] O.J. 1978, C103.
[64] *Infra*, Chapter 22.
[65] Signed February 29, 1968, Suppt. 2/69 Bulletin EC together with a later protocol (75/464, O.J. 1975, L204/28) on interpretation by the Court of Justice.

having their statutory registered office in the territories to which the Convention applies (Art. 1), and to legal persons of public or private law, established under the same conditions, having as their aim or necessary object an economic activity normally exercised for reward (Art. 2). Article 8 of the Convention provides that recognition is not to be denied or restricted merely because the law in accordance with which an entity is established does not grant it the legal status of a body corporate; thus for example the *Offene Handelsgesellschaft* (OHG) of German law qualifies. But contracting States may declare that they will not apply the Convention to entities having their real registered office outside the Convention territories, and having no genuine link with the economy of one of the territories. Exceptionally, a contracting State may in addition require certain special requirements of its own legislation to be complied with where the entity to be recognised has its real registered office on its own territory (Art. 4). "Real registered office" is defined by Article 5 as meaning the place where the entity's central administration is established.

17—48   The effect of recognition is such that the recognised entity is to have in the recognising State the capacity accorded to it by the law under which it is established (Art. 6), but the recognising State may refuse certain rights and powers which it does not grant to similar entities governed by its own law, but this is not to result in the withdrawal of the capacity to contract, or to accomplish other legal acts or to sue or to be sued (Art. 7, first para.). The limitations arising from restrictions thus imposed may not be invoked by the recognised entity (Art. 7, second para.). The application of the Convention is made subject to accepted principles of public policy (Art. 9).

A Convention is proposed respecting the bankruptcy of individuals and of companies (*i.e.* involving compulsory winding-up of insolvent companies), supplementary to the Convention on Jurisdiction and the Enforcement of Civil and Commercial Judgements,[66] to be drawn up with a view to securing uniform effect throughout the Community of adjudications in bankruptcy, etc.[67]

A Convention has also been discussed and drafts proposed on the merger of EEC companies.

The European company

17—49   It is of course theoretically possible to set up by treaty a legal entity or corporation not possessing the nationality of any State, though in practice at least in the past it has usually been thought more convenient to incorporate such essentially international institutions such as the Bank for International Settlements under a system of municipal law - in that case Swiss law.

---

[66] September 27, 1968; Cmnd. 7395. *cf.* also para. 23–09.
[67] *Cf.* also para. 23–09.

But even the theoretical possibility of establishing a non-national company does not exist for private enterprise, as opposed to States. The creation of the Common Market has not so far altered this situation.

7—50   In 1966, however, the Commission responded to a French proposal for the adoption of a uniform company law by each of the Six with a suggestion for the establishment by convention of a system of European company law under which European companies might be incorporated.[68] The Sanders Committee, appointed to consider this suggestion, reported in favour of the plan whereby European companies might be brought into existence by the merger of companies incorporated under different systems of national law; as holding companies associated with such companies, or by direct registration as European companies. The plan envisaged a body of European company law under the aegis of the Court of Justice of the Communities.[69] A feature of it was a somewhat ill-defined scheme for employee participation in European companies. It was rejected, however, by the Commission in favour of the latter body's own proposal made under Article 235 of the EEC Treaty.[70]

7—51   This proposal did not allow for the establishment of European companies by direct registration, but contemplated rather that they should come into existence exclusively through the merger of companies incorporated under the laws of two or more Member States. Though no tax advantages such as would prejudice the revenue of any Member State are envisaged for the European company, it was hoped that these entities would benefit from the proposed directive on the taxation of mergers[71] and that they would be free to adopt a system of consolidated accounting allowing a loss made in one country of the Community to be set off against a profit made elsewhere before submission of a tax return to the country of domicile. This would be subject to adequate safeguards for the shareholders. Another feature of the proposal was the reservation to shareholders of concerns merged into European companies of an option to be bought out at a fair price.

7—52   The most controversial aspect of this proposal was, as with the proposal for a fifth Directive on the structure of public limited companies, the extent of employee participation. A good number of changes were made to this and other aspects of the proposal by the European Parliament, and in response to the Parliament's suggestions, a new proposal was adopted by the Commission in

[68] Suppt. 9/10 Bulletin EC 1966.
[69] Etudes Concurrence No.6, 1967, Brussels.
[70] J.O. 1970, C124/1, Suppt 8/70 Bulletin EC 1970.
[71] *Infra*, Chapter 22.

1975.[72] In this new proposal, the right to form an "SE" (Societas Europaea) is to be limited to companies who are recognised pursuant to the Convention on the Mutual Recognition of Companies and Bodies Corporate. (Essentially the purpose of the proposal is to permit transnational mergers.) The proposal in its Table 4 provides for the creation of a Board of Management and a Supervisory Board on the German model, the latter to be composed of representatives of shareholders (one-third), representatives of workers (one-third) and members co-opted by these two groups (one-third). Article 137 requires the employees' representatives to be elected by the employees. It is possible for a maximum of two such representatives (if their total is more than three, otherwise one), not to be employees of the SE; in other words, some Trade Union officials may be elected.

Other forms of European co-operation in the field of company law

17—53   In 1971, the Commission proposed a regulation[73] on the formation of joint undertakings between *public* departments or services which would receive Community financial backing and have legal personality in all the Member States. This is to be contrasted with a 1973 proposal for a regulation for the setting up of a "European co-operative group" to encourage co-operation in the private sector - in the nature of a partnership between Community undertakings governed by contract.[74]

---

[72] Suppt 4/75 Bulletin EC 1975.

[73] J.O. 1971, C107/15 and see written question 147/74, O.J. 1974, 95/21.

[74] J.O. 1972, C131/15, Proposal of December 21, 1973, Suppt 1/74 Bulletin EC, O.J. 1974, C14.

Chapter 18

CAPITAL

18—01 The free movement of capital, dealt with by Articles 67 to 73, together forming Chapter IV of Title III of Part Two of the Treaty, is the fourth of the four freedoms fundamental to the Community. The "equivalent" of Articles 48, 52 and 59 is to be found in Article 67 which provides for the abolition of all restrictions on the movement of capital belonging to persons resident in Member States and of discrimination based on residence or nationality or on the place where capital is invested. Unlike the other provisions however, Article 67 contains a proviso - the restrictions, etc., need only be abolished "to the extent necessary to ensure the proper functioning of the Common Market."

18—02 Two opposing views have been taken of this proviso. On the one hand it is argued that Article 3 (c) specifically includes the abolition of obstacles to the free movement of capital on a par with the other freedoms. Hence it follows that there must be a common market in capital. The proviso therefore refers to the common market in capital, and not to the other freedoms. There is some slight support for this view in Case 7/78 *R.* v. *Johnson et al.*[1] On this basis all capital movements should be freed unless perhaps they are of a purely speculative nature in which case they might actually harm the common market in capital.

On the other hand it is argued that the proviso refers to the other freedoms, from which it would follow that capital movements need only be liberated to the extent necessary to guarantee those freedoms. This would arguably reduce the need for liberalisation considerably, although it has already been seen that some services, such as banking and insurance, cannot be entirely freed until the restrictions on capital movements are lifted.

On either interpretation, the discretionary element makes it highly unlikely that Article 67, para. 1, could be directly applicable.[2]

18—03 Furthermore, the question of capital movements being closely connected with national economic policies, the obligation to liberalise these movements is primarily in the hands of the Member

---

[1] [1978] E.C.R. 2247.
[2] *Cf.* Article 90 (2) and Case 10/71 *Ministère Public* v. *Muller-Hein* [1971] E.C.R. 723 and see Article 5 (3) of the First Directive: "The restrictions on capital movements under the rules for establishment in a Member State shall be abolished pursuant to this Directive only in so far as it is incumbent upon the Member States to grant freedom of establishment in implementation of Articles 52 to 58 of the Treaty." (Directive of May 11, 1960, *infra,* note 4).

States. This is in line with the terms in which the stipulations of the title on Economic Policy (Arts. 103 to 116) are expressed. Part of that title, in particular the chapter on balance of payments (Arts. 104 to 109) relates also to free movement of capital. The exercise of powers under Articles 108 and 109 in particular may result in some limitation on free movement of capital (see *infra*, paras. 24-11 - 24-19). The powers relating specifically to capital movements contained in the Treaty as a whole are not sufficient to meet the needs of the Community and measures have been taken in this field under Article 100 (harmonisation of laws) to fill in some of the gaps. The proposals for Economic and Monetary Union could, if implemented, have led to complete freedom of capital movement, and the responsibilities of the Community in this area would then have been much greater than they are at present.[3]

A two-fold approach is adopted for freeing capital movements; the first object of the chapter on capital, already mentioned, is expressed to be the elimination of restrictions on movement of capital and discriminations based on nationality or residence or place of investment (Art. 67). This is complemented by a second object (set out in Art. 70) of co-ordinating the exchange policies of Member States *vis-à-vis* third countries with a view to avoiding the distortions and deflections of capital movements between the Community and third States, which would otherwise follow upon a simple dismantling of internal controls pursuant to Article 67.

18—04   Articles 67 to 73 do not define free movement of capital, nor do the implementing directives contain any such definition. But the lists, nomenclature and explanatory notes annexed to the First Directive for the implementation of Article 67 of May 11, 1960,[4] indicate what capital movements are covered by the directive and thus, indirectly, by the notion of free movement of capital.

It appears that the latter notion involves the abolition of exchange control restrictions, of any discriminatory laws and regulations regarding the nationality or residence of parties concerned and of any residual restrictions not necessarily discriminatory but which hinder capital flows. Capital includes both long-term direct investment capital, and short-term capital, invested in Treasury bills and other securities normally dealt in on the money market, and any capital falling in between these two extremes. The Community has, however, failed to free all types of capital movement, as will emerge below. In Case 7/78 *R.* v. *Johnson*,[5] the Court held that current coins are means of payment covered by

---

[3] See generally, *infra*, para. 24–21.
[4] J.O. 1960, 921, O.J. 1959–62, 49 as amended by Directive 63/21, J.O. 1963, 62, O.J. 1963–64, 5 and Annex I (VII) (3) of the Act of Accession of the UK, Ireland and Denmark. Greece is granted deferrals: Articles 49 to 56 of the Act of Accession.
[5] *Supra*, note 1.

Articles 67 to 73 or by Articles 104 to 109 and not goods covered by Articles 30 to 34 and 36.

Article 67

18–05 Article 67 (1) strikes at restrictions based on residence as well as nationality. This is because national exchange control regulations are generally based on residence. The explanatory notes at the end of the First Directive leave to national exchange control regulations the definition of resident and non-resident status. The criterion of residence comprehends others besides "nationals," but nationals may of course be non-residents. It is now generally accepted that besides residents of a State, all those persons established in that State, especially as defined by Article 58, benefit from the free movement of capital and Article 5 (3) of the First Directive creates a direct link between freedom of establishment and free movement of capital.

18–06 The First Directive implementing Article 67[6] issued under Article 69 is designed to secure the abolition of restrictions on the movement of capital belonging to residents of Member States. A decision taken by the Council on the same day[7] applies Article 67 to 73 EEC to Algeria and the French overseas departments. The directive was modified slightly by Directive 63/21[8] and by the Acts of Accession.[9]

The directive divides capital movements into four groups (annexed as Lists A to D). List A covers direct investments, investments in real estate and personal capital movements such as gifts, inheritances, royalties, insurance payments and remittances. Article 1 of the directive requires Member States to grant all foreign exchange authorisations necessary for such capital movements between residents of Member States. An authorisation is still required to prevent fraudulent inclusion within this category of transactions properly outside it. Member States are required to authorise these capital movements at the normal exchange rates (Art. 1 (2)) and the Monetary Committee (set up under Art. 105 EEC) is entrusted with the task of following the exchange rates applied so as to ensure that no disparities occur.

List B covers the acquisition of securities quoted on a stock exchange; Article 2 of the directive allows complete freedom in respect of such transactions and transfers, but without the monetary conversion safeguard incorporated in Article 1 (2). Member States have a duty merely "to endeavour to ensure that transfers are made at rates which do not show appreciable and lasting differences from those ruling for payments relating to current

[6] *Supra*, note 4.
[7] Decision of May 11, 1960, J.O. 1960, 919.
[8] *Supra*, note 4.
[9] *Ibid.*

transactions." The Commission has a power to make recommendations after consulting the Monetary Committee.

18—07   List C relates notably to the issue of shares on a stock exchange, the acquisition of securities not quoted on a stock exchange, and to long and medium-term credits and to related securities. Article 3 requires Member States to grant the required foreign exchange authorisations with the reservation that:

> "Where such free movement of capital might form an obstacle to the achievement of the economic policy objectives of a Member State, the latter may maintain or re-introduce the exchange restrictions on capital movements which were operative on the date of entry into force of this directive [in the case of new Member States, the date of accession]. It shall consult the Commission on the matter." (Art. 3 (2)).

18—08   List D covers the remaining types of capital movement, *e.g.* those in short-dated Treasury paper and short-term credits, bank deposits and the like, and personal capital movements, loans and sureties not covered in the other list, as well as the physical import an export of financial assets (which would include tourist allowances). No liberalisation is required for List D but Article 6 requires Member States to endeavour not to introduce within the Community any new exchange restrictions affecting capital movements which were free at the date of entry into force of the directive (or the date of accession) nor to make existing provisions more restrictive. This standstill provision is not a simple repetition of the standstill Clause in Article 71, first para. of the Treaty, relating only to new (*i.e.* post-1957) restrictions, for the operative date here is that of the entry into force of the directive for the Member State concerned.

Article 5 of the directive permits Member States to verify the nature and bona fides of transactions and transfers, so that capital frauds may be kept in check. Their ability so to do, is, however, already implicit in the maintenance of authorisations even for movements in List A. However, Community customs rules cannot be used for this purpose.[10]

18—09   The second directive, Directive 63/21[11] deletes a safeguard provision relating to List B. The only country which took advantage of this was Italy. The Second Directive also amends and expands the lists so as to include, for example, transfers of workers' savings and annual transfers of blocked funds within List A. No further

---

[10] Case 65/79 *Procureur de la République* v. *Châtain* [1980] E.C.R. 1345.
[11] *Supra,* note 4.

measures in relation to the abolition of restrictions on the movement of capital have been promulgated.

18—10   Article 67 (1) EEC provides further for the abolition of discrimination based on the place of investment of capital. Progress here has been slight. In April 1964 the Commission made proposals on the elimination of such discrimination, but these were not adopted, nor were its revised proposals of 1967, although progress in this field is of paramount importance.[1][2]

Article 67 (2) concerns current payments connected with the movement of capital; restrictions on these payments were required to be abolished by the end of the first stage. Since these payments had already been liberalised by all the Member States in the context of the Bretton Woods Agreement of 1944 (Article VIII) this paragraph has never been of any importance. Invisible transactions not connected with the movement of goods, services, capital or persons (*i.e.* not already liberalised under Article 106) are covered by Directive 63/474.[1][3]

Article 68

18—11   Article 68 (1), requiring Member States to be as liberal as possible in granting "such exchange authorisations as are still necessary after the entry into force of this Treaty" was originally designed as a safeguard against delayed issue of a directive implementing Article 67. Even now that directives have been issued, this paragraph must be regarded as encouraging further voluntary liberalisation of exchange authorisations, although the more general terms of Article 71, second para. (*infra*), cover the same ground and more. Neither article prohibits the re-introduction of restrictions, but Article 67 and Article 71, first para., place considerable limits on this. Article 6 of the First Directive[1][4] merely calls on Member States to "endeavour not to introduce" any new exchange restrictions affecting capital movements which had already been liberalised on the entry into force of the directive for that State.

18—12   Article 68 (2) requires the domestic rules governing the operation of the capital market and the credit system to be applied in a non-discriminatory manner to the movements of capital liberalised in accordance with the provisions of the chapter. These rules do not necessarily relate directly to capital movements, but may have that effect. If operated in a discriminatory fashion, these rules may come within the prohibition of Article 67 (1). Like paragraph 1, paragraph 2 of Article 68 sets out a rule of general application,

[12] See the Segré Report, the Development of a European Capital Market, Commission, Brussels 1966.
[13] J.O. 1963, 2240, O.J. 1963–64, 45.
[14] *Supra,* note 3.

not requiring implementation by directive. The obligation of non-discrimination is probably directly applicable.

Article 68 (3) constitutes a derogation from the principles of free movement of capital outlined in Article 67; under its provisions neither the Member States nor their public authorities may obtain financing through loans placed in another Member State without prior agreement of that State. The exception is limited to the raising of loans, there being no bar to capital transactions and transfer for other purposes, such as currency swap agreements or the financing of the institutions of the Community under Articles 207 and 208. Article 68 (3) is expressed not to preclude the European Investment Bank from borrowing on the capital markets of Member States, as provided for by Article 22 of the Protocol on its statute.

Article 69

18—13   Article 69 sets out the procedure for the issue of directives implementing the provisions of Article 67. These are issued by the Council acting now by qualified majority on a proposal from the Commission, which must in this case consult the Monetary Committee provided for in Article 105. The limitation built into Article 69 that the Council may issue only the "necessary" directives is a cross-reference to the corresponding limitation in Article 67 (1).

Article 70

18—14   Article 70 forms the other side of the two-fold approach to free movement of capital, providing for proposals from the Commission to the Council for directives on the progressive co-ordination of all aspects of exchange policies *vis-à-vis* third States. The directives are to be issued by unanimous vote. Clearly, a common attitude to movements of capital between the Community and third States is necessary if the benefits of internal free movement are not to be lost, but there is now felt to be a need for something more than simple co-ordination, although, in issuing the directives the Council is required to endeavour to attain the highest possible degree of liberalisation (Art. 70 (1)).

Paragraph 2 of Article 70 contemplates the situation where differences remain in the exchange policies of Member States despite measures taken under paragraph 1. It permits a Member State to take appropriate safeguard measures after consulting with the other Member States and with the Commission, if the free circulation rules lead to capital movement deflection.

18—15   The question arises in connection with Article 70 (2) whether the capital deflection can be merely apprehended or has to be actual before a Member State may take appropriate safeguard measures. The phrase used in the English text, "could lead persons

. . . to use," seems to suggest that there need only be a potential risk, as does the French *inciteraient . . . à utiliser*, but the German *Benutzen* seems to require some concrete evidence of deflection. Nevertheless, the consultation requirement restricts the use of such safeguards, and should the Council find that the measures taken by a particular Member State restrict the free movement of capital within the Community to an extent greater than that required to meet the situation, it may, acting by a qualified majority on a proposal from the Commission, decide that the State concerned shall amend or abolish the measures.

8—16   Council Directive 72/156[15] based on Articles 70 and 103 (conjunctural policy), is designed to regulate international capital flows and to neutralise their undesirable effects on domestic liquidity. The directive requires Member States to take powers to control deposits and interest rates on the money market, and to control loans which Community residents contract with non-Community residents, if need be by derogating from Article 3 (1) of the First Directive.[16] The directive also permits measures to be taken to control the net external liability of credit institutions and to fix compulsory reserve margins, in particular for the holdings of non-residents.

Article 71

8—17   Article 71 acts as a standstill provision in respect of restrictions dealt with by Article 67. Member States are required by this article to endeavour to avoid introducing any new exchange restrictions on movement of capital and associated current payments, and are also to endeavour not to make existing rules more restrictive. As far as the article deals with current payments, it is of minor significance, since all restrictions on such had been abolished prior to the entry into force of the Treaty. The phrasing of the article reflects the general level of obligation within this chapter; it does not lay down an absolute rule - Member States are only to endeavour to avoid introducing any new restrictions. The ambit of the article has been cut down by the subsequent standstill clause contained in the First Directive.

The second paragraph of Article 71 is similar to provisions found elsewhere in the Treaty, affording Member States the possibility of going beyond the degree of liberalisation of capital provided for in the preceding articles, in so far as their economic situation, in particular their balance of payments, permits. The Commission may, after consulting the Monetary Committee, make recommendations to Member States on this subject.

[15] J.O. 1972, L91/13; O.J. 1972, 296.
[16] *Supra,* note 3.

Article 72

18—18   By Article 72, Member States are required to keep the Commission informed of any movements of capital to and from third countries which come to their knowledge. Article 72 was intended to provide the source material on the basis of which to establish measures to be taken under both Articles 70 and 105. But in practice the article has not proved very useful. Only those capital movements which come to the attention of the Member States have to be reported to the Commission - an implicit acceptance of the principle of bankers' secrecy. In 1965 the Commission made proposals for the issue of a decision to be taken on the basis of Article 213, which enables the Commission to be given powers to collect information necessary for the performance of its tasks, so that a uniform and obligatory rule regarding disclosure of information on capital movements could be issued. The proposal was never adopted. The Commission is also empowered by Article 72 to give opinions on the subject of capital movement (*cf.* the general power to deliver opinions under Article 155, second hyphen.)

Article 73

18—19   Article 73 (1) requires the Commission to authorise Member States to take safeguard measures should capital movements lead to disturbances on the national capital markets. The conditions and details of these measures are laid down by the Commission itself, after consulting the Monetary Committee, subject only to amendment or revocation by the Council, acting by qualified majority. It will be noted that the Article 73 (1) safeguards are not confined to combating the disturbances brought on as a result of measures of liberalisation.

     Article 73 (2) enables a Member State in difficulties to take measures unilaterally where this is justified on grounds of secrecy or urgency. It must, however, inform the Commission and the other Member States of such measures by the date of their entry into force at the latest, and the Commission may, after consulting the Monetary Committee, require the amendment or abolition of the measures taken. It is somewhat surprising that the Commission has the last word over the presumably more important matters dealt with under Article 73 (2), but not under Article 73 (1). It would appear that such a result may not have been intended.

18—20   Articles 108 and 109, which relate to safeguards where the balance of payments is threatened, are fairly similar to the provisions of Article 73, and indeed would be applicable were the disturbances such as to effect the balance of payments of a Member State.[17]

[17] Safeguard measures have been taken under both Articles, see *infra,* para. 24–19.

Part 5

COMMUNITY POLICIES

Chapter 19

TRANSPORT POLICY

—01   The provisions relating specifically to transport in the EEC Treaty
are Article 61, and Title IV of Part Two of the Treaty-Policy of
the Community - entitled "Transport" (Arts. 74 to 84).

Article 61 (1) states that "freedom to provide services in the
field of transport shall be governed by the provisions of the Title
relating to transport." The question arises as to the applicability of
the Treaty in general to the specific area of transport. Article 61 is
in the chapter on services, and since, economically speaking,
transport constitutes a service, a provision in that chapter is
necessary, if transport is to be exempted from its general provisions. This does not of itself indicate that the general rules are
of application in the absence of specific provisions to the contrary but nor does it leave the matter free from doubt.

The matter was resolved by the Court in Case 167/73 *Commission* v. *French Republic*.[1] It was held there that "far from
involving a departure from [the general rules, including the objectives of the Treaty], the object of the rules relating to the common
transport policy is to implement and complement them by means
of common action. Consequently the said general rules must be
applied insofar as they can achieve these objectives."

The Treaty Provisions (Articles 74 to 84)

Types of transport covered

—02   Article 84 (1) states that the provisions of the transport title
apply to rail, road and inland waterway transport. Paragraph 2
stipulates that the Council may decide whether, to what extent
and by what procedure provisions may be laid down for sea and
air transport. The juxtaposition of the two paragraphs suggests
that the matters referred to in paragraph 2 are not covered already
by paragraph 1, but it is nowhere made clear whether this is so.[2]
Further, Article 84 appears to exclude from its ambit other forms
of transport, such as transport by pipeline or vacuum tube, but
again there is no clear statement to this effect.

Article 74

—03   Article 74 provides that the objectives of the Treaty are, in
matters governed by the transport title, to be pursued by Member

---

[1] [1974] E.C.R. 359, 370.
[2] This nevertheless seems to have been the assumption of the Court in Case 167/73
supra, note 1.

States in the framework of a common transport policy.

Article 75

19—04   Article 75 provides powers for the elaboration of the common transport policy mentioned above, and gives some indication of the contents of that policy. The Council, now acting by a qualified majority on Commission proposals and after consulting the Economic and Social Committee and the Parliament, lays down the basic rules "taking into account the distinctive features of transport." Where the application of Community transport provisions would be liable to have serious effects on the standard of living and employment in certain areas, and on the operation of transport facilities, they are to be adopted by the Council acting unanimously (Art. 75 (3)).

19—05   Article 75 (1) indicates two specific areas to be covered by the transport policy before the end of the transitional period, namely:

> "(a) common rules applicable to international transport to or from the territory of a Member State or passing across the territory of one or more Member States.

> (b) the conditions under which non-resident carriers may operate transport services within a Member State."

The Council has also to lay down:

> "(c) any other appropriate provisions."

This last clause (which is applicable even after the transitional period) has enabled the Community to develop the notion of transport policy.[3] Article 75 has been used as the legal basis for most of the subsidiary legislation issued in the transport field, except where a specific provision exists elsewhere in the transport title. The Commission also based its arguments that it was for the Community to negotiate international transport agreements upon this clause; the Court endorsed this view in Case 22/70 *Commission* v. *Council* (AETR)[4] and again in the *Laying-up fund* case.[5]

In 1975-6 a difficult situation arose in connection with the United Nations Code of Conduct on Liner Conferences which three Member States had signed although the Commission was attempting to create a common position for the Community.[6] In the face of the infringement procedure under Article 169 the States agreed not to ratify the Code, but a regulation was even-

---

[3] Case 97/78 *Schumalla* [1978] E.C.R. 2311.
[4] [1971] E.C.R. 263.
[5] Opinion 1/76, given pursuant to Article 228 (1) of the EEC Treaty, [1977] E.C.R. 741, *infra,* para. 29–05.
[6] See 10th General Report (1976) point 451.

tually issued concerning ratification of or accession to the Code by Member States.[7]

Article 76

9—06   Article 76 prohibits Member States from making their national transport legislation more restrictive *vis-à-vis* carriers from other Member States pending the introduction of common rules unless such measures are unanimously approved by the Council. To assist with the implementation of the standstill clause, the Council instituted a procedure for prior examination and consultation in respect of legislative changes proposed by Member States in the transport sector.[8] Under this decision, Member States proposing legislation which may interfere substantially with the implementation of the common transport policy must notify the Commission and at the same time inform the other Member States. Other, peripheral matters, need not be notified, although the Commission may be kept abreast of events informally. The Commission is then required to address an opinion or recommendation to the Member State concerned, indicating whether it considers the measure proposed compatible with the common transport policy. Other Member States have an opportunity to comment. As both Article 76 EEC and this decision are operative in the context of the progressive implementation of a common transport policy, the need for both will be reduced as the policy is implemented.

Article 77

9—07   Article 77, stating aids to transport to be compatible with the Treaty "if they meet the needs of co-ordination of transport or if they represent reimbursement for the discharge of certain obligations inherent in the concept of a public service," is not an exception to the general provisions on aids found in Article 92 to 94 in the chapter on competition.[9] Aids to transport have been a consistent feature of governmental economic policies, since transport costs are a major input factor in the overall cost of goods and also services, and thus it was felt necessary to allow at least certain types of aid in this sector. Article 77 gives a side-light on the priorities envisaged for a common transport policy, in that although the second category of aids was the one most usually to be applied, the authors specifically included aids granted to co-ordinate transport, thus establishing co-ordination a major objective of any efficient transport policy as early as 1957.

[7] Regulation 954/79, O.J. 1979, L121/1.
[8] Decision of March 21, 1962, J.O. 1962 720; O.J. 1959–62, 96, amended by Decision 73/402, O.J. 1973, L347/48.
[9] Case 156/77 *Commission* v. *Belgium* [1978] E.C.R. 1881.

297

19—08   Regulation 1191/69[10] cuts down the scope of the article particularly in relation to aids granted to cover public service obligations. Article 1 (1) of the regulation requires Member States to terminate all obligations inherent in the concept of a public service as defined in the regulation imposed on transport by rail, road or inland waterway. This is in accordance with the market economy philosophy of the EEC, since it was found that Member States were becoming over-liberal in giving aids on the pretext of meeting a public service obligation. The regulation does permit aids to be given to ensure the provision of adequate transport services (Arts. 1 (2) and 14) and it does not apply to passenger transport rates and conditions imposed in the interests of particular categories of persons (Art. 1 (3)): this idea is clarified in Article 3 which states that the services should be the least costly mode to the community and the adequacy of such services is to be assessed having regard to the public interest and the possibilities of substitution and the rates and conditions. Financial burdens devolving on transport undertakings as a result of the maintenance of public service obligations are subject to compensation arrangements laid down in the regulation.

19—09   Regulation 1107/70[11] applies Articles 92 to 94 to road, rail or inland waterway transport. It was designed to remove confusion regarding the scope of co-ordination measures and the public service obligations not covered by Regulation 1191/69. Articles 3 and 4 which specify the possible circumstances when an aid may be granted are therefore expressed to be without prejudice to that regulation and Regulation 1192/69 and Decision 75/327 (*infra*. para. 19-27 and 19-28). Compliance with the regulation is ensured by the Commission, assisted in this task by an advisory committee.

Article 78

19—10   Article 78 of the Treaty, which ordains that any measure taken in connection with transport "shall take account of the economic circumstances of carriers" is regarded by those desirous of minimising the application of the rest of the Treaty rules to transport as acknowledging the special nature of the transport sector, which thus demands special treatment by the Community. The better view is that the article is simply a statement that transport undertakings and particularly railway undertakings are in a special economic situation in view of their structure and infrastructure and obligations of public services. The article has in fact proved of little practical importance.

[10] J.O. 1969, L156/1; O.J. 1969, 276.
[11] J.O. 1970, L130/1; O.J. 1970, 360, amended by Regulation 1473/75, O.J. 1975, L152/1.

Article 79

19—11   Article 79 is designed to eliminate discrimination which takes the form of carriers charging different rates and imposing different conditions for the carriage of the same goods over the same transport links on grounds of the country of origin or of destination of the goods in question, and may be considered one of the special provisions mentioned by Article 7 (the general rule against discrimination); since Article 79 (1) only mentions carriage of goods, Article 7 must be held to apply to any discrimination relating to carriage of persons. These discriminations were to be eliminated by the end of the second stage; Article 79 (3) required the Council to lay down rules for the implementation of Article 79 (1) within two years of the entry into force of the Treaty. This was done by Regulation 11 of 1960,[12] which obliges Member States to notify the Commission of any tariffs or agreements on transport rates or conditions which vary according to the country of origin or destination of the goods in question (Art. 5). These discriminations are prohibited by Article 4 which reiterates Article 79. As under Article 79 (4), the Commission is empowered by Article 14 of the regulation to exercise a power of scrutiny and control over compliance with the regulation, although it is in the first place the Member States who are responsible for ensuring such compliance. The Commission has a power to call for information from firms, reinforced by a power to impose administrative penalty payments (Arts. 17-19). The scope of the regulation is not perhaps very wide, for Article 79 (1) of the Treaty, re-enacted by Article 4 (1) of the regulation, only proscribes discrimination in the carriage of "the same goods over the same transport links," which narrows the scope of the prohibitions to exactly similar circumstances of transport.

Articles 80 and 82

19—12   Article 80 prohibits the Member States from setting rates and conditions involving any elements of support or protection in the interest of one or more particular undertakings or industries, unless authorised by the Commission. The second paragraph of the article goes on to require the Commission to examine such rates, taking into account "the requirements of an appropriate regional policy," "the needs of under-developed areas and the problems of areas seriously affected by political circumstances." This last consideration relates to the problems of West Berlin, Upper Franconia and the *Zonenrandgebiet*.[13] Article 82 provides in addition that the provisions of the transport title are not to prevent the application of German domestic measures to compensate for the economic disadvantages caused by the division

[12] J.O. 1960, 1121; O.J. 1959–62, 6.
[13] The area of the Federal Republic of Germany bordering the German Democratic Republic.

of Germany, and thus the title provides two safeguards for Germany. Article 82 is probably slightly wider, however, and is not in any case logically identical: Article 80 (2) is directed to the Commission, whilst Article 82 is directed to the Federal Republic (*cf.* the similar provisions of Art. 92 (2) (*c*) in the general chapter on aids). Taking into account the considerations mentioned in Article 80 (2), and after consulting the Member States concerned, the Commission is empowered to "take the necessary decisions" (Art. 80 (2), second sub-para.) to allow or suppress the subsidies and protective measures mentioned in Article 80 (1). The Commission cannot apparently take decisions on "tariffs fixed to meet competition," for these are excluded from the ambit of Article 80 (1) by Article 80 (3). Tariffs which subsidise one form of transport so as to enable it to compete with another are included within the term "tariffs fixed to meet competition."

Article 81

19–13   Article 81 requires Member States to endeavour to reduce costs of charges or dues in respect of frontier crossings on a progressive basis. Although the article refers only to a reduction of these dues, the ultimate aim is complete elimination of such charges, for with the elimination of internal customs duties these charges can become substantial barriers to trade, and yet have no economic value to the transporter. The transporters in turn are required to pass on no more than a reasonable charge, having regard to the cost actually incurred. The Commission is given a power to make recommendations for the application of these provisions. The provision is probably now of marginal importance in view of the wide interpretation given to the provisions on elimination of measures having equivalent effect to quantitative restrictions (*supra*, para. 13-20).

Article 83

19–14   Article 83 sets up a Transport Advisory Committee, consisting of experts designated by the governments of Member States, to be attached to the Commission. The composition was made more specific by Article 1 of the Rules of Procedure of the Transport Committee of September 15, 1958:[14] each government designates one or two transport experts from among senior officials of the national administration. In addition governments may designate not more than three experts in, respectively, road, rail and inland waterway transport. Alternates are permitted (Art. 2). Members and their alternates are appointed in their personal capacity (Arts. 3 and 4). The Committee has an advisory role and its powers are expressed to be without prejudice to the powers of the transport section of the Economic and Social Committee (Art. 83 EEC).

[14] J.O. 1958, 509; O.J. 1957–58, 72.

The very inclusion in the Treaty of Article 82 setting up the Advisory Committee is an indication that the transport sector was regarded as being of importance, since the Treaty contains few specific provisions for the establishment of advisory bodies (see generally *supra*, paras. 3-45 *et seq*.

The Common Transport Policy

19—15 An action programme for transport was drawn up in 1962[15] which envisaged the achievement of a common market in the supply of transport services as an adjunct to the achievement of the other freedoms provided for in the Treaty. Although much was done during the period prior to 1970 (the end of the original transitional period) even those basic freedoms had only been partially achieved, and the following few years saw very little further progress. However, the prospect of Economic and Monetary Union held out by the Paris summit of 1972,[16] together with the declarations on other policies and the avowed intent to achieve wider goals such as improvement in the quality of life, was the cue for the Commission to attempt a new start in transport. It resulted in a Communication to the Council[17] on the development of the common transport policy. This envisaged building on the progress so far, with the ultimate aim of achieving a genuine common market and at the same time starting the process leading towards common action in such areas as transport infrastructure and integration of the various forms of transport. In 1974 the Council indicated that it intended to take the guidelines into account, "embodying them where appropriate in practical measures."[18] The subsequent years have seen some real progress towards the stated goals, but there is still a long way to go; indeed, there is still no common market in the supply of transport services.

Transport by Road, Rail and Inland Waterway

1. Access to the Market: licensing controls and quotas

19—16   Prior to the establishment of the EEC the Member States had bilateral agreements with each other providing for the reciprocal

[15] *Action programme for the common transport policy,* May 23, 1962, (Doc VII/Com (62) 88, final). For early proposals see notably *Memorandum on the orientation to be given to the common transport policy* (Schaus Memorandum) of April 10, 1961, (Doc VII/Com (61) 50, final); Decision 65/271, J.O. 1965, 1500; O.J. 1965–66, 67 on the harmonisation of certain provisions affecting competition in transport by rail, road and inland waterway; the accord of the Council of Ministers of June 22, 1965, on the general principles of the transport market (Plan Jacquet): Bulletin No. 8, 1965, p. 86; *Options in tariff policy* (Allais report): EEC Transport Series No. 1 1965; Decision 67/790, J.O. 1967, 322/4; O.J. 1974, (2nd) IV 23 on certain measures of common transport policy; Communication on the common organisation of the transport market, September 16, 1971.
[16] October 19 and 20, 1972, Bulletin EC 10–1972, p. 14; Cmnd. 5109, paras. 1 *et seq.*
[17] Bulletin EC Suppt. 16/73.
[18] 8th General Report (1974) point 349.

admission of predetermined numbers of commercial vehicles to each other's territories. These arrangements were uniform neither as to quantity nor as to their conditions of operation. The Commission pressed for the elimination of these bilateral agreements and the adoption of a Community licensing system whereby vehicles from Member States would be granted a licence to operate transport services on all routes between all Member States (the Community quota to be divided between all Member States). Such a system was adopted at the same time as the rate bracket publicity system (*infra*). Where bilateral quotes still exist they are governed by Decision 80/48,[19] laying down standard criteria and linked to the issue of transport authorisations in accordance with Directive 65/269 *infra*. The quota systems are to be distinguished from the TIR system simplifying formalities connected with international transport for operations guaranteed by national issuing associations and conducted in type-approved vehicles under the 1975 TIR convention.[20]

Services completely liberalised

19–17   A first Council directive of July 23, 1962,[21] freed certain limited types of road transport from the bilateral quota system, *e.g.* frontier traffic up to a distance of 25 kilometres from a frontier internal to the Community, provided the length of the journey does not exceed 100 kilometres; postal services; and carriage of goods by vehicles not exceeding six tons unloaded weight and various specialised occasional services. Council Directive 65/269[22] provided standard types of form authorising intra-Community carriage of goods by road on a vehicle-by-vehicle basis, either for single journeys or over a period of time. Common rules regarding international carriage of passengers by coach and bus were laid down by Regulation 117/66,[23] introducing a complete liberalisation for occasional services (Art. 5). The implementation of proposals on liberalisation of shuttle and regular services, envisaged by Articles 7 and 8, was achieved by Regulations 516 and 517/72.[24] Common rules have also been introduced for combined road-rail transport, where the road vehicle carrying the goods is itself transported by rail across state borders.[25]

Services subject to a quota

19–18   A system of quotas for carriage of goods by road, under which

[19] O.J. 1980, L18/21.
[20] Convention of November 14, 1975, Regulation 2112/78, O.J. 1978, L252/1.
[21] J.O. 1962, 2005; O.J. 1959–62, 267, as last amended by Directive 80/49, O.J. 1980, L18/23.
[22] J.O. 1965, 1469; O.J. 1965–66, 64, last amended by Directive 73/169, O.J. 1973, L181/20.
[23] J.O. 1966, 2688; O.J. 1965–66, 177.
[24] J.O. 1972, L67/13 and 19; O.J. 1972, 137 and 143.
[25] Directive 75/130, O.J. 1975, L48/31.

Member States would be obliged to offer a given number of licences allowing operations throughout the EEC, was introduced in 1968.[26] The basic regulation now in force is Regulation 3164/76.[27] The total quota and quotas for each Member State are revised annually.

The initial system was devised as a temporary expedient pending total liberalisation, but was permanently adopted by the Council in November 1975. Provided the number of quotas continues to increase at a substantial rate this would eventually lead to a *de facto* liberalisation. But it is worth noting that in 1973 the quotas accounted for only 3 per cent. of total intra-Community traffic.[28]

Operators

9—19   A natural accompaniment to the quota arrangement are the directives on admission to the occupation of transport operator.[29]

2. Transport rates

9—20   A system for controlling the rates for the carriage of goods was thought to be essential, at least as far as *road* transport was concerned, because of the dangers of undercutting or abuse of a dominant position which might accompany the gradual liberalisation of transport services. The original Member States had diverse national systems of rate regulation varying from a Dutch free rate to a German fixed rate. The compromise adopted in Regulation 1174/68[30] entailed a bracket tariff system, under which rates were fixed by bilateral negotiation but allowed to vary within a certain bracket (23 per cent. of the maximum rate). The system was supposed to be a temporary expedient, but the regulation was extended almost annually until 1977 when a revised scheme was introduced[31] allowing Member States to agree either on compulsory bracket tariffs as provided for under the 1968 scheme or non-obligatory reference tariffs - the latter clearly constituting a step in the direction of more freedom of competition in rates. This new scheme is experimental. It envisages adoption of a new scheme at the end of its five year life. Road hauliers' associations were given the opportunity to draw up drafts for the introduction or amendment of tariffs subject to time limits.[32] Disputes on reference tariffs may be settled by a procedure which may culminate in a decision by the Commission

---

[26] Regulation 1018/68, J.O. 1968, L175/13.
[27] O.J. 1976, L357/1. Amended with 1981 quotas, to take account of Greek accession by Reg. 305/81, O.J. 1981, L34/1.
[28] Bulletin EC 6–1973 point 2404.
[29] Directives 74/561 and 562, O.J. 1974, L308/18 and 23; and 77/796, O.J. 1977, L334/37.
[30] J.O. 1968, L194/1; O.J. 1968, 411, last amended by Regulation 3181/76, O.J. 1976, L359/13.
[31] Regulation 2831/77; O.J. 1977, L334/22.
[32] *Ibid.* Article 6 and Decision 78/934, O.J. 1978, L326/8.

(Art. 7). The Commission has similar powers regarding compulsory tariffs (Article 13). Derogations from compulsory tariffs are permitted in limited clearly defined circumstances (Article 14). The reference tariffs and the compulsory tariffs are required to be published (Article 20).

19—21   Specific powers in relation to railway tariffs exist only under the ECSC Treaty. The ECSC Treaty treats transport as a complementary matter. It regards as a crucial problem the reflection in the retail price of goods of the additional cost factor of transport charges; thus, Article 70 of the ECSC Treaty enunciates the principle of non-discrimination in transport tariffs and, in keeping with the minimalist philosophy of the Treaty as a whole (see Art. 5, ECSC, last para.), implements this by prescribing publicity or notification to the High Authority of tariff rates. However, the fifth paragraph of Article 70 states that: "subject to the provisions of this Article, and to the other provisions of this Treaty, transport policy . . . shall continue to be governed by the laws or regulations of the individual Member States." The other applicable portions of the Treaty are Article 4 (*b*) which prohibits measures or practices which discriminate between producers, between purchasers or between consumers, especially in prices and delivery terms or transport rates and conditions, and the provisions in Article 60 (1) regarding publication of prices and conditions. Paragraph 10 of the Convention on Transitional Provisions created a Commission of Experts to study the suppression of discriminations prohibited in Article 70, the establishment of through (or direct) international tariffs, and rates and conditions for carriage of coal and steel by the different modes of inland transport.

19—22   The arrangements for through international tariffs, including those for transit by rail across the territories of Austria and Switzerland, were established gradually as from 1955 by the following agreements:

Agreement of the Representatives of the Member States of March 21, 1955, on the establishment of through international railway tariffs.[33]
Supplementary Agreement of March 16, 1956.[34]
Second Supplementary Agreement of March 23, 1959.[35]
Third Supplementary Agreement of November 22, 1973.[36]
Fourth Supplementary Agreement of December 6, 1979.[37]
Agreement of July 28, 1956, on the introduction of through

[33] J.O. 1955, 701; O.J. 1952–58, 25.
[34] J.O. 1956, 130; O.J. 1952–58, 40.
[35] J.O. 1959, 431; O.J. 1952–58, 53.
[36] O.J. 1973, L347/64.
[37] O.J. 1979, L315/17.

international railway traffs for the carriage of coal and steel through Swiss territory.[38]

Supplementary Protocol of October 14, 1974.[39]

Agreement of July 26, 1957, on the introduction of through international railway tariffs for the carriage of coal and steel through the territory of the Austrian republic.[40]

Supplementary Protocol of October 10, 1974.[41]

Agreement of February 1, 1958, on freight rates and conditions of carriage of coal and steel on the Rhine.[42]

Special measures have been taken to permit support tariffs for the transport of coal and steel in the Saarland[43] and to permit reduced tariffs for the transport of iron ore by rail from Lorraine and western France to Belgium, Luxembourg and the Saar,[44] the aim being to avoid disturbances in employment in those areas.

9—23   The efforts of the High Authority to obtain publication of national transport tariffs pursuant to the third paragraph of Article 70 ECSC received a setback, Cases 20 and 25/59, *Italy* v. *High Authority*[45] and *Netherlands* v. *High Authority*[46] holding that the High Authority had no power, express or implied, to implement Article 70 by means of decisions. Thus it might not challenge the Member States' failure to fulfil the obligation to publish by taking a substantive decision under Article 88 which limits the High Authority to a finding that a Member State has failed to fulfil its obligations. High Authority Recommendation 1/61[47] concerning publication of transport rates recognises that executive authority in the matter remains with the Member States, but nevertheless indicates what measures should be taken to comply with the Community obligation.

This approach was upheld by the Court of Justice when challenged in *Government of the Netherlands* v. *High Authority*.[48] The Court held that Article 70, third para., was an obligatory rule to be observed by the Member States and thus the High Authority was entitled to issue recommendations to secure its observance.

3. Harmonisation in the taxation, social and technical fields

9—24   A timetable for action on harmonisation in the taxation, social

[38] J.O. 1957, 223, O.J. (2nd) VIII 3, Cmnd. 5892.

[39] O.J. 1979, L12/15. Cmnd. 5892.

[40] J.O. (ECSC) 1958, 78; O.J. (2nd) VIII 8. Supplemented J.O. 1961, 1237; O.J. (2nd) VIII 14, amended 1966, J.O. 1966, 3837 and all in O.J. 1979, L12 and Cmnd. 5891.

[41] O.J. 1979, L12/27, Cmnd. 5891.

[42] J.O. 1958, 49; O.J. 1952–58, 53.

[43] 78/975/ECSC, O.J. 1978, L330/34.

[44] 75/356/ECSC, O.J. 1975, L159/71 extended to 1983 by Decision 78/103, O.J. 1978, L38/20.

[45] [1960] E.C.R. 325.

[46] [1960] E.C.R. 355.

[47] J.O. 1961, 469; O.J. 1959–62, 69.

[48] Case 29/61 [1962] E.C.R. 213.

and technical fields was laid down by Decision 65/271,[49] on the harmonisation of certain provisions affecting competition in transport by rail, road and inland waterway. It deals in particular with taxation questions, certain kinds of State intervention and social questions.

(a) *Taxation*

19—25 Decision 65/271 called for the elimination of double taxation on international transport vehicles, the standardisation of duty-free franchise on motor spirit in commercial vehicles, the adoption of a uniform basis for the calculation of tax on goods vehicles and cargo-carrying inland waterway vessels. The taxation of carriage of goods was to be harmonised in step with the VAT system. So far the only action taken pursuant to Decision 65/271 is Directive 68/297,[50] providing for a 50 litre per vehicle per journey running fuel franchise, exempt from excise duty in other Member States. A more general proposal on reorganisation of taxation of vehicles and fuel, first put forward in 1968,[51] was agreed to "in principle" by the Council in 1978.[52]

(b) *State intervention*

19—26 Decision 65/271 calls for the termination of obligations inherent in the concept of a public service imposed on transport undertakings in so far as they are not essential in order to ensure the provision of adequate services, for the payment of compensation to transport undertakings in respect of public service burdens and "social" transport rates imposed by Member States, for the normalisation of railway accounts, for harmonisation of provisions governing financial relations between railway undertakings and States, and for proposals for the implementation of Article 77 of the Treaty.

Regulation 1191/69,[53] on action by Member States concerning the obligations inherent in the concept of a public service in transport by rail, road and inland waterway, has already been discussed (*supra*, 19-08).

19—27 Regulation 1192/69[54] institutes common rules for the "normalisation" of national railway accounts. This consists in determining the financial burdens borne, or the benefits enjoyed, by railway undertakings, by reason of any provision laid down by law, regulation or administrative action, by comparison with their position if they were to operate under the same conditions as

[49] J.O. 1965, 1500; O.J. 1965–66, 67.
[50] J.O. 1968, L175/15; O.J. 1968, 313.
[51] J.O. 1968, C95/41.
[52] Bulletin EC 6 1978 point 2.1.106.
[53] J.O. 1969, L156/1; O.J. 1969, 276.
[54] J.O. 1969, L156/8; O.J. 1969, 283.

other transport undertakings and payment of compensation in respect of the burdens or benefits thus disclosed.

Provision also exists in relation to accounting for expenditure on infrastructure in respect of transport by rail, road and inland waterway.[55] Certain types of infrastructure expenditure are excluded, *e.g.* those relating to minor railways, agricultural or forestry roads; waterways which can only carry vessels up to 250 metric tons, and waterways of maritime character. As far as the United Kingdom is concerned, the only waterways of maritime character appended to the list provided for by Regulation 281/71[56] are the Gloucester and Sharpness Canal and the Weaver Navigation. (The Manchester Ship Canal is thus excluded.)

9—28　　In 1975 the Council adopted a decision on the improvement of the situation of railway undertakings and harmonisation of the rules governing financial relations between undertakings and the State[57] which aims at achieving financial balance of railway undertakings by a date to be fixed in accordance with Article 15. This was followed by Regulation 2183/78[58] laying down uniform costing principles for railway undertakings and Regulation 2830/77[59] on a standard form of balance sheet for railway undertakings.

(c) *Social provisions*

9—29　　Lastly, Decision 65/271 calls for harmonisation of laws, regulations and administrative provisions relating to working conditions in the three surface modes of transport (excluding pay, etc.) of provisions on manning, and on working and rest periods.

9—30　　Various committees have been set up to assist the Commission in its tasks relating to social questions in various transport fields; there are now a Joint Advisory Committee on social questions for road transport,[60] a Joint Advisory Committee for inland navigation; and a Joint Advisory Committee for the railway industry.[61] The composition of the Committees is balanced between employers and transport employees; their function is to give opinions on topics referred to them by the Commission.

9—31　　The major piece of legislation in the social field relating to transport is Regulation 543/69[62] on road transport. This establishes

---

[55] Regulation 1108/70, J.O. 1970, L130/4; O.J. 1970, 363.
[56] J.O. 1971, L33/11; O.J. 1971, 57 as adapted by Annex I (IV) (5) to the 1972 Act of Accession.
[57] Decision 75/327, O.J. 1975, L152/3.
[58] O.J. 1978, L258/1.
[59] O.J. 1977, L334/13.
[60] Decision 65/362, J.O. 1965, 2184.
[61] Decision 67/745, J.O. 1967, L297/13.
[62] J.O. 1969 L77/49; O.J. 1969, 170.

various standards and lays down control procedures relating to the age of drivers, composition of crews, driving periods and rest periods, applicable to road transport anywhere within the Community. The regulation does not apply to carriage by small vehicles, by vehicles of an essentially public character (police, military, fire, utilities, etc.), and by vehicles used for regular passenger services with a route of not more than 50 kilometres (Art. 4). A regulation of this kind was clearly required, and indeed one of the reasons why road transport is cheaper than other forms is that working conditions are often primitive (although pay may be high) and drivers are encouraged to drive long, unbroken periods in order to make maximum use of the vehicle.

This regulation was amplified in particular by Regulation 1463/70[63] which requires the installation of recording equipment (tachographs) on passenger and goods vehicles, other than those referred to in Article 4 of Regulation 543/69 (see previous para.) and vehicles used for regular passenger services with a route of more than 50 kilometres. Subject to limited derogations the use of recording equipment was to be compulsory at the latest by January 1, 1978, and the failure in particular of the United Kingdom government to observe the regulation led to findings of infringement under Article 169.[64] Ratification of the European Road Transport Agreement[65] by the Member States acting on behalf of the Community following the important Case 22/70 *Commission* v. *Council* discussed *supra*, required some amendment to Regulation 543/69.[66]

The social legislation together with amendments made over the years is now conveniently codified.[67]

d) *Harmonisation in technical fields*

19—32   A large number of directives has now been issued under Article 100 relating to technical standards for road vehicles, including type approval.[68] These do not form an integral part of the common transport policy as such. Technical standards relating to axle weights and dimensions of road vehicles do, however, intimately concern the common transport policy, for national rules on the subject are clearly barriers to trade. Although proposals have from time to time been made on this subject, no legislation has yet been enacted. Attempts to link it with the extension of the quota system ended with separate decisions being made as regards the latter.

[63] J.O. 1970, L164/1; O.J. 1970, 42 amended by Regulation 2828/77, O.J. 1977, L334/5.
[64] Case 128/78 *Commission* v. *United Kingdom* [1979] E.C.R. 419.
[65] O.J. 1978, L95/1, implemented by Regulation 2829/77, O.J. 1977, L334/11.
[66] Regulation 2829/77, *supra* note 65.
[67] O.J. 1979, C73/1.
[68] Directive 70/156 J.O. 1970, L42/1; O.J. 1970, 96.

4. Competition

19—33   The title on transport contains no specific provisions on competition. It was originally considered, therefore, that the rules on competition set out in Articles 85 and 86 of the Treaty, and implemented under Regulation 17/62,[69] made under Article 87 of the Treaty, would apply to transport as well. Within 10 months of the issue of Regulation 17/62, however, the Council issued a further regulation on competition, Regulation 141/62,[70] exempting transport from the application of Regulation 17. The preamble to Regulation 141 clearly indicates that transport was considered to be a special case: it reads in part as follows:

> "Whereas in pursuance of the common transport policy, account being taken of the distinctive features of the transport sector, it may prove necessary to lay down rules governing competition different from those laid down or to be laid down for other sectors of the economy, and whereas Regulation 17 should not therefore apply to transport. . . ."

19—34   In fact, it appears from Article 2 of the regulation that appropriate provisions for road, rail and inland waterway transport were to be adopted, and thus by Article 3, the regulation was to expire on December 31, 1965, in so far as it applied to these three modes of transport. Regulation 1017/68 applying rules of competition to transport by rail, road and inland waterway was not in fact adopted until July 19, 1968.[71] As a result of the decision in Case 167/73 (*supra*, para. 19-01), it is now clear that the Treaty provisions on competition apply to all forms of transport except to the extent that special measures (such as the bracket tariffs described above) have been adopted in the context of the transport policy. The position would therefore appear to be that while the Treaty provisions apply to all forms of transport, the implementing Regulation 17/62 does not apply to *any* form while Regulation 1017/68 applies only to the forms mentioned. (This leaves air and sea transport without implementing regulations but subject to the competition provisions.)

5. Infrastructure

19—35   The 1962 action programme had concentrated on the achievement of a common market in transport services although it did envisage some limited common action as well, chiefly in the form of investment surveys and studies. The 1973 action programme,[72]

---

[69] J.O. 1962, 204, *infra* Chapter 20.

[70] O.J. 1962, 2751.

[71] Regulation 1017/68, J.O. 1968, L175/1; O.J. 1968, 302. Supplemented by Regulation 1629/69, J.O. 1969 L209/1; O.J. 1969, 371 and 1630/69, J.O. 1969, L209/11; O.J. 1969, 381.

[72] Bulletin EC, Suppt 16/73.

as already mentioned, went much further in envisaging common action to attain in the transport sector the goals which find general expression in other policies (*e.g.* protection of the environment, conservation of energy and regional growth), particularly as regards transport infrastructure.

19—36   As early as 1964 a decision was adopted instituting mechanisms for the survey of infrastructure costs for transport by rail, road and inland waterways.[73] These and other decisions[74] assisted the Commission in co-ordinating Community infrastructure investment. A decision of 1966[75] set up procedures for consultation in respect of transport infrastructure investment. Work began after the 1973 programme was published on studies leading to harmonisation of the charges for the use of infrastructure, but it was not until 1976 that the Commission put to the Council a batch of measures concerning consultations, studies and guidelines for infrastructure which led in 1977/78 to the introduction of a more efficient procedure for consultation on transport infrastructure,[76] including the setting up of a Committee on Transport Infrastructure. In its 1979 Memorandum "The Role of the Community in the Development of Transport Infrastructure"[77] the Commission looks to the Council to adopt a regulation on Community financial assistance in respect of transport infrastructure. Immediate tasks are the identification of relevant transport links.[78] Studies had already been instituted concerning such subjects as information on passenger transport demand trends between large European conurbations (completed 1976) and the forward survey of the requirements of the goods transport sector between 1985 and 2000, the first phase of which was completed in 1977.[79]

2. *Sea and Air Transport*

19—37   Article 84 of the Treaty left it to the Council of Ministers to decide whether and to what extent the provisions should be laid down for sea and air transport, but it needed the accession of the three new Member States in 1973, together with the Court's decision in the *French seamen* case,[80] to persuade even the Commission to start taking action in this field. Since 1974 the Commission has been investigating the structure of competition in the European air transport industry. First steps towards a

[73] Decision 64/389, J.O. 1964, 1598; O.J. 1974, (2nd) IV, 18; Decision 65/270, J.O. 1965, 1473; O.J. 1974, (2nd) IV 20 and Decision 70/108, J.O. 1970, L23/24; O.J. 1970, 64.
[74] *e.g.* Decision 78/546, O.J. 1978, L168/29 on regional statistics for road transport.
[75] Decision 66/161, J.O. 1966, 583; O.J. 1965–66, 77.
[76] Decision 78/154, O.J. 1978, L54/16.
[77] Bulletin Suppt 8/79, cover heading "A Transport Network for Europe," outline of a policy.
[78] *Ibid.*
[79] 11th General Report (1977) point 372.
[80] *Supra*, note 1.

Community air transport policy include decisions on consultations in international civil aviation and on noise limitation.[81] As concerns sea transport, there has been a gradual move towards a common position on various issues currently of concern in world shipping, such as the Code of Conduct for Liner Conferences;[82] International Conventions on safe containers and safety in shipping;[83] and the share of world shipping being taken by Eastern countries.[84] A decision of 1977 instituted a consultation procedure on relations between Member States and third countries in shipping matters and on a common stance within international organisations.[85] On the domestic level directives have been issued on the pilotage of vessels by deep sea pilots[86] and minimum requirements for tankers entering or leaving EEC ports.[87]

[81] Decision 80/50 and Directive 80/51, O.J. 1980, L18/24 and 26.
[82] Regulation 954/79, O.J. 1979, L121/1.
[83] Recommendations on ratification of the International Convention on safe containers and Convention on safety in shipping O.J. 1979, L125/18 and 194/17. Also, Convention on standards of training certification and watchkeeping of seafarers O.J. 1979, L33/31 and Convention for the safety of fishing vessels, O.J. 1980, L259.
[84] Decision 78/774, O.J. 1978, L258/35.
[85] Decision 77/587, O.J. 1977, L239/23.
[86] Directive 79/115, O.J. 1979, L33/32.
[87] Directive 79/116, O.J. 1979, L33/33 amended by Directive 79/1034, O.J. 1979, L315/16.

Chapter 20

COMPETITION POLICY

20—01 Articles 85-94 EEC provide for the establishment of a Competition Policy applying both to "undertakings" (*i.e.* natural or legal persons) and to the authorities of the Member States. Articles 85 and 86 set out substantive rules for undertakings. Article 85 (1) imposes a prohibition on restrictive trade practices in the form of agreements, concerted practices or decisions between undertakings, and any agreement so prohibited is void under Article 85 (2).[1] Prohibited agreements *may* be exempted from paragraph (1) if they satisfy certain conditions laid down in paragraph (3). A general scheme for the administration of both Articles 85 and 86 is laid down by Regulation 17/62,[2] the operation of which is described below.[3] Article 86 imposes a general prohibition on abuses of a dominant position in the common market or a substantial part of it. Articles 87 to 89 contain provisions for the implementation of Articles 85 and 86 and set out some rules for the sharing of responsibilities as between Community authorities and those of Member States. Article 90 describes the extent to which the rules of the Treaty, and in particular the competition rules are to be applied to some types of public undertaking. Article 91 contains rules on intra-Community dumping, now spent, although there is a corresponding transitional provision in Article 131 of the Greek Act of Accession. Dumping by third states is considered *infra* para. 30-18. Articles 92 to 94 relate to state aids to undertakings. These provisions are considered separately in the next chapter.

Rules Applicable to Undertakings - Articles 85-90

Scope of Application

1. Relationships with other policies

20—02 Agriculture was not subject to the Community rules initially[4] but became subject to them as a result of Regulation 26/62.[5] However, the application of the rules was not to hinder the functioning of national or common market organisations or the attain-

---

[1] Subject to the limited scope of "provisional validity" discussed *infra,* paras. 20–46 to 20–48.
[2] J.O. 1962, 204; O.J. 1959–1962, 87.
[3] Paras. 20–44 *et seq.*
[4] See Article 42 EEC.
[5] J.O. 1962, 993; O.J. 1959–1962, 129.

ment of the agricultural policy's objectives.[6] Of course, national market organisations have now virtually disappeared,[7] being replaced by common organisations. In so far as they have been replaced, their justification has ceased and the competition rules apply without qualification to any national rules still in existence.[8] This subject is discussed *supra*, para. 15-10. The application of the rules on competition to transport is considered *supra*, paras. 19-33 and 19-34. Regulation 1017/68 made transport by road, rail and inland waterway subject to the competition rules although notice is taken in the regulation of the special position and structure of the transport industry in the Community. The position of sea and air transport is still uncertain but following Case 167/73[9] the Commission began an investigation into the state of competition in those sectors, particularly air transport within the Community, which is still continuing.

2. Territorial scope

20—03   Both Articles 85 and 86 require that to be prohibited, a practice must both take place "within the common market" and "affect trade between Member States." Article 86 additionally requires that the above must affect at least "a substantial part of the common market."

(a) *"Within the common market"*

20—04   The articles do not actually require the parties to be present within the common market but the extent to which the *practice* must take place there is not clear. In most cases where a party has been physically outside the Common Market, it has been found that it nevertheless *"acted"* within the Common Market, *e.g.* by making an agreement which was *intended* to cover its sales activities on Common Market territory and which would be implemented by a subsidiary, or agent.[10] This may perhaps be also regarded as an acceptance of the "effects" doctrine by virtue of which a party may be held liable because the effect of his action is felt within the territory but it seems clear that the effect must at least be intended.

The converse situation must also be considered, *i.e.* where the parties act within the Common Market but their actions relate to practices intended only to have effect outside the EEC. It appears that the *intention* to affect competition within the EEC

---

[6] Set out in Article 39 EEC.
[7] *Supra,* paras. 15–07 to 15–09.
[8] *Groupement d'exportation du Léon & Soc. d'Investissements et de Co-operation agricoles,* O.J. 1978, L21/23.
[9] [1974] E.C.R. 359.
[10] Cases 48/69 *et seq. ICI* v. *Commission* [1972] E.C.R. 619.
[11] And see also Megret, Waelboeck *et al,* Le droit de la CEE, Vol. 4 Concurrence, p.111. But *cf. Taiwanese Mushroom Packers, J.O.* 1972, C111/13.

need not be present - the Commission will have jurisdiction if the effect is felt in a significant way within the EEC.[12]

(b) *"Affect trade between Member States"*

20—05   Clearly where one or both parties act outside the EEC it will be necessary to examine the effect on inter-state trade because of the presence of this requirement.[13] But the requirement exists equally where both parties act within the EEC. It is thus an "internal" territorial requirement, as well as a jurisdictional requirement as regards parties outside the EEC.

In the early days of the Treaty it had been suggested that the inclusion of this requirement meant that the practice should have a "detrimental" effect on trade. Certainly the Dutch and Italian texts gave some ground for supposing this was so. Other writers argued that the requirement was *only* territorial - provided the practice affected trade it did not matter whether the effect was "detrimental" or "beneficial" (*e.g.* increasing the volume of exports from one Member State to another).

20—06   The Court in Cases 56 and 58/64, *Grundig*,[14] was faced with this issue for the first time. Grundig had challenged a decision by the Commission which had found an infringement of Article 85 on the basis that Grundig and Consten had entered into an agreement under which Consten acquired the exclusive right to sell Grundig's products in France under the trademark "GINT." The Commission argued that by conferring exclusivity on Consten, the parties had altered the normal pattern of trade between France and Germany in that imports of Grundig's products could only now enter France via Consten rather than through various distributors. The Court ruled that this was sufficient to establish that trade between Member States had been affected. But it also indicated that any effect on trade was "detrimental," because it distorted the concept of a single market.

The effect of this ruling was of course to deprive the requirement of any "substantive" force it might have had. Its importance was further diminished by the Court's ruling in the same case and in another almost simultaneous decision, LTM/MBU,[15] that the effect need not be actual - a potential effect was sufficient. Only rarely did the Commission consider that the effect on trade was not established and that a practice was legitimate despite an effect on competition.[16]

20—07   In *Commercial Solvents Co.* v. *Commission*[17] an effect on trade

[12] *Rieckermann* J.O. 1968, L276/25; [1968] C.M.L.R. D78.
[13] See, *e.g.* Case 28/77 *Tepea* v. *Commission* [1978] E.C.R. 1391.
[14] Case 56 and 58/64 *Consten and Grundig—Verkaufs GmbH* v. *Commission* [1966] E.C.R. 299.
[15] Case 56/65 *Société Technique Minière* v. *Maschinenbau Ulm* [1966] E.C.R. 235.
[16] See *Cobelaz* J.O. 1968, L276/13; [1968] C.M.L.R. D45.
[17] Cases 6 & 7/73 [1974] E.C.R. 223.

was found on the following facts:

The Italian subsidiary of an American company refused to make available a raw material aminobutanol to an Italian competitor who used the raw material in manufacturing a drug, ethambutol, which the supplier also wished to manufacture. The abuse, a refusal to supply, appeared to concern only the Italian market. The Court found, however, that the withholding of supplies would have "repercussions on the competitive structure within the Common Market."

0—08   Following these rulings the Commission began to *assume* an effect on trade if competition was affected or if an abuse of a dominant position had occurred. The Court however, emphasised the need in *Hugin*[18] to prove an effect on interstate trade where a Swedish cash register manufacturer was the supplier of parts to United Kingdom customers for these machines. Similarly, in *Tepea*[19] the Court disapproved of a fine imposed in the following circumstances:

A British manufacturer had, prior to United Kingdom accession and continuing after that date, an agreement with a Dutch distributor for the exclusive sale of his product in the Netherlands. It was not established that this agreement had any *appreciable* effect on trade in the product as between the Netherlands and the other five original Member States, but the Commission had fined the parties with respect to both pre-Accession and post-Accession conduct.

The Court ruled that the fine was not permissible as concerned the former because there was no appreciable effect on inter-state trade, but did not alter the size of it because the period prior to accession to which the fine was expressed to apply was so short.

It is therefore clear that the requirement is still considered an important element. The effect must be appreciable and proved. On the other hand, it would never be safe to assume that a practice or abuse which appeared to take place within only one state was outside the scope of Articles 85 and 86 for that reason alone.

It is probably easier to discover the effect on inter-state trade under Article 85 because the *parties'* behaviour can be examined. Under Article 86 on the other hand the effect on trade can depend on assessing the impact on a market in which many other participants are involved.

(c) "*a substantial part of the Common Market*"

0—09   This requirement, found only in Article 86, again does not seem to have been a serious obstacle to the establishment of an infringement. Thus a region of a larger Member State (West Germany) has

[18] Case 22/78 [1979] E.C.R. 1869.
[19] *Supra,* note 13.

been found to be a substantial part of the Common Market.[20]
A small Member State also falls within its ambit and even Luxembourg may not be too small.[21]

This phrase seems to refer to the "product" market as well as to the "geographical" extent of the market because what is substantial may depend not only on area but also on the importance of economic activity within that area as opposed to the Community as a whole.

Thus if demand for a particular product exists predominantly in the Netherlands, the highest areas of consumption within the Netherlands may be a substantial part of the Common Market. However, it will be necessary to examine the effect on trade between Member States in such cases. This requirement has been categorised as a form of *"de minimis"* rule.[22]

3. Personal scope

20—10   Both Articles 85 and 86 are limited to the activities of "undertakings." This term has never been defined in the context of the rules on competition but it may be inferred from Court decisions that it is co-extensive with "economic units" where the persons or organisations making up that unit do not have freedom to act independently and for their own account in the market place.[23] Thus, a parent and its wholly-owned subsidiary may be separate "undertakings" where the subsidiary is able to conduct its own affairs in the market place, and the same may be true even of divisions within a single legal entity but a principal-agent relationship is to be regarded as a single undertaking.[24] It should be emphasised that although even divisions of a single corporate legal entity may be regarded as undertakings, their "cohesive" behaviour in, say, dividing up markets would not infringe Article 85 because normally there can be no competition between them capable of restriction.[25]

20—11   It appears that the term "undertaking" implies at least the carrying on of some commercial activity.[26] This would exclude trade unions from the application of the competition rules, because generally unions only represent the interests of their members, who in turn only carry on commercial activity through the undertakings which employ them. The term "undertaking" does not preclude the activity of a single individual.[27]

---

[20] Cases 40–48, 50, 54–56, 111 and 114/73 *Suiker Unie and others* v. *Commission* [1975] E.C.R. 1663.

[21] Case 6/72 *Europemballage and Continental Can* v. *Commission* [1973] E.C.R. 215.

[22] See Wyatt & Dashwood, *The Substantive Law of the EEC*, pp. 296 *et seq.*

[23] Case 48/69 *ICI, supra,* note 10 Case 40, *etc.,*/73, *Suiker, supra,* note 20.

[24] Cases 40, *etc.* /73, *Suiker, supra,* note 20. Case 15/74 *Centrafarm BV* v. *Sterling Drug Inc.* [1974] E.C.R. 1147.

[25] *Infra,* see, *e.g. Christiani and Nielsen* J.O. 1969 L165/12, [1965] C.M.L.R. D36.

[26] Case 155/73 *Sacchi* [1974] E.C.R. 409.

[27] *Reuter/BASF* J.O. 1976, L254/40; [1976] 2 C.M.L.R. D44; *Unitel Film-und Fernseh-Produktionsgesellschaft* O.J. 1978, L157/39; [1978] 3 C.M.L.R. 306.

Article 85 also applies to "associations of undertakings." They too must at least represent "undertakings" as described above. But it appears that the actual members of the association need not themselves be the undertakings or their representatives.[28]

The use of the term "undertakings" does not of itself preclude the application of Articles 85 and 86 to organisations which form part of a governmental activity, provided that the organisation's activity is commercial in nature. They must probably also be able to exercise an independent will.[29]

"Public" undertakings, to the extent that they are engaged in economic activity, are subject to the general rules of the Treaty including the competition provisions. This seems to be implicit from the provisions of Article 90 (1) of the Treaty which provides as follows:

> "In the case of public undertakings and undertakings to which Member States grant special or exclusive rights, Member States shall neither enact nor maintain in force any measure contrary to the rules contained in this Treaty, in particular to those rules provided for in Article 7 and Articles 85 to 94."

20—12   This provision is probably best regarded as designed to prevent trading and manufacturing undertakings whose general policy is directed by a Member State's authorities from relying on the provisions of national law or on governmental directives which may cause them to take anti-competitive actions.[30]

The application of the competition rules to such undertakings would carry with it the right for individuals to invoke Articles 85 and 86 in national proceedings against their anti-competitive practices. However, this right must be placed in doubt by the ambiguity of the term "public undertakings."[31] A national court, called upon to determine whether a body incorporated by statute, such as the United Kingdom National Enterprise Board, is caught by Articles 85 and 86 may decline to decide whether it is an "undertaking." These doubts must be reinforced by Article 90 (2) which states:

> "Undertakings entrusted with the operation of services of general economic interest or having the character of a revenue-producing monopoly shall be subject to the rules contained in this Treaty, in particular to the rules on competition, in so far as the application of such rules does not obstruct the performance, in law or in fact, of the particular tasks assigned to them. The development of trade must not be affected to such an extent as would be contrary to the interests of the Community."

[28] *Pabst and Richarz* v. *BNIA* O.J. 1976, L331/24; [1976] 2 C.M.L.R. D63.
[29] See *infra.* paras. 20–24 to 26.
[30] See Case 94/74 *IGAV* v. *ENCC* [1975] E.C.R. 699 and 83/78 *Pigs Marketing Board* v. *Redmond* [1978] E.C.R. 2347.
[31] To be construed strictly; Case 127/73 *BRT* v. *SABAM* [1974] E.C.R. 313.

20—13   The vagueness of this provision apparently led the Court of Justice in 1971 to decide that it confers no rights on individuals.[32]

It must be admitted, however, that an individual would not rely on this provision, but on Articles 85 and 86 if invoking the competition rules against a public undertaking. It would be up to the latter therefore to raise Article 90 (2) as a possible defence.[33] A national Court would assess the status of the undertaking, decide whether or not Articles 85 and 86 are applicable and whether its activities are impeded by EEC rules. If the latter is the case, there is no infringement of the competition rules.

4. Application in time

20—14   This issue has been the source of considerable confusion, particularly in respect of Article 85. The Court held in Case 13/61[34] that neither Articles 85 nor 86 applied directly before the coming into force of the implementing administrative Regulation 17/62, on March 13, 1962, and although the Member States could have enforced them prior to that date, none of them chose to do so. The foregoing ruling does not therefore preclude the application of the rules by administrative bodies in respect of conduct occurring prior to the date mentioned. Article 85 prohibits the anti-competitive *effect* of agreements, which does not seem to preclude the prohibition of agreements existing before the entry into force of the Treaty provided the effect was still present after that date. The Court held as much in *Sirena*,[35] where the agreement in question had been made during the Second World War - the assignment of a trademark - which had the effect of partitioning the Common Market when it came into existence and could have been a contributing factor to a restriction on competition. This radical approach has subsequently been abandoned, and the Court would now require at least evidence of a concerted practice aimed at perpetuating the effect of the agreement.[36]

5. The Scope of the Prohibitions - general considerations

(a) *Collusion between undertakings under Article 85*

20—15   The prohibition set out in Article 85 covers both legally binding contracts and looser arrangements ("concerted practices") between undertakings which have the effect of harming competition.

20—16   **The nature of the arrangement - "agreements," "decisions" and "concerted practices."** The most significant practical aspect of controversy surrounding this terminology is the extent of col-

---

[32] Case 10/71 *Ministère public* v. *Hein, née Muller* [1971] E.C.R. 723.
[33] Case 127/73 *supra*, note 31.
[34] *De Geus* v. *Bosch* [1962] E.C.R. 45.
[35] Case 40/70 *Sirena* v. *Eda* [1971] E.C.R. 69.
[36] Case 51/76 *EMI* v. *CBS* [1976] E.C.R. 811.

lusion required to constitute an infringement. In *ICI*[37] the Court held that a concerted practice may exist where there is a "form of co-ordination between undertakings, which, without having reached the stage where an agreement properly so-called has been concluded, knowingly substitutes practical cooperation between them for the risks of competition."[38] In *Suiker*[39] the Court appeared to go even further in holding that a concerted practice need not require the "working out of an actual plan." In fact the two cases mentioned above suggest that where price fixing and, to a lesser extent, market sharing, are involved, the existence of a concerted practice can be established by circumstantial evidence, and there is a very heavy burden placed on the accused parties to rebut the inferences from that evidence. The Court takes the view that where the market conditions appear to be different from those which would be expected, from all the facts, to prevail, it may be presumed that a concerted practice accounts for the distortion.[40]

20—17   **"Horizontal" and "vertical" arrangements.** Article 85 does not limit itself to arrangements between competitors (horizontal agreements). Hence in *Grundig*[41] the Court held that an agreement between a manufacturer and a distributor (a vertical agreement) was caught, even though the parties were not necessarily competitors. Although this decision was controversial at the time, it has become a fundamental tenet of policy that because the competition rules aim to preserve competition, it does not really matter how the undertakings involved go about distorting it. Even if they maintain that an arrangement is beneficial to competition, as between one of the parties to an arrangement and *other* competitors not party to it, there is nevertheless a distortion and therefore an infringement. The proper course of action is to seek an exemption under Article 85 (3).

20—18   **The nature of "competition" protected by the Treaty.** Economic competition is usually thought of as competition between the suppliers of goods or services, and most decisions taken under Article 85 are concerned, one way or another, with such competition. However the rules also protect competition in the obtaining of supplies[42] or in research and development[43] or other aspects of an undertaking's activity.

When examining the competition which is alleged to be restricted,

[37] *Supra,* note 10.
[38] *Ibid.* p. 655.
[39] *Supra,* note 20.
[40] *ICI, supra,* note 10.
[41] *Supra,* note 14.
[42] See, *e.g.* Socemas J.O. 1968 L201/7 [1968] C.M.L.R. D28. *Intergroup Trading* O.J. 1975 L212/23; [1975] 2 C.M.L.R. D14.
[43] See, *e.g. Henkel/Colgate* J.O. 1972 L14/14.

there is nothing in Article 85 to suggest that the effect on the relevant competition should be significant, or, put another way, Article 85 does not specifically state that it is protecting "workable" competition. However, the rulings of the Court of Justice and the policy of the Commission show that agreements which affect only a small fraction of the competition in the market place or which restrict a type of competition which is of secondary importance to the interests of enhancing the principal form of competition will escape the prohibition of Article 85 (1).

20—19   Thus in *Völk* v. *Vervaecke*[44] the Court ruled that an agreement between a manufacturer and a distributor which affected only a fraction of the competition in the products concerned would escape the prohibition. A qualification, however, must be made to this ruling, namely that in assessing the competition affected, regard must be had to all the circumstances surrounding the agreement. Thus where an agreement forms part of a whole network of similar agreements, there may be an infringement.[45]

It will be appreciated that it becomes at that point very difficult for one or even both parties to assess whether they are committing an infringement or not. The Commission has attempted to give some guidance here by issuing, to date, two notices concerning minor agreements,[46] the second of which amended the first and provides that in general if the aggregate turnover of the participating undertakings is less than 50 million ECU *and* their combined market share is less than 5 per cent., the agreement will not be in infringement of Article 85 (1). It must be emphasised that the notices are for guidance only, and decisions to date suggest that only agreements which fall *well* within the limits set out in them will have a chance of escaping the prohibition.[47] If the market is divided up between many competitors, a market share of less than 2 per cent. may be significant.[48]

20—20   Competition as to price is the principal area of "competition" governed by Article 85 but is not necessarily always paramount. In *SABA*[49] the Commission exempted arrangements under which SABA, an audio equipment manufacturer, set up a distribution network designed to promote its product as high quality goods, and the effect of this was to suppress some price competition because high turnover supermarkets could not guarantee the expertise in selling and after sales service. One such supermarket, "Metro" challenged the Commission's decision.[50]

[44] Case 5/69, [1969] E.C.R. 295.
[45] Case 23/67 *Brasserie de Haecht* v. *Wilkin & Janssen* (No.1) [1967] E.C.R. 407.
[46] May 27, 1970, J.O. 1970, C64/1 [1970] C.M.L.R. D15; O.J. 1977, C313/3, [1978] 3 C.M.L.R. 648.
[47] See, *e.g. SAFCO* J.O. 1972, L13/44; [1972] C.M.L.R. D83.
[48] *Floral Düngemittel* O.J. 1980, L39/51; [1980] 2 C.M.L.R. 285.
[49] O.J. 1976, L28/19; [1976] 1 C.M.L.R. D61.
[50] Case 26/76 *Metro-SB-Grossmärkte* v. *Commission* [1977] E.C.R. 1875.

The Court held *inter alia* that competition in quality was the primary area of competition, so that restrictions on price competition did not necessarily constitute an infringement, let alone require exemption.[51]

(b) *Abuse of a dominant position*

—21   **"Dominant position."** In early cases[52] the Court, in laying down basic rules for determining the existence of a dominant position, referred to the power to impede the maintenance of effective competition. This definition perhaps laid undue emphasis on a positive ability to prevent others from competing and subsequent definition by the Commission[53] concentrated on the power to behave independently. Such a definition was approved by the Court in Case 28/76 *United Brands*:[54]

> "The dominant position referred to in this Article relates to a position of economic strength enjoyed by an undertaking which enables it to prevent effective competition being maintained on the relevant markets by giving it the power to behave to an appreciable extent independently of its competitors, customers and ultimately of its consumers."[55]

How does one determine whether such a dominant position exists? Two steps must be gone through. First, what is the relevant market? Secondly, does the undertaking have the ability to behave independently in that market?

—22   **The relevant market.** Geographically, the market will be limited in terms of delivery costs, feasibility of transportation, the need to provide after sales service and other similar factors. These factors must be considered objectively; the fact that an undertaking does not compete in a wide geographical area does not mean that the market is limited to the area in which it actually competes.

Other factors, such as the nature of governmental controls[56] and the habits of consumers, may also be relevant.[57] The area must form a substantial part of the common market (see *supra*, para. 20-09).

The establishment of the relevant *product* market is more difficult, involving essentially an assessment of the substitutability of one product for another, a factor which depends in turn on the assessment of the "cross-elasticity of demand," *i.e.* whether

---

[51] However, such findings will be exceptional.
[52] See especially Case 78/70 *Deutsche Grammophon* v. *Metro* [1971] E.C.R. 487.
[53] See the definition repeated from the appealed decision in Case 6/72 *Europemballage and Continental Can* v. *Commission, supra,* note 21.
[54] *United Brands Company* v. *Commission* [1978] E.C.R. 207.
[55] *Ibid.* at p. 277.
[56] *Ibid.*
[57] Cases 40, *etc.,*/73, *Suiker, supra,* note 10.

purchasers will switch to an alternative product when a small increase in price takes place. Conversely the same product may have different end uses, so that to take a given product may not of itself be a narrow enough definition of the product market. For instance, in Case 85/76 *Hoffman - La Roche*,[58] the Court considered that two types of vitamin pill with different uses also shared some end uses. The fact that the pills were not always used for the purposes for which they were interchangeable was sufficient for the Court to establish them as belonging to different product markets. However it may be asked whether the product market should not have been limited to "a pill for a particular end-use." Again in *United Brands*[59] the Court held that bananas were not part of a wider market for fruits because there were some uses for which they were not replaceable.

20–23   A market may be limited to a particular brand in an extreme case. Where for instance purchasers of cash registers can only obtain spare parts for those machines from one supplier, as in *Hugin*[60] the Court held that the relevant market was the market for those parts. Of course this does not preclude others from manufacturing those parts but the obstacles to entry to such a market may be too great (both legal - patent and design copyright - and practical - the lack of an economy of scale compared with the manufacturer of the machine who will be making parts both for original equipment and for spares).

Where an independent market is artifically created by the temporary disappearance of competitors, *e.g.* by the consequences of the actions of overseas governments, it is conceivable that the market in question could be limited to the products of a single supplier even if normally other suppliers compete. However, it is difficult to establish that this has happened.[61]

20–24   **The power to behave independently.** A mixture of three approaches is used by the Court and Commission[62] in discovering whether an undertaking has the power to behave independently:

Market share. This is the most important factor. To date the cases where a dominant position was found involved undertakings who had a monopoly[63] or market shares of over 50 per cent[64] whilst competitors held very small shares. Where the share was less (as in *United Brands* where it was between 40-45 per cent.) the Court will turn to the other factors.

[58] *Hoffman La Roche* v. *Commission* [1979] E.C.R. 461.
[59] *Supra*, note 54.
[60] Case 22/78 *Hugin* v. *Commission* [1979] E.C.R. 1869. See also 26/75 *General Motors* v. *Commission* [1975] E.C.R. 1367.
[61] Case 77/77 *BP et al* v. *Commission* [1978] E.C.R. 1513.
[62] See, *e.g.* the Commission's remarks in the *Continental Can* decision J.O. 1972, L7/25; [1972] C.M.L.R. D11.
[63] Cases 5, 6 & 7/73 *Commercial Solvents Corporation* v. *Commission* [1974] E.C.R. 223.

0—25   *The structure of the market.* Although an undertaking may not have a large market share, the cost for potential competitors of entering the market (*e.g.* high investment in technology or advertising) may enable the undertaking to ignore the threat of *new* competitors. (Existing competitors may also not be able to afford the costs of increasing their market share.)

0—26   *Behaviour in the market place.* This approach demands an examination of the behaviour of the undertaking over a considerable period, to see whether it did in fact ignore or avoid competition. The Court in *United Brands,*[65] when examining the latter's behaviour, observed that the company had been trading at a loss from time to time and that there had also on occasion been lively price competition in the market. However, United Brands had not lost market share over the period under investigation.

It seems unlikely that the latter two criteria would ever be used to establish a dominant position in the absence of a substantial market share. There are constant references on the cases back to the *support* which these tests might give, but neither could be conclusive on its own.

Exemptions under Article 85 (3)

0—27 The conditions under which an exemption may be granted by virtue of Article 85 (3) are classified in terms of two positive and two negative requirements. The two positive requirements, are that:

- that the agreement etc, should contribute to the improvement in the production or distribution of goods or to the promotion of technical or economic progress.
- The agreement should allow a fair share of the resulting benefit to consumers.

The two negative conditions are that the agreement does not:

- impose on the undertakings concerned restrictions which are not indispensable to the attainment of these objectives.
- afford such undertakings the possibility of eliminating competition in respect of a substantial part of the products in question.

0—28   **The positive conditions:** *Improvements in the existing state of the market.* The agreement must "objectively constitute an improvement on the situation that would otherwise exist." The fundamental principle here is that fair and undistorted competition is the best

[64] Case 6/72, *Continental Can, supra,* note 21.
[65] *Supra,* note 54.

guarantee of regular supply on the best terms.[66] In practice the Commission has only attempted to make an appraisal of the benefits of competition versus the agreement in cases where exemption has been refused.[67] Hence agreements which are claimed to confer benefits merely by virtue of restricting competition will never qualify for exemption.[68] However, where the alternative to restrictions on competition is likely to be the disappearance of the weaker competitors altogether, an exemption may exceptionally be granted.[69]

The Commission invariably lays down a time limit to the exemption, usually in the region of 5-10 years,[70] although exceptionally a longer period has been allowed; in one instance a 15 year period was considered necessary for a long term research project.[71] Conditions are also frequently attached to the grant, such as a requirement to report at varying intervals.[72]

20-29. Improvements in production have been found to result from specialisation agreements,[73] research and development agreements[74] and in some cases, distribution agreements.[75] Such improvements take the form of a reduction in costs or an improvement in quality resulting from economies of scale, or the elimination of duplication of costs. Improvements in distribution are generally the primary benefit of exclusive distribution agreements, trade fairs and selective dealer networks.[76] Economic progress is obviously a very broad term, but it has been used by the Commission to describe improvements in the way the market functions or in the structure of an industry.[77]

20-30 *Consumers must be allowed a fair share of the resulting benefit.* "Consumer" embraces not only the end user but intermediate users as well.[78] A consumer will usually benefit from the exempted arrangement for the same reasons that the arrangement is exempted. The Commission therefore concentrates on ensuring that the benefits do indeed reach the consumer. The best way of doing so is to grant exemption only where it is clear that lively competition

---

[66] *Bayer/Gist—Brocades* O.J. 1976, L30/13; [1976] 1 C.M.L.R. D98, D109.

[67] See, *e.g. NCH,* J.O. 1972, L22/16; [1973] C.M.L.R. D257.

[68] See, *e.g. Groupement des fabricants de papiers peints* O.J. 1974, L237/3 [1974] 2 C.M.L.R. D102.

[69] *Transocean Marine Paint Association,* O.J. 1974, L19/18; [1974] 1 C.M.L.R. D11.

[70] Thus, for instance, the block exemption for exclusive distribution agreements was originally good for five years but was renewed in 1972 for 10 years. Reg. 2591/72, J.O. 1972, L276/15; O.J. 1972 (December 9-28) 7.

[71] As in *KEWA,* O.J. 1976, L30/13; [1976] 1 C.M.L.R. D98.

[72] See, *e.g. Bayer/Gist Brocades supra,* note 66.

[73] *e.g. Prym* O.J. 1973, L296/24; [1972] C.M.L.R. D250.

[74] *e.g. Bayer/Gist-Brocades supra,* note 66.

[75] *e.g. BMW* O.J. 1975, L29/1; [1975] 1 C.M.L.R. D44.

[76] See *infra,* paras. 20-36 and 20-41.

[77] See, *e.g. Davidson Rubber* J.O. 1972, L143/31; [1972] C.M.L.R. D52.

[78] *Kabelmetall/Luchaire,* O.J. 1975, L222/34; [1975] 2 C.M.L.R. D40.

continues to exist between the parties to the arrangement on the one hand, and other competitors on the other.[79] Where such competition does not exist, the agreement may nevertheless be exempted if the consumers themselves can exert the necessary pressure to prevent abuses,[80] or if the Commission can impose and maintain stringent conditions of operation.

1—31   *The two negative conditions.* The mention of "negative" requirements has the effect of placing certain limitations on the Commission's discretion. The first condition gives the Commission the power to require the deletion of objectionable clauses. It appears that if the arrangement would not be acceptable to the parties at all without the presence of the clauses which might strictly speaking be irrelevant to its purpose, those clauses should be considered indispensable.[81]

The second "negative" requirement can only be considered after a consideration has been made of the relevant market, both from the point of view of the product and of geographical extent. As such, considerations similar to those which have to be taken into account when considering whether a firm has a dominant position under Article 86 come into play. Geographically the entire Common Market has been considered as the relevant area,[82] and even the world market has been taken into account.[83]

Generally speaking the relevant product market has not been considered in depth except where the elimination of competition has been the principal ground for the refusal of exemption. It is possible that, following the *Metro*[84] case, much more attention will have to be paid to this consideration.[85]

Policy with Respect of Particular Practices

Price fixing between competitors and attendant practices such as the sharing of current information on prices are the most obvious forms of anticompetitive behaviour. However, many other practices have come under the scrutiny of the Commission, and some of the more common practices are described below.

1. Market sharing

1—32   As the acquisition of market share is the immediate object of

---

[79] See, *e.g. Rank/Sopelem*, O.J. 1975, L29/20; [1975] 1 C.M.L.R. D72.

[80] Thus in *United Reprocessors*, O.J. 1976, L51/7; [1976] 2 C.M.L.R. D1 the consumers were the largely monopolised electricity supply organisations of the Member States.

[81] See, *e.g. Davidson Rubber; supra*, note 77; *Europair/Durodyne* O.J. 1975, L29/11; [1975] 1 C.M.L.R. D62.

[82] *Lightweight Paper*, J.O. 1972, L182/24; [1972] C.M.L.R. D94.

[83] *Bayer/Gist-Brocades, supra*, note 66.

[84] *Supra*, note 52.

[85] In Cases 19 & 20/74 *Kali und Salz and Kali-chemie* v. *Commission* [1975] E.C.R. 499 the Court disagreed with the Commission's conclusions relating to the elimination of competition because the product market which had been taken into account was not justified in terms of the facts stated in the Commission's decision.

competitive action in the market place, attempts to divide up the market between competitors not unnaturally are virtually never condoned. Hence, agreements between producers and between wholesalers or both expressly or impliedly aimed at preserving traditional markets are virtually never capable of being exempted.[86] Exceptionally, however, the Commission has taken the view that market sharing agreements may be exempted when the participants in the practice are medium-sized or small undertakings which risk being forced out of business by bigger concerns unless they can count on the absence of competition from firms of their own size.[87] Agreements between larger firms, even if likely to preserve jobs in a recessionary period and to retain the possibility of competition when an economic upturn takes place, will not be exemptable.[88]

Market sharing is an "activity" which is frequently based upon a "concerted practice" rather than an actual agreement. It is therefore important for undertakings to look not only at the extent of co-operation between them but also at the behaviour of the market if they wish to avoid any inference of market sharing, since the establishment of a concerted practice depends so greatly on circumstantial evidence.[89]

2. Refusals to sell

20—33   Except where refusals to sell or deal except on stringent terms such as cash with order are the result of concerted action by suppliers, there will not normally be an infringement of the competition rules unless the supplier in question is in a dominant position. When a dominant position does exist the supplier should take great care to ensure that any refusal to sell at any rate to regular customers[90] is based upon purely objective grounds, as for instance the uncreditworthiness of a customer, and is not an attempt to force the customer out of business or otherwise to manipulate the market place. Thus, where the sole supplier of a basic chemical refuses to sell to a manufacturer of an end product using that chemical who is or may be in direct competition with the supplier in the latter product, an abuse of a dominant position will be established.[91]

20—34   A refusal to deal except on certain terms, the object of which is

---

[86] See, *e.g. Stoves and Heaters,* O.J. 1975, L159/22; [1975] 2 C.M.L.R. D1 and cases 40–48, etc/73, etc, *Suiker Unie, supra,* note 20.
[87] *Transocean Marine Paint, supra,* note 69.
[88] The history of the man-made fibres producers cartel is a good illustration of this. Although proposed by a number of manufacturers to preserve a scaled down man-made fibres industry in Europe and receiving the blessing of some Commissioners it nevertheless was condemned by the majority.
[89] *Supra,* para. 20–16.
[90] Case 77/77 *BP* v. *Commission* [1978] E.C.R. 1511.
[91] Cases 6 and 7/73 *Commercial Solvents Corporation, supra,* note 17.

to keep prices up by restricting the number of customers or the competition between customers is equally an abuse, and is all the more serious if the effect is of dividing up the common market along national lines. A good example of this is the *United Brands* case[92] where the supplier, United Brands, sold bananas in an unripened state only to distributors who were also "ripeners." Because bananas in a ripened state must be consumed quickly, this practice resulted in distributors being able to sell only in their local areas. Were it not for an obligation to ripen the bananas, they could have shipped into more distant markets and the result would have been a levelling out of the discrepancies found to exist between prices in various Member States. This principle could equally be applied to other industries if the supplier requires his cutomers to manufacture "in-house" rather than allowing them to sell on to others if desired. Such practices would also fall within Article 85 since each *customer* would be party to an agreement with his supplier effectively restricting competition with other customers and with the supplier especially if the practice formed part of a network of agreements.[93]

Again it should be emphasised that such refusals may be objectively justified, *e.g.* in an attempt to maintain quality and to preserve the reputation of a trademark (it being assumed that the latter would otherwise be in danger, and the result of a loss of reputation significant).[94]

3. Discrimination between customers

—35   Discrimination between customers as to terms may also constitute an abuse of a dominant position if not based on objective reasons such as those mentioned above. Thus, where a supplier in a dominant position sells to undertakings at different prices or on different terms for delivery, time of payment, etc, he must be able to show that the discrimination was objectively based and not for instance designed to force smaller suppliers out of business by attacking the latter's market with prices which are so low that they cannot be met. (This practice is known as predatory pricing.)

Discrimination between customers as to the prices charged can be legitimate if it takes the form of discounting or rebating so as to reflect cost savings justified by the volume of sales. It has not yet been determined to what extent the cost savings must be capable of proof. Volume discounts or rebates are not truly discriminatory because the customers are differentiated by the different volumes they have agreed to take. On the other hand fidelity rebates, which are related to the faithfulness of the customer rather than the volume of purchases are prima facie contrary to

---

[92] *Supra*, note 54.
[93] See Case 23/67 *Brasserie de Haecht* v. *Wilkin-Janssen* (No. 1) [1967] E.C.R. 407 and also *Distillers Co. Ltd.* O.J. 1978, L50/16; [1978] 1 C.M.L.R. 400.
[94] *United Brands, supra,* note 54 and *Hoffman La Roche* v. *Commission, supra,* note 58.

Articles 86 and 85 (the latter even if the rebate is forced on the *supplier*: there is nevertheless an agreement, which, by giving a customer an incentive to stay with a particular supplier, restricts competition).

4. Distribution agreements

20—36 These agreements theoretically may infringe Article 85 because they tie up a customer to a supplier for a relatively long period, and the effect of such a relation would be to discourage the customer from approaching other suppliers. Alternatively they may, where the customer is the more powerful party, prevent the supplier from approaching other customers. There is thus a potential effect on competition between customers or suppliers respectively. There is also the possibility of an effect on competition between the two parties. Where for instance a manufacturer could make direct sales into the territory of an appointed distributor, exclusivity conferred on the distributor will prevent him from doing so. Even in the absence of exclusivity, however, the parties may, by the terms of their agreement, harm competition. Thus, if the distributor is entitled to compensation for direct sales into his territory by his supplier and the supplier is capable of making such sales and indeed is permitted to do so by the agreement, there is a restriction on competition.[95] Against this, however, must be balanced the cost to the distributor of building up a market through advertising and other sales efforts. Whether a compensation provision such as that described above is legitimate thus depends on the circumstances of the particular market and in particular on whether the distributor is in effect launching a new product.

20—37 *Exclusive* distribution agreements were exempted by Regulation 67/67[96] because of the beneficial effects they may have, particularly in launching a new product.

Essentially, in order to benefit from the exemption these agreements must relate to goods for which there is lively alternative competition; there must be no restriction on sales outside the territory assigned to the distributor (which territory can be limited only by reference to non-national barriers, and must not exceed an area in which more than 100 million Community inhabitants live). However, the distributor may be restricted from *soliciting* sales outside his territory since one of the justifications for granting the block exemption was to encourage greater penetration of particular markets by smaller competitors.

Agreements that do not fulfil the terms of Regulation 67/67

---

[95] *BP Kemi/DDSF,* O.J. 1979, L286/32; [1979] 3 C.M.L.R. 685.
[96] Reg. 67/67, J.O. 1967, 849; O.J. 1967, 10 as amended by Reg. 2591/72 J.O. 1972, L276/15, O.J. 1972 (December 9–28) 7 extending its term to December 31, 1982.

may be exempted by individual decision if justified.[97] It is unlikely, however, that exemption will ever be granted for agreements which prohibit or discourage the distributor from selling outside his territory when he has an order placed on him by a foreign customer, if the object is to segment the common market.[98]

5. Specialisation agreements

)—38   Specialisation agreements clearly have the effect of restricting competition between competitors although their manner of implementation often resembles a merger of business assets followed by cross-licensing to sell the products in which each participant has agreed to specialise.

Such agreements can have clear benefits of the kind listed in Article 85 (3), and the desirability to further them led to the establishment of a block exemption, in the form of Regulation 2779/72.[99] This regulation exempts agreements between undertakings having less than 10 per cent. of the relevant market in any one Member State and a joint turnover of less than 150 million ECU. The conditions require that the parties remain free to market and manufacture other products and to sell goods covered by the agreement which are not supplied by the manufacturer who has taken over their manufacture, although stipulations for minimum stocks and spares or after-sales service and guarantee are acceptable.

6. Joint sales/purchase agreements

0—39   This type of agreement clearly will restrict competition in sales or supplies unless it allows the parties to sell or purchase independently if they choose (the joint sales/purchase agency becoming a sort of distributor). A careful examination of the agreement must be made to ascertain whether it has a significant discouraging effect on independent competition. It might be argued that the very existence of the agency may have that effect, but the Commission has not so far taken that view.[1]

7. Co-operation agreements not directly related to purchase or supply

0—40   Co-operation in matters such as accounting, transport and advertising restricts competition in those areas and may theoretically be subject to Article 85 (1). The Commission took the view

---

[97] See, *e.g. Goodyear Italiana,* O.J. 1975, L38/10; [1975] 1 C.M.L.R. D31.
[98] See, *e.g. Distillers Co. Ltd.* O.J. 1978, L50/16; [1978] 1 C.M.L.R. 400, confirmed by the Court of Justice in Case 30/78 *Distillers Co. Ltd.* v. *Commission* (July 10, 1980).
[99] J.O. 1972, L292/23; O.J. 1972, (December 28–30) 80, renewed by Reg. 2903/77, O.J. 1977, L338/14.
[1] See *CFA* J.O. 1968, L276/29; [1968] C.M.L.R. D68, *Cobelaz* O.J. 1968, L276/13; [1968] C.M.L.R. D45.

originally that they will normally not do so unless they are instrumental in restricting competition in the market place.[2] This initial view must be regarded now with some scepticism since the attitude to one item at least covered by the Commission's notice of 1968 on the subject has changed, namely research and development. In *Henkel/Colgate*[3] the Commission found that a research and development agreement infringed Article 85 (1). Such agreements may be exempted provided that the parties do not restrict themselves as to the use of the results of their co-operation, though more recent decisions indicate that some restrictions or duties (*e.g.* in the field of patent licensing) may be acceptable.[4]

8. Trade fairs

20–41 Trade fairs and exhibitions are an essential element of doing business, especially for small firms wishing to sell in a large geographical market. The rules of such fairs often prohibited exhibition at rival fairs as a condition of participation. Such prohibitions affect not only competition between the organisations which run the fairs but also between the participants. When submitted for review by the Commission the rules of such fairs have frequently been amended,[5] especially with respect to the length of the period during which exhibiting at other fairs is prohibited.

9. Mergers, takeovers and joint ventures

20–42 A merger of two or more competitors whereby each ceases to be a separate entity and a new legal person is created does not come within the prohibition of the competition rules at present (although Article 66, ECSC does require pre-notification and approval of all "concentrations" involving coal and steel firms). There are, however, two types of "concentration" which may fall under existing EEC prohibitions. First, mergers which do not involve the disappearance of the parties may infringe Article 85 (1) if the arrangement is a disguised device for restricting competition between two potentially "continuing" competitors. A joint venture which amounts usually to an agreement to pool certain resources for specific purposes by way of a form of "partnership" usually falls into this category if it is not designed to be permanent,[6] and hence will require exemption, which will usually be granted if the parties are to cease collaboration at the end of

---

[2] Notice of July 29, 1968, J.O. 1968, C75/3; [1968] C.M.L.R. D5.

[3] J.O. 1972, L14/14. See also *ACEC/Berliet* J.O. 1968, L201/17; [1968] C.M.L.R. D35.

[4] *Bayer/Gist-Brocades* O.J. 1976, L30/13; [1976] 1 C.M.L.R. D98; *KEWA* O.J. 1976, L51/15; [1976] 2 C.M.L.R. D15; *GEC/Weir* O.J. 1977, L327/26; [1978] 1 C.M.L.R. D42.

[5] *e.g. Cecimo* O.J. 1969, L69/13; [1969] C.M.L.R. D1.

[6] *e.g. Vacuum Interrupters* O.J. 1977, L48/32; [1977] 1 C.M.L.R. D67; *Bayer/Gist, supra*, note 4.

the project and do not restrict themselves in their use of the results of the collaboration.

On the other hand, the formation of a permanent union, if genuine, and involving a genuine and irreversible transfer of control to a single management will escape the prohibition of Article 85 (1).[7]

0—43 Secondly, *takeovers* may be subject to Article 86 if the acquiring party has abused a dominant position in acquiring the shares or interests of the party taken over. Thus in *Continental Can*,[8] the acquiring party, Europemballage, had a dominant position in the metal packing and containers market in Germany through its German subsidiary, Schmalbach-Lubeckawerke. The object of taking over its rival in the Dutch market, Thomassen & Drijver Verblifa, was found to be that of eliminating competition, although the Commission's decision was annulled by the Court for lack of sufficient evidence of a dominant position.

The principle of the decision that a dominant position could be abused in this way is open to criticism because it is not really possible to say that the taking over of a rival is an abuse of the dominant position held in another related market. It was the size of the acquirer in general that enabled it to effect the takeover, and in that sense it could have used resources not in any way related to it dominant position in any particular market. It must be queried whether the arrangement could have been questioned if the parties had structured it as a merger rather than a takeover, especially as Thomassen & Drijver agreed to the takeover. Furthermore, a legal régime which makes control of takeovers subject to competition rules only when the company making the takeover has a dominant position is clearly unsatisfactory. In 1973 the Commission proposed a regulation providing for a general system of takeover control,[9] which would supplement the existing Treaty provisions. Early adoption of this proposal seems unlikely.

The Enforcement and Administration of Competition Policy

0—44 The broad provisions of Articles 85 and 86 are implemented principally by Regulation 17 of 1962[10] (referred to as Regulation 17) adopted pursuant to Article 87 (1) of the Treaty, which gives the Council broad powers to adopt regulations and directives.

[7] See Annual General Report 1977, pp. 31–34 and *De Laval/Stork* O.J. 1977, L215/11; [1977] 2 C.M.L.R. D69, where the agreement failed to amount to a true merger but was exempted under Article 85 (3); *SHV/Chevron* O.J. 1975, L38/14; [1975] 1 C.M.L.R. D68.
[8] *Supra*, note 21.
[9] O.J. 1973, C92/1.
[10] J.O. 1962, 204; O.J. 1959–62, 87.

(a) The direct applicability of Articles 85 and 86

20–45   Article 1 of Regulation 17 settled any doubts which might have existed about the direct applicability of Articles 85 and 86 by declaring:

> " . . . agreements, decisions and concerted practices of the kind described in Article 85 (1) of the Treaty and the abuse of a dominant position in the market, within the meaning of Article 86 of the Treaty, shall be prohibited, *no prior decision to that effect being required.*"

(b) Direct applicability of Article 85 (1) and consequences under Article 85 (2): provisional validity

20–46   Although Article 85 (2) renders void agreements prohibited under para. (1), the Court in Case 13/61 *Bosch,*[11] was unwilling to accept that agreements existing prior to the date of entry into force of Regulation 17 were automatically void, even if Article 1 of the latter regulation could be regarded as merely declaratory. Regulation 17 in fact contains a number of provisions conferring different treatment on such agreements (see Articles 5, 6 and 7). The Court stated:

> "It follows [from the effect of Article 6 (2) and Article 5 (1) of Regulation 17] that the authors of the Regulation seem to have envisaged also that at the date of its entry into force there would be subsisting agreements to which Article 85 (1) applied but in respect of which decisions under Article 85 (3) had not yet been taken, without such agreements thereby being automatically void."

> "The opposite interpretation would lead to the inadmissible result that some agreements would have been automatically void for several years without having been so declared by any authority, and even though they might ultimately be validated subsequently with retroactive effect."[12]

The effect of this judgment is that neither Article 85 nor 86 was applicable until the coming into force of Regulation 17 unless action had been taken to enforce them by the authorities of the Member States. Any agreement, etc., not prosecuted (and none was) was therefore valid and legitimate in terms of EEC law up until March 13, 1962.

20–47   The effect of the *Bosch* ruling would, without more, have been to create a lacuna between the entry into force of Regulation 17 and the grant of exemption (if a grant was made pursuant to

[11] [1962] E.C.R. 45.
[12] [1962] E.C.R. 45, 52.

332

notification). This was further complicated by the fact that the Commission had the power to declare the agreement exempt retrospectively to the coming into effect of Regulation 17.[13] Hence the Court decided in *Bosch* that duly notified agreements in existence on March 13, 1962, were "provisionally valid." (Agreements falling within Article 5 (2) of Regulation 17 were "valid"). Such agreements are known as "old agreements." The same principles apply to agreements, etc., which fall within Article 85 as a result of accession of the three new Member States on January 1, 1973, and of Greece of January 1, 1981. Hence those principles continue to be relevant. Although the doctrine of "provisional validity" was subject to a good deal of criticism and may have been doubted in subsequent cases, there seems little doubt from a more recent decision that it does survive. In *de Bloos* v. *Bouyer*[14] the Court held:

> "During the period between notification and the date on which the Commission takes a decision, courts before which proceedings are brought relating to an old agreement duly notified or exempted from notification must give such an agreement the legal effects attributed thereto under the law applicable to the contract, and those effects cannot be called into question by any objection which may be raised concerning its compatibility with Article 85 (1)."[15]

20—48   Provisional validity lasts only for as long as the Commission has not made a decision to exempt or not to exempt the agreement. Placing the agreement on a "dead" file: in other words, simply deciding not to take any action in respect of an agreement, and notifying the parties of that action, will also have the effect of removing "provisional validity,"[16] although the result may subsequently be "full" validity if a national court decides that the agreement does not infringe Article 85. *New agreements, i.e.* those which were not in existence on March 13, 1962 or (in the case of agreements falling under Article 85 by virtue of accession), January 1, 1973, or January 1, 1981, as the case may be, are not provisionally valid.[17] In such cases the national court, if called upon to implement Article 85 (2), should normally stay proceedings and await the Commission's decision on exemption. This would not be necessary where the agreement has not been notified or clearly has no chance of being exempted.

(c) The "negative clearance" (Article 2)

20—49   Article 2 of Regulation 17 empowers the Commission to certify

[13] Reg. 17/62, Article 6 (2), *infra.*
[14] Case 59/77 [1977] E.C.R. 2359.
[15] *Ibid.* p.2371.
[16] Case 99/79 *Lancôme & Cosparfrance* v. *Etos & Albert Heijn Supermart* [1980] 2 C.M.L.R. 164.
[17] Case 48/72 *Brasserie de Haecht* (No.2) [1973] E.C.R. 77.

that agreements do not come within the ambit of either Article 85 (1) or Article 86 of the EEC Treaty. This procedure was not envisaged by the Treaty, but forms part of the Community strategy for dealing expeditiously with the huge number of agreements potentially subject to Articles 85 and 86. Other devices are the use of block exemptions, "test cases" and Notices, mentioned below.

Parties seeking to establish officially that their activities do not infringe the rules of competition must apply for clearance to the Commission. Clearance will be given only if, on the basis of the facts known to it, the Commission finds no grounds for action under Article 85 (1) or 86. This does not amount to a finding that the agreement does not infringe these articles but only that there is no present evidence that it does. Originally the Commission required firms to submit separate forms, depending on whether they sought a negative clearance or an exemption under Article 85 (3) (Form A for negative clearance, Form B for exemption applications). It emerged in practice that firms wished their agreements to be considered for both types of exoneration, *i.e.* for negative clearance first and then, if unsuccessful, for exemption. It was thus considered administratively more efficient to combine the two forms into a Form A/B since both applications concerned exactly the same facts.[18]

20—50   According to Article 2, application for negative clearance must be by "the undertakings or associations of undertakings concerned." Article 1 of Regulation 27/62 makes it clear that notification can be effected by any undertaking party to the agreement.

Because of the lack of finality of the negative clearance it has been argued that the clearance does not amount to a formal "decision" within the meaning of Article 189.[19] This is likely to be a significant issue if another party to the agreement desires to challenge the Commission's action (as for instance when it is involved in national proceedings where it is seeking to invoke Article 85 (2)). Theoretically a national court could come to a contrary decision since it may have other facts at its disposal, from which it would follow that the Commission's action does not have any legal consequences and is therefore not a "decision."[20] Furthermore, even on the same facts a national court would possibly refer the same to the Court under Article 177 and get a different answer. It seems therefore unlikely that persons party to the agreement could compel the Commission to issue a negative clearance, since Article 175 clearly requires that a decision be requested. Non-parties are certainly precluded because the clearance desired is not addressed to them.[21]

---

[18] See now Regulation 1133/68, J.O. 1968, L189/1; O.J. 1968, 400.
[19] See, *e.g.* Megret, Waelbroeck, *le Droit de la CEE,* Vol.4, Concurrence, page 116.
[20] See paras. 6–18 *et seq.*
[21] See Case 125/78 *GEMA* v. *Commission* [1979] E.C.R. 3173.

(d) The finding of infringement (Article 3)

20—51   Article 3 (1) empowers the Commission to take a legally binding decision requiring termination of infringements of Articles 85 and 86 EEC. The Commission may also adopt interim measures.[22] It appears from *Grundig*[23] that the Commission decision can only strike at the whole agreement where it violates Article 85 or 86 in its entirety. Where this is not the case the decision should only strike at the parts which are incompatible with the Treaty. The Commission may itself set in motion the procedures for investigating whether there is an infringement, or it may be requested to do so. A decision under Article 3 (1) will also be taken in consequence of a refusal of a negative clearance or a refusal of an exemption under Article 85 (3), where the agreement is not voluntarily abandoned.

Article 3 (2) states that Member States and natural or legal persons may apply to the Commission to start proceedings under paragraph 1. Member States do not have to assert a particular interest, but natural and legal persons must claim a legitimate interest, meaning that they must be able to justify that claim. A legitimate interest will be constituted by evidence that the complainant is in some measure affected by the practice complained of. Form C has space for declaration of legitimate interest.

Probably the degree of interest required is much the same as that required to intervene in an action before the Court.[24] A person who has complained is directly and individually concerned by any decision taken to exempt or ban the agreement and may challenge it.[25]

20—52   It appears, however, that the complainant has no right to require the Commission to take a decision should it fail to do so.[26] If the Commission takes action on its own initiative the legitimacy of the initial complaint is irrelevant.[27] Article 3 (3) empowers the Commission to make recommendations to undertakings or associations involved in practices which infringe Article 85 or 86 with a view to bringing about a voluntary modification of the practices in question so that they no longer infringe the Community rules. If a modification is satisfactory a negative clearance or exemption may be given; otherwise the Commission will take a decision under Article 3 (1) of the regulation.

Once an agreement is notified[28] the parties will become immune from fines until an adverse decision is taken or a notification is made under Article 15 (6) that the Commission does not

---

[22] Case 792/79 R *Camera Care* v. *Commission* [1980] E.C.R. 119.
[23] *Supra*, note 9, p. 313.
[24] Case 41/73, etc. *SA Générale Sucrière et al* v. *Commission* [1973] E.C.R. 1465.
[25] See Case 26/76 *Metro SB Grossmärkte* v. *Commission* [1977] E.C.R. 1875.
[26] *GEMA* note 21, *supra*.
[27] See Case 26/76 *Metro, supra,* note 25.
[28] *Infra.* para. 20–53.

consider that the agreement can qualify for an exemption. Because of the legal effect on the parties, such a notification is considered by the Court to be a decision.[29]

(e) The grant of an exemption

20—53 *Notification*

Article 4 (1) states that:

"Agreements, decisions and concerted practices of the kind described in Article 85 (1) of the Treaty which come into existence after the entry into force of this regulation and in respect of which the parties seek application of Article 85 (3) must be notified to the Commission. Until they have been notified, no decision in application of Article 85 (3) may be taken."

The terms of the paragraph are self-explanatory. There is no duty to notify, but there is a clear incentive to do so, for no exemption can be granted without notification.

The only agreements which need not be notified are those listed in paragraph 2 of the article (see further below), although they may in fact be notified if desired, with the same legal consequences.

20—54 As already stated, notification for the purposes of Article 4 (1) follows the same procedure as that for the applications for negative clearances. The agreement once notified enjoys a privileged status in that even if the Commission eventually takes an adverse decision on it, no fine for violation of Article 85 (1) may be imposed in respect of the period between notification and decision.

Agreements which have been the subject to a block exemption need not be notified. In addition, however, Article 4 (2) exempts certain agreements (whether new or old) from notification. These agreements are deemed to have special features which may make them less prejudicial to the development of the common market. The exempted agreements are:

20—55 (1) So-called national agreements, which concern firms from one Member State only, and relate neither to imports nor to exports;[30]

(2) Agreements between two undertakings only, which do no more than:

---

[29] Cases 8–11/66 *Cimenteries CBR* v. *Commission* [1967] E.C.R. 75.

[30] Agreements relating to goods which had previously been imported do not normally relate to imports or exports: Case 63/75 *Fonderies Roubaix Wattrelos* v. *Roux* [1976] E.C.R. 111. On the other hand, the fact that an agreement does not relate to imports or exports does not preclude the application of Article 85 (1) (as indeed Article 4 (2) of Reg. 17 must suggest): Case 43/69 *Bilger* v. *Jehle* [1970] E.C.R. 127.

(a) Impose restrictive conditions on the resale of goods the subject of the agreement. This may include restrictions on fixing resale prices;

(b) Impose restrictions on the exercise of industrial property rights, methods of manufacture or know-how, grant of such rights being the subject of the agreement;

(3) Agreements having as their sole object:

(a) The development or uniform application of standards or types; or

(b) Joint research and development;[31]

(c) Specialisation in the manufacture of products, including agreements necessary for the achievement thereof;

- where the products which are the subject of specialisation do not, in a substantial part of the Common Market, represent more than 15 per cent. of the volume of business done in identical products or those considered by the consumers to be similar by reason of their characteristics, price and use, and;

- where the total annual turnover of the participating undertakings does not exceed 200 million ECUs.

Time limit of exemption and other conditions

20—56   Article 6 (1) provides that Commission decisions exempting agreements under Article 85 (3) shall not take effect from an earlier date than the date of notification (although the decision may have retroactive effect to that date or a later date).

Article 6 (2) states that the Commission may make exceptions to the rule in paragraph 1 in respect of agreements which do not formally require notification under Regulation 17/62, and old agreements which have been notified within the time limits set.

20—57   Article 8, para. 1, states that an exemption may be given for a specific time period only and may be subject to conditions and obligations. The Commission frequently requires to be kept informed of relevant matters occurring in the context of the agreement as a condition of granting exemption, and may thus keep the circumstances under review. The exemption may be renewed on application if the conditions of Article 85 (3) are still satisfied. The Commission may revoke or amend the decision of exemption where (a) there has been a fundamental change in the factual situation underlying the agreement, (b) in case of breach of any obligation imposed on the parties by the Commission's decision, (c) where the decision is based on incorrect information or was induced by deceit, or (d) the exemption is abused by the parties to the agreement. The Commission may attack such an abuse without upsetting the exemption already granted.[32]

---

[31] As amended by Regulation 2822/71, J.O. 1971, L285/49.
[32] Cases 32 & 36–82/78 *BMW Belgium* v. *Commission* [1980] 1 C.M.L.R. 370

(f) Procedure

20—58   The Commission's procedure usually moves along the following path once it has decided to take action against an agreement, practice or abuse.

First, an investigation must take place.

Articles 11 to 14 of Regulation 17 confer investigative powers on the Commission. Such powers are obviously necessary if the Community competition policy is to work. Article 11 (1) is quite wide in its purview:

> "In carrying out the duties assigned to it by Article 89 and by provisions adopted under Article 87 of the Treaty, the Commission may obtain all necessary information from the Governments and competent authorities of the Member States and from undertakings and associations of undertakings."

20—59   It represents little more than a particular application of the general power contained in Article 213 of the Treaty. The article also contains provisions to compel firms to supply the required information. If a firm does not comply with a formal request for information within a time limit set, the Commission can proceed to a formal decision requiring the information. This decision specifies a further time limit for reply, and must state that under Article 16 (1) (c) the Commission has the power to impose periodic penalty payments to compel production of complete and correct information. The decision must also mention that the furnishing of incorrect information may be penalised. Article 11 thus clearly envisages a two-stage process.

The Commission's use of information received is limited by the provisions of Article 20 of Regulation 17, which lays down that any information given to the Commission, whether under Article 11, 12, 13 or 14, shall be used only for purposes relevant to the investigation in hand. In addition the Community and the national authorities involved are under an obligation not to infringe the code of professional secrecy by making public information disclosed to them under the above-mentioned articles (Art. 20 (2)). But general information may be made public (Art. 20 (3)).

20—60   Article 11 is designed to empower the Commission to make specific requests for particular information from States and firms; Article 12 gives the Commission general authority to investigate the situation in any part of the economy where it fears a breach of Articles 85 and 86 of the EEC Treaty, while Article 14 permits the Commission to carry out on-the-spot investigations at any firm, in pursuance of its duties under this regulation. Again, the Commission may do so without a formal decision to that effect. However, unlike the procedure under Article 11 it is not obliged to make a formal request first. A decision may be validly adopted which is notified to the undertaking concerned when Commission officials arrive at the offices of the undertaking. Hence, the undertaking is not entitled to any prior warning of a visit.[33] Article 13 allows the Commission to authorise the national cartel bodies to perform this function on its behalf. The investigations of the Commission under Articles 11 and 14 must be carried out only for the purposes of provisions adopted under Article 87, in carrying out duties assigned to it by Article 89, but this is not a real limitation. There seems nevertheless to be an incipient doctrine of privilege.[34]

20—61 When the investigation has been completed, a notification may be made under Article 15.[35] The Commission will subsequently deliver to the undertakings concerned a "statement of objections" (if it intends to take an adverse decision). The parties are given the opportunity to respond in writing and to be heard in the matter.[36] Third parties having a sufficient interest may also be heard. Third parties who have complained are entitled to notification by the Commission where the latter considers that there are insufficient grounds for granting the application, and this then entitles the complainant to make further comments in writing. After the hearing the Commission must consult with the Advisory Committee on Restrictive Practices and Monopolies. The opinion of the Committee is confidential. Finally, the Commission will adopt its formal decision.

The above procedure may be curtailed at any stage if the parties come to an amicable arrangement, in which case the result is usually a press release to that effect.

(g) Penalties for non-compliance

20—62 Article 15 (2) empowers the Commission to impose fines of between 1,000 to 1 million ECU or of up to 10 per cent. of the turnover in the previous year for infringement of Article 85 (1) or Article 86 or a breach of the conditions subject to which an Article 85 (3) exemption is granted. Periodic fines may be imposed under Article 16 ranging from 50 to 1,000 ECU per day to be calculated from the date of the decision.[37] Fines may only be imposed where the act was done intentionally or negligently[38] and should take account of all relevant factors including the national legislative background.[39]

---

[33] Case 136/79 *National Panasonic (UK) Ltd.* v. *Commission* [1980] E.C.R. 2033.
[34] *AM & S Europe Ltd.* O.J. 1979, L199/31; [1979] 3 C.M.L.R. 376.
[35] *Supra,* para. 30–52.
[36] Regulation 99/63, J.O. 1963, 2268; O.J. 1963–1964, 47.
[37] The fine will be fixed in terms of a national currency once calculated in ECU and will not thereafter vary, cases 40–48, etc/73, *SA Générale Sucrière et al* v. *Commission* [1973] E.C.R. 1465.
[38] Reg. 17, Article 15.
[39] Cases 40, etc/73 *Suiker Unie* [1975] E.C.R. 1663.

The imposition of fines is now subject to a limitation period: The Commission may not impose fines in respect of infringements which took place, or, in the case of a continuing infringement, ceased to take place more than five years before the commencement of action by the Commission provided that the action has been notified to at least one of the parties.[40] The effect of the action is to start time running afresh, but no fine may be imposed after a period equal to twice the limitation period has elapsed without the Commission having imposed a fine or a penalty. The mere fact that a practice has ceased has no effect on the power of the Commission to impose fines.[41]

20—63   Fines may be imposed on undertakings which have their principal place of business outside the EEC if they have acted within the EEC, although clearly this power must be subject to the extent of the undertaking's assets within the EEC.[42]

Fines are enforced through the national authorities of the Member States.[43] In England the Commission registers the decision with the High Court, and it then has the same force and effect as a judgment of the High Court.[44]

The Court has complete jurisdiction to review the level of fines and increase, diminish or annul them if not satisfied with the Commission's action. In practice it has never increased a fine, but has in many cases reduced a fine[45] or annulled it because the substance of the decision was at fault.[46]

In assessing the size of a fine, regard must be had to three basic elements:[47]

- the nature and gravity of the infringement (*e.g.* did an agreement partition the common market along national lines)
- the degree of intention of the parties in committing the infringement
- the duration of the infringement.

The maximum fine will only be levied in the case of an intentional infringement of the gravest kind and of considerable duration.[48]

(h) Review of decisions

20—64   The Commission's decisions are subject to review under the

---

[40] Regulation 2988/74, Articles 1 and 2 (1); O.J. 1974, L319/1.
[41] Cases 41, 44 and 45/69 *ACF Chemiefarma, Buchler & Boehringer* v. *Commission* [1970] E.C.R. 661, 733, 769.
[42] *Supra.* See para. 20–04 regarding territorial jurisdiction.
[43] Article 192 EEC.
[44] European Communities (Enforcement of Community Judgments) Order 1972 (SI 1972 No. 1590).
[45] As in *United Brands, supra*, note 54.
[46] As in *Grundig, supra*, para. 20–06, note 14.
[47] *Pioneer HiFi Equipment* [1980] 1 C.M.L.R. 457.
[48] Case 19/77 *Miller International Schallplatten* v. *Commission* [1978] E.C.R. 131.

normal procedures of Article 173 and the Court has jurisdiction also to review fines.[49] The Court has no specific power to review the facts but it can nevertheless carry out a very full review of the evidence to ascertain whether the facts as found support the Commission's conclusion.[50]

(i) General investigations into sectors of the economy

20—65　　The definition of the scope of application of Articles 85 and 86 to the various branches of the economy was clearly not considered to be an important function, and it was in any case considered in some quarters that such definitions would derogate from the desired uniformity of rules. Article 12 of the regulation nevertheless provides for the carrying out of inquiries to determine whether there is a breach of Articles 85 or 86 in the sector as a whole. But this does not seem to be directed to the same problem.

(j) Relationship between national law and the competition rules

20—66　　Regulation 17 does not set out any clear guide to the relationship of national and Community competition laws. The furthest it goes is to lay down certain rules concerning the overlapping of action by the authorities (Article 9). Article 9 defines the respective areas of competence of the national authorities and of the Commission. So long as the Commission has not "initiated any procedure" under Articles 2, 3, or 6 of Regulation 17, the national authorities remain competent to apply Articles 85 (1) and 86. They are free to apply the provisions of Community law up to the time when the Commission begins to act in the matter, but the grant of exemption is in the hands of the Commission exclusively.

　　The term "initiation of a procedure" has never been fully defined but would appear to cover the case where the Commission has taken some action as a result of a notification. The "authorities of the Member States" may include national courts, but they remain free to apply Article 85 (2) regardless of Regulation 17 because the power in such a case derives from the Treaty itself.[51]

20—67　　Of more importance is the relationship between EEC and national competition law, and in particular, the possibility of incompatibility between a decision to exempt on the part of the Commission and a decision to prohibit by one of the Member States. In *Walt Wilhelm*[52] the Court indicated that:

　　" . . . should it prove that a decision of a national authority regarding an agreement would be incompatible with a decision

[49] *Supra* paras. 11–18 *et seq.*
[50] As it did for example in Case 27/76 *United Brands, supra,* note 54.
[51] Cases 127/73 *SABAM* v. *Fonior* [1974] E.C.R. 51; 37/69 *Anne Marty SA* v. *Estee Lauder SA* [1981] 2 C.M.L.R. 143.
[52] Case 14/68 *Wilhelm* v. *Bundeskartellamt* [1969] E.C.R. 1.

adopted by the Commission at the culmination of the procedure initiated by it, the national authority is required to take proper account of the effects of the latter decision.

Where, during national proceedings, it appears possible that the decision to be taken by the Commission at the culmination of a procedure still in progress concerning the same agreement may conflict with the effects of the decision of the national authorities, it is for the latter to take the appropriate measures."[53]

This statement is not easily applied in practice. It can be argued that national authorities cannot proceed to prohibit any agreement which has been exempted by the Commission,[54] but it may also be argued that they may continue to do so unless the exemption forms part of an overriding Community policy.[55] The fact that the Commission has indicated that there is no need for it to take action does not prevent Member States from applying stricter national law.[56]

Greek Accession

20–68   Provisions similar to those applied on the Accession of the United Kingdom are applied by Article 21 of the Act of Accession in conjunction with Annex I, section 5. The competition provisions thus apply from January 1, 1981, to agreements affecting trade between Greece and the other Member States.

---

[53] *Ibid.* and p.14.
[54] *Ibid.*
[55] Markert, (1974) 11 C.M.L.R. 92, p.99.
[56] Case 253/78 & 1–3/79 *Procureur de la République* v. *Giry and Guèrlain et al.* [1981] 2 C.M.L.R. 99.

Chapter 21

AIDS - ARTICLES 92 - 94

21–01 A Community rule on aids is necessary in order to avoid the distortions of Community competition which might result from grants of assistance to certain areas or industries without reference to Community requirements as a whole. The Community rule established by Articles 92 to 94 making up section 3 of the Chapter on competition consists of a general provision that aids which distort competition are incompatible with the common market (Art. 92 (1)). This prohibition is subject to exceptions, by which certain defined aids are recognised as compatible with the common market (Art. 92 (2)), certain defined aids can be considered compatible (Art. 92 (3)), and, exceptionally, other aids can be considered compatible if approved unanimously by the Council (Art. 92 (3) (*d*)).

General supervision of aids is in the hands of the Commission.

Article 92

21–02 Articles 92 lays down the basic Community rule on the subject of aids. However, this rule is not expressed in absolute terms, for in the first place it applies only "save as otherwise provided in this Treaty." Other Treaty provisions on aids are found in Articles 42, 77, 82 and 223. Article 42 allows the Council to authorise special agricultural aids,[1] while Articles 77 and 82 envisage certain aids to the transport sector.[2] Although Article 30 could on a broad interpretation be considered as prohibiting "aids" which act in effect as barriers to trade by facilitating domestic sales, the Court has ruled that aids do not as such fall within Article 30 but the aspects of the aid which are not necessary for the attainment of its object or for its proper functioning and which contravene this prohibition may for that reason be held to be incompatible with Article 30: but the fact that an aspect of aid is incompatible with Article 30 does not invalidate the aid as a whole or for that reason vitiate the system of financing the aid.[3] There are similar rulings in relation to other articles.[4]

[1] Thus subordinating Articles 92 to 94: Case 177/78 *Pigs and Bacon Commission* v. *McCarren* [1979] E.C.R. 2161; Case 72/79 *Commission* v. *Italy* [1980] E.C.R. 1411.
[2] In Case 156/77 *Commission* v. *Belgium* [1978] E.C.R. 1881, however, the Court ruled that Article 77 cannot exempt aid to transport from the general system of the Treaty concerning aid granted by Member States. Reg. 1473/75, O.J. 1975, L152/1, stipulates that Articles 92 to 94 are to apply to aid granted to transport.
[3] Case 74/76 *Iannelli* v. *Meroni* [1977] E.C.R. 557.
[4] Cases 91/78 *Hansen* v. *HZA Flensburg* [1979] E.C.R. 935 (Article 37) and 73/79 *Commission* v. *Italy* [1980] E.C.R. 1233 (Article 95).

Article 223 makes it clear that the Treaty is without prejudice to the right of a Member State to take necessary measures for "the protection of the essential interests of its security which are connected with the production of or trade in arms, munitions and war material." This permits Member States to subsidise ordnance factories and the like, Articles 92 and 94 notwithstanding.

21—03   In principle the aids provisions do not apply to the coal and steel sector in view of Article 232 of the EEC Treaty ("the provisions of this Treaty shall not affect the provisions of" the ECSC Treaty) and of Article 4 (c) of the ECSC Treaty which prohibits subsidies or aids granted by States in any form whatsoever.

However, Article 67 (2) ECSC shows that this prohibition is not absolute,[5] while the Commission seems to have taken the view that the EEC provisions may be applicable,[6] at least where an aid is not specific to coal and steel.[7]

The principle of incompatibility: definition of "aid"

21—04   Subject to the saving discussed in the previous section, Article 92 (1) declares incompatible with the common market:

> "any aid granted by a Member State or through State resources in any form whatsoever which distorts or threatens to distort competition by favouring certain undertakings or the production of certain goods insofar as it affects trade between Member States."

Though the Treaty does not define aid, in response to a written question in the European Parliament, the Commission indicated that it considered that aid could manifest itself in the form of subsidies, tax exemptions, interest rate reductions, loan guarantees on favourable terms, provision of buildings or land free or on favourable terms; provision of goods or services on preferential terms; loss indemnities, or any other measure having equivalent effect.[8]

The one element of definition which Article 92 does give is that aids are "granted by a Member State *or through State resources in any form whatsoever.*" Thus, Article 92 embraces aids granted by semi-public agencies or local authorities as well as by central

---

[5] Case 30/57 *Steenkolenmijnen* v. *H.A.* [1961] E.C.R. 1.
[6] On the basis of Cases 59/70 *Netherlands* v. *Commission* [1971] E.C.R. 639 and 70/72 *Commission* v. *Germany* [1973] E.C.R. 813.
[7] See Comp. Rep. EC. 1971 sec. 189 *et seq.* and, *e.g.* Decision 257/80 ECSC, O.J. 1980, L29/5.
[8] W.Q. 48/63, J.O. 1963, 2235. The Commission has now developed a substantial jurisprudence on the basis of Article 93. See *passim* the Commission's Reports on Competition Policy (Comp. Rep. EC) published annually in conjunction wth its annual General Report. Important policy statements are contained in these Reports. Formal decisions taken under Article 93 (2) are listed in Comp. Rep. EC 1976, p.195, 1979, p.172 and 1980 p.205.

government. However, a measure characterised by the fixing of minimum retail prices with the objective of favouring distributors of a product at the exclusive expense of consumers cannot constitute an aid, because it is not granted with State resources.[9] Where State financial resources are used, the question whether the use of them amounts to an aid must be settled by reference to the *effects* rather than the alleged purpose.[10] The fact that the assistance is financed by a general levy on the industry which benefits from the assistance does not preclude the characterisation of that assistance as an aid.[11]

21—05   The immediate beneficiary of the aid is not necessarily the undertaking or producer of goods; thus, in Decision 66/556[12] the Commission objected to an aid to purchasers of French-manufactured gliders. The reduction in price acted as a stimulus to sales and indirectly to production.

Nor do export-orientated aids escape the prohibition. In 6/69 *Commission* v. *France*[13] a preferential discount rate available for exports constituted an aid incompatible with the common market. In Case 730/79 *Philip Morris*[14] the Court upheld the Commission's finding that an aid which would in effect increase export capacity would affect trading conditions to an extent contrary to the common interest.

Further, although the effects on trade between Member States may not in themselves be substantial, it may be that the disturbance it creates is increased by a method of financing it which could render the scheme as a whole incompatible with a single market and the common interest.[15]

21—06   There is no clear guidance as to the application of the aid provisions to shareholdings, increases in capital, etc., in state-owned enterprises. The Commission earlier took the view that Articles 92 to 94 apply equally to state-owned enterprises but that their incidence in the circumstances described would have to be looked at on a case by case basis given that government decision-making in this area is as much political as economic.[16] As a step towards clarifying the relationship of government to state-owned enterprises, the Commission issued Directive 80/723,[17] on the tran-

---

[9] Case 82/77 *Openbaar Ministerie* v. *van Tiggele* [1978] E.C.R. 25. *cf.* also Case 61/79 *Ammin. delle Finanze* v. *Denkavit Italiana* [1980] E.C.R. 1205. (Refund of tax imposed contrary to Community law not an aid).

[10] Case 173/73 *Italy* v. *Commission* [1974] E.C.R. 709.

[11] Case 78/76 *Steinike & Weinlig* v. *Germany* [1977] E.C.R. 595, para. 22.

[12] J.O. 1966, 3141.   [13] [1969] E.C.R. 523.

[14] (September 17, 1980). See also Commission Decision of March 20 1981 on SX 70 and discussion of *Philip Morris* in Comp. Rep. EC 1980 sec. 214.

[15] Case 47/69 *France* v. *Commission* [1970] E.C.R. 487.

[16] W.Q. 48/63, *supra,* note 8, see also Comp. Rep. EC 1972 sec 122 ff: Decision 72/34, J.O. 1972 L10/22 and Comp. Rep. EC 1978, secs. 227 *et seq.*

[17] O.J. 1980, L195/35.

345

sparency of financial relations between Member States and public undertakings. The validity of the directive was challenged by France, Italy and the United Kingdom on technical rather than substantive grounds, objecting that Article 90 (3), the legal basis for the directive, could not be construed as conferring the necessary general law-making power.[18]

Direct applicability

21—07   The Court has held that Articles 92 to 94 give the Commission a wide measure of discretion[19] and that therefore there must be a decision under Article 93 (2) or Article 94 or a failure to comply with Article 93 (2) before the question of any direct applicability of Article 92 can arise.[20]

Derogations from the principle of incompatibility: aids which are compatible with the common market

21—08   Article 92 (2) sets out a list of aids which are compatible with the common market, without additional formality. Sub-paragraph (a) concerns "aids having a social character": this does not relate to social security and welfare payments by the national authorities to individuals, but rather to aids granted to firms in order to meet a governmental social objective, *e.g.* keeping down the price of bread.

Under sub-paragraph (b) aids which compensate for natural disasters or "exceptional occurrences" are compatible with the common market. Although this clause would seem to cover only "Acts of God" and the like, it appears that in the initial stages the Commission was willing to give a wide interpretation to "exceptional occurrences," and approved a German plan for assistance to be given to the lead and zinc mines, which had suffered considerable financial losses. The Commission supported its argument by referring to the peculiar distortions in the world market for these base metals. However, more recent decisions have indicated that such aids should be designed to produce lasting achievements and be directed to regional or sectoral problems; in other words, they would no longer fall under this particular heading.[21]

21—09   Sub-paragraph (c) relates to the general agreement amongst the Member States on the signing of the EEC Treaty that special provision should be made to assist those areas of Germany known as the *Zonenrandgebiet*, which border on East Germany and Czechoslovakia. Provision was made in Article 82 of the Treaty

[18] Cases 188 to 190/80.
[19] Cases 77/72 *Capolongo* v. *Maya* [1973] E.C.R. 611; 74/76, *supra,* note 3; 78/76, *supra,* note 11, 730/79, *supra,* note 14.
[20] *Ibid.*
[21] See, *e.g.* Decision 72/34, J.O. 1972, L10/22 (Belgian aids for companies in difficulties).

for the application of measures in the transport sector to compensate for the economic disadvantages of this area, and the clause here merely amplifies this, permitting aids of any kind to assist the economy of these districts.

It is to be noted that all the aids listed in paragraph 2, although definitively compatible with the common market, must nevertheless be notified to the Commission in accordance with the provisions of Article 93 (1) and (3).

Aids which may be considered to be compatible with the common market

1—10   Paragraph 3 of the article provides that certain aids "may be considered to be compatible with the common market." The procedure for approval involved here must be deduced from the provisions of Article 93. There is no actual provision stating that the Commission shall take a positive decision if it approves an aid as coming within the categories set out in this paragraph. If after consideration of the aid in question, the Commission is of the opinion that it qualifies under Article 92 (3), then it informs the Member State concerned in an unpublished communication but reserves to itself (Art. 93 (1)) the power to review its decision at any time.[22]

The various types of aid set out in Article 92 (3) are as follows:

1—11   Category (a) comprises aids for regions where there is an abnormally low standard of living or serious under-employment. The category is self-explanatory, but no satisfactory criteria for determining what is an abnormally low standard of living have been evolved. This category is, however, seldom used to justify aids, since category (c) (below) embodies a much more generous definition, under which it is possible to subsume most regional problems, whether social, economic or industrial. Category (b) allows aids to be used for a project of common European interest, *i.e.* which involve more than one Member State directly or indirectly. This would include a road tunnel under the Alps, a hydro-electric scheme in Luxembourg, whose power serves Germany, France and/or Belgium, and presumably the Channel Tunnel. The category also permits aids where a serious disturbance in the economy of a Member State has occurred. This was used in the 1975 recession.[23] Category (c) is the most important category in that it is wider in scope than either of the two categories already mentioned. It is around this category that the Community

---

[22] *Cf.* The Decision that a German investment grant scheme for coal producing areas in North-Rhine Westphalia, begun in 1968, should no longer be deemed compatible with the Common Market, because the conditions under which the aid was authorised were no longer fulfilled: Decision 71/121, J.O. 1971, L57/19. See cases cited *supra,* note 19 as to the nature of the discretion.

[23] See Comp. Rep. EC 1975, secs. 130 *et seq.*

aid policy has developed. It permits aids to be granted "to facilitate the development of certain economic activities or of certain economic areas, where such aid does not adversely affect trading conditions to an extent contrary to the common interest." It will be apparent that the category includes *sectoral* aids, *i.e.* aids which benefit a particular industry or branch of it, as well as *regional* aids.

21—12   *Sectoral aids* have been approved in particular for the benefit of shipbuilding, textiles, the film industry and aircraft manufacture. The Commission emphasises that these aids should be selective; designed to stimulate competitive development and re-organisation of firms with a competitive future; be transparent (*i.e.* quantifiable and undisguised) and be designed to have the least effect on intra-Community competition.[24] Shipbuilding has been the subject of directives aimed at the elimination of discriminatory assistance but designed to boost the ailing sectors of the industry.[25] The directives have provided for the reduction of production aids, the grant of export aids only within the scheme laid down by the OECD, the achievement of transparency and consultative procedures particularly with respect to ad hoc assistance.

For the textile industry guidelines were first laid down in July 1971 and these have been used to bring national systems within the broader rules of the Treaty. The application of sectoral aids to shipbuilding, textiles and steel (where the Commission has invoked the Coal and Steel Treaty provisions together with Articles 92 - 94 EEC[26]) has formed part of a more general industrial policy for the relevant sectors.

21—13   *Regional aids* granted by Member States (as opposed to Community aid as part of the regional policy) have been the subject of progressive co-ordination since the late 1960s with the first formal guidelines adopted in 1971.[27] In 1975 the procedures for co-ordination were finally extended to the entire territory of the Community.[28] New guidelines were adopted in a Commission communication of December 21, 1978, to apply from January 1, 1979.[29] The communication seeks to co-ordinate ceilings of aid intensity; expresses reservations in principle as to the compatibility of operating aids, *i.e.* those not conditional on initial investment or job creation - structural aids; emphasises regional specificity, *i.e.* aids should not cover the whole of national territory

---

[24] Comp. Rep. EC 1971, secs. 164 *et seq*. See also communication of 25 May, 1978, Comp. Rep. EC 1978, secs. 172–176, com (78) 221 final.
[25] See currently Directive 81/363, O.J. 1981, L 137/39 on aids to shipbuilding extended to March 31, 1981.
[26] See *supra*, para. 21–03.
[27] First Resolution on Regional Aids, J.O. 1971, C111/1.
[28] Communication of June 27, 1973, Comp. Rep. EC 1973, secs. 80 *et seq*.
[29] O.J. 1979, C31/9 and see also Comp. Rep. EC 1978, secs. 151 *et seq*.

but only designated areas; and points out potential sectoral repercussions of regional aid. Community co-ordination continues on the existing basis, amended and supplemented by the Annex to the communication.

1—14   *General Aid Schemes* are to be distinguished from regional aid schemes. General aid schemes which pursue vague objectives such as general economic growth or modernisation and which can amount to a general subsidy to all sectors of the economy and all areas of national territory are in principle ruled out by the Commission on the ground that they do not relate to "certain" activities or "certain" regions; that they are not quantifiable; may jeopardise the Community arrangements for sectoral aids and may escape the detailed supervision implied by Article 93.[30] The Commission therefore requires to be informed of the detailed application of such schemes if they are approved in the first place. Exceptionally, however, general schemes may be authorised for short periods under Article 92 (3) (*b*). (serious disturbances).[31]

1—15   *Employment subsidies* create difficulties similar to general aids because of their non-specific, production rather than structural - orientated character.[32]

Paragraph 3 of Article 92 provides a final category (d) of aids which may be considered to be compatible with the common market, namely "such other categories of aid as may be specified by decision of the Council acting by a qualified majority on a proposal from the Commission." No such proposals have been made.

Administration of the Provisions on Aids

1—16   Article 93 lays down procedures for dealing with both existing and new systems of aid.[33] By paragraph 1, the Commission has the task of co-operating with the Member States to "keep under constant review" all *existing* forms of aid. It has power to propose amendments required by changing economic circumstances, so that aids remain compatible with the common market and do not distort competition to any degree. By paragraph 3 Member States are required to submit plans to *grant* or *alter* aids before their implementation so that the Commission may comment. The notification requirement applies whether or not the Member State considers the aid compatible with the common market. If the Commission considers an existing or proposed aid is not compatible with the common market having regard to Article 92, in

[30] See generally Comp. Rep. EC 1972, secs. 116 *et seq.*, 1979, secs. 183 *et seq.* and especially 1980 secs. 212 to 217 discussing *Philip Morris, supra*, note 14.
[31] *Ibid.*
[32] Comp Rep. EC 1976, secs. 233 *et seq.*
[33] Commission practice is described in the Annual Reports on Competition Policy: *supra*, note 8.

that it distorts competition, the Commission is to initiate the procedure provided for in paragraph 2. The Member State concerned may not put its proposed measures into effect until this procedure has resulted in a final decision.

The Article 93 (2) procedure is in effect an Article 169 procedure but with some important differences. As with Article 169, Article 93 (2) envisages an opportunity to comment, followed if the Member State has still not modified or abolished its aid or its proposal and the Commission still finds its objections valid, by Commission action. Under Article 169 this action takes the form of an opinion, which has to be confirmed by a reference to the Court before it has legal effects. However, under Article 93 (2) the Commission takes a decision that the aid is not compatible with the common market or is being misused. This decision is directly binding on the Member State. A Member State not wishing to comply therefore has itself to appeal to the Court under Article 173 within the relevant time-limit: it cannot wait to be taken to Court by the Commission or another Member State under Article 93 (2).[34]

21–17   The Commission or another Member State can reinforce the Commission decision by a direct reference to the Court under Article 93 (2), in derogation from Articles 169 and 170, if the Member State granting or altering or proposing to grant the aid does not comply with the decision within the prescribed time (if any).[35] If a failure to comply with the decision subsequently appears an Article 169 or 170 action may be appropriate.[36]

Alternatively (or indeed before the Commission initiates the Article 93 (2) procedure but probably not once a decision has been taken), the Member State concerned may refer the matter to the Council for a unanimous decision. This has the effect of staying the Article 93 (2) procedure if it has been initiated for three months or until the Council has acted. This procedure has been invoked on a number of occasions.[37]

Once a plan has been submitted to the Commission, no particular limit is set by the Treaty as to the length of time in which a decision must be made. The Court has held, however, that in defining its attitude, the Commission should be guided by the time limits set out in Articles 173 and 175. When this two month period has expired, the Member State may implement its proposal, but "legal certainty" requires that the Member State should notify its implementation to the Commission. The aid will at that

[34] Cases 156/77, *supra*, note 2 and 31/77R and 53/77R *Commission* v. *UK* [1977] E.C.R. 921. See also Gilmour, note 36, *infra*.
[35] Case 70/72, *supra*, note 6.
[36] Case 6/69 *Commission* v. *France, supra*, note 13. See Gilmour, 18 C.M.L. Rev. 63.
[37] J.O. 1960, 1972; J.O. 1968, L76; in the agricultural sector it was apparently invoked in favour of UK sugar in 1973 and subsequently in favour German barley.

point become a system of "existing" aid.[38] This means also that there need be no formal decision if the Commission does not wish to prohibit or amend the proposal.[39] If a decision is made, it will only take effect on condition that the Commission indicates to the Member States which aspects of the aid it considers to be incompatible.[40]

1—18   The decision that aid shall be abolished need fix no particular time limit.[41] It may entail repayment of an aid paid in contravention of Community law.[42] The Court has held that only the last sentence of Article 93 (3) is directly applicable.[43] This provides that the Member State concerned shall not put its proposed measures into effect until the Article 93 (2) procedure has resulted in a final decision. But Article 93 does not preclude a national court from referring a question on the interpretation of Article 92 to the Court of Justice if it considers a decision thereon is necessary to enable it to give judgment. But in the absence of a decision under Article 93 (2) or (3) or Article 94 the national court has no jurisdiction to decide on the compatibility of an aid with Article 92.[44]

Article 94 gives the Council power to issue regulations for the implementation of Article 93 but none have ever been adopted.

[38] Case 120/73 *Lorenz* v. *Federal Republic of Germany & Land Rheinland/Pfalz*, [1973] E.C.R. 1471. Case 121/73 *Markmann* v. *Federal Republic of Germany & Land Schleswig Holstein* [1973] E.C.R. 1495. Case 122/73 *Nordsee Deutsche Hochseefischerie GmbH* v. *Federal Republic of Germany & Land Rheinland/Pfalz* [1973] E.C.R. 1511. Case 141/73 *Lohrey* v. *Federal Republic of Germany & Land Hessen* [1973] E.C.R. 1527.

[39] *Ibid.*

[40] Case 70/72 *Commission* v. *Federal Republic of Germany* [1973] E.C.R. 813.

[41] Case 70/72, *supra,* note 6 and 173/73, *supra,* note 10.

[42] *Ibid.*

[43] Cases 6/64 *Costa* v. *ENEL* [1964] E.C.R. 585; 77/72, *supra,* note 19 and *Lorenz,* etc. *supra,* note 38.

[44] Case 78/76, *supra,* note 11.

Chapter 22

TAXATION

22—01 Chapter 2 in Title 1, "Common Rules," in Part Three of the Treaty, "Policy of the Community," entitled "Tax Provisions," is the basis for the greater part of Community action on taxation. Harmonisation of direct taxation must, however, be carried out under Article 100. The chapter is included in the "Common Rules," indicating that the purpose of the Community taxation rules is to ensure that disparities in national tax structures do not distort the balance of competition or hinder the operation of the customs union. The maintenance of discrimination in taxation systems has a similar effect to the retention of customs barriers, and therefore taxation of goods and services inside the common market is to be on a basis of non-discrimination as between Member States.[1]

Indirect Taxation

Article 95

22—02   Article 95 provides that:

"No Member State shall impose, directly or indirectly, on the products of other Member States any internal taxation of any kind in excess of that imposed directly or indirectly on similar domestic products."

"Furthermore, no Member State shall impose on the products of other Member States any internal taxation of such a nature as to afford indirect protection to other products."

The third paragraph provides for repeal or amendment of any provisions of national legislation which conflict with the principles set out in the first two paragraphs by January 1, 1962, the start of the second stage of the transitional period.

22—03   Paragraph 1 prohibits all discriminatory fiscal treatment of the same or similar products as between domestic and non-domestic goods because it is presumed that such discrimination will have a protective effect in favour of the domestically produced product. Paragraph 2 deals with the situation where a system of taxation which is not necessarily discriminatory as between same or similar

---

[1] See generally the Commission's report on the way ahead: "Report on the Scope for Convergence of Tax Systems in the Community," Bulletin EC Suppt. 1/80.

products nevertheless has a protective effect in favour of other goods. Clearly, even under this paragraph, the goods in question must be in competition with the products protected, for otherwise it is difficult to see how the protection could arise (see *infra*, para. 22-09).

In Case 57/65 *Lütticke* v. *Hauptzollamt Saarelouis*[2] the plaintiff in the domestic action claimed that a demand for payment of a compensatory tax in place of turnover tax on the import of powdered milk from Luxembourg was invalid, since domestic powdered milk was exempt from turnover tax. This being so, the compensatory tax was, so the plaintiff argued, illegal under Article 95. The *Finanzgericht* referred the matter to the Court of Justice, asking whether Article 95, first para., had direct effects and created rights for the individual to which national courts should give effect. The Court stated that:

> The first paragraph of Article 95 sets forth, as a general and permanent rule of Community law that Member States shall not impose on the products of other Member States any internal taxation in excess of that imposed on similar domestic products. Such a system, often adopted by the Treaty to ensure the equal treatment of nationals within the Community under national legal systems, constitutes in fiscal matters the indispensable foundation of the Common Market.[3]

2–04   Furthermore the Court found that Article 95, first para., fulfilled the requirements for direct applicability, the time condition in the third paragraph of the article being a simple suspensive condition, which in no way detracted from the directly applicable character of the first paragraph, after the time for the fulfilment of that condition had elapsed.

As a result of this decision there ensued a flood of domestic actions in Germany, all contesting the imposition of compensatory taxes on imports at a level higher than that applied to similar domestic products. In Case 28/67 *Molkerei-Zentrale* v. *Hauptzollamt Paderborn*,[4] the *Bundesfinanzhof*, the highest German taxation court, asked the Court of Justice for a preliminary ruling on whether it still held to the opinion given in the *Lütticke* case, pointing out that if this was so, individuals had a more extensive right of enforcement in respect of this provision than the Community had itself, since the *Lütticke* decision obliges national courts to treat the individuals concerned in a taxation dispute as if the Member State had already performed its duties under Article 95, whereas the Community could only require the State to proceed to fulfil those obligations.

[2] [1966] E.C.R. 205.
[3] *Ibid.* p.210.
[4] [1968] E.C.R. 143.

The Court of Justice affirmed the directly applicable character of Article 95 and stated that:

> "It is not possible to base an argument—contrary to the interpretation of Article 95 as it follows from the judgment in Case 57/65—on a comparison of the rights conferred by this provision on individuals, on the one hand, and the powers conferred on the Community institutions on the other. ... In fact proceedings by an individual are intended to protect individual rights in a specific case, whilst intervention by the Community authorities has as its object the general and uniform observance of Community law.[5]

The elements of Article 95 (1)

"Directly or indirectly"

22—05   The Court went on in the above case to clarify the meaning of the phrase "internal taxation . . . imposed directly or indirectly on similar domestic products."

"Directly or indirectly imposed" refers to taxation actually imposed. In particular, indirect imposition refers to the taxes charged on the domestic product at all stages of manufacture and distribution, but not, it would seem, where the imposition becomes insignificant through remoteness.

"Taxation imposed indirectly on a product" must be interpreted, however, as including a charge imposed on the international transport of goods by road according to the distance covered on the national territory and the weight of the goods in question.[6] Internal taxation may also impose a heavier burden on products from other Member States than on domestic products if it is used exclusively or principally to finance aids for the sole benefit of domestic products.[7]

"Similar products"

22—06   In order to establish that the products are similar under Article 95, para. 1., it appears that the goods must be placed in the same classification for the purposes of taxation, the levying of customs duties or for statistical purposes.[8] Summarising its earlier case-law in the infringement proceedings in respect of spirits against France, Italy and Denmark,[9] the Court reiterated that "similar" is to be interpreted widely, that similar products are those which have similar characteristics and meet the same needs from the point of view of consumers and that products covered are not therefore

[5] *Ibid.* p.153.
[6] Case 20/76 *Schöttle* v. *FA Freudenstadt* [1977] E.C.R. 247.
[7] See especially Case 73/79 *Commission* v. *Italy* [1980] E.C.R. 1533.
[8] Case 27/67 *Fink-Frucht* v. *HZA München* [1968] E.C.R. 223.
[9] Case 168/78 *Commission* v. *France* [1980] E.C.R. 347 and also Cases 169 & 171/78.

ones which are strictly identical, but which have similar and comparable uses.

The discrimination

2—07   The different treatment accorded to the domestic and foreign product may not be obvious. It may be concealed by the use of a different basis of assessment, such as in Case 16/69 *Commission v. Italy*[10] where a tax was levied on imports of "eaux de vie" on the basis of a presumed alcohol content, while the domestic product was taxed on actual alcohol content. It may also be concealed by a different classification of the goods[11] or by a different method of levying the charge.[12] In Case 45/75 *Rewe-Zentrale*[13] the Court held that in ascertaining whether a discrimination was operating, it was necessary to compare the taxation imposed on products which are at the same stage of marketing, have the same characteristics and meet the same needs from the point of view of consumers; and in looking at the manner of levying the charge a discrimination existed where the end result was the existence of different price levels to consumers. It follows that Article 95 may not be infringed by special tax advantages granted to a part of a given sector, provided these advantages are extended without discrimination to goods coming from other Member States.[14] Equally, a domestic system of taxation which embraces products for export on an equal footing is not for that reason discriminatory.[15] But nor, for that matter, is "reverse discrimination" against domestic products prohibited.[16]

In the above-mentioned cases the Court has frequently emphasised that the interpretation it is asked to give does not resolve the issue: it is still for the national court to decide, on the facts, whether the tax contravenes Article 95.[17] Furthermore, it cannot make any statement as to how the national authorities should go about making necessary corrections, or be responsible for solving severe difficulties within the national fiscal system brought about by its ruling.[18]

2—08   In the infringement proceedings against France, the Court in Case

[10] [1969] E.C.R. 377. See also Cases 54/72 *FOR* v. *VKS* [1973] E.C.R. 193; 20/76, *supra*, note 6; 74/76 *Ianelli & Volpi* v. *Meroni* [1977] E.C.R. 557.
[11] Cases 28/69 *Commission* v. *Italy* [1970] E.C.R. 187; 45/75 *Rewe-Zentrale* v. *HZA Landau* [1976] E.C.R. 181.
[12] Cases 77/69 *Commission* v. *Belgium* [1970] E.C.R. 237; 54/72, *supra*, note 10; 127/75 *Bobie* v. *HZA Aachen* [1976] E.C.R. 1079; 20/76, *supra*, note 6.
[13] Case 45/75, *supra*, note 11.
[14] Case 21/79 *Commission* v. *Italy* [1980] E.C.R. 1; Cases 168, 169 & 171/78, *supra*, note 9.
[15] Cases 142/77 *Statens Kontrol* v. *Larsen* [1978] E.C.R. 1543; 27/74 *Demag* v. *FA Duisburg-Süd* [1974] E.C.R. 1037.
[16] Case 86/78 *Peureux* v. *Services Fiscaux* [1979] E.C.R. 897.
[17] Case 77/76 *Cucchi* v. *Avez* [1977] E.C.R. 987.
[18] Cases 34/67 *Lück* v. *HZA Köln* [1968] E.C.R. 245; 68/79 *Just* v. *Ministry for Fiscal Affairs* [1980] E.C.R. 501.

168/78[19] was of course itself obliged to come to a view as to whether Article 95 had been infringed. In that case it was unable to determine whether or not the products concerned were "similar," but declared that the French taxation system was clearly contrary to the second paragraph, concerning indirect protection. The factual basis was even further from being agreed in Case 170/78 *Commission* v. *United Kingdom*,[20] where any finding of infringement of Article 95 turned on whether or not there was a competitive relationship between wine and beer, and further what an appropriate tax ratio might be between the two. Accordingly the Court ordered the parties to re-examine the subject-matter of the dispute in the light of the legal considerations set out in the judgment. These considerations seem to have included acceptance that there is at least some competitive relationship between wine and beer and that any future trends in this direction, particularly having regard to habits in other Member States, should be allowed for by a neutral tax system.

Article 95, second paragraph

22–09 In Case 27/67 *Fink-Frucht* v. *HZA München*[21] the Court held that the second paragraph of Article 95 was also directly applicable. Nevertheless, the indirect protection prohibited by the article may be more difficult to identify and quantify. As the Court held in *Fink-Frucht* itself, it strikes at an internal tax which weighs more heavily on a competing product although the two products in question are insufficiently similar to come within Article 95, first paragraph. A tax is to be regarded as contravening the prohibition if it is *capable* of having an indirect protective effect, whereas the test in the first paragraph is that the burden borne by the imported product must not be *in excess of* that borne by similar domestic products. It follows that neither paragraph purports to prohibit internal taxation on imported goods which have no competition with a domestic product.[22] The purpose of taxing such products is to place in a comparable fiscal situation all categories of products, whatever their origin.[23]

The relationship between Article 95 and Articles 12 and 13

22–10 It is important to determine which of these articles applies because under Article 95 the prohibition extends only to discrimination, *viz.* the tax is not prohibited altogether, but only to the extent that it discriminates against foreign products, while under Articles 12 and 13 it is altogether prohibited. For this reason the Court has always held that a charge cannot be both a

---

[19] *Supra*, note 9.
[20] [1980] E.C.R. 417.
[21] *Supra*, note 8. Confirmed by Cases 168, 169 & 171/78, *supra*, note 9.
[22] Case 31/67 *Stier* v. *HZA Hamburg* [1968] E.C.R. 235.
[23] *Ibid.*

tax and a customs duty or charge having equivalent effect.[24] To distinguish between them, however, is often a difficult matter because the true nature of the charge may be heavily "disguised."

For example, a particular form of tax may be levied on an industry with the purpose of raising revenue to support aid to that industry or to its customers or suppliers. Provided that the tax is levied on domestic products, the levying of a tax on imports, the manufacturers of which could not benefit from the charge, would not normally be regarded as a charge equivalent to a customs duty unless the purpose of the reimbursement to the domestic industry were to make good the charge previously imposed.[25]

Thus if the charges are not made good in full, or are reimbursed directly in the form of subsidies on raw materials, they could not be regarded as falling within Articles 12 and 13, although they may well contravene Article 95.[26] The underlying test is clearly whether, in all the circumstances, the charge has the effect of acting as a customs duty rather than as part of a system of internal taxation.[27] Turnover taxes (including now VAT) imposed on all products whether domestic or imported are, by their nature, mainly fiscal and when they are imposed on imports their purpose is to put all types of goods, whatever their origin, into one and the same fiscal situation.[28]

The relationship between Article 95 and Articles 30 et seq

2—11   The reasoning of the Court has been very similar to that described above as to the inapplicability to the situations to which Article 95 applies of Articles 30 *et seq.* on the abolition of quantitative restrictions and measures having equivalent effect.[29]

Article 96

2—12   Article 96 provides the complement to Article 95 in the aim of achieving an indirect taxation system in the Community which does not discriminate between home-produced and imported goods. Article 95 forbids the taxing of imports at a higher rate than that imposed on domestic goods, while Article 96 prohibits refunds on exports to other Member States in excess of the internal taxes actually imposed. The Court of Justice examined

---

[24] Cases 10/65 *Deutschmann* v. *Germany* [1965] E.C.R. 469; 57/65, *supra,* note 2; 94/74 *IGAV* v. *ENCC* [1975] E.C.R. 699; 35/76 *Simmenthal* v. *Ammin. delle Finanze* [1976] E.C.R. 1871.

[25] Cases 77/72 *Capolongo* v. *Maya* [1973] E.C.R. 611; 94/74 *IGAV* v. *ENCC, supra,* note 24.

[26] Cases 105/76 *Interzuccheri* v. *Ditta Rezzano e Cavassa* [1977] E.C.R. 1029; 73/79 *Commission* v. *Italy* [1980] E.C.R. 1533.

[27] Case 94/74 *IGAV* v. *ENCC, supra,* note 24.

[28] Case 7/67 *Wöhrmann* v. *HZA Bad Reichenhall* [1968] E.C.R. 177.

[29] Case 27/67 *supra,* note 8 and Cases 2 & 3/69 *Diamantarbeiders* v. *Brachfeld* [1969] E.C.R. 211; 74/76, *supra,* note 10.

the role of Article 96 in Case 45/64 *Commiss.̮n* v. *Italy*.[30] The Italian system of drawback (export refunds) permitted compensation for tax levied on the *firms* in addition to tax levied on the goods exported. The Court held drawbacks in respect of taxes not levied *on the goods themselves* (whether directly or indirectly) to be contrary to Article 96. It considered that "indirectly" referred to those charges which were borne by the goods during their various manufacturing stages. The Court was, however, prepared to accept a system of flat-rate rebates on exports, since it is difficult to calculate the exact tax burden incurred by a particular product under a turnover tax system.[31]

Article 96 deals only with the case where exported goods enjoy a more favourable treatment than the domestically consumed product. It would not therefore appear to prohibit discrimination aimed at making exported goods uncompetitive, although if a tax is levied solely on exports (as opposed to merely refunding a tax normally refundable) it may constitute a charge having equivalent effect to an export duty.[32]

Article 97

22—13   This article is now of historical interest only since it laid down special rules in relation to turnover taxes based on a cumulative system. Where Member States levied compensating taxes on imports and granted refunds on exports as part of this system they were permitted to establish average rates for the products concerned. All the Member States now operate a VAT system and such matters are dealt with in that context.[33]

Article 99

22—14   Article 99, requiring the Commission to "consider how the legislation of the various Member States concerning turnover taxes, excise duties and other forms of indirect taxation . . . can be harmonised in the interest of the common market" is the basis for all harmonisation work on indirect taxation. Any harmonisation of direct taxation must be carried out under Article 100[34] (general provision on approximation of laws).

Article 99, second para., requires the Commission to submit proposals to the Council on the harmonisation of indirect taxation. The Council is to act unanimously, without prejudice to the power to issue directives contained in Articles 100 and 101. Under Article 99, the Council may use any type of instrument, although it has in fact only used directives.

[30] [1965] E.C.R. 857.
[31] *Infra*, para. 22–13.
[32] Case 27/74 *Demag* v. *Finanzamt Duisburg-Süd* [1974] E.C.R. 1037.
[33] *Infra*.
[34] *Infra*, Chapter 23.

Value added tax

2—15   Disparities between the Member States' systems of indirect taxation were considered to be a much greater hindrance to the creation of the common market than were the differing systems of direct taxation; hence the singling out of indirect taxation in Article 99. The Commission deemed the harmonisation of indirect taxation so important that it set up three working groups to establish the requirements of a non-discriminatory system of indirect taxation as early as 1962; as a result of these inquiries it was concluded that a non-cumulative multi-stage tax would be the best for operations inside a common market. This form of taxation, already in existence in France, is referred to as the value added system. Amongst its advantages may be mentioned the fact that it is economically neutral, *i.e.* it does not differentiate between goods produced by a vertically integrated firm and goods produced by the combined efforts of a line of specialist firms.

In response to this report, the Commission published a draft directive relating to the general modalities of VAT.[35] This draft was revised and refined.[36] To this a draft second directive was added, setting out detailed rules of application of the tax.[37] The two directives in their final form were issued as Directives 67/227 and 228.[38] It was originally hoped that the VAT system would be fully operative throughout the Community by January 1, 1970, but economic and political difficulties necessitated the postponement of the operation of VAT in both Belgium and Italy. A third directive, 69/463,[39] was issued to postpone the date for the implementation of the entire system to January 1, 1972. The Belgian VAT entered into force on January 1, 1971, and Italy introduced the tax on January 1, 1973, having obtained a further stay until that date.[40] VAT is now in force throughout the Community.

The VAT directives

2—16   The two directives, (67/227 and 228), laid down the basic principles and the fundamental mechanics for the operation of the system of value added tax. The tax system is defined by Article 2 of the First Directive in the following terms:

"The principle of the common system of value added tax involves the application to goods and services of a general tax on consumption exactly proportional to the price of the goods and services, whatever the number of transactions

[35] Suppt. to Bulletin 12 1962 Doc. IV Com(62)217.
[36] Suppt. to Bulletin 7 1964 Doc. IV Com(64)144.
[37] Suppt. to Bulletin 5 1965 Doc. IV Com(65)144.
[38] J.O. 1967, 1301, 1303; O.J. 1967, 14, 16.
[39] J.O. 1969, L320/34; O.J. 1969, (II) 551.
[40] Directive 72/250, J.O. 1972, L162/18.

which take place in the production and distribution process before the stage at which tax is charged.

On each transaction, value added tax, calculated on the price of the goods or services at the rate applicable to such goods or services, shall be chargeable after deduction of the amount of value added tax borne directly by the various cost components.

The common system of value added tax shall be applied up to and including the retail trade stage."

VAT is therefore a "general tax on consumption," applicable up to and including the retail stage (although many national systems in fact make exceptions for small retailers whose gross annual turnover is less than a specified sum). It is also a tax which, unlike the cascade system of taxation, is economically neutral, in that it is applied in respect of the price of goods and services, irrespective of whether they have passed through several hands before reaching the consumer, or have emerged from a completely integrated producer.

The First Directive does not lay down any aim of establishing common rates for the tax, common classification of goods and services for taxation purposes, or common exemptions from the tax, and neither were these provided for in the Second Directive, which was envisaged by Article 3 of the First Directive as concerning "the structure of, and the procedure for applying, the common system of value added tax."

22–17   The Second Directive has now been repealed and superseded by Directive 77/388[41] which lays down a uniform basis of assessment for VAT. (The implementing United Kingdom legislation is contained in the Finance Act 1977, s. 14 and Sched. 6.) The primary importance of the adoption of Directive 77/388 is that it makes possible the implementation at long last of the "own resources" provision that 1 per cent. of Member States' VAT should be paid directly to the Community. The latter was made conditional on the adoption of the uniform basis.

Article 2 of Directive 77/388 lays down a general rule regarding transactions which are to be subject to VAT, namely the provision of goods and services by taxable persons within the territory of each Member State, and the importation of goods. Services supplied across national boundaries are treated as supplied in the supplier's country but many of the most common services such as

[41] O.J. 1977, L145/1, Article 37. This was the "6th directive" on turnover taxes, but numbers 3–5 all concerned various extensions of time for implementation. Directive 77/388 was itself the subject of an extension since only two Member States (including the UK) had actually implemented it by the stated date (see Directive 78/583, O.J. 1978, L194/16).

those of the professions are excepted from this rule and deemed to be supplied in the territory where the customer has his principal place of business (Article 9). A taxable person is defined to mean any person who independently carries out in any place any economic activity specified in paragraph 2 of Article 4 which includes "all activities of producers, traders and persons supplying services." There are detailed rules on all aspects of the charge except the rate, including the taxable amount, accountable persons, deductions and exemptions.

2—18   Article 35 envisages further directives which should lead eventually to the need to abandon charges on the importation of goods and refunds on exports in intra-Community trade. Such an objective is still a long way from attainment because there is no likelihood of achieving harmonised rates at present.

Article 32 provided that the Council should have, before December 31, 1977, laid down a "Community taxation system" to be applied to used goods, works of art, antiques and collectors' items. A proposal[42] to this effect was rejected in its entirety by the Economic and Social Committee in 1978. In May 1979 the Commission amended its proposal,[43] but no directive has yet been adopted. A proposal for a tenth directive has also been published, relating to the hiring out of moveable tangible property.[44] A directive has been adopted on the refund of VAT to persons not established in the territory of the Member State levying the tax.[45] Article 145 and more particularly Annex XII of the Act of Accession requires Greece to implement the VAT system by the end of 1983.

Excise duties

2—19   Article 99 provides for the harmonisation not only of turnover taxes, but also of excise duties and other forms of indirect taxation, these being applied in particular to oil and petrol, beer, wines and spirits and tobacco. Following the adoption of the programme leading to Economic and Monetary Union by 1980 the Commission put forward proposals for the progressive harmonisation of these taxes throughout the Community in line with the hoped-for harmonisation of the rates for VAT. The failure to achieve the latter has been mirrored by the very slow progress made with regard to excise duties. A subsequent "action programme" put before the Council in July 1975 urged *inter alia* the adoption of measures to this end as a matter of priority, the abolition of trade frontiers within the Community being dependent on common rates in excise duties as well as for VAT.

[42] O.J. 1978, C26/2.
[43] O.J. 1979, C136/8.
[44] O.J. 1979, C116/4.
[45] Directive 79/1072, O.J. 1979, L331/11.

To date, in spite of continuing discussions, the only measures adopted are two directives on the progressive harmonisation of duties on manufactured tobacco. Directive 72/464[46] provided for a first stage of five years[47] during which uniform methods of levying the tax were to be adopted, involving duty calculated partly on a proportion of the retail selling price and partly on a specific amount per unit. For cigarettes the specific duty was to be not lower than 5 per cent. nor higher than 75 per cent. of the aggregate amount of the proportional excise duty and the specific excise duty levied on cigarettes.[48] Articles 10A and 10B provided for a second stage when the maximum rate was to be reduced to 55 per cent. of the aggregation of the proportional excise duty, specific duty *and* turnover tax (VAT). There was a 30 month exceptional period for the United Kingdom in respect of the taxation of high tar cigarettes. The second stage expired at the end of 1980. This may lead to the adoption of a final stage during which

> "the same ratio shall be established for cigarettes in all Member States between the specific excise duty and the sum of the proportional excise duty and the turnover tax, in such a way that the range of retail selling prices reflects fairly the difference in the manufacturers' delivery prices."[49]

Relief from excise duties and VAT for international travellers

22—20   It has been pointed out already that both excise duty and VAT are levied also on importations. Member States all granted certain exemptions from them for the personal luggage of travellers (*temporary* imports being already generally exempted) and these provisions have now been harmonised. Directive 69/169[50] as last amended by Directives 78/1032 and 1033[51] provides that for imports into the Community from third countries exemption from VAT is granted for items of a non-commercial character worth up to 40 ECU. For intra-Community travel the exemption is 180 ECU *in toto*.

Excise duty exemption limits are also specified, those for intra-Community trade generally being up to twice those for travel from third countries.

These exemptions apply only to goods purchased in another Member State or third country, the purpose of the directive being to cut down the risk of double taxation where the goods have already borne tax in the country of purchase. It does not therefore apply to duty-free sales, the exemptions in these cases still being

---

[46] J.O. 1972, L303/1; O.J. 1972, (December 31)3.
[47] *Ibid.* Article 7.
[48] *Ibid.* Article 8.
[49] *Ibid.* Article 4.
[50] J.O. 1969, L133/6; O.J. 1969, (I) 232.
[51] O.J. 1978, L366/28; O.J. 1978, L366/31.

within the control of Member States. (The Commission has on occasion indicated the desirability of abolishing these concessions). The directive also requires Member States to ensure that people domiciled in Member States do not obtain remission of taxes for goods benefiting from these exemptions on exportation. Hence, VAT for instance is not remittable on purchases below a specified amount in value.[52] Remissions of VAT (but not excise duty) are otherwise permitted, under certain conditions.

22—21   Directives 74/651[53] and 78/1035[54] make provision for exemptions from taxes of goods of a non-commercial character sent from other Member States and third states respectively.

Exemptions from excise duty in relation to fuel in the tanks of motor vehicles are discussed in the context of transport policy. The Commission has also made proposals regarding the elimination of double taxation resulting from taxes involved:

- in putting cars for business purposes on the road and on the movement and possession thereof;
- in the importation of personal effects by individuals moving house between Member States.

Other forms of indirect taxation

22—22   Directive 69/335[55] provides for the harmonisation of charges "on contributions of capital to capital companies" (*viz.* limited liability companies), and by Article 1 of Directive 73/80[56] the charge was to be, from January 1, 1976, 1 per cent. The only other type of indirect taxation to have been the subject of proposals to date has been a proposal for a directive on taxes on transactions in securities which would provide for the partial harmonisation of the structures of these taxes, eliminating discrimination based on the type of security or on the place of residence of the parties.

Direct Taxes

22—23   The EEC Treaty does not by and large deal with direct taxation in specific terms. It would appear that in 1957 they were not viewed as factors which would inhibit the formation of a common market and they did not therefore receive special treatment in the Treaty. Articles 95 to 97 and 99 deal solely with indirect taxation, and only Article 98 concerns itself with direct taxes, the article defining such taxes negatively as "charges other than turnover taxes, excise duties and other forms of indirect taxation." The article prohibits the granting of remissions and repayments of these other charges

[52] See Article 6 (3) of Directive 69/169.
[53] O.J. 1974, L354/57 as amended by Directive 78/1034; O.J. 1978, L366/33.
[54] O.J. 1978, L366/34.
[55] J.O. 1969, L249/25; O.J. 1969, (II) 412.
[56] O.J. 1973, L103/15.

in respect of exports to other Member States, and the imposition of countervailing charges in respect of imports from other Member States, in the absence of prior approval granted for a limited period by the Council acting by a qualified majority on a proposal from the Commission. It is clear that such drawbacks and counter-vailing charges are unacceptable within a common market for they constitute a patent subsidy to exporting industries and protect domestic industry. The article was apparently inserted to take account of the difficulties experienced by France following devaluation of the franc.

The approval mechanism to gain a derogation from the article has never been used.

22—24   In the absence of specific provisions, harmonisation of direct taxes must be based on Article 100, providing for the approximation of laws by means of directives. It was made apparent by the Segré Report, *Development of a European Capital Market*,[57] that unequal fiscal conditions whereby each Member State maintained its own different taxes and rates of tax on income prohibited the emergence of a European capital market. The specific obstacles were stated to be:

(a) the double taxation of investments placed abroad;
(b) the preferential treatment of investments made in the country where the taxpayer is domiciled and conversely the discriminatory taxation by the taxing State of investments made by a non-resident;
(c) the discriminatory taxation of institutional investors; and
(d) the discrepancies between the national tax collection systems, which consequently favoured certain types of investment as opposed to others.

The ideas in the Report were taken up and reworked by the Commission into a Programme for the harmonisation of direct taxes[58] which contained a five-point plan to ensure fair competition, free movement of capital and investment, and industrial reorganisation and to co-ordinate national fiscal policies. The plan aimed to:

(1) harmonise the system of corporation tax throughout the Community;
(2) approximate the bases of assessment for taxes on company profits (*i.e.* establish common accounting principles);
(3) approximate the tax arrangements applicable to parent companies and subsidiaries, to company mergers and winding-up operations;
(4) harmonise the system of withholding taxes on dividends and interest payments; and

[57] EEC Commission, Brussels 1966.
[58] Suppt. to Bulletin 8, 1967.

(5) organise a multilateral convention to avoid double taxation phenomena which remained despite the measures mentioned above.

As a result of the above considerations the Commission in 1969 submitted proposals for directives on the taxation of mergers and similar transactions and on the taxation of parent and subsidiary companies, the aim being to avoid double taxation.[59] Neither proposal was adopted, despite the Commission's re-emphasising the need for these in its taxation action programme of 1975. That action programme was followed by proposals for directives on corporation tax, with the adoption of a tax credit system for the taxation of dividends[60] and on the elimination of double taxation of transactions between subsidiaries and parents located in different Member States by a process of arbitration between the authorities concerned.[61]

Mutual assistance between the Member States

22—25   The only Community legislation to date touching on direct taxation has been the adoption of a directive concerning mutual assistance by the competent authorities of the Member States in the field of direct taxation[62] and, since 1979, value added tax.[63]

[59] J.O. 1969, C39/1. The proposed directive, which would introduce a common tax regime for mergers and for international transfer of assets, is of interest here also, as is another (J.O. 1969, C39/7) respecting the taxation of companies and their subsidiaries where parent company and subsidiary are situated in the territories of different Member States. Article 5 of this proposal would do away with withholding tax upon dividends remitted to parent companies holding not less than 20 per cent. of the share capital of the subsidiary. Article 7 would permit the presentation of consolidated accounts in the case of a participation of at least 50 per cent.
[60] O.J. 1975, C253/2.
[61] O.J. 1976, C301/4.
[62] Directive 77/799, O.J. 1977, L336/15.
[63] O.J. 1979, L331/8.

Chapter 23

APPROXIMATION AND HARMONISATION OF LAWS

23—01 Paragraph (*h*) of Article 3 of the EEC Treaty specifies "The approximation of the laws of Member States to the extent required for the proper functioning of the common market" as an activity to be undertaken by the Community for the sake of the general purpose of establishing the common market, set out in Article 2. "Approximation of Laws" is further the heading and subject-matter of the third and last chapter in Title I, "Common Rules," of Part Three of the Treaty, which deals with the policy of the Community. An identical or similar process in specific contexts is envisaged by numerous other articles throughout the Treaty.

23—02 The different expressions "approximation," "harmonisation" and "co-ordination," to be found in these various provisions are not particularly happy, especially in their English versions. It is not thought, however, that their variety implies, as has been suggested, any particular order of things, or that "co-ordination" involves, for instance, something less than "harmonisation" or "approximation." Nor is it considered that the draftsman has, by ringing the changes upon these expressions, meant to distinguish between the case where Member States are called upon, for instance, to adopt identical laws, and that in which it is sufficient that their laws do not conflict.

23—03 Perhaps the only distinction that may validly be drawn is this: that where a completely uniform Community rule is envisaged, terminology implying harmonisation, etc., is not used, and a power to issue directly applicable instruments (regulations) is generally conferred. Where, conversely, it is intended to leave to Member States liberty to legislate in a given area, but where a greater or less degree of adjustment is nevertheless necessary if the objectives of the Treaty are to be met, the Treaty speaks in terms of harmonisation, co-ordination, etc., and generally confers a lesser power of Community action, usually by directive, *i.e.* laying down the ends to be achieved, but leaving the choice of means to the Member States. The scope left to national action may, however, be quite limited where the directive is very detailed. The Treaty in fact rarely gives a specific power to issue regulations, that power being more usually subsumed under a general power to take any type of action. Two provisions do in fact confer a power to issue directives or regulations (Arts. 49 and 87). But neither is a true exception to the suggested distinction, since these articles contemplate a common rule on certain matters, while on others harmonisation is all that is necessary. Nevertheless, no directives have been issued pursuant to Article 87, whereas both regulations and directives have been issued on the legal basis of Article 49, generally in complementary pairs.[1]

The Chapter on Approximation of Laws (Articles 100 to 102)

23—04 It is perhaps slightly anomalous that the chapter heading "Approximation of Laws" should come within the Title "Common Rules," since what it aims at is the reconciliation in one way or another of existing national laws rather than the adoption of a new and uniform law throughout the Community. It is not only laws which, by virtue of Article 100, are to be subjected by directive to the process of approximation, but all "such provisions laid down by law, regulation or administrative action in Member States as directly affect the establishment or functioning of the common market," the Assembly and Economic and Social Committee being consulted if any directive promulgated involves for its implementation the amendment of the legislation of one or more Member States.

Possibly this wording, wide though it be, does not embrace unwritten administrative practice, as does Article 49; no doubt, however, Article 235 could be prayed in aid to justify a directive aimed at the approximation of any such practices.

Presumably where a matter is not the subject of any provision "laid down by law, regulation or administrative action" in any of the Member States, Article 100 cannot be relied upon to establish a rule where none existed before. On the other hand, a Member State desirous of introducing a new rule which may cause distortion of the conditions of competition in the common market is under an obligation, under Article 102 (*infra*), to consult the Commission.

23—05 Article 100, though not of infinite scope, is nevertheless wider than Article 101, which deals not with the approximation generally of national provisions directly affecting the establishment or functioning of the common market, but merely with differences between such provisions which the Commission finds to be causing a distortion of conditions of competition requiring elimination. Where this situation arises the Commission has a duty to consult the Member States concerned. If such consultation does not result in an agreement putting an end to the distortion in question, the Council is, on the proposal of the Commission, to issue any necessary directives, and Commission and Council may take any other appropriate measures for which the Treaty provides.

Article 100 has commonly been invoked in conjunction with other provisions of the Treaty, for instance with Article 43, for

---

[1] See, *e.g.* Regulation 1612/68, J.O. 1968, L257/2; O.J. 1968, 475, complemented by Directive 68/360, J.O. 1968, L257/13 O.J. 1968, 485.

purposes of agricultural standardisation and harmonisation[2] the latter article making no specific mention of approximation of national provisions. It has similarly been used together with Article 99 in connection with the VAT Directives (*supra*, para. 22-16), harmonisation in this context being deemed essential to the Community and best achieved with the assistance of the Economic and Social Committee and the European Parliament in their consultative capacity.

23—06   Action taken under Article 100 alone has related in particular to matters where the Treaty has not provided specific or sufficient powers in other substantive chapters. Notably this is the case as regards customs matters, where, as has already been indicated,[3] the substantive provisions allow only for recommendations. A framework for the issue of these directives was provided by the General Programme of May 28, 1969, on the elimination of technical barriers to trade.[4] The need for action by directive in this field has been to some extent cast in doubt by the Court's ruling in the *Cassis de Dijon*[5] case where Article 30 was held to curtail the application of national laws laying down standards to imports from the other Member States.

23—07   The stipulations of Article 101 respecting the remedying of distortion of conditions of competition arising through differences between existing national provisions are reinforced by those of Article 102, to which allusion has already been made. By this article a Member State wishing to introduce a new legislative, etc., provision must consult the Commission if there is reason to fear that the result will be distortion within the meaning of Article 101. The Commission is then, after consultation with the Member States, to recommend appropriate preventative measures. Should the State making the innovation fail to comply with the Commission's recommendations, the other Member States are relieved of any obligation to amend their own provisions under Article 101. If, further, the Member State ignoring the Commission's recommendation causes distortion detrimental to itself alone, that article is expressed not to apply.

In 6/64 *Costa* v. *ENEL*[6] a preliminary ruling on the interpretation of Article 102 was requested from the Court of Justice. The Court held that the article was not directly applicable, so that

---

[2] See generally Chapter 15, *supra*.
[3] *Supra*, para. 13–17.
[4] J.O. 1969, C76/1. Over 100 Directives have now been adopted under this head, many of them related to the motor vehicles industry. And see generally, House of Lords Select Committee on the European Communities, "Approximation of Laws under Article 100 of the EEC Treaty," HL 131, April 18, 1978 and HL Deb., Vol 394, cols. 848 to 911.
[5] Case 120/78 *Rewe-Zentrale* v. *Bundesmonopolverwaltung* [1979] E.C.R. 649.
[6] [1964] E.C.R. 585.

the question whether Italy had any obligation thereunder to consult the Commission in relation to legislation nationalising electricity undertakings was not examinable at the suit of an individual.

Other Provisions

3—08 The existence in the Treaty, outside the articles of the chapter specifically headed "Approximation of Laws," of provisions expressly or impliedly stipulating in particular contexts for the same or for similar processes has been referred to already. In particular the following Treaty articles are relevant: Articles 27, 43, 49, 54, 56, 57, 66, 75, 99, 111, 112, 113, 117 and 118.

Upon a consideration of the Weinkamm Report on progress in legislative approximation up to 1965,[7] the European Parliament adopted a resolution[8] advocating a general programme of harmonisation, the transfer of certain responsibilities therefor from Council to Commission, the extension of the process of harmonisation to the realm of penal law, the establishment of arrangements for reciprocal recognition and execution of judgments, and the necessity of taking into account the evolution of Community law in revising municipal law. This resolution did not fail to emphasise the importance of utilising the Parliament itself as a legislative body. Since that report, however, there has been a noticeable increase in hostility to a general harmonisation policy both on the part of the national electorates (where opposition to harmonisation often fails to appreciate that the Community organs are usually not introducing complicated rules for the first time but are merely altering existing rules) and on the part of the Council, whose slow progress in adopting directives was a source of friction with the Commission, although significant steps forward were taken in 1976.[9]

There has been an increasing tendency to incorporate new directives, and to adapt old ones, within the framework of new policies, such as the energy and environmental areas. This may lead to a renewed interest in harmonisation, since it may in future be possible to justify directives on grounds which are less esoteric than the elimination of distortions to competition and appear to lead in a more positive direction.

Approximation under Treaty or Convention: Article 220

3—09 Article 220 of the Treaty provides that the Member States shall, so far as is necessary, negotiate with each other with a view to securing for their respective nationals four particular types of benefit, namely: national treatment generally, relief from double taxation,

[7] EP Doc. 54/65.
[8] J.O. 1965, 2035.
[9] See, *e.g.* 10th Annual General Report, point 110.

mutual recognition of judgments and arbitral awards. Though the negotiations which this article contemplates need not be negotations for a treaty or convention, but might equally well lead to parallel legislation, for instance, the article has been resorted to for the conclusion of two conventions, each having associated with it a supplementary protocol, concluded later,[10] conferring jurisdiction in relation to it upon the Court of Justice.[11] The first convention, which was signed on February 29, 1968, is on the Mutual Recognition of Companies and Bodies Corporate[12] and the second, signed on September 27, 1968, deals with Jurisdiction and the Enforcement of Civil and Commercial Judgments;[13] the first three new Member States acceded to the latter convention in 1978[14] though it is not yet in force as between all those States and all the original six States, ratifications still being outstanding in some cases. A Convention on the Law Applicable to Contractual Obligations, designed to complement the Judgments Convention, was opened for signature on June 19, 1980.[15]

23—10   The conventions which have been concluded, as well as other possible conventions falling within the ambit of Article 220, may call for significant modifications in the law both of the six original States and of all the new Member States. There is a proposal presently under consideration regarding bankruptcy.[16]

---

[10] June 3, 1971.
[11] Suppt. 4/71—Bulletin EC, O.J. 1975, L204/28.
[12] Suppt. 2/69—Bulletin EC. See also *supra,* para. 17–36.
[13] O.J. 1978, L304; E.C. No. 46 (1978) Cmnd. 7395.
[14] *Ibid.* The text of the Accession Convention appends the texts of the 1968 Convention and the 1971 Protocol. The interpretative Reports by Mr.P.Jenard on the 1968 Convention and the 1971 Protocol (O.J. 1979, C59/1 and 66) and by Prof.P.Schlosser on the Accession Convention (O.J. 1979, C59/71) are particularly important and may be referred to in applying the instruments (*cf.* Clause 3 (3) of the Civil Jurisdiction and Judgments Bill.)
[15] O.J. 1980, L266. See also Report on the Convention in O.J. 1980, C282.
[16] Proposed text published by the Dept. of Trade, London, August 1979.

Chapter 24

ECONOMIC POLICY

24—01 In the broad sense, economic policy is a term used to describe the pursuit by governments of economic objectives (such as full employment or stable prices) through the use of economic instruments (such as taxation, public expenditure and control over money supply). Clearly such policies have a profound effect on the functioning of the common market, so it is not surprising that the Treaty has something to say about how states manage their economies. It is also perhaps not surprising that it does not, on the other hand, purport to substitute Community action for national action. Nevertheless the Member States have taken some steps towards common action, outside the immediate framework of the Treaty. The following examination of the role of the Community in economic policy divided into two parts: 1. the existing Treaty provisions and measures taken in furtherance of them; 2. the objective of Economic and Monetary Union ("EMU").

24—02 Title II of Part Three of the Treaty, "Policy of the Community," is entitled "Economic Policy." It contains three chapters, Chapter 1: Conjunctural Policy (Art. 103); Chapter 2: Balance of Payments (Arts. 104 to 109); and Chapter 3, Commercial Policy (Arts. 110 to 116). In the strict sense of the term, "economic policy" does not extend to the third chapter, and Commercial Policy is considered in connection with the foreign relations of the Community in general (*infra*, Part 6).

In the context of a customs union, where individual States are not permitted to apply the usual methods of economic control unilaterally (*e.g.* increase or introduction of duties or quotas, subsidies and the like), and where free movement of goods, labour and capital in any case lessens the effect of applying permissible restrictive controls, basic economic problems seem both more difficult to control at a national level, and more likely to spread to the other members of the customs union. Therefore it was deemed necessary to insert provisions into the Treaty tending towards the co-ordination of national economic policies and providing some form of mutual co-operation between Member States in case of economic difficulty. However, in inserting such provisions, it was necessary to strike a balance between the need to leave the basic powers of the Member States over their economic policies unimpaired, and the necessity for Community action and control. Chapters 1 and 2 of this title contain phrases such as:

371

"Member States shall regard their conjunctural policies as a matter of common concern" (Art. 103 (1));
" . . . Member States shall co-ordinate their economic policies" (Art. 105 (1));
"Each Member State shall treat its policy with regard to rates of exchange as a matter of common concern" (Art. 107 (1)).

These indicate that the balance of initiative of action rests with the Member States, subject to their general duty to ensure fulfilment of their obligations arising out of the Treaty—Article 5 EEC. But Article 103 (2) and (3) provide, with regard to measures to be taken on conjunctural policies, for Council decisions (*lato sensu*) and for directives.

Economic Policy in general (Articles 103-5)

Treaty provisions

24—03   In ordinary usage a distinction is drawn between short-term or conjunctural policy and medium-term policy, the former being a description of measures taken on an annual or more frequent basis (*e.g.* the raising or lowering of interest rates), while the latter would describe longer term objectives over a period of five or so years. The Treaty, however, seems to draw a distinction between "conjunctural policy" on the one hand and "economic policy" on the other. The former is covered by Article 103 and the general tenor of it suggests that "conjunctural policy" is being employed to describe measures taken to meet sudden crises. It does not require mere "co-ordination" of policy but imposes an obligation on the Member States to treat their conjunctural policies as a matter of common concern. It gives the Council a power of decision (para. 2) and a power to issue directives (para. 3[1]); it talks of taking measures "appropriate to the situation" and paragraph (4) talks of "difficulty . . . in the supply of certain products."

"Economic policy" (including presumably "short-term policy") is covered by Articles 104 and 5. Article 104 requires each Member State to "pursue the economic policy needed to ensure the equilibrium of its overall balance of payments and to maintain confidence in its currency, while taking care to ensure a high level of employment and a stable level of prices;" Article 105 requires co-ordination of those policies.

In practice the measures relating to *co-ordination* of policy have also been based to some extent on Article 103, this being inevitable since there can be no rigid distinction between a crisis measure on the one hand and more general policy on the other. The use of Article 103 in the context of co-ordination moreover offers greater

---

[1] As to the nature of these powers of decision see Case 5/73 *Balkan Import-Export GmbH* v. *HZA Berlin Packhof* [1973] E.C.R. 1091. Article 103 confers "wide powers of appraisal": Case 43/72 *Merkur* v. *Commission* [1973] E.C.R. 1055.

scope for stronger measures, and for the transfer of decision-making to the Community, because it is more specific about the role of the Community institutions.

Relationship of Articles 103-5 with other areas of the Treaty

24—04   The decision-making power of Article 103 is expressed to be without prejudice to any other measures provided for in the Treaty. Thus "conjunctural policy" decisions relating to agriculture must be adopted according to the rules governing the agricultural policy, *viz.* at the Community level only.[2] On the other hand, where measures required in respect *inter alia* of agricultural goods are not specifically provided for by the relevant Treaty provisions, Article 103 can be, and has been, used as a basis for action. Thus, the introduction of monetary compensatory amounts[3] following the widening of currency margins was initially based on this provision.[4] The other provisions do not pose problems of overlap with other Treaty provisions.

Secondary legislation

24—05   During the transitional period, very little action was taken in the direction of co-ordination of policy, although this was not a serious matter since at that time the economies of the Six were largely moving in the same direction anyway.[5] However, with the end of the transitional period an increasing number of economic problems began to emerge to which Member States began to react in diverging ways; the accession of the first three new Member States brought further complications since their economic development was in some ways quite different from the Six; and hard on the heels of accession in 1973 came the oil crisis bringing with it severe inflation and rising unemployment. The various states coped with these problems with varying degrees of success but the result was a divergence of policy during the period following the 1974 recession. As the Community began to pull out of the recession, conditions for closer co-ordination became more favourable, but the varying vulnerabilities of the Member States to oil price fluctuations continues to act as a negative influence.

Against this rather unencouraging background, the attempts by the Member States to establish a permanent system of co-ordinated economic policy were bound to be only partially successful.

Short term policy

24—06   A decision of 1969 provided for prior consultation on economic

---

[2] Case 5/73, *supra*, note 1, and Case 31/74 *Filippo Galli* [1975] E.C.R. 47.
[3] *Supra*, para. 15–69.
[4] Regulation 974/71, J.O. 1971, L106/1; O.J. 1971, 257. See also Case 5/73, *supra*, and 9/73 *Schlüter* v. *HZA Lörrach* [1973] E.C.R. 1135.
[5] But see recommendations on the restoration of equilibrium on several occasions. J.O 1965, 985; J.O. 1966, 4059; J.O. 1967, 159/6.

measures to be organised between Member States through the monetary, conjunctural and budgetary policy committees,[6] and a decision in 1971 provided for the strengthening of this co-ordination by requiring the Council to hold three meetings per year to examine the economic situation in the Community and to lay down obligatory guidelines for the Member States to follow including ones concerning national budgetary matters.[7]

The next move towards greater co-ordination came in 1974 when the Council took a decision "on· the attainment of a high degree of convergence of the economic policies of the EEC."[8] Convergence of course is not the same as co-ordination, which implies only that each Member State takes action which *complements* the action of the other states. *Convergence* involves a move towards "harmonisation" of policy. The decision was taken with EMU in mind,[9] and required, as before, three meetings per year by the Council at which the Commission should present proposals for legislation and the Council would adopt guidelines. An annual report was to be adopted. Meetings would be held regularly to enure that the guidelines were observed and Member States could demand consultation within the Council in the event of serious problems. This decision was followed by a directive "on stability, growth and full employment"[10] which laid down fairly specific objectives and measures to be taken to achieve them. At the same time it was decided to merge the various specialist committees into an Economic Policy Committee.[11]

24—07 These actions were not altogether successful, although this is perhaps not surprising in view of the economic situation at the time. Thus the Parliament observed that the Council had not adhered to the provisions of the 1974 decision on convergence.[12]

After a gap of four years during which efforts to combat the various economic problems were only partially successful, a new initiative was launched at the Copenhagen European Council (summit)[13] in April 1978. A common economic strategy was agreed in principle; this was defined more closely at the Bremen summit[14] and implemented on July 24.[15] In essence this common strategy aimed at a "concerted" effort to overcome the recession by dovetailing an expansionary policy by some states with a more restrictive policy for other states. This was followed by a decision in 1979 amending the 1974 decision on convergency[16]

[6] Decision 69/227, J.O. 1969, L183/41.
[7] Decision 71/141, J.O. 1971, L73/14, O.J. 1971 (I) 174.
[8] Decision 74/120, O.J. 1974, L63/16 amended by Decision 79/136, O.J. 1979, L35/8.
[9] *Infra*, paras. 24–21 *et seq.*
[10] Directive 74/121, O.J. 1974, L63/19.
[11] Decision 74/122, O.J. 1974, L63/21.
[12] O.J. 1974, C140.
[13] Bulletin EC 4—1978, point 1.2.2.
[14] Bulletin EC 6—1978, point 1.5.2.
[15] Decision 78/658, O.J. 1978, L220/27 on adaptation of public budgets.
[16] Decision 79/136, O.J. 1979, L35/8.

requiring henceforth a two and-a-half yearly report on the economic situation.

Medium term policy

4—08   The decisions on convergency mentioned above dealt also with medium term policy, but the most significant development in this area has been the adoption to date of four five-year policies, the last having been adopted in 1977.[17] This aims primarily at the restoration of full employment through

- an active, regionally and sectorally balanced, growth policy;
- a sustained effort by the two sides of industry to take account of overall economic constraints in their attitude to incomes;
- an active and forward-looking employment policy to achieve a better balance between labour supply and demand.

Measures to deal with sudden crises

4—09   It has already been pointed out that Article 103 appears to permit stronger *Community* action in relation to crises or "conjunctural problems." It might have been expected that the oil crises would at least have given rise to Community action under this head. In fact the *Community* has been almost totally unable to take action, the effect being to place differing burdens on the Member States.[18] Only within the context of the Tokyo Summit of 1979 has the Community agreed to restrict the increase in oil imports together with similar commitments made by the United States, Japan and Canada.

This inaction was condemned by the Court, which stated that the absence of appropriate rules revealed "a neglect of the principle of Community solidarity . . . and a failure to act . . . is all the more serious since Article 103 (4) provides in terms that 'the procedures provided for in this article shall also apply if any difficulty should arise in the supply of certain products'."[19] Article 103 was, however, used in relation to the currency problems associated with the CAP.[20] The oil-stocks directive[21] was also adopted on the basis of Article 103.

Balance of Payments and Rates of Exchange

4—10   Equilibrium in the balance of payments is an objective of economic policy, and the rate of exchange of the national currency is an instrument of policy which is particularly used in achieving that

---

[17] Decision 77/294, O.J. 1977, L101/1.
[18] See generally Chapter 28, *infra.*
[19] Case 77/77 *Benzine en Petroleum Handelsmaatschappij BV and others* v. *Commission* [1978] E.C.R. 1513, 1525.
[20] *Supra,* para. 15–69.
[21] *Infra,* para. 28–12.

particular goal. Both were singled out for special treatment by the Treaty because the latter's main concern is with the free flow of trade between Member States. Such freedom could be seriously impaired by measures taken which affect payments for goods.

Article 106 - freedom of payments

24–11   Although this Article can be regarded as embodying a "fifth" freedom, (as it itself acknowledges), it is to be found in the section of the Treaty dealing with the balance of payments since the liberalisation of payments clearly weakens the Member States' control over monetary movements and, therefore, over the balance of payments. In Case 7/78 *R.* v. *Thompson, Johnson and Woodiwiss*[21a] the Court declared that the aim of Article 106 (1) "is to ensure that the necessary monetary transfers may be made both for the liberalisation of movements of capital and for the free movement of goods, services and persons." Despite the article's relationship to the other freedoms it is unlikely that any of its paragraphs could be regarded as directly applicable.[21b]

The burden of implementing the Article is placed on the Member States themselves as it is in the other Articles concerned with economic policy, rather than upon the Community institutions, which share the task of implementing the four other freedoms. Paragraph 1, first sub-paragraph, contains an undertaking on the part of the Member States to authorise in the appropriate currencies, any payments connected with the movement of goods, services or capital and also any transfers of capital and earnings associated with those freedoms and with free movement of persons to the extent that those four freedoms have been attained. The second sub-paragraph contains a declaration of intention to undertake further liberalisation than that required, if possible.

In so far as movement of goods, services and capital are hindered only by restrictions on related payments, paragraph 2 requires such restrictions to be abolished by application of the measures relating to goods, services and capital. Article 106 (2) contains no power to issue directives for this purpose, but such a measure was envisaged by the General Programme on services. Directive 63/340,[21c] based on Article 63 and Article 106 (2), requires such restrictions to be abolished, and Member States are to grant all foreign exchange authorisations needed for the transfer of such payments (Art. 1). The directive does not apply to transport services, nor does it apply to foreign exchange allowances for tourists (Art. 3 of the directive), but many of the restrictions had already been eliminated by Member States, so the effect of the directive was only of a

[21a] [1978] E.C.R. 2247.
[21b] See *Miliangos* v. *George Frank (Textiles) Ltd.* [1976] A.C. 443; *Contra, Schorsch Meier GmbH* v. *Hennin* [1975] QB. 416.
[21c] J.O. 1963, 1609.

residual nature. Article 106 (3) of the Treaty requires Member States not to introduce any new restrictions on transfers connected with the invisible transactions listed in Annex III[21d] which includes freight charges, commission fees, subscriptions, claims for damages, etc. Some of these are covered by the dispositions in paragraphs 1 and 2 and some by the chapter on the free movement of capital, but the others are to be abolished along the lines laid down in the chapter on services. Certain of these, notably bank charges, membership fees and fines, were dealt with by Directive 63/474,[22] requiring Member States to enable the transfers relating to such transactions to be made at the exchange rates prevailing for payments relating to current transactions. By 1964 an almost complete liberalisation of payments had been achieved by virtue of a combination of Article 67 (2), Directive 63/340 and Directive 63/474, except in the field of transport, and for tourist allowances.

4—12   The provisions already mentioned obviously encompass this particular subject-matter. Article 105, however, goes on to set up a "Monetary Committee" to help co-ordinate policy "in the monetary field," and Article 107 requires the Member States to treat their policy with regard to rates of exchange as a matter of common concern. Paragraph (2) appears to indicate, as with Article 103, that the use of this phrase implies a stronger obligation than mere co-ordination since in requiring Member States to obtain permission from the Commission to take preventive measures if one Member State breaks its obligations under Article 104[23] it implies that they may not otherwise act unilaterally. This is reinforced by the provisions of Articles 108 and 109 which lay down Community procedures for dealing with balance of payments problems. Article 108 allows the Commission to investigate the position of a Member State which "is in difficulties or is seriously threatened with difficulties as regards its balance of payments . . . " and to recommend measures. If the measures are inadequate, the matter can be referred to the Council which may grant assistance in terms of credits, international action or measures to assure that quantitative restrictions imposed on goods from third countries do not lead to a deflection of trade. If *that* is insufficient, the Commission may authorise protective measures to be taken. Article 109 deals with sudden crises in the balance of payments. It allows a Member State to take unilateral protective measures if nothing has been done under Article 108 (2). But those measures must then be scrutinised by the Commission, which can recommend assistance under Article 108. The Council

---

[21d] Cmnd. 7460, p.122.

[22] J.O. 1963, 2240.

[23] *Supra*, para. 24–03.

may grant such assistance and "amend, suspend or abolish the protective measures referred to above."

Secondary legislation

Background

24—13   The "economic history" of the Community has already been outlined. Events since the end of the transitional period meant that as in the field of economic policy in general it would have been surprising if the Member States had taken the broad injunctions of Articles 105 and 107 a great distance along the road towards greater co-ordination. However, there were some encouraging signs, and the EMS[24] constitutes a major step forward.

Rates of exchange

24—14   After a period of relative stability in exchange rates during the 1960s when rates were fixed according to the "Bretton Woods" agreement of 1944, 1971 saw the first indications that radical change was beginning. The chief problem then was the decline of the dollar. New parities had to be fixed following pressures for revaluations of the DM in particular, and this led to the Smithsonian agreements of that year where a drastic realignment of currencies was agreed. The ensuing crises of 1973, in particular the further devaluation of the dollar, led to the floating of the pound in June 1973. Other European currencies were by them trading within fixed limits against each other and "in concert" against the dollar (the so-called "snake in the tunnel"), in accordance with the Basle agreement of April 1972. In early 1974, with the crisis deepening, the French franc was allowed to float, seriously weakening the credibility of the snake. The franc rejoined the snake in July 1975, but left again in March 1976. The Italian lira, British and Irish pounds continued to float. In 1978, the proposals for a European Monetary System (EMS) encouraged the hope that floating currencies might soon be abandoned. The implementation of the EMS was delayed until April 1979. Since that date it has managed to hold together in spite of continuing turmoil in the world monetary system.

Balance of payments

24—15   The fluctuations in the fortunes of the various currencies mirror to some extent the fortunes of the various countries' balance of payments. Since 1970 the situation has been characterised by, on the one hand, a strong or satisfactory balance of payments situation for the countries which had always remained in the "snake" and a

[24] *Infra*, para. 24–24.

chequered career for the others. Britain and Italy in particular had colossal deficits between 1973 and 1976, but from then the situation began rather erratically to improve. The surpluses of the stronger currencies ensured that the Community as a whole was generally in surplus with the rest of the world at any rate until the end of the 1970s.

Co-ordination of policy in the monetary field

4—16   It has already been seen that the Treaty itself provides for the establishment of a Monetary Committee, but as early as 1964 a Decision was taken to set up a Committee of Governors of the Central Banks[25] which along with the Monetary Committee[26] could exercise co-ordination of national policies. The Monetary Committee is governed by rules adopted in 1958[27] and must be consulted on matters falling within Articles 69, 71, 73 (1) and (2), 107 (2), 108 (1) and 109 (3). The Council and Commission may request the opinion of the Committee in other cases, and the latter has in any event "the power and the obligation" to draw up opinions on its own initiative wherever it considers such to be necessary.

I Short Term Financial Support

(i) European Monetary Co-operation Fund (FECOM)

4—17   The Community's involvement in support for exchange rates, as opposed to the international structure, already well established, really dates from 1973 and the setting up of the European Monetary Co-operation Fund.[28] The functions of the Fund are to promote:- the proper functioning of the progressive narrowing of the margins of fluctuation of the Community currencies; interventions in Community currencies on the exchange markets; and settlements between Central Banks, leading to a concerted policy on reserves.

The regulation setting up the Fund provided expressly only for a "first stage" in its development, which involved primarily taking over the administration of the monetary support mechanisms agreed by the Governors of the Central Banks in February 1970 and March 1972 (short term and very short term support) and Rules of Procedure were adopted on June 28, 1973. Those arrangements were designed to allow FECOM to grant short and very short term credits to the extent of 15 bn u.a. It was hoped

[25] Decision 64/300, J.O. 1964, 1206; O.J. 1964, 141 and Dec. 71/142, J.O. 1971, L73/14; O.J. 1971, 75 on strengthening co-operation between central banks.
[26] Decision 64/301, J.O. 1964, 1207; O.J. 1964, 143. Decision 64/229, J.O. 1964, 1205; O.J. 1964, 140.
[27] March 18, 1958, J.O. 1958, 390; O.J. 1952–1958, 60 amended by Decision of April 2, 1962, O.J. 1962, 1064; O.J. 1959–62, 131 and Decision 76/332 O.J. 1976, L84/56.
[28] Regulation 907/73, O.J. 1973, L89/2. Located in Luxembourg with an office in Brussels—Decision 73/208, O.J. 1973, L207/46.

that within a very short time the Fund's functions could be increased by giving it the backing of 20 per cent. of the Central Banks' reserves, which would be pooled for the purpose. However, in spite of some increased flexibility in the original "first stage" provisions, the pooling of reserves plan did not get off the ground until the introduction of the EMS, some six years later.

(ii) Community loans

Financial support for dealing with balance of payments deficits through loans began in 1975 with the adoption of framework regulations.[29] The aim of these arrangements was to provide temporary assistance to those Member States which were suffering as a result of the oil crisis by allowing the Community to borrow on the financial markets so as to on-lend to Member States in difficulty. If the Member State has difficulty in repaying the loans, the deficiencies must be made up by the other Member States in agreed proportions. The total loans contracted by the Community are not to exceed 6,000 million ECU. The beneficiary Member State must observe economic policy conditions laid down by the Council and supervised by the Commission. The Community first made use of this facility in 1976 with loans of 1,000 million EUA to Italy and 300 million EUA to Ireland.[30]

A further loan power was adopted in 1978[31] to empower the Community to promote investment in the energy, industry and infrastructure sectors. The overall envelope of 1,000 million ECU is now in principle fully committed.[32]

In 1979 the Council adopted a regulation[33] providing for interest subsidies in favour of beneficiaries of loans under the 1978 scheme or of loans granted by the European Investment Bank directly from its own resources. These subsidies are intended to aid investments in the less prosperous Member States, provided that they are full members of the EMS system (*infra*). Ireland and Italy were designated as immediate beneficiaries of these measures.[34]

II *Medium Term Financial Assistance*

24–18   Arrangements have existed since 1971[35] under which Member

[29] Regulation 397/75, O.J. 1975, L46/1 and Regulation 398/75, O.J. 1975, L46/3 implementing Regulation 397/75; both replaced by Regulation 682/81, O.J. 1981 L73/1, doubling the total envelope.
[30] Decision 76/322, O.J. 1976, L77/12.
[31] Decision 78/870, O.J. 1978, L298/9. (Referred to as the New Community Instrument: NCI) and see Dec. 80/1108, O.J. 1980, L326/19.
[32] Decision 79/486, O.J. 1979, L125/16 & Decs. 80/739 & 1103, O.J. 1980, L205/19 & 326/19.
[33] Reg. 1736/79, O.J. 1979, L200/1.
[34] Dec. 79/691, O.J. 1979, L200/19.
[35] Dec. 71/143, J.O. 1971, L73/15; O.J. 1971, 76 amended Dec. 75/785, O.J. 1975, L330/50; Dec. 78/1041, O.J. 1978, L379/3; Dec 80/1264, O.J. 1980 L375/16.

States are obliged to make available medium-term credits (subject to ceilings) granted in the form of mutual assistance by directive or decision under Article 108 (2), in order to enable the beneficiary to meet balance of payments difficulties. The grant of mutual assistance is subject to the observance of economic policy guidelines. The principal beneficiary of these arrangements has been Italy.[36]

III The Application of Articles 107 to 109

—19 The observance of the requirements in these articles to consult with other Member States and with the Commission before making any changes in rates of exchange has been unsatisfactory on the whole. On several occasions following the disruption of monetary affairs in the early 1970s Member States did not give adequate warning of changes.[37] Articles 108 and 109 have been used chiefly in respect of Italy which needed Community backing for an import deposit scheme to stem imports and restore a grave crisis in its balance of payments, in 1974.[38] Derogations from the requirements on the free movement of capital were necessary as regards the United Kingdom,[39] until the abolition of exchange controls by the latter in October 1979. Measures have also been taken under these powers in favour of Ireland.[40]

Economic and Monetary Union

—20 The actions described above fall firmly into the category of co-ordination of national policies rather than Community action, even though taken by Community institutions and having the character of Community legislation, for they do not involve the *transfer* to the *Community* of the decision making process of economic policy, nor of its instruments. An economic and monetary union involves such a *transfer*: in its perfected state, "EMU" would entail a single economic policy and a single currency unit.

From the end of the transitional period the thoughts of European leaders began to turn towards the prospect of economic and monetary union. Many reasons might be advanced for such a view. "EMU" could be seen as the next step towards political integration; or as a logical and necessary development of co-ordination of policy, for co-ordination cannot be viewed in a vacuum - the Member States would have to agree on a *direction* for their co-ordination; or as necessary for the preservation of the common market - if national economies began to diverge significantly, the

[36] Dir. 74/637, O.J. 1974, L330/10, last amended Dec. 78/840, O.J. 1978, L291/12.
[37] *e.g.* the decision to float the French franc in late 1973.
[38] Decision 74/287, O.J. 1974, L152/18. See also Decision 76/446, O.J. 1976, L120/30 and Decision 76/614, O.J. 1976, L196/20.
[39] Decision 75/487, O.J. 1975, L211/29; repealed and replaced by Decision 78/154, O.J. 1978, L45/30.
[40] Decision 78/152 & 153, O.J. 1978, L45/28 & 29.

Member States would, if they still possessed the power of unilateral decision making, be bound to take action which affected the flow of goods (*e.g.* an import deposit scheme). Such arguments tend to demonstrate the instability of the common market as a concept when deprived of common action in other areas which affect it.

24—21   The notion of "EMU" found its first expression in the communiquê following the Hague Summit of December 1969. This declared support for the development of a plan for EMU, and in March 1970 the Council set up the "Werner" Committee to investigate the possibilities.[41] The Werner Report duly followed in October 1970. The Commission, in that same month, then submitted proposals for the establishment of EMU by stages in the light of the Report and these proposals were in the main adopted by the Council in a resolution of March 22 1971.[42] The aim enunciated by the Council was to achieve EMU by 1980.

The general aim of the resolution was the creation of an economic and monetary union, so that the main economic policy decisions would be taken at Community level. A consequence would be the adoption of a single currency for the Community. The resolution envisaged a 10 year period for the achievement of various aims explained in fairly extensive detail. By the end of this period the Community would

1. constitute a zone within which persons, goods, services and capital will move freely and without distortion of competition, without, however, giving rise to structural or regional imbalances, and in conditions which would allow persons exercising economic activity to operate on a Community scale;

2. form an individual monetary unit within the international system, characterised by the total and irreversible convertibility of currencies, the elimination of fluctuating margins of rates of exchange, and the irrevocable fixing of parity rates—all of which are indispensable conditions for the creation of a single currency—and including a Community organisation of the Central Banks;

3. hold the powers and responsibilities in the economic and monetary field enabling its Institutions to organise the administration of the union. To this end, the required economic policy decisions would be taken at Community level and the necessary powers would be given to the Institutions of the Community.

24—22   The resolution set out in fairly specific terms the action deemed necessary in order to attain these aims in the first phase (January 1, 1971, to December 31, 1973), while leaving the period from then

[41] J.O. 1970, L94/9.
[42] J.O. 1971, L28/1. This resolution, with Arts. 5 and 107 of the Treaty, is not directly applicable at the present stage: Case 9/73, *supra*, note 4.

to the finalisation of the Economic and Monetary Union vague and uncharted: it provided for:

(1) reinforcement of co-ordination of short-term economic policies:

(2) greater harmonisation in taxation structures, tending towards the alignment of VAT and excise duty rates throughout the Community;

(3) greater movement of capital and co-ordination of financial market policies;

(4) greater efforts to solve regional and structural problems;

(5) reinforcement of co-ordination in monetary and credit policies, by means of consultation at the level of the Committee of the Governors of the Central Banks and the Monetary Committee;

(6) adoption of common Community attitudes in monetary relations with third countries;

(7) narrowing of margins of fluctuation in parities between the Member States' currencies; and

(8) drawing up of a report on the role and organisation of a European Monetary Co-operation Fund.

This first phase was only partially successful: the decisions relating to mutual short term assistance[43] and to the convergency of economic policies[44] were taken in the context of EMU as well as "co-ordination" under Articles 103-9. Measures relating to regional policy were also taken (*infra*, Chapter 26). Despite the looming recession at the end of 1973 the Council resolved to push ahead into the second stage, which would go beyond mere co-ordination and begin the process towards centralisation. A few measures were adopted in early 1974 (mentioned above), but the process ground to a halt during that year.

4—23 The Commission set up a committee of 15 to look at what had happened, and this reported in 1975 (the Marjolin Committee). It regarded the efforts since 1969 as having failed due to adverse economic developments and a lack of understanding as to what was involved.[45] A new group was then set up to work out what kind of economic policy should be pursued by the Memer States, (the "Optica" group) and this concluded that there should be an emphasis on achieving a concerted budgetary and incomes policy, leading eventually to a unified currency unit. The Commission put forward new proposals based on these conclusions in 1976 and again in 1977 but it was not until the Copenhagen summit in April 1978 that the first "breakthrough" came with the Franco-German proposal for the establishment of a "European Monetary System" (EMS). The support of the other Member States (except the

[43] *Supra,* paras. 24–17 *et seq.*
[44] *Supra,* paras. 24–06 *et seq.*
[45] Bulletin EC 4–1975 point 2201; see also Bulletin EC Suppt. 5/75.

United Kingdom) was forthcoming at the start, faltered close to the date of launch (January 1, 1979), but eventually the EMS came into operation on March 13, 1979, following insistence by France that its adoption be linked with a reform of the agricultural MCAs.[46]

Operation of the EMS[47]

24—24   As between currencies the operation does not differ markedly from the old "snake." Each currency has a margin of 2.25 per cent. fluctuation in each direction against every other currency in the system. This 4.5 per cent. margin is largely theoretical because if one currency were to reach the ceiling or floor against another currency, the intervention measures to bring it back to the "central rate" would probably cause it, through a variety of factors, to reach its floor or ceiling against another currency before it had again attained parity. The margin of fluctuation is thus probably around 3.5 per cent for the majority of currencies; less for the strongest and weakest.

Where the EMS goes further than the "snake," however, is in tying the fluctuation of each currency also to a central unit known as the European Currency Unit (ECU). This is composed of fractions of the participating national currencies, weighted to represent the percentage shares of trade as between Member States. The weightings can be changed but this is unlikely to happen frequently. The amounts of each currency in the ECU basket are DM: 0.828; UKL: 0.0885; FF: 1.15; LIT: 109.00: HFL: 0.286; BFR: 3.66; LFR: 0.140; DKR: 0.217; IRL: 0.00759.[48]

24—25   To obtain the value of the ECU in a national currency, a conversion of the indicated fractions of the other participating currencies is made, currently as follows in relation to Sterling:

---

[46] Bulletin EC 12 1978, point 1.1.1. to 1.1.12.; Cmnd. 7419; Regs. 3180 and 3181/78, O.J. 1978, L379/1 & 2. See also House of Lords Select Committee on the European Communities. "European Monetary System," HL (61) July 24, 1979.
[47] *Supra,* note 46 for texts.
[48] Reg. 3180/78, *supra,* note 46.

Economic and Monetary Union

Currency	Rate of exchange	Value of fraction
DM	3.975	20.83p
FF	9.2075	12.49p
LIT	1792	6p
HFL	4.36	6.6p
BFR	63.65	5.8p
LFR	63.65	0.2p
DKR	11.45	1.9p
IRL	1.0545	0.7p
UKL	—	8.85p
ECU		63.37p

Theoretically a currency should not deviate by more than 75 per cent. of 2.25 per cent in either direction against a central exchange rate fixed for the ECU at the same time as the central rates for currencies between themselves were agreed. This limit is known as the divergence threshold. In fact in all cases it will be less than 75 per cent. of 2.25 per cent. because one element of the ECU does not vary, *i.e.* the fraction of its value supplied by the currency in question. Thus, even where all other currencies are stretched to the limit against that currency, it may not have diverged by 2.25 per cent. against the ECU but by a lesser amount depending on its percentage share. The greater the share, the less the maximum divergence, hence the lower the divergence threshold. At present the divergence thresholds are as follows:
BFR: 1.53%; DKR: 1.635%; DM: 1.325%; FF: 1.35%; HFL: 1.5075%; IRL: 1.655%; LIT: 4.0725%.
(The margin for the Italian lira is greater because of its 12 per cent. fluctuation limit.) The object of this second aspect of the EMS is primarily to encourage corrective policy measures before currencies reach the limits of their parity grids so that the frequency with which these limits are reached should be reduced. Whenever under "the snake" a currency slipped to the floor, it was incumbent on the central bank of that currency to intervene by buying it in through obtaining foreign currency by swop arrangement or credit from FECOM. Under EMS, a currency which has reached the

divergence threshold will have in fact begun to show a tendency to diverge from the mainstream pattern of currency movements. The presumption is that the authorities can then (and ought to) intervene to pull it back into line, whether it is increasing in value or declining in value, thereby introducing more objective criteria against which action should be taken and making the burden of adjustment more equal in respect of both relatively strong and relatively weak currencies.

24—26   The ECU will eventually also be used as an accounting device for making settlements between central banks and as against credits given by a new European Monetary Fund to replace FECOM. The Fund will have deposited with it 20 per cent. of each Member State's gold and dollar reserves, and Member States will obtain and repay credits in ECU whose value is calculated against those two units. The EMF will be able to extend credits to the total of 25 bn ECU rather than the 15 bn EUA under the former FECOM system. It has now replaced the EUA as the accounting unit in all EEC legislation.[49]

The EMS was reviewed on September 17, 1979, by the Council and no changes were found to be necessary. However, shortly afterwards a devaluation of the Danish Kroner took place, followed by a further devaluation in November 1979. Although the EMS was due for a strengthening after two years in operation, it now seems likely that any such move will be postponed for at least two years.

[49] Regulation 3308/80, O.J. 1980, L345/1 and see *supra*, para. 3–76.

Chapter 25

SOCIAL POLICY

—01   The content of "social policy" varies somewhat from one country to another depending on the extent to which governments are involved in the subject-matter it may encompass. As a general rule the term describes at least the policy adopted with regard to all aspects of working conditions, *i.e.* non-discrimination (race, colour, sex); health and safety; vocational training and general measures to assist the unemployed; help for disadvantaged (*e.g.* handicapped) workers; regional and sectoral problems; and industrial relations. Because of the close connection with one of the foundations of the Treaty - *viz.* the free movement of workers - social policy receives special treatment, and the Community is given instruments of policy which allow it to some extent to have a policy of its own, superimposed or dovetailing with that of the Member States. But it also plays a role as a promoter of co-operation between the Member States.

—02   The provisions of the Treaty on social matters are contained in Articles 117 to 128, together forming Title III of Part Three of the Treaty—Policies of the Community—entitled "Social policy." The title is itself divided into two chapters—Chapter 1, "Social Provisions" and Chapter 2, "The European Investment Bank." The individual articles in Chapter 1 do not, apart from Article 119, which relates to equal pay between male and female labour, contain any provisions imposing obligations either on the Community or Member States. The theory inherent in the chapter is that social progress will come about incidentally to progress in other spheres; this is indicated by the phrasing of Article 117, whereby "Member States agree upon the need to promote improved working conditions. . . . They believe that such a development will ensue not only from the functioning of the common market, . . . but also from the procedures provided for in this Treaty. . . ." These procedures are in particular those relating to the free movement and social security of workers (Arts. 48 to 51), the equal pay provision (Art. 119), the creation of the European Social Fund (Arts. 123 to 127), and the formulation of a common policy on vocational training (Art. 128). Tangentially involved are those provisions which erect common policies in specific areas, such as agriculture and transport, *e.g.* Articles 39 (1) (*b*) and 41 (*a*) and Article 75. The first article of Chapter 1, Article 117, records the agreement of the Member States "upon the need to promote improved working conditions and an improved standard of living for workers, so as to make possible their har-

monisation while the improvement is being maintained" (first
para.). The second paragraph records the belief of the Member
States that the development referred to in the first paragraph
"will ensue not only from the functioning of the common market,
which will favour the harmonisation of social systems, but also
from the procedure provided for in this Treaty and from the
approximation of provisions laid down by law, regulation or
administrative action."

Article 118

25—03   Article 118 lists the particular fields (namely employment,
labour law and working conditions, vocational training, social
security, industrial safety, and hygiene, and the right of association
and collective bargaining) in which the Commission is given the
task of promoting close co-operation between the Member States
so that the aspirations of Article 117 may be achieved. The
Commission's powers cover other matters outside the list, but are
without prejudice to other provisions of the Treaty, and are to be
in conformity with its general objectives. Article 118 embodies
no binding engagement or undertaking by Member States, but is a
simple attribution of competence to the Commission in the matter
of promotion, the ultimate responsibility in these affairs remaining
with the Member States. The Commission is to act in close contact
with the Member States by making studies, delivering opinions and
arranging consultations both on problems arising at national level
and those of concern to international organisations. Before delivering the opinions provided for, the Commission is to consult the
Economic and Social Committee. Generally, the Commission has
had recourse to the power under Article 155 to make recommendations. (These are nevertheless issued after consultation with
the Economic and Social Committee.)

Article 119

25—04   Article 119 of the EEC Treaty stands alone in the "Social
Provisions" chapter in imposing a definite obligation on the
Member States to conform to its provisions by a specific date—the
end of the first stage of the period of transition on December 31,
1961. The first paragraph of Article 119 contains a clear statement
of principle—Member States shall ensure and subsequently maintain the application of the principle that men and women should
receive equal pay for equal work. For this purpose, the second
paragraph defines "pay" as meaning "the ordinary basic or minimum wage or salary and any other consideration, whether in cash
or in kind, which the worker receives, directly or indirectly, in
respect of his employment from his employment." The third
paragraph explains that pay without discrimination based on sex
means:

"(*a*) that pay for the same work at piece rates shall be calculated on the basis of the same unit of measurement;

(*b*) that pay for work at time rates shall be the same for the same job."

Direct applicability

–05   This article was held directly applicable by the Court in the second *Defrenne*[1] case. The decision came as a surprise to many commentators because, although the article is sufficiently close to several others in its formulation, the effect of direct applicability would be in theory to give all persons who could show they had not received equal pay since 1962 the right to claim it. To avoid this consequence, the Court tempered its decision with political and economic realism by declaring its decision as applicable only from the date thereof (*i.e.* April 8, 1976).

Implementation

–06   The equal pay principle has an honourable international legal pedigree in that it was incorporated into the preamble to Part XIII of the 1919 Treaty of Versailles, which contains the original constitution of the ILO, and was reiterated in the 1944 Declaration of Philadelphia which renewed the mandate of the ILO. ILO Convention No. 100, of June 29, 1951, enunciates the principle in terms of equal pay for work of equal value. The European Social Charter, formulated under the guidance of the Council of Europe, states that "the contracting parties undertake . . . to recognise the right of men and women workers to equal pay for work of equal value" (Art. 4 (3)), although this Charter has had little legal effect to date. The principle in Article 119 is more concise, "equal pay for equal work," and the definition in the second paragraph is borrowed from the ILO Convention, but no clarification is given on the meaning of the phrase "directly or indirectly" used in the second paragraph in defining what constitutes pay received. It was thought that this referred to deferred payments of wages or salary, such as pensions and this question was specifically posed in 80/70 *Defrenne* v. *Belgium*[2] where differential pension rights were given to staff of Sabena (the Belgian national airline), dependent on their work and sex; air hostesses were compulsorily retired at 40 without having been able to accumulate pension privileges accorded to other staff. The Court of Justice decided that a pension is not wholly a payment by the employer, there also being contribution from the worker

---

[1] Case 43/75 *Gabrielle Defrenne* v. *SABENA* [1976] E.C.R. 455.
[2] [1971] E.C.R. 445. Direct applicability expanded upon in Cases 129/79, *Wendy Smith* v. *McCarthy's* [1980] E.C.R. 1275, 68/80 *Worringham and Humphreys* v. *Lloyd's Bank Ltd.* [1981] 2 C.M.L.R. 1, 96/80, *Jenkins* v. *Kingsgate* [1981] 2 C.M.L.R. 24.

(but surely this is in reality payment he actually forgoes) and contributions from the relevant national authority, and that the worker's title to payment did not therefore depend upon the employer's contribution to the pension fund, but is merely based on the fulfilment by the worker of certain criteria, usually of age, and the payment of a certain number of contributions by the worker himself. Therefore, the principle of Article 119 did not apply to state pensions or other social security benefits, although it might apply to privately financed pension schemes.

25—07   In establishing whether discrimination has occurred, it is necessary to compare the services performed by a woman against those performed by a man. Thus it is not possible to claim that discrimination has occurred where a particular job has always been performed by a woman, even if there is evidence that a man would be offered a higher wage or salary. On the other hand, it is legitimate to compare the salary offered to a woman who is taking over from a man with the latter's salary, experience and qualifications being equal.[3]

In the third *Defrenne*[4] case the Court held that Article 119 cannot be interpreted as prescribing, in addition to equal pay, equality in respect of other working conditions applicable to men and women. In particular, the fact that the fixing of certain conditions of employment - such as a special age limit - may have pecuniary consequences is not sufficient to bring them within the field of application of Article 119, "which is based on the close connexion which exists between the nature of the services provided and the amount of remuneration." There is therefore as yet no general Community prohibition on sex discrimination although the third *Defrenne* case itself holds that elimination of sex discrimination is part of fundamental rights which is in turn one of the general principles of Community law. Such a prohibition does therefore apply in relation to Community rules (*e.g.* Staff Regulations).[5] Directives (*infra*, para. 25-19) have been issued in furtherance of the principle of equality of treatment.

Article 120

25—08   This article provides simply that "Member States shall endeavour to maintain the existing equivalence between paid holiday schemes." Disparities in such schemes were considered potentially to be a distorting factor in the same way as disparities in legislation relating to the rights of women. In fact it was discovered that the schemes in the various original six Member States were largely the same, hence it was necessary only to require the main-

---

[3] Case 129/79 *McCarthys Ltd.* v. *Wendy Smith* [1980] E.C.R. 1275. See also Case 96/80 *Jenkins* v. *Kingsgate, supra* note 1 (part-time workers).
[4] Case 149/77, *Gabrielle Defrenne* v. *SABENA* [1978] E.C.R. 1365.
[5] *e.g.* Case 257/78 *Devred* v. *Commission* [1979] E.C.R. 3767.

tenance of this equivalence. Subsequent developments have tended to show a disregard for this article.

Articles 121 and 122

5—09   Article 121 enables the Council to assign to the Commission "tasks in connection with the implementation of common measures, particularly as regards social security for the migrant workers referred to in Articles 48 to 51." The article is self-explanatory as regards the delegation of tasks to the Commission, but no definition is given of "implementation of common measures." It must be assumed that the expression covers all general and particular objects of the Treaty in social affairs.

Article 122, first para., requiring the Commission to include a separate chapter on social developments within the Community in its annual report to the Assembly (now called the European Parliament), reflects one aspect of the general duty of the Commission contained in Article 156 to publish an annual report, which by Article 143 must be discussed by the European Parliament. The specific provision in Article 122, that the report should include a separate chapter on social development, seems unique, as nowhere else does the Treaty list obligatory chapter headings for the annual reports. The Commission also publishes a separate annual report on social questions, covering the same ground in greater depth. This too is stated to be published pursuant to Article 122. The second paragraph of Article 122 is in some sense the reciprocal of the first, for it empowers the Assembly to invite the Commission to draw up reports on any particular problems concerning social conditions; the two paragraphs thus institutionalise the dialogue which exists outside the article.

Articles 123-127

5—10   These articles deal with the European Social Fund, discussed below.

Article 128

5—11   Article 128 provides that the Council should lay down general principles for the implementation of a common vocational training policy. The developments in this field are dealt with below.

I The Instruments of Policy

(a) The European Social Fund

Scope

5—12   The European Social Fund ("ESF") was set up by the Treaty to make finance available to cope with changing social and employment situations within the Community. Thus Article 123 provides that the Fund has the "task of rendering the employment of workers easier and of increasing their geographical and occupational mobility within the Community," in order to "improve employment opportunities for workers in the common market and to contribute thereby to raising the standard of living." However, Article 125 effectively limited the intervention of the Fund to two actions - *viz.* vocational training and resettlement allowances on the one hand, and temporary aid for workers employed by an undertaking which is converting to another business, the workers being laid off during the period of conversion.

Article 126 provided that the rules set out in Article 125 could be changed to widen the scope of the Fund at the end of the transitional period. This was duly done by Decision 71/66[6] which came into force on May 1, 1972 after the necessary administrative and financial rules had been made.[7] The decision was subsequently amended by Decision 77/801.[8]

25—13   Under present arrangements the Fund's resources may be used to "grant assistance for members of the labour force who, having benefited from a measure taken within the scope of the Fund, are to pursue activities as employed or self-employed persons."[9] Its areas of intervention are placed into two categories. Article 4 on the one hand allows for action when the employment situation is affected by *Community* action or where that situation calls for joint action to improve the balance of supply and demand for labour at *Community* level. Article 5, on the other hand, allows the Fund to assist operations within the framework of the employment policies of the *Member States* provided those operations are aimed at one of four objectives:

-   assistance in less developed and declining regions
-   adaptation to technological progress
-   transformation of the business of undertakings
-   assistance for the entry or re-entry of the handicapped into economic activity.

These very broad areas of activity are defined in greater detail by implementing Regulation 2396/71[10] as amended substantially by Regulation 2893/77.[11] Essentially these regulations provide that Article 5 alone may be used in providing assistance for operations designed to eliminate long term structural unemployment or to retrain workers (at least 60 per cent. of Article 5

[6] J.O. 1971, L28/15, O.J. 1971, (I) 52.
[7] Regulations 858/72, J.O. 1972, L101/3; O.J. 1972 (II) 353, amended by Regulation 2894/77, O.J. 1977, L337/5.
[8] O.J. 1977, L337.
[9] Decision 71/66, Article 3, as amended.
[10] J.O. 1971, L249/54; O.J. 1971, 924.
[11] O.J. 1977, L337/1.

appropriations); provided that generally the assistance forms part of a specific programme directed at remedying the causes of the imbalance of employment.

5—14   Articles 4 *and* 5 allow for assistance concerning aid:

- to cover the cost of training persons in occupational knowledge
- to facilitate mobility of workers and integration of such workers in their new environment
- to make access to employment for handicapped and older workers
- to promote better conditions of employment in various specified regions.

In addition these articles may be used, if the Council agrees, for other purposes, especially assistance for the unemployed.[12]

Article 7 of Regulation 2396/71 also empowers the Commission to use funds appropriated for the purpose to participate in pilot schemes. Article 4 of Decision 71/66 can only be used when the Council has adopted a specific decision, whilst the Commission is given the power to operate Article 5. Decisions under Article 4 have included assistance:

- for persons leaving agriculture[13];
- for persons affected by employment difficulties[14];
- for persons occupied in the textile and clothing industries[15];
- for migrant workers[16];
- for women[17]

Assistance under the last four items has been extended to be available to January 1, 1983.[18] Assistance under the old fund continued for some years but has now ceased.

Administration

5—15   For operations undertaken by public authorities, the Fund may only contribute up to 50 per cent. of expenditure and for private sector projects it may match the amount of the project borne by any public authority. Its contribution may be increased by 10 per cent. in the case of operations in regions of structural unemployment[19] (such as Northern Ireland). Applications for grants must

[12] See, *e.g.* aid for young people, Regulation 3039/78, O.J. 1978, L361/3.
[13] Decision 72/428, J.O. 1972, L291/158; O.J. 1972 (28–30 December), 73.
[14] Decision 75/459, O.J. 1975, L199/36.
[15] Decision 76/206, O.J. 1976, L39/39. These three decisions were amended by Decision 77/802, O.J. 1977, L337/10 to take account of the reforms of the ESF mentioned above.
[16] Decision 74/327, O.J. 1974, L185/20, extended to 1981 by Decision 77/803, O.J. 1977, L337/12.
[17] Dec. 77/804, O.J. 1977, L337/14.
[18] Dec. 80/1117, O.J. 1980, L332/17.
[19] Reg. 2895/77, O.J. 1977, L337/7.

be made to the employment authorities of the Member States (United Kingdom Department of Employment, Ireland Department of Labour) which then forward them to the Commission. The Commission adopts guidelines each year, and as the number of applications increases, so the need for priorities becomes more pressing. More detailed rules on applications and administrative matters are to be found in two decisions of 1978.[20]

The amount in the Fund is allocated on an annual basis and has been steadily increasing over the years.

Decisions are taken after consultation with the Social Fund Committee and usually in batches, three or four times a year.

(b) Articles 54-56 of the ECSC

Scope

25—16   By Article 56, the Commission is given the power to finance programmes of investment for any industry whether coal or steel or otherwise, which aim at the reabsorption into gainful employment of the redundant workers in the coal and steel industries. The Commission is also authorised to grant non-repayable aids in the form of, for example, tide-over, resettlement or retraining allowances to workers who had either to suffer temporary unemployment while their employer was converting his establishment to a new type of production, or who became unemployed and were forced to move to find suitable employment elsewhere, or who, after becoming unemployed, found it necessary to undergo a period of retraining to learn a new trade or skill which would give them the opportunity of a job. Article 56 as originally formulated only envisaged the financing of new schemes in the context of technical innovations (in the context of the coal and steel industries) being responsible for causing widespread redundancies. After the coal crisis of the mid-1950s it became obvious that market forces other than technical advances were responsible for making workers in the coal and steel industries redundant. These forces were basically the increased use of alternative fuels and materials, so much so that it became necessary to amend Article 56 to take account of the situation. The amendment consists in the addition of a new paragraph 2 to the unamended provisions of the article (now para. 1). (This is the only ECSC article to be revised under the *petite révision* provisions of Article 95 ECSC. The other Community Treaties contain no such provision.) By paragraph 2 the Commission is now empowered to finance investment programmes in situations where fundamental changes not directly connected with the establishment of the coal and steel common market may lead some undertakings permanently to discontinue, curtail or change their activities; the Commission may also provide allowances for undertakings to enable them to con-

[20] Dec. 78/742 O.J. 1978, L248/1 and Dec. 78/706 O.J. 1978, L238/20.

tinue paying such of their workers as may have to be temporarily laid off as a result of the undertaking's change of activity in addition to the types of allowances payable under paragraph 1. The relative freedom of action of the Commission was to a certain extent due to the fact that unlike the ESF, the Commission enjoys its own financial resources and because it deals with only two sectors of the economy. The ECSC also undertakes programmes of house-building to assist displaced workers or to ameliorate housing conditions generally, by virtue of the powers granted to it in Article 54.

Administration

6—17   The administration of the assistance available under these articles is described in Chapter 26 on regional policy.

II Policy

Action programmes

—18   The formulation of a coherent policy on social matters could really get off the ground only after the reforms of the ESF introduced in 1971, when, indeed, a policy became necessary. This led to the formulation of the first general social action programme in 1973, in response to a call by the heads of government at the Paris summit of 1972.

This first general action programme presented to the Council in 1973 set out general considerations and objectives and listed a number of concrete actions which should be completed by the end of 1974. The Council accepted the programme in January 1974[21] and also set forth a number of longer term priorities including:

- a comprehensive programme for migrant workers;
- a common policy on vocational training;
- a programme for the progressive involvement of workers in the life of firms;
- pilot schemes as a means of combating poverty.

The years following saw the attainment of most of the short term objectives and the drawing up of further action programmes for the employment of handicapped persons in an open market economy (1973) and for migrant workers (1974 and 1976). The main achievements to date are summarised here.

Action to promote equal treatment for women

6—19   The 1973 action programme envisaged the drawing up of a directive concerning the application of Article 119. The directive

[21] O.J. 1974, C13/1.

was adopted in 1975,[22] and other directives have since been adopted in relation to the equal treatment of women as regards access to employment, vocational training and promotion and working conditions[23] and in social security matters.[24] Member States have been slow to implement the first mentioned directive.

Other action in this field has included:

- the setting up of a documentation and information centre on women's employment;
- progress reports on the implementation of Article 119 (1970 and 1974);
- the setting up of a specialised department to deal with the problems of employment for women;
- special assistance from the social fund for the employment of women.[25]

Action to relieve unemployment

25—20   This is an area where the Member States have remained jealous of their powers and duties to take action, so Community action has had to concentrate on problems of a more structural kind, in particular on vocational training for persons made redundant in given industries. About 95 per cent. of the assistance of the new social fund has been disbursed for this purpose[26] and in fact an action programme on vocational training had been adopted as early as 1972.[27]

The principles of a common policy on vocational training mentioned in Article 128 were laid down by a 1963 decision.[28] The decision lists 10 such principles; the first principle contains a definition of a common vocational training policy as meaning "a coherent and progressive common action which entails that each Member State shall draw up programmes and ensure that these are put into effect in accordance with the General Principles" contained in the decision. Further, "it shall be the responsibility of the Member States and the competent bodies of the Community to apply such General Principles within the framework of the Treaty." The second principle indicates the objectives of the policy as being generally to ensure the correct and adequate operation of training facilities, and, *inter alia*, to promote basic and advanced vocational training and where appropriate, retraining, suitable to the various stages of working life. The third principle refers to the importance of training as well as to the forecasting

---

[22] Directive 75/117, O.J. 1975, L45/19 on approximation of the laws of the Member States relating to the application of the principle of equal pay for men and women.
[23] Directive 76/207, O.J. 1976, L39/40.
[24] Directive 79/7, O.J. 1979, L6/24.
[25] Decision 77/804, O.J. 1977, L337/14.
[26] See 7th General Report (1974), point 221.
[27] See 6th General Report (1974), point 200.
[28] Decision 63/266, J.O. 1963, 1338; O.J. 1957–1964, 25.

and information services. The fourth, fifth and sixth principles indicate that the role of the Commission in this matter is to initiate measures, to carry out research, to encourage direct exchanges of information, and to collate information. The Commission is assisted in these tasks by a Tripartite Advisory Committee. The seventh principle indicates that the training of teachers and instructors should be developed, while the eighth principle envisages the eventual harmonisation of levels of vocational training, to facilitate the eventual interchange between Member States of qualified personnel. The tenth principle states that the financing of measures taken to implement the common vocational training policy may be jointly undertaken.

5—21   The development of the new fund with its broader scope of course meant that the above principles would have to be revised and elaborated. In 1977, therefore, the Advisory Committee[29] began preparation of new guidelines. The Community also set up a Community Vocational Training Centre[30] in Berlin, which was opened in March 1977 and should contribute towards the formation of a genuine common policy.

Special attention has been paid to the problems of young people under the age of 25. In 1975 the Social Fund provisions were applied to give assistance to young people in employment difficulties[31] and in 1977 the Commission adopted a recommendation on the vocational preparation for unemployed young people.[32] This was followed in 1978 by a Council regulation on a new form of aid from the Social Fund which supplements the assistance given by the Fund for training programmes.[33]

Other actions in the field of unemployment have included:

- a resolution on the reorganisation of working time (in the context of work sharing)[34];
- a resolution on so-called alternance training (schemes combining training with work experience). The resolution (Council) asks the Commission to look into ways the ESF might be able to provide assistance[35];
- the setting up of a Standing Committee on Employment[36];
- a directive on the consequences of mass dismissals[37];
- the gradual working out of a Community wide clearing house for job vacancies (known as SEDOC).

[29] Rules of procedure Decision 63/688, J.O. 1963, 3090; O.J. 1963–64, 86, amended Decision 68/189, J.O. 1968, L91/26; O.J. 1968, 79.
[30] Regulation 337/75, O.J. 1975, L39.
[31] Decision 75/459, O.J. 1975, L199/36.
[32] Recommendation 77/467, O.J. 1977, L180/18.
[33] Regulation 3039/78, O.J. 1978, L361/3.
[34] O.J. 1980, C2/1.
[35] O.J. 1980, C1/1.
[36] Decision 70/532, J.O. 1970, L273/25; O.J. 1970, 863.
[37] Directive 75/129, O.J. 1975, L48/29.

Actions to combat poverty

25—22   In 1974 the Commission began drawing up pilot schemes to combat poverty which would qualify for aid under Article 7 of Regulation 2396/71;[38] these were approved by the Council in 1975[39] and extended in 1977.[40]

Handicapped workers

25—23   This has been one of the more successful areas of action. The Council in 1974 approved the use of Article 4 of the Social Fund for aid to handicapped workers,[41] the setting up of a general industrial safety committee and the adoption of an action programme.[42] The first concrete step came with the granting of aid from the Fund for occupational rehabilitation in the form of pilot schemes and of choosing rehabilitation centres and bodies to help devise and teach new methods. Action has continued along these lines.

Migrant workers

25—24   The 1974 decision on the opening up of the Social Fund applied also to migrant workers, and the subsequent action programme aimed in particular at achieving voting rights in local elections by 1980, and improvements in social security for non-Community nationals. In 1976 the Commission put forward a proposal for a directive on illegal immigration and employment[43] but it has not yet found favour with the Council. A directive on the education of children of migrant workers was adopted, in 1977.[44]

Industrial relations

25—25   The role of the Communities in industrial relations has been strictly limited to furthering understanding between workforce and management through the setting up of sectoral committees and the introduction of annual tripartite conferences (Community, employers' and workers' representatives) to discuss the economic situation. A proposal for a directive on conflicts of laws in industrial relations has not yet been adopted.

25—26   At the end of the life of the old Commission before Greek accession, highly controversial proposals were brought forward on procedures for informing and consulting the employees of trans-

---

[38] *Supra*, para. 25–13.
[39] Decision 75/458, O.J. 1975, L199/34.
[40] Decision 77/779, O.J. 1977, L322/28.
[41] *Supra*, para. 25–14.
[42] O.J. 1974, C80/30.
[43] O.J. 1976, C34.
[44] O.J. 1977, L199.

national undertakings as a whole.[45] It remains to be seen whether this will be pursued by the new Commission.

Working conditions

5–27   The 1973 action programme envisaged the setting up of a general industrial safety committee and extension of the competence of the Mines Safety and Health Committees; both these actions were duly carried out, in the latter case by giving the MSHC competence over offshore oil drilling rigs.

Other actions in this area have included:

- the establishment of a foundation for the improvement of
- living and working conditions (1974)[46];
- research projects on, *e.g.* industrial safety;
- a recommendation on the adoption of a 40-hour week[47];
- proposals on the reform of the organisation of work[48];
- a Council directive on safety standards for health protection against ionising radiation[49];
- the first meeting of the Community's Ministers of Health in 1977;
- a cataloguing of occupational diseases[50] and a recommendation on occupational hygiene[51];
- establishment of an advisory committee on safety, hygiene and health protection at work[52];
- a directive on the provision of safety signs at work[53].
- a directive on the protection of workers from risks associated with exposure to chemical, biological and physical agents at work[54];
- a directive on the protection of employees in the event of the insolvency of their employer.[55]

[45] Vredeling Proposals: O.J. 1980, C297; Bulletin EC Suppt. 3/80.
[46] Regulation 1365/75, O.J. 1975, L139/1.
[47] O.J. 1975, L199/32.
[48] See Parliament Resolution on this at O.J. 1977, C163.
[49] Directive 76/579, O.J. 1976, L187/1 as amended by Directive 80/836, O.J. 1980, L246.
[50] J.O. 1962, 2188.
[51] J.O. 1962, 2181.
[52] Decision 74/325, O.J. 1974, L185/15.
[53] Directive 77/576, O.J. 1977, L229/12 as amended by Directive 79/640, O.J. 1979, L183/11.
[54] Directive 80/1107, O.J. 1980 L327/8.
[55] Directive 80/987, O.J. 1980, L283/23.

Chapter 26

REGIONAL POLICY

26—01 The EEC Treaty declares in its preamble that the Contracting Parties were "anxious to strengthen the unity of their economies and to ensure their harmonious development by reducing the differences existing between the various regions and the backwardness of the less favoured regions." Yet there are no explicit provisions in the Treaty regarding the establishment of a coherent regional policy. Such a policy became increasingly necessary following the end of the transitional period, bearing in mind that the loss of control on the part of Member States to protect deprived areas through traditional measures such as import controls and the loss of some power positively to assist such regions, would slowly lead to an even greater discrepancy between poor and wealthy areas; and as already mentioned, the reduction of such divergencies was to be a Community concern. Furthermore, in the event of the formation of an economic and monetary union, a *regional* policy would be vital since *economic* policy would not of itself be able to take regional (state) variations into account to a significant extent. Hence, from the end of 1969 onwards the Commission began to make proposals for the development of a Community regional policy. These proposals found support from the Council in the Paris Summit of October 1972, and Community involvement in a substantial way in regional policy really dates from that point.

I The Instruments of Policy

(1) The European Regional Development Fund

Legal framework

26—02   The Commission was asked to draw up a report analysing the regional problems existing in the enlarged Community,[1] which was published in May 1973.[2] At the same time a regulation was drawn up aimed at setting up a Regional Development Fund and a Committee which would administer a common policy and co-ordinate national policies. Unfortunately agreement could not be reached in the Council by the original deadline of December 1973 but towards the end of 1974 an "operational decision" was taken and in 1975 a regional fund and regional committee

---

[1] 7th General Report, 1973 points 291 *et seq.*
[2] Bulletin EC Suppt. 8/73.

400

were set up by Regulation 724/75[3] and Decision 75/185[4] respectively.

The original fund totalled 1,300m ua, to be paid out over the three years 1975-8 (300m ua in 1975, 500m ua in 1976 and 500m ua for 1977) and had to be distributed in accordance with national quotas. In 1978, a new fund fell to be agreed henceforth on an annual basis. The new budgetary procedures in the Parliament meant that that body was in a position to have the final say (subject to the "ceiling") on the amount to go into the ERDF for 1979, this being a non-obligatory item. Despite the use of the conciliation procedure, the Council could not agree with the Parliament's amendments to the amount and for a while the two sides were deadlocked. Eventually a compromise was reached,[5] with the Parliament accepting a smaller sum but compensation being made through the interest relief under the new European Monetary System.[6] The 1979 regulation[7] also provided for a change in national quotas and the introduction of a 5 per cent. non-quota section.

Administration of the fund

5—03   Aid is only available in respect of areas qualifying for national regional assistance,[8] but in respect of the 5 per cent. non-quota section aid may be given for other areas, provided that the Member State concerned has also given, or gives assistance. The Fund contributes to the national programmes within strictly defined percentage limits, usually a maximum of 20 per cent. for investment in industrial, artisan or service activities and up to 30 per cent. for infrastructure. The investments themselves must exceed 50,000 ECU and be designed to achieve creation or maintenance of at least 10 jobs (in the case of industrial investment) or to fulfil infrastructure projects carried out by local authorities. Investments may benefit from the Fund's assistance only if they form part of a regional development programme submitted to the Commission, and this programme will contribute to the correction of imbalances within the common market.[9] Applications for aid can be made only by national authorities and the money is paid to them: in the case of the United Kingdom this is the Department of Trade for private sector applications and the Department of the

[3] O.J. 1975, L73/1, amended by Reg. 214/79, O.J. 1979, L35/1; consolidation O.J. 1979, C36.
[4] O.J. 1975, L73/47.
[5] A supplementary budget was adopted: O.J. 1979, L124/1.
[6] *Supra*, para. 24–23.
[7] Regulation 214/79 O.J. 1979, L35/1, amended by Reg. 3325/80, O.J. 1980, L349/10 laying down the national quotas taking into account Greek accession.
[8] Regulation 724/75, Art. 3. See also Commission Opinion 97/534 and Recommendation 79/535 on national regional development programmes, dealing with form, presentation and content, O.J. 1979, L143/7 and 9.
[9] Regulation 724/75, Article 6 as amended.

Environment for public infrastructure projects. Decisions on aid are usually taken in batches during the year[10] after consultation with the Fund Committee. This procedure is clearly designed to minimise the "visibility" of the Community fund, but from 1977 publicity hoardings on the sites of major infrastructure projects were permitted, and the Commission carries out spot checks to make sure Community money is being properly employed.[11]

Research

26—04   The inception of the regional policy entailed a great deal of groundwork research. The initial 1973 study already mentioned was followed by many projects covering such matters as the building up of information through the preparation of harmonised employment statistics, analysis of investments in less prosperous regions, and pilot studies and specific studies requested by Member States for given regions. In 1976 the Regional Policy Committee set up a working group with the task of preparing a co-ordinated programme of research, and the importance of studies was under-lined by 1977 guidelines.[12] In 1978 the Commission was drawing up long term study programmes in collaboration with the regional policy committee, giving priority to the tasks set forth in the guidelines.

(2) The ECSC Funds

26—05   The coal and steel industries originally formed the basis of a separate and earlier Treaty because they were regarded as the basic industries in the peace- and war-time economies of the Member States. Since that time they have been in decline throughout Western Europe and this has led to a decline in the prosperity of the regions in which they were based. Thus the present malaise in these industries might be regarded as essentially a regional problem; and the involvement of the Communities is all the more important because the problems have a natural tendency to straddle national borders. The ECSC Treaty in Article 2 aims at raising the standard of living in Member States and at ensuring the most rational dis-tribution of products at the highest possible level of productivity, while safeguarding continuity of employment and avoiding the provoking of fundamental and persistent disturbances in the economies of Member States.

Substantive powers relating to regional activity are contained in Article 54 ECSC, providing for assistance in the form of loans and guarantees to the financing of works and installations which contribute directly and primarily to increasing production, or facilitating the marketing of products over which the Commission

[10] See, *e.g.* Regs. 2615–9/80, O.J. 1980, L271.
[11] 11th General Report (1977) point 275.
[12] *Infra*, note 15.

has jurisdiction. The funds here are raised on the one hand from the levy imposed by the Commission on the coal and steel industries and on the other by loans floated on national financial markets. More significant, however, is Article 56 which enables the Commission, on application by the governments concerned, to finance new projects and to provide re-adaptation where regional problems appear as a result of unemployment. As originally drafted, this article was too narrow in scope to deal with the grave structural crisis in 1958, and was revised then successfully under the Article 95 procedure of the ECSC Treaty. Funds are also available for housebuilding and modernisation of dwellings for workers.

26—06   Applications for industrial loans and for grants for technical assistance are made directly to the Commission (Luxembourg). Housebuilding loans applications are made through employers and then centralised by regional committees which determine priorities and make financing proposals. The Commission makes the final decisions. In other cases applications are made through the national ministries involved.

(3) Other EEC provisions

26—07   A number of other Treaty provisions have something to say regarding regional matters. Perhaps the most directly relevant are the provisions setting up European Investment Bank (Article 129 *et seq*), the provisions relating to structural policy within the agricultural policy, and the Social Fund.

The Investment Bank makes or guarantees loans to private undertakings or public authorities for industrial investment and public infrastructure projects, and the promotion of regional development is given priority. Normally the Bank will not finance more than half the cost; loans are generally for 7 - 12 years, and normally the minimum lent is 1 million ECU. Smaller-scale projects may be financed through global loans given to intermediary banks.

Interest rates are close to those prevailing on the capital markets since the Bank finances itself by borrowing there, and normally no reduction in rates is permissible. However, the ERDF provides for a small reduction on interest rates in relation to regional infrastructure grants by making up the difference. Applications may be made direct to the Bank or through other banks.

26—08   The agricultural policy, of course, provides for structural reorganisation, and this may be regarded as a regional matter since, like the coal and steel industries, agriculture is essentially a regional activity and in some cases is the only significant activity in a depressed region (such as the Mezzogiorno in Italy). The "guidance" given to agriculture under the EAGGF is considered *supra* in the chapter on agriculture. The European Social Fund and the provisions on government aids to industry, which both have regional policy aspects, are also considered elsewhere.[13]

Finally, the introduction of the EMS has important consequences for regional development, since some countries, notably Ireland and southern Italy, virtually constitute development regions in their own right and would be bound to suffer from holding to a stable rate of exchange if their economies were not capable of sustaining the rate. Thus it was agreed that a transfer of resources through "interest relief" should take place, amounting in each case to some 200m ECU.[14]

II Policy of the Community

26—09   The first significant step towards a co-ordinated regional policy at the Community level was taken in June 1978 when the Council agreed in principle to a resolution dealing both with the reforms to the fund mentioned above and with a common approach to the guidelines for Community regional policy.[15] The agreement entailed three actions in the direction of a common policy:

the establishment of a comprehensive system of analysis and policy formulation. This requires the Commission to prepare a regular report on the social and economic development of the regions of the Community and to present it to the Council every two and-a-half years; the Council would use this as a basis for discussing the priorities and guidelines proposed by the Commission.

regional impact assessment of Community policies. Here the objective is to ensure that the regional impact of other policies is taken into account in their formulation.

co-ordination of national regional policies, leading to a balanced distribution of economic activities from a Community point of view.

26—10   Despite these promising steps, a truly Community policy remains a long way off. The quota system of the regional fund coupled with the award of grants on the basis of (albeit now more co-ordinated) national policies and regional demarcations means that the Fund is still largely only a device for a very small transfer of resources from richer to poorer Member States. Furthermore, the existence of the various different mechanisms for granting aid, with different objectives and bodies administering them in some cases, and largely directed by national governments through their control of applications means that it is still not possible to regard them as implementing a single common policy. The non-quota

[13] *Supra*, chapters 25 and 21, respectively.
[14] *Supra*, para. 24–17.
[15] Bulletin EC. 6 1978, points 1.2.1–1.2.9.; Bulletin EC Suppt. 2/77 and Council Resolution of February 7, 1979, O.J. 1979, C36/10.

section of the Fund, the only truly *Community* fund for regional purposes, was a significant step in the direction of such a policy but remains a small element in the overall fund.

Chapter 27

ENVIRONMENTAL POLICY

Background

27—01 Member States have for a long time exercised control over particular forms of industrial pollution, but there was in many cases no general policy aimed at protecting or improving the environment. The position is now changing. Environmental movements sprang up in the 1960s, prompted by a general realisation that whilst material prosperity grew and flourished, irreparable harm was being caused to the environment in many ways, and that as a result economic growth might actually be causing a decline in living standards on levels other than a purely economic one. Since the EEC Treaty aims at improving the living standards of the peoples of the Member States primarily through economic growth,[1] it became clear, at the end of the transitional period, when a fundamental appraisal of the future direction of the common market had to be made, that the Community should have its own policy in this field if it was to avoid serious confrontation with national environmental policy through an over zealous and blinkered pursuit of purely economic aims. Hence, at the 1972 Paris summit the Member States took the bold step of declaring their desire for a Community policy in this field and asked the Commission to draw up an "action programme" which would form the basis of the policy. In legal terms, this step was founded largely on a gloss on the interpretation of Article 2 of the Treaty with the aid of Articles 100 and 235: the legal foundation for Community action remains even today a matter of controversy,[2] but the growth of legislation since 1973 is a reality which even the fiercest opponents of Community action have to concede.

27—02 The action programme demanded by the Council of Ministers and Member States was produced by the Commission in 1973 and adopted by the Council on 22nd November.[3] It comprised essentially a statement of general principles, a framework for

---

[1] Article 2 EEC.

[2] House of Lords Select Committee on the European Communities, 22nd Report 1978–79 and minutes of July 3, 1979 (HL (68)). Although see now Case 92/79 *Commission* v. *Italy* [1980] E.C.R. 1115, 1122: "It is by no means ruled out that provisions on the environment may be based upon Article 100 of the Treaty. Provisions which are made necessary by considerations relating to the environment and health may be a burden upon the undertakings to which they apply and if there is no harmonisation of national provisions on the matter, competition may be appreciably distorted."

[3] O.J. 1973, C 112/1.

action and a detailed timetable in respect of each type of action. In many cases the timetables were not met,[4] but much was achieved. A second action programme was adopted in 1977[5] which largely aimed to carry on the work envisaged in the first programme with some elaborations.

The Community Policy

27—03 At the outset it must be remembered that although undoubtedly the Community is implementing its own policy, the Member States have their own policies (now highly developed in some cases), so that to a large extent one is talking about "harmonisation" of national laws. Moreover, the enforcement of legislation remains in the hands of Member States. It was therefore necessary that a system be set up which would allow the Commission to review national laws already in existence and also to monitor new laws. A survey of national legislation on the environment was commissioned,[6] and the Member States agreed to supply information on new laws as a matter of course.[7]

The 1973 action programme's framework for action[8] comprised three main heads:

1. action to reduce and prevent pollution and nuisances;
2. action to improve the environment
3. common action at the international level.

As the third head relates simply to "external" action concerning the first two heads, the Community's achievements at the international level will be examined in those contexts.

1. Reduction and prevention of pollution and nuisances

27—04 Because action in this area is so recent, much background research was required and continues to be necessary on procedures and criteria for measuring pollution and nuisances, for gathering of information on the environment, and evaluating the economic impact on industry of environmental legislation. At this general level, a decision of 1976[9] set up a common procedure for the establishing and constant updating of an inventory of sources of information on the environment; a 1975 decision established a common procedure for the exchange of information between surveillance and monitoring networks relating to some forms of atmospheric pollution.[10] The programme adopts the principle that the polluter pays the costs of control, etc, and more concrete

---

[4] See "State of the Environment: First Report" (1977), p. 10.
[5] O.J. 1977, C 139/1, (for 1977 to 1981).
[6] Published by Graham & Trotman, 1976 for the Commission.
[7] Agreement of March 5, 1973, O.J. 1973, C 9.
[8] *Supra* note 3.
[9] Decision 76/161, O.J. 1976, L31/8.
[10] Decision 75/441, O.J. 1975, L 194/32.

form was given to this by a 1975 recommendation[11] which lays down common rules, regardless of where the pollution has its effect. Recommendation 79/3[12] sets out methods of evaluating the cost of pollution control to industry.

Besides the general research mentioned above, the programme provided for a great deal of research into pollution of various kinds, and particularly regarding the iron and steel, chemical and pulp and paper industries. Initial framework decisions were adopted in 1973[13] followed by subsequent decisions extending and amending them[14] and in 1976 a new research programme.[15] Decisions setting up "concerted projects" have covered such areas as the analysis of micropollutants in water,[16] the physico-chemical behaviour of atmospheric pollutants[17] and the treatment of sewage sludge.[18] Action has been taken to disseminate the conclusions of such research.[19] A more general effort has been made to try and make the population more aware of environmental problems.

27–05   The programme recognised that the control of pollution and nuisances involves a number of different types of action. First, many products which are usually regarded as indispensable to life in a modern industrial society have harmful effects which must be minimised. In this respect many of the directives adopted pursuant to the harmonisation of legislation provisions have been adapted to take environmental impact into account, and others have been adopted with that object in mind. In particular, the Council has amended the directive on the classification, packaging and labelling of dangerous substances[20] so as to introduce a requirement that new substances be notified to national authorities before being placed on the market. The purpose of this notification is to permit assessment of the impact on the environment of such substances.

Secondly, it is necessary to lay down quality objectives in respect of various natural resources which may be polluted by a great many different harmful agents.

Directives under this head have concentrated on quality standards for water, *i.e.* the quality of:

- surface water intended for drinking water[21];

[11] O.J. 1975, L194/1.
[12] O.J. 1979, L5/28.
[13] Decisions 73/126, O.J. 1973, L153/11; 73/174, O.J. 1973, L189/30; 73/180, O.J. 1973, L189/43.
[14] Decisions 75/514, O.J. 1975, L231/19; 75/518, O.J. 1975, L231/27.
[15] Decision 76/311, O.J. 1976, L74/36.
[16] Decision 78/888, O.J. 1978, L311/6 (cost project: see also Appendix 3, Part 1).
[17] Decision 78/889, O.J. 1978, L311/10 (cost project).
[18] Decision 79/311, O.J. 1979, L72/35 (cost project).
[19] Regulation 2380/74, O.J. 1974, L255/1.
[20] 67/548, J.O. 1967, L196/1; O.J. 1967, 234. 6th Amendment Directive 79/831, O.J. 1979, L259/10.
[21] Directive 75/440, O.J. 1975, L194/26.

- bathing water[22];
- freshwater supporting fish life[23];
- shellfish waters[24];
- water intended for human consumption.[25]

Attention is now also being turned to quality standards for the atmosphere, with the adoption of a directive on air quality standards for sulphur dioxide and suspended particulate matter in the atmosphere.[26]

7—06 The exchange of information on atmospheric pollution mentioned above aims at achieving, eventually, qualities of purity in the air, and discussions on air quality standards for lead were converted into a programme for the biological screening of the population for lead.[27]

Thirdly, the control and prevention of pollution by waste and other discharges naturally received a high priority. Directives have been adopted on the disposal of waste oils,[28] waste in general (a framework directive),[29] waste in the titanium dioxide industry[30] ("red mud") toxic and dangerous waste,[31] and the disposal of polychlorinated biphenyls and terphenyls.[32] The Commission has also concerned itself with the recycling of waste.

The discharge of oil by accident or deliberately at sea has been the subject of a resolution setting up an action programme following the Amoco Cadiz disaster off the Brittany coast.[33] A number of conventions governing marine pollution and the pollution of rivers from various sources have been concluded by the Community or are close to conclusion[34] and the Community is represented in a number of international organisations dealing with this problem. The discharge of dangerous substances into the aquatic environment (Community internal waters) is dealt with by Directive 76/464.[35]

---

[22] Directive 76/160, O.J. 1976, L31/1.
[23] Directive 78/659, O.J. 1978, L222/1.
[24] Directive 79/923, O.J. 1979, L281/47.
[25] Directive 80/778 O.J. 1980, L229/11.
[26] Directive 80/779 O.J. 1980, L229/30.
[27] Directive 77/312, O.J. 1977, L105/10.
[28] Directive 75/439, O.J. 1975, L194/23.
[29] Directive 75/442, O.J. 1975, L194/39.
[30] Directive 78/176, O.J. 1978, L54/19.
[31] Directive 78/319, O.J. 1978, L84/43.
[32] Directive 76/403, O.J. 1976, L108/41.
[33] O.J. 1978, C 162.
[34] Decision 75/437 & 438 concluding the Convention for the Prevention of Marine Pollution from land-based sources, O.J. 1975, L194/5 & 22; Decision 77/585 concluding the Convention and Protocol for the protection of the Mediterranean from pollution by dumping, O.J. 1977, L240/1; Decision 77/586 concluding the Convention for the protection of the Rhine against chemical pollution, O.J. 1977, L240/35. The Council has also recommended ratification by Member States of the 1973 MARPOL Convention for the prevention of marine pollution from ships O.J. 1978, L194/17.
[35] Directive 76/464, O.J. 1976, L129/23.

A more specific directive on the protection of groundwater against pollution by certain dangerous substances has been adopted as envisaged by Article 4 of Directive 76/464.[36]

So far as the atmosphere is concerned, directives have been issued to date dealing with noise (sound levels of motorcycles,[37] noise emission of construction plant and equipment[38] and noise emissions from subsonic aircraft[39]) and concerning chlorofluoro-carbons in the environment (relating primarily to aerosol sprays),[40] and to some extent lead (lead content in petrol).[41]

It should be remembered, fourthly, that the Communities have an involvement in the nuclear industry through Euratom and a good deal has been done in the direction of protecting both workers and the public from the dangers of radiation.[42]

2. Improvement of the environment

27–07   The improvement of the environment involves such matters as protection of the natural environment, environmental problems caused by the depletion of natural resources, urban development and improvement of amenities and improvement of the working environment.

So far legislative action has concentrated on the first of the areas mentioned above. Even before the adoption of the 1973 programme the Commission had already submitted draft directives on mountain and hill farming and farming on poor areas.[43] These have been followed by a number of other measures: action to support afforestation,[44] the protection of wild birds[45] (with listings of protected species, rules on marketing of certain species and methods of killing and capture); and residues of pesticides.[46] Other directives already mentioned may also be regarded as con-tributing to the protection of the natural environment (*e.g.* the purity of water intended to support fish life). The Commission has been proceeding with an ecological mapping project.[47]

---

[36] Directive 80/68, O.J. 1980, L20/43.
[37] Directive 77/212, O.J. 1977, L66/33.
[38] Directive 79/113, O.J. 1979, L33/15.
[39] Directive 80/51, O.J. 1980, L18/26.
[40] Directive 80/372, O.J. 1980, L90/45.
[41] Directive 78/611, O.J. 1978, L197/19.
[42] Resolution on energy and the environment, O.J. 1975, C168/2. Decision 75/406, O.J. 1975, L178/28 adopting an indirect action programme for the management and storage of radioactive waste. Directive 76/579, O.J. 1976, L187/1 laying down revised basic safety standards for the health protection of the general public and workers against the dangers of ionising radiation, as amended by Directive 79/343, O.J. 1979, L83/18. Decision 76/309, O.J. 1976, L74/32 adopting a research and training programme (1976–80) for the EAEC in the field of biology and health protection.
[43] Directive 75/268, O.J. 1975, L128/1.
[44] Regulation 269/79, O.J. L38/1.
[45] Directive 79/409, O.J. 1979, L103/1.
[46] Directive 76/895, O.J. 1976, L340/26.
[47] Thirteenth General Report (1979), point 282.

Action in the other areas has been largely concentrated on research up till now. A European Foundation for the Improvement of Living and Working Conditions was established in Dublin in 1975.

Chapter 28

ENERGY AND THE COMMUNITIES

28—01   The production and use of energy in the Communities was a major
pre-occupation of the "founding fathers," both in 1950-52 when
the ECSC Treaty was concluded (coal being both an energy source
as well as a raw material in the steel industry) and in 1956-57
when the EEC and Euratom Treaties were concluded. The EEC
Treaty nevertheless contains nothing specific in relation to energy
whilst the other two Treaties deal respectively with coal and
nuclear power, but without any clear direction as to an integrated
energy policy. During the 1960s, with plentiful and cheap supplies
of oil, this meant that both the latter Treaties really took a "back
seat," Euratom in particular, and all attention was focused on the
EEC Treaty. At the end of the transitional period the Member
States became increasingly aware that some form of common
action in the energy area generally would be needed chiefly
because of the over-dependence on imported oil. Thus at the Paris
summit of 1972 the Member States requested the Commission to
draw up a comprehensive set of proposals for a common energy
policy. The legal basis of the action at least by the Commission
was, as in other areas, to be the general objectives of the EEC
Treaty plus Articles 100 and 235. The Council has sometimes
acted *qua* Council of Ministers and sometimes *qua* European
Council. The existence of the other Treaties with limited specific
powers meant that the legal grounds for common action were
probably stronger here than, *e.g.* in the fields of environmental or
regional policy. The Community in the meantime was being
overtaken by events. The change in the oil supply situation created
by the new-found unity and resulting concerted actions of the oil-
producing (OPEC) countries together with the Middle East conflict in 1973, led to shortages of crude oil and rising domestic
prices. The formation of a common energy policy ceased to be
merely desirable and became a necessity.

28—02   The Copenhagen summit in the autumn of 1973 failed to
produce a solid front in the face of pressure by the Middle East
suppliers. Consequently the Member States each adopted their
own measures for dealing with the crisis. The Netherlands found
itself boycotted altogether for a while by Arab suppliers. Moreover
the Council began by rejecting the Commission's first set of

proposals.[1] A second set was eventually adopted,[2] but progress on implementing them has been slow and it was considered by 1978 that the objectives were unlikely to be achieved by the 1985 deadline.[3] The progress that has been made is outlined below. The general strategy will be examined first, and then the measures actually taken will be outlined.

I The Energy Strategy of the Community[4]

(a) Energy conservation

3—03 The strategy here aims at reducing the growth of energy consumption without reducing the growth of the gross national product, the elimination of wastage being the chief instrument. The aim was to reduce Community energy consumption by 1985 to 10 per cent. below 1973 estimates.

(b) Types of energy source

3—04 The strategy envisaged a 50 per cent. dependence on nuclear energy by the end of the century. This would entail the encouragement of electricity consumption which should reach 35 per cent. by 1985 with nuclear energy covering half the supply. Oil consumption should be confined to specific uses such as motor fuel and for petrochemicals so that by 1985 it would be at a level barely higher than the 1973 level, and the rest of electricity demand would be covered by solid fuels, coal in particular, output of which should remain at 250 million metric tonnes. This would require considerable improvements in production and preparation techniques. Emphasis should also be placed on the use of natural gas which by 1985 could cover a quarter of energy needs. However, because the demand for oil would remain high for a long time, encouragement should be given to prospecting for and developing domestic resources. Other energy sources such as solar power it was recognised would not be significant even by the end of the century.

(c) Measures for dealing with shortages

8—05 The strategy envisaged the consolidation of measures designed to ensure buffer stocks of oil,[5] and a comprehensive programme to build up information on imports and exports of oil and on prices. Competition in the supply of oil should be strictly enforced:

---

[1] 9th General Report 1974, point 335.
[2] "Towards a new energy policy strategy for the Community," (June 5, 1974), Suppt. 4/74 and Bulletin EC 5–1974, points 1201–1212. Resolution of the Council, September 17, 1974, Bulletin EC 9–1974, points 1401 *et seq.* O.J. 1975, C153/1, 2, 6 (implementation).
[3] See 12th General Report 1978, point 375.
[4] Bulletin EC Suppt. 4/74.
[5] *Infra.* para. 28–12.

prices in oil-derived products should be "harmonised" and transparency achieved so as to ensure that competition is Community-wide. Seasonal swings in demand should also be ironed out.

(d) Foreign relations

28—06   The strategy did not envisage a single approach to actual trading arrangements with third countries (suppliers) but did argue that bilateral agreements should be subject to prior consultation at Community level. The Community countries should try to speak with a single voice in multilateral negotiations.

(e) Research

28—07   The development of the strategy would necessitate research into alternative sources, into prospecting for conventional sources internally (uranium, oil in particular), and into the technology of energy creation (such as for coal). The strategy was amended later particularly in relation to the oil consumption target, which was reduced downwards to 15 per cent. from 10 per cent.[6]

The amended strategy outlined above was largely reiterated by the European Council at its 1978 and 1979 meetings. Besides re-emphasising the overall goals, the Council resolved that by 1985 dependence on imported oil should be reduced to 50 per cent., net oil imports should be limited and the ratio between the rate of increase in energy consumption and the rate of increase in gross domestic production should be reduced to 0.8. The Bremen meeting in July 1978 also stressed the need for worldwide co-operation.

28—08   Two Council Resolutions of June 9, 1980[7] take note of a Commission Communication of June 14, 1979, on "Community energy objectives for 1990 and convergence of the policies of the Member States." The first resolution recalls the 1978 and 1979 European Council conclusions and goes on to state that the adequate and secure availability of energy on a satisfactory economic basis is a prerequisite for the pursuit of the Community's economic and social objectives. It describes as essential more progress in the priority areas such as energy conservation, rational use of energy and the reduction of oil consumption and imports. For the purposes of enabling the Community to "determine the convergence of national policies in relation to Community objectives" the operative paragraphs call on Member States to submit their annual energy plans up to 1990 to the Commission. The Commission will examine these plans in the light of guidelines for the Community as a whole, which confirm a 0.7 average ratio of the rate of growth in gross primary energy consumption to the

---

[6] Bulletin EC 11–1974, points 2266 *et seq.*
[7] O.J. 1980, C149/1 and 3.

rate of growth in GDP. In addition these guidelines aim at reduction of Community oil consumption to 40 per cent. of gross primary energy consumption; coverage of 70 to 75 per cent. of primary energy requirements from coal or nuclear generated electricity; encouragement of use of renewable (alternative) energy sources and pursuit of an energy pricing policy aimed at achieving Community energy objectives. The Commission is invited to submit an annual report and to make any necessary recommendations and proposals.

The second resolution,[8] concerning new lines of action by the Community in the field of energy saving, expressly approves the Community target of an 0.7 average ratio of the rate of growth in gross primary energy consumption to the rate of growth in GDP. It goes on to propose guidelines to be adopted for national energy-saving programmes and calls for speeding up of work on measurement of energy consumption and performance standards, especially for domestic equipment.

II Progress in Implementation of the Strategies

28—09   The co-ordination of action on energy was improved by the setting up of an Energy Committee, composed of representatives of the Member States and chaired by the Commission.[9] As with the Regional Policy Committee it acts as a medium between Community and Member States in supplying information and drafting proposals.

(a) Energy conservation

28—10   On June 26, 1975, the Council passed a resolution[10] on a short-term target for the reduction of oil consumption by 9 per cent. as compared with 1973. A series of Council regulations in 1976 dealt with ways of promoting the rational use of energy by promoting the thermal insulation of buildings, improving the heating systems of existing buildings, better driving habits, better use of energy in public transport and by the suitable labelling of household appliances.[11] The latter was eventually transformed into a directive designed to help the public choose energy efficient appliances.[12] In December 1977 the Council adopted a directive on the performance, maintenance and regulation of heat generators and the insulation of the distribution system in new buildings.[13] In October of that year three recommendations were also adopted

---

[8] *Ibid.*
[9] Decision of 5.2.74: this decision does not appear to have been published in the Official Journal.
[10] Bulletin EC 6–1975, point 2280.
[11] Recommendations 76/492–6, O.J. 1976, L140.
[12] Directive 79/530, O.J. 1979, L145/1 and implementing Directive 79/531, O.J. 1979, L145/7 (electric oven).
[13] Directive 78/170, O.J. 1978, L52/32.

relating to: the regulating of the level of heating, the efficient use
of energy in industrial undertakings and the setting up of national
advisory bodies to be consulted on combined heat and power
production in district heating.[14] The Energy Committee was
directed to hold meetings devoted exclusively to conservation.
A decision of November 7, 1977,[15] permits the Commission to
set up a target for reducing the consumption of petroleum products by up to 10 per cent. for a period of two months in the
event of supply difficulties in a Member State. In 1978 the Council
was finally persuaded to give financial support for demonstration
projects in the field of energy saving.[16]

These very modest achievements are unlikely to make a great
contribution to the target set at Bremen, or in the earlier strategy.

(b) Types of energy source

28—11   The policy described in the strategy to develop alternative
energy sources to oil has met with a little more enthusiasm in
terms of action at Community level. Perhaps the most significant
development in the field of nuclear energy so far has been the
Council decision of March 29, 1977, authorising the Commission
to borrow up to 500 million ua to help finance the building of
new nuclear power stations.[17] Other measures to further the
nuclear power policy have been limited, but in 1975 the Parliament authorised a grant of 1 million ua towards prospecting for
uranium in Europe, (at that time acting against the wishes of the
Council) and a larger sum (5 million ua) was granted in 1977.
Nothing of significance has been done to encourage the proposed
switch to electricity although a resolution was adopted in 1978 to
the effect that the Commission should be informed about siting of
new power stations.[18] In order to reduce the use of oil in power
stations, the Council in 1975 adopted a directive, which requires
Member States to subject the building of oil-fired power plants
to official approval, and to restrict that approval to specific,
clearly defined cases.[19] At the same time the use of natural gas
was to be similarly restricted.[20] Positive measures to stimulate the
use of solid fuels have taken the form of support for coal prices.[21]
Aid for coking coal production and sales (primarily in connection
with the steel industry) would, it was hoped, also help to create a

[14] Recommendations 77/712, 3, 4, O.J. 1977, L295.
[15] Decision 77/706, O.J. 1977, L292/9. Commission implementing Dec. 79/639, O.J. 1979,
L183/1.
[16] Reg. 1303/78, O.J. 1978, L158/6 and Reg. 725/79, O.J. 1979, L93/1.
[17] Decision 77/270, O.J. 1977, L88/9.
[18] Bulletin EC 10–1978, point 2.1.113.
[19] Directive 75/405, O.J. 1975, L178/26.
[20] Directive 75/404, O.J. 1975, L178/24.
[21] Decision 72/443/ECSC, O.J. 1972, L297/45 on the alignment of prices for the sale of
coal in the common market.

healthy coal industry.[22] Finally, in 1978 the Council adopted a framework regulation on the granting of financial support for projects to exploit alternative energy sources.[23]

(c) Measures for dealing with shortages

8—12 Action had been taken long before the development of the energy strategy in 1973-75 in this field. In 1968 a directive had been adopted imposing an obligation on Member States to maintain minimum stocks of crude oil and petrol[24] for 65 days' consumption. This was amended in 1972 to 90 days.[25] Minimum stocks requirements now apply also to fossil fuel for power stations.

Beginning in 1972 a system has been established requiring Member States to notify the Commission of imports of crude oil and natural gas, and of investment projects in the energy area.[26] In 1973 the Council adopted a directive on measures to mitigate the effects of difficulties in the supply of crude oil and petroleum products.[27] This directive required Member States to give all necessary authority for drawing on reserve stocks, to impose restrictions on consumption and to regulate prices. The Commission would be required to convene a meeting of representatives of the Member States so as to co-ordinate such action. In view of the urgency the directive allowed the Member States only two months to introduce the necessary measures.

8—13 Two types of measure can be discerned in the various acts adopted since 1973 to help deal with temporary shortages. First, a monitoring system has been introduced[28] which requires Member States to record all imports of crude oil and petroleum product by a registration system. The information is then passed on to the Commission. A slightly different monitoring system also operates as regards prices, enabling the sharing of such information amongst the Member States.[29]

Secondly, in order to improve security of supplies, and in development of the 1973 directives mentioned above, Member States have been required to introduce a licensing system, under which intra-Community exports of crude oil and petroleum

[22] Decision 73/287/ECSC, O.J. 1973, L259/36, last amended and extended to December 31, 1981, by Dec. 1613/77, O.J. 1977, L180/8.
[23] Reg. 1302/78, O.J. 1978, L158/3 and Regs. 726–729/79, O.J. 1979, L93.
[24] Directive 68/414, J.O. 1968, L308/14; O.J. 1968, 586. See also Decision 68/416, J.O. 1968, L308/19; O.J. 1968, 591.
[25] Directive 72/425, J.O. 1972, L291/154; O.J. 1972, (December 28–30) 69.
[26] Regulation 1055, 6/72, J.O. 1972, L120 and implementing Reg. 1068/73, O.J. 1973, L113/1 and 3254/74, O.J. 1974, L349/1 and 2677/75, O.J. 1975, L275/1.
[27] Directive 73/238, O.J. 1973, L228/1.
[28] See now Regs. 1893/79, O.J. 1979, L220/1; 2592/79, O.J. 1979, L297/1; 649/80, O.J. 1980, L73/1.
[29] Dir. 76/491, O.J. 1976, L140/4 and Dec. 77/190, O.J. 1977, L61/34, amended by Dec. 79/607, O.J. 1979, L170/1.

products are to be licensed with the possibility of withdrawal of licences in times of shortage.[30] For exports to third countries there is a notification requirement only, which applies to quantities of 100,000 metric tons or more of crude oil and petroleum products or natural gas equivalent exported by a person or undertaking in one year.[31]

The Commission took action against a number of oil companies which it claimed had abused a dominant position during the Dutch crisis of 1973-74, but the Court annulled the decision on the ground that no dominant position existed where, because of shortages, retailers became wholly dependent on their regular suppliers and could not have obtained oil from other sources.[32] This action by the Commission can be seen as an attempt to implement the strategy's aim to encourage competition.

Tariff concessions under the CCT were made for petroleum products to prevent shortages arising because of tariff barriers.[33]

(d) Research

28—14   A Community energy research and development programme was adopted in 1975.[34] A substantial number of research projects have been authorised in the period since 1973 in such fields as nuclear physics, hydrocarbons and the use of solar energy, and recycling of raw materials, but perhaps the most significant has been the decision establishing the Joint European Torus ("JET") nuclear fusion project at Culham in Oxfordshire.[35]

---

[30] Decision 77/186, O.J. 1977, L61/23. And Decision 78/890, O.J. 1978, L311/13 in application of Decision 77/186. Decision 79/397, O.J. 1979, L97/15 (systems of authorisation for trade in crude oil provided for initially by Decisions 79/126 and 79/135, O.J. 1979, L32/39.
[31] Reg. 388/75, O.J. 1975, L45/1 and Reg. 2678/75, O.J. 1975, L275/8.
[32] Case 77/77 *Benzine en Petroleum Handelsmaatschappij BV* v. *Commission* [1978] E.C.R. 1513.
[33] Regulation 1773/77, O.J. 1977, L195/5.
[34] Decision 75/510, O.J. 1975, L231/1 amended by Dec. 77/54, O.J. 1977, L10/28. A programme of research into the use of solar energy and recycling of raw materials was adopted at the same time Dec. 75/517, O.J. 1975, L231/25, amending Decision 73/176, O.J. 1973, L189/34. For hydrocarbons sector see Reg. 3056/73, O.J. 1973, L312/1.
[35] Decision 78/471 O.J. 1973, L151/10.

Part 6

EXTERNAL RELATIONS

Chapter 29

EXTERNAL RELATIONS

Introductory

9—01 Article 210 provides that "The Community shall have legal personality." As the Court held in Case 22/70 *Commission* v. *Council (AETR)*[1]:

> "This provision means that in its external relations the Community enjoys the capacity to establish contractual links with third countries over the whole field of objectives defined in Part One of the Treaty."

This Community international legal personality, which is reflected in Community capacity or competence to act in international relations, derives from a limitation of sovereignty or a transfer of powers from the Member State to the Community, as elaborated in Case 6/64 *Costa* v. *ENEL*.[2] The Member States who are the constituent parts of the Community are therefore represented by the Community where competence exists. In most cases this competence is an exclusive one in the sense that the transfer of powers to the Community precludes the Member States from acting concurrently or so as to impede Community action (*infra*, paras. 29-43 *et seq.*).

For most purposes the Commission represents the Community, in accordance with Article 211. However, agreements are concluded by the Council (Articles 114 and 228, *infra*). In somewhat exceptional cases, the Member States may represent the Community (Case 22/70 *AETR*, *infra*, para. 29-49).

9—02 Having international legal personality, the Community is a subject of public international law.[3] As such, provisions of international law may have the effect of binding it directly. Thus the Court held in *International Fruit Company*[4] that the provisions of the GATT have the effect of binding the Community, within the area of Community competence. This is because the Member States were parties and by conferring commercial policy powers on the Community were deemed to wish to bind the Community by the same obligations under the GATT. Thus, no concept of

---

[1] [1971] E.C.R. 263.
[2] [1964] E.C.R. 585.
[3] See, *e.g.* G le Tallec, *The Commercial Policy of the EEC,* (1976) ICLQ 732, pp; 732 to 734.
[4] Cases 21 to 24/72 *International Fruit Company* v. *Produktschap voor Groenten en Fruit* [1972] E.C.R. 1219.

succession is involved. The Court held that rules of international law binding the Community may be invoked to contest the validity of Community rules, provided the international law rule is directly applicable.[5] In several cases in which this type of question has been raised, it has nevertheless concluded that the rule of international law in question is not directly applicable.[6] Community contractual obligations have been treated for most purposes as being no different from other Community acts.[7] These quasi-contractual aspects of international law are to be distinguished from the question whether the principles of international law and notably the law of treaties form part of the sources of Community law. This is considered *supra*, para. 6-29.

29–03   By expressly referring to a corresponding provision in the Treaty of Rome, the Community is regarded as undertaking precisely the same obligation in an agreement with third countries.[8] It may be, nevertheless, that the content of the obligation will vary because of the manner in which it is envisaged that it be implemented.[9] The Member States are under no obligation to extend to third countries the binding principles governing their relations *inter se.*[10]

Fundamental rights have been considered on a rather different plane, being regarded as "an integral part of the principles of law protected by the Court of Justice."[11] The question whether the Community is bound by, or should become a party to, the European Convention on Human Rights, may have become academic in view of some of the Court's more recent decisions, which appear to apply the principles if not the terms of the European Convention to Community situations.[12] The statement in Case 41/74 *Van Duyn* v. *Home Office* that "it is a principle of international law, which the EEC Treaty cannot be assumed to disregard in relations between Member States, that a State is precluded from refusing its own nationals the right of entry or residence"[13] appears to be inspired by the European Convention and its Protocols. It has no

---

[5] *Ibid:* Art. XI of GATT: and Case 9/73 *Schlüter* v. *HZA Lörrach* [1973] E.C.R. 1135; Art. II of GATT and agreement under Art. XVIII of GATT: and Case 38/73 *Nederlandse Spoorwegen* [1975] E.C.R. 1439; GATT and Brussels Nomenclature Convention of December 15, 1950; see also *infra*, para. 31–38.

[6] *Ibid.* See also discussion of *AG* v. *Burgoa, infra,* para. 29–41.

[7] Cases 181/73 *Haegeman* v. *Belgian State* [1974] E.C.R. 449, 87/75 *Bresciani* v. *Amministrazione Italiana delle Finanze* [1976] E.C.R. 129.

[8] Cases 87/75 *Bresciani* v. *Amministrazione Italiana* [1976] E.C.R. 129; 65/79 *Chatain* (the Sandoz case) [1980] E.C.R. 1345.

[9] Cases 65/75 *Razanatsimba* [1977] E.C.R. 2229; 225/75 *Procureur* v. *Bouhelier* [1979] E.C.R. 3151. See also Cases 270/80 and 172104/81 (not yet decided).

[10] Cases 51/75 *EMI* v. *CBS (UK) Ltd.* [1976] E.C.R. 811; 86/75 *EMI* v. *CBS Grammofon A/S* [1976] E.C.R. 871; 96/75 *EMI* v. *CBS Schallplatten GmbH* [1976] E.C.R. 913. Case 65/79 *Chatain* (Sandoz) [1980] E.C.R. 1345.

[11] Case 11/70 *Internationale Handelsgesellschaft* v. *EVSt* [1970] E.C.R. 1125.

[12] See *supra*, paras. 6–31 *et seq.*

[13] [1974] E.C.R. 1337, 1351.

foundation in customary law and is, indeed, out of line with the Court's general approach to ordinary rules of customary international law discussed above.

Clearly the relationship between Community law and international law is at an early stage of elaboration. The doctrines of direct applicability and that a Community contractual obligation is a Community act may serve for many types of international obligation, but are of doubtful utility in relation to more general international obligations.

9—04   It may be asked whether there are any limitations on the international legal personality of the Community. The traditional view that the personality of an international organisation is at best limited has evolved substantially.[14] But the Community has in any event adopted the view that it is not like other international organisations and prefers to characterise itself as an intergovernmental organisation. This attitude is justified from at least one point of view: for most purposes in external relations the Community exercises "real powers stemming from a limitation of sovereignty or a transfer of powers from the States to the Community."[15] To this extent the Community acts like a federal state and not like a conventional international organisation which is more or less independent of its Member States. In international agreements it participates on an equal footing with other sovereign states.

9—05   Nevertheless, there is at least one limitation and that is the scope of the Treaty itself. The Treaty has proved susceptible of very elastic interpretation by the Court. In Opinion 1/76 *Laying-up Fund*,[16] the Court nevertheless found that the Member States had in the negotiations for the laying-up fund, produced results "which are incompatible with the requirements implied by the very concepts of the Community and its common policy." The Court's particular concern was that the proposed statute of the Fund:

> "constitutes both a surrender of the independence of action of the Community in its external relations and a change in the internal constitution of the Community by the alteration of essential elements of the Community structure as regards both the prerogatives of the institutions and the position of the Member States *vis-à-vis* one another."

The Court's substantive objections were that the draft statute purported to exclude both the Community as such and certain Member States from participation in a body falling in principle

[14] See, *e.g.* le Tallec, *supra*, note 3 and D.P.O'Connell, *International Law* (2nd ed.), Vol. 1, pp. 94 to 106.
[15] Case 6/64 *Costa* v. *ENEL* [1964] E.C.R. 585, 593.
[16] [1977] E.C.R. 741. See similarly Ruling 1/78 *Physical Protection* [1978] E.C.R. 2151.

within the scope of the common transport policy and further that the draft statute would purport to oust the jurisdiction of the European Court. Presumably such results, if desired, could be attained only by amending the Treaty.

29—06   The powers under which the Community conducts its external relations are various. It possesses general and particular powers to conclude agreements, bilateral or multilateral, with third countries and with international organisations. These powers may be express or implied. It also possesses internal powers, to give effect to its international obligations and also to regulate trade with third countries more generally.

The express powers of the EEC Treaty respecting external affairs are to be found in Chapter 3 - Commercial Policy (Arts. 110 to 116), within Title II, "Economic Policy," of Part Three; in Part Four - Association of the Overseas Countries and Territories (Arts. 131 to 136); and in various Articles within Part Six - General and Final Provisions -that is to say Articles 227 to 231, 234, 237, 238. The dispositions referred to cover the main areas of external relations: commercial and trade relations; association with other States; co-operation with international organisations; and admission of third States to membership of the Community.

29—07 These topics are dealt with in this Part as follows:

External relations powers (Paras. 29-10 *et seq.*)

- The Common Commercial Policy
- Association with the EEC
- International Organisations, Conventions and Negotiations
- Admission of New Member States
- Other Express Powers
- Implied Powers and "Competence"

29—08 *The external relations of the Community in practice (Chapter 30)*

- Common Commercial Policy: internal rules
- Co-ordination of Relations with Third Countries
- Development Policies
- Status and Representation

29—09 *Survey of agreements (Chapter 31)*

- Agreements between the Community and Third Countries
- Participation of the Community in International Organisations
- General Multilateral Conventions to which the Community is a Party

Political co-operation, strictly a process taking place outside the system of the Treaty, referred to under the heading of Co-ordination of Relations with Third Countries (*infra*, para. 30-28), is considered in Chapter 4, *supra*.

The Common Commercial Policy - Articles 110 to 116 EEC

—10   The necessity for a common commercial policy derives from the fact that unlike the ECSC, the EEC is founded on a full customs union and therefore presents a common face to exporters from third countries.

Although the terms of the chapter on commercial policy appear to link the content of the common commercial policy with the customs union and the movement of goods, it has been cogently argued that there is no reason why the definition of commercial policy should be so limited. The chapter is to be found in a title of general import: "Economic Policy," and nowhere else in the Treaty is there are express attribution of powers for the conduct of external relations with reference to general economic affairs. Therefore, this chapter is considered to be of general relevance to Parts One, Two and Three of the Treaty. Emphasis is placed on the expressed aim of the Member States, by establishing the customs union between themselves, "to contribute, in the common interest, to the harmonious development of world trade, the progressive abolition of restrictions on international trade and the lowering of customs barriers" (Art. 110). They are to do this according to the guidelines laid down in the succeeding articles.

9—11   Article 110 itself is a general policy statement, outlining the aim of a common Community trade policy. It has no distinct legal force, but it gives some indication of the intended scope of the common commercial policy outlined in the succeeding articles, and required by the second paragraph to "take into account the favourable effect which the abolition of customs duties between Member States may have on the increase in the competitive strength of undertakings in those States." Further indications of the potential scope of the commercial policy may be derived from Articles 111 and 113 (*infra*).

Article 111, which applied during the original transitional period, refers specifically to Community tariff negotiations, to the adjustment of national tariff agreements in relation to the introduction of the common customs tariff, to national liberalisation lists and the abolition or reduction of national quantitative restrictions. Article 113, which sets up the permanent regime, refers to the common commercial policy as being based on uniform principles "particularly in regard to changes in tariff rates, the conclusion of tariff and trade agreements, the achievement of uniformity in measures of liberalisation, export policy and measures to protect trade such as those taken in cases of dumping or subsidies." But despite attempts to clarify the notion, the content of the common commercial policy remains controversial. In Opinion 1/75 the

Court nevertheless indicated that a broad and evolving interpretation was to be applied.[17]

29—12   As the Court said in Opinion 1/78 *Natural Rubber*[18]:

" . . . it would no longer be possible to carry on any worthwhile common commercial policy if the Community were not in a position to avail itself also of more elaborate means devised with a view to furthering the development of international trade. It is therefore not possible to lay down, for Article 113 of the EEC Treaty, an interpretation the effect of which would be to restrict the common commercial policy to the use of instruments intended to have an effect only on the traditional aspects of external trade to the exclusion of more highly developed mechanisms such as appear in the agreement envisaged. A 'commercial policy' understood in that sense would be destined to become nugatory in the course of time. Although it may be thought that at the time when the Treaty was drafted liberalisation of trade was the dominant idea, the Treaty nevertheless does not form a barrier to the possibility of the Community's developing a commercial policy aiming at a regulation of the world market for certain products rather than at a mere liberalisation of trade.

Article 113 empowers the Community to formulate a commerical 'policy', based on 'uniform principles' thus showing that the question of external trade must be governed from a wide point of view and not only having regard to the administration of precise systems such as customs and quantitative restrictions. The same conclusion may be deduced from the fact that the enumeration in Article 113 of the subjects covered by commercial policy (changes in tariff rates, the conclusion of tariff and trade agreements, the achievement of uniformity in measures of liberalisation, export policy and measures to protect trade) is conceived as a non-exhaustive enumeration which must not, as such, close the door to the application in a Community context of any other process intended to regulate external trade. A restrictive interpretation of the concept of common commercial policy would risk causing disturbances in intra-Community trade by reason of the disparities which would then exist in certain sectors of economic relations with non-member countries." (paras. 44 and 45).

29—13   It seems further that where agreements have other aspects

---

[17] Opinion 1/75 *Export Credits* [1975] E.C.R. 1355. See also 8/73 *HZA Bremerhaven* v. *Massey Ferguson* [1973] E.C.R. 2897.
[18] [1979] E.C.R. 2871.

besides the commercial policy aspect (*e.g.* economic policy, strategic reserves or official development assistance) the commercial policy aspect will not for that reason be overridden: "the negotiation of these clauses must therefore follow the system applicable to the agreement considered as a whole" (para. 56) and the scope "of the provisions relating to commercial policy . . . cannot be restricted in the light of more general provisions relating to economic policy and based on the idea of mere co-ordination" (para. 49).

Paradoxically, however, the Court was able to find that separate participation in the rubber agreement by Member States would be justified to the extent that the latter were to finance the so-called economic clauses. Nevertheless, there seems to be a clear echo here of the definition propounded by Judge Pescatore that "the commercial policy [means] all measures intended to regulate economic relations with the outside world."[19]

9—14   Whatever the precise scope of the commercial policy, it will be apparent that the policy necessarily has two aspects: arrangements concluded with third countries, (usually called contractual or sometimes conventional arrangements) and internal measures of commercial policy arrived at without regard to a particular international obligation (usually referred to as autonomous measures). These autonomous measures may of course need to take into account wider international obligations but they may also be in direct response to international negotiations falling short of a binding agreement.

The principal powers to enter into contractual arrangements and to adopt autonomous measures are contained in Article 111, which applied during the original transitional period, and in Article 113, which provides for the definitive regime. Because of the nature of the commercial policy there is no particular priority between internal measures and external measures: it may be appropriate to enter into obligations with third states before an internal regime is established.[20] The reverse is nevertheless the more normal case.

Article 111: Co-ordination and common action

9—15   By Article 111 (1) Member States were to "coordinate their trade relations with third countries so as to bring about, by the end of the transitional period, the conditions needed for implementing a common policy in the field of external trade." During

---

[19] 1961 (II) Hague Recueil 90, cited in G le Tallec, *The common commercial policy of the EEC*, (1976) ICLQ 732 at 738. This article is itself interesting for an early expression of the Commission views. See also the intervention by M. Waelbroeck in "les Relations Exterieures de la C.E. Unifieé," Bruges, p. 263 as to the relationship of services to the commercial policy.

[20] Opinion 1/75, *supra.* note 17.

the transitional period the Commission was to submit proposals to
the Council regarding the procedure for common action during
that period and regarding the achievement of uniformity in the
commercial policies of the Member States, the Council acting
unanimously during the first two stages, and by qualified majority
thereafter (para. 3). Responsibility for co-ordination was thus
imposed equally on the Member States and on the institutions of
the Community. A similar dual responsibility was imposed by
paragraphs 4 and 5 of Article 111. By paragraph 4 Member
States were required in consultation with the Commission to:

> "take all necessary measures, particularly those designed to
> bring about an adjustment of tariff agreements in force with
> third countries, in order that the entry into force of the
> common customs tariff shall not be delayed."

By paragraph 5, first sub-para., Member States were to:

> "aim at securing as high a level of uniformity as possible
> between themselves as regards their liberalisation lists in
> relation to third countries or groups of third countries.
> To this end, the Commission shall make all appropriate
> recommendations to Member States."

By the second sub-paragraph Member States abolishing or reducing
quantitative restrictions in relation to third countries were required
to inform the Commission beforehand and to accord the same
treatment to other Member States.

Article 113: Uniform principles

29–16   The ground work for the introduction of a common commercial
policy, provided for in Article 111, is regarded as complete by
Article 113 which provides that after the original transitional
period had ended "the common commercial policy shall be based
upon uniform principles." At first sight, and read with Article 111,
this phrase might be taken to imply a continuation of national
policies, but on a uniform basis. In fact, for the contractual
aspects of the commercial policy the Community is now exclusively
competent,[21] while for the autonomous aspects the scope for
national action is limited.[22]
    Paragraph 2 confers a very broad power on the Community to
deal with both aspects: "The Commission shall submit proposals
to the Council for implementing the common commercial policy."
The Council acts by qualified majority (para. 4).

---

[21] *Ibid.*
[22] Cases 37 and 38/73 *Diamentarbeiders* v. *Indiamex* [1973] E.C.R. 1609; 41/76
Donckerwolcke [1976] E.C.R. 1921.

Articles 111 and 113

The negotiation of Community commercial agreements

29—17   During the transitional period the Commission was, by Article 111 (2) to "submit to the Council recommendations for tariff negotiations with third countries in respect of the common customs tariff." The Council (acting in accordance with para. 3, *supra*) was to authorise the Commission to open negotiations which were to be conducted in consultation with a special committee ("the Article 111 Committee") appointed by the Council to assist the Commission in this task and within the framework of such directives as the Council might issue to it, again acting in accordance with paragraph 3.

Now that the transitional period has expired:

> "Where agreements with third countries need to be negotiated, the Commission shall make recommendations to the Council, which shall authorise the Commission to open the necessary negotiations.
> The Commission shall conduct these negotiations in consultation with a special committee appointed by the Council to assist the Commission in this task and within the framework of such directives as the Council may issue to it."
> (Art. 113 (3)).

29—18   Thus, the powers of the Commission to negotiate agreements with third countries are now much wider than they were, but it is still to act in consultation with a special committee ("the Article 113 Committee," the successor to the Article 111 Committee) appointed by the Council to assist it in this task, and within the framework of such directives as the Council may issue to it. The Article 113 Committee has a number of manifestations. As a committee of national directors of trade policy it resembles COREPER in dealing with commercial policy questions generally. There are, however, Article 113 committees for particular negotiations and also to oversee the running of individual agreements. A very similar committee system exists for third country association under Article 238 (*infra*, para. 29-26). In practice, however, COREPER tends to overshadow the activities of the Article 113 Committees.

The directives issued by the Council, often called mandates, are in effect negotiating instructions which may be more or less precise. Even in the absence of a mandate the Commission may hold exploratory talks, so long as it does not negotiate. Commission co-operation agreements seem to have been concluded on this informal basis.[23]

---

[23] *e.g.* exchanges of letters on co-operation on environmental matters with *USA* of July 1, 1974, (SEC (74) 2518 (final) and *Canada* of November 6, 1975, (SEC (74) 2132 (final) and *Switzerland* of December 18, 1975, (SEC (75) 4081).

29—19   Under both Articles 111 and 113 the Commission is responsible only for negotiations. By Article 114:

> "The agreements referred to in Article 111 (2) and in Article 113 shall be concluded by the Council on behalf of the Community, acting unanimously during the first two stages and by a qualified majority thereafter."

Conclusion under Article 114 parallels the procedure laid down generally in Article 228 (1), *q.v. infra*, para. 29-36.

"Agreement," for the purposes of Article 113, is to be interpreted broadly: "in its reference to an 'agreement,' the second sub-paragraph of Article 228 (1) of the Treaty uses the expression in a general sense to indicate any undertaking entered into by entities subject to international law which has binding force, whatever its formal designation."[24] It is clear from the context of the opinion that an understanding or gentlemen's agreement comes within this definition.

The distinction between Article 113 Agreements and Association Agreements under Article 238 is not well defined. Generally speaking, Article 238 is used alone or in addition to Article 113 where the agreement contains provisions going beyond trade matters to aid and labour and social questions. But no test is decisive.

29—20   Of course the mere existence of the powers in Article 113 does not automatically terminate bilateral trade agreements concluded previously by Member States: see *infra*, para. 30-25 on the procedures whereby these agreements are maintained in force. Some of these agreements are at first sight primarily of historical interest. However, the three nineteenth century friendship, commerce and navigation agreements between the United States (with which the Community has no general trade agreement) and the United Kingdom[25] still form the basis for the latter's enjoyment of certain m.f.n. trade rights in the United States. The majority of the United Kingdom's trade arrangements are nevertheless now governed by Community agreements.

Article 112

29—21   Article 112 is concerned with the harmonisation by Member States of their systems of aids for exports to third countries. Under paragraph 1 this was to be effected by the end of the transitional period, the Council issuing any necessary directives, acting unanimously until the end of the second stage and by a qualified majority thereafter, on a proposal from the Commission.

---

[24] Opinion 1/75, *supra*, note 17.
[25] See Decision 79/880, O.J. 1979, L 270/60. See similarly Decision 79/882, O.J. 1979, L 272/25.

Such harmonisation was clearly necessary, for the incidence of export aids is reflected in export prices, and differences between national systems of aids would result in an imbalance in export prices and would affect the relative competitiveness of the exports. The notion of export aid includes export credits.[26]

Article 112 (2) exempts drawbacks of customs duties and equivalent charges, and repayments of internal indirect taxation (*cf.* Art. 96 for intra-Community trade) from the incidence of paragraph 1 in so far as they do not exceed the actual amount imposed, directly or indirectly, on the products exported. Matters falling within Article 112 are now governed by Article 113.

Article 115

29—22   Article 115 provides for safeguards both during and after the transitional period. The operative paragraph of the article reads:

> "In order to ensure that the execution of measures of commercial policy taken in accordance with this Treaty by any Member State is not obstructed by deflection of trade, or where differences between such measures lead to economic difficulties in one or more of the Member States, the Commission shall recommend the methods for the requisite co-operation between Member States. Failing this, the Commission shall authorise Member States to take the necessary protective measures, the conditions and details of which it shall determine." (first para.)

Priority is to be given to measures which cause the least disturbance to the functioning of the common market (third para.). Now that the transitional period has expired Member States may no longer take unilateral action even in case of urgency, as was permitted under the second paragraph.[27] The obligation to take into account the need to expedite the introduction of the CCT (third paragraph) has lost its force now that the CCT is fully in place.

Action under Article 115 may be taken to protect the Community or a Member State against imports of particular products from a particular country.

In theory, when a complete commercial policy is instituted, a safeguard clause benefiting individual Member States will become obsolete. The prime importance of the article at present is in relation to textiles where there is no Community agreement with the supplier country. It is most commonly used to prevent goods which cannot reach one Member State directly, because of autonomous restrictions applying there, from reaching that

---

[26] Opinion 1/75, *supra*, note 17 and see further *infra*, para. 29–22.

[27] Case 41/76 *Donckerwolcke* v. *Procureur* [1976] E.C.R. 1921; 27/78 *Amministrazione delle Finanze* v. *Rasham* [1978] E.C.R. 1761; 179/78 *Procureur* v. *Rivoira* [1979] E.C.R. 1147. Commission prior authorisation system, O.J. 1980, L 16.

Member State via another Member State where the same restrictions do not apply.[2 8]

Article 115 is to be interpreted strictly.[2 9] The Court will examine closely the need for Article 115 action[3 0].

Article 116

29—23   This article is considered below, para. 29-28, in the section on relations with international organisations.

Association with the EEC

Part Four of the Treaty

29—24   When the EEC was set up some of its members still maintained special relations with dependent or newly independent territories, mainly in Africa. Part Four of the Treaty (Arts. 131 to 136) set out the guidelines for an association of the dependent territories with the EEC, elaborated upon in an implementing Convention annexed to the Treaty. The territories enjoying Part Four Association were listed in Annex IV. This list was extended with the accession of the new Member States in 1973. The purpose of this association is expressed to be to promote the economic and social development of the countries and territories concerned and to establish close economic relations between them and the Community as a whole (Art. 131, second para.):

> "In accordance with the principles set out in the Preamble to this Treaty, association shall serve primarily to further the interests and prosperity of the inhabitants of these countries and territories in order to lead them to the economic, social and cultural development to which they aspire" (third para.).

The objectives of the association which was founded on a series of customs unions between each of the associated countries and the Six (Art. 133) were:

1. Community treatment for trade with the countries and territories concerned;

[2 8] Written Question 1621/79, O.J. 1980, C 60/18, and Decision 80/605, O.J. 1980, L 164/20. It may also be relevant to *public supply*; see Commission statement and Council Resolution of July 22, 1980, O.J. 1980, C 211/1 and 2; and to *hydrocarbons*; Written Question 257/73, O.J. 1973, C 114/5. See also Commission Decision 80/47, O.J. 1980, L 16/14, which establishes surveillance and protective measures which Member States may be authorised to take with a view to preventing evasion of QRs or VRAs where goods from Third Countries are in free circulation in another Member State.   [2 9] See, *e.g.* Case 52/77 *Cayrol* v. *Rivoira* [1977] E.C.R. 2261.

[3 0] Case 62/70 *Bock* v. *Commission* [1971] E.C.R. 897; 29/75 *Kaufhof* v. *Commission* [1976] E.C.R. 431, 442; 41/76 *Donckerwolcke* v. *Procureur* [1976] E.C.R. 1921 and see generally C. Reich, *La Politique Commerciale Commune de la CEE et le Contrôle de l'Utilization de l'Article 115 de la Traité CEE* (1978) RTDE 3 and P. Vogelenzang, "Two Aspects of Article 115" (1981) 18 C.M.L.Rev. 169.

2. equality of treatment for the rest of the EEC with that accorded to the former metropolitan territory;
3. contributions to investment for development;
4. for investments financed by the Community, participation in tenders and supplies to be open on equal terms to all natural and legal persons who are nationals of a Member State or of one of the countries and territories; and,
5. in principle, freedom of establishment between the Member States and the countries and territories (Art 132).

29—25 The practical arrangements largely provided for in the implementing convention, which was concluded for five years, have been periodically revised to parallel the Yaoundé and Lomé agreements;[31]

Article 227, on the territorial application of the EEC Treaty, confirms the application of Articles 131 to 136 to the overseas countries and territories, paragraph 3 stating the special arrangements set out in Part Four of the Treaty to apply to the overseas countries and territories listed in Annex IV. As paragraph 2 of that article makes clear, Part Four Association does not apply to the French Overseas Departments.[32]

Article 238

29—26 The Treaty contains in Article 238 a quite general disposition on association providing for the conclusion of association agreements with a third State, a union of States or an international organisation, involving reciprocal rights and obligations, common action and special procedures.

This article was used when new association arrangements were negotiated with the countries previously associated under Part Four of the Treaty which had become independent during the period of validity of the latter association arrangements.

Article 238 has led to difficulties of interpretation; basically it is an empowering article. It has to be inferred that the Community has power to conclude such agreements only within the scope of its competence, and that therefore outside that scope the Member States retain their own powers to conclude such agreements. The article itself contemplates that "where such agreements call for amendments to this Treaty," *e.g.* where their potential scope goes wider than the existing powers of the Community, "these amendments shall first be adopted in accordance with the procedure laid down in Article 236."[33] In practice this latter procedure has never been used, but rather where the Community lacked powers in respect of certain aspects of the projected agreement the

[31] *Infra*, para. 30–33.
[32] See *supra*, paras., 5–04 *et seq.* on Art. 227 generally.
[33] *i.e.* amendment of the EEC Treaty.

Member States have joined with the Community, sometimes at the negotiation stage, and always at the conclusion stage, to create a so-called mixed agreement (*infra*, para. 29-50). The agreement is concluded by the Council on behalf of the Community acting unanimously after consulting the Assembly (Article 238, second para.). Thus the Assembly is involved only after the agreement has been negotiated. This is, however, more than is provided for in the chapter on commercial policy, where no participation of the Assembly is specified at all.

29—27   These deficiencies are to some extent remedied by the Luns-Westerterp procedure, designed to cover agreements under Article 113 and Article 238. Under this procedure the Assembly must be informed of the negotiations through the appropriate parliamentary committees, first, by the Commission while negotiations are in progress and secondly, by the Council when the negotiations have been completed and the agreement signed, but before it enters into force. The Assembly also has the right to hold an orientation debate before negotiations with a third country are begun.[34]

International Organisations, Conventions and Negotiations

29—28   Article 116 provides for co-ordination of action "within the framework of international organisations of an economic character." During the original transitional period Member States were merely to consult each other with a view to concerting action to be taken and adopting uniform attitudes "as far as possible." Now that the transitional period has ended, they are required, in respect of all matters of particular interest to the common market, to proceed only by common action. To this end the Commission is empowered to submit proposals to the Council, which is to act by a qualified majority, concerning the scope and implementation of such action.

Article 116 would appear to be of general application and not to be restricted to the scope of the common commercial policy, the common action within the framework of economic organisations being called for "in respect of *all* matters of particular interest to the common market." Notwithstanding the reference to *organisations*, Article 116 probably also applies to conventions and conferences also[35]: practice on the article is limited because the normal ad hoc co-ordination procedures usually take place without reference to any Treaty provision (*infra*, paras. 31-35 *et seq.*).

29—29   The article assumes that Member States will retain their membership of these international organisations as individual states; as

---

[34] See House of Lords, Select Committee on the European Community, Session 1976–1977, 40th Report, p. 5.
[35] Cases 3, 4 and 6/76 *Kramer et al* [1976] E.C.R. 1279.

the Court held in Opinion 1/78 *Natural Rubber*:[36] "Article 116 was conceived with a view to evolving common action by the Member States in international organisations of which the Community is not part."[37] Where, within an international organisation to which Article 116 does apply, an international agreement is to be elaborated "it is the provisions of the Treaty relating to the negotiation and conclusion of agreements . . . which apply and not Article 116," presumably where there is Community competence.

Where the Community has competence, whether alone or with the Member States, the Community has sought and in many cases obtained separate membership on its own behalf in a growing number of international bodies and conventions (see *infra*, para. 31-35 *et seq.*). Article 116 would appear to be subject to Article 229 to 231 in so far as these relate to maintenance of appropriate relations or co-operation with specialised agencies having an economic character, and with GATT, the Council of Europe and the OEEC (now the OECD).

29–30   By Article 229:

> "It shall be for the Commission to ensure the maintenance of all appropriate relations with the organs of the United Nations, of its specialised agencies and of the General Agreement on Tariffs and Trade.
>
> The Commission shall also maintain such relations as are appropriate with all international organisations."

Clearly, the residuary provision of the second paragraph gives the Commission a very wide margin of discretion in determining what relations shall be established or maintained.

Articles 230 and 231 concern the establishment respectively of all appropriate forms of co-operation by the Community with the Council of Europe, and of close co-operation with the OEEC (now OECD), the details of the latter to be determined by common accord.

The procedure for the conclusion of agreements with international organisations, with the exception of association agreements under Article 238 (above), is laid down in Article 228 (see below). Article 238 has never been used in relation to international organisations.

29–31   The status of the Community in the individual organisations and conferences (considered *infra*, paras. 31-35 *et seq.*) depends first, on the rights enjoyed by the Community in the individual organisations and secondly, on Community competence for the

[36] [1979] E.C.R. 2871.
[37] See also *Kramer, supra.* note 35.

subjects considered. Other things being equal the Community is normally represented on matters within its competence by the Commission, although in areas of uncertain or mixed competence this role may be filled by the Presidency or by the Presidency and the Commission acting in consultation. Where the Community is not a member of the organisation the Presidency usually covers all aspects of Community competence. The Community position is usually arrived at ad hoc on the basis of co-ordination among the Member States represented and the Commission, possibly on the basis of guidelines agreed in COREPER or relevant Council Committees in Brussels. Where there is a Community position Member States do not speak except in support of the common position. Otherwise they speak having regard for the results of the co-ordination. If no result is reached Member States are free to speak but must not prejudice future Community positions. There is theoretically no obligation to co-ordinate on matters not of Community competence although the extent of the obligation in Article 116 (*supra*, para. 29-28) to proceed only by common action in respect of all matters of particular interest to the Common Market within the framework of international organisations of an economic character cuts down this freedom somewhat. In practice Member States have chosen to pursue co-ordination and adopt common positions within the United Nations itself even on matters falling clearly outside Community competence. This is largely a function of the political co-operation mechanisms. In other areas, especially in technical bodies, pressure to co-ordinate views or to adopt a common position has been resisted by the larger Member States.

Admission of New Member States

29—32 Article 237 EEC with which Article 206 Euratom is identical, lays down the conditions and procedure for the admission of a third country to membership of the Community. The prior conditions are:

(a) the applicant must be a European State (although what constitutes a European State is not uncontroverted);
(b) the applicant must apply to the Council;
(c) the Council must agree unanimously on the application after obtaining the opinion of the Commission (first para.).

Conduct of the negotiations is not mentioned specifically by this article, and although the Commission argued that it should be for it to negotiate on behalf of the Community and the Member States, the negotiations relating to the applications of Denmark, Ireland, Norway and the United Kingdom made in 1970, were conducted neither by the Commission nor the original Member States, but by the Council. This pattern was followed with Greece. Prior to each of the negotiation sessions, the Council met to agree on common positions to present to the applicant countries.

9—33   By the first sentence of the second paragraph of Article 237 "the conditions of admission and the adjustments to this Treaty necessitated thereby shall be the subject of an agreement between the Member States and the applicant State."[38] In respect of the applications just referred to this agreement is constituted by the Treaty and Act of Accession of January 22, 1972, concerning the accession of Denmark, Ireland and the United Kingdom (Norway did not accede and references to Norway were subsequently deleted) to both the EEC and Euratom and corresponding instruments of May 28, 1979, for Greece.[39]

As respects accession to the ECSC Treaty, the opening sentences of Article 98 ECSC are substantially similar to the first paragraph of Article 237 EEC, but the former article goes on to provide that "the Council shall also determine the terms of accession, likewise acting unanimously." Provision for the accession of the applicant States to the ECSC was therefore made by decisions of the Council of the Communities, taken the same day the Treaties of Accession were signed and expressed in substantially similar terms. The Acts of Accession are expressed to be annexed to these decisions as well as to the Treaty of Accession.

Article 237 EEC, second paragraph requires "this agreement" (*i.e.* the Treaties of Accession), to be submitted for ratification by all the contracting States in accordance with their respective constitutional requirements. Article 98 ECSC does not call for ratification of the Council decision, since thereunder accession is effected by a Community act rather than by a wholly international agreement.

Both Spain and Portugal have applied to join the Community. Negotiations continue. With Portugal the Community has concluded an agreement on "pre-accession aid,"[40] designed, in terms of the agreement itself, "in order to undertake measures of common interest to prepare and facilitate the harmonious integration of the Portuguese economy into the Community economy." 150M ECU is made available in the form of ElB loans and a further 125M ECU in the form of grant aid. The loans are for investment projects, the grants are for restructuring and infrastructure. The emphasis is on regional development. For grant aid the Community will in most cases meet half the cost. Mech-

[38] Since the conditions of admission are defined in the context of the Article 237 procedure the Court has no jurisdiction to determine these conditions judicially in advance: Case 93/78 *Matteus* v. *Doego* [1978] E.C.R. 2203; nor, conversely, do the accession arrangements, which call for acceptance of existing Community rules, validate measures which are incompatible with Treaties establishing the Communities: Case 185/73 *HZA Bielefeld* v. *König* [1974] E.C.R. 607.
[39] See *supra*, Chapter 2, notes 6, 7 and 12.
[40] Reg. 3323/80, O.J. 1980, L349/1.

anisms follow the pattern for other EIB loans and for Community aid agreements.

Acceding States and External Relations

29—34 Articles 4 and 5 of the Acts of Accession contain general provisions on the application of the *"acquis"* (*i.e.* that which has already been achieved) in external relations by the new Member States.

Community-alone agreements or conventions with a third State or States, an international organisation or with a national of a third State are to be binding on the new Member States under the conditions laid down in the original Treaties and in the Acts (Art. 4 (1) of the Acts). New Member States are thus bound at once in most cases.

By contrast, new Member States only "undertake to accede" to mixed agreements and to related agreements concluded by the original Member States (Art. 4 (2) of the Acts). The Community and the existing Member States are to assist the new Member States in this respect. The formula covering the internal agreements concluded by the existing Member States for the purpose of implementing the agreements or conventions referred to in paragraph (2) is different again: new Member States "accede [to them] by this Act and under the conditions laid down therein" (para. 3). The detailed provisions referred to here in relation to the 1973 Act of Accession are largely spent.[41] The arrangements in Articles 115 to 123 of the Greek Act of Accession are along similar lines.

29—35 By Article 4 (4) of the Acts of Accession new Member States are to take appropriate measures, where necessary, to adjust their positions in relation to international organisations and international agreements to which one of the Communities or to which other Member States are also parties, to the rights and obligations arising from their accession to the Communities. This is without prejudice, however, to Article 5 of the Acts of Accession, which provides that Article 234 of the EEC Treaty shall apply, for the new Member States, to agreements or conventions concluded before accession (see *infra*, para. 29-39 on Article 234).

Articles 115 to 123 of the Greek Act of Accession provide the detailed rules. Under Article 115 Greece will apply the Commercial Policy import rules over the five year transitional period. It will align with the GSP over the same period. Subject to transitional protocols, Greece will apply the agreements with the EFTA, Magrheb and Mashreq countries, Cyprus, Malta, Spain and

---

[41] For discussion of 1972 arrangements see 1st edition of this work, paras. 37–59 to 37–68. For *Greece* initial arrangements on certain customs matters are provided for in O.J. 1980, C 259.

Turkey and also the textiles agreements under the GATT Multi-fibre agreement. It will apply Lomé II from accession.[42]

Other Express Powers

Article 228

9—36 Where the EEC Treaty provides for the conclusion of agree-ments[43] between the Community and one or more States or an international organisation, Article 228 lays down a general rule, requiring such agreements to be negotiated by the Commission and, subject to the powers vested in the Commission in this field, to be concluded by the Council, after consulting the Assembly where required by the Treaty. Conclusion normally takes the form of a decision, apparently in the form laid down in Article 189, but usually described as *sui generis*, annexing the agreement as signed. If the decision precedes signature it will constitute authority for signature of the annexed draft, otherwise, signature is authorised by a separate Council decision. Conclusion is the equivalent of a governmental ratification by a State.

In each of the major areas involving external relations, (commercial policy, association agreements, and relations with international organisations), the Treaty contains specific provisions, which would appear in practice to override Article 228.

9—37 However, Article 228 (1) contains an element additional to Articles 111, 113, 237 or 238, in that the second paragraph establishes a means for determining whether the content of a proposed agreement is compatible with the provisions of the Treaty. The Council, Commission or a Member State may, prior to the conclusion of an agreement, obtain the opinion of the Court of Justice on the question. Where the opinion of the Court is adverse the agreement may enter into force only in accordance with Article 236 (Treaty amendment). The procedure for obtaining an opinion has been invoked three times under the EEC Treaty and once under the corresponding provision of the Euratom Treaty.[44] In Opinion 1/78 EEC *Natural Rubber*[45] the Court, referring to its earlier opinions "emphasised that under the pro-cedure of Article 228, like that of Article 103 of the EAEC Treaty, it is possible to deal with all questions which concern the compatibility with the provisions of the Treaty of an agreement envisaged." Amongst other things, the distribution of powers of the institutions of the Community could therefore be considered.

---

[42] See generally Chapter 31 on these agreements.
[43] *Cf.* para. 29–19, *supra*.
[44] Opinion 1/75 *Export Credits* [1975] E.C.R. 1355. Opinion 1/76 *Laying-up Fund* [1977] E.C.R. 74. Ruling 1/78 EAEC *Physical Protection* [1978] E.C.R. 2151. Opinion 1/78 EEC *Natural Rubber* [1979] E.C.R. 2871.
[45] *Supra*, note 44.

The fact that negotiation on the draft international rubber agreement were not complete again did not deter the Court.

29—38   In Opinion 1/75 *Export Credits*[46] the Court had to consider admissibility. It found that the OECD understanding on an export credits standard for local costs was an "agreement envisaged" within the meaning of Article 228 (1) because there was sufficient evidence that the understanding was such as to bind the contracting parties and was in all but final form. Furthermore, the fact that the understanding was conceived as a Member States alone agreement did not for that reason invalidate the Commission's request for an opinion, on the ground that Article 228 (1) talks of agreements to be concluded by the Community and by Member States.

Article 228 (2) provides that "Agreements concluded under these conditions shall be binding on the institutions of the Community and on Member States." This paragraph is generally considered to apply to all "Community alone" agreements: Article 228 (1) being considered merely to reiterate *mutatis mutandis* the other provisions of the Treaty relating to the conclusion of agreements, differences of detail being allowed for by the words "subject to the powers vested in the Commission in this field" and "where required by this Treaty." But the other articles authorising the negotiation and conclusion of agreements contain nothing comparable to Article 228 (2). Such a provision is appropriate since international agreements do not constitute a category of binding acts within Article 189 EEC. In 21-24/72 *International Fruit Co.* v. *Produktschap voor Groenten en Fruit*[47] and 181/73 *Haegeman* v. *Belgium*[48] the Court held that agreements concluded under the conditions laid down in Articles 228 and 238 are acts of one of the institutions for the purposes of Article 177. Article 228 (2) is also useful in making it clear that the Community is to be regarded as having international responsibility through its institutions (*cf. supra*, para. 29-01) for its acts, and that the Member States enjoy no species of limited liability in respect of "Community alone" agreements which will enable them to repudiate them at will.

In special cases an agreement may be concluded by the Member States, acting "on behalf of the Community;" see *infra*, para. 29-40.

Article 234

29—39   This article is not a power: rather it regulates the relationship of the EEC Treaty to other international obligations. It provides that the prior international rights and obligations of Member

[46] *Ibid.*
[47] [1972] E.C.R. 1219.
[48] [1974] E.C.R. 449.

States shall not be affected by the Treaty (first paragraph) but calls on Member States to take all appropriate steps to eliminate any incompatible aspects of such agreements. The watershed date for the application of Article 234 is the date of the entry into force of the Treaty of Rome (January 1, 1958) for the original Member States and the date of accession for the new Member States. It must be assumed that the operative date may be later where Community policies are applied to given sectors for the first time at a later date (*e.g.* under Article 84 (2) - Sea and Air Transport).

In Case 10/61 *Commission* v. *Italy*[49] the Court said:

> "The applicant replies that the terms 'rights and obligations' in Article 234 refer, as regards the 'rights', to the rights of third countries and, as regards the 'obligations', to the obligations of Member States and that, by virtue of the principles of international law, by assuming a new obligation which is incompatible with rights held under a prior treaty a State *ipso facto* gives up the exercise of these rights to the extent necessary for the performance of its new obligations. The applicant's interpretation is well founded and the objection raised by the defence must be dismissed. In fact, in matters governed by EEC Treaty, that Treaty takes precedence over agreements concluded between Member States before its entry into force, including agreements made within the framework of GATT."

9–40   The view of the applicant (the Commission) is probably an accurate expression of the position in international law if it means that a Member State can invoke a prior obligation but not a prior right under Article 234. The Court's own conclusion may be too sweeping: a Member State may owe a duty to a third country by virtue of a prior obligation in a matter governed by the EEC Treaty which may consist in conducting its relations with Member States on that matter in a particular way. The Court's own conclusion would be a correct reflection of international law in relation to agreements concluded among Member States alone.

It may be thought that Article 234 (and corresponding provisions in the Acts of Accession) is becoming a dead letter with time. The Member States nevertheless frequently invoke it in argument with the Commission. Furthermore, a view is developing that the article should be applied along the lines of the GATT Grandfather Clause (Paragraph 1 (*b*) of the Protocol of Provisional Application). Effectively this would mean that Article 234 can be invoked in relation to a subsequent agreement also, if that agreement is only a novation or represents a "rolling over" of a prior agreement. For instance, the agreements establishing commodity organisations and communications organisations are renewed at

[49] [1962] E.C.R. 1. Confirmed, Case 812/79 *AG* v. *Burgoa* (October, 14, 1980).

regular intervals. In Case 34/79 *R.* v. *Henn and Darby*[50] the Court ruled that:

> 'In so far as a Member State avails itself of the reservation relating to the protection of public morality provided for in Article 36 of the Treaty, the provisions of Article 234 do not preclude that State from fulfilling the obligations arising from the Geneva Convention, 1923, for the suppression of traffic in obscene publications and from the Universal Postal Convention (renewed at Lausanne in 1974, which came into force on 1 January 1976).''

This ruling does not deal with the point directly, but given that the point was argued before the Court and dealt with by the Advocate General (who did not accept the view argued for) the Court's ruling can only be described as introducing an element of constructive ambiguity.

29—41   The question what is an agreement for the purposes of Article 234 may probably be looked at in very wide terms although this is an exception provision.[51]

Article 234 does not bind the institutions of the Community although they are bound not to impede the performance of prior treaty obligations. It follows that Article 234 creates no directly applicable rights for individuals in such prior treaties.[52] In Case 812/79 *AG* v. *Burgoa*[53] the Court nevertheless held that the framework of relations between the Community and Spain, which included certain Community fisheries regulations, were:

> "superimposed on the regime previously applied in those zones in order to take account of the general development of international law in the field of fishing on the high seas."[54]

It is not clear that this ruling was essential to the case and its precise scope must remain doubtful. Nevertheless, it seems to lie inside the rule of customary international law (and codified in the Vienna Convention on the Law of Treaties) that it is open to two parties to a multilateral convention to vary or suspend the operation of the convention as between themselves.

29—42   In applying agreements entered into prior to joining the Community, Member States are required to take into account the third paragraph of Article 234, by which:

> "[   ] Member States shall take into account the fact that the advantages accorded under this Treaty by each Member

---

[50] [1979] E.C.R. 3795.
[51] *Cf.* Opinion 1/75 *Export Credits* [1975] E.C.R. 1355.
[52] Case 812/79, *supra*, note 49.
[53] *Ibid.*
[54] *Ibid.*

State form an integral part of the establishment of the Community and are thereby inseparably linked with the creation of common institutions, the conferring of powers upon them and the granting of the same advantages by all the other Member States."

This somewhat roundabout formulation in effect calls for preferential treatment to be granted to the Community, in view of its special status *vis-à-vis* individual Member States. This is necessary in order, apparently, to avoid the implication that third States enjoying most-favoured-nation status are entitled to avail themselves of the advantages accorded to each other by the Member States.

Implied Powers and Co.npetence

>—43 At least until the end of the original transitional period it was generally supposed that in external relations the Community only had such powers as were expressly conferred upon it: in the absence of express powers none were to be implied. This view was rudely shattered, at least in so far as some observers were concerned[55] by the decision of the Court in Case 22/70 *Commission* v. *Council*[56], the celebrated AETR or ERTA case.

The background to the case was as follows. Discussions had been going on sporadically for many years, most recently within the UN Economic Commission for Europe, for a European Agreement concerning the work of crews engaged in international road transport or European Road Transport Agreement (ERTA - in French AETR). Adoption by the Community of Regulation 543/69 covering much of the same ground served to re-awaken interest in finalising the agreement. At this stage, the Council, in the course of its meeting on March 20, 1970, nevertheless decided that the six original Member States should complete the negotiations, albeit on the basis of "common action, co-ordinating their position in accordance with the usual procedures, in close association with the Community institutions." The Commission sought annulment of the proceedings of the Council relating to the negotiation and conclusion of the AETR by the Member States. It took the view that Article 75 of the Treaty, which confers wide powers with a view to implementing the common transport policy, must apply to external relations just as much as to internal measures and that the agreement should, therefore, be concluded under Article 228. Although the Commission failed on the merits (the negotiations were well advanced before Regulation 543/69 was adopted) the Court laid down the general principle that the existence of Community common rules pre-

---

[55] See, *e.g.* "*La Cour de Justice a-t-elle outrepassé ses compétences?*" Le Monde, April 27, 1971 attributed to Puissochet.
[56] [1971] E.C.R. 263.

cludes Member States from undertaking obligations with third
countries which affect those rules.

29—44   The Court reached this at the time surprising conclusion,
taking the view that Article 210, which confers on the Community international legal capacity, relates to all the substantive
provisions of the Treaty and to measures adopted with a view to
implementing common policies envisaged by the Treaty. The
Court held further that this power was exclusive in all external
matters affecting the application of the Community legal system,
the internal measures being inseparable from the external aspect.
It was reinforced in this view in relation to AETR because both
Article 75 and Regulation 543/69 make reference to relations
with third countries:

> "In particular, each time the Community, with a view to
> implementing a common policy envisaged by the Treaty,
> adopts provisions laying down common rules, whatever form
> these may take, the Member States no longer have the
> right, acting individually or even collectively, to undertake
> obligations with third countries which affect those rules"
> (para. 17)

> If [Articles 3 (e) and 5] are read in conjunction, it follows
> that to the extent to which Community rules are promul-
> gated for the attainment of the objectives of the Treaty, the
> Member States cannot, outside the framework of the Com-
> munity institutions, assume obligations which might affect
> those rules or alter their scope" (para. 22).

29—45   This ruling is frequently referred to as the *"AETR doctrine."*
The mechanics of it are that adoption of Community common
rules applying internally carry with it an exclusive external
relations power in the same area. Adoption of or the existence
of internal rules is frequently referred to as conferring *"Community competence"* in external relations.
    Whether or not there was actual or potential Community
competence assumed considerable importance as a result of the
AETR case in debates within the Community on the elaboration
of new policies and the extension of existing ones. It was equally
relevant to the conclusion of agreements by Member States.
    For some time, it was the accepted wisdom that if there were
no internal common rules, there was no Community competence.
(There was scope for argument as to what were common rules
for the purposes of the *AETR* doctrine, but it seems to have been
accepted that this concept extended beyond directly applicable
instruments, at least to directives, but probably not *e.g.* to an
action programme enshrined in a resolution). The ruling of the

Court in Opinion 1/75 *Export Credits*[57] was regarded as not prejudicing this view, because it related to the commercial policy.

—46   There the Commission argued that conclusion of the OECD Local Costs understanding was a matter for exclusive Community competence. The Member States, citing *AETR*, argued that this could only be so if there were corresponding internal rules and pointed out that the then Community rules on export credits matters were at best limited in extent. The Court in effect by-passed these arguments, holding that the subject-matter of the understanding fell clearly within the commercial policy and was as such a matter for exclusive Community competence under Articles 113 and 114. Nevertheless, in Opinion 1/76 *Laying-up Fund*,[58] the Court made it clear that the existence of common rules was not necessarily the prerequisite for the exercise of Community competence: "the power to bind the Community *vis-a-vis* third countries nevertheless flows by implication from the provisions of the Treaties creating the internal power and in so far as the participation of the Community is, as here, necessary for the attainment of one of the objectives of the Treaty."

—47   Community competence in external relations, therefore, exists where there is an internal power to act whether or not it has been exercised and participation in an agreement is necessary. The language in which this necessity is described is similar to that used in Article 235, but the threshold, namely that Community objectives cannot be met through other powers, is probably not quite equivalent because it does not depend upon the absence of other powers. The reference to internal powers here is more problematic: arguably what is referred to is a substantive power, *e.g.* Article 75 (transport policy) or even Article 235 (general power).

Opinion 1/76 does not deal with the question where powers lie if Community competence is not or has not been exercised. Cases 3, 4 and 6/76 *Kramer et al*,[59] a slightly earlier decision, provides some clarification. That case concerned Article 102 of the 1972 Act of Accession, which provided that from the sixth year after accession at the latest the Council should determine conditions for fishing having regard to conservation requirements. The question arose as to what powers were still enjoyed by Member States pending action under Article 102. The Court held that "the Community not yet having fully exercised its functions in the matter . . . the Member States had the power to assume commitments. . . . " It nevertheless described this power as transitional, expiring with the deadline in Article 102 at the latest and

[57] [1975] E.C.R. 1355.
[58] [1977] E.C.R. 741.
[59] [1976] E.C.R. 1279.

indeed possibly as soon as the Community institutions initiate the procedure for implementing Article 102.[60]

29—48   It therefore appears from *AETR*, the *Laying-up Fund* opinion and *Kramer* that Member States retain a transitional power in areas where there are no common internal rules *and* the Community has not exercised its external competence directly. It seems to follow that if the Member States acting collectively within the Community and in the absence of common rules, choose not to exercise the Community external relations power they may do so, preserving their national powers intact. But if common rules already exist, the Member States are not permitted to act other than through the Community. Article 5 would seem to require Member States not to frustrate an agreed exercise of Community competence, *e.g.* by concluding a long-term agreement when Community negoitations were at a preliminary stage. It also seems to be the basis for the statement in *Kramer*

> "that as soon as the Community institutions have initiated the procedure for implementing the provisions of the said Article 102, and at the latest within the period laid down by that article, those institutions and the Member States will be under a duty to use all the political and legal means at their disposal in order to ensure the participation of the Community in the Convention and in other similar agreements."[61]

This would seem to translate into a duty to seek a Community accession clause in new or renegotiated agreements which are the subject of exclusive or mixed Community competence but it probably does not go so far as to require the Member States to seek renegotiation of an already well-established agreement, *e.g.* GATT.

29—49   Even where the Community has not replaced the Member States for one technical reason or another, they may be required to proceed by way of common action under Article 116 as in *AETR*. In the event, the Member States ratified or acceded to AETR acting "on behalf of the Community."[62]
There may also be a duty of consultation on measures adopted by a Member State to comply with one of its international obligations even in the absence of substantive Community rules. Thus in Case 141/78 *France* v. *United Kingdom*[63] the Court found a duty

---

[60] In fact the deadline may have been extended *de facto* by the Hague Resolution of October 30, 1976, Annex VI, as to which see *supra.* para. 15–79 and Cases141/78 *France* v. *Commission* [1979] E.C.R. 2923; 32/79 *Commission* v. *UK* [1981] 1 C.M.L.R. 219, and 804/79 *Commission* v. *UK* (May 5, 1981).
[61] [1976] E.C.R. 1279, paras. 44/45.
[62] Reg. 2829/77, O.J. 1977, L 334/11, Art. 2.
[63] *Supra.* note 60.

to seek the approval of the Commission under Annex VI of the Hague Resolution before taking implementing measures under the then applicable North-East Atlantic Fisheries Convention.

–50   Of course, matters are not invariably clear-cut: there may be matters dealt with by an international agreement which fall clearly within Community competence, but other aspects may appear more naturally to relate to the powers and responsibilities of the Member States. A practice grew up with the first association agreements of providing for participation both by the Community acting in its own right and by the Member States acting individually. Agreements concluded in this form were called "mixed" agreements, involving "mixed competence." Although the Commission seems initially to have accepted the institution of mixed agreements, it seems to have adopted a somewhat hostile attitude towards them particularly in the light of the *Export Credits* Opinion[64] which upheld exclusive Community competence in relation to the commercial policy. In two subsequent opinions, the Court has nevertheless given its blessing to mixed agreements. In Ruling 1/78 *Physical Protection*,[65] an opinion given under Article 103 of the Euratom Treaty, but on similar principles, such a finding was natural because Article 102 of the Euratom Treaty, which has no equivalent in the EEC Treaty, expressly envisages agreements "to which, in addition to the Community, one or more Member States are parties." There the Court further found that it was neither necessary nor indeed possible, since they change over time, to define the precise division of powers reflected by a mixed agreement.

–51   In Opinion 1/78 *Natural Rubber*[66] the Court was able to countenance separate participation by the Member States in an agreement otherwise within the commercial policy in so far as the so-called economic clauses of the agreement were to be financed by the Member States. Separate participation was also accepted even in an agreement the subject of exclusive Community competence where a given Member State participates exclusively on behalf of a dependent territory not covered by the EEC Treaty.
       The importance of the mixed procedure for the future is nevertheless open to question because the finding that "the negotiation and execution" of clauses admittedly not involving Community competence "must . . . follow the system applicable to the agreement considered as a whole" apparently because they were of "an altogether subsidiary and ancillary nature . . . closely connected with the objective of the agreement." This and the finding in relation to strategic reserves (*supra*, para. 29-12) imply that if the

[64] [1975] E.C.R. 1355.
[65] [1978] E.C.R. 2151.
[66] [1979] E.C.R. 2871.

overall objective of the agreement can be described as involving commercial policy then all aspects of the agreement should follow common commercial policy procedures.

These opinions and Case 22/70 themselves show that differences as to whether or not Community competence exists are for determination by the Court and that the Court has adopted a pragmatic approach. Radical though the decision seemed at the time the *AETR* case lacked a certain symmetry in making an external relations power dependent on the creation of an internal policy. This may have seemed logical at the time, when the majority of the policies were provided for in the Treaty itself, but the elaboration of so-called second generation policies, based in some instances on Article 235 (the general power to act where no other is provided) and going well beyond the limited framework of the Treaty, called for the more systematic approach of the *Laying-up Fund* opinion, which rightly recognises that there is no inevitable priority of internal measures over the exercise of external powers: on the contrary, within national legal systems, many developments have resulted from international conventions.

29--52   Short of a decision by the Court, there are frequently differences within the Community over where competence lies. Usually an ad hoc solution is found safeguarding the legal position. In at least one case an express clause was inserted preserving the power of Member States to enter into bilateral arrangements on matters covered by the agreement.[67]

---

[67] Article III (4) of The EEC/Canada Framework Agreement of July 6, 1976, O.J. 1976, L 260/3.

Chapter 30

THE EXTERNAL RELATIONS OF THE COMMUNITY
IN PRACTICE

The Common Commercial Policy: Internal Rules

-01   The original transitional period for the implementation of the EEC Treaty having expired, the common commercial policy is now based on uniform principles with regard to both import and export policy (Art. 113). Although complete uniformity has yet to be achieved, substantial progress has been made. It was relatively easy for the Community to establish its policy with regard to tariffs, since the setting up of the common customs tariff enabled it to present one face to the rest of the world in tariff matters. It must thus be remembered that Articles 18 to 29 of the Treaty, on the setting up of the CCT, are closely related to the common commercial policy, the establishment of the former being a fundamental prerequisite to the latter. The implementation of the common agricultural policy and the consequent setting up of individual market organisations also contributed to the common commercial policy, each regulation setting up a market organisation containing dispositions relating to external trade in the products subject to it. The area of principal application of commercial policy internal rules relates to quantitative restrictions and associated measures on imports. Tariff measures are considered *supra*, paras. 13-12 *et seq.*

Commercial Policy import Rules

-02   Article XI of GATT calls for the general elimination of quantitative restrictions. There are two exceptions to this rule, Article XII and Article XIX. Under Article XII a contracting party may restrict the quantity or value of merchandise permitted to be imported in order to safeguard its external financial position and its balance of payments. The import restrictions so instituted must not exceed those necessary (and the GATT has to accept the determination of the IMF on whether they are necessary) to protect a country's monetary reserves. Article XIX allows for emergency action on imports of particular products in rather more general circumstances. The criterion here is that a product is being imported into the territory of a contracting party in such increased quantities and under such conditions as to cause or threaten serious injury to domestic producers in that territory of like or directly competitive products. Exporting countries affected are free to take "substantially equivalent" retaliatory action (which does not have to be, and normally would not be, on the same product).

Article XIX does not state that safeguard action should be undertaken only on a non-discriminatory basis but the article is so interpreted in GATT. It is considered that the non-discriminatory requirement is implicit from the general most-favoured-nation obligation in Article I and (in so far as quantitative restrictions are used as safeguard measures) from Article XIII entitled "non-discriminatory administration of quantitative restrictions." The Community pressed unsuccessfully in the MTNs for agreement that henceforth Article XIX action may, in appropriate circumstances, be taken selectively.[1] The Community rules discussed in the following account take account of GATT obligations.

30—03   Imports into the Community are treated differently according to whether they come from:

(a) *preferential trading partners*: *i.e.* those with which the Community has concluded association or preferential trade agreements. These include the Lomé ACP countries, the Mediterranean countries and the EFTA members. Broadly speaking, the Lomé and Mediterranean agreements provide for tariff free access to the Community market for industrial goods and varying degrees of tariff free or reduced rate access for agricultural goods. The EFTA agreements provide for tariff free access for industrial goods but there is no provision for agriculture (see *infra*, para. 30-34 on the Community's Generalised Scheme of Tariff Preferences (GSP)).

(b) *other third countries other than State Traders*: A number of these countries, including Yugoslavia, Argentina, Brazil, Uruguay, Mexico, India and Canada, have concluded non-preferential agreements with the Community providing for trade on a reciprocal most-favoured-nation basis. Most of the remainder enjoy m.f.n. treatment under GATT.

(c) *State Trading Countries*: *i.e.* Albania, Bulgaria, Hungary, Poland, Romania, Czechoslovakia, Soviet Union, German Democratic Republic, People's Republic of China, North Korea, Vietnam and Mongolia.

(d) There may also be *voluntary restraint agreements* and;

(e) *Textiles* are treated somewhat separately.

(a) **Preferential trading partners**

30—04   In general terms imports from preferential trading partners are free of quantitative restrictions. Where QRs exist the arrangements for them are set out in the agreements by which the privilege is established and any changes, *i.e.* the introduction of new restric-

---

[1] See *"Modalities of Application of Article XIX"* of GATT, L/4679, July 5, 1978, (GATT Secretariat) and G.M. Meier, "Externality law and Market Safeguards: Applications in the GATT Multilateral Trade Negotiations." (1977) *Harvard International Law Journal*, p.491.

tions or reductions in the size of the quotas, are governed by the provisions of the safeguard clauses of the agreements. On the internal Community side there is normally a Community regulation which sets out how and under what conditions the safeguard is to be invoked or applied. Unilateral action by a Member State to invoke these rights is possible, but must be endorsed by the Commission and/or Council within a short time. (GSP is discussed *infra*, para. 30-34). For preferential tariff treatment applied by the Community on January 1, 1981 see O.J. 1981, C122.

(b) **Other third countries other than State trading countries**

05   Imports from these countries are either liberalised throughout the Community (*i.e.* subject to certain exceptions, free from quantitative restrictions on entry into the Community) or "not liberalised." Goods which are not liberalised may be: not currently subject to restriction when imported into the Community; subject to restriction when imported into one or more of the Member States, under measures taken nationally (but under a Community procedure); or subject to restriction under measures taken by the Community. (The distinction between liberalised and non-liberalised goods is somewhat arbitrary, relating to whether or not any Member State had restrictions on those goods at a particular date when the first rules for the common import regime were laid down). For agricultural goods there are particular regimes. The general regime covers all industrial goods and complements the agricultural rules.

The basic regulation for liberalised and non-liberalised goods is now Regulation 926/79.[2]

06   Under Article 1 (1) "importation into the Community of products included in the common liberalisation list contained in Column 1 of Annex I and originating in any third country or territory included in the list of countries contained in Annex II shall be free, that is to say not subject to any quantitative restriction." For non-liberalised products (Annex I, column 2) importation is free of any quantitative restriction in the same way in the Member States indicated (Art. 1 (2)).

Article 2 provides for amendment of the Annexes. This article envisages extension of the lists. In particular the revocation of national quantitative restrictions triggers a procedure aimed at including the product in the common liberalisation list (Arts. 2 (2), 5 (4) and 17). Most of the regulation is concerned with imposing restrictions on products previously liberalised at the Community level.

07   Title II (Arts. 3 to 6) sets out a Community information and

---

[2] O.J. 1979, L131/15: Annex 1 updated to May 1, 1980, in O.J. 1980, C173. Although China is no longer classified as a state trading country in this regulation a special regime applies to it under Regulation 2532/78, O.J. 1978, L306/1.

consultative procedure. This is triggered by a Member State informing the Commission that particular trends appear to call for measures of surveillance or protective measures (Art. 2 (1)). Consultations, at the initiative of a Member State or the Commission, follow within eight working days (Art. 4). Consultations must be held if surveillance or protective action is to be taken. The forum for these consultations is an advisory committee of the Member States, chaired by the Commission (Art. 5) although consultation may take place in writing, subject to a right to seek oral consultation in the next five to eight working days (*ibid.*). Once measures have been taken under Title III or IV they are subject to consultation procedures under Article 15 which may lead to the Commission revoking its own decision or proposing revocation of any Council action taken.

30—08   *Title III (Arts. 7 to 11): Surveillance.* Surveillance may be instituted where developments in the market in respect of a product threaten to cause injury to Community producers of like or directly competing products *and* the interests of the Community so require (Art. 7 (1)). Surveillance may be either retrospective or prior to importation. In the latter event the goods can be imported only on production of an import document (Art. 8). Import documents must be freely issued on application but are of limited validity. National surveillance may be imposed if prior Community surveillance is refused (Art. 9). Similar conditions apply. There is usually no great difficulty either about getting agreement to institute Community surveillance or about imposing surveillance at national level as provided for in Article 9, since surveillance is essentially a system of keeping check, watching trends and appreciating risks. Unless otherwise provided, surveillance measures lapse at the end of the second half calendar year after they were imposed.

30—09   *Title IV (Arts. 12 to 15): Protective Measures.* A more direct protective measure is the introduction or modification of quantitative restrictions. The normal procedure is for the Member State which wants restrictions to ask for them. If the Commission agrees with the request, it proposes a regulation which establishes quantitative restrictions for the Member State or States, or the whole Community, and the regulation is adopted by the Council. The Commission may adopt interim measures by Commission regulation pending Council action. If the Commission declines to propose restrictions the applicant Member State can refer the matter to the Council which decides by qualified majority.

The principal powers to impose Community protective measures are Article 12, which describes the interim procedures, and Article 13 which deals with the longer term action to be taken by the

Council. Under both, measures may apply for the whole of the Community or a region of it. The criterion for action is fear of substantial injury to Community producers of like or directly competing products (the GATT test). Article 13 can in addition be used, *e.g.* to prevent a particular third country producer from using up an entire quota made available to third countries as a group or under the GSP arrangements.[3] The Council's powers to act under Article 13 are quite general. The Commission interim measures under Article 12 may consist in limiting the period of validity of prior Community surveillance, imports documents or requiring import authorisation on terms and conditions laid down by the Commission pending action, if any, by the Council under Article 13 (Art. 12 (1)). Under Article 12 the Commission can be called upon to act within the five working days (para. 4) and its decisions take effect immediately (para. 1). They can be referred to the Council by any Member State within one month (para. 5). The Council can confirm, amend or revoke the Commission's decision. Inaction on the referral for three months means revocation (para. 6).

—10   For liberalised products and, from January 1, 1982, non-liberalised products also (Art. 17 (6) and (9)), Article 14 allows individual Member States to impose import restrictions unilaterally on an interim basis pending endorsement by the Commission and/or the Council under the Article 12 and 13 machinery. Grounds are again fear of substantial injury (as under Article 12 and 13) or any appropriate protective clause contained in a pre-Community commercial policy bilateral agreement between that Member State and the sending third country which has been kept in force.[4] The action taken here by the Member State must be autonomous: discussions with the other party are permitted but not negotiations or the conclusion of an agreement, since these matters now fall to the Community under Article 113. Action under either limb of Article 14 triggers the five-day period for Commission action under Article 12 (4). Normally any Commission decision would override the national measures immediately, but if the Member State refers the Commission decision to the Council first its own measures remain in force until Article 12 (6) has run its course (Art. 14 (4)). In relation to fear of substantial injury Article 14 is limited in validity until December 31, 1981, by which time it is to be amended by Council decision. The predecessor Article 14 in Regulation 1439/74[5] was correspondingly limited and was not in fact amended. The view was therefore taken that it remained in force.

National procedures for the adjustment of rules on non-liberalised

---

[3] *Infra,* para. 30–34.
[4] *Infra,* para. 30–25.
[5] O.J. 1974, L159/1.

goods are to be abolished from December 31, 1981, (Art. 17 (9)). Thereafter they will be subject to Title IV except for the right of a Member State to refer the Commission decision to the Council. The effect of this change will be largely to assimilate non-liberalised goods to those on the common liberalisation list, so far as concerns states not maintaining limitations.

(c) State trading Countries

30—11 Regulation 925/79[6] establishes common rules for imports from state trading countries. The system is closely related to that established by Regulation 926/79. In principle products covered by the Annex are not subject to quantitative restrictions but following a Community information and consultation procedure surveillance or protective measures may be imposed in respect of those products. Where a product is liberalised throughout the Community there are two choices: either it can be added to the Annex listing free imports from state trading countries or, if no Member State objects, the product can be added to the common liberalisation list now contained in Regulation 926/79 (Art. 2).

Because of the economic structure of state trading countries and the consequent impact on the cost of goods, consultation is triggered not only where trends in imports appear to call for protective measures, but where any unusual or exceptional activity is detected at the stage of granting import authorisation (Art. 3).

30—12 Surveillance (Art. 6) can be imposed "where Community interests so require." Procedures are similar to and to some extent linked to those provided for in Regulation 926/79 for non-liberalised products. Even at the surveillance stage, however, powers are provided to limit the period of validity of import documents or to provide for insertion of a revocation clause or to make the grant of import documents subject to the prior notification and prior consultation procedure of Article 4 (3) (Art. 6 (1) (c)). There is in this case only Community surveillance. There is no provision for national surveillance of products covered.

The powers to take protective measures are again divided between Commission interim measures (Art. 7), Council measures (Art. 8) and Member State interim measures (Art. 9). The criteria for taking protective measures are the same as under Regulation 926/79, Article 12 (1) (*b*).

Like Regulation 926/79, Regulation 925/79 is to be amended by December 31, 1981, notably by introducing a Community import document for state traders (Art. 11).

30—13 Pending the conclusion of trade agreements between the Community and the various state trading countries, the Community now operates a *quota system* for *non-liberalised* products, under

[6] O.J. 1979, L131/1.

Regulation 3286/80,[7] which involves "communitarisation" of national quotas in respect of products imported from state trading countries. Under this regulation what were formerly national quotas are converted into annual Community quotas in respect of each state trading country for each Member State. It is expressly stated in Article 3 (1) of the regulation that the annual Council decision laying down the quotas to be opened shall not affect Member States' rules governing the opening and administration of quotas. Where products are subject to QRs in a single Member State the Member State may extend the quota or open import facilities if no quota has been laid down (Art. 4 (1) (*a*)). Where products are subject to QRs in more than one Member State the interested Member State can take unilateral action within certain limits (Art. 4 (1) (*b*)). In other cases a Member State must initiate a process of amending the import arrangements applicable to a given state trading country, or countries, by notifying the other Member States and the Commission (Art. 7). If no consultations are requested in response to this notification, the Member States may implement the proposed amendment of import arrangements within five days (Art. 9). Consultation may have the effect of delaying adoption of the proposed amendment but the amendment can only be blocked by submitting a proposal to the Council taking account of the objections raised in the course of consultations (Art. 9 (4)). In urgent cases, measures to restrict import facilities by withdrawing liberalisation or abolishing or reducing a quota may be brought into effect after notification but without prior consultation.

—14   Article 4 (3) provides that once the opening of Community negotiations with a third country has been authorised, Member States may no longer put into effect autonomous amendments to their import terms in respect of that country without authorisation by the Council.

(d) Voluntary Restraint Arrangements (VRAs)

—15   In certain circumstances the Community or Member States prefer to avoid formal imposition of quotas. Instead some form of voluntary restraint on the part of the exporter is sought. Negotiation of such voluntary restraints at government to government level is for the Community represented by the Commission. This does not rule out the possibility of discussions between the Member States and the third country but it does exclude a formal bilateral agreement. The Member State may, however, formally request the Commission to negotiate on its behalf. The autonomous increase of imports of products subject to a VRA are governed by Regulation 1471/70[8] which provides that where the

---

[7] O.J. 1980, L353/1. See Dec. 80/1278 O.J. 1980, L376/1 for 1981 quotas.
[8] Reg. 1471/70. J.O. 1970, L164/41.

Community decides to propose or to accept that a third country practising voluntary restraint in respect of exports to the Community may increase its exports to the Community the decision is to be taken in accordance with the management committee procedure laid down in Article 11 of Regulation 1023/70 (*supra*), establishing the common procedure for administering quantitative quotas, and having due regard to certain listed factors.[9]

Interim Protective Measures: QRs and VRAs

30–16   Where direct import of a product is subject to QRs or VRAs in one Member State there may be a danger of trade deflection through other Member States. In these circumstances Decision 71/202[10] and Decision 73/55[11] permit the Member State concerned to make importation subject to the granting of an import authorisation under certain conditions. If trade deflection in fact proves likely the Member State concerned can withhold the import authorisation and ask for action under Article 115.

(e) Textiles

30–17   As textiles are governed by the GATT Arrangement regarding International Trade in Textiles (the so-called Multifibre Agreement),[12] they are something of a special case. Article 2 (1) of the Multifibre Agreement requires all existing unilateral quantitative restrictions, bilateral agreements and any other quantitative measures in force which have a restrictive effect to be notified to the Textile Surveillance Body (TSB). Article 2 (2) and (3) then envisages some dismantling of restrictive arrangements. Article 3 prohibits new restrictions on trade in textile products or the intensification of existing restrictions unless such action is justified under the GATT or under Article 3 itself. Article 3 provides essentially for restrictions in the case of disruption of the national market by imports. The right of the Community to take action under the Multifibre Agreement or under Regulation 926/79 may be limited by the commitments accepted in a given bilateral agreement on trade in textile products between the Community and the given country. Recent agreements with low-cost suppliers have provided for bilateral quota ceilings. Those bilateral quotas are reflected in Community quantitative limits, imports of other listed products from listed countries being free in principle.[13] Imports of textile products from state trading countries are

---

[9] For a list of VRAs see W.Q. 295/77; O.J. 1977, C270/10 and Appendix 3.
[10] J.O. 1971, L121/26.
[11] O.J. 1973, L80/22.
[12] Arrangement regarding international trade in textiles, Geneva December 20, 1973, Cmnd. 6205, extended by Decision 77/806, O.J. 1977, L348/59.
[13] Regulation 3059/78, O.J. 1978, L365/1, last amendment by Regulation 2143/79, O.J. 1979, L248/1. China: Regulation 3061/79 O.J. 1979, L345/1.

governed by separate arrangements.[14] There are also separate arrangements for GSP beneficiaries.[15]

Imports

▶—18   Article VI (2) of GATT permits contracting parties to levy an anti-dumping duty on any dumped product. This must not be greater in amount than the margin of dumping. Normally this is based upon the difference between the price on the export market and the price charged on the manufacturer's home market. Paragraph 3 permits the imposition of countervailing duties to an amount equal to the estimated bounty or subsidy determined to have been granted, directly or indirectly, on the manufacture, production or export of a product in the country of origin or exportation. The term "countervailing duty" is to be understood to mean a special duty levied for the purpose of offsetting any bounty or subsidy bestowed, directly or indirectly, upon the manufacture, production or export of any merchandise. Under paragraph 6 (*a*) of Article VI no contracting party shall levy any anti-dumping or countervailing duty on the importation of any product unless it determines that the dumping or subsidisation will cause or threaten material injury to an established domestic industry, or will retard materially the establishment of a domestic industry.

Additional GATT rules were adopted at the conclusion of the 1973 to 1979 Multilateral Trade Negotiations in the form of an Agreement on the interpretation and application of Article VI, XVI and XXIII of GATT - dealing with subsidies and countervailing duties - and an agreement on implementation of Article VI - the new Anti-Dumping Code.[16]

▶—19   The Community rules, adopted to take account of the new GATT rules, are contained in Regulation 3017/79[17] for EEC products and the very similar Council Recommendation 3018/79/ECSC[18] for ECSC products. Dumping and countervailing is now a matter of exclusive Community competence. Article 2, Part A, of the EEC regulation sets out the basic principle that an anti-dumping duty is to be applied to any dumped product whose entry for consumption in the Community causes injury. A product is to be considered dumped if its export price to the Community is less than the normal value of the like product. Parts B to F of Article 2 then set out rules for determining normal value, export price, methods of comparison, like product and dumping margin.

[14] See Regulation 3286/80 O.J. 1980, L353/1.
[15] Regulation 3320/80, O.J. 1980, L351/1 (1981 quotas).
[16] Concluded on behalf of the Community by Council Decision 80/271, O.J. 1980, L71/72 & 90.
[17] O.J. 1979, L339/1. And see generally C. Stanbrook, *A Manual on the EEC Anti-Dumping Law and Procedure,* (1980 EBP).
[18] O.J. 1979, L339/15.

Article 3 provides for countervailing duties to off-set any subsidy on any product whose entry for consumption in the Community causes injury. The annex contains a non-exhaustive list of subsidies. Article 3 (3) exempts refunds of duties or taxes on export goods from countervailing duties. Article 4 lays down mechanisms for determining injury under both Article 2 and 3. The criterion is one of material injury, actual or potential, to an established or nascent industry.

30—20 Provision is made for individuals to initiate the procedures under the regulation by written complaint (Art. 5). Consultation within an advisory committee of the Member States, chaired by the Commission, follows the complaint (Art. 6). If there appears to be a prima facie case, investigations are initiated by the Commission, which may result in the imposition by regulation (Art. 13) of anti-dumping or countervailing duties. There duties may be provisional (Art. 11) or as a result of definitive action (Art. 12). Proceedings may equally be terminated with a finding that protective measures are unnecessary (Art. 9) or on the basis of a satisfactory undertaking from the supplier (Art. 10).

The regulation is expressed to be without prejudice to any special rules in agreements with third countries or in Community agricultural regulations or any Community special measures provided they do not run counter to GATT obligations. These special measures may not by-pass the basic regulation.[19]

The anti-dumping and countervailing powers complement those on common rules for imports (*supra*): surveillance or other protective measures may be a preliminary to action under this instrument.

Powers in relation to exports

30—21 Regulation 2603/69[20] establishing common rules for exports is very similar in structure to Regulation 926/79. In principle exports are free (Art. 1) subject to a fairly short list of exceptions (Art. 11). Surveillance (Art. 5) or protective measures may be imposed following the usual Community information and consultative procedure (Arts. 2 to 4). Commission interim measures (Art. 6) may be taken in order to prevent a critical situation from arising on account of a shortage of essential products or to remedy such a situation. Definitive measures may be taken where the interests of the Community so require, the Council acting on the same grounds as under Article 6, or to meet international undertakings (Art. 7).

---

[19] See, *e.g.* Reg. 3171/80, O.J. 1980, L331/25 and see ball bearing cases: 113/77 *NTN Toyo Bearing Co.* v. *Council* [1979] E.C.R. 1185; 118/77 *ISO* v. *Council* [1979] E.C.R. 1277.

[20] O.J. 1969, L324/25.

Provisions common to imports and exports

0—22   Regulation 1023/70[21] sets up a Community system for the allocation between Member States of autonomous and contractual quantitative import and export quotas on products other than agricultural products subject to a market organisation (Art. 13). The quota for the whole Community is fixed by the Council (Art. 2) but the individual Member State allocations are made by the Commission and the Quota Administration Committee acting as a normal management committee upon criteria laid down by the Council (Arts. 2 and 11).

Quotas fixed by the Member States themselves, whether unilaterally or by agreement, are not covered by the regulation. Such quotas may still exist for products not covered by Regulation 926/79.

Export credits

0—23   Some action has been taken in relation to export aids, referred to in Article 112. A decision of the Council of September 27, 1960,[22] set up a policy co-ordination group in this connection for credit insurance, credit guarantees and financial credits. The Group is to put forward suggestions for harmonisation and generally to consider matters in this area. It consists of representatives from the Member States and the Commission. Under the action programme for the Community in matters of common commercial policy, established by Council decision of September 25, 1962,[23] the Commission established a list of all existing export aids. Council Decision 65/53[24] revised the consultation procedure previously applicable in the field of credit insurance, etc., to facilitate harmonisation of the systems throughout the Community. On the basis of this preparatory work, the Community has now issued instruments respecting the adoption of common credit insurance techniques for various types of operations, and rules on export guarantees.[25] The Commission seems not to be contemplating common rules in this area. There are, however, international understandings in this area and notably the OECD

---

[21] J.O. 1970, L124/1.

[22] J.O. 1960, 1359.

[23] J.O. 1962, 2353.

[24] J.O. 1965, 255.

[25] Directive 70/509, J.O. 1970, L254/1, on the adoption of a common credit insurance policy for medium and long-term transactions with public buyers: Directive 70/510, J.O. 1970, L254/26, on the adoption of a common credit insurance policy for medium and long-term operations with private buyers: Decision 70/552, J.O. 1970, L284/50, on the rules applicable in the fields of export guarantees and finance for export, to certain sub-contracting in other member countries of the European Communities or in non-member countries; and Directive 71/86, J.O. 1971, L36/14, on the harmonisation of basic provisions in respect of guarantees for short-term transactions (political risks) with public buyers or with private buyers.

Gentlemen's Agreement on Export Credits.[26] In Opinion 1/75 *Export Credits*[27] dealing with the understanding on a local costs standard the Court had no difficulty in holding that the Community had powers under the commercial policy to adopt internal rules and to conclude agreements with third countries relating to systems of aid for exports. It went on to hold that these powers are exclusive, at least in a field such as that governed by the understanding in question, this despite the argument that action in respect of export credits is for Member States and not the Community. It may nevertheless be supposed that the opinion is not unlimited in scope: it presumably does not extend to export credits granted as part of official development assistance (ODA).

Co-ordination of Relations with Third Countries

30—24 The EEC Treaty makes no provision for the co-ordination of the bilateral agreements of Member States with third countries (multilateral agreements are considered *supra*, para. 29-28). This lacuna was filled by the Council Decision of October 9, 1961,[28] obliging Member States to communicate details of all negotiations concerning commercial relations to the other Members and to the Commission, and instituting a system of prior consultation between the Member States and the Commission. This is reinforced by another decision of the same date,[29] aimed at standardising the duration of trade agreements with third countries. No new trade agreement was to be extended in duration beyond the end of the original transitional period (Art. 1) pending the establishment of the common commercial policy. The Council had already laid it down by decision of July 20, 1960[30] that Member States should insist on the insertion of a clause guaranteeing the benefits of any bilateral agreement to all Member States of the Community, so avoiding potential conflicts with the progressive implementation of the common commercial policy. By Article 2 of the second decision of October 9, 1961, agreements not containing an "EEC clause" nor a clause providing for annual notice were not, subject to Article 1 (*supra*), to be valid for more than one year.

30—25 During the transitional period, this system operated well. For the definitive period Article 113 requires that trade agreements shall be negotiated by the Commission on behalf of the Community. Provisions needed for the transition from the old to new procedure were laid down by Decision 69/494.[31] Difficulties

---

[26] To which the Community adhered in March 1977. Current arrangements date from February 22, 1978.
[27] [1975] E.C.R. 1355.
[28] J.O. 1961, 1273.
[29] J.O. 1961, 1274.
[30] W.Q. 78, J.O. 1960, 1965.
[31] J.O. 1969, L326/29.

arise here because certain countries do not recognise the Community as an international legal person and will not therefore undertake trade negotiations with it.

The decision establishes a system of notification (Art. 1) and consultation between States and the Commission prior to the renegotiation or extension, express or tacit, of any agreements or arrangements concerning commercial relations (Art. 2). Article 3 permits the express or tacit extension of such agreements for up to one year where they do not hinder the implementation of the common commercial policy. Where the agreement has a reservation clause or a clause providing for annual notice of termination, extension may be authorised for a longer period. If the agreement seems likely to hinder the common commercial policy, the renegotiation of the agreement is to be governed by Title II (Art. 4). Title II sets out the system of Community negotiations, which is merely the Article 113 procedure in expanded form. However, Title III makes provision for the situation where such negotiating procedure is not appropriate, notably in respect of State trading countries. In the latter case negotiations may, after consultations, be conducted by Member States (Art. 12) but they must follow the recommendations put forward by a special committee of representatives of the Member States, set up by the first decision of October 9, 1961.[32] The result of the negotiations must be reported to the Commission and the other Member States; if no objections are lodged by Member States and if the Commission approves, the agreement may be concluded; otherwise it may be concluded only after authorisation by the Council, acting by qualified majority on a proposal from the Commission (Art. 13). The Title III derogation was to have terminated on December 31, 1973, but in the absence of agreements with the Eastern European countries, bilateral agreements were permitted on the precedent of a Franco-Soviet agreement of May 26, 1969, the last expiring on December 31, 1975.[33]

0—26   The Council has authorised the tacit extension of a number of trade agreements acting under Article 113 EEC and 3 of Decision 69/494.[34]

So much for trade agreements. Whereas new trade agreements have become a matter of exclusive Community competence, and the renewal of old bilateral agreements is a matter for Community procedures, economic co-operation agreements fall into a separate category. Member States are free to conclude economic co-operation agreements provided they do not incorporate matters falling within the common commercial policy (most obviously tariffs and quantitative restrictions). The borderline is obviously

---

[32] *Supra*, note 28.
[33] Decision 69/265 J.O. 1969, L206/33 and W.Q. 466/74 O.J. 1975, C19/15 and Decision 74/34, O.J. 1974, L30/1 and Decision 74/482, O.J. 1974, L226/1.
[34] See, *e.g.* Decision 80/379, O.J. 1980, L93/26.

a fine one. Agreements with state trading countries have manifested more of the commercial policy characteristics than have others with non-state traders.[35]

A consultative procedure in this area too was instituted by Decision 74/393[36] which covers economic and industrial co-operation agreements and associated measures in so far as these measures may affect common policies or in particular trade (Art. 1). It is interpreted as not applying to agreements concerned purely with scientific co-operation or assistance to developing countries without economic concessions (technical assistance agreements). Financial agreements are subject to a separate procedure.

30—27   Member States are to inform the Commission and the Member States about negotiations and are to forward the texts of co-operation agreements in final form but before signature (notification procedure). Consultations take place on the request of any Member State or the Commission within the usual type of committee of representatives of the Member States chaired by the Commission. Matters relating to the responsibilities of the Policy Co-ordination Group for credit insurance, credit guarantees and financial credits are referred to that Group.[37]

During an initial period the consultation procedure was applied in practice only to agreements with state trading countries and oil producing countries.

Political Co-operation

30—28   Because of its very close links with the work of the European Council in other fields, political co-operation in foreign affairs is considered in chapter 4; European Council : Political Co-operation.

Development Policies

30—29 The Community's present development co-operation policies are now manifested through a wide range of legal instruments but the basis for the current approach is the Commission Memorandum on a Community Development Co-operation Policy of July 27, 1971.[38] This envisaged a coherent policy towards the various elements of the then state of the Community's external relations. First concrete steps were considered to be the adaptation of the agreements in the Mediterranean Basin to take account of the enlargement of the Community; renewal on a broader basis of the agreements with Morocco and Tunisia, and the development and

---

[35] See W.Q. 486/80, O.J. 1980, L213/13 and 939/79, O.J. 1979, C316/58 and 156/11.
[36] O.J. 1974, L208/23.
[37] J.O. 1960, 1339.
[38] Bulletin Suppt. 5/1971. See also Stevens, C. (ed.), *EEC and the Third World, A Survey* (Hodder & Stoughton, 1981).

reinforcement of the Community's policy towards the Mediterranean in general; negotiations for the extension of Yaoundé II and Arusha II; developments in the context of generalised preferences, food aid, participation in UNCTAD III, and participation in work under the second Development Decade; and finally, implementation of measures decided on by the Council following study of the Commission's Memorandum on Latin American problems.[39] Further, the Commission advocated various generalised measures designed to facilitate exports from developing countries and to provide the latter with development aid and technical assistance.

0—30   In the "Memorandum from the Commission on a Community Policy on Development Co-operation" of February 2, 1972,[40] described as a programme for initial action, reference was made to "Measures to benefit exports from developing countries," involving action on commodities, notably coffee, cocoa and sugar; action to promote the export trade of developing countries with the Community: gradual abolition of excise duties on tropical produce; and protection of the guarantee of origin of foodstuffs. The programme also referred to "other measures favouring economic development of developing countries," which should be taken especially in order to intensify public aid and ensure its regularity, to ease the financial conditions attached to aid, to institute Community untying of public aid, to harmonise aid action, and to encourage regional co-operation between developing countries.

0—31   With a view to carrying out this programme the Council adopted nine resolutions and a recommendation on: improvement of the GSP; commodity agreements; volume of official aid for development (ODA); conditions attaching to ODA; debt burden of developing countries, geographical allocation of aid (the recommendation); regional integration among LDCs; promotion of exports from LDCs; co-ordination and harmonisation of Member States' national policies on development co-operation, and financial and technical aid to non-associated LDCs.[41]

These ideas are reflected in the Commission's more general communication entitled Development Aid: Fresco of Community Action Tomorrow.[42] The Fresco recognises that the problems of under-development are very diverse and that given limited resources emphasis should be on the most needy (both Associated and Non-Associated), financial and technical co-operation enjoying priority.

0—32   These various strands are being implemented through the Association and Co-operation Agreements in particular under

[39] Council Doc. 5/913/2/70 (COMER 211) Rev.2.
[40] Bulletin Suppt. 2/1972.
[41] Bulletin 7/8/1974.
[42] Com (74) 1725 final; Bulletin Suppt. 8/1974; E.P. Doc. 42/75.

Lomé[43] and the Mediterranean Agreements.[44] New trade and co-operation agreements are now being negotiated with countries outside these umbrellas, notably with India.[45] Besides these general agreements reference must be made to bilateral agreements under the GATT,[46] MFA,[47] the food-aid programme[48] and the GSP[49] and to the various comodity agreements[50] and the Common Fund.[51] The Community also makes contributions from its budget to bodies concerned with international development and to non-associated countries.[52] A composite table of Preferential Tariff Treatment applied by the Community as at January 1, 1981, was published in O.J. 1981, C122. It is not the place here to analyse the North South Dialogue. Suffice it to say that the Community has been active, with the Member States in the sixth, seventh and eighth special sessions of the United Nations on Development issues. In the Paris Conference on International Economic Co-operation (CIEC) the Community in the shape of the Presidency and the Commission spoke for the Member States on all issues since the number of places for Western delegations was limited. Member States, participating in a single Community delegation, could comment on specific issues if so invited, but this facility was little used. As will be apparent from the foregoing account, the Community's development policies cover a very broad range of topics. The legal aspects present themselves in a somewhat partial and fragmented fashion. Apart from those aspects mentioned above and considered elsewhere, three specific areas call for further discussion; the implementing arrangements for Part Four Association, the GSP and Food Aid.

Part Four association

30—33   The Treaty provisions here are discussed *supra*, para. 29-24. The implementing arrangements are contained in successive Council decisions on the association of the overseas countries and territories with the European Economic Community,[53] designed to parallel the successive Yaoundé/Lomé Association Agreements.[54]

---

[43] *Infra,* Chapter 31.
[44] *Ibid.*
[45] *Ibid.*
[46] *Ibid.*
[47] *Ibid.*
[48] *Infra,* para. 30–35.
[49] *Infra,* para. 30–34.
[50] *Infra,* Chapter 31.
[51] *Ibid.*
[52] See Fourteenth General Report (1980) point 590.
[53] Currently Decision 80/1186, O.J. 1980, L361/1 (parallels Lomé II).
[54] *Infra,* Chapter 31.

Generalised Scheme of Tariff Preferences (GSP)

0—34 Introduced in July 1971, the Community's scheme of generalised preferences in favour of developing countries[55] has been renewed for the post-1980 period.[56] Principal criticisms to date have been that the original system principally benefitted a rather small group of the intended beneficiaries, in practice only covered a limited proportion of trade and was in any event unduly complex in its administration.[57] It is hoped that these criticisms are met in the new system. The new scheme's differential application of preferential treatment may meet the first two criticisms.

Food aid

0—35 Principally an emanation of the policies designed to dispose of food surpluses,[58] the Community food aid programme now covers, in addition to grains under the International Wheat Agreement and associated Food Aid Convention[59] a wide range of high protein and high calorie foods. The programme is directed to coping with international emergencies and disaster relief, medium term dietary supplementation and in particular to meet the "food gap" in many developing countries and thus to contribute to economic and social development. Food aid is provided direct in many instances and also through international relief and humanitarian agencies.[60]

The so-called programme is still very piecemeal, being based as to most commodities on Article 43 (agriculture) for the autonomous arrangements, and on Article 113 (commercial policy) for most contractual arrangements.[61]

Status and Representation

0—36 An aspect of the Community's enjoyment of international legal

[55] Originally Regs. 1308 to 1314/71, O.J. 1971, L142, with annual updatings.
[56] Regs. 3320/80 (textiles), 3321/80 (agricultural products), 3322/80 (multi-annual scheme in respect of industrial products) and Decision 80/1185 ECSC (steel products), all in O.J. 1980, L354. See also House of Lords Select Committee on the European Communities, Generalised Scheme of Tariff Preferences (GSP), session 1979–80, 61st Report July 22, 1981, (332).
[57] For criticisms see, *e.g.* R.N. Cooper, "The European Community's System of Generalised Tariff Preferences: A critique," 8 *Journal of Development Studies*, p.379; B. S. Hurni, "Evolution of the Generalised System of Preferences of the European Communities; a Perspective" (1976) J.W.T.L. 383; A. Weston, "How sensitive is the EEC's Generalised System of Preferences?" *1980 Overseas Development Institute Review*.
[58] See G. Marendo, "Bases juridiques communautaires de l'aide alimentaire aux pays en voie de développement" (1973) RTDE, p.623.
[59] *Infra*, Chapter 31.
[60] See generally *L'aide alimentaire de la Communauté*, X/607/74–8.
[61] See note 58 *supra*. For current arrangements see, *e.g.* Regs. 1310/80, 1311/80 (*Skimmed Milk Powder*), 1312/80, 1313/80, (*milk fats*) and Decision 80/541 (*Cereals*) O.J. 1980, L134. See also Fourteenth Annual Report (1980) point 593.

personality is that it necessarily requires premises in the Member States and arrangements to cover it personnel and those having dealings with it. This is considered under two headings; location of the institutions of the Communities; and privileges and immunities, both in Chapter 5, *supra*.

A further aspect to be mentioned is that the Community also sends representatives to third countries. In those circumstances they usually receive the Vienna Convention level of privileges and immunities. The Community has delegations (effectively diplomatic missions) in Canada, Japan and the United States and Colombia (for South America) and also at the seat of the OECD in Paris, and at the United Nations in Geneva and in New York. There are also delegations in most of the ACP States, dealing principally with co-operation under Lomé. Besides these there is an information office in Turkey.

Chapter 31

SURVEY OF AGREEMENTS

N.B. All References are given in Appendix 3

31—01 Since the accession of the first new Member States in 1973 the scope and range of matters covered by international agreements to which the Community is a party (either acting alone or with the Member States) has expanded enormously.[1]

In this survey the main agreements[2] are considered under the following headings:

(1) Agreements between the Community and third countries
(2) Participation of the Community in international organisations
(3) General multilateral conventions to which the Community is a party.

Largely because many of the agreements have been subject to successive amendments, the references to the agreements discussed are omitted from this survey. References to the agreements, and their amendments, are to be found in Appendix 3.

Agreements between the Community and Third Countries

31—02 This category of agreement is essentially bilateral in character in that these agreements purport to regulate the relations (principally trade) between the Community on the one hand and the other party or parties on the other. The multilateral agreements in this group (notably the Lomé Convention) distinguish themselves from the agreements in category 3 in that they are concluded under the auspices of the Community rather than of some other international organisation or conference, typically within the United Nations system.

While it cannot necessarily be said that the Community has a coherent policy towards third countries as a group, or even towards all groups of third countries, the agreements with countries in given parts of the world show definite common characteristics. The agreements are therefore considered in the following groups.

(1) EFTA countries
(2) Mediterranean countries

---

[1] For position to January 1, 1972, *cf.* 1st ed. of this work.

[2] Main agreements: this survey leaves out of account ephemeral agreements (duration 12 months or less) such as annual tariff agreements and minor amendments of main agreements. Bilateral GATT tariff agreements are also omitted. For full picture of agreements in force with a particular country see Appendix 3.

    (A) Mediterranean countries in Europe
      (1) Trade Agreements
      (2) Association Agreements
    (B) Mediterranean countries in Africa and Asia
    (3) State trading countries
    (4) Lomé Convention
    (5) Trade agreements with Asian countries
    (6) Latin American countries
    (7) North American countries
    (8) Sectoral Agreements

31—03   It is helpful to bear in mind two points in this survey:

(1)   trade agreements concluded under Articles 113 and 114 are
Community alone agreements; agreements going wider than trade
matters have in practice been mixed agreements; and
(2)   all general agreements in categories 1 to 4 and 8 are preferential: that is to say, they offer tariff concessions over and above
the CCT and GSP. General trade agreements in categories 5 to 7
above are non-preferential. A composite table of Preferential
Tariff Treatment applied by the Community on January 1, 1980,
was published in O.J. 1980, C244.

EFTA Countries

31—04   The European Free Trade Association (EFTA) was established by
European countries which did not participate in the founding of
the European Economic Community. EFTA was in large measure
the response of those countries to the EEC. The EFTA association
is much looser than the EEC customs union. It is limited to providing for tariff-free access for industrial products originating in
EFTA countries. It does not extend to trade in agricultural goods.
    The United Kingdom, Denmark and Ireland, all originally EFTA
countries, acceded to the Community on January 1, 1973, at the
same time necessarily terminating their EFTA participation. With
a view to avoiding any disruption in relations between the EFTA
and EEC groupings preferential trade agreements were negotiated
between the Community and each of the so-called EFTA non-
candidate   countries   (*Austria,   Iceland,   Portugal,   Sweden,
Switzerland* (with *Liechtenstein*) - July 22, 1972; *Finland* - October
5, 1973, and, since she did not in the event accede to the EEC,
Norway - May 14, 1973). These agreements were for the most part
designed to enter into force on January 1, 1973, the date the new
Member States acceded to the EEC. That with Finland entered
into force on January 1, 1974, while that with Norway entered
into force on July 1, 1973.

31—05   The basic provisions of the EFTA agreements are identical.
Differences arise in the treatment of individual products, for the
most part covered in annexed Protocols. Discussion in the ensuing

paragraphs is based on the article numbers of the EEC/Austria Agreement. (The numbers of articles in the agreements with Iceland and Portugal are displaced by the interpolation of additional articles attracting additional Protocols of lists of products, etc.).

Each of the agreements provides for free trade in industrial products and processed agricultural products (Art. 2). Agricultural products *per se* are excluded although the parties "declare their readiness to foster . . . the harmonious development of trade in agricultural products . . . " (Art. 15 (1)). Tariff disarmament for the products covered and originating in the EFTA country or the Community, as the case might be, was to take place progressively. All customs duties and all charges having equivalent effect on imports and exports were, with a few exceptions, abolished by July 1, 1977.

Tariff treatment for particular goods (including agricultural products) is defined in Protocols 1 and 2, and in some cases additional Protocols, tailored to each EFTA country. Subject to this, quantitative restrictions and measures having equivalent effect on imports and exports were to be abolished by January 1, 1975 (Art. 13).

l—06   The tariff arrangements are supported by freedom of payments (Art. 19) and a variety of specific clauses on non-discrimination (veterinary and health rules, Art. 15 (2); internal taxation, Art. 18; application of rules on *ordre public*, Art. 20), but conversely once tariff disarmament is complete, products from the EFTA country may not enjoy more favourable treatment than that applied by the Member States between themselves (Art. 16).

These basic trade provisions are backed up by a number of general clauses for the most part reflecting provisions in the EEC Treaty: a saving for defence interests (Art. 21; *cf.* Art. 223 EEC); full faith and credit clause (Art. 22; *cf.* Art. 5 EEC); competition rules (Art. 23; *cf.* Arts. 85, 86 and 92 EEC); safeguards (Art. 24; *cf.* Art. 226 EEC and agricultural safeguard clauses); anti-dumping (Art. 25; *cf.* Reg. 3017/79[3]); a safeguard in respect of serious disturbances in any sector of the economy or risk of serious deterioration in the economic situation of a region (Art. 26; *cf.* Art. 92, paras. 2 and 3, EEC) and a balance of payments safeguard (Art. 28; *cf.* Arts. 108 and 109 EEC).

l—07   A Contracting Party may take safeguard measures immediately under Article 28 and, in "exceptional circumstances requiring immediate action" under Articles 24, 25 and 26 and in respect of export aids. In other circumstances, consultations are required first within the Joint Committee established to administer and implement the agreement under Article 29 (Art. 27). The Joint Committee also administers the skeletal competition rules (Art. 27

[3] O.J. 1979, L339/1 *supra*, para. 30–18.

(3) (*a*)). The EFTA agreements being "Community alone" agreements, the Joint Committee is composed of representatives of the Community on the one hand, and of representatives of the EFTA country on the other (Art. 30).

The Joint Committee is the forum for exchange of information and consultation concerning the application of the agreement. No other disputes settlement machinery is provided for, but consultation takes place at the request of either party (Art. 29 (2)). The Joint Committee meets on request of either Party and in any event once a year (Art. 31). It acts by mutual agreement (Art. 30).

31—08   Each Party presides in turn over the Joint Committee (Art. 31), which adopts its own rules of procedure (Art. 29 (3)). The Committee has power to make recommendations and to take decisions in the cases provided for in the agreement (notably in Art. 27) (Art. 29 (1)).

Although terminable on 12 months notice (Finland three months) (Art. 34) the agreements are concluded for an unlimited period. Provision is made for negotiations to widen the scope of the agreements (*e.g.* by extension to agriculture or to cover free movement of persons) (Art. 32). Protocols have been concluded to take account of Greek accession to the Community.

Portugal has applied for community membership. There is a pre-accession aid agreement, discussed *supra*, para. 29-33.

Mediterranean Countries in Europe

Trade agreements

31—09   The Community concluded a preferential Trade Agreement with *Spain* in 1970 and an accession protocol in 1973. Since that date no new arrangements have been made although negotiations for Spanish accession to the Community were opened in February 1979.[4] The agreement has expired.

The agreement is very similar in form to the Association Agreements with *Malta* and *Cyprus*, but was a pure trade agreement, so there was no provision for moves to a further stage. The Association Council, here called a Joint Committee, consisted of representatives of "the Community" on the Community side, this being a Community alone agreement concluded under Article 113.

The Community concluded Trade Agreements with *Yugoslavia* in 1970 and 1973. A new Co-operation Agreement was concluded on April 2, 1980, together with an Interim Agreement and Protocol pending entry into force of the Co-operation Agreement.

Association agreements

31—10   The Community concluded its first substantive agreements with

[4] Commission Opinion Bulletin Suppt. 9/78.

third countries in this group, Greece and Turkey. With the accession of Greece to the Community present members of the category are Turkey, Malta and Cyprus.

The Agreement of July 9, 1961, establishing an Association with *Greece*[5] now overtaken by accession of Greece to the Community,[6] formed the model for that with Turkey, with adaptations in the light of that first experience and having regard to the particular circumstances of Turkey.

31—11   The association agreement with *Greece* provided for the establishment of a customs union between the Community and Greece over a transitional period of 12 years. Provision was made for the free movement of goods along the lines of Title I of Part Two of the EEC Treaty: Articles 6 to 11 provided for free movement of goods in general; Articles 12 to 19 provided for the elimination of customs duties as between the contracting parties: Articles 20 and 21 provided for the adoption by Greece of the CCT and Articles 22 to 31 provided for the elimination of quantitative restrictions as between the parties. The agreement also contained special provisions relating to agriculture, in effect obliging Greece to adopt the Community's common agriculture policy, which must itself take account of Greek interests and problems (Arts. 32 to 43). The agreement further provided for free movement of persons and services (Arts. 44 to 50) as well as laying down rules relating to competition, taxation and the approximation of laws (Arts. 51 to 57). Articles 58 to 64 required the co-ordination of aims in the field of economic policy and called for freedom for payments and capital movements. It may be seen that the agreement was largely based on the EEC Treaty itself, this being indicative of the fact that the eventual aim of the association was always admission of Greece to full membership of the Community. Free access for Greek industrial goods and most agricultural goods was attained by July 1, 1968.

31—12   The agreement provided for a Council of Association, composed of members of the governments of Member States, of members of the Council and Commission, and of members of the Greek Government. No other institutions were mentioned although Article 67 (2) provided for the establishment of an ad hoc Court of Arbitration to settle disputes unresolved by the Council of Association. In addition to the above, a joint parliamentary committee was set up to assist in co-operation between the European Parliament and the Greek Parliament.

Protocol No. 19 annexed to the Agreement, the Financial Protocol, provided for Community loans to the Greek Government up to 125 million dollars, to be used for investment in Greece, particularly in infrastructure.

---

[5] J.O. 1963, 293.
[6] *Supra,* para. 29–32.

Following the Greek *coup d'état* in April 1967 the Association was limited to current affairs only.[7] The Agreement was, however, re-activated in August 1974, following the return to democracy. An accession protocol was concluded on April 28, 1975, and a new financial protocol on February 28, 1977.

31—13   *Turkey* followed Greece's example in concluding an association agreement with the Community. This was signed by the Member States, the Council and Turkey on September 12, 1963.

It aims at the progressive establishment of a customs union, but the timetable envisaged is slower than that for Greece; three phases of association are provided for: a preparatory phase lasting 12 to 22 years depending on the products involved, and a final phase. The conditions for the implementation of the transitional period were detailed in an Additional Protocol of November 23, 1970. A supplementary Accession Protocol and interim agreement (valid until entry into force of the Supplementary Protocol) were concluded on July 30, 1973.

As in the Greek Agreement, the provisions regarding the implementation of the customs union, and elimination of quantitative restrictions, are based on the principles of the EEC Treaty. Turkey has enjoyed free access for most industrial and 90 per cent. of agricultural exports since 1971. Financial Protocols to the original Agreement and to the Additional and Supplementary Protocols provide for financial aid to Turkey.

The Agreement sets up a Council of Association, composed as under the Greek agreement and with the same duties, but there is no provision for an ad hoc arbitration court.

31—14   The Association Agreements with *Malta* and *Cyprus* are less ambitious than those with Greece and Turkey. The stated aim here is to eliminate obstacles as regards the main body of trade between the Community and the associated country. The agreements detail the preferences extended and back these up with the usual provisions on rules of origin, non-discrimination, dumping, freedom of payments, serious disturbances, etc. There are no provisions on free movement of persons, etc. The agreements are supervised by a Council of Association which consists of Members of the Council (since these are mixed agreements) and the Commission on the Community side. The Council takes decision by common agreement. There is no provision in terms for disputes settlement.

These agreements provide for two successive stages, each in principle of five years, the second "providing for a further elimination of obstacles to trade . . . and the adoption by [the Associated Country] of the common customs tariff." In fact, this programme proved too ambitious. Neither agreement has moved to the second stage. Instead the first stage was extended and supplementary

[7] Fifth General Report (1971), p.309.

Protocols concluded providing for development co-operation and funding, principally in the form of EIB loans, over a period of five years (Malta 26 MUA; Cyprus 30 MUA in aggregate).

Besides the Protocols extending the first stage and the Financial Protocols, there are two further protocols in the case of Cyprus; a Supplementary Protocol and Protocol Relating to Agricultural Products, whose stated aim is to align the arrangements with Cyprus with those worked out for other Mediterranean countries under the Community's global policy, while at the same time taking account of the special difficulties resulting from partition.

Mediterranean Countries in Africa and Asia

—15   The Community has concluded Co-operation Agreements with the Mashreq and Magrheb countries and with Egypt and Israel. In accordance with the global Mediterranean policy,[8] the content of these agreements is very similar.

In the case of each of the *Magrheb* countries (*Algeria, Morocco, Tunisia*) there is a Co-operation Agreement of April 1976. Common provisions detail rules on m.f.n., non-discrimination, originating products, payments, dumping and safeguards, in principle applicable to both sides. The agreements are supervised by a Co-operation Council reflecting the mixed character of the agreement by including Council and Commission representation on the Community side. Provision is also made for compulsory settlement of disputes by arbitration.

No additional trade concessions are made by the Magrheb countries in the Co-operation Agreements beyond the provision on m.f.n. and non-discrimination. Provision is made for economic, technical and financial co-operation. Protocol No. 1 provides for Community financing, principally in the form of loans, but with about a quarter of the funds in the form of grants. This funding is to be available until October 31, 1981. That date will no doubt have to be extended.

In addition the Agreements provide that workers from the Magrheb will receive Community treatment in regard to terms and conditions of employment and benefits but not the right to seek work. These provisions are reciprocal for Community workers in the Magrheb.

The Co-operation Agreements were to be subject to review in 1978 and 1983, in the light of experience.

1—16   The arrangements with the *Mashreq* Countries (*Syria, Lebanon, Jordan*, and for these purposes, *Egypt*) are materially identical with those for the Magrheb. However, the Co-operation Agreements contain no provisions on labour and no compulsory arbitration clause, the only disputes mechanism being consultation in the Co-operation Council. The review dates for these agreements are

[8] Commission communication to the Council of September 22, 1972 ("Les relations entre la Communauté et les pays du bassin méditerranéen").

1979 and 1984; the financial Protocols run in principle to October 31, 1981.

31—17   The arrangements with *Israel*, growing out of an agreement dating from 1964, are based on a 1975 reciprocal preferential agreement providing for a standstill on new customs duties and QRs and charges and measures having equivalent effect. In addition to the usual provisions on non-discrimination, payments, safeguards and dumping there are outline competition rules similar to those in the EFTA Agreements. The agreement was in effect turned into a Mediterranean Co-operation Agreement by an Additional Protocol and Financial Protocol of 1977 instituting economic, technical and financial co-operation funded by loans. The Joint Committee provided for by the 1975 Agreement became a Co-operation Council established on a mixed agreement basis. No disputes settlement machinery is provided for as such. Review of the agreement is next to take place in 1983 (Art. 22) in the light of experience. Article 26 allows for extension to fields not covered by the 1975 Agreement and Protocols, following consultations and new agreements.

State Trading Countries

31—18 Negotiations with the Council for Mutual Economic Assistance (CMEA or COMECON) have been going on sporadically since 1972. With China no longer in this category for most purposes and Yugoslavia enjoying a wider trade agreement, the main country currently falling within this category is *Romania*, with which the Community has an agreement on trade in textiles, and agreements of July 28, 1980, establishing a Joint Committee, and on industrial products. The latter supplements the m.f.n. treatment now accorded to Romania as a result of its accession to GATT notably by placing a freeze on new QRs on products covered by the agreement and by according certain quotas on products which are subject to QRs. Serious injury/consultation mechanisms are provided. The Joint Committee, established by the separate agreement, is to oversee Community/Romania trade generally and to ensure the proper functioning of any agreements, in particular the trade agreement. The Committee can adopt recommendations by mutual agreement. VRAs have been concluded with certain countries on sheepmeat and goatmeat (see Appendix 3).

Lomé Convention[9]

31—19 The Second Lomé Convention of October 31, 1979, grew out of the Yaoundé Agreements concluded with the old Part Four Association countries after independence, as enlarged following

---

[9] For comment and criticisms see K.R. Simmonds "The Second Lomé Convention: the innovative features," 17 C.M.L. Rev. 1980 415–436 and C.H. Kirkpatrick, "Lomé II," 1980 J.W.T.L. 352.

accession of the United Kingdom and Denmark in 1973 in the first Lomé Convention. The new Convention has to be seen as a five-year step in a continuing relationship. The Second Lomé Convention, a mixed agreement, extends non-reciprocal preferences to some 58 African, Caribbean and Asian (ACP) countries for the five year duration of the agreement. The Community receives in return non-discriminatory m.f.n. treatment (Art. 9). For most ACP products access to the Community is duty free (Art. 2). Nevertheless, this provision does not affect a very large new volume of trade since ACP products for the most part benefit from GSP or m.f.n. Where agricultural goods are covered by variable levies, special preferential arrangements are to be made (Art. 2 (2)). (A separate exchange of letters extends preferential quotas on beef and veal to Botswana, Kenya, Madagascar and Swaziland.) Quantitative restrictions and measures having equivalent effect are also eliminated (Art. 3). The usual provisions apply on *ordre public*, Community preference, origin and safeguards (Arts. 5 to 16). Under Title I—Trade Co-operation—Chapter 1, Trade Arrangements, and Chapter 2, Special Undertakings on Rum and Bananas, are backed up by Chapter 3, Trade Promotion. Trade promotion measures are to include technical and financial assistance across the whole spectrum from production to final distribution of products. A maximum of 40 million EUA is allocated as the Community contribution to financing of this type of activity (Art. 22).

—20   Next, Title II deals with export earnings from commodities. The principal limb here is the stabilisation of earnings or STABEX scheme (Arts. 23 to 47) in respect of export commodities representing in most cases at least 6.5 per cent. of a given ACP country's export earnings (2 per cent. in the case of the least developed, island and landlocked ACP States: Arts. 46 and 47). All the products covered are agricultural except iron ore, which is to be covered only for the duration of Lomé II. The system is funded with 550 million EUA managed by the Commission (Art. 31) available in equal annual instalments but with provision for carry-over (Art. 32) and for anticipation on the next year's funds (Art. 34).

An ACP state becomes eligible for a STABEX transfer if its actual earnings from a benefiting product falls at least 6.5 per cent. below a reference level fixed for each ACP State and each product (Arts. 36 and 37: 2 per cent. in the case of the least developed, landlocked and island ACP States: Arts. 46 & 47). A replenishment obligation is then attracted during the seven years following the year of payment (Arts. 42 and 43). Replenishment is required only if certain earnings thresholds are surpassed, so it may be that replenishment will be partial or else the requirement waived (Art. 44). It is waived in respect of the least developed (Art. 46).

31—21   Chapter 2 makes special provision for sugar, annexing Protocol 3 of Lomé I to Lomé II as Protocol 7, thereby continuing the guaranteed price and quota arrangements (Art. 48). For mineral products Title III provides a parallel MINEX system of project and programme aid with an allocation of 280 million EUA (Art. 51). Here the trigger figures are 15 per cent of export earnings (10 per cent. in the case of the least developed, landlocked and island ACP States) and a substantial fall in production or export capacity defined as 10 per cent. (Arts. 53 and 52). This system is coupled with provision on technical and financial assistance via EIB funding for the development of mining and energy potential of the ACP States (Arts. 57 to 59).

Title IV, investments, speaks in rather general terms of encouraging investment. By the joint declaration contained in Annex IV of the Final Act, the benefit of Investment Protection and Promotion Agreements with one Member State of the Community is to be extended to others on request with a minimum of formality.

31—22   Title V, industrial co-operation, extends the Lomé I arrangements. These are supervised by a committee on industrial co-operation, supervised by the Committee of Ambassadors (Art. 78). The Centre for Industrial Development (Art. 7) set up under Lomé I is to assist in attainment of the objectives of industrial co-operation. Its functions relate principally to information gathering and dissemination and to provision of advisory services (Art. 84).

Title VI on agricultural co-operation parallels Title V, laying down rural development and agricultural expansion objectives. A Technical Centre for Agricultural and Rural Co-operation (Art. 88) performs functions similar to the Centre for Industrial Development.

31—23   Financial assistance is provided for under Title VII, Financial and Technical Co-operation. The objective here is the very broad one of promoting economic and social development (Art. 91). For Lomé II the overall amount of the Community's financial assistance is fixed at 5,227 million EUA (Art. 95), which includes the amounts allocated under Titles II and III for STABEX and MINEX. Of the remainder, 3,772 million EUA is to come from the European Development Fund (EDF)[10]; 2,928 million EUA in the form of grants, the rest as loans and risk capital. The remaining 685 million EUA is to be in the form of EIB loans. The ACP

---

[10] The EDF (in fact the 5th EDF) is established by the Community internal agreement of November 20, 1979, on the Financing and Administration of Community Aid (EC No.16 (1980) Cmnd. 7898, p.218), which sets out the amount to be borne by each Community Member State and conferring administration duties on the Commission assisted by an EDF Committee of representatives of the Governments of the Member States. The same Agreement provides for co-ordination of the role of the EIB notably through a similar Committee, the Article 22 Committee.

states expressed disappointment in the amounts made available, describing them as inadequate (Annex XLIII concerning Art. 95). Community financing may take the form of co-financing (Arts. 96 to 108). Special treatment is to be accorded to the least developed ACPs (Art. 106). A condition of Community financing is that participation in invitations to tender and contracts is to be open on equal terms to all Community and ACP nationals and firms (Art. 125).

·24   Title VIII, general provision concerning the least developed, landlocked and island ACP states, defines which these states are and ties together the various specific provisions for their benefit.

Title IX deals in Chapter 1 with current payments and capital movements. In the first place the parties agree to refrain from taking action which would impede the operation of the substantive provisions of the Convention. In particular, there is a non-discrimination and m.f.n. provision (Art. 157). This is couched in best endeavours terms, but subject to international monetary rules being observed where exceptions have to be made. Chapter 2 makes provision on establishment and services, for non-discrimination on the basis of reciprocity (Art. 160). There is no provision in the convention as such on workers but Annex XV, the Joint Declaration on Workers residing legally in a Member State or an ACP State, grants non-discriminatory treatment in respect of working conditions and pay and social security benefits, but not for free movement itself (*cf.* comparable provisions in the Mediterranean Agreements).

—25   Title X provides for the institutions, which are the Council of Ministers, the Committee of Ambassadors and the Consultative Assembly. The Council of Ministers is composed of the Members of the Council of the European Communities and of members of the Commission on the one hand and of a member of the Government of each of the ACP States on the other (Art. 164). The operation of the Council of Ministers follows the usual Association Council pattern. It acts by mutual agreement (Art. 167). The posture taken within the Council of Ministers by the Community representatives is governed by the internal Agreement of November 20, 1979, on the measures and procedures required for implementation of the Second ACP-EEC Convention of Lomé.[11] The Community common position is to be adopted by the Council, acting unanimously, after consulting the Commission (Art. 1 (1)). Where national competence is involved implementation is for the Member States (Art. 2). By Article 5 the Member States agree to refer internal disputes to the European Court. Decisions of the Council of Ministers are binding on the parties, who are obliged to implement them (Art. 168 (3)). The Council of Ministers

[11] E.C. No.16 (1980); Cmnd. 7895, p.215.

may, where necessary, delegate any of its powers to the Committee of Ambassadors, in effect modelled on COREPER. The Consultative Assembly (Art. 175) is, in effect, an inter-parliamentary committee. It does have power to adopt resolutions but its only substantive power and duty is to consider the annual report of the Council of Ministers.

31—26   Article 175 makes provision for compulsory settlement of disputes by arbitration if discussions fail within the Council of Ministers or a good offices procedure established by the Council is unsuccessful.

Allowance is made (Art. 181) for appropriate measures of adaptation and transition in the case of accession to the Community of new Member States. More importantly, provision is made for accession to Lomé II itself. Arrangements have been negotiated for the accession of *Zimbabwe*.

Trade Agreements with Asian Countries

31—27   In this region the Community has concluded non-preferential (*i.e.* m.f.n.) trade co-operation agreements with *India* (1973 - being revised), *Sri Lanka* (1975) *Pakistan* and *Bangladesh* (1976). It has most recently concluded such an agreement with the ASEAN members - *Indonesia, Malaysia, Philippines, Singapore* and *Thailand*. The functioning of the Co-operation Agreements is supervised by a Joint Commission which also supervises any sectoral agreements (*e.g.* on jute and coir products or handicrafts, etc.). The Commissions have power to make recommendations to the respective authorities. These agreements are clearly very limited in scope but they do expand somewhat on the benefits available notably under the GSP. The ASEAN agreement is a little more concrete than the earlier agreements on the co-operation aspects, designed to promote the development and diversification of reciprocal trade in the commercial field and in the economic field to encourage investment, technological and scientific progress, the opening up of new sources of supply and new markets and new employment opportunities. There is also a promise to expand development co-operation. The agreements are valid for five years and thereafter from year to year (two year periods in the case of ASEAN).

31—28   As its title implies the 1978 Trade Agreement with *China* lacks the co-operation elements of the agreements with other Asian countries. This is a straight non-preferential (*i.e.* m.f.n.) agreement coupled with expressions of willingness to expand mutual trade. From the Community exporter's point of view the important elements here are a commitment to ensure that Community exporters have the possibility of participating fully in opportunities for trade with China (Art. 4 (1)), an undertaking to promote trade visits and contacts (Art. 6) and to permit payments in convertible currencies (Art. 8). Further, there is a stipulation that trade in goods and the provision of services shall be effected at market-related prices and rates (Art. 7). This is the key element for taking China out of the state trader category. The agreement is monitored by a Joint Committee for Trade, with a power of recommendation.

Latin America

—29   Sectoral agreements apart (notably on textiles) the Community has concluded agreements in this region only with *Argentina* (1971), *Brazil* and *Urugary* (1973) and *Mexico* (1975). The agreement with Argentina was allowed to expire at the end of 1980, since Argentina felt her interests to be covered in the new GATT arrangement on beef and veal. A new framework agreement with Brazil was signed on September 18, 1980. It is not yet in force. Negotiations with the countries of the Andean Pact (*Bolivia, Colombia, Ecuador, Peru* and *Venezuela*) are stalled.

The existing agreements with South American countries are all of a pattern: they are non-preferential (*i.e.* m.f.n.) trade agreements, as usual complementing the benefits of the GSP so far as these are available. They provide for mutual co-operation in agriculture (mainly consultation and study of problems) within the Joint Committee supervising the agreements. The Joint Committees have power to make suggestions serving the objectives of the agreements. Special provision is made in these agreements on beef and veal exports. Special consideration is also given to Brazilian cocoa butter and soluble coffee (*i.e.* instant). The agreements annex rather circumspect declarations on investments, asserting in the case of Uruguay and Brazil that non-discriminatory treatment is available. The agreements were concluded for initial periods of three years and are continued in force from year to year.

The m.f.n. agreement with *Mexico* (1975) is similar to those with the South American countries, but notably lacks the specific agricultural provisions. It was concluded for an initial period of five years.

North America

1—30   A Community alone Framework Commercial and Economic Co-operation Agreement was concluded with *Canada* in 1976. This agreement is unprecedented in including in a Community alone agreement matters outside strict Community competence (hence conclusion under Article 235 as well as Article 113). Because the provisions on economic co-operation potentially impinge on national competence the position is reserved by Article III (4) which preserves the powers of the Member States to undertake bilateral activities (including concluding agreements) in the field of economic co-operation.

The agreement provides for m.f.n. treatment (Art. I) and commercial co-operation including consultations within the Joint Co-operation Committee which is set up to promote and keep under review the various commercial and economic co-operation activities envisaged (Art. IV). Economic co-operation (Art III) is to cover industry, science and technology, supply and markets, employment, regional problems and environment. It is generally to contribute to the development of the respective economies and standards of living. This is to be achieved through the fostering of commercial and financial links and participation and techno-logical and scientific exchanges.

The agreement is valid for an initial period of five years: there-after from year to year.

Sectoral Agreements

31—31 Besides the general agreements with individual countries or groups of countries there are frequently related agreements on annual tariff quotas or prices for particular products. These are not con-sidered separately here.

In addition the Community has concluded agreements with third countries regulating particular sectors, specifically *fisheries, sheepmeat and goatmeat*, and *textiles*. Agreements with certain developing country suppliers on jute, cois, silks, handicrafts, etc., are listed in Appendix 3.

Fisheries

31—32 Until recently the Community has been unable to agree on the conclusion of fisheries agreements but has been dependent on autonomous arrangements. However, in 1980 the Community was able to conclude agreements with *Sweden, Spain, The Faroe Islands, Senegal, Guinea Bissau, Norway* and *Canada*, to add to those already concluded with the *United States* (see further *supra*, para. 15-79). These concern access to the waters of the third countries in question, and govern licensing of vessels, etc.

Sheepmeat and goatmeat sector

31—33 In parallel with the establishment of the market organisations in this sector (*supra*, para. 15-65) the Commission negotiated volun-tary restraint agreements with a number of third country suppliers (see Appendix 3). The agreements establish varying ceilings for sendings to the Community, and extend a corresponding tariff quota, or more properly limitation in applicable agricultural levy, of 10 per cent. *ad valorem*. The agreements are without prejudice to the rights of the parties under GATT. They entered into force on October 20, 1980 and run until March 31, 1984, thereafter from year to year.

Textiles

-34   Acting under the GATT Multifibre Agreement (*supra*, para. 30-17) the Community has concluded bilateral agreements with a number of low-cost suppliers valid until the expiry of the multifibre Agreement itself on December 31, 1982. Under these agreements the exporter undertakes to exercise restraint and the Community undertakes to admit specified textiles in principle quota free subject to subsequent imposition of quantitative limits if the totals for earlier years are exceeded by certain percentages. The annual levels are adjustable. Quantitative limits for Community regions (the United Kingdom is a region) are envisaged in appropriate circumstances.

Cottage-industry products as defined in the agreements are excluded from the limitation system. The agreements are governed by consultation procedures. The agreements override any other right to impose quantitative restrictions, *i.e.* under Article XIX of GATT or Article 3 of the MFA. Measures having equivalent effect are prohibited.

Textiles agreements on this pattern currently in force have been concluded with *Macao, Pakistan, Thailand, Korea, Argentina, Sri Lanka, Bangladesh, Singapore, Indonesia, Guatemala, Peru, Haiti, Uruguay, Hong Kong* and *the Philippines*.

Participation of the Community in International Organisations

United Nations

—35   The Community was granted observer status by General Assembly Resolution 3208 (XXIX). It is represented by the Presidency and a Commission representative depending on competence (*cf. supra*, para. 29-43 *et seq*.). The Commission has its own delegation in New York. Co-ordination of the positions of the Member States has become very close irrespective of where competence lies on a particular issue.[12] The Presidency often delivers agreed statements on behalf of the Member States on matters of national competence.

The Community also has observer status in ECOSOC, its status being as in the General Assembly. It has observer status in UNCTAD along similar lines. The Commission has claimed exclusive Community competence for a growing number of the commodity negotiations[13] under UNCTAD and thus claims the right to represent the Community alone. It is participating with the Member States in the Common Fund.[14]

The Community has observer status in the United Nations conference on the Law of the Sea. It claims competence for a

---

[12] and see W.Q. 688/75, O.J. 1976, C158/4.
[13] *Infra*, para. 31–42.
[14] See generally UNCTAD: Agreement on the Common Fund, 1980 J.W.T.L. 541.

number of matters. Statements on matters within Community competence are nevertheless made by the Presidency. The Community seeks a Community clause in any resulting convention.

Specialised agencies of the United Nations

31—36   The EEC early on established relations with the ILO by means of an Agreement of July 7, 1958, under Article 229, signed by the President of the Commission and the Director General of the ILO. It provides for co-operation in the form of consultation, exchange of information and technical assistance, but it establishes no new organs through which to channel this co-operation.

     Apparently the Commission has concluded agreements along similar lines with a number of other Specialised Agencies.[15] The Community as such enjoys observer status in a number of the Specialised Agencies. Representation is along the usual lines.

OECD

31—37   The Commission participates in the Committees of the OECD and speaks on matters of exclusive Community competence. Member States are free to speak where there is no Community position.

GATT

31—38   The Court has held that in so far as the Community has assumed the powers previously exercised by Member States in the area governed by the GATT, the provisions of the GATT have the effect of binding the Community.[16] The Community is not, however, a party to the GATT so it is difficult to see how a third country could invoke it except by arguing that the Community must be taken to have succeeded to the obligations of the individual Member States by a process of subrogation. The Community's position has, however, been made somewhat clearer by Community conclusion (with the Member States) of the agreements resulting from the Tokyo Round of Multilateral Trade Negotiations (MTNs)[17]. It also participated in the earlier Dillon and Kennedy Rounds and in other multilateral and bilateral agreements under GATT.[18] A question now of purely historic interest was the

[15] E.P. Doc. 47/67.

[16] See *supra*, para.29.02 and 30.01. For criticism of the court decisions see M. Waelbroeck, "Effect of GATT within the Legal Order of the EEC," 1974 J.W.T.L. 614.

[17] Decision 80/271, O.J. 1980, L71 annexing the agreements and see generally "Symposium on the Multinational Trade Agreements," *Law and Policy in International Business* (1979), Vol.11 No.4 and (1980), Vol.12 No.1. See on Public Supply Contracts Dir. 80/767, O.J. 1980, L215/1. See Regulation 1224/80, O.J. 1980, L134/1 for rules on valuation of goods for customs purposes.

[18] *e.g.* on textiles (*supra*, para. 31—34) and under Article XXVIII (negotiations on tariff alterations). Quite a number of minor tariff adjustment agreements have been concluded under this head. See, *e.g.* Decision 80/461, O.J. 1980, L111/17 (Canada).

compatibility of the EEC Treaty system itself with GATT. GATT clearance has also been sought for Community preferential agreements with third countries.[19]

Subjects dealt with by GATT are almost entirely within the common commercial policy. The Commission therefore acts on behalf of the Member States on most matters. Member States retain powers in the Budget Committee.

General Multilateral Conventions

Transport, energy and environment

–39 In the transport sector, where Community has competence, most actions in the external relations field have in fact been by common action under Article 116 or Article 84 (2) rather than by Community participation.[20] The Commission is an observer in the work of the Central Commission for the Navigation of the Rhine, the European Conference of Ministers of Transport (ECMT) and the Berne Union Railway Conference. It also attends European Civil Aviation Conference (ECAC) meetings.

–40 The Community has signed the Berne Convention on the Conservation of European Wildlife and Habitat of September 19, 1979, and the Bonn Convention on the Conservation of Migratory Species of Wild Animals of July 23, 1979. Community participation in the 1973 Washington Convention on trade in endangered species is proposed. Community accession is proposed for the Bonn Agreement on North Sea Oil Pollution, the Barcelona Convention on Mediterranean Pollution, the Oslo Convention on Marine Pollution by Dumping, but not for the London Convention on the same subject. The Community is a party to the Paris Convention on Marine Pollution from Land Based Sources and the ECE Convention on Long-Range Transboundary Air Pollution. Competence is not exclusive in any of these areas.

The Community has observer status in the International Energy Agency. The Agreement on an International Energy Programme provides for Community accession.

Customs conventions

–41 The assumption here has been that the sujbect-matter is mixed and that the Community should participate with the Member States (*e.g.* TIR and the 1974 Kyoto Convention on Customs Procedures). Nevertheless the conclusions to be drawn from Opinion 1/78 *Natural Rubber*[21] may affect the picture.

---

[19] See W.Q. 456/71 J.O. 1972, C23/11; see, *e.g.* Regs. 2829/77, O.J. 1977, L334/11.
[20] (AETR) and 954/79, O.J. 1979, L121/1 (UN Liner Code of Conduct).
[21] *Supra,* para.29–43 *et seq.*

Commodity agreements

31—42 The Community participates in all the Commodity Agreements elaborated under UNCTAD auspices. For the most part participation has been mixed, *i.e.* together with the Member States. For some of the more recent agricultural commodity agreements, however, where there is already exclusive competence by virtue of the existence of a common organisation of the market, participation has been by the Community acting alone (*e.g.* sugar), albeit certain Member States (notably the United Kingdom) have participated as well, acting on behalf of their dependent territories to which the EEC does not apply. The position on competence has been complicated somewhat by the Court's ruling in Opinion 1/78 *Natural Rubber*[22] that "the negotiation and execution" of clauses admittedly not involving Community competence "must . . . follow the system applicable to the agreement considered as a whole." The implications of this decision have not yet fully been worked through.

The Community participated, on a basis of mixed competence, in the establishment of the Common Fund for Commodities.

[22] *Ibid.*

APPENDIX 1

TREATY PROVISIONS HELD DIRECTLY APPLICABLE

Arts. 9 & 12	Cases 2 & 3/69 *Diamantarbeiders* v. *Brachfeld* [1969] E.C.R. 211.
Art. 12	Case 26/62 *Van Gend en Loos* v. *Nederlandse Administratie der Belastingen* [1963] E.C.R. 1.
Arts. 9 & 13 (2)	Case 33/70 *SACE* v. *Ministry of Finance* [1970] E.C.R. 1215.
Art. 13 (2)	Case 79/72 *Capolongo* v. *Maya* [1973] E.C.R. 611.
Arts. 9 & 16	Case 18/71 *Eunomia* v. *Italy* [1971] E.C.R. 811.
Art. 16	Case 45/76 *Comet* v. *Produktschap* [1976] E.C.R. 2043.
Art. 30	Case 74/76 *Iannelli* v. *Meroni* [1977] E.C.R. 557.
Arts. 31 and 32 (1)	Case 13/68 *Salgoil* v. *Italy* [1968] E.C.R. 453.
Art. 37 (1)	Case 59/75 *Manghera* [1976] E.C.R. 91.
Art. 37 (2)	Case 6/64 *Costa* v. *ENEL* [1964] E.C.R. 585.
Art. 48	Case 41/74 *Van Duyn* [1974] E.C.R. 1337.
Art. 52	Case 2/72 *Reyners* v. *Belgium* [1974] E.C.R. 631.
Art. 53	Case 6/64 *Costa* v. *ENEL* [1964] E.C.R. 585.
Arts. 59 (1) and 60 (3)	Case 33/74 *Van Binsbergen* [1974] E.C.R. 1299.

Appendix 1

Art. 85	Case 13/61 *De Geus* v. *Bosch* [1962] E.C.R. 45. Case 127/73 *BRT* v. *SABAM* [1974] E.C.R. 51.
Art. 86	Case 127/73 *BRT* v. *SABAM* [1974] E.C.R. 51. Case 155/73 *Sacchi* [1974] E.C.R. 409.
Art. 92 (1)	Case 77/72 *Capolongo* v. *Maya* [1973] E.C.R. 611.
Art. 93 (3), last sentence	Case 6/64 *Costa* v. *ENEL* [1964] E.C.R. 585.
Art. 95 (1)	Case 57/65 *Lütticke* v. *HZA Saarlouis* [1966] E.C.R. 205.
Art. 95 (2)	Case 27/67 *FinkFrucht* v. *HZA München Landsbergerstrasse* [1968] E.C.R. 223.
Art. 95	Case 45/75 *Rewe* v. *HZA Landau* [1976] E.C.R. 181.
Art. 119	Case 43/75 *Defrenne* v. *Sabena* [1976] E.C.R. 455. Extensions in 129/79, *Smith* v. *McCarthy's* [1980] E.C.R. 1275, 69/80 *Worringham & Humphreys* v. *Lloyds Bank* [1981] 2 C.M.L.R. 1, 96/80, *Jenkins* v. *Kingsgate* [1981] 2 C.M.L.R. 24.

Treaty provisions held not directly applicable

Art. 5	Cases 78/70 *DGG* v. *Metro* [1971] E.C.R. 482; 51 to 54/71 *International Fruit Co* [1971] E.C.R. 1107.
Arts. 32, last sentence & 33	Case 13/68 *Salgoil* v. *Italy* [1968] E.C.R. 453.
Art. 90 (2)	Case 10/70 *Muller/Hain* [1971] E.C.R. 723.
Art. 93 (3) *except* last sentence	Case 6/64 *Costa* v. *ENEL* [1964] E.C.R. 585.
Art. 97	Case 28/67 *Molkerei Zentrale* [1968] E.C.R. 143.
Art. 102	Case 6/64 *Costa* v. *ENEL* [1964] E.C.R. 585.

EUROPEAN COURT: BASES OF JURISDICTION

Bases of Jurisdiction Contained in the EEC Treaty

The EEC Treaty contains the following bases of jurisdiction[1] :

Legal Basis	Grounds of Jurisdiction	Plaintiff	Defendant
Article 93 (2), 2nd para.	Direct reference in derogation from Articles 169 and 170 for failure to comply with a decision of the Commission on abolition of aids	Commission, any interested State	Member State
Article 157 (2), 3rd para. repealed by Article 19 of the Merger Treaty, but re-enacted by Article 10 of the same	Application for a ruling that a Commission Member be compulsorily retired under Article 160 (Article 13) of the Merger Treaty) or be deprived of pension rights or other benefits	Council, Commission	(Commission Member)
Article 160, repealed by Article 19 of the Merger Treaty, but re-enacted as to first paragraph by Article 13 of the same	Application for compulsory retirement of Commission Member (power of provisional suspension not re-enacted)	Council, Commission	(Commission Member)
Article 169	Action for failure to fulfil an obligation	Commission	Member State
Article 170	Same	Member State	Member State
Article 172	Jurisdiction in	(Any party)	(Commission)

[1] Plaintiffs and defendants listed in brackets are not referred to as such explicitly in the relevant Article.

Legal Basis	Grounds of Jurisdiction	Plaintiff	Defendant
	regard to penalties laid down in regulations		
Article 173, 1st para.	Action seeking review of legally binding acts of Council or Commission	Member State, Council, Commission	Council, Commission
Article 173, 2nd para.	Same, the category of acts being restricted to decisions addressed to the plaintiff or acts of direct and individual concern to him	Any natural or legal person	Council, Commission
Article 175, 1st para.	Action for failure to act	Member State, the other institutions	Council, Commission
Article 175, 3rd para.	Action for failure to address to the plaintiff a binding act	Any natural or legal person	Council, Commission
Article 177	Application for a preliminary ruling	(Reference by municipal court)	—
Article 178	Jurisdiction in disputes relating to the compensation for damage provided for in Article 215, 2nd para.	(Any party)	(Community institutions)
Article 179	Jurisdiction in disputes between the Communnity and its servants	(Servants, Community institutions)	(Community institutions, Servants)
Article 180	Jurisdiction in relation to the European Investment Bank	—	—
Article 180 (a)	Article 169-type action	Board of Directors of the Bank	Member State

Legal Basis	Grounds of Jurisdiction	Plaintiff	Defendant
Article 180 (b)	Article 173-type action	Member State, Commission, Board of Directors of the Bank	Board of Governors of the Bank
Article 180 (c)	Article 173-type action for non-compliance with the procedure laid down in Article 21 (2), (5), (6) and (7) of the Statute of the Bank	Member State, Commission	Board of Directors of the Bank
Article 181	Jurisdiction pursuant to any arbitration clause in a contract concluded by or on behalf of the Community	(Any party) (Community institution)	(Any party) (Community institution)
Article 182	Jurisdiction in disputes submitted under a special agreement	Member State	Member State
Article 184	Plea (or exception) of illegality	Any party	Council, Commission
Article 225, 2nd para.	Direct reference in derogation from Articles 169 and 170, for improper use of Articles 223 and 224 (defence etc.)	Commission, Member State	Member State
Article 228 (1), 2nd sub-para.	Opinion of the Court as to whether an agreement envisaged is compatible with the provisions of the Treaty	(Reference by Council, Commission or Member State)	—

Bases of Jurisdiction in the ECSC Treaty

Article 10, 11th para. repealed by Article 19 of the Merger Treaty	Declaration of annulment of abusive use of veto on appointments to the High Authority	A Government	A Government

489

Appendix 2

Legal Basis	Grounds of Jurisdiction	Plaintiff	Defendant
Article 12, repealed by Article 19 of the Merger Treaty, replaced by Article 10 of the same	Application for compulsory retirement of High Authority Members	High Authority, Council	(High Authority Member)
Article 33, 1st para.	Action seeking review of legality	Member State,	High Authority
Article 33, 2nd para.	Same, category of acts being limited to individual decisions, and to general decisions involving misuse of powers affecting the plaintiff	Council Under-takings or Associations	High Authority
Article 34	Proceedings for damages for failure to comply with judgment of annulment of act involving a fault rendering the Community liable	(Under-takings or groups of under-takings)	High Authority
Article 35	Action for failure to act or for abstention from acting	(Any party)	High Authority
Article 37	Action against express or implied decision refusing to recognise a situation potentially of a nature to provoke fundamental and persistent disturbances in the economy	(Member State)	High Authority
Article 38	Application for declaration of nullity of Assembly or Council act	Member States, High Authority	Assembly, Council
Article 40, as amended by Article 26 of the Merger Treaty	Jurisdiction to order reparation from the Community	(Any party)	(Community institution)

Appendix 2

Legal Basis	Grounds of Jurisdiction	Plaintiff	Defendant
Article 41	Jurisdiction to give preliminary rulings on the validity of High Authority or Council acts	(Reference by national court or tribunal)	—
Article 42	Equivalent to Article 181 EEC		
Article 43, 1st para.	Jurisdiction where provided for in any provision supplementing the Treaty	—	—
Article 43, 2nd para.	Jurisdiction where conferred by the law of a Member State	—	—
Article 47, 4th para.	Actions for compensation under Article 40 for breach of professional secrecy by the High Authority	(Any party)	High Authority
Article 63	Right of action impugning restriction or prohibition on dealings imposed following finding of discrimination by the High Authority	Purchaser	High Authority
Article 66 (5), 2nd para.	Unlimited jurisdiction, by way of derogation from Article 33, to assess whether transaction amounts to concentration	Any person directly concerned	High Authority
Article 88, 2nd para.	Action against a decision establishing a failure to fulfil an obligation	Member State	High Authority
Article 88, 4th para.	Action against decisions taken by way of sanction	Member State	High Authority
Article 89, 1st para.	Provision for (optional) jurisdiction of the Court where no other procedure for settlement provided	Member State	Member State

Legal Basis	Grounds of Jurisdiction	Plaintiff	Defendant
Article 89, 2nd para. Article 95	Equivalent to Article 182 EEC Submission of proposed amendments to the Treaty for opinion of the Court (*petite révision*)	Council and the High Authority	—

Bases of Jurisdiction in the Euratom Treaty

Legal Basis	Grounds of Jurisdiction	Plaintiff	Defendant
Article 12, 4th para.	Application to the Court in licensing matters	Licensee	Commission
Article 18, 2nd para.	Appeals against the decisions of the arbitration committee	The parties	The parties
Article 21, 3rd para.	Reference to the Court for failure to grant a licence	Commission	Member State
Article 38, 3rd para.	Direct reference to the Court by way of derogation from Articles 141 and 142 for failure to comply with Commission directives on radioactivity levels	Commission, Member State	Member State
Article 81, 3rd para.	Power of President to issue decision ordering compulsory inspection	(application by Commission)	—
Article 82, 4th para.	Direct reference to the Court by way of derogation from Articles 141 and 142 for failure to comply with Commission directive calling on Member States to end infringements relating to records on nuclear materials	Commission, Member State	Member State
Article 83 (2)	Special provisions in relation to actions impugning sanctions	Persons, Undertakings, (and Commission or any Member State)	Commission

492

Legal Basis	Grounds of Jurisdiction	Plaintiff	Defendant
Article 126	Equivalent to Article 157 EEC		
Article 129	Equivalent to Article 160 EEC		
Article 141	Equivalent to Article 169 EEC		
Article 142	Equivalent to Article 170 EEC		
(Article 144)	(Unlimited jurisdiction given in relation to Articles 12 and 83)	—	—
Article 145	Action to establish infringement of the Treaty to which Article 83 does not apply	Commission	Persons, Under-takings
Article 146	Equivalent to Article 173 EEC		
Article 148	Equivalent to Article 175 EEC		
Article 150	Equivalent to Article 177 EEC		
Article 151	Equivalent to Article 178 EEC		
Article 152	Equivalent to Article 179 EEC		
Article 153	Equivalent to Article 181 EEC		
Article 154	Equivalent to Article 182 EEC		
Article 156	Equivalent to Article 184 EEC		

APPENDIX 3

COMMUNITY AGREEMENTS IN FORCE OR VALID AFTER JANUARY 1 1981

Part 1: Community Bilateral Agreements
Part 2: General Multilateral Agreements with Community Participation

(Bilateral Agreements with International Organisations Listed in Part 1)

PART 1

Community Bilateral Agreements

Annual quota agreements and agreements under GATT excluded
    Line 1: Country
    Line 2: Subject
    Line 3: Place and date of signature
    Line 4: Date of entry into force
    Line 5: Duration
    Line 6: References
    Line 7: Amendments if any

Listings *alphabetical* by country, then by *date* within each country. Amendments listed under agreement amended.

ACP (African, Caribbean and Pacific) States

See Lomé

Algeria

Co-operation Agreement (and ECSC Agreement)
Algiers, April 26, 1976
November 1, 1978 (and January 1, 1980)
Terminable on 6 months notice
Cmnd. 6938, EC 1977/23; O.J. 1978, L 263/1

Andean Group

No Agreement

494

Argentina

Nuclear Energy
Buenos Aires, September 4, 1962
November 6, 1963
20 years
J.O. 1963, 2986, O.J. 2nd V p. 3

Trade Agreement
November 8, 1971
January 1, 1972
Expired 1980
J.O. 1971, L249/19, O.J. 2nd I (2), 289

Trade in Textiles
Brussels, September 18, 1979
January 1, 1981
Applicable from January 1, 1978 to December 31, 1982
Cmnd. 7838, E.C. 1980/8; O.J. 1979, L 298/1

Trade in Mutton and Lamb
October 20, 1980
Until March 31, 1984; subject to one year's notice of termination
O.J. 1980, L 275/14

Arusha

See LOMÉ

ASEAN (Indonesia, Malaysia, Philippines, Singapore, Thailand)

Co-operation Agreement
Kuala Lumpur, March 7, 1980
October 1, 1980
Five years; thereafter for periods of two years, subject to 6 months
notice
Cmnd. 7980, E.C. 1980/31; O.J. 1980, L 144

Australia

Trade in Mutton, Lamb and Goatmeat
Brussels, November 14, 1980
October 20, 1980
Until March 31, 1984; subject to one year's notice of termination
O.J. 1980, L275/20, Cmnd. 8208, E.C. 1981/25

Austria

ECSC Railway Tariffs
Luxembourg, July 26, 1957
Unlimited
J.O. 1958, 78: Cmnd. 5891, E.C. 1975/30; O.J. 2nd VIII, 8; O.J. 1979, L12
   Supplementary Agreement November 29, 1960, Cmnd. 5891; O.J. 1961, 1237; O.J. 2nd VIII, 14
   Accession Protocol October 10, 1974, Cmnd. 5891; O.J. 1979, L12
   Amendment O.J. 1978, C23/2

EFTA Non-Candidate Agreement
Brussels, July 22, 1972
January 1, 1973
Terminable on 12 months notice
Cmnd. 5159, Misc. 1972/49; J.O. 1972, L300/1
   Supplementary Protocol May 29, 1975, Cmnd. 6213, E.C. 1975/124; O.J. 1975, L 106/1
   Amendments (Exchanges of Letters) November 29, 1976 and December 8, 1976,
      Cmnd. 6784, E.C. 1977/11; O.J. 1976, L 298/1 & 338/1
   Derogation (Exchange of Letters) June 14, 1977, Cmnd. 7689, E.C. 1979/22; O.J. 1977, L 139/1
   Amendment (Exchange of Letters) June 12, 1979, Cmnd. 7727, E.C. 1979/27; O.J. 1978, L 302
   Derogation O.J. 1980, L 371/42
   Amendment O.J. 1980, L 385/2
   Additional Protocol November 28, 1980 O.J. L 357/2, Cmnd. 8190, E.C. 1981/22

ECSC Agreement
Brussels, July 22, 1972
January 1, 1973
Terminable on 12 months notice
Cmnd. 5663, T.S. 1974/45; O.J. 1973, L 350
   Additional Protocol (Accession) November 28, 1980, Cmnd. 8224, E.C. 1981/28

Community Transit (and Accession Protocol)
Brussels, November 30, 1972 (and January 1, 1974)
January 1, 1974 (and January 2, 1974)
Terminable on six months' notice
Cmnd. 6092, E.C. 1975/70; O.J. 1972, L 294/86 and O.J. 1974, L 58/3
   Amendment (Exchange of Letters) June 29, 1977, Cmnd. 7012, E.C. 1977/41; O.J. 1977, L151/87.

Amendment June 23, 1980, Cmnd. 8052, E.C. 1980/43; O.J. 1980, L 155/3
Amendments (Exchanges of letters), O.J. 1981, L 167/114, 124

Trade with Greece and Turkey
Vienna, June 11, 1975
May 1, 1976
Terminable of six months' notice
Cmnd. 6476, E.C. 1976/13; O.J. 1975, L 188/1
  Amendment O.J. 1981, L 107/3

Mutton and Goatmeat (VRA)
January 1, 1981
March 31, 1984 and thereafter from year to year
O.J. 1981, L 137/2

Extension of the Application of the Rules on Community Transit
Brussels, July 12, 1977
March 1, 1978
Terminable on six months' notice
O.J. 1977 L142/1; Cmnd. 7023, E.C. 1977/44
  Greek text O.J. 1981 L 147/2

Bangladesh

Agreements on Silks and on Handicrafts
Brussels, October 24, 1974
January 30, 1975
Unlimited
Cmnd. 6379, E.C. 1976/3 and Cmnd. 6391, E.C. 1976/5; O.J. 1977 L 307

Commercial Co-operation
Luxembourg October 19, 1976
December 1, 1976
Five years; thereafter from year to year; terminable on six months' notice
Cmnd. 6782, E.C. 1977/8; O.J. 1976, L 319/1

Trade in Textile Products
Dacca, July 23, 1979
August 1, 1980
Applicable from January 1, 1978 to December 31, 1982
Cmnd. 7840, E.C. 1980/10; O.J. 1979, L 298/38

Jute Products
Brussels, November 20, 1980
March 1, 1981
Applicable from January 1, 1980 to December 31, 1983
O.J. 1981, L 43/2, Cmnd. 8256, E.C. 1981/30

Appendix 3

Bank for International Settlements

Mobilisation of Claims
Unlimited
O.J. 1978, L 316/21

Brazil

Atomic Energy
Brazilia, June 9, 1961
June 24, 1965
20 years
J.O. 1969, L79/7; O.J. 2nd V, 10

Trade Agreement
Brussels, December 19, 1973
August 1, 1974
3 years, thereafter from year to year
O.J. 1974, L102/23; Cmnd. 5760, E.C. 19/1974
Financial Agreement
Brussels, September 18, 1980

Trade in Textile Products
Brussels, January 23, 1980
Applicable from January 1, 1978 to December 31, 1982
Cmnd. 8007, E.C. 1980/36; O.J. 1980, L 70/1

Canada

Atomic Energy
Brussels, October 6, 1959
November 18, 1959
10 years; thereafter terminable on six months' notice
J.O. 1959, 1165; CT IX 11
   Amendment (Safeguards), January 16, 1978, O.J. 1978, L65/16

Framework Agreement
Ottawa, July 6, 1976
October 1, 1976
Terminable on one years' notice, after five years
Cmnd. 6646, E.C. 1976/26; O.J. 1976, L 260/1

E.C.S.C. Products
Brussels, July 26, 1976
Coterminous with Framework Agreement
Cmnd. 6632, E.C. 1976/24; O.J. 1976, L 260/28

Fisheries
Brussels, June 28, 1979
Cmnd. 7804, E.C. 3/1980; O.J. 1979, L312/1
Extension O.J. 1980, L63/21
Extension and amendment O.J. 1980, L 226/52 & 54

Canada

(Atomic Energy of Canada Ltd.)
Euratom Co-operation
November 3, 1980
See O.J. 1981, C 103/7, W.Q. 1831/80

Central Commission for the Navigation of the Rhine

Co-operation; Exchange of Letters
June 6, 1961
Immediately
Unlimited
J.O. 1961, 1027; O.J. 1974 (2nd) I (2) 350

China (People's Republic of)

Trade Agreement
Brussels, April 3, 1978
June 1, 1978
Five years; thereafter from year to year; subject to termination on
six months' notice
Cmnd. 7301, E.C. 1978/34; O.J. 1978, L 123/1

CMEA (COMECON)

No agreement

Cost Projects

11 Cmnd. 5283, T.S. 1973/47
11 bis O.J. 1980, L.350/46
43 Cmnd. 7677, T.S. 1979/76
50/51/52 Cmnd. 5284, T.S. 1973/38
53 Cmnd. 5265, T.S. 1973/8
61a Cmnd. 5257, T.S. 1973/36
61a bis Cmnd. 5196, E.C. 1981/23, O.J. 1980, L 39/18
64b Cmnd. 5264, T.S. 1973/37
64b bis Cmnd. 7973, E.C. 1980/30, O.J. 1980, L 39/24
68 Cmnd. 5122, T.S. 1972/114
68 bis O.J. 1979, L 72/35
90 Cmnd. 7990, E.C. 1980/33, O.J. 1980, L39/30
91 O.J. 1980, L 350/55

Appendix 3

Cyprus

Association Agreement (with Accession Protocol)
Brussels, December 12, 1972
June 1, 1973
Extended until March 31, 1981
Cmnd. 5694, E.C. 1974/13; O.J. 1973, L 133
  Additional Protocol and Financial Protocol, September 15, 1977, Cmnd. 7228, E.C. 1978/31;
    O.J. 1977, L 339/1 and Cmnd. 7490. T.S. 1979/31; O.J. 1978, L332/1
  Supplementary Protocol and Protocol on Agricultural Products, May 11, 1978
    Cmnd. 7315, E.C. 1978/35; O.J. 1978, L 172/1 & 350/1
  Transitional Protocol February 7, 1980
    O.J. 1980, L 84/1

Denmark (Faroes)
Fisheries
Brussels, March 15, 1977
Applied provisionally from January 1, 1977
10 years, thereafter for periods of six years
Cmnd. 7759, E.C. 1980/1; O.J. 1980, L 226/12

Egypt

Co-operation Agreement (and ECSC Agreement)
Brussels, January 18, 1977
November 1, 1978 and January 1, 1980
Terminable on 12 months' notice
Cmnd. 7820, T.S. 1980/22; O.J. 1978, L 266 (and O.J. 1979, L316)

Eurocontrol

October 6, 1981
See 14th Gen. Rep. E.C., point 432

Faroes (See Denmark)

Food and Agriculture Organisation (FAO)

Exchange of Letters
December 1961
J.O. 1962, 1356; CT IX, 49

Finland

EFTA Non-candidate Agreement
Brussels, October 5, 1973
January 1, 1974
Terminable on three months' notice; may be continued in operation for nine months after termination

Cmnd. 5669, E.C. 1974/5; O.J. 1973, L 328/1
Rectification June 26, 1974, Cmnd. 5940, E.C. 1975/4; O.J. 1974, L 163/1
Supplementary Protocol, May 29, 1975, Cmnd. 6217, E.C. 1975/125, O.J. 1975, L 106/4
Amendments (Exchanges of Letters) November 29 and December 8, 1976
Cmnd. 6777, E.C. 1977/3, O.J. 1976, L 298/8 & 338/4
Derogation O.J 1977, L 139/4
Amendment December 8, 1978, Cmnd. 7559, E.C. 1979/13; O.J. 1978, L302/13
Accession Protocol, November 6, 1980, Cmnd. 8159, E.C. 1981/13; O.J. 1980, L 357/28
Derogation O.J. 1980, L 371/44
Amendment O.J. 1980, L 385/5

ECSC Agreement
Brussels, October 5, 1973
January 1, 1975
Terminable on three months' notice; may be continued in operation nine months after termination
Cmnd. 5960, T.S. 54/1975; O.J. 1974, L 348
Additional Protocol Brussels, November 6, 1980, Cmnd. 8169, E.C. 18/1981

Duty-free quotas
Brussels, April 18, 1980
Immediately
Cmnd. 8028, E.C. 1980/39; O.J. 1980, L 76
Amendment September 19, 1980, Cmnd. 8135, E.C. 1981/5

Greece

Association Agreement
Athens, July 9, 1961
In Force November 1, 1962
December 31, 1980
J.O. 1963, 293, O.J. 1974 (2nd) I (1), 3; Cmnd. 7621, T.S. 66/1979, O.J. 1978, L161
Convention on implementation (administrative co-operation) *ibid*
Financial Protocol *ibid*
Convention on Implementation of Arts 7 - 8 ibid
Accession Protocol of April 28, 1975 Cmnd. 7621, T.S. 66/1979; O.J. 1978, L161/1
Financial Protocol of February 28, 1977 Cmnd. 7389, T.S. 91/1978; O.J. 1978, L225/25

Greece (Switzerland acceding)

Concerted Action Project in the Field of Registration of Congenital Abnormalities
December 14, 1979
August 1, 1980
See now *Switzerland*
Cmnd. 7878, E.C. 1980/12, O.J. 1979, L205/28

Guatemala

Trade in Textiles
Brussels, November 7, 1979
Applicable from January 1, 1978 to December 31, 1982
Cmnd. 7910, E.C. 1980/17; O.J. 1979, L 350/1

Guinea-Bissau

Fisheries
Brussels, February 27, 1980
Applicable provisionally from date of signature
Applicable for two years from entry into force; thereafter from year to year
Cmnd. 7993, E.C. 1980/34; O.J. 1980 L 58/73 & O.J. 1980, L226/33

Haiti

Trade in Textile Products
Brussels January 15, 1980
Applicable from January 1, 1978 to December 31, 1982
Cmnd. 7989, E.C. 1980/32; O.J. 1980, L 70/67

Hong Kong

Trade in Textile Products
Brussels, February 12, 1980
Applicable from January 1, 1978 to December 31, 1982
Cmnd. 8008, E.C. 1980/37; O.J. 1980, L 95/1

Hungary
Sheepmeat and Goatmeat (VRA)
Applicable from January 1, 1981 to March 31, 1984, thereafter for periods of 2 years O.J. 1981, L150/7

Iceland

EFTA Non-Candidate Agreement
Brussels, July 22, 1972
April 1, 1973
Terminable on 12 months' notice

Cmnd. 5182, Misc. 1972/50; J.O. 1972, L 301
 Supplementary Protocol May 29, 1975, Cmnd. 6216, E.C.
 1975/127; O.J. 1975, L 106/7
 Amendment June 29, 1976, Cmnd. 6737, E.C. 1977/1; O.J.
 1976 L 217/1
 Amendments (Exchanges of Letters) November 29 and
 December 8, 1976
  Cmnd. 6794, E.C. 1977/13; O.J. 1976, L 298/15 & 338/7
 Amendment   O.J. 1977, L 139/7
 Amendment   O.J. 1980, L 123/1
 Accession Protocols Brussels November 6, 1980, Cmnd. 8167,
 E.C. 1981/16; O.J. 1980, L 357/54
 Derogation O.J. 1980, L 371/48
 Amendment O.J. 1980, L 385/8

ECSC Agreement
Brussels, July 22, 1972
January 1, 1974
Terminable on 12 months' notice
Cmnd. 5806, T.S. 1975/1, O.J. 1973, L350
 Additional Protocol Brussels November 6, 1980, Cmnd. 8168,
 E.C. 17/1981

Sheepmeat and Goatmeat (VRA)
January 1, 1981 until March 31, 1984, thereafter from year to
year
O.J. 1981 L 137/8

India

Commercial Cooperation
Brussels, December 17, 1973
April 1, 1974
5 years; thereafter from year to year; terminable on six months'
notice
Cmnd. 5746; E.C. 9/1974; O.J. 1974, L 82/1

Cane Sugar
Brussels, July 18, 1975
July 18, 1975
Indefinite
Cmnd. 6273, E.C. 1975/143; O.J. 1975, L 190/35

Indonesia

Trade in Textiles
Brussels, September 4, 1979
Applicable from January 1, 1978 to December 31, 1982
Cmnd. 7884, E.C. 1980/14; O.J. 1979, L 350/27

Appendix 3

International Atomic Energy Agency (IAEA)

Co-operation Agreement
Vienna, December 1, 1975
January 1, 1976
Terminable on six months' notice
Cmnd. 6872, E.C. 1977/14; O.J. 1975, L 329/28

International Atomic Energy Agency (IAEA) and the United Kingdom

Safeguards
Vienna, September 6, 1976
August 14, 1978
Linked to Treaty of July 1, 1968 on the non-proliferation of nuclear weapons
Cmnd. 7388, T.S. 1978/90; O.J. 1978, L 51/1

International Bureau of Weights and Measures

Exchange of Letters (Euratom)
November 18, 1965
Unlimited
J.O. 1966, 614; CT IX 75: O.J. 2nd V, 8

International Development Association (IDA)

Special Action Programme
Brussels, May 2, 1978
January 1, 1979
Until repayment of all Special Action Credits
Cmnd. 7572, T.S. 1979/54; O.J. 1979, L 43/13

International Labour Organisation

Cooperation Agreement (ECSC)
August 14, 1953
Unlimited
J..O. 1953, 167; CT VII, 1

Co-operation Agreement
July 7, 1958
Unlimited
J.O. 1959, 521; CT VII, 1

Co-operation (Euratom)
January 26, 1961
Unlimited
J.O. 1961; 473; CT IX, 27

Israel

Agreement
Brussels, May 11, 1975
July 1, 1975
Terminable on 12 months' notice
Cmnd. 6249, E.C. 1975/136; O.J. 1975, L 136/1
    Additional Protocol and Financial Protocol, February 8, 1977
        Cmnd. 7025, E.C. 1977/48; O.J. 1978, L 270
    Second Additional Protocol, O.J. 1981, L 102/1

ECSC Products
Brussels, May 11, 1975
May 1, 1978
Terminable on 12 months' notice
Cmnd. 7261, T.S. 1978/68; O.J. 1975, L 165

Jordan

Co-operation Agreement (and ECSC Agreement)
Brussels, January 18, 1977
November 1, 1978 (and January 1, 1980)
Terminable on 12 months' notice
Cmnd. 7819, T.S. 1980/21; O.J. 1978, L 268 (and O.J. 1979, L316)

Korea (Republic of)

Trade in Textile Products
Brussels, September 12, 1979
February 1, 1980
Applicable from January 1, 1978 to December 31, 1982
Cmnd. 7836, E.C. 1980/7, O.J. 1979, L 298/67

Laos

Silks and Handicrafts
Brussels, May 23, 1975
July 22, 1975
Unlimited
Cmnd. 6337, E.C. 1975/145; O.J. 1977, L 307
Cmnd. 6338, E.C. 1975/146; O.J. 1977, L 307

Lebanon

Co-operation Agreement (and ECSC Agreement)
Brussels, May 3, 1977
November 1, 1978 and January 1, 1980
Terminable on 12 months' notice
Cmnd. 7842, T.S. 1980/29; O.J. 1978, L 267 (and O.J. 1979, L316)

Lomé Convention

Second ACP-EEC Convention of Lomé and Agreement on Products within the Province of the ECSC
Lomé, October 31, 1979
January 1, 1981
Applicable from March 1, 1980 to February 28, 1985
Cmnd. 7895, E.C. 1980/16; O.J. 1980, L 347

Macao

Trade in Textile Products
Brussels, July 19, 1979
Applicable from January 1, 1978 to December 31, 1982
Cmnd. 7801, E.C. 1980/2; O.J. 1979, L 298/106

Malta

Association Agreement
Valletta, December 5, 1970
April 1, 1971
Extended to March 31, 1981
J.O. 1971, L 61/1; Cmnd. 6640, E.C. 1976/21
 Protocol and Financial Protocol March 4, 1976, Cmnd. 6640, E.C. 1976/21, O.J. 1976, L 111/1
 Agreement Extending the First Stage, February 27, 1976, Cmnd. 6641, E.C. 1976/22; O.J. 1976, L 81/1
 Additional Protocol October 27, 1977, Cmnd, 7555, E.C. 1979/12; O.J. 1977, L 304/1

Mexico

Trade Agreement
Brussels, July 15, 1975
November 1, 1975
Five years, thereafter from year to year
Cmnd. 6394, E.C. 1976/6; O.J. 1975, L 247/10

Morocco

Co-operation Agreement (and ECSC Agreement)
Rabat, April 27, 1976
November 1, 1978 (and January 1, 1980)
Terminable on six months' notice
Cmnd. 6920, E.C. 1977/22; O.J. 1978, L 264

Wines entitled to a Designation of Origin
Brussels, March 12, 1977
April 1, 1977
Part of Co-operation Agreement
Cmnd. 7046, E.C. 1977/49; O.J. 1977, L 65/1

New Zealand

Trade in Mutton, Lamb and Goatmeat
Brussels, October 17, 1980
October 20, 1980
March 31, 1984; subject to one years' notice of termination
O.J. 1980, L 275/28, Cmnd. 8207, E.C. 1980/24

Norway

EFTA Non Candidate Agreement
Brussels, May 14, 1973
July 1, 1973
Terminable on 12 months' notice
Cmnd. 5556, E.C. 1974/3; O.J. 1973, L 171
   Rectification December 21, 1973, Cmnd. 5958, E.C. 1975/32;
   O.J. 1973, L 357/1
   Amendments (Exchanges of Letters) November 29, 1976 and
   December 8, 1976
      Cmnd. 6793, E.C. 1977/12; O.J. 1976, L 298/22 & 338/10
   Derogation O.J. 1977, L 139/10
   Amendment December 28, 1978, Cmnd. 7564, E.C. 1979/16;
   O.J. 1978, L 303
   Accession Protocol November 6, 1980, Cmnd. 8145, E.C.
   1981/7; O.J. 1980, L 357/79
   Derogation O.J. 1980, L 371/51
   Amendment O.J. 1980, L 385/11

ECSC
Brussels, May 14, 1973
January 1, 1975
Terminable on 12 months' notice
Cmnd. 5961, T.S. 1975/55; O.J. 1974, L 348
   Additional Protocol, Brussels, November 6, 1980, Cmnd 8164,
   E.C. 14/1981

Customs Arrangements: Fishery Products
Brussels, May 31, 1974
May 31, 1974
Cmnd. 5831, E.C. 1974/18; O.J. 1977, L 310/27

Fisheries
Brussels, February 27, 1980
Applied provisionally from date of signature
Ten years from date of entry into force; thereafter for periods of
six years
Cmnd. 8058, E.C. 1980/50; O.J. 1980, L 226/48

Duty-free quotas
Brussels, April 29, 1980
Immediately
Cmnd. 8029, E.C. 1980/40; O.J. 1980, L 76

Pakistan

Commercial Co-operation
Brussels, June 1, 1976
July 1, 976
Five years, thereafter from year to year; terminable on six months'
notice
Cmnd. 6596, E.C. 20/1976; O.J. 1976, L168

Trade in Textile Products
Islamabad, July 7, 1979
February 1, 1980
Applicable from January 1, 1978 to December 31, 1981; may be
extended by mutual agreement to December 31, 1982
Cmnd. 7811, E.C. 1980/4; O.J. 1979, L 298/143

Peru

Trade in Textile Products
Brussels, November 22, 1979
September 1, 1980
Applicable from Janaury 1, 1978 to December 31, 1982
Cmnd. 7911, E.C. 1980/18; O.J. 1979, L 350/59

Philippines

Trade in Textile Products
Brussels, October 29, 1980
Applicable from January 1, 1978 to December 31, 1982
Cmnd. 8174, E.C. 1981/20; O.J. 1980, L 371/2

Poland

Sheepmeat and Goatmeat (VRA)
January 1, 1981
March 31, 1984, thereafter from year to year
O.J. 1981, L 137/13

Portugal

EFTA Non-Candidate Agreement
Brussels, July 22, 1972
January 1, 1973
Terminable on 12 months' notice
Cmnd. 5164, Misc. 1972/51; O.J. 1972, L 301

Agreements of December 20, 1972, January 30, 1974 and June 26, 1974
    Cmnd. 5825, E.C. 1975/9; O.J. 1974, L 36/1 & L 181/1
Agreement December 18, 1973, Cmnd. 5991, E.C. 1975/43; O.J. 1974, L 37/7
Supplementary Protocol May 29, 1975, Cmnd. 6214, E.C. 1975/126; O.J. 1975, L 106/10
Additional Protocol and Financial Protocol September 20, 1976
    Cmnd. 7526, T.S. 1979/35, O.J. 1978, L 274
Amendment November 29, 1976, Cmnd. 6789, E.C. 1977/9
Derogation, June 14, 1977; O.J. 1977, L 139/13
1977, L 139/13
Amendment July 10, 1979, Cmnd. 7769, E.C. 1979/23; O.J. 1978, L302
Supplementary Protocol December 19, 1979, Cmnd. 8026, E.C. 1980/38; O.J. 1979, L 348/43
Agreement relating to Article 9 of the Supplementary Protocol, September 30, 1980, Cmnd. 8124, E.C. 1981/2, O.J. 1980, L 245/2
Exchange of Letters (Pre-accession aid) O.J. 1980, L 349/2
Derogation O.J. 1980, L 371/54

ECSC Agreement
Brussels, July 22, 1972
January 1, 1974
Terminable on 12 months' notice
Cmnd. 5736, T.S. 1974/47; O.J. 1973, L 350

Romania

Trade in Industrial Products (and Agreement on the establishment of the Joint Committee)
Bucharest, 28 July, 1980
January 1, 1981
Five years, thereafter from year to year
Cmnd. 8141, E.C. 1981/6; O.J. 1980, L 352

Sheepmeat and Goatmeat (VRA)
January 1, 1981
March 31, 1984, thereafter from year to year
O.J. 1981, L 137/21

Senegal

Fishing off the Coast
Brussels, June 15, 1979
Applied provisionally from date of signature
Two years from entry into force; thereafter from year to year
Cmnd. 8062, E.C. 1980/47; O.J. 1980, L 226/17

Appendix 3

Singapore

Trade in Textile Products
Brussels, October 30, 1979
June 1, 1980
Applicable from January 1, 1978 to December 31, 1982
Cmnd. 7879, E.C. 1980/13; O.J. 1979, L 350/99

Spain

Controlled Nuclear Fusion
Three Years
O.J. 1980, L 190/23

Fisheries
Brussels, April 15, 1980
Applied provisionally from date of signature
Five years from date of entry into force; thereafter for additional
periods of five years.
Cmnd. 8134, E.C. 1981/4; O.J. 1980, L 322/4

Sri Lanka

Silks
Brussels, May 23, 1975
June 1, 1975
Unlimited
Cmnd. 6332, E.C. 1975/144

Commerical Co-operation
Brussels, July 22, 1975
December 1, 1975
Five years; thereafter from year to year; terminable on six months'
notice
Cmnd. 6355, E.C. 1975/140; O.J. 1975, L 247/1

Trade in Textile Products
Colombo, July 24, 1979
March 1, 1980
Applicable from January 1, 1978 to December 31, 1982
Cmnd. 7839, E.C. 1980/9; O.J. 1979, L 298/184

Sweden

EFTA Non-Candidate Agreement
Brussels, July 22, 1972
January 1, 1973
Terminable on 12 months' notice
Cmnd. 5180, Misc. 1972/52; O.J. 1972, L 300/97

Supplementary Protocol May 29, 1975, Cmnd. 6215, E.C.
1975/123; O.J. 1975, L 106/13
Amendments (Exchanges of Letters) November 26 and
December 8, 1975
    Cmnd. 6775, E.C. 1977/5; O.J. 1976, L 298/36 & 338/13
Derogation   O.J. 1977, L 139/16
Rectification   O.J. 1978, L 210/1
Amendment September 27, 1978, Cmnd. 7485, E.C. 1979/3;
O.J. 1978, L 303/14
Derogation O.J. 1980, L 371/57
Accession Protocol November 6, 1980, O.J. 1980, L 357/105
Amendment O.J. 1980, L 385/14

ECSC Agreement
Brussels, July 22, 1972
January 1, 1974
Terminable on 12 months' notice
Cmnd. 5657, T.S. 1974/44; O.J. 1973, L 350
    Additional Protocol Brussels November 6, 1980, Cmnd. 8165,
    E.C. 15/1981

Fisheries
Brussels, March 21, 1977
Applied provisionally from date of signature
Ten years from date of entry into force; thereafter for periods of
six years
Cmnd. 8056, E.C. 1980/48; O.J. 1980, L226/2

Salmon
Brussels, November 21, 1979
Applied provisionally from date of signature
Tied to that of 1977 agreement on fisheries
Cmnd. 8057, E.C. 1980/49; O.J. 1980, L 226/8 & O.J. 1979,
L 297&23

Duty-free Quotas
Brussels, June 16, 1980
Rectification
Cmnd. 8055, E.C. 1980/46; O.J. 1980, L 76/13

Switzerland

Consultation (ECSC)
May 7, 1956
Renewed tacitly for periods of five years from February 10,
1958 unless terminated on three months' notice
J.O. 1957, 85; CT VII, 21

ECSC Railways Tariffs

Luxembourg, July 28, 1956
June 1, 1957
Indefinite
Cmnd. 5892, E.C. 1975/29; J.O. 1957, 223, O.J. (2nd) VIII, 3
    Accession Protocol October 10, 1974, *Ibid* and O.J. 1979, L12

Clock and Watch Industry
Brussels, July 20, 1972 (and Agreement of June 30, 1967)
January 1, 1973
Terminable on 12 months' notice
Cmnd. 6075, E.C. 1975/69; O.J. 1974, L 118/11
    Amendment O.J. 1977, C253/1

EFTA Non Candidate Agreement
Brussels, July 22, 1972
January 1, 1973
Terminable on 12 months' notice
Cmnd. 5509, T.S. 1974/3; O.J. 1972, L 300
    Supplementary Protocols May 29, 1975, Cmnd. 6226, E.C.
    1975/130; O.J. 1975, L 106/16 & 19
    Amendment December 14, 1976, Cmnd. 6757, E.C. 1977/2,
    O.J. 1976, L 298/43
    Amendments November 29, 1976 and December 8, 1976,
    Cmnd. 6778, E.C. 1977/4; O.J. 1976, L 298 & 328/58 & 338/16
    Derogation   O.J. 1977 L 139/19
    Amendment September 27, 1978, Cmnd. 7487, E.C. 1979/4,
    O.J. 1978, L 303/25
    Accession Protocol July 17, 1980, Cmnd. 8146, E.C. 1981/8;
    O.J. 1980, L 357/131
    Derogation O.J. 1980, L 371/60
    Amendment O.J. 1980, L 385/17

ECSC Agreement
Brussels, July 22, 1972
January 1, 1974
Terminable on 12 months' notice
Cmnd. 5737, T.S. 1974/49; O.J. 1973, L 350
    Additional Protocol Brussels July 17, 1980, Cmnd. 8157, E.C.
    11/1981
    Supplementary Protocol, Brussels July 17, 1980, Cmnd. 8158,
    E.C. 1981/12

Community Transit (with Accession Protocol)
Brussels, November 23, 1972 (and December 4, 1973)
January 1, 1974
Terminable on six months' notice
Cmnd. 6093, E.C. 1975/68, J.O. 1972, L 294/1, O.J. 1973, L
365/209

Amendment June 29, 1977, Cmnd. 7013, E.C. 1977/42; O.J. 1977, L 151/1
Amendment June 23, 1980, Cmnd. 8053, E.C. 1980/44; O.J. 1980, L 155/12
Amendment O.J. 1981, L 108/104 & 114

Extension of EURONET
Brussels, September 28, 1979
Upon signature
Until December 31, 1983
Cmnd. 8030, E.C. 1980/41; O.J. 1979, L 214/18 & 234/12

Switzerland (and Austria)

Extension of the Application of the Rules on Community Transit
Brussels, July 12, 1977
March 1, 1978
Terminable on six months' notice
Cmnd. 7023, E.C. 1977/44; O.J. 1977 L 142/1
   Greek text O.J. 1981, L 147/2

Switzerland (and Greece)

Concerted Action Project in the Field of Registration of Congenital Abnormalities
December 14, 1979
Accession August 1, 1980
Extended to December 31, 1981
Cmnd. 7878, E.C. 1980/12, O.J. 1981, L113/44

Syria

Co-operation Agreement (and ECSC Agreement)
Brussels, January 18, 1977
November 1, 1978 (and January 1, 1980)
Terminable on 12 months' notice
Cmnd. 7821, T.S. 1980/23; O.J. 1978, L 269 (and O.J. 1979, L 316)

Thailand
Trade in Textile Products
Pattaya, July 21, 1979
February 1, 1980
Applicable from January 1, 1978 to December 31, 1982
Cmnd. 7837, E.C. 1980/6; O.J. 1979, L 298/223

Tunisia

Co-operation Agreement (and ECSC Agreement)

Tunis, April 25, 1976
November 1, 1978 (and January 1, 1980)
Cmnd. 6894, E.C. 1977/18; O.J. 1978, L 265

Tunisia

Wines entitled to a Designation of Origin
Brussels, October 23, 1978
November 1, 1978
Part of Co-operation Agreement
Cmnd. 7484, E.C. 1979/2; O.J. 1978, L 296

Turkey

Association Agreement
Ankara, September 12, 1963
December 1, 1964
Unspecified
J.O. 1964, 3687, O.J. 1977, L 361
   Additional Protocols November 23, 1970, J.O. 1972, L 293/1;
      O.J. 1977, L 361
   Accession Agreement and Financial Agreement June 30, 1973,
      Cmnd. 5548, E.C. 1974/1; O.J. 1977, L 361
   Amendment November 23, 1973, Cmnd. 5933, E.C. 1975/27;
      O.J. 1974, L34/7
   Financial Protocol May 12, 1977, Cmnd. 7709, T.S. 1979/87;
      O.J. 1979, L 67/14

ECSC Agreement
Brussels, November 23, 1970
January 1, 1973
J.O. 1972, L 293/63; O.J. 1977, L 361
   Supplementary Protocol June 30, 1973, *ibid.*

United Kingdom

Privileges of the Joint European Torus (JET) Project
Brussels, May 3, 1978
June 1, 1978
Cmnd. 7255, T.S. 1978/66

United Kingdom

See also IAEA

Uruguay

Trade Agreement
Luxembourg, April 2, 1973
August 1, 1974
Three years; thereafter from year to year
Cmnd. 5894, E.C. 1975/7; O.J. 1973, L 333/1

Trade in Textile Products
Brussels, January 28, 1980
Applicable from January 1, 1978 to December 31, 1982
Cmnd. 8006, E.C. 1980/35; O.J. 1980, L 70/38

Trade in Mutton and Lamb
Brussels, October 17, 1980
October 20, 1980
Until March 31, 1984; subject to one year's notice of termination
O.J. 1980, L 275/37

United States of America

Euratom Agreement
May 29/June 19, 1958
August 27, 1958
Unlimited
J.O. 1959, 309, CT IX, 1

Peaceful uses of Atomic Energy
November 8, 1958
February 19, 1959
Until December 31, 1985
J.O. 1959, 312; CT IX, 3
   Additional Agreement June 11, 1960, J.O. 1961, 668; CT IX, 21
   Amendment to Agreement, May 21/22, 1962, J.O. 1862, 2038; CT IX 37
   Amendment to Agreement, May 21/22, 1962, J.O. 1962, J.O. 1962, 2045; CT IX 43
   Ibid. August 22/27, 1963, J.O. 1964, 2586, CT IX 47
   Ibid. September 20, 1972, Cmnd. 5392, Misc. No. 22 (1973)

Fisheries
Washington, February 15, 1977
June 9, 1977
Until July 1, 1984; may be extended
Cmnd. 7018, E.C. 1977/38; O.J. 1977, L 141/1

United States (Nuclear Regulatory Commission)

Co-operation (Euratom)
March 19, 1979
See O.J. 1981, C 103/7, W.Q. 1831/80

Yaoundé (see now Lomé)

Yugoslavia
Co-operation Agreement (with ECSC Agreement)

Belgrade, April 2, 1980
Unlimited; terminable on six months' notice
Cmnd. 8088, E.C. 1980/52, O.J. 1980, L 130

Interim Agreement
Brussels, May 6, 1980
July 1, 1980
Until entry into force of the Co-operation Agreement or until
June 30, 1985
Cmnd. 8120, E.C. 1981/1; O.J. 1980, L 130/2
   Amendment to Annex A, O.J. 1980, L 196/2
   Exchange of letters O.J. 1981, L 147/6

Interim Protocol
Brussels, May 6, 1980
July 1, 1980
Until entry into force of the Co-operation Agreement or until
June 30, 1985
Cmnd. 8133, E.C. 1981/3; O.J. 1980, L 130/99

Sheepmeat and Goatmeat (VRA)
January 1, 1981
March 31, 1984, thereafter from year to year
O.J. 1981, L 137/30

Zimbabwe

Interim Agreement
Luxembourg, November 4, 1980
January 1, 1981
Until entry into force of the main agreement
O.J. 1980, L 372/2, Cmnd. 8218, E.C. 1981/26

Accession to Lomé II
Luxembourg, November 4, 1980
Cmnd. 8150, E.C. 1981/9

ECSC Products
Luxembourg, November 4, 1980
With accession to Lomé II
Until February 28, 1985
Cmnd. 8151, E.C. 1981/10

Appendix 3

PART 2

General Multilateral Agreements with Community Participation

Only includes agreements mentioned in *Official Journal*, with corresponding Command Paper (Cmnd.) references, unless Cmnd. shows Community participation

Line 1: title
Line 2: date of opening for signature of instrument
Line 3: references

Listings in *date order*

Arrangement Concerning Certain Diary Products

Geneva, January 12, 1970
May 14, 1970
C.T. VIII - 3, 117

European Agreement Concerning the Work of Crews of Vehicles engaged in International Road Transport (AETR)

Geneva, July 1, 1970
O.J. 1977, L334/11; Cmnd. 7401, T.S. 1978/103

International Wheat Agreement 1971

Washington, March 29, 1971
O.J. 1974, L. 219/24; Cmnd. 4953, T.S. 1972/21
   Sixth Extension O.J. 1981, L155/25

Agreement on the Establishment of a European Informatics Network (Euratom)

Brussels, November 23, 1971
February 1, 1973
Cmnd. 5283, T.S. 1973/47

Convention on International Trade in Endangered Species of Wild Fauna and Flora

Washington, March 3, 1973
Cmnd. 6647, T.S. 1976/101

GATT Protocol relating to Milk Fat

Geneva, April 2, 1973
Cmnd. 3412, T.S. 1973/93; O.J. 1973, L 153/19

International Convention on the Simplification and Harmonisation of Customs Procedures

Kyoto, May 18, 1973
O.J. 1975, L100/1; O.J. 1980, L 100/27; Cmnd. 5938, T.S. 1975/36

Arrangement on International Trade in Textiles

Geneva, December 20, 1973
O.J. 1974, L 118/1; Cmnd. 6205, Misc. 1975/18
  Protocol extending the arrangement, December 14, 1977, O.J. 1977, L 348/59
    Cmnd. 7259, Misc. 1978/19

Convention for the Prevention of Marine Pollution from land-based Sources

Paris, June 4, 1974
Cmnd. 7251, T.S. 1978/64

European Agreement on the Exchange of Tissue-typing Reagents

Strasbourg, September 17, 1974
O.J. 1977, L 295/7; Cmnd. 7558, T.S. 1979/51

Fifth International Tin Agreement

New York, July 1, 1975
O.J. 1976, L222/1 & 288/26; Cmnd. 7033, T.S. 1977/10

International Cocoa Agreement 1975

New York, November 10, 1975
O.J. 1976, L 321; O.J. 1979, L 44/13; Cmnd. 7544, T.S. 1979/43

TIR Convention

Geneva, November 14, 1975
O.J. 1978, L 252/1; Cmnd. 6492, Misc. 1976/22

International Coffee Agreement 1976

New York, January 1, 1976
O.J. 1976, L309; O.J. 1979, L248/10; Cmnd. 7079, T.S. 1978/12

International Coffee Agreement

New York, January 31, 1976
O.J. 1976, L 309/28, O.J. 1979, L 248/10; Cmnd. 7079, T.S. 1978/12

Protocol to the Agreement on the Importation of Educational, Scientific and Cultural Materials

November 26, 1976
O.J. 1979; L 134/13; Cmnd. 8100, Misc. 1980/25

Convention of Future Multilateral Co-operation in the Northwest Atlantic Fisheries

Ottawa, October 24, 1978
O.J. 1978, L378/1; O.J. 1981, L69/1; Cmnd. 7569, Misc. 1979/9

GATT: Multilateral Agreements resulting from the 1973 to 1979 Trade Negotiations (MTNs)

Geneva, June 30, 1979
O.J. 1980, L 71

Amendment to the 1950 Brussels Convention on Classification of Goods in Customs Tariffs

Entered into force July 1, 1979
Cmnd. 7579, T.S. 1979/57

International Olive Oil Agreement 1979

Madrid, July 1, 1979
Provisionally in force January 1, 1980
O.J. 1979, L327/1

International Natural Rubber Agreement 1979

New York, January 2, 1980
Cmnd. 8018, Misc. 1980/21; O.J. 1980, L 213/1

Food Aid Convention 1980

Washington, March 11, 1980
July 1, 1980
Cmnd. 8009, Misc. 1980/20

International Convention on the Physical Protection of Nuclear Material

Vienna and New York March 3, 1980
O.J. 1980, L 149/41; Cmnd. 8112, Misc. 1980/27

Agreement Establishing the Common Fund for Commodities

New York, October 1, 1980
Cmnd. 8192, Misc. 1981/7

V

INDEX

Index

International Law, *See* External
    Relations.
International Labour Organisation (ILO),
    25–26, 31–36
    Convention No. 111, 6–32
International Law
    community legal order and, 7–03
International Monetary Fund (IMF),
    30–02
International Terrorism, Declaration on,
    Iran, 4–04
Ireland
    EEC, accession to, 1–01,1–02 *et seq.*
Israel
    EEC, Reciprocal Preference Agreement
    with, 31–17

Joint European Torus (" JET"), 28–14
Judgments—*See under* Convention on
    Jurisdiction and Enforcement of Civil
    and Commercial Judgments *and*
    Court of Justice.
Jurisdiction, Convention on. *See under*
    Convention on Jurisdiction.

Legislation, Community. *See* Acts of the
    Institutions *and* Community Law.
Legislation, national. *See* National
    Legislation.
Lomé Convention, 13–19 *et seq.*, 29–25,
    29–35, 30–03, 30–32 *et seq.*, 30–36,
    31–02. *See also* External Relations
    institutions, 31–25
    Committee of Ambassadors, 31–25
    Consultative Assembly, 31–25
    Council of Ministers, 31–25
    STABEX, 31–20, 31–23
    sugar, 15–30, 15–77
    Zimbabwe, accession to, 31–26
Luxembourg, accords of, 3–16, 3–37, 3–38,
    3–63

Magrheb Countries
    EEC, Interim and Co-operation
    Agreements with, 31-15
Malta
    Association Agreement with, 31–14
Mansholt, Sicco, 15–72
Marjolin Committee, 24–23
Mashreq Countries
    EEC, Interim and Co-operation
    Agreements with, 31–16
Member States
    aids, provision of, 21–17
    Common Customs Tariff, and, 13–19
    decisions of, 6–23 *et seq.*
    courts, jurisdiction of, 9–01
    disputes between, 9–01
    international law, obligations under
    29–39
    obligations of, 12–05 *et seq.*
    economic policies, co-ordination of,
    12–07
    sovereignty, limitation of, 7–03 *et seq.*,
    7–14
    territorial definition of, 5–04 *et seq.*
    Berlin, 5–09
    Gibraltar, 5–05

Member of States—*cont.*
    third countries, relations with, 30–24 *et
    seq.*
Member States, Actions Against, 3–12,
    11–01 *et seq.*
    breach, form of, 11–02
    commission, by, 11–01 *et seq.*
    ECSC Treaty, under, 11–15
    judgment, effect of, 9–05, 11–14
    Member State, by, 11–13
    procedure, 11–06 *et seq.*
    Court, reference to, 11–10 *et seq.*
    Member State, action by, 11–13
    pre-contentious, 11–07
    reasoned opinion, 11–08 *et seq.*
Merger Treaty, 3–02, 3–05
Mexico
    EEC, agreement with, 31–29
Migrant Workers. *See* Social Policy *and*
    Social Security.
Milk Products
    market organisation in, 15–31 *et seq.*
    community-produced products,
    15–32
    third countries, trade with, 15–33
    structural policy, 15–76
    turnover tax, 11–02
    U.K., Community regulations in, 15–34
Monaco
    application of EEC to, 5–05
    Common Customs Tariff, 5–05
Monetary Committee, 3–16, 3–54, 24–11
Monetary Compensatory Amounts, *See*
    under CAP (Common Agricultural
    Policy).
Monopolies, State, 13–27 *et seq.*
    agricultural policy, and, 13–32 *et seq.*
    commercial character, 13–28 *et seq.*
    competition policy, and, 13–33
    discrimination, elimination of, 13–30
    quantitative restrictions, and, 13–30
Motor Vehicles,
    technical harmonisation, 19–32

Nationality, discrimination on grounds of,
    prohibited, 12–08 *et seq.*, 16–08 *et seq.*,
    19–14, 22–07 *et seq.*
National Legislation, Harmonisation of,
    23–01 *et seq.*
    competition, distortion of, and, 23–05
    convention, by, 23–09 *et seq.*
    customs legislation, 13–17 *et seq.*
    economic policies, 12–05, 12–07
    environmental policies, 27–03
    harmonisation, definition of, 23–02 *et
    seq.*
    provisions, relationship with, 23–08
    trade, technical barriers to, 23–06
    treaty, by, 23–09
Non-contractual Liability
    causation, 11–55
    damage, 11–56
    fault, need to prove, 11–48 *et seq.*
    limitation of actions, 11–57
    monetary compensatory amounts, and,
    15–70
    normative injustice, 11–51 *et seq.*
    vicarious liability, 11–46